CIMA

MANAGEMENT

PAPER F2

FINANCIAL MANAGEMENT

Our text is designed to help you study **effectively** and **efficiently**.

In this edition we:

- **Highlight** the **most important elements** in the syllabus and the **key skills** you will need

- **Signpost** how each chapter links to the syllabus and the learning outcomes

- **Provide** lots of **exam alerts** explaining how what you're learning may be tested

- **Include examples** and **questions** to help you apply what you've learnt

- **Emphasise key points** in **section summaries**

- **Test your knowledge** of what you've studied in **quick quizzes**

- **Examine your understanding** in our **exam question bank**

- **Reference all the important topics** in the **full index**

SUITABLE FOR EXAMS UP TO NOVEMBER 2014

First edition 2009

Fifth edition 2013

ISBN 9781 4453 7130 6
(Previous ISBN 9781 4453 9606 4)

eISBN 9781 4453 7130 6

British Library Cataloguing-in-Publication Data
A catalogue record for this book is available from the British
Library

Published by

BPP Learning Media Ltd
BPP House, Aldine Place,
London W12 8AA

www.bpp.com/learningmedia

Printed in the United Kingdom by Polestar Wheatons
Hennock Road
Marsh Barton
Exeter
EX2 8RP

Your learning materials, published by BPP Learning Media
Ltd, are printed on paper sourced from sustainable,
managed forests.

The contents of this book are intended as a guide and not professional
advice. Although every effort has been made to ensure that the contents
of this book are correct at the time of going to press, BPP Learning
Media makes no warranty that the information in this book is accurate or
complete and accept no liability for any loss or damage suffered by any
person acting or refraining from acting as a result of the material in this
book.

We are grateful to the Chartered Institute of Management Accountants
for permission to reproduce past examination questions. The suggested
solutions in the exam answer bank have been prepared by BPP Learning
Media Ltd.

Contents

How our Study Text can help you pass

Streamlined studying	• We show you the best ways to study efficiently • Our Text has been designed to ensure you can easily and quickly navigate through it • The different features in our Text emphasise important knowledge and techniques
Exam expertise	• **Studying F2** on page xi introduces the key themes of the syllabus and summarises how to pass • We highlight throughout our Text how topics may be tested and what you'll have to do in the exam • We help you see the complete picture of the syllabus, so that you can answer questions that range across the whole syllabus • Our Text covers the syllabus content – no more, no less
Regular review	• We frequently summarise the key knowledge you need • We test what you've learnt by providing questions and quizzes throughout our Text

Our other products

BPP Learning Media also offers these products for the F2 exam:

Practice and Revision Kit	Providing lots more question practice and helpful guidance on how to pass the exam
Passcards	Summarising what you should know in visual, easy to remember, form
Success CDs	Covering the vital elements of the F2 syllabus in less than 90 minutes and also containing exam hints to help you fine tune your strategy
i-Pass	Providing computer-based testing in a variety of formats, ideal for self-assessment
Interactive Passcards	Allowing you to learn actively with a clear visual format summarising what you must know

You can purchase these products by visiting www.bpp.com/cimamaterials

CIMA Distance Learning

BPP's distance learning packages provide flexibility and convenience, allowing you to study effectively, at a pace that suits you, where and when you choose. There are four great distance learning packages available.

Online classroom live	Through live interactive online sessions it provides you with the traditional structure and support of classroom learning, but with the convenience of attending classes wherever you are
Online classroom	Through pre-recorded online lectures it provides you with the classroom experience via the web with the tutor guidance & support you'd expect from a face to face classroom
Basics Plus	A guided self study package containing a wealth of rich e-learning & physical content
Basics Online	A guided self study package containing a wealth of rich e-learning content

You can find out more about these packages by visiting www.bpp.com/cimadistancelearning

BPP LEARNING MEDIA

Features in our Study Text

 Section Introductions explain how the section fits into the chapter

 Key Terms are the core vocabulary you need to learn

KEY TERM

 Key Points are points that you have to know, ideas or calculations that will be the foundations of your answers

KEY POINT

 Exam Alerts show you how subjects are likely to be tested

 Exam Skills are the key skills you will need to demonstrate in the exam, linked to question requirements

 Formulae To Learn are formulae you must remember in the exam

LEARN

 Exam Formulae are formulae you will be given in the exam

EXAM

 Examples show how theory is put into practice

 Questions give you the practice you need to test your understanding of what you've learnt

 Case Studies link what you've learnt with the real-world business environment

CASE STUDY

 Links show how the syllabus overlaps with other parts of the qualification, including Knowledge Brought Forward that you need to remember from previous exams

 Website References link to material that will enhance your understanding of what you're studying

 Further Reading will give you a wider perspective on the subjects you're covering

 Section Summaries allow you to review each section

Streamlined studying

What you should do	In order to
Read the Chapter and Section Introductions	See why topics need to be studied and map your way through the chapter
Go quickly through the explanations	Gain the depth of knowledge and understanding that you'll need
Highlight the Key Points, Key Terms and Formulae To Learn	Make sure you know the basics that you can't do without in the exam
Focus on the Exam Skills and Exam Alerts	Know how you'll be tested and what you'll have to do
Work through the Examples and Case Studies	See how what you've learnt applies in practice
Prepare Answers to the Questions	See if you can apply what you've learnt in practice
Revisit the Section Summaries in the Chapter Roundup	Remind you of, and reinforce, what you've learnt
Answer the Quick Quiz	Find out if there are any gaps in your knowledge
Answer the Question(s) in the Exam Question Bank	Practise what you've learnt in depth

Should I take notes?

Brief notes may help you remember what you're learning. You should use the notes format that's most helpful to you (lists, diagrams, mindmaps).

Further help

BPP Learning Media's *Learning to Learn Accountancy* provides lots more helpful guidance on studying. It is designed to be used both at the outset of your CIMA studies and throughout the process of learning accountancy. It can help you **focus your studies on the subject and exam**, enabling you to **acquire knowledge, practise and revise efficiently and effectively**.

Syllabus and learning outcomes

Paper F2 Financial Management

The syllabus comprises:

Topic and Study Weighting

A	Group Financial Statements	35%
B	Issues in Recognition and Measurement	20%
C	Analysis and Interpretation of Financial Accounts	35%
D	Developments in External Reporting	10%

Learning Outcomes		
Lead	**Component**	**Syllabus content**
A	**Group financial statements**	
1 Prepare the full consolidated statements of a single company and the consolidated statements of financial position and comprehensive income for a group (in relatively complex circumstances)	(a) Prepare a complete set of consolidated financial statements in a form suitable for a group of companies	(i) Relationships between investors and investees, meaning of control and circumstances in which a subsidiary is excluded from consolidation
	(b) Demonstrate the impact on group financial statements where: there is a non-controlling interest; the interest in a subsidiary or associate is acquired or disposed of part way through an accounting period (to include the effective date of acquisition and dividends out of pre-acquisition profits); shareholdings, or control, are acquired in stages; intra-group trading and other transactions occur; the value of goodwill is impaired	(ii) The preparation of consolidated financial statements (including the group cash flow statement and statement of changes in equity) involving one or more subsidiaries, sub-subsidiaries and associates (IAS 1 (revised), 7 and 27, IFRS 3)
		(iii) The treatment in consolidated financial statements of minority interests, pre- and post-acquisition reserves, goodwill (including its impairment), fair value adjustments, intra-group transactions and dividends, piece-meal and mi-year acquisitions, and disposals to include sub-subsidiaries and mixed groups
	(c) Apply the concept of a joint arrangement and how the two types (joint operations and joint ventures) are accounted for	(iv) The accounting treatment of associates and joint ventures (IAS 28 and 31) using the equity method and proportional consolidation method

Learning Outcomes				
Lead		**Component**		**Syllabus content**
2	Explain the principles of accounting for capital schemes and foreign exchange rate changes	(a)	Explain the principles of accounting for a capital reconstruction scheme or a demerger	(i)	Accounting for reorganisations and capital reconstruction schemes
		(b)	Explain foreign currency translation principles, including the distinction between functional and presentation currency and accounting for overseas transactions and investments in overseas subsidiaries	(ii)	Foreign currency translation (IAS 21), to include overseas transactions and investments in overseas subsidiaries
		(c)	Explain the correct treatment for foreign loans financing foreign equity investments		
B	**Issues in recognition and measurement**				
1	Discuss accounting principles and their relevance to accounting issues of contemporary interest	(a)	Discuss the problems of profit measurement and alternative approaches to asset valuations	(i)	The problems of profit measurement and the effect of alternative approaches to asset valuation; current cost and current purchasing power bases and the real terms system; Financial Reporting in Hyperinflationary Economies (IAS 29)
		(b)	Discuss measures to reduce distortion in financial statements when price levels change		
		(c)	Discuss the principle of substance over form applied to a range of transactions	(ii)	The principle of substance over form and its influence in dealing with transactions such as sale and repurchase agreements, consignment stock, debt factoring, securitised assets, loan transfers and public and private sector financial collaboration
		(d)	Discuss the possible treatments of financial instruments in the issuer's accounts (ie liabilities versus equity, and the implications for finance costs)	(iii)	Financial instruments classified as liabilities or shareholders funds and the allocation of finance costs over the term of the borrowing (IAS 32 and 39)
		(e)	Discuss circumstances in which amortised cost, fair value and hedge accounting are appropriate for financial instruments, the principles of these accounting methods and considerations in the measurement of fair value	(iv)	The measurement, including methods of determining fair value, and disclosure of financial instruments (IAS 32 and 39, IFRS 7)
		(f)	Discuss the recognition	(v)	Retirement benefits, including pension schemes – defined benefit schemes and defined contribution schemes, actuarial deficits and surpluses (IAS 19)

Learning Outcomes

Lead		Component		Syllabus content	
		and valuation issues concerned with pension plans (including the treatment of remeasurement gains and losses) and share-based payments		(vi)	Share-based payments (IFRS 2): types of transactions, measurement bases and accounting determination of fair value
C	**Analysis and interpretation of financial accounts**				
1	Produce a ratio analysis from financial statements and supporting information	(a)	Interpret a full range of accounting ratios	(i)	Ratios in the areas of performance, profitability, financial adaptability, liquidity, activity, shareholder investment and financing, and their interpretation
		(b)	Discuss the limitations of accounting ratio analysis and analysis based on financial statements	(ii)	Calculation of Earnings per Share under IAS 33, to include the effect of bonus issues, rights issues and convertible stock
				(iii)	The impact of financing structure, including use of leasing and short-term debt, on ratios, particularly gearing
				(iv)	Limitations of ratio analysis (eg comparability of businesses and accounting policies)
2	Evaluate performance and position	(a)	Analyse financial statements in the context of information provided in the accounts and corporate report	(i)	Interpretation of financial statements via the analysis of the accounts and corporate reports
		(b)	Evaluate performance and position based on analysis of financial statements	(ii)	The identification of information required to assess financial performance and the extent to which financial statements fail to provide such information
		(c)	Discuss segmental analysis, with inter-firm and international comparisons taking account of possible aggressive or unusual accounting policies and pressures on ethical behaviour	(iii)	Interpretation of financial obligations included in financial accounts (eg redeemable debt, earn-out arrangements, contingent liabilities)
				(iv)	Segment analysis: inter-firm and international comparison (IFRS 8)
		(d)	Discuss the results of an analysis of financial statements and its limitations	(v)	The need to be aware of aggressive or unusual accounting practice ('creative accounting'), eg in the areas of cost capitalisation and revenue recognition, and threats to the ethics of accountants from pressure to report 'good results'
				(vi)	Reporting the results of analysis

D	Developments in external reporting		
1	Discuss contemporary developments in financial and non-financial reporting	(a) Discuss pressures for extending the scope and quality of external reports to include prospective and non-financial matters, and narrative reporting generally	(i) Increasing stakeholder demands for information that goes beyond historical financial information and frameworks for such reporting, including as an example of national requirements and guidelines, the UK's Business Review and the Accounting Standard Board's best practice standard, RS1, and the Global Reporting Initiative
		(b) Explain how information concerning the interaction of a business with society and the natural environment can be communicated in the published accounts	(ii) Environmental and social accounting issues, differentiating between externalities and costs internalised through, for example, capitalisation of environmental expenditure, recognition of future environmental costs by means of provisions, taxation and the costs of emissions permit trading schemes
		(c) Discuss social and environmental issues which are likely to be most important to stakeholders in an organisation	(iii) Non-financial measures of social and environmental impact
		(d) Explain the process of measuring, recording and disclosing the effect of exchanges between a business and society – human resource accounting	(iv) Human resource accounting
			(v) Major differences between IFRS and US GAAP, and progress towards convergence
		(e) Discuss major differences between IFRS and US GAAP, and the measures designed to contribute towards their convergence	

Studying F2

1 What's F2 about

The Paper F2 syllabus is in four parts:

- Group financial statements
- Issues in recognition and measurement
- Analysis and interpretation
- Developments in external reporting.

1.1 Group financial statements

This is given a weighting of 35%. However, there could be as many as 45 marks available. It is important, therefore, that you study all aspects of this topic in full.

It is vital that you get a good grasp of the basics and the principles. There are a lot of easy marks available for basic consolidation techniques. You should not, however, concentrate on the 'hows' of the calculation to the exclusion of the 'whys', which will always be tested in some form. For example, you may be asked to explain a group structure and then to produce consolidated financial statements. Your explanation will help directly in your calculation.

You should focus most of your efforts on the consolidated statements of financial position and profit or loss and other comprehensive income.

1.2 Issues in recognition and measurement

This part of the syllabus involves explaining the problems of profit measurement and alternative approaches to asset valuations. Thus you will need to understand the weaknesses of historical cost accounting and the advantages, disadvantages and basic mechanics of alternative approaches. You will also need to apply relevant accounting standards, all of which are covered in this Study Text. This section is worth 20%.

1.3 Analysis and interpretation

With a weighting of 35%, this is an important area, unsurprisingly, given that the title of the paper is Financial Management, rather than Financial Accounting. There will generally be two analysis and interpretation questions on each paper. They will take slightly different forms, one being a conventional ratio analysis report and another discussing, for example, the impact of adopting a particular accounting policy.

Discussion is every bit as important as calculation in this section. The examiner has indicated that candidates spend too much time calculating ratios and too little time evaluating them. Credit is often given for different conclusions drawn, provided these can be backed up with sensible arguments.

Conversely, you should not 'waffle' in analysis questions, something the examiner has also criticised. Practice is the key in this area. You should try every question in the Study Text and Revision Kit, even if you end up only doing answer plans for some of them.

1.4 Developments in external reporting

Worth 10%, this section is not as important as group accounts or analysis. However, it is a good way to earn marks. You will not have to know exposure drafts.

The main focus at the moment is on harmonisation, for example with US GAAP. Paper F2 is based only on International Financial Reporting Standards, and you may well have to discuss the advantages of these and the practical problems of implementing them. Other topical issues include environmental accounting, or the Operating and Financial Review. Questions on these areas are fairly straightforward; again, structuring your answers is the key.

2 What's required

2.1 Knowledge

The exam requires you to demonstrate knowledge as much as application. Bear in mind this comment from the examiner, from her report on an exam under the old syllabus:

> *At the top end, some candidates scored very highly indeed, producing a full complement of excellent answers. However, a substantial minority of candidates appeared to have virtually no useable knowledge of the syllabus.*

2.2 Explanation

As well as stating your knowledge, you will also sometimes be asked to demonstrate the more advanced skill of explaining the requirements of accounting standards. Explaining means providing simple definitions and covering the reasons why regulations have been made and what the problems are that the standards are designed to counter. The examiner has stated that the key to remember is '**because**'. If you have answered the '**because**' element, then this is a full answer. You'll gain higher marks if your explanations are clearly focused on the question and you can supplement your explanations with examples.

2.3 Calculations

The examiner does not usually set purely numerical questions. It is more likely that you will have to use calculations to support your explanations or arguments. It goes without saying that all workings should be shown and referenced. Not only is it professional, but it enables the examiner to give you credit by following through your answer if you make a mistake early on.

2.4 Interpretation and recommendation

As discussed above, you may have to interpret and draw conclusions from any figures or ratios you have calculated. Your arguments should be logical and structured.

You must also be aware of the key verbs used by the examiner in the exam. These are reproduced in full in the exam question and answer bank.

2.5 What the examiner means

The table below has been prepared by CIMA to help you interpret the syllabus and learning outcomes and the meaning of exam questions.

You will see that there are 5 levels of Learning objective, ranging from Knowledge to Evaluation, reflecting the level of skill you will be expected to demonstrate. CIMA Certificate subjects were constrained to levels 1 to 3, but in CIMA's Professional qualification the entire hierarchy will be used.

At the start of each chapter in your study text is a topic list relating the coverage in the chapter to the level of skill you may be called on to demonstrate in the exam.

Learning objectives	Verbs used	Definition
1 Knowledge		
What are you expected to know	• List	• Make a list of
	• State	• Express, fully or clearly, the details of/facts of
	• Define	• Give the exact meaning of
2 Comprehension		
What you are expected to understand	• Describe	• Communicate the key features of
	• Distinguish	• Highlight the differences between
	• Explain	• Make clear or intelligible/state the meaning of
	• Identify	• Recognise, establish or select after consideration
	• Illustrate	• Use an example to describe or explain something
3 Application		
How you are expected to apply your knowledge	• Apply	• Put to practical use
	• Calculate/ compute	• Ascertain or reckon mathematically
		• Prove with certainty or to exhibit by practical means
	• Demonstrate	
	• Prepare	• Make or get ready for use
	• Reconcile	• Make or prove consistent/compatible
	• Solve	• Find an answer to
	• Tabulate	• Arrange in a table
4 Analysis		
How you are expected to analyse the detail of what you have learned	• Analyse	• Examine in detail the structure of
	• Categorise	• Place into a defined class or division
	• Compare and contrast	• Show the similarities and/or differences between
	• Construct	• Build up or compile
	• Discuss	• Examine in detail by argument
	• Interpret	• Translate into intelligible or familiar terms
	• Prioritise	• Place in order of priority or sequence for action
	• Produce	• Create or bring into existence
5 Evaluation		
How you are expected to use your learning to evaluate, make decisions or recommendations	• Advise	• Counsel, inform or notify
	• Evaluate	• Appraise or assess the value of
	• Recommend	• Propose a course of action

3 How to pass

3.1 Cover the whole syllabus?

Ideally, yes. The examiner has stated that any syllabus topic could be examined. In view of the weighting, however, it makes sense to focus most of your efforts on groups and financial analysis. Leaving topics out is not advisable, but if you are forced to do this through lack of time, then make sure you do not leave out any aspects of these very important topics. At least get an overview of any topic not covered, by skim reading or reading Passcards.

3.2 Practise

Our text gives you ample opportunity to practise by providing questions within chapters, quick quiz questions and questions in the exam question bank at the end. In addition the BPP Practice and Revision Kit provides lots more question practice. It's particularly important to practise:

- Ten mark questions, mostly knowledge based with some calculations.
- Longer scenario questions, of the type to be found in Section B

3.3 Develop time management skills

The examiner has identified time management as being a problem, with some candidates not leaving themselves enough time to do the shorter calculations. Particularly therefore towards the end of your course, you need to practise all types of question, only allowing yourself the time you will be given in the exam.

3.4 Develop business awareness

Candidates with good business awareness can score well in a number of areas.

- Reading articles in CIMA's *Financial Management* magazine and the business press will help you understand the practical rationale for accounting standards and make it easier for you to apply accounting requirements correctly

- Looking through the accounts of major companies will familiarise you with the contents of accounts and help you comment on key figures and changes from year-to-year

4 Brought forward knowledge

The examiner may test knowledge or techniques you've learnt at lower levels. As F2 is part of the Financial pillar, the content of paper F1 will be significant.

The exam paper

Format of the paper

		Number of marks
Section A:	Five compulsory medium answer questions, each worth 10 marks. Short scenarios may be given, to which some or all questions relate	50
Section B:	One or two compulsory questions. Short scenarios may be given, to which questions relate	50
		100

Time allowed: 3 hours, plus 20 minutes reading time

CIMA guidance

Good answers demonstrate knowledge and show understanding in the application thereof. Reading the scenario where applicable should give you clues on what issues or tools to use.

Weaker answers tend to repeat book knowledge without applying it to the question set. Candidates who fail reveal a lack of knowledge or depth in their understanding.

The key to passing this paper is to understand the concepts and techniques in the syllabus and show you can apply these to whatever situation presents itself in the exam.

Students should be able to:

- Prepare consolidated accounts and explain the accounting principles associated with this area, such as changes part way through an accounting period

- Appropriately employ relevant accounting standards

- Evaluate a business entity's financial statements and provide analysis of performance

- Explain the problems of profit measurement and alternative approaches to asset valuations

- Discuss and evaluate current developments in external reporting

Numerical content

The paper is approximately half numerical and half written. Both numerical and discursive parts are likely to be included in all sections of the paper.

Breadth of question coverage

Short scenarios may be given in Section A and some questions may be wholly discursive. Section B questions may be scenario-based and areas across the syllabus may be covered in one question.

Knowledge from other syllabuses

Candidates should also use their knowledge brought forward from paper F1.

May 2013 exam paper

Section A

1   Defined benefit pension plan

2   Goodwill, consolidated retained earnings and NCI

3   Ratio and trend analysis

4   Financial instruments

5   Human resource accounting

Section B

6   Consolidated statement of profit or loss and other comprehensive income and statement of changes in equity with NCI, foreign currency translation and impairment of goodwill

7   Analysis of financial performance and position for a potential investor and discussion of further information that would be useful in making the investment decision

March 2013 exam paper

Section A

1   Defined benefit pension plan and share-based payment

2   Goodwill, consolidated retained earnings, NCI and business combinations achieved in stages

3   Earnings per share with changes in capital structure, ratio analysis

4   Financial instruments

5   Environmental reporting

Section B

6   Consolidated statement of cash flows; bonus issue of shares

7   Analysis of performance and position for an expanding company using ratios; limitations of financial analysis based on published annual reports

November 2012 exam paper

Section A

1   Defined benefit pension plan; hyperinflation

2   Goodwill, consolidated retained earnings and NCI

3   Ratio analysis for working capital and liquidity

4   Financial instruments; foreign currency translation

5   International harmonisation; *Conceptual Framework*

Section B

6   Consolidated statement of financial position with NCI; financial instruments

7   Analysis of performance and position for a potential investor; discussion of further information that would be useful in making the investment decision; limitations of financial ratios

September 2012 exam paper

Section A

1   Defined benefit pension plan and share-based payment

2   Consolidated statement of cash flows with associate and NCI

3   Analysis of key financial indicators for a potential investor; limitations of financial analysis

4   Financial instruments

5   Human resource accounting and narrative reporting

Section B

6   Consolidated statement of financial position; discussion of treatment of business combinations achieved in stages; financial instruments

7   Analysis of performance and position for a potential investor using ratio analysis and earnings per share; discussion of further information that would be useful in making the investment decision

May 2012 exam paper

Section A

1   Defined benefit pension plan and share-based payment

2   Goodwill, consolidated retained earnings and NCI

3   Statement of cash flows and report for potential investor

4   Financial instruments

5   Human resource accounting

Section B

6   Consolidated statement of profit or loss and other comprehensive income and statement of changes in equity; discussion of treatment of investments in step acquisitions

7   Analysis of performance and position for a potential investor and discussion of further information that would be useful in making the investment decision

March 2012 exam paper

Section A

1   Share-based payments

2   Foreign exchange gain or loss; consolidated statement of profit or loss and other comprehensive income

3   Global Reporting Initiative

4   Financial instruments

5   Operating segments

Section B

6   Disposal of shares in subsidiary; consolidated statement of financial position

7   Analysis of financial performance including calculating ratios; contingent liabilities

November 2011 exam paper

Section A

1   Consolidated statement of financial position including joint arrangements

2   Sale of land; whether to consolidate another entity's results

3   Basic and diluted earnings per share

4   Financial instruments; pensions

5   Convergence and its benefits

Section B

6   Consolidated statement of profit or loss and other comprehensive income; IAS 21
7   Report analysing financial performance including calculating ratios; limitations of ratio analysis

September 2011 exam paper

Section A

1   Consolidated statement of financial position

2   Financial instruments; share options

3   Environmental reports

4   Substance over form; inflation accounting

5   Ratio analysis

Section B

6   Consolidated statement of cash flows
7   Report analysing financial performance including calculating ratios; earnings per share

May 2011 exam paper

Section A

1   Defined benefit pension plan and share-based payment

2   Consolidated statement of changes in equity with step acquisition

3   Discussion of usefulness of segment reporting

4   Financial instruments

5   Discussion of advantages and drawbacks of including voluntary narrative disclosures in the annual report

Section B

6   Consolidated statement of profit or loss and other comprehensive income and statement of financial position for a group with a foreign subsidiary
7   Analysis of performance and position for a potential investor and discussion of further information that would be useful in making the investment decision

March 2011 exam paper

Section A

1   Consolidated statement of profit or loss and other comprehensive income with subsidiary and associate

2   Discussion on human resource accounting

3   Share-based payment and defined benefit pension plan

4   Financial instruments

5   Financial analysis of a statement of cash flows

Section B

6   Consolidated statement of financial position with mid-year acquisition and fair value adjustments

7   Analysis of performance and position for an individual contemplating accepting employment with an entity, and discussion of limitations of ratio analysis

November 2010 exam paper

Section A

1   Share-based payment

2   Discussion on human resource accounting

3   Consolidated statement of profit or loss and other comprehensive income with subsidiary and associate

4   Financial instruments

5   Financial analysis (with pre-calculated ratios)

Section B

6   Consolidated statement of financial position with step acquisition

7   Analysis of performance and position in the context of a loan application

May 2010 exam paper

Section A

1   Classification of investments
2   Substance over form; share-based payments
3   Earnings per share
4   Consolidated statement of financial position workings: goodwill, consolidated retained earnings, NCI
5   Convergence between IFRS and US GAAP

Section B

6   Consolidated statement of profit or loss and other comprehensive income
7   Report on expansion plan, including ratio analysis

Specimen exam paper

Section A

1   Consolidated statement of profit or loss and other comprehensive income
2   Environmental reporting
3   Financial instruments, including accounting adjustments; share-based payments
4   Off-balance sheet finance; consolidated statement of financial position
5   Asset valuation and changing prices

Section B

6   Consolidated statement of cash flows
7   Report on a takeover target, including ratio analysis

ISSUES IN RECOGNITION AND MEASUREMENT

Part A

SUBSTANCE OVER FORM AND REVENUE RECOGNITION

This is a very topical area and has been for some time. Companies (and other entities) have in the past used the **legal form** of a transaction to determine its accounting treatment, when in fact the **substance** of the transaction has been very different. We will look at the question of **substance over form** and the kind of transactions undertaken by entities trying to avoid reporting true substance in Sections 1 and 2.

The main weapon in tackling these abuses is the IASB's *Framework for the Preparation and Presentation of Financial Statements* because it applies **general definitions** to the elements that make up financial statements. We will look at how this works in Section 3.

Sections 4 and 5 deal with examples of common abuses and a standard brought in to counter one form: **revenue recognition.**

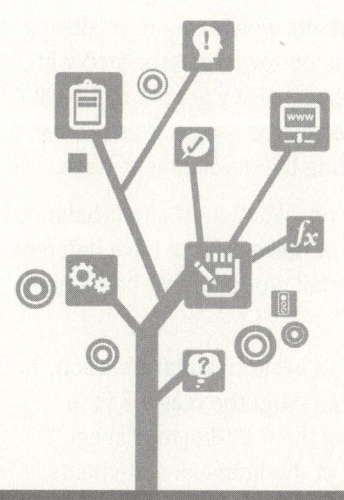

topic list	learning outcomes	syllabus references	ability required
1 Off-balance sheet finance explained	B1	B1 (ii)	Application
2 Substance over form	B1	B1 (ii)	Application
3 The IASB's *Framework for the preparation and presentation of financial statements*	B1	B1 (ii)	Application
4 Common forms of Substance over form	B1	B1 (ii)	Application
5 Revenue recognition	B1	B1 (ii)	Application

1   Off-balance sheet finance explained

Introduction

'Off-balance sheet transactions' are transactions which are not fully disclosed in the statement of financial position. Such transactions may involve the **removal of assets** from the statement of financial position, as well as liabilities, and they are also likely to have a significant impact on profit or loss.

KEY TERM

OFF-BALANCE SHEET FINANCE is the funding or refinancing of a company's operations in such a way that, under legal requirements and traditional accounting conventions, some or all of the finance may not be shown in its statement of financial position.

1.1 Why off-balance sheet finance exists

Why might company managers wish to enter into such transactions?

(a) In some countries, companies traditionally have a lower level of gearing than companies in other countries. Off-balance sheet finance is used to **keep gearing low**, probably because of the views of analysts and brokers.

(b) A company may need to keep its gearing down in order to stay within the terms of **loan covenants** imposed by lenders.

(c) A quoted company with high borrowings is often expected (by analysts and others) to declare a **rights issue** in order to reduce gearing. This has an adverse effect on a company's share price and so off-balance sheet financing is used to reduce gearing *and* the expectation of a rights issue.

(d) Analysts' short term views are a problem for companies **developing assets** which are not producing income during the development stage. Such companies will match the borrowings associated with the developing assets, along with the assets themselves, off-balance sheet. They are brought back into the statement of financial position once income is being generated by the assets. This process keeps return on capital employed higher than it would have been during the development stage.

(e) In the past, groups of companies have excluded **subsidiaries** from consolidation in an off-balance sheet transaction because they carry out completely different types of business and have different characteristics. The usual example is a leasing company (in say a retail group) which has a high level of gearing. This exclusion is now disallowed.

You can see from this brief list of reasons that the overriding motivation is to avoid **misinterpretation**. In other words, the company does not trust the analysts or other users to understand the reasons for a transaction and so avoids any effect such transactions might have by taking them off-balance sheet. Unfortunately, the position of the company is then misstated and the user of the financial statements is misled.

You must understand that not all forms of 'off-balance sheet finance' are undertaken for cosmetic or accounting reasons. Some transactions are carried out to **limit or isolate risk**, to reduce interest costs and so on. In other words, these transactions are in the best interests of the company, not merely a cosmetic repackaging of figures which would normally appear in the statement of financial position.

1.2 The off balance sheet finance problem

The result of the use of increasingly sophisticated off-balance sheet finance transactions is a situation where the users of financial statements do not have a proper or clear view of the **state of the company's affairs**. The disclosures required by national company law and accounting standards did not in the past provide sufficient rules for disclosure of off-balance sheet finance transactions and so very little of the true nature of the transaction was exposed.

Whatever the purpose of such transactions, **insufficient disclosure** creates a problem: if transactions were accounted for merely by recording their **legal form**, the accounting may not reflect the **real economic effect** of the transaction.

This problem has been debated over the years by the accountancy profession and other interested parties and some progress has been made (see the later sections of this chapter). However, company collapses during recessions have often revealed much higher borrowings than originally thought, because part of the borrowing was off-balance sheet.

IAS 8 *Accounting policies, changes in accounting estimates and errors* requires that an entity's accounting policies 'reflect the **economic substance** of transactions, other events and conditions, and not merely the **legal form**.'

Section summary

The subject of **off-balance sheet finance** is a complex one which has plagued the accountancy profession. In practice, off-balance sheet finance schemes are often very sophisticated and these are beyond the range of this syllabus.

2 Substance over form   5/10, 9/11

Introduction

This is a very important concept. It is used to **determine accounting treatment** in financial statements through accounting standards and so prevent off-balance sheet transactions. The following paragraphs give examples of where the principle of substance over form is enforced in various accounting standards.

KEY TERM

SUBSTANCE OVER FORM The principle that transactions and other events are accounted for and presented in accordance with their substance and economic reality and not merely their legal form.

2.1 IAS 18 *Revenue*

Revenue and expenses from the sale of goods is recognised when the conditions set out in IAS 18 are met. Generally, recognition should be when it is probable that **future economic benefits** will flow to the entity and when these benefits can be **measured reliably**.

The application of IAS 18 is a crucial part of the substance over form concept. We will discuss the standard in more detail in Section 5 below.

2.2 IAS 17 *Leases*

In IAS 17, there is an explicit requirement that if the lessor transfers substantially all the **risks and rewards of ownership** to the lessee, then, even though the legal title has not necessarily passed, the item being leased should be shown as an asset in the statement of financial position of the lessee and the amount due to the lessor should be shown as a liability.

2.3 IAS 24 *Related party disclosures*

IAS 24 requires financial statements to disclose fully any material transactions undertaken with a related party by the reporting entity, **regardless of any price charged**.

2.4 IAS 11 *Construction contracts*

In IAS 11, there is a requirement to account for **attributable profits** on construction contracts under the accruals basis of accounting. However, there may be a problem with realisation, since it is arguable whether we should account for profit which, although attributable to the work done, may not have been invoiced to the customer. The convention of substance over form is applied to justify ignoring the strict legal position.

2.5 IFRS 10 *Consolidated financial statements*

IFRS 10 *Consolidated financial statements* requires **structured entities** (previously known as '**special purpose entities**') to be consolidated in group consolidated financial statements.

We will look at this again in Section 4.4, and the topic of structured entities will be discussed in more detail in Chapter 6.

You may also hear the term **creative accounting** used in the context of reporting the substance of transactions. This can be defined simply as the manipulation of figures for a desired result. Remember, however, that it is very rare for a company, its directors or employees to manipulate results for the purpose of fraud. The major consideration is usually the effect the results will have on the company's share price.

Some areas open to abuse (although some of these loopholes have been closed) are given below and you should by now understand how these can distort a company results.

(a)   Income recognition and cut-off

(b)   Impairment of purchased goodwill

(c)   Manipulation of reserves

(d)   Revaluations and depreciation

(e)   Window dressing – transactions undertaken, eg loans repaid just before the year end and then reversed in the following period.

(f)   Changes in accounting policy

Exam alert

The May 2010 exam included a 5 mark part question on determining the economic substance of a transaction.

Question 1.1	Creative accounting

Learning outcomes B1

Creative accounting, off balance sheet finance and related matters (in particular how ratio analysis can be used to discover these practices) often come up in articles in the financial press. Find a library, preferably a good technical library, which can provide you with copies of back issues of such newspapers or journals and look for articles on creative accounting.

Section summary

Substance over form means that a transaction is accounted for according to its economic reality rather than its legal form.

3   The IASB's *Framework for the preparation and presentation of financial statements*   11/11

Introduction

As noted above, the IASB's *Framework for the preparation and presentation of financial statements* (referred to throughout this Text thereafter as *'Framework'*) states that accounting for items according to substance and economic reality and not merely legal form is a key determinant of reliable information

(a)   For the majority of transactions there is **no difference** between the two and therefore no issue.

(b)   For other transactions **substance and form diverge** and the choice of treatment can give different results due to non-recognition of an asset or liability even though benefits or obligations result.

The *Framework* is due to be replaced by the *Conceptual Framework for Financial Reporting*, which is currently being developed by the IASB. We will look at the *Conceptual Framework* in chapter 17. For the purposes of the exam, all references to the *Framework* relate to the *Framework for the preparation and presentation of financial statements*. However, you should be aware of the new developments with regards to the *Conceptual Framework*.

Full disclosure is not enough: all transactions must be **accounted for** correctly, with full disclosure of related details as necessary to give the user of accounts a full understanding of the transactions.

3.1 Relationship to IFRSs

The interaction of the *Framework* **with other standards** is also an important issue. Whichever rules are the more specific should be applied, given that IFRSs should be consistent with the *Framework*.

Leasing provides a good example: straightforward leases which fall squarely within the terms of IAS 17 should be accounted for without any need to refer to the *Framework*, but where their terms are more complex, or the lease is only one element in a larger series of transactions, then the *Framework* comes into play. In addition, the *Framework* implicitly requires that its general principle of substance over form should apply in the application of other existing rules.

3.2 Basic principles

The first step in determining whether a transaction should be recorded or disclosed in the financial statements is deciding whether the transaction concerned meets the definition of an **element** of the financial statements according to the Framework, or changes an existing element.

If the definition of an element is met, the transaction will be recognised if it meets the **recognition criteria**, as described in Section 3.4 below.

3.3 Definitions

The elements of the financial statements are defined as follows in the *Framework*.

KEY TERMS

An ASSET is a resource **controlled** by an entity as a result of **past events** and from which **future economic benefits** are expected to flow to the entity.

A LIABILITY is a **present obligation** of the entity arising from **past events**, the settlement of which is expected to result in an **outflow** from the entity of resources embodying economic benefits. *(Framework)*

Identification of **who has the risks** relating to an asset will generally indicate **who has the benefits** and hence **who has the asset**. If an entity is in certain circumstances unable to avoid an **outflow of benefits**, this will provide evidence that it has a liability.

The definitions given in the IASB *Framework* of income and expenses are not as important as those of assets and liabilities. This is because income and expenses are **described in terms of changes in assets and liabilities**, ie they are secondary definitions.

KEY TERMS

INCOME is increases in economic benefits during the accounting period in the form of inflows or enhancements of assets or decreases of liabilities that result in increases in equity, other than those relating to contributions from equity participants.

EXPENSES are decreases in economic benefits during the accounting period in the form of outflows or depletions of assets or incurrences of liabilities that result in decreases in equity, other than those relating to distributions to equity participants. *(Framework)*

The real importance, then, is the way the *Framework* defines assets and liabilities. This forces entities to acknowledge their assets and liabilities regardless of the legal status.

3.4 Recognition

KEY TERM

RECOGNITION is the process of incorporating in the statement of financial position or statement of profit or loss and other comprehensive income an item that meets the definition of an element and satisfies the criteria for recognition set out below. It involves the depiction of the item in words and by a monetary amount and the inclusion of that amount in the statement of financial position or statement of profit or loss and other comprehensive income totals.

The next key question is deciding **when** an asset or a liability has to be recognised in the statement of financial position. Where a transaction results in an item that meets the definition of an asset or liability, that item should be recognised in the statement of financial position if:

(a)   it is **probable** that any **future economic benefit** associated with the item will flow **to** or **from the entity**, and

(b)   the item has a cost or value that can be **measured reliably**.

This effectively prevents entities abusing the definitions of the elements by recognising items that are vague in terms of likelihood of occurrence and measurability. If this were not in force, entities could **manipulate the financial statements** in various ways, eg recognising assets when the likely future economic benefits cannot yet be determined.

Probability is assessed based on the situation at the end of the reporting period. For example, it is usually expected that some customers of an entity will not pay what they owe. The expected level of non-payment is based on past experience and the receivables asset is reduced by a percentage (the general bad debt provision).

Measurement must be reliable, but it does not preclude the use of **reasonable estimates**, which is an essential part of the financial statement preparation.

Even if something does not qualify for recognition now, it may meet the criteria **at a later date**.

3.5 Other standards

The *Framework* provides the general guidance for reporting the substance of transactions and preventing off balance sheet finance. The IASB has developed guidance for specific transactions. These were mentioned in Section 2 and they are covered in various parts of this text. You should consider the particular off-balance sheet finance problem they tackle as you study them.

- IAS 17 *Leases* (covered in Paper F1)
- IAS 18 *Revenue* (see Section 5)
- IAS 39 *Financial instruments: Recognition and Measurement* (in respect of the recognition and derecognition of financial assets and liabilities, such as loans. See Chapter 2)

Other areas where the *Framework* is important include:

- IFRS 10 *Consolidated financial statements* (see Chapter 6)
- IAS 24 *Related party disclosures* (covered in Paper F1)
- Harmonisation (see Chapter 17)
- Human resource accounting (see Chapter 18)

Section summary

Important points to remember from the *Framework* are:

- **Substance over form**
- Definitions of **assets** and **liabilities**
- Definition of **recognition**
- **Criteria** for recognition

4 Common forms of substance over form

Introduction

How does the theory of the *Framework* **apply in practice**, to real transactions? The rest of this section looks at some complex transactions that occur frequently in practice.

We will consider how the principles of the *Framework* would be applied to these transactions.

- Consignment inventory
- Sale and repurchase agreements/sale and leaseback agreements
- Factoring of receivables/debts
- Loan transfers/securitised assets

4.1 Consignment inventory

Consignment inventory is an arrangement where inventory is held by one party (say a dealer) but is owned by another party (for example a manufacturer or a finance company). Consignment inventory is common in the motor trade and is similar to goods sold on a 'sale or return' basis.

To identify the correct treatment, it is necessary to identify the point at which the dealer acquired the risks and benefits of the asset (the inventory item) rather than the point at which legal title was acquired.

4.1.1 Summary of indications of asset status

The following lists out some indications as to which company, the manufacturer or the dealer, has the risks and benefits of the asset. We will use the example of the automobile business for illustrative purposes.

Indications that ownership of the inventory belongs to the manufacturer	Indications that ownership of the inventory belongs to the dealer
Benefits:	
Price fixed at the date of legal transfer	Price fixed at delivery date
Manufacturer can require dealer to return inventory	Manufacturer cannot require dealer to return inventory
Dealer pays penalty for distance driven on test vehicles	Dealer can use vehicles for test purposes without penalty
Risks:	
Dealer has a right to return obsolete inventory	Dealer has no right of return
Dealer does not pay finance charge on slow-moving inventory	Dealer pays a finance charge
Manufacturer pays for the insurance	Dealer pays for the insurance
Dealer invoiced for financing when the dealer sells the inventory to third parties	Dealer invoiced for financing on the delivery of the inventory

4.1.2 Required accounting

The following apply where it is concluded that the inventory **is in substance an asset** of the dealer.

(a) The inventory should be recognised as such in the dealer's statement of financial position, together with a corresponding liability to the manufacturer.

(b) Any deposit should be deducted from the liability and the excess classified as a trade payable.

Where it is concluded that the inventory is **not in substance an asset** of the dealer, the following apply.

(a) The inventory should not be included in the dealer's statement of financial position until the transfer of risks and rewards has crystallised.

(b) Any deposit should be included under 'other receivables'.

Exam alert

If journal entries are required in the exam, you must write them out in the following format:

DEBIT   X

CREDIT   X

Being [narrative description of what the journal relates to, ie depreciation of property, plant and equipment for the year]

Question 1.2	Recognition

Learning outcomes B1

Daley Motors Co owns a number of car dealerships throughout a geographical area. The terms of the arrangement between the dealerships and the manufacturer are as follows. For each of terms below, state whether the asset and related liability should be recognised by Daley Co.

(a) Legal title passes when the cars are either used by Daley Co for demonstration purposes or sold to a third party.

(b)   The dealer has the right to return vehicles to the manufacturer without penalty. (Daley Co has rarely exercised this right in the past.)

(c)   The transfer price is based on the manufacturer's list price at the date of delivery.

(d)   Daley Co makes a substantial interest-free deposit based on the number of cars held.

4.2 Sale and repurchase agreements

These are arrangements under which the company sells an asset to another person on terms that allow the company to **repurchase the asset** in certain circumstances. A common example is the sale and repurchase of maturing whisky inventories.

The key question is whether the transaction is a **straightforward sale**, or whether it is, in effect, a **secured loan**. It is necessary to look at the arrangement to determine who has the rights to the economic benefits that the asset generates, and the terms on which the asset is to be repurchased.

If the seller keeps the right to the risks and benefits of the **use of the asset**, and the repurchase terms are such that the **repurchase is likely** to take place, the transaction should be accounted for as a **loan**. The repurchase of the asset would be recorded as a loan repayment.

4.2.1 Summary of indications of the sale of the asset

The following summary is helpful.

Indications that ownership of the asset has been transferred	Indications that ownership of the asset has not been transferred (secured loan)
Normal customer	Unusual customer (ie financial institution)
Sale price at market value	Sale price is less than **market value** at date of sale.
Normal timing	Unusual timing (eg a vineyard 'sells' unmatured wine and buys it back just in time to sell it to the public)
Option to repurchase the asset that is unlikely to be exercised, or offers no advantage over the rest of the market.	Obligation for **seller to repurchase** asset, or option to repurchase that is likely to be exercised
Risk of **changes in asset value** borne by buyer	Risk of **changes in asset value** borne by seller such that buyer receives solely a lender's return (eg repurchase price equals sale price plus costs plus interest)
Nature of the asset is such that it will be used over the life of the agreement, and seller has no rights to **determine its use**. Seller has no rights to determine asset's development or future sale.	Seller retains right to **determine asset's use**, development or sale, or rights to associated profits.

4.2.2 Required accounting

Where the substance of the transaction is that of a **secured loan**:

(a)   The seller should continue to recognise the original asset and record the proceeds received from the buyer as a liability.

(b)   Interest, however designated, should be accrued.

(c)   The carrying amount of the asset should be reviewed for impairment and written down if necessary.

The table below shows a comparison between the accounting treatment of a normal sale and that of a secured loan.

Accounting treatment	
Normal sale	**Secured loan**
If selling property, plant and equipment:	*When selling asset:*
Derecognise asset from statement of financial position and recognise profit/loss on disposal in profit or loss.	Keep asset in statement of profit or loss. Record sales proceeds as loan.
If selling inventory:	*Each year:*
Record revenue from sale	Record interest as finance cost in profit or loss and increase value of loan.
If selling property, plant and equipment:	*When selling asset:*
DEBIT Cash	DEBIT Cash
CREDIT Property, plant and equipment	CREDIT Loan
DEBIT/CREDIT Profit/loss on disposal	*Each year:*
If selling inventory:	DEBIT Finance cost
DEBIT Cash	CREDIT Loan
CREDIT Revenue	

4.2.3 Sale and leaseback transactions

A sale and leaseback transaction involves the sale of an asset and the leasing back of the same asset. The lease payment and the sale price are usually negotiated as a package.

The accounting treatment depends upon the type of lease involved. If the transaction results in a **finance lease**, then it is in substance a loan from the lessor to the lessee (the lessee has sold the asset and then leased it back), with the asset as security. In this case, any 'profit' on the sale should not be recognised as such, but should be deferred and amortised over the lease term.

If the transaction results in an **operating lease** and the transaction has been conducted at fair value, then it can be regarded as a normal sale transaction. The asset is derecognised and any profit on the sale is recognised. The operating lease instalments are treated as lease payments, rather than repayments of capital plus interest.

Question 1.3	Sale and repurchase

Learning outcomes B1

X Co are brandy distillers. They normally hold inventories for six years before selling it.

A large quantity of two-year old inventories has been sold to a bank at cost. The normal selling price is cost + 100% profit. X Co has an option to buy back the brandy in four years' time at a price which represents the original sale price plus interest at current market rates.

Required

Explain how the sale of the inventory transaction should be treated in X Co's financial statements in accordance with IFRS. Prepare any necessary journal entries to record the sale of the inventory in X Co's financial statements.

4.3 Factoring of receivables

Where debts or receivables are factored, the original creditor **sells the debts to the factor**. The sales price may be fixed at the outset or may be adjusted later. It is also common for the factor to offer a credit facility that allows the seller to draw upon a proportion of the amounts owed (ie to receive cash immediately).

In order to determine the correct accounting treatment, it is necessary to consider whether the risks of the debts has been passed on to the factor, or whether the factor is, in effect, providing a loan on the security of the receivables.

If the seller has to **pay interest** on the difference between the amounts advanced to him and the amounts that the factor has received, and if the seller bears the **risks of non-payment** by the debtor, then the indications would be that the transaction is, in effect, a loan.

4.3.1 Summary of indications of appropriate treatment

The following summarises some indications of whether the ownership of the debts have passed from the seller (the original creditor) to the factor, or whether they remain with the seller.

Indications the debts belong to the seller	Indications that the debts do not belong to the seller
Finance cost varies with speed of collection of debts.	Transfer is for a single non-returnable fixed sum.
There is full recourse to the seller for losses (ie debts over a certain age are returned to the seller for repayment).	There is no recourse to the seller for losses (ie. bad debts cannot be returned to the seller for repayment).
Seller pays a finance charge on outstanding debts.	Seller does not pay a finance charge on outstanding debts.

4.3.2 Accounting treatment

Where the ownership of the receivables has been transferred from the seller to the factor, the receivables should be removed from its statement of financial position.

Where the seller retains ownership of the receivables, an asset representing the receivables balance should be shown in the statement of financial position of the seller within assets, and a corresponding liability in respect of the proceeds received from the factor should be shown within liabilities.

The interest element of the factor's charges should be recognised as it accrues and included in profit or loss with other interest charges. Other factoring costs should be similarly accrued.

Accounting treatment	
Seller transfers ownership of receivables to factor	**Seller retains ownership of receivables**
Derecognise receivables from statement of financial position.	Keep receivables in seller's statement of financial position.
	Record factor proceeds as a **loan**.
When selling receivables:	*When selling receivables:*
DEBIT Cash	DEBIT Cash
CREDIT Trade receivables	CREDIT Loan
No further journals.	*If factor collects cash from customers:*
	DEBIT Loan
	CREDIT Trade receivables
	If factor returns debts to seller:
	DEBIT Loan
	CREDIT Cash
	And
	DEBIT Bad debt expense
	CREDIT Trade receivables

Question 1.4

Debt factoring

Learning outcomes B1

Apple Co sells all of its trade receivables to Factor Co, the terms of the arrangement being as follows.

(a)   Factor Co administers the sales ledger of Apple Co charging 1% of factored debts.

(b)   Factor Co maintains a ledger detailing transactions with Apple Co. The account is debited with any amounts advanced to Apple Co (the amount is restricted to 75% of all factored debts) and credited with amounts collected by Factor Co from debtors.

(c)   Interest is charged on a daily basis at national base rate + 3%.

(d)   Any debts not recovered after 90 days are transferred back to Apple Co for immediate cash payment.

(e)   On termination the balance on the factoring account is settled in cash.

Required

Explain the accounting treatment and the journal required in Apple Co's financial statements when they sell the receivables to Factor Co.

4.4 Structured entities (special purpose entities)

KEY TERM

A STRUCTURED ENTITY is an entity that has been designed so that voting or similar rights are not the dominant factor in deciding who controls the entity, such as when any voting rights relate to administrative tasks only and the relevant activities are directed by means of contractual arrangements. (IFRS 12 *Disclosures of interests in other entities*.)

BPP
LEARNING MEDIA

At first glance, these entities do not appear to be subsidiaries. However, if they meet the definition of **control** according to IFRS 10 *Consolidated financial statements*, they behave like subsidiaries in substance, and should therefore be consolidated.

KEY POINT

The syllabus also mentions the question of control in **structured entities**. This will be dealt with in Chapter 6.

4.5 Loan transfers/securitised assets

These are similar to the **factoring of receivables**, such as loans receivable being transferred to a third party or to a **structured entity** (set up for that specific purpose) as part of a financing scheme.

Whether the debts should be derecognised and cash received treated as a loan depends on which party bears the risks and benefits of ownership.

Benefits include the future cash flows from payments of principal and interest.

Risks would include credit risk, slow payment risk, variable interest rate risk, early redemption risk and moral risk (moral obligation to fund any losses on the loans).

Section summary

We have looked at some of the **major types** of substance-over-form transactions, including factoring, sales and leaseback, and consignment inventory.

5 Revenue recognition   **11/11**

Introduction

Accruals accounting is based on the **matching of costs with the revenue they generate**.

5.1 Introduction

It is crucially important in accruals accounting that we can establish the point at which revenue may be recognised in the statement of profit or loss so that the correct treatment can be applied to the related costs. For example:

- The costs of producing an item of finished goods should be carried as an asset in the statement of financial position until such time as it is sold.

- When the item is sold, a **sale is recorded in profit or loss** (the revenue from the sale recognised and the related costs expensed) as the **asset is derecognised in the statement of financial position**.

Which of these two treatments should be applied cannot be decided until it is clear at what moment the sale of the item takes place.

The decision has a **direct impact on profit**, since it would be unacceptable to recognise the profit on sale until a sale had taken place in accordance with the criteria of revenue recognition.

Revenue is generally recognised as **earned at the point of sale**, because at that point four criteria will generally have been met.

(a)   The goods or service have been **provided to the buyer**.

(b)   The buyer has **recognised his liability** to pay for the goods or services provided. The converse of this is that the seller has recognised that ownership of goods has passed from himself to the buyer.

(c)   The buyer has indicated his **willingness to hand over cash** or other assets in settlement of his liability.

(d)   The **monetary value** of the goods or services has been established.

At earlier points in the business cycle, there will not in general be **firm evidence** that the above criteria will be met. Until work on a product is complete, there is a risk that some flaw in the manufacturing process will necessitate its writing off; even when the product is complete there is no guarantee that it will find a buyer.

At later points in the business cycle, for example when cash is received for the sale, the recognition of revenue may occur quite some time after related costs were charged. Revenue recognition would then depend on fortuitous circumstances, such as the cash flow of a company's customers, and might fluctuate misleadingly from one period to another.

There are times when revenue is **recognised at other times than at the completion of a sale** – for example, in the recognition of profit on long-term construction contracts. Under IAS 11 *Construction contracts,* contract revenue and contract costs associated with the construction contract should be recognised as revenue and expenses respectively, by reference to the stage of completion of the contract activity at the end of the reporting period.

(a)   Because of the length of time taken to complete such contracts, if we defer recording revenue and costs until completion, this may cause the statement of profit or loss and other comprehensive income to be skewed by the contracts which have been completed by the year end, rather than reflecting a fair view of the company's activities throughout the year.

(b)   Revenue in this case is recognised when production on, say, a section of the total contract is complete, even though no sale can be made until the whole is complete.

5.2 IAS 18 Revenue

IAS 18 governs the recognition of revenue in specific (common) types of transaction. Generally, recognition should be when it is probable that **future economic benefits** will flow to the entity and when these benefits can be **measured reliably**.

Income, as defined by the IASB's *Framework* (see Section 3.3 above), includes both revenues and gains. Revenue is income arising in the ordinary course of an entity's activities and it may be called different names, such as sales, fees, interest, dividends or royalties.

Exam alert

You may typically be asked to discuss how a transaction should be accounted for in accordance with the principles of IAS 18 *Revenue* and the *Framework*. As the examinable transactions tend to involve sale of goods, it is important to know the revenue recognition criteria for the sale of goods under IAS 18.

5.3 Scope

IAS 18 covers the revenue from specific types of transaction or events.

- **Sale of goods** (manufactured products and items purchased for resale)
- **Rendering of services**
- Use by others of entity assets yielding **interest, royalties and dividends**

For your exam, the first type of transaction is the most important one. When the entity has transferred the risks and rewards of ownership, in substance the asset no longer belongs to the entity and therefore the asset should be derecognised (ie removed from the books), and a sale should be recorded.

Interest, royalties and dividends are included as income, because they arise from the use of an entity's assets by other parties.

KEY TERMS

INTEREST is the charge for the use of cash or cash equivalents or amounts due to the entity.

ROYALTIES are charges for the use of non-current assets of the entity, eg patents, computer software and trademarks.

DIVIDENDS are distributions of profit to holders of equity investments, in proportion with their holdings, of each relevant class of capital.

The standard specifically **excludes** various types of revenue arising from leases, insurance contracts, changes in value of financial instruments or other current assets, natural increases in agricultural assets and mineral ore extraction.

5.4 Definitions

KEY TERMS

REVENUE is the gross inflow of economic benefits during the period arising in the course of the ordinary activities of an entity when those inflows result in increases in equity, other than increases relating to contributions from equity participants. (*IAS 8*)

FAIR VALUE is the price that would be received to sell an asset or paid to transfer a liability in an orderly transaction between market participants at the measurement date. (*IFRS 13*)

Revenue **does not include** sales taxes, value added taxes or goods and service taxes which are only collected for third parties, because these do not represent an economic benefit flowing to the entity. The same is true for revenues collected by an agent on behalf of a principal. Revenue for the agent is only the commission received for acting as agent.

5.5 Measurement of revenue

When a transaction takes place, the amount of revenue is usually decided by the **agreement of the buyer and seller**. The revenue is actually measured, however, as the **fair value of the consideration received**, which will take account of any trade discounts and volume rebates.

5.6 Identification of the transaction

Normally, each transaction can be looked at **as a whole**. Sometimes, however, transactions are more complicated, and it is necessary to break a transaction down into its **component parts**. For example, a sale may include the transfer of goods and the provision of future servicing, the revenue for which should be deferred over the period the service is performed.

At the other end of the scale, **seemingly separate transactions must be considered together** if apart they lose their commercial meaning. An example would be to sell an asset with an agreement to buy it back at a later date. The second transaction cancels the first and so both must be considered together. We looked at sale and repurchase in paragraph 4.2.

5.7 Sale of goods

Revenue from the sale of goods should only be recognised when **all** these conditions are satisfied.

(a)   The entity has transferred the **significant risks and rewards** of ownership of the goods to the buyer

(b)   The entity has **no continuing managerial involvement** to the degree usually associated with ownership, and no longer has effective control over the goods sold

(c)   The amount of revenue can be **measured reliably**

(d)   It is probable that the **economic benefits** associated with the transaction will flow to the entity

(e)   The **costs incurred** in respect of the transaction can be measured reliably

The transfer of risks and rewards can only be decided by examining each transaction. Mainly, the transfer occurs at the same time as either the **transfer of legal title**, or the **passing of possession** to the buyer – this is what happens when you buy something in a shop.

If **significant risks and rewards remain with the seller**, then the transaction is *not* a sale and revenue cannot be recognised – for example, if the receipt of the revenue from a particular sale depends on the buyer selling on the goods.

It is possible for the seller to retain only an **'insignificant' risk of ownership** and for the sale and revenue to be recognised. The main example here is where the seller retains the title to the goods, only to ensure collection of what is owed on the goods. This is a common commercial situation, and when it arises the revenue should be recognised on the date of sale.

The probability of the entity receiving the revenue arising from a transaction must be assessed. Sometimes, the probability of receiving economic benefits only arises when an uncertainty is removed – for example, government permission for funds to be received from another country. Only when the uncertainty is removed should the revenue be recognised. This is in contrast with the situation where revenue has already been recognised but where the **collectability of the cash** is brought into doubt. Where recovery has ceased to be probable, the amount should be recognised as an expense, *not* an adjustment of the revenue previously recognised. These points also refer to services and interest, royalties and dividends below.

Matching should take place, ie the revenue and expenses relating to the same transaction should be recognised at the same time. It is usually easy to estimate expenses at the date of sale (eg warranty costs, shipment costs, etc). Where they cannot be estimated reliably, then revenue cannot be recognised; any consideration which has already been received is treated as a liability.

Example: accounting for sale

A washing machine sells for $500 with a one-year warranty. The dealer knows from experience that 15% of these machines develop a fault in the first year and that the average cost of repair is $100. He sells 200 machines. How does he account for this sale?

Solution

He will recognise revenue of $100,000 ($500 × 200) and an associated expense of $3,000 ($100 × 200 × 15%).

Section summary

Revenue recognition is straightforward in most business transactions, but some situations are more complicated and some give opportunities for manipulation.

Chapter Roundup

✓ The subject of **off-balance sheet finance** is a complex one which has plagued the accountancy profession. In practice, off-balance sheet finance schemes are often very sophisticated and these are beyond the range of this syllabus.

✓ **Substance over form** means that a transaction is accounted for according to its economic reality rather than its legal form.

✓ Important points to remember from the *Framework* are:

- **Substance over form**
- Definitions of **assets** and **liabilities**
- Definition of **recognition**
- **Criteria** for recognition

✓ We have looked at some of the **major types** of off-balance sheet finance, including factoring, sale and leaseback and consignment inventory.

✓ Revenue recognition is straightforward in most business transactions, but some situations are more complicated and give some opportunities for manipulation.

Quick Quiz

1   Why do companies want to use off-balance sheet finance?

2   How does the *Framework* describe substance over form?

3   What is a quasi subsidiary?

4   How has the use of quasi subsidiaries been curtailed?

5   What are the common features of transactions whose substance is not readily apparent?

6   When should a transaction be recognised?

Answers to Quick Quiz

1   The overriding motivation is to avoid misinterpretation. However, users are often misled.

2   The principle that transactions and other events are accounted for and presented in accordance with their substance and economic reality rather than merely their legal form.

3   An entity that does not fulfil the definition of a subsidiary but is directly or indirectly controlled by the reporting entity and gives rise to benefits that are in substance no different from those arising if it were a subsidiary.

4   By IFRS 10 – the definition of a subsidiary based on **power** rather than ownership.

5   (a)   The legal title is separated from the ability to enjoy benefits.

(b)   The transaction is linked to others so that the commercial effect cannot be understood without reference to the complete series.

(c)   The transaction includes one or more options under such terms that it is likely the option(s) will be exercised.

6   When it is probable that a future inflow or outflow of economic benefit to the entity will occur and the item can be measured in monetary terms with sufficient reliability.

Answers to Questions

1.1 Creative accounting

Well done if you did this research.

1.2 Recognition

(a) Legal form is irrelevant

(b) Yes: only because rarely exercised (otherwise 'no')

(c) Yes

(d) Yes: the dealership is effectively forgoing the interest which could be earned on the cash sum

1.3 Sale and repurchase

Although legally X Co has sold the inventories, they have not transferred the risks and benefits and in substance, this is not a true sale but a loan. The following unusual terms of the agreement support the conclusion that this is a secured loan:

(a) Unusual customer (bank)

(b) Unusual timing/price (sold two-year-old goods at cost and usually sell six-year-old at cost plus 100% mark up)

(c) Option to buy back on maturity of brandy (keep benefits)

(d) Option likely to be exercised given that this represents X Co's inventories in trade

(e) The bank receives a lender's return.

As a result:

(a) Inventories should remain on X Co's statement of financial position at cost

(b) An equivalent amount reflected as a liability:

DEBIT   Cash

CREDIT   Loan

Being recording sale of inventories as a loan.

(c) The interest should be recognised as a finance cost in profit or loss over the four years of the agreement:

DEBIT   Finance cost

CREDIT   Loan

Being interest accrued on the loan.

1.4 Debt factoring

On the sale of the receivables, Factor Co has the legal title. However, in substance, Apple Co retains the risks inherent in the receivables:

(a) Debts older than 90 days can be returned by the factor to Apple Co so Apple Co keeps the bad debt risk.

(b) Apple Co has to pay the factor interest on outstanding balances so Apple Co retains the slow movement risk.

The receivables should stay on the statement of financial position of Apple Co until they either go bad or the factor collects the amounts owing from the customers.

Any amounts advanced by the factor should be shown as a loan:

DEBIT   Cash

CREDIT   Loan

Being recognition of factor proceeds as a loan.

Now try this question from the Exam Question Bank

Number	Level	Marks	Time
Q1	Examination	10	18 mins

FINANCIAL INSTRUMENTS

 Financial instruments sounds like a daunting subject, and indeed this is a complex and controversial area. The numbers involved in financial instruments are often huge, but don't let this put you off. In this chapter we aim to simplify the topic as much as possible and to focus on the important issues.

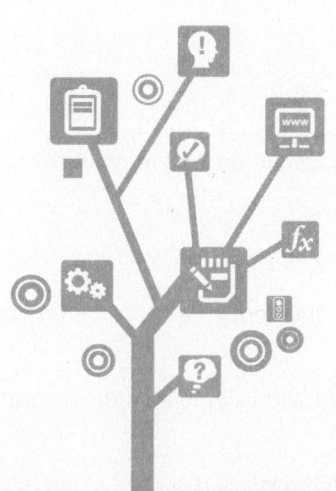

topic list	learning outcomes	syllabus references	ability required
1 Financial instruments	B1	B1 (iii), (iv)	Application
2 Presentation of financial instruments	B1	B1 (iii), (iv)	Application
3 Recognition of financial instruments	B1	B1 (iii), (iv)	Application
4 Measurement of financial instruments	B1	B1 (iii), (iv)	Application
5 Hedging	B1	B1 (iii), (iv)	Application
6 Disclosure of financial instruments	B1	B1 (iii), (iv)	Application

1 Financial instruments

Introduction

If you read the financial press you will probably be aware of **rapid international expansion** in the use of financial instruments. These vary from straightforward, traditional instruments, eg bonds, through to various forms of so-called 'derivative instruments'.

Exam alert

IAS 39 is being replaced by IFRS 9 *Financial Instruments,* currently a work in progress. However, IFRS 9, which will not come into force until 2015, is not examinable in 2013.

1.1 Background

The dynamic nature of international financial markets has resulted in the widespread use of a variety of financial instruments. Prior to the issue of IAS 32, many financial instruments were '**off-balance-sheet**', being neither recognised nor disclosed in the financial statements while still exposing the shareholders to significant risks.

Why was a project to create a set of accounting standards for financial instruments was considered necessary?

(a)   The **significant growth of financial instruments** over recent years has outstripped the development of guidance for their accounting.

(b)   The topic is of **international concern**.

(c)   There have been recent **high-profile disasters** involving derivatives (eg Barings) which, while not caused by accounting failures, have raised questions about accounting and disclosure practices.

These are three Standards on financial instruments:

(a)   IAS 32 *Financial instruments: Presentation*, which deals with:

(i)   The classification of financial instruments between liabilities and equity
(ii)   Presentation of certain compound instruments

(b)   IFRS 7 *Financial instruments: Disclosures*, which revised, simplified and incorporated disclosure requirements previously in IAS 32.

(c)   IAS 39 *Financial instruments: Recognition and measurement*, which deals with:

(i)   Recognition and derecognition
(ii)   The measurement of financial instruments
(iii)   Hedge accounting

1.2 Classifications (IAS 32)

Financial instruments fall into three categories, summarised in the diagram below.

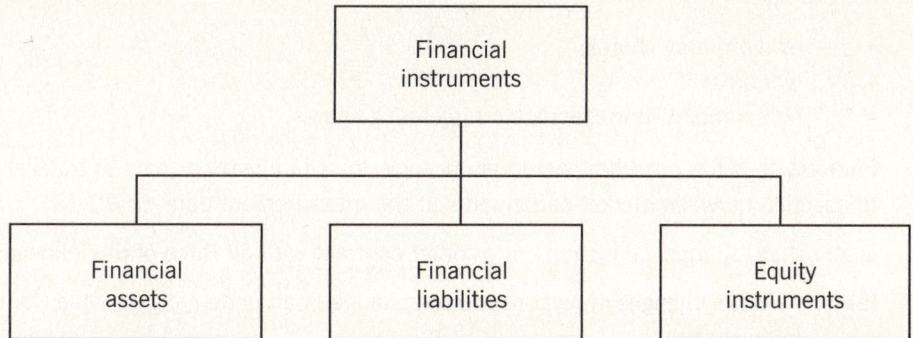

Financial liabilities are treated as 'debt' in financial analysis and equity instruments as 'equity'. Their classification is therefore fundamental to the accuracy of the gearing calculation.

1.3 Definitions

The most important definitions are common to all three Standards.

KEY TERMS

FINANCIAL INSTRUMENT. Any contract that gives rise to both a financial asset of one entity and a financial liability or equity instrument of another entity.

FINANCIAL ASSET. Any asset that is:

(a)   cash

(b)   an equity instrument of another entity

(c)   a contractual right:

(i)   to receive cash or another financial asset from another entity; or

(ii)   to exchange financial assets or financial liabilities with another entity under conditions that are potentially favourable to the entity; or

(d)   a contract that will or may be settled in the entity's own equity instruments.

For example:

- trade receivables;
- options;
- shares (as an investment).

FINANCIAL LIABILITY. Any liability that is:

(a)   a contractual obligation:

(i)   to deliver cash or another financial asset to another entity, or

(ii)   to exchange financial assets or financial liabilities with another entity under conditions that are potentially unfavourable to the entity; or

(b)   a contract that will or may be settled in the entity's own equity instruments.

For example:

- trade payables;
- debenture loans (payable);
- mandatorily redeemable preference shares;
- cumulative irredeemable preference shares;
- forward contracts standing at a loss.

KEY TERMS

EQUITY INSTRUMENT. Any contract that evidences a residual interest in the assets of an entity after deducting all of its liabilities.

For example:

- own ordinary shares;
- warrants;
- non-cumulative irredeemable preference shares.

FAIR VALUE is the price that would be received to sell an asset or paid to transfer a liability in an orderly transaction between market participants at the measurement date. (*IFRS 13*)

DERIVATIVE. A financial instrument or other contract with all three of the following characteristics:

(a)   its value changes in response to the change in an underlying variable (for example, share price or interest rate)

(b)   it requires little or no initial net investment; and

(c)   it is settled at a future date.

Exam alert

These definitions are very important – particularly for financial assets, financial liabilities and equity instruments – so learn them.

We should clarify some points arising from these definitions. Firstly, one or two terms above should be themselves defined.

(a)   A '**contract**' need not be in writing, but it must comprise an agreement that has 'clear economic consequences' and which the parties to it cannot avoid, usually because the agreement is enforceable in law.

(b)   An '**entity**' here could be an individual, partnership, incorporated body or government agency.

The definitions of **financial assets and financial liabilities** may seem rather circular, referring as they do to the terms financial asset and financial instrument. The point is that there may be a chain of contractual rights and obligations, but it will lead ultimately to the receipt or payment of cash *or* the acquisition or issue of an equity instrument.

Financial instruments include both of the following.

(a)   **Primary instruments**: eg receivables, payables and equity securities

(b)   **Derivative instruments**: eg financial options, futures and forwards, interest rate swaps and currency swaps, **whether recognised or unrecognised**

IAS 32 makes it clear that the following items are *not* financial instruments.

- **Physical assets**, eg inventories, property, plant and equipment, leased assets and intangible assets (patents, trademarks etc)

- **Prepaid expenses**, deferred revenue and most warranty obligations

- Liabilities or assets that are **not contractual** in nature

- Contractual rights/obligations that **do not involve transfer of a financial asset**, eg commodity futures contracts, operating leases

Question 2.1	Why not?

Learning outcomes B1

Can you give the reasons why the first two items listed above do not qualify as financial instruments?

Contingent rights and obligations meet the definition of financial assets and financial liabilities respectively, even though many do not qualify for recognition in financial statements. The reason for this is the contractual rights or obligations exist because of a past transaction or event (eg assumption of a guarantee).

1.4 Derivatives

A **derivative** is a financial instrument that **derives** its value from the price or rate of an underlying item. As seen above, it has three characteristics, as follows.

(a)   Its value changes in response to an underlying variable eg share price or interest rate.

(b)   It requires little or no initial net investment.

(c)   It is settled at a future date.

Common **examples** of derivatives include:

(a)   **Forward contracts**: agreements to buy or sell an asset at a fixed price at a fixed future date

(b)   **Futures contracts**: similar to forward contracts except that contracts are standardised and traded on an exchange

(c)   **Options**: rights (but not obligations) for the option holder to exercise at a pre-determined price; the option writer loses out if the option is exercised

(d)   **Swaps**: agreements to swap one set of cash flows for another (normally interest rate or currency swaps).

The nature of derivatives often gives rise to **particular problems**. The **value** of a derivative (and the amount at which it is eventually settled) depends on **movements** in an underlying item (such as an exchange rate). This means that settlement of a derivative can lead to a very different result from the one originally envisaged. A company which has derivatives is exposed to **uncertainty and risk** (potential for gain or loss) and this can have a very material effect on its financial performance, financial position and cash flows.

Yet, because a derivative contract normally has **little or no initial cost**, under traditional accounting it **may not be recognised** in the financial statements at all. Alternatively, it may be recognised at an amount which bears no relation to its current value. This is clearly **misleading** and leaves users of the financial statements unaware of the **level of risk** that the company faces. IAS 32 and 39 were developed in order to correct this situation.

1.5 Overview

•   Three accounting standards are relevant:

   –   **IAS 32**: *Financial instruments: Presentation*
   –   **IFRS 7**: *Financial instruments: Disclosures*
   –   **IAS 39**: *Financial instruments: Recognition and measurement*

•   The definitions of **financial asset, financial liability** and **equity instrument** are fundamental to the standards.

•   Financial instruments include:

   –   **Primary** instruments
   –   **Derivative** instruments

Section summary

Financial instruments can be very complex, particularly **derivative instruments**, although **primary instruments** are more straightforward.

The important definitions to learn are:

- **Financial asset**
- **Financial liability**
- **Equity instrument**

2 Presentation of financial instruments

Introduction

The presentation of financial instruments is covered by IAS 32.

2.1 Objective

The objective of IAS 32 is to 'establish principles for presenting financial instruments as liabilities or equity and for offsetting financial assets and financial liabilities.'

2.2 Scope

IAS 32 should be applied in the presentation of **all types of financial instruments**, whether recognised or unrecognised.

Certain items are **excluded**.

- Interests in subsidiaries (IFRS 10: Chapter 6)
- Interests in associates and joint ventures (IAS 28: Chapter 9)
- Interests in joint arrangements (IFRS 11: Chapter 9)
- Pensions and other post-retirement benefits (IAS 19: Chapter 3)
- Insurance contracts
- Contracts for contingent consideration in a business combination
- Contracts that require a payment based on climatic, geological or other physical variables
- Financial instruments, contracts and obligations under share-based payment transactions (IFRS 2: Chapter 4)

2.3 Liabilities and equity   5/11

The main thrust of IAS 32 here is that financial instruments should be presented according to their **substance, not merely their legal form**. In particular, entities which issue financial instruments should classify them (or their component parts) as **either financial liabilities, or equity**.

The classification of a financial instrument as a liability or as equity depends on the following.

- The substance of the contractual arrangement on initial recognition
- The definitions of a financial liability and an equity instrument

How should a **financial liability be distinguished from an equity instrument**? The critical feature of a **liability** is an **obligation** to transfer economic benefit. Therefore a financial instrument is a financial liability if there is a **contractual obligation** on the issuer either to deliver cash or another financial asset to

the holder or to exchange another financial instrument with the holder under potentially unfavourable conditions to the issuer.

The financial liability exists **regardless of the way in which the contractual obligation will be settled**. The issuer's ability to satisfy an obligation may be restricted, eg by lack of access to foreign currency, but this is irrelevant as it does not remove the issuer's obligation or the holder's right under the instrument.

Where the above critical feature is *not* met, then the financial instrument is an **equity instrument**. IAS 32 explains that although the holder of an equity instrument may be entitled to a *pro rata* share of any distributions out of equity, the issuer does *not* have a contractual obligation to make such a distribution.

Although substance and legal form are often **consistent with each other**, this is not always the case. In particular, a financial instrument may have the legal form of equity, but in substance it is in fact a liability. Other instruments may combine features of both equity instruments and financial liabilities.

For example, many entities issue **preference shares** which must be **redeemed** by the issuer for a fixed (or determinable) amount at a fixed (or determinable) future date. In such cases, the issuer has an **obligation**. Therefore the instrument is a **financial liability** and should be classified as such.

Another example is **cumulative irredeemable preference shares**. While the issuer does not redeem the preference shares, there is an obligation on the issuer to pay fixed dividends. If the entity has insufficient retained earnings in a given year, the dividends still must be paid in future years. Again, because the issuer has an obligation, the instrument should be classified as a financial liability.

The classification of the financial instrument is made when it is **first recognised** and this classification will continue until the financial instrument is removed from the entity's statement of financial position.

2.4 Contingent settlement provisions

An entity may issue a financial instrument where the way in which it is settled depends on:

(a)   The occurrence or non-occurrence of uncertain future events, or

(b)   The outcome of uncertain circumstances,

that are beyond the control of both the holder and the issuer of the instrument. For example, an entity might have to deliver cash instead of issuing equity shares. In this situation, it is not immediately clear whether the entity has an equity instrument or a financial liability.

Such financial instruments should be classified as **financial liabilities** unless the possibility of settlement is remote.

2.5 Settlement options

When a derivative financial instrument gives one party a **choice** over how it is settled (eg, the issuer can choose whether to settle in cash or by issuing shares) the instrument is a **financial asset** or a **financial liability** unless **all the alternative choices** would result in it being an equity instrument.

2.6 Compound financial instruments   5/11

Some financial instruments contain both a liability and an equity element. In such cases, IAS 32 requires the component parts of the instrument to be **classified separately**, according to the substance of the contractual arrangement and the definitions of a financial liability and an equity instrument.

One of the most common types of compound instrument is **convertible debt**. This creates a primary financial liability of the issuer and grants an option to the holder of the instrument to convert it into an equity instrument (usually ordinary shares) of the issuer. This is the economic equivalent of the issue of conventional debt plus a warrant to acquire shares in the future.

Although in theory there are several possible ways of calculating the split, the following method is recommended:

(a)   Calculate the value for the liability component.

(b)   Deduct this from the instrument as a whole to leave a residual value for the equity component.

The reasoning behind this approach is that an entity's equity is its residual interest in its assets amount after deducting all its liabilities.

The **sum of the carrying amounts** assigned to liability and equity will always be equal to the carrying amount that would be ascribed to the instrument **as a whole**.

Example: valuation of compound instruments

Rathbone Co issues 2,000 convertible bonds at the start of 20X2. The bonds have a three year term, and are issued at par with a face value of $1,000 per bond, giving total proceeds of $2,000,000. Interest is payable annually in arrears at a nominal annual interest rate of 6%. Each bond is convertible at any time up to maturity into 250 common shares.

When the bonds are issued, the prevailing market interest rate for similar debt without conversion options is 9%. At the issue date, the market price of one common share is $3. The dividends expected over the three year term of the bonds amount to 14c per share at the end of each year. The risk-free annual interest rate for a three year term is 5%.

Required

What is the value of the equity component in the bond?

Solution

The liability component is valued first, and the difference between the proceeds of the bond issue and the fair value of the liability is assigned to the equity component. The present value of the liability component is calculated using a discount rate of 9%, the market interest rate for similar bonds having no conversion rights, as shown.

	$
Present value of the principal: $2,000,000 payable at the end of three years ($2m × 0.772)*	1,544,000
Present value of the interest: $120,000 payable annually in arrears for three years ($120,000 × 2.531)*	303,725
Total liability component	1,847,720
Equity component (balancing figure)	152,280
Proceeds of the bond issue	2,000,000

* These figures can be obtained from discount and annuity tables.

The split between the liability and equity components remains the same throughout the term of the instrument, even if there are changes in the **likelihood of the option being exercised.** This is because it is not always possible to predict how a holder will behave. The issuer continues to have an obligation to make future payments until conversion, maturity of the instrument or some other relevant transaction takes place.

2.7 Treasury shares

If an entity **reacquires its own equity instruments**, those instruments ('treasury shares') shall be **deducted from equity**. No gain or loss shall be recognised in profit or loss on the purchase, sale, issue or cancellation of an entity's own equity instruments. Consideration paid or received shall be recognised directly in equity.

2.8 Interest, dividends, losses and gains

As well as looking at statement of financial position presentation, IAS 32 considers how financial instruments affect the profit or loss (and movements in equity). The treatment varies according to whether interest, dividends, losses or gains relate to a financial liability or an equity instrument.

(a)   Interest, dividends, losses and gains relating to a financial instrument (or component part) classified as a **financial liability** should be recognised as **income or expense** in profit or loss.

(b)   Distributions to holders of a financial instrument classified as an **equity instrument** should be **debited directly to equity** by the issuer.

(c)   **Transaction costs** of an equity transaction shall be accounted for as a **deduction from equity** (unless they are directly attributable to the acquisition of a business, in which case they are accounted for under IFRS 3).

You should look at the requirements of IAS 1 *Presentation of financial statements* for further details of disclosure, and IAS 12 *Income taxes* for disclosure of tax effects.

2.9 Key points

- Financial instruments issued to raise capital must be classified as **liabilities** or **equity**

- The **substance** of the financial instrument is more important than its **legal form**

- The **critical feature of a financial liability** is the contractual obligation to deliver cash or another financial instrument

- **Compound instruments** are split into equity and liability parts and presented accordingly

- **Interest, dividends, losses and gains** are treated according to whether they relate to an equity instrument or a financial liability

Section summary

Financial instruments must be classified as **liabilities** or **equity** according to their **substance.**

The critical feature of a financial liability is the **contractual obligation to deliver cash** or another financial asset.

Compound instruments are split into **equity** and **liability** components and presented accordingly in the statement of financial position.

3   Recognition of financial instruments   9/12, 11/12

Introduction

IAS 39 *Financial instruments: Recognition and measurement* establishes principles for recognising and measuring financial assets and financial liabilities.

3.1 Scope

IAS 39 applies to **all entities** and to **all types of financial instruments except** those specifically excluded, as listed below.

(a)   Investments in **subsidiaries, associates, and joint arrangements** that are accounted for under IFRS 10, IAS 27 or IAS 28.

BPP
LEARNING MEDIA

(b)   Employers' rights and obligations **under employee benefit plans** covered in IAS 19

(c)   **Forward contracts** for a sale that will result in a **business combination** at a later date

(d)   Rights and obligations under **insurance contracts** (although IAS 39 applies where the insurance contract principally involves the transfer of financial risks and derivatives embedded in insurance contracts)

(e)   Equity instruments **issued by the entity** eg ordinary shares issued, or options and warrants

(f)   Financial instruments, contracts and obligations under **share based payment transactions,** covered in IFRS 2

(g)   Rights to **reimbursement payments** to which IAS 37 *Provisions, Contingent Liabilities and Contingent Assets* applies

3.2 Initial recognition

Financial instruments should be recognised in the statement of financial position when the entity becomes a party to the **contractual provisions of the instrument**.

KEY POINT

An important consequence of this is that all derivatives should be in the statement of financial position.

Notice that this is **different** from the recognition criteria in the *Framework*, which states items are normally recognised when there is a probable inflow or outflow of resources and the item has a cost or value that can be measured reliably.

3.3 Example: initial recognition

An entity has entered into two separate contracts.

(a)   A firm commitment (an order) to buy a specific quantity of iron.

(b)   A forward contract to buy a specific quantity of iron at a specified price on a specified date, provided delivery of the iron is not taken.

Contract (a) is a **normal trading contract**. The entity does not recognise a liability for the iron until the goods have actually been delivered. (Note that this contract is not a financial instrument because it involves a physical asset, rather than a financial asset.)

Contract (b) is a **financial instrument**. Under IAS 39, the entity recognises a financial liability (an obligation to deliver cash) on the **commitment date**, rather than waiting for the closing date on which the exchange takes place.

Note that planned future transactions, no matter how likely, are not assets and liabilities of an entity – the entity has not yet become a party to the contract.

3.4 Derecognition

Derecognition is the removal of a previously recognised financial instrument from an entity's statement of financial position.

An entity should derecognise a **financial asset** when:

(a)   The **contractual rights** to the cash flows from the financial asset **expire,** or

(b)   The entity **transfers substantially all the risks and rewards of ownership** of the financial asset to another party.

Question 2.2   Risks and rewards

Learning outcomes B1

Can you think of an example of a situation in which:

(a)   An entity has transferred substantially all the risks and rewards of ownership?

(b)   An entity has retained substantially all the risks and rewards of ownership?

Exam alert

The principle here is that of **substance over form**.

When a financial asset is derecognised, there are three steps to follow.

   Revalue at fair value.

   Recognise proceeds.

   Derecognise financial asset.

Example: Derecognition

In July 20X8 AB sold 12,000 shares for $16,800 (their market value at that date). It had purchased the shares through a broker in 20X7 for $1.25 per share. The quoted price at the 20X7 year end was $1.32 - $1.34 per share. The broker charges transaction costs of 1% purchase/sale price.

What were the journal entries to record the derecognition?

Solution

The shares were originally recorded at their cost of $15,150 in 20X7 and revalued to market value at the 20X7 year end with a gain of $690 reported in other comprehensive income:

	$	
20X7 Purchase ((12,000 × $1.25) + (1% × $15,000))	15,150	other comprehensive income 20X5
Fair value gain at 31.12.20X7 β	690	
Fair value at 31.12.20X7 (12,000 × $1.32 bid price)	15,840	

At the date of the derecognition in July 20X8, the shares must first be remeasured to their fair value (i.e. the sales price as they were sold at market price) and the gain is reported in other comprehensive income ('items that will not be reclassified to profit or loss'):

DEBIT   Financial asset (16,800 − 15,840) $960

CREDIT   Other comprehensive income $960

On derecognition, the transaction costs are charged to profit or loss:

DEBIT	Cash (16,800 – (1% × 16,800))	$16,632
DEBIT	Profit or loss (1% × 16,800)	$168
CREDIT	Financial asset	$16,800

A **financial liability** should be removed from the statement of financial position when, and only when, it is **extinguished** – that is, when the obligation specified in the contract is either **discharged** or **cancelled** or **expires**.

Exam alert

No gain or loss will arise on the derecognition of an investment unless it is sold at a price different to fair value.

Section summary

IAS 39 *Financial instruments: recognition and measurement* is a recent and most controversial standard.

The IAS states that all financial assets and liabilities should be recognised in the statement of financial position, including derivatives.

4 Measurement of financial instruments   11/10, 3/11, 9/12

Introduction

Financial assets are initially measured at the **fair value** of the consideration given or received (ie, **cost**) **plus** (in most cases) **transaction costs** that are **directly attributable** to the acquisition or issue of the financial instrument.

4.1 Introduction

The diagram below summarises how different types of financial assets are measured. We will look at the initial and subsequent measurement of each type of financial asset one by one.

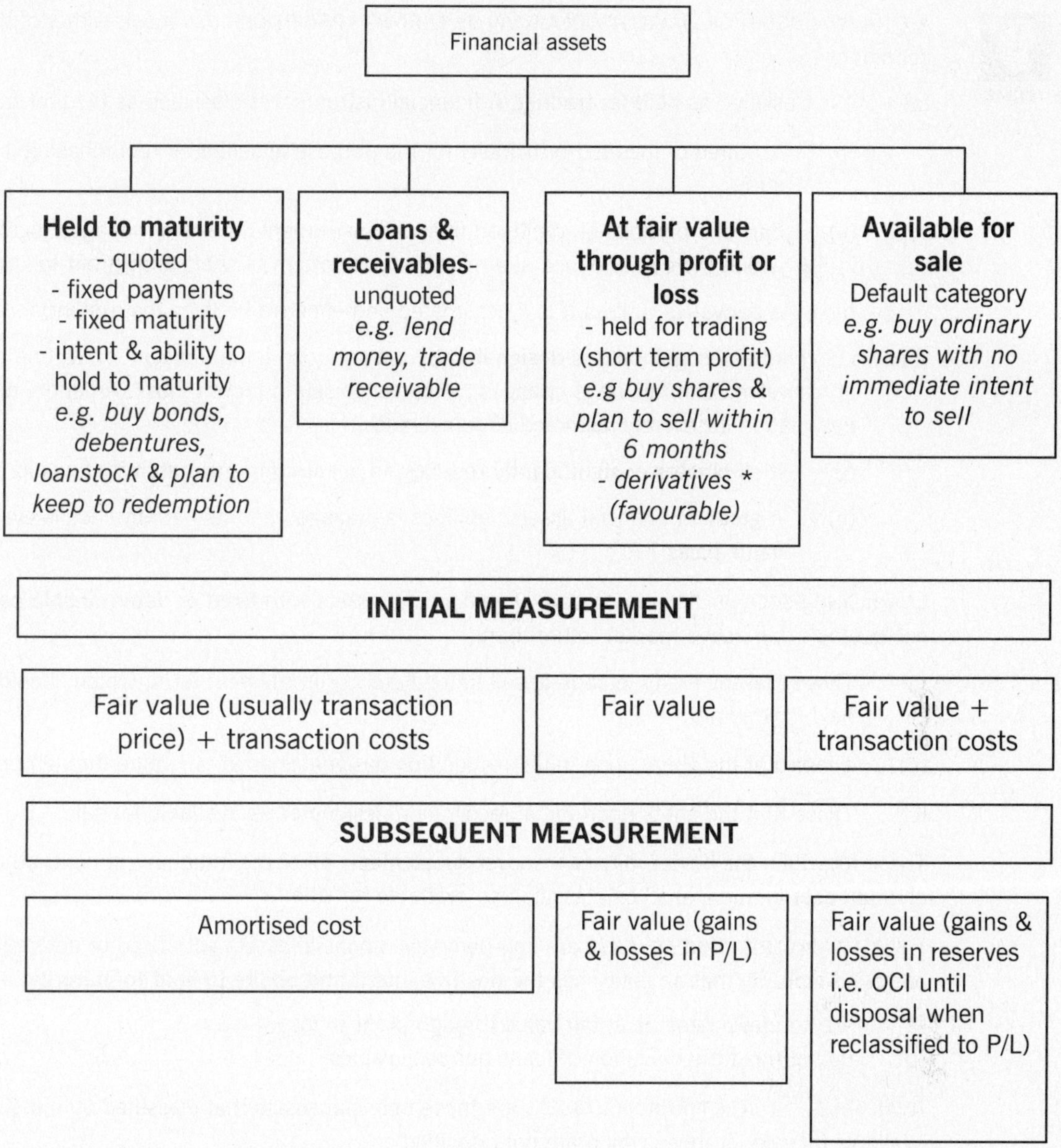

```
                          ┌──────────────────────┐
                          │   Financial assets    │
                          └──────────────────────┘
```

| Held to maturity
- quoted
- fixed payments
- fixed maturity
- intent & ability to hold to maturity
e.g. buy bonds, debentures, loanstock & plan to keep to redemption | Loans & receivables-
unquoted
e.g. lend money, trade receivable | At fair value through profit or loss
- held for trading (short term profit)
e.g buy shares & plan to sell within 6 months
- *derivatives * (favourable)* | Available for sale
Default category
e.g. buy ordinary shares with no immediate intent to sell |

INITIAL MEASUREMENT

| Fair value (usually transaction price) + transaction costs | Fair value | Fair value + transaction costs |

SUBSEQUENT MEASUREMENT

| Amortised cost | Fair value (gains & losses in P/L) | Fair value (gains & losses in reserves i.e. OCI until disposal when reclassified to P/L) |

4.1.1 Initial measurement

Financial assets are measured at fair value plus transaction costs, except when they are designated as **at fair value through profit or loss**.

Where a financial instrument is designated as **at fair value through profit or loss** (this term is explained below). In this case, **transaction costs** are **not** added to fair value at initial recognition.

The **fair value** of the consideration is normally the **transaction price** or market prices. If market prices are not reliable, the fair value may be **estimated** using a valuation technique (for example, by discounting cash flows).

4.1.2 Subsequent measurement

As you can see in the diagram above, IAS 39 classifies financial assets into four categories. These are defined here. Note particularly the criteria for a financial asset or liability **at fair value through profit and loss**.

A FINANCIAL ASSET OR LIABILITY AT FAIR VALUE THROUGH PROFIT OR LOSS meets either of the following conditions:

(a) It is classified as **held for trading**. A financial instrument is classified as held for trading if it is:

    (i) Acquired or incurred principally for the purpose of selling or repurchasing it in the short term

    (ii) Part of a portfolio of identified financial instruments that are managed together and for which there is evidence of a recent actual pattern of short-term profit-taking, or

    (iii) A derivative (unless it is a designated and effective hedging instrument).

(b) Upon initial recognition it is **designated** by the entity on initial recognition as one to be measured at fair value, with fair value changes being recognised in profit or loss. An entity may only use this designation in severely restricted circumstances:

    (i) It **eliminates** or **significantly reduces an accounting mismatch** that would otherwise arise.

    (ii) A **group** of financial assets/liabilities is managed and its performance is evaluated **on a fair value basis**.

LOANS AND RECEIVABLES are non-derivative financial assets with **fixed or determinable payments** that **are not quoted in an active market**, other than:

(a) Those that the entity intends to sell immediately or in the near term, which should be classified as held for trading

(b) Those that the entity upon initial recognition designates as at fair value through profit or loss, or

(c) Those that the entity upon initial recognition designates as available-for-sale.

Those for which the holder may not recover substantially all of the initial investment, other than because of credit deterioration, shall be classified as **available for sale**.

HELD-TO-MATURITY INVESTMENTS are non-derivative financial assets with fixed or determinable payments and fixed maturity that an entity has the **positive intent and ability to hold to maturity**, and that:

(a) are not designated as at fair value through profit or loss

(b) do not meet the definition of loans and receivables.

AVAILABLE-FOR-SALE FINANCIAL ASSETS are those financial assets that classified on initial recognition as available for sale, or those which are not classified as:

(a) Loans and receivables originated by the entity,

(b) Held-to-maturity investments, or

(c) Financial assets at fair value through profit or loss.   *(IAS 39)*

After initial recognition, all financial assets should be **remeasured to fair value**, without any deduction for transaction costs that may be incurred on sale or other disposal, except for:

(a) Loans and receivables – measured at amortised cost

(b) Held to maturity investments – measured at amortised cost

(c) Investments in equity instruments that do not have a quoted market price in an active market and whose **fair value cannot be reliably measured** (and derivatives indexed to such equity instruments) – measured at **cost**

Loans and receivables and **held to maturity investments** should be measured at **amortised cost** using the **effective interest method**.

KEY TERMS

AMORTISED COST of a financial asset or financial liability is the amount at which the financial asset or liability is measured at initial recognition minus principal repayments, plus or minus the cumulative amortisation of any difference between that initial amount and the maturity amount, and minus any write-down (directly or through the use of an allowance account) for impairment or uncollectability.

The EFFECTIVE INTEREST METHOD is a method of calculating the amortised cost of a financial instrument and of allocating the interest income or interest expense over the relevant period.

The EFFECTIVE INTEREST RATE is the rate that exactly discounts estimated future cash payments or receipts through the expected life of the financial instrument to the net carrying amount of the financial asset or liability.   (*IAS 39*)

Example: amortised cost

On 1 January 20X1 Abacus Co purchases a debt instrument for its fair value of $1,000. The debt instrument is due to mature on 31 December 20X5. The instrument has a principal amount of $1,250 and the instrument carries fixed interest at 4.72% that is paid annually. (The effective interest rate is 10%.)

How should Abacus Co account for the debt instrument over its five year term?

Solution

Abacus Co will receive interest of $59 (1,250 × 4.72%) each year and $1,250 when the instrument matures.

Abacus must allocate the discount of $250 and the interest receivable over the five year term at a constant rate on the carrying amount of the debt. To do this, it must apply the effective interest rate of 10%.

The following table shows the allocation over the years:

Year	Amortised cost at beginning of year $	Profit or loss: Interest income for year (@10%) $	Interest received during year (cash inflow) $	Amortised cost at end of year $
20X1	1,000	100	(59)	1,041
20X2	1,041	104	(59)	1,086
20X3	1,086	109	(59)	1,136
20X4	1,136	113	(59)	1,190
20X5	1,190	119	(1,250+59)	–

Each year the carrying amount of the financial asset is increased by the interest income for the year and reduced by the interest actually received during the year.

Investments whose **fair value cannot be reliably measured** should be measured at **cost**.

The proforma and double entries for recording amortised cost are as follows:

Financial asset

	$	Post to:		
Balance b/d	X		DEBIT	(↑) Financial asset
			CREDIT	(↓) Cash
			(if initial recognition at start of year)	
Finance income (effective interest × b/f)	X	P/L	DEBIT	(↑) Financial asset
			CREDIT	(↑) Finance income
Interest received (coupon × par value)	(X)		DEBIT	(↑) Cash
			CREDIT	(↓) Financial asset
Balance c/d	X	SOFP		

Financial liability

	$	Post to:		
Balance b/d	X		DEBIT	(↑) Cash
			CREDIT	(↑) Financial liability
			(if initial recognition at start of year)	
Finance cost (effective interest × b/f)	X	P/L	DEBIT	(↑) Finance cost
			CREDIT	(↑) Financial liability
Interest paid (coupon × par value)	(X)		DEBIT	(↓) Financial liability
			CREDIT	(↓) Cash
Balance c/d	X	SOFP		

4.1.3 Classification

There is a certain amount of flexibility in that **any** financial instrument can be designated as fair value through profit or loss. However, this is a **once and for all choice** and has to be made on initial recognition. Once a financial instrument has been classified in this way, it **cannot be reclassified**, even if it would otherwise be possible to measure it at cost or amortised cost.

In contrast, it is quite difficult for an entity **not** to remeasure financial instruments to fair value.

Exam alert

Notice that derivatives **must** be remeasured to fair value. This is because it would be misleading to measure them at cost.

For a financial instrument to be held to maturity it must meet several extremely narrow criteria. The entity must have a **positive intent** and a **demonstrated ability** to hold the investment to maturity. These conditions are not met if:

(a)   The entity intends to hold the financial asset for an undefined period

(b)   The entity stands ready to sell the financial asset in response to changes in interest rates or risks, liquidity needs and similar factors (unless these situations could not possibly have been reasonably anticipated)

(c)   The issuer has the right to settle the financial asset at an amount significantly below its amortised cost (because this right will almost certainly be exercised)

(d)   It does not have the financial resources available to continue to finance the investment until maturity

(e)   It is subject to an existing legal or other constraint that could frustrate its intention to hold the financial asset to maturity

In addition, an **equity** instrument is **unlikely** to meet the criteria for classification as held to maturity.

There is a **penalty** for selling or reclassifying a 'held-to-maturity' investment other than in certain very tightly defined circumstances. If this has occurred during the **current** financial year or during the **two preceding** financial years, **no** financial asset can be classified as held-to-maturity.

If an entity can no longer hold an investment to maturity, it is no longer appropriate to use amortised cost and the asset must be re-measured to fair value. **All** remaining held-to-maturity investments must also be re-measured to fair value and classified as available-for-sale (see above).

4.1.4 Gains and losses

Instruments at **fair value through profit or loss**: gains and losses are recognised **in profit or loss**.

For **available for sale** financial assets: gains and losses are recognised in **reserves (ie other comprehensive income)**. When the asset is disposed of and derecognised, the cumulative gain or loss previously recognised in other comprehensive income should be **reclassified to profit or loss**.

Financial instruments carried at **amortised cost**: gains and losses are recognised **in profit or loss** as a result of the amortisation process and when the asset is derecognised.

Financial assets and financial liabilities that are **hedged items**: special rules apply (discussed later in this chapter).

Question 2.3	Finance cost 1

Learning outcomes B1

On 1 January 20X3 Deferred issued $600,000 loan notes. Issue costs were $200. The loan notes do not carry interest, but are redeemable at a premium of $152,389 on 31 December 20X4. The effective finance cost of the debentures is 12%.

What is the finance cost in respect of the loan notes for the year ended 31 December 20X4?

A $72,000
B $76,194
C $80,613
D $80,640

Question 2.4	Exam standard example

Learning outcomes B1

Palermo, a public limited company, has requested your advice for the following financial instrument transactions:

(a)   Palermo purchased a deep discount bond during the previous accounting period on 1.1.20X0 for $157,563 plus $200 transaction costs. Interest of 4% is payable annually on 31 December. The bond will be redeemed on 31.12.20X4 for $200,000 (its par value). The bond will be held until redemption. The effective interest rate of the bond is 9.5%

(b)   Palermo issued 60,000 redeemable $1 preference shares on 1.1.20X1 paying an annual (cumulative) dividend of 7% per annum, redeemable in ten years' time.

(c)   Palermo purchased 12,000 shares in ABC Co through a broker on 1 July 20X0 for $1.25 a share. The market price at 31 December 20X0 was $1.32 a share. On 30 September 20X1, Palermo sold the shares in ABC for $16,800. The broker charges transaction costs of 1% purchase/sale price.

(d)   On 1 November 20X1, Palermo took out a speculative forward contract to buy coffee beans for delivery on 30 April 20X2 at an agreed price of $6,000 intending to settle net in cash. Due to a surge in expected supply, a forward contract for delivery on 30 April 20X2 would have cost $5,000 at 31 December 20X1.

Required

Explain how the above transactions should be accounted for in the year ending 31 December 20X1, showing relevant calculations where appropriate.

4.2 Impairment and uncollectability of financial assets

At each year end, an entity should assess whether there is any objective evidence that a financial asset or group of assets is impaired.

Question 2.5	Impairment

Learning outcomes B1

Give examples of indications that a financial asset or group of assets may be impaired.

Where there is objective evidence of impairment, the entity should **determine the amount** of any impairment loss. Examples of indications of impairment include:

- Financial difficulty of issuer
- Breach of contract in repayments
- Granting a concession to a borrower not normally given
- High probability of bankruptcy of borrower

4.2.1 Financial assets carried at amortised cost

For **loans and receivables** and **held-to-maturity investments**, the impairment loss is the **difference** between the asset's **carrying amount** and its **recoverable amount**.

The asset's recoverable amount is the present value of estimated future cash flows, discounted at the financial instrument's **original** effective interest rate.

The amount of the loss should be **recognised in profit or loss.** The carrying amount of the asset is either reduced directly or through the use of an allowance account.

If the impairment loss decreases at a later date (and the decrease relates to an event occurring **after** the impairment was recognised) the reversal is recognised in profit or loss. The carrying amount of the asset must not exceed the original amortised cost.

4.2.2 Financial assets carried at cost

Unquoted equity instruments are carried at cost if their fair value cannot be reliably measured. The impairment loss is the difference between the asset's **carrying amount** and the **present value of estimated future cash flows**, discounted at the current market rate of return for a similar financial instrument.

Such impairment losses cannot be reversed.

4.2.3 Available for sale financial assets

Available for sale financial assets are carried at fair value and gains and losses are recognised directly in equity.

Where an available-for-sale financial asset suffers an impairment loss, the loss is charged first against any cumulative **gains** on fair value adjustments previously recognised in equity (and is shown as an expense in other comprehensive income), and then to profit or loss.

If there are cumulative **losses** held in equity, they are reclassified ('recycled') from equity to profit or loss in addition to the impairment loss.

The impairment loss is the difference between its **acquisition cost** (net of any principal repayment and amortisation) and **current fair value** (for equity instruments) or recoverable amount (for debt instruments), less any impairment loss on that asset previously recognised in profit or loss.

Impairment losses relating to equity instruments cannot be reversed. Impairment losses relating to debt instruments may be reversed if, in a later period, the fair value of the instrument increases and the increase can be objectively related to an event occurring after the loss was recognised.

Example: impairment

Broadfield Co purchased 5% debentures in X Co on 1 January 20X3 (their issue date) for $100,000. The term of the debentures was 5 years and the maturity value is $130,525. The effective rate of interest on the debentures is 10% and the company has classified them as a held-to-maturity financial asset.

At the end of 20X4 X Co went into liquidation. All interest had been paid until that date. On 31 December 20X4 the liquidator of X Co announced that no further interest would be paid and only 80% of the maturity value would be repaid, on the original repayment date.

The market interest rate on similar bonds is 8% on that date.

Required

(a)   What value should the debentures have been stated at just before the impairment became apparent?

(b)   At what value should the debentures be stated at 31 December 20X4, after the impairment?

(c)   How will the impairment be reported in the financial statements for the year ended 31 December 20X4?

Solution

(a)   The debentures are classified as a held-to-maturity financial asset and so they would have been stated at amortised cost:

	$
Initial cost	100,000
Interest at 10%	10,000
Cash at 5%	(5,000)
At 31 December 20X3	105,000
Interest at 10%	10,500
Cash at 5%	(5,000)
At 31 December 20X4	110,500

(b)   After the impairment, the debentures are stated at their recoverable amount (using the **original** effective interest rate of 10%):

$$80\% \times \$130,525 \times 0.751 = \$78,419$$

(c)   The impairment of $32,081 ($110,500 − $78,419) should be recorded:

DEBIT	Profit or loss	$32,081	
CREDIT	Financial asset		$32,081

Being impairment of held-to-maturity financial asset

4.3 Subsequent measurement of financial liabilities

After initial recognition, all financial liabilities should be measured at **amortised cost**, with the exception of financial liabilities at fair value through profit or loss (including most derivatives). These should be measured at **fair value**, but where the fair value **is not capable of reliable measurement**, they should be measured at **cost**.

4.4 Recap

- On initial recognition, financial instruments are measured at fair value plus transaction costs, except when they are designated as at fair value through profit or loss.

- Subsequent measurement depends on how a financial asset is **classified**.

- Financial assets at **fair value through profit or loss** are measured at **fair value**; gains and losses are recognised in **profit or loss**.

- **Available for sale** assets are measured at **fair value**; gains and losses are taken to **equity**, through other comprehensive income.

- **Loans and receivables** and **held to maturity** investments are measured at **amortised cost**; gains and losses are recognised in **profit or loss**.

- Financial **liabilities** are normally measured at **amortised cost**, unless they have been classified as at fair value through profit or loss.

Section summary

Financial assets should initially be measured at cost = fair value.

Subsequently they should be re-measured to fair value except for

(a) Loans and receivables not held for trading
(b) Other held-to-maturity investments
(c) Financial assets whose value cannot be reliably measured

5 Hedging   11/10

Introduction

IAS 39 **requires hedge accounting** where there is a **designated hedging relationship** between a hedging instrument and a hedged item.

5.1 Definitions

Companies enter into hedging transactions in order to reduce business risk. Where an item in the statement of financial position or future cash flow is subject to potential fluctuations in value that could be detrimental to the business, a hedging transaction may be entered into. The aim is that where the item hedged makes a financial loss, the hedging instrument would make a gain and *vice versa*, reducing overall risk.

KEY TERMS

HEDGING, for accounting purposes, means designating one or more hedging instruments so that their change in fair value is an offset, in whole or in part, to the change in fair value or cash flows of a hedged item.

A HEDGED ITEM is an asset, liability, firm commitment, or forecasted future transaction that:

(a) exposes the entity to risk of changes in fair value or changes in future cash flows, and that
(b) is designated as being hedged.

A HEDGING INSTRUMENT is a designated derivative or (in limited circumstances) another financial asset or liability whose fair value or cash flows are expected to offset changes in the fair value or cash flows of a designated hedged item.

(A non-derivative financial asset or liability may be designated as a hedging instrument for hedge accounting purposes only if it hedges the risk of changes in foreign currency exchange rates.)

HEDGE EFFECTIVENESS is the degree to which changes in the fair value or cash flows of the hedged item attributable to a hedged risk are offset by changes in the fair value or cash flows of the hedging instrument.   *(IAS 39)*

In simple terms, entities hedge to reduce their exposure to risk and uncertainty, such as changes in prices, interest rates or foreign exchange rates. Hedge accounting recognises hedging relationships by allowing (for example) losses on a hedged item to be offset against gains on a hedging instrument.

Generally only assets, liabilities etc that involve external parties can be designated as hedged items. The foreign currency risk of an intragroup monetary item (eg payable/receivable between two subsidiaries) may qualify as a hedged item in the group financial statements if it results in an exposure to foreign exchange rate gains or losses that are not fully eliminated on consolidation. This can happen (per IAS 21) when the transaction is between entities with different functional currencies.

In addition, the foreign currency risk of a highly probable group transaction may qualify as a hedged item if it is in a currency other than the functional currency of the entity and the foreign currency risk will affect profit or loss.

The **standard** identifies three types of **hedging relationship**.

KEY TERMS

FAIR VALUE HEDGE: These hedge against the change in value of an asset or liability that could affect the profit or loss (eg hedging the fair value of fixed rate debentures due to changes in interest rates)

CASH FLOW HEDGE: These hedge against the risk of a change in value of future cash flows that could affect profit or loss (eg hedging a variable rate interest income stream)

(a)   is attributable to a particular risk associated with a recognised asset or liability (such as all or some future interest payments on variable rate debt) or a highly probable forecast transaction (such as an anticipated purchase or sale), and that

(b)   could affect profit or loss.

HEDGE OF A NET INVESTMENT IN A FOREIGN OPERATION: These hedge against changes in the value of an entity's investment in a foreign operation.

IAS 21 defines a net investment in a foreign operation as the amount of the reporting entity's interest in the net assets of that operation.   *(IAS 39)*

5.2 Conditions for hedge accounting

Adopting the hedge accounting provisions of IAS 39 is mandatory where a transaction qualifies as a hedge. To qualify the relationship needs to show it satisfies the following conditions.

(a)   It was **designated at its inception** as a hedge with full documentation of how this hedge fits into the company's strategy

(b)   The hedge has been and is expected to be **'highly effective'** (ie the ratio of the gain or loss on the hedging instrument compared to the loss or gain on item being hedged is within the ratio 80% to 125%)

(c)   The hedge effectiveness can be **reliably measured**.

5.3 Accounting treatment

5.3.1 Fair value hedges

All gains and losses on **both** the **hedged item** and **hedging instrument** are recognised immediately in **profit or loss**.

5.3.2 Cash flow hedges

The gain or loss on the effective portion of the hedge (ie up to the value of the loss or gain on cash flow hedged) is recognised in other comprehensive income ('items that may be reclassified subsequently to profit or loss'). This is transferred to profit or loss when the cash flow itself is recognised in profit or loss.

Any excess is recognised immediately in profit or loss.

5.3.3 Hedges of net investments in a foreign operation

The hedge is accounted for in the same way as for a cash flow hedge (but gains or losses on the hedge are not transferred to profit or loss, until the disposal of the foreign operation).

Example: hedging

On 1 September 20X7, the directors of JKL entered into a contract to buy some inventories for 400,000 florins for delivery and payment on 30 June 20X9. JKL's functional currency is the dollar.

The directors were concerned about how the fluctuation in the exchange rate could affect the amount that they would have to pay and so on the same date entered into a forward contract to buy 400,000 florins on 30 June 20X9 at a rate of $1 = 4 florins.

Relevant forward exchange rates for delivery on 30 June 20X9 are:

At 1 September 20X7 $1 = 4 florins

At 31 December 20X7 $1 = 3.8 florins

At 31 December 20X8 $1 = 3.7 florins

Required

(a)   Show how the forward contract should be accounted for in the company's statement of profit or loss and other comprehensive income and statement of financial position for the year ending 31 December 20X8, including comparatives:

     (i)   if it does not meet the criteria to be classified as a hedge

     (ii)   if it is to be classified as a hedge.

     In part (ii) you should assume that the hedge is fully effective.

(b)   Explain what happens to inventories purchase and the hedge in 20X9.

Tutorial note:

A foreign currency forward contract is valued as follows:

	$
Price of contract in $ at year end	X
Price of contract in $ at inception	(X)
Value of/gain on contract	X

Solution

(a)

	(a)(i) Not a hedge		(a)(ii) Cash flow hedge	
	20X8 $	20X7 $	20X8 $	20X7 $
STATEMENT OF PROFIT OR LOSS AND COMPREHENSIVE INCOME (EXTRACT)				
Finance income:				
Gain on forward contract (W1)	2,845	5,263	–	–
Other comprehensive income (items that may be reclassified subsequently to profit or loss)				
Gain on forward contract	–	–	2,845	5,263
STATEMENT OF FINANCIAL POSITION (EXTRACTS)				
Financial assets:				
Forward contract (W1)	8,108	5,263	8,108	5,263
Equity:				
Cash flow hedge reserve (W1)	–	–	8,108	5,263

In part (a)(i) the forward contract is held at fair value through profit or loss, as all derivatives that are not held for hedging fall into this category.

In part (a)(ii) the hedge is a cash flow hedge, because it is trying to minimise fluctuations in cash outflows to acquire the inventories.

Workings

1   *Gain on forward contract at 31 December 20X7:*

Price of contract at 31.12.20X7 (400,000/3.8)		$105,263
Price of contract at 1.9.20X7 (400,000/4)		$100,000
Gain on contract		$5,263
DEBIT Forward contract	5,263	
CREDIT Profit or loss (a)		5,263
or CREDIT Cash flow hedge reserve (b)		5,263

2   *Additional gain on forward contract at 31 December 20X8:*

Price of contract at 31.12.20X8 (400,000/3.7)		$108,108
Price of contract at 31.12.20X7 (400,000/3.8)		$105,263
Gain on contract		$2,845
DEBIT Forward contract	2,845	
CREDIT Profit or loss (a)		2,845
or CREDIT Cash flow hedge reserve (b)		2,845

(b)   When the inventories are purchased they will be recorded at the exchange rate ruling on 30 June 20X9, and, being a non-monetary item, will not subsequently be restated.

The cumulative gain $8,108 plus/net of any gain/loss on the forward contract in 20X9, will be transferred to cost of sales when the inventories are sold, thereby compensating the extra cost of the inventories recognised in cost of sales due to the exchange rate movement between 1 September 20X7 and their date of delivery 30 June 20X9.

5.4 Recap

- **Hedge accounting** means designating one or more instruments so that their change in fair value is **offset** by the change in fair value or cash flows of another item.

- **Hedge accounting** is permitted in certain circumstances, provided the hedging relationship is **designated at inception**, **measurable** and actually **effective**.

- There are three types of hedge: **fair value** hedge; **cash flow** hedge; hedge of a **net investment in a foreign operation**.

- The accounting treatment of a hedge **depends on its type**.

Section summary

Hedging is allowed in certain strictly defined circumstances.

6 Disclosure of financial instruments

Introduction

The IASB maintains that users of financial instruments need information about an entity's exposures to risks and how those risks are managed, as this information can **influence a user's assessment of the financial position and financial performance of an entity** or of the amount, timing and uncertainty of its **future cash flows**.

There have been new techniques and approaches to measuring risk management, which highlighted the need for guidance.

Accordingly, IFRS 7 *Financial instruments: Disclosures* was issued in 2005.

6.1 Objective

The objective of IFRS 7 is to require entities to provide disclosures in their financial statements that enable users to evaluate:

(a)   The **significance** of financial instruments for the entity's financial position and performance

(b)   The **nature and extent of risks** arising from financial instruments, and how the entity manages those risks.

The principles in IFRS 7 complement the principles for recognising, measuring and presenting financial assets and financial liabilities in IAS 32 *Financial instruments: Presentation* and IAS 39 *Financial instruments: Recognition and measurement*.

6.2 Classes of financial instruments and levels of disclosure

The entity must group financial instruments into classes **appropriate to the nature of the information presented**. An entity must decide, based on its circumstances, how much detail it provides. Sufficient information must be provided to permit reconciliation to the line items presented in the statement of financial position.

6.2.1 Statement of financial position

The following must be disclosed.

(a)   **Carrying amount** of financial assets and liabilities (by IAS 39 category).

(b)   Special disclosures about financial assets and financial liabilities designated to be measured **at fair value through profit and loss**, including disclosures about credit risk and market risk, changes in fair values attributable to these risks and the methods of measurement.

(c)   **Reason for any reclassification** of financial instruments from one category to another.

(d)   The **carrying amount** of financial assets the entity has **pledged as collateral** for liabilities or contingent liabilities and the associated terms and conditions.

(e)   Reconciliation of movement in the allowance account for credit losses (bad debts) by class of financial assets.

(f)   The **existence of multiple embedded derivatives**, where compound instruments contain these.

(g)   Defaults on loans payable.

6.2.2 Statement of profit or loss and other comprehensive income

The entity must disclose the following items of **income, expense, gains or losses**, either on the face of the financial statements or in the notes.

(a)   **Net gains/losses** on financial instruments recognised in profit or loss by IAS 39 category (broken down as appropriate: eg interest, fair value changes, dividend income).

(b)   Total effective **interest income/expense** (for items **not** held at fair value through profit or loss).

(c)   Impairments losses by class of financial asset.

6.2.3 Other disclosures

Other disclosures must be made relating to **hedge accounting**, as follows:

(a)   Accounting policy for the measurement basis of financial instruments.

(b)   Description of each hedge.

(c)   Description of each financial instrument designated as **hedging instruments** and their fair value at the reporting date.

(d)   The **nature of the risks** being hedged.

(e)   For **cash flow hedges**, periods **when the cash flows will occur** and when will affect profit or loss.

(f)   For fair value hedges, details of fair value changes of the hedging instrument and the hedged item.

(g)   The **ineffectiveness recognised in profit or loss** arising from cash flow hedges and net investments in foreign operations.

Disclosures must be made relating to **fair value** by class of financial instrument, in a way that allows comparison to statement of financial position value in the statement of financial position. (Financial assets and liabilities may only be offset to the extent that their carrying amounts are offset in the statement of financial position.)

Example: fair value disclosures

Background

On 1 January 20X1 an entity purchases for $15 million financial assets that are not traded in an active market. The entity has only one class of such financial assets.

The transaction price of $15 million is the fair value at initial recognition.

After initial recognition, the entity will apply a valuation technique to establish the financial assets' fair value. This valuation technique includes variables other than data from observable markets.

At initial recognition, the same valuation technique would have resulted in an amount of $14 million, which differs from fair value by $1 million.

The entity has existing differences of $5 million at 1 January 20X1.

Solution

Application of requirements

The entity's 20X2 disclosure would include the following:

Accounting policies

The entity uses the following valuation technique to determine the fair value of financial instruments that are not traded in an active market: [description of technique, not included in this example]. Differences may arise between the fair value at initial recognition (which, in accordance with IAS 39, is generally the transaction price) and the amount determined at initial recognition using the valuation technique. Any such differences are [description of the entity's accounting policy].

In the notes to the financial statements

As discussed in note X, the entity uses [name of valuation technique] to measure the fair value of the following financial instruments that are not traded in an active market. However, in accordance with IAS 39, the fair value of an instrument at inception is generally the transaction price. If the transaction price differs from the amount determined at inception using the valuation technique, that difference is [description of the entity's accounting policy]. The differences yet to be recognised in profit or loss are as follows:

	31 Dec 20X2 $m	31 Dec 20X1 $m
Balance at beginning of year	5.3	5.0
New transactions		1.0
Amounts recognised in profit or loss during the year	(0.7)	(0.8)
Other increases		0.2
Other decreases	(0.1)	(0.1)
Balance at end of year	4.5	5.3

Disclosures of fair value are **not required** if carrying value is a reasonable approximation to fair value, or if fair value cannot be measured reliably.

6.3 Nature and extent of risks arising from financial instruments

In undertaking transactions in financial instruments, an entity may assume or transfer to another party one or more of **different types of financial risk** as defined below. The disclosures required by the standard show the extent to which an entity is exposed to these different types of risk, relating to both recognised and unrecognised financial instruments.

Credit risk	The risk that one party to a financial instrument will cause a financial loss for the other party by failing to pay for its obligation.
Liquidity risk	The risk that an entity will encounter difficulty in paying its financial liabilities. (Loans payable are financial liabilities, other than short-term trade payables on normal credit terms.)
Market risk	The risk that the fair value or future cash flows of a financial instrument will fluctuate because of changes in market prices.

6.3.1 Qualitative disclosures

For each type of risk arising from financial instruments, an entity must disclose:

(a)   The **exposures to risk** and how they arise,

(b)   Its objectives, policies and processes for managing the risk and the methods used to measure the risk,

(c)   Any **changes** in (a) or (b) from the previous period.

6.3.2 Quantitative disclosures

For each financial instrument risk, **summary quantitative data** about risk exposure must be disclosed. This should be based on the information provided internally to key management personnel. More information should be provided if this is unrepresentative.

Information about **credit risk** must be disclosed by class of financial instrument:

(a)   Maximum exposure at the year end

(b)   Any collateral pledged as security

(c)   In respect of the amount disclosed in (b), a description of collateral held as security and other credit enhancements

(d)   Information about the credit quality of financial assets that are neither **past due** nor impaired

(e)   Financial assets that are past due or impaired, giving an age analysis and a description of collateral held by the entity as security.

(f)   Collateral and other credit enhancements obtained, including the nature and carrying amount of the assets and policy for disposing of assets not readily convertible into cash.

For **liquidity risk** entities must disclose:

(a)   A maturity analysis of financial liabilities
(b)   A description of the way risk is managed

Disclosures required in connection with **market risk** are:

(a)   Sensitivity analysis, showing the effects on profit or loss of changes in each market risk
(b)   Additional information if the sensitivity analysis is not representative of the entity's risk exposure

6.4 Capital disclosures

Certain disclosures about **capital** are required. An entity's capital does not relate solely to financial instruments, but has more general relevance. Accordingly, those disclosures are included in IAS 1, rather than in IFRS 7.

Section summary

IFRS 7 specifies the **disclosures** required for financial instruments. The standard requires qualitative and quantitative disclosures about exposure to risks arising from financial instruments and specifies minimum disclosures about credit risk, liquidity risk and market risk.

Chapter Roundup

✓ Financial instruments can be very complex, particularly **derivative instruments**, although **primary instruments** are more straightforward.

✓ The important definitions to learn are:

- **Financial asset**
- **Financial liability**
- **Equity instrument**

✓ Financial instruments must be classified as **liabilities** or **equity** according to their **substance.**

✓ The critical feature of a financial liability is the **contractual obligation to deliver cash** or another financial asset.

✓ **Compound instruments** are split into **equity** and **liability** components and presented accordingly in the statement of financial position.

✓ **IAS 39** *Financial instruments: recognition and measurement* is a recent and most controversial standard.

✓ The IAS states that **all financial assets and liabilities** should be **recognised in the statement of financial position, including derivatives**.

✓ **Financial assets** should **initially** be measured at **cost = fair value**.

✓ Subsequently they should be **re-measured to fair value** except for

(a) Loans and receivables not held for trading
(b) Other **held-to-maturity investments**
(c) **Financial assets** whose value **cannot be reliably measured**

✓ **Hedging** is allowed in certain strictly defined circumstances.

✓ **IFRS 7** specifies the **disclosures** required for financial instruments. The standard requires quantitative and qualitative disclosures about exposure to risks arising from financial instruments and specifies minimum disclosures about credit risk, liquidity risk and market risk.

Quick Quiz

1 Which four issues are dealt with by IAS 32?

2 What items are *not* financial instruments according to IAS 32?

3 What is the critical feature used to identify a financial liability?

4 How should compound instruments be presented in the statement of financial position?

5 When should a financial asset be de-recognised?

6 How are financial instruments initially measured?

7 What is hedging?

8 Name the three types of hedging relationship identified by IAS 39.

Answers to Quick Quiz

1 Classification; presentation; offsetting and disclosure

2 Physical assets; prepaid expenses; non-contractual assets or liabilities; contractual rights not involving transfer of assets

3 The contractual obligation to deliver cash or another financial asset to the holder

4 By calculating the present value of the liability component and then deducting this from the instrument as a whole to leave a residual value for the equity component

5 Financial assets should be derecognised when the rights to the cash flows from the asset expire or where substantially all the risks and rewards of ownership are transferred to another party.

6 At fair value plus transaction costs, except when they are designated as at fair value through profit or loss (in which case, at fair value).

7 Hedging, for accounting purposes, means designating one or more hedging instruments so that their change in fair value is an offset, in whole or in part, to the change in fair value or cash flows of a hedged item.

8 Fair value hedge; cash flow hedge; hedge of a net investment in a foreign operation

Answers to Questions

2.1 Why not?

Refer to the definitions of financial assets and liabilities given above.

(a) **Physical assets**: Control of these creates an opportunity to generate an inflow of cash or other assets, but it does not give rise to a present right to receive cash or other financial assets.

(b) **Prepaid expenses, etc**: The future economic benefit is the receipt of goods/services rather than the right to receive cash or other financial assets.

(c) **Deferred revenue, warranty obligations**: The probable outflow of economic benefits is the delivery of goods/services rather than cash or another financial asset.

2.2 Risks and rewards

IAS 39 includes the following examples:

(a) (i) An unconditional sale of a financial asset

(ii) A sale of a financial asset together with an option to repurchase the financial asset at its fair value at the time of repurchase

(b) (i) A sale and repurchase transaction where the repurchase price is a fixed price or the sale price plus a lender's return

(ii) A sale of a financial asset together with a total return swap that transfers the market risk exposure back to the entity

2.3 Finance cost 1

C The premium on redemption of the preferred shares represents a finance cost. The effective rate of interest must be applied so that the debt is measured at amortised cost (IAS 39).

At the time of issue, the loan notes are recognised at their net proceeds of $599,800 (600,000 – 200).

The finance cost for the year ended 31 December 20X4 is calculated as follows:

	B/f $	Interest @ 12% $	C/f $
20X3	599,800	71,976	671,776
20X4	671,776	80,613	752,389

2.4 Exam standard example

Item (a)

The bond is a financial asset 'held to maturity'. It is therefore held at amortised cost calculated as follows.

Total finance income:
Coupon receipts (5 × 4% × 200,000)   40,000
Deep discount income (200,000 – (157,563 + 200))   <u>42,237</u>
Total income   <u>82,237</u>

Spread using effective interest rate of the bond, 9.5%, as follows.

	$
Cash – 1.1.20X0 (157,563 + 200)	157,763
Interest 20X0 (9.5% × 157,763)	14,988
Coupon received (4% × 200,000)	(8,000)
At 31.12.20X0	164,751
Interest 20X1 (9.5% × 164,751)	15,651
Coupon received (4% × 200,000)	(8,000)
At 31.12.20X1	172,402

Item (b)

Despite being called 'shares', the redeemable preference shares are, in substance, debt and are therefore accounted for as a financial liability.

They are held at amortised cost as a company's own shares cannot be classified as held for trading. They will be shown under non-current liabilities. The annual 'dividend' payments of 7% × 60,000 × $1 = $4,200 will be classified as interest payable.

Item (c)

Unless held for short-term profit-making, shares held as an investment fall into the category 'available-for-sale' financial assets. They are originally recorded at their cost (plus transaction costs) on 1 July 20X0 and revalued to fair value at the year end (31/12/X0) with a gain of $690 reported in other comprehensive income ('items that may be reclassified subsequently to profit or loss'):

	$
Fair value at 31.12.X0 (12,000 shares × $1.32)	15,840
Cost (1.1.X0) [(12,000 shares × $1.25 = $15,000) + (1% × $15,000)]	(15,150)
Fair value gain (to other comprehensive income)	690

When the shares are sold, this fair value gain is reclassified from other comprehensive income to profit or loss and a profit on derecognition is recognised:

	$
Proceeds ($16,800 – (1% × $16,800))	16,632
Less: carrying value of financial asset	(15,840)
	792
Fair value gain reclassified from OCI	690
Total gain to be recognised in profit or loss	1,482

Item (d)

A forward contract to be settled net in cash and not held for hedging purposes is accounted for at fair value through profit or loss.

The value of the contract at inception is zero.

The value of the contract at the year end is:

	$
Market price of forward contract at year end for delivery on 30 April 20X2	5,000
Palermo's forward price	(6,000)
Loss (as Palermo have to pay $1,000 more under their forward than they would at year end prices)	(1,000)

A financial liability of $1,000 is therefore recognised with a corresponding charge of $1,000 to profit or loss.

2.5 Impairment

IAS 39 lists the following:

(a) Significant financial difficulty of the issuer

(b) A breach of contract, such as a default in interest or principal payments

(c) The lender granting a concession to the borrower that the lender would not otherwise consider, for reasons relating to the borrower's financial difficulty

(d) It becomes probable that the borrower will enter bankruptcy

(e) The disappearance of an active market for that financial asset because of financial difficulties

---

Now try this question from the Exam Question Bank

Number	Level	Marks	Time
Q2	Introductory	10	18 mins

EMPLOYEE BENEFITS

An increasing number of companies and other entities now provide a **pension and other benefits** in addition to salaries and wages as part of their employees' remuneration package. In view of this trend, it is important that there is standard best practice for the way in which employee benefit costs are **recognised, measured, and presented** in the sponsoring entities' accounts.

Note that IAS 19 was revised in June 2011.

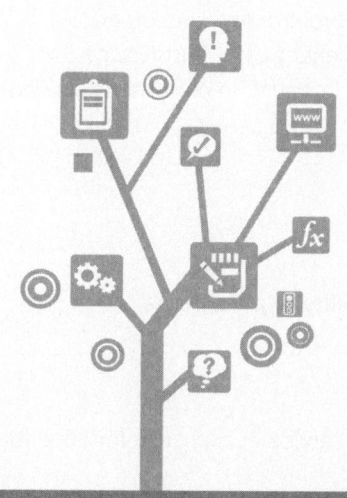

topic list	learning outcomes	syllabus references	ability required
1 IAS 19 *Employee benefits*	B1	B1 (v)	Application
2 Short-term employee benefits	B1	B1 (v)	Application
3 Post-employment benefits	B1	B1 (v)	Application
4 Defined contribution plans	B1	B1 (v)	Application
5 Defined benefit plans: recognition and measurement	B1	B1 (v)	Application
6 Defined benefit plans: other matters	B1	B1 (v)	Application
7 Other long term benefits	B1	B1 (v)	Application
8 Disclosures	B1	B1 (v)	Application
9 Other issues	B1	B1 (v)	Application

1 IAS 19 *Employee benefits*   11/11

Introduction

When a company or other entity employs a new worker, that worker will be offered a **package of pay and benefits**. Some of these will be short-term and the employee will receive the benefit at about the same time as he or she earns it, for example basic pay, overtime etc. Other employee benefits are **deferred**, however, the main example being retirement benefits (ie a pension).

1.1 The conceptual nature of employee benefit costs

The cost of these deferred employee benefits to the employer can be viewed in various ways. They could be described as **deferred salary** to the employee. Alternatively, they are a **deduction** from the employee's true gross salary, used as a tax-efficient means of saving. In some countries, tax efficiency arises on retirement benefit contributions because they are not taxed on the employee, but they are allowed as a deduction from taxable profits of the employer.

1.2 Accounting for employee benefit costs

Accounting for **short-term employee benefit costs** tends to be quite straightforward, because they are simply recognised as an expense in the employer's financial statements of the current period.

Accounting for the cost of **deferred employee benefits** is much more difficult. This is because of the large amounts involved, as well as the long time scale, complicated estimates and uncertainties. In the past, entities accounted for these benefits simply by charging the statements of profit or loss and other comprehensive income of the employing entity on the basis of actual payments made. This led to substantial variations in reported profits of these entities and disclosure of information on these costs was usually sparse.

1.3 IAS 19 *Employee benefits*

IAS 19 is intended to prescribe the following.

(a)   When the cost of employee benefits should be **recognised as a liability or an expense**
(b)   The **amount** of the liability or expense that should be recognised

As a basic rule, the standard states the following.

(a)   A **liability** should be recognised when an employee has provided a service in exchange for benefits to be received by the employee at some time in the future.

(b)   An **expense** should be recognised when the entity enjoys the economic benefits from a service provided by an employee regardless of when the employee received or will receive the benefits from providing the service.

The basic problem is therefore fairly straightforward. An entity will often enjoy the **economic benefits** from the services provided by its employees in advance of the employees receiving all the employment benefits from the work they have done, for example they will not receive pension benefits until after they retire.

1.4 Categories of employee benefits

The standard recognises four categories of employee benefits, and proposes a different accounting treatment for each. These four categories are as follows.

1   **Short-term** benefits including:

   - Wages and salaries
   - Social security contributions
   - Paid annual leave
   - Paid sick leave
   - Paid maternity/paternity leave
   - Profit shares and bonuses
   - Paid jury service
   - Paid military service
   - Non-monetary benefits, eg medical care, cars, free or subsidised goods

2   **Post-employment benefits**, eg pensions and post-employment medical care and post-employment insurance

3   **Other long-term benefits**, eg profit shares, bonuses or deferred compensation payable later than 12 months after the year end, sabbatical leave, long-service benefits and long-term disability benefits

4   **Termination benefits**, eg early retirement payments and redundancy payments

Benefits may be paid to the employees themselves, to their dependants (spouses, children, etc) or to third parties.

1.5 Definitions

IAS 19 uses a great many important definitions. This section lists those that relate to the different categories of employee benefits.

KEY TERMS

EMPLOYEE BENEFITS are all forms of consideration given by an entity in exchange for service rendered by employees or for the termination of employment.

SHORT-TERM EMPLOYEE BENEFITS are employee benefits (other than termination benefits) that are expected to be settled wholly before twelve months after the end of the annual reporting period in which the employees render the related service.

POST-EMPLOYMENT BENEFITS are employee benefits (other than termination benefits and short-term employee benefits) that are payable after the completion of employment.

OTHER LONG-TERM EMPLOYEE BENEFITS are all employee benefits other than short-term employee benefits, post-employment benefits and termination benefits.

TERMINATION BENEFITS are employee benefits provided in exchange for the termination of an employee's employment as a result of either:

(a)   an entity's decision to terminate an employee's employment before the normal retirement date, or

(b)   an employee's decision to accept an offer of benefits in exchange for

---

Section summary

IAS 19 *Employee benefits* is a long and complex standard covering both short-term and long-term (post-employment) benefits. The complications arise when dealing with **post-employment benefits**.

2 Short-term employee benefits

Introduction

Accounting for short-term employee benefits is fairly straightforward, because there are **no actuarial assumptions** to be made, and there is **no requirement to discount** future benefits (because they are all, by definition, payable no later than 12 months after the end of the accounting period).

2.1 Recognition and measurement

The rules for short-term benefits are essentially an application of **basic accounting principles and practice**.

(a) **Unpaid short-term employee benefits** as at the end of an accounting period should be recognised as an accrued expense. Any short-term benefits **paid in advance** should be recognised as a prepayment (to the extent that it will lead to, eg a reduction in future payments or a cash refund).

(b) The **cost of short-term employee benefits** should be recognised as an **expense** in the period when the economic benefit is given, as employment costs (except insofar as employment costs may be included within the cost of an asset, eg property, plant and equipment).

2.2 Short-term absences

There may be **short-term accumulating compensated absences**. These are absences for which an employee is paid, and if the employee's entitlement has not been used up at the end of the period, they are carried forward to the next period. An example is paid holiday leave, where any unused holidays in one year are carried forward to the next year. The cost of the benefits of such absences should be **charged as an expense** as the employees render service that increases their entitlement to future compensated absences.

There may be **short-term non-accumulating compensated absences**. These are absences for which an employee is paid when they occur, but an **entitlement to the absences does not accumulate**. The employee can be absent, and be paid, but only if and when the circumstances arise. Examples are maternity/paternity pay, (in most cases) sick pay, and paid absence for jury service.

2.3 Measurement

The cost of accumulating paid absences should be measured as the additional amount that the entity expects to pay as a result of the unused entitlement that has accumulated at the end of the reporting period.

Example: unused holiday leave

A company gives its employees an annual entitlement to paid holiday leave. If there is any unused leave at the end of the year, employees are entitled to carry forward the unused leave for up to 12 months. At the end of 20X9, the company's employees carried forward in total 50 days of unused holiday leave. Employees are paid $100 per day.

Required

State the required accounting for the unused holiday carried forward.

Solution

The short-term accumulating compensated absences should be recognised as an expense in the year when the entitlement arises, ie in 20X9 with a corresponding accrual. The amount would be the 50 unused holiday days multiplied by the daily salary of $100 ie $5,000 in total (providing that all 50 days' holiday are likely to be taken in the following year).

Question 3.1
Sick leave

Learning outcomes B1

Plyman Co has 100 employees. Each is entitled to five working days of paid sick leave for each year, and unused sick leave can be carried forward for one year. Sick leave is taken on a LIFO basis (ie firstly out of the current year's entitlement and then out of any balance brought forward).

As at 31 December 20X8, the average unused entitlement is two days per employee. Plyman Co expects (based on past experience which is expected to continue) that 92 employees will take five days or less sick leave in 20X9, the remaining eight employees will take an average of 6½ days each.

Required

State the required accounting for sick leave for the year ended 31 December 20X8.

2.4 Profit sharing or bonus plans

Profit shares or bonuses payable within 12 months after the end of the accounting period should be recognised as an expected cost when the entity has a **present obligation to pay it**, ie when the employer has no real option but to pay it. This will usually be when the employer recognises the profit or other performance achievement to which the profit share or bonus relates. The measurement of the constructive obligation reflects the possibility that some employees may leave without receiving a bonus.

Example: profit sharing plan

Mooro Co runs a profit sharing plan under which it pays 3% of its net profit for the year to those employees who have not left during the year. Mooro Co estimates that this will be reduced by staff turnover to 2.5% in 20X9.

Required

Which costs should be recognised by Mooro Co for the profit share in 20X9?

Solution

Mooro Co should recognise a liability and an expense of 2.5% of net profit.

Section summary

There are **no specific disclosure requirements for short-term employee benefits** in the standard.

3   Post-employment benefits   3/11, 5/11, 11/11, 5/12, 9/12, 11/12, 3/13

Introduction

Many employers provide post-employment benefits for their employees after they have stopped working. **Pension schemes** are the most obvious example, but an employer might provide post-employment death benefits to the dependants of former employees, or post-employment medical care.

3.1 General

Post-employment benefit schemes are often referred to as '**plans**'. The 'plan' receives regular contributions from the employer (and sometimes from current employees as well) and the money is invested in assets, such as stocks and shares and other investments. The post-employment benefits are paid out of the income from the plan assets (dividends, interest) or from money from the sale of some plan assets.

3.2 Definitions

IAS 19 sets out the following definitions relating to classification of plans.

KEY TERMS

DEFINED CONTRIBUTION PLANS are post-employment benefit plans under which an entity pays fixed contributions into a separate entity (a fund) and will have no legal or constructive obligation to pay further contributions if the fund does not hold sufficient assets to pay all employee benefits relating to employee service in the current and prior periods.

DEFINED BENEFIT PLANS are post-employment benefit plans other than defined contribution plans.

MULTI-EMPLOYER PLANS are defined contribution plans (other than state plans) or defined benefit plans (other than state plans) that:

(a)   Pool the assets contributed by various entities that are not under common control, and

(b)   Use those assets to provide benefits to employees of more than one entity, on the basis that contribution and benefit levels are determined without regard to the identity of the entity that employs the employees concerned.

There are two types or categories of post-employment benefit plan, as given in the definitions above.

(a)   **Defined contribution plans**. With such plans, the employer (and possibly current employees too) pay regular contributions into the plan of a given or 'defined' amount each year. The contributions are invested, and the size of the post-employment benefits paid to former employees depends on how well or how badly the plan's investments perform. If the investments perform well, the plan will be able to afford higher benefits than if the investments performed less well.

(b)   **Defined benefit plans**. With these plans, the size of the post-employment benefits is determined in advance, ie the benefits are 'defined'. The employer (and possibly current employees too) pay contributions into the plan, and the contributions are invested. The size of the contributions is set at an amount that is expected to earn enough investment returns to meet the obligation to pay the post-employment benefits. If, however, it becomes apparent that the assets in the fund are insufficient, the employer will be required to make additional contributions into the plan to make up the expected shortfall. On the other hand, if the fund's assets appear to be larger than they need to be, and in excess of what is required to pay the post-employment benefits, the employer may be allowed to take a 'contribution holiday' (ie stop paying in contributions for a while).

It is important to make a clear distinction between the following.

- **Funding** a defined benefit plan, ie paying contributions into the plan
- **Accounting for** the cost of funding a defined benefit plan

The key difference between the two types of plan is the nature of the 'promise' made by the entity to the employees in the scheme:

(a) Under a **defined contribution** plan, the 'promise' is to pay the agreed amount of contributions, Once this is done, the entity has no further liability and no exposure to risks related to the performance of the assets held in the plan.

(b) Under a **defined benefit** plan, the 'promise' is to pay the amount of benefits agreed under the plan. The entity is taking on a far more uncertain liability that may change in future as a result of many variables and has continuing exposure to risks related to the performance of assets held in the plan. In simple terms, of the plan assets are insufficient to meet the plan liabilities to pay pensions in future, the entity will have to make up any deficit.

3.3 Multi-employer plans

These were defined above. IAS 19 requires an entity to **classify** such a plan as a defined contribution plan or a defined benefit plan, depending on its terms (including any constructive obligation beyond those terms).

For a multi-employer plan that is a **defined benefit plan**, the entity should account for its proportionate share of the defined benefit obligation, plan assets and cost associated with the plan in the same way as for any other defined benefit plan and make full disclosure.

When there is **insufficient information** to use defined benefit accounting, then the multi-employer plan should be accounted for as a defined contribution plan and additional disclosures made (that the plan is in fact a defined benefit plan and information about any known surplus or deficit).

3.4 Recap

- There are two categories of **post-retirement benefit plans**:

  - Defined contribution plans
  - Defined benefit plans

- **Defined contribution plans** provide benefits commensurate with the fund available to produce them.

- **Defined benefit plans** provide promised benefits and so contributions are based on estimates of how the fund will perform.

- **Defined contribution plans costs** are easy to account for and this is covered in the next section.

Section summary

There are two types of post-employment benefit plan:

- Defined contribution plans

- Defined benefit plans

4 Defined contribution plans 11/12

Introduction

Defined contribution plans produce benefits based on contributions made.

4.1 Accounting

A typical defined contribution plan would be where the employing company agreed to contribute an amount of, say, 5% of employees' salaries into a post-employment plan.

Accounting for payments into defined contribution plans is straightforward.

(a)   The **obligation** is determined by the amounts to be contributed for that period.

(b)   There are no actuarial assumptions to make.

(c)   If the obligation is settled in the current period (or at least no later than 12 months after the end of the current period) there is **no requirement for discounting**.

IAS 19 requires the following.

(a)   **Contributions** to a defined contribution plan should be recognised as an **expense** in the period they are payable (except to the extent that labour costs may be included within the cost of assets).

(b)   Any liability for **unpaid contributions** that are due as at the end of the period should be recognised as a **liability** (accrued expense).

(c)   Any **excess contributions** paid should be recognised as an asset (prepaid expense), but only to the extent that the prepayment will lead to, eg a reduction in future payments or a cash refund.

In the (unusual) situation where contributions to a defined contribution plan do not fall due entirely within 12 months after the end of the period in which the employees performed the related service, then these should be **discounted**. The discount rate to be used is discussed below in paragraphs 5.22 and 5.23.

4.2 Disclosure requirements

The financial statements must disclose the amount recognised as an **expense** in the period. Where required by IAS 24, the entity should disclose information about contributions to defined contribution plans for key management personnel.

Section summary

Defined contribution plans are simple to account for as the benefits are defined by the contributions made.

5 Defined benefit plans: recognition and measurement
3/11, 5/11, 11/11, 5/12, 9/12, 11/12, 3/13, 5/13

Introduction

Defined benefit plans produce benefits set out at the start of the plan. The annual pension will be calculated with a formula. For example:

(Final salary/60) x number of years worked

5.1 Introduction

Accounting for defined benefit plans is much more complex. The complexity of accounting for defined benefit plans stems largely from the following factors.

(a)   The future benefits (arising from employee service in the current or prior years) **cannot be estimated exactly**, but whatever they are, the employer will have to pay them, and the liability should therefore be recognised now. To estimate these future obligations, it is necessary to use **actuarial assumptions**.

(b)   The obligations payable in future years should be valued, by discounting, on a **present value** basis. This is because the obligations may be settled in many years' time.

(c)   If actuarial assumptions change, the amount of required contributions to the fund will change, and there may be **remeasurement gains or losses**. A contribution into a fund in any period is not necessarily the total for that period, due to actuarial gains or losses.

IAS 19 defines the following key terms to do with defined benefit plans.

KEY TERMS

The NET DEFINED BENEFIT LIABILITY (ASSET) is the deficit or surplus, adjusted for any effect of limiting a net defined benefit asset to the asset ceiling.

The DEFICIT OR SURPLUS is:

(a)   the present value of the defined benefit obligation less

(b)   the fair value of plan assets (if any).

The ASSET CEILING is the present value of any economic benefits available in the form of refunds from the plan or reductions in future contributions to the plan.

The PRESENT VALUE OF A DEFINED BENEFIT obligation is the present value, without deducting any plan assets, of expected future payments required to settle the obligation resulting from employee service in the current and prior periods.

PLAN ASSETS comprise:

(a)   Assets held by a long-term employee benefit fund; and

(b)   Qualifying insurance policies

ASSETS HELD BY A LONG-TERM EMPLOYEE BENEFIT FUND are assets (other than non-transferable financial instruments issued by the reporting entity) that:

(a)   are held by an entity (a fund) that is legally separate from the reporting entity and exists solely to pay or fund employee benefits; and

(b)   are available to be used only to pay or fund employee benefits, are not available to the reporting entity's own creditors (even in bankruptcy), and cannot be returned to the reporting entity, unless either:

(i)   the remaining assets of the fund are sufficient to meet all the related employee benefit obligations of the plan or the reporting entity; or

(ii)   the assets are returned to the reporting entity to reimburse it for employee benefits already paid.

A QUALIFYING INSURANCE POLICY is an insurance policy issued by an insurer that is not a related party (as defined in IAS 24 *Related party disclosures*) of the reporting entity, if the proceeds of the policy:

(a)   can be used only to pay or fund employee benefits under a defined benefit plan; and

(b)   are not available to the reporting entity's own creditors (even in bankruptcy) and cannot be paid to the reporting entity, unless either:

    (i)   the proceeds represent surplus assets that are not needed for the policy to meet all the related employee benefit obligations; or

    (ii)   the proceeds are returned to the reporting entity to reimburse it for employee benefits already paid.

FAIR VALUE is the price that would be received to sell an asset in an orderly transaction between market participants at the measurement date.

5.2 Outline of the method

An outline of the method used for an employer to account for the expenses and obligation of a defined benefit plan is given below. The stages will be explained in more detail later.

Determine the deficit or surplus:

    (a)   An **actuarial technique** (the **Projected Unit Credit Method**), should be used to make a reliable estimate of the amount of future benefits employees have earned from service in relation to the current and prior years. The entity must determine how much benefit should be attributed to service performed by employees in the current period, and in prior periods. Assumptions include, for example, assumptions about employee turnover, mortality rates, future increases in salaries (if these will affect the eventual size of future benefits such as pension payments).

    (b)   The benefit should be **discounted** to arrive at the present value of the defined benefit obligation and the current service cost.

    (c)   The **fair value** of any **plan assets** should be deducted from the present value of the defined benefit obligation.

The surplus or deficit determined in Step 1 may have to be adjusted if a net benefit asset has to be restricted by the **asset ceiling**.

Determine the amounts to be recognised in **profit or loss**:

    (a)   **Current service cost**
    (b)   Any **past service cost** and **gain or loss on settlement**
    (c)   **Net interest** on the **net defined benefit liability (asset)**

Determine the **remeasurements** of the **net defined benefit liability (asset)**, to be recognised in other **comprehensive income** (items that will not be **reclassified to profit or loss**):

    (a)   **Actuarial gains and losses**

    (b)   **Return on plan assets** (excluding amounts included in net interest on the net defined benefit liability (asset))

    (c)   Any change in the effect of the **asset ceiling** (excluding amounts included in net interest on the net defined benefit liability (asset))

5.3 Constructive obligation

IAS 19 makes it very clear that it is not only its legal obligation under the formal terms of a defined benefit plan that an entity must account for, but also any **constructive obligation** that it may have. A constructive obligation, which will arise from the entity's informal practices, exists when the entity has no realistic alternative but to pay employee benefits, for example if any change in the informal practices would cause unacceptable damage to employee relationships.

5.4 The projected unit credit method

With this method, it is assumed that each period of service by an employee gives rise to an **additional unit of future benefits**. The present value of that unit of future benefits can be calculated, and attributed to the period in which the service is given. The units, each measured separately, build up to the overall obligation. The accumulated present value of (discounted) future benefits will incur interest over time, and an interest expense should be recognised.

These calculations are complex and would normally be carried out by an actuary. In the exam, you will be given the figures but the following example (from IAS 19) is included to explain the method.

Example: projected unit credit method

A lump sum benefit is payable on termination of service and equal to 1% of final salary for each year of service. The salary in year 1 is $10,000 and is assumed to increase at 7% (compound) each year. The discount rate used is 10% per year. The following table shows how the obligation builds up for an employee who is expected to leave at the end of year 5, assuming that there are no changes in actuarial assumptions. For simplicity, this example ignores the additional adjustment needed to reflect the probability that the employee may leave the entity at an earlier or later date.

Year	1	2	3	4	5
	$	$	$	$	$
Benefit attributed to:					
Prior years	0	131	262	393	524
Current year (1% × final salary)	131	131	131	131	131
Current and prior years	131	262	393	524	655
Opening obligation	-	89	196	324	476
Interest at 10%	-	9	20	33	48
Current service cost	89	98	108	119	131
Closing obligation	89	196	324	476	655

Notes

1. *The opening obligation is the present value of the benefit attributed to prior years.*
2. *The current service cost is the present value of the benefit attributed to the current year.*
3. *The closing obligation is the present value of the benefit attributed to current and prior years.*

5.5 Actuarial assumptions

Actuarial assumptions are needed **to estimate the size of the future (post-employment) benefits** that will be payable under a defined benefits scheme. The main categories of actuarial assumptions are as follows.

(a) **Demographic assumptions** are about mortality rates before and after retirement, the rate of employee turnover, early retirement, claim rates under medical plans for former employees, and so on.

(b) **Financial assumptions** include future salary levels (allowing for seniority and promotion as well as inflation) and the future rate of increase in medical costs (not just inflationary cost rises, but also cost rises specific to medical treatments and to medical treatments required given the expectations of longer average life expectancy).

The standard requires actuarial assumptions to be neither too cautious nor too imprudent: they should be **'unbiased'**. They should also be based on **'market expectations'** at the year end, over the period during which the obligations will be settled.

5.6 The statement of financial position

In the statement of financial position, the amount recognised as a **net defined benefit liability** (which may be a negative amount, ie an asset) should be the following.

(a)   The **present value of the defined obligation** at the year end, **minus**

(b)   The **fair value of the assets of the plan** as at the year end (if there are any) out of which the future obligations to current and past employees will be directly settled.

The earlier parts of this section have looked at the recognition and measurement of the defined benefit obligation. Now we will look at issues relating to the assets held in the plan.

5.7 Plan assets

Plan assets are:

(a)   Assets such as stocks and shares, held by a fund that is legally separate from the reporting entity, which exists solely to pay employee benefits.

(b)   Insurance policies, issued by an insurer that is not a related party, the proceeds of which can only be used to pay employee benefits.

Investments which may be used for purposes other than to pay employee benefits are not plan assets.

The standard requires that the plan assets are measured at fair value, as 'the price that would be received to sell an asset in an orderly transaction between market participants at the measurement date'. You may spot that this definition is slightly different to the revised definition in accordance with IFRS 13 *Fair value measurement* (see Chapter 5). The two standards were being updated around the same time so the definitions are currently out of step, but this should make no difference to the practicalities you will have to deal with in questions, where the fair value is normally stated in the scenario information.

IAS 19 includes the following **specific requirements**:

(a)   The plan assets should exclude any contributions due from the employer but not yet paid.

(b)   Plan assets are reduced by any liabilities of the fund that do not relate to employee benefits, such as trade and other payables.

5.8 The statement of profit or loss and other comprehensive income

All of the gains and losses that affect the plan obligation and plan asset must be recognised. The **components of defined benefit cost must be recognised as follows** in the statement of profit or loss and other comprehensive income:

Component	*Recognised in*
(a) **Service cost**	Profit or loss
(b) **Net interest on the net defined benefit liability**	Profit or loss
(c) **Remeasurements of the net defined benefit liability**	Other comprehensive income (not reclassified to P/L)

5.9 Service costs

These comprise:

(a)   **Current service cost**, this is the increase in the present value of the defined benefit obligation resulting from employee services during the period. The measurement and recognition of this cost was introduced in Section 5.1.

(b)   **Past service cost**, which is the change in the obligation relating to service in **prior periods**. This results from amendments or curtailments to the pension plan, and

(c)   Any **gain or loss on settlement.**

The detail relating to points (b)and (c) above will be covered in a later section. First, we will continue with the basic elements of accounting for defined benefit pension costs.

5.10 Net interest on the defined benefit liability (asset)

In Section 5.1 we looked at the recognition and measurement of the defined benefit obligation. This figure is the discounted **present value** of the future benefits payable. Every year the discount must be 'unwound', increasing the present value of the obligation as time passes through an interest charge.

5.10.1 Interest calculation

IAS 19 requires that the interest should be calculated on the **net defined benefit liability (asset)**. This means that the amount recognised in profit or loss is the net of the interest charge on the obligation and the interest income recognised on the assets.

The calculation is as follows:

The **net defined benefit liability/(asset)** should be determined as at the **start** of the accounting period, taking account of changes during the period as a result of contributions paid into the plan and benefits paid out.

Many exam questions include the assumption that all payments into and out of the plan take place at the end of the year, so that the interest calculations can be based on the opening balances.

In the exam, **interest** will need to be **calculated separately** on the opening defined benefit obligation and the opening **plan assets** to be able to find the remeasurement gains/losses as a balancing figure (see paragraph 5.11 below) as follows:

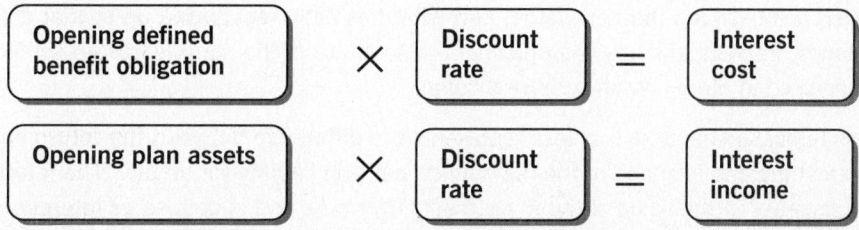

Then the **net interest cost** (or income) is posted to **profit or loss** and represents the **financing effect** of paying for benefits in advance (if there is a net pension asset and surplus ie net interest *income*) or in arrears (if there is a net pension liability and deficit ie net interest *cost*).

5.10.2 Discount rate

The **discount rate** adopted should be determined by reference to **market yields** on high quality fixed-rate corporate bonds. In the absence of a 'deep' market in such bonds, the yields on comparable government bonds should be used as reference instead. The maturity of the corporate bonds that are used to determine a discount rate should have a term to maturity that is consistent with the expected maturity of the post-employment benefit obligations, although a single weighted average discount rate is sufficient.

The guidelines comment that there may be some difficulty in obtaining a **reliable yield for long-term maturities**, say 30 or 40 years from now. This should not, however, be a significant problem: the present value of obligations payable in many years time will be relatively small and unlikely to be a significant proportion of the total defined benefit obligation. The total obligation is therefore unlikely to be sensitive to errors in the assumption about the discount rate for long-term maturities (beyond the maturities of long-term corporate or government bonds).

5.11 Remeasurements of the net defined benefit liability 5/11

Remeasurements of the net defined benefit liability/(asset) comprise:

(a)   Actuarial gains and losses;

(b)   The return on plan assets, (excluding amounts included in net interest on the net defined benefit liability/(asset)); and

(c)   Any change in the effect of the asset ceiling, (excluding amounts included in net interest on the net defined benefit liability/(asset)).

The gains and losses relating to points (a) and (b) above will arise in every defined benefit scheme so we will look at these in this section. The asset ceiling is a complication that is not relevant in every case, so it is dealt with separately, later in the chapter.

5.11.1 Remeasurement gains or losses on defined benefit obligation

At the end of each accounting period, a new valuation, using updated assumptions, should be carried out on the obligation. Remeasurement ('actuarial') gains or losses arise because of the following.

*   **Actual events** (eg employee turnover, salary increases) differ from the actuarial assumptions that were made to estimate the defined benefit obligations

*   The effect of **changes to assumptions** concerning benefit payment options

*   **Estimates are revised** (eg different assumptions are made about future employee turnover, salary rises, mortality rates, and so on)

*   The effect of changes to the **discount rate**

Remeasurement gains and losses are recognised in **other comprehensive income**. They are **not reclassified to profit or loss** under the 2011 revision to IAS 1 (see Chapter 17).

5.11.2 Remeasurement gains or losses on plan assets

A new valuation of the plan assets is carried out at each period end, using current fair values. Any **difference between the new value, and what has been recognised up to that date** (normally the opening balance, interest, and any cash payments into or out of the plan) is treated as a '**remeasurement**' and recognised in other comprehensive income.

This remeasurement gain or loss represents the **difference between the return on the plan assets and the interest income** included in the net defined pension liability (or asset). The **return** on the plan assets is the increase in the value of the investments over time and is defined as **interest, dividends and other income** derived from the plan assets together with **realised and unrealised gains or losses** on the plan assets, less any costs of managing plan assets and tax payable by the plan itself.

 Example

At 1 January 20X2 the fair value of the assets of a defined benefit plan were valued at $1,100,000 and the present value of the defined benefit obligation was $1,250,000. On 31 December 20X2, the plan received contributions from the employer of $490,000 and paid out benefits of $190,000.

The current service cost for the year was $360,000 and a discount rate of 6% is to be applied to the net liability/(asset).

After these transactions, the fair value of the plan's assets at 31 December 20X2 was $1,500,000. The present value of the defined benefit obligation was $1,553,600.

Required

Calculate the remeasurement gains or losses on the defined benefit obligation and plan assets and illustrate how this pension plan will be treated in the statement of profit or loss and other comprehensive income and statement of financial position for the year ended 31 December 20X2.

Solution

It is always useful to set up a working reconciling the assets and obligation:

	Assets $	*Obligation* $
Fair value/present value at 1/1/X2	1,100,000	1,250,000
Interest (1,100,000 × 6%)/(1,250,000 × 6%)	66,000	75,000
Current service cost		360,000
Contributions received	490,000	
Benefits paid	(190,000)	(190,000)
	1,466,000	1,495,000
Remeasurement gain on plan assets through OCI (balancing figure)	34,000	–
Remeasurement loss on defined benefit obligation through OCI (balancing figure)	-	58,600
Closing fair value/present value at 31/1/X2	1,500,000	1,553,600

The following accounting treatment is required.

(a)   In the **statement of profit or loss and other comprehensive income**, the following amounts will be recognised:

In **profit or loss:**

	$
Current service cost	360,000
Net interest on net defined benefit liability (75,000 – 66,000)	9,000
	369,000

In **other comprehensive income:**

	$
Remeasurement gain on plan assets	34,000
Remeasurement loss on defined benefit obligation	(58,600)
	24,600

(b)   In the **statement of financial position**, the net defined benefit liability of $53,600 (1,553,600 – 1,500,000) will be recognised.

5.12 Recap

The recognition and measurement of defined benefit plan costs are complex issues.

• Learn and understand the definitions of the various elements of a defined benefit pension plan

• Learn the **outline of the method of accounting** (see paragraph 5.2)

• Learn the recognition method for the:

   – Statement of financial position
   – Statement of profit or loss and other comprehensive income

• The examiner often uses the term 'plan liabilities' rather than 'defined benefit obligation'. Either can be used in the exam.

Section summary

Defined benefit plans are much more difficult to deal with as the benefits are promised so they define the contributions to be made.

Future benefits are attributed to services performed by employees using the **projected unit credit method**.

Discount rates used should be determined by reference to market yields on high-quality fixed-rate corporate bonds.

Actuarial assumptions made should be unbiased and based on market expectations.

Remeasurement gains or losses, which form part of the return on plan assets, arise due to differences between **the year end valuation of the defined benefit obligation and plan assets** and their **accounting value**. They are required to be recognised in **other comprehensive income**.

6 Defined benefit plans: other matters

Introduction

This section looks at the special circumstances of curtailments and settlements. These complications are less likely to appear in exam questions than the matters covered in the earlier sections of this chapter.

We have now covered the basics of accounting for defined benefit plans. This section looks at the special circumstances of past service costs, curtailments and settlements.

6.1 Past service cost and gains and losses on settlement

Exam skills

You should know how to deal with past service costs and curtailments and settlements.

In paragraph 5.9 we identified that the total service cost may comprise not only the current service costs but other items, past service cost and gains and losses on settlement. This section explain these issues and their accounting treatment.

6.1.1 Past service cost

Past service cost is the change in the present value of the defined benefit obligation resulting from a plan **amendment** or **curtailment**.

A plan **amendment** arises when an entity either introduces or withdraws, a defined benefit plan or **changes the benefits payable** under an existing plan. As a result, the entity has taken on additional obligations that it has not hitherto provided for (or reduced its obligation to its employees). For example, an employer might decide to introduce a medical benefits scheme for former employees. This will create a new defined benefit obligation, that has not yet been provided for.

A **curtailment occurs when an entity significantly reduces the number of employees covered by a plan**. This could result from an isolated event, such as closing a plant, discontinuing an operation or the termination or suspension of a plan.

Past service costs can be either **positive** (if the changes increase the obligation) or **negative** (if the change reduces the obligation).

6.1.2 Accounting for past service cost

An entity should **remeasure the obligation** (and the related plan assets, if any) using current actuarial assumptions, before determining past service cost or a gain or loss on settlement.

Past service costs are recognised at the earlier of the following dates:

(a)   When the plan amendment or curtailment occurs, and

(b)   When the entity recognises related restructuring costs (in accordance with IAS 37, see Chapter 18) or termination benefits.

6.1.3 Gains and losses on settlement

A **settlement** occurs either when an employer enters into a transaction to eliminate part or all of its post-employment benefit obligations (other than a payment of benefits to or on behalf of employees under the terms of the plan and included in the actuarial assumptions).

A curtailment and settlement might **happen together**, for example when an employer brings a defined benefit plan to an end by settling the obligation with a one-off lump sum payment and then scrapping the plan.

The gain or losses on a settlement is the difference between:

(a)   The **present value of the defined benefit obligation** being settled, as valued on the date of the settlement; and

(b)   The **settlement price**, including any plan assts transferred and any payments made by the entity directly in connection with the settlement.

6.1.4 Accounting for past service cost and gains and losses on settlement

An entity should **remeasure the obligation** (and the related plan assets, if any) using current actuarial assumptions, before determining past service cost or a gain or loss on settlement.

The rules for recognition for these items are as follows.

Past service costs are recognised at the earlier of the following dates:

(a)   When the plan amendment or curtailment occurs, and

(b)   When the entity recognises related restructuring costs (in accordance with IAS 37, see Chapter 18) or termination benefits.

6.1.5 Accounting for gains and losses on settlement

An entity should recognise a **gain or loss** on settlement in **profit or loss** when the **settlement occurs**.

6.2 Asset ceiling test

When we looked at the recognition of the net defined benefit liability/(asset) in the statement of financial position at the beginning of Section 5 the term 'asset ceiling' was mentioned. This term relates to a threshold established by IAS 19 to ensure that any defined benefit asset (ie a pension surplus) is carried at **no more than its recoverable amount**. In simple terms, this means that any net asset is restricted to the amount of cash savings that will be available to the entity in future.

6.3 Net defined benefit assets

A net defined benefit asset may arise if the plan has been overfunded or if actuarial gains have arisen. This meets the definition of an asset (as stated in the *Framework*) because **all** of the following apply.

(a)   The entity **controls a resource** (the ability to use the surplus to generate future benefits).

(b)   That control is the **result of past events** (contributions paid by the entity and service rendered by the employee).

(c)   **Future benefits** are available to the entity in the form of a reduction in future contributions or a cash refund, either directly or indirectly to another plan in deficit.

The **asset ceiling** is the **present value** of those future benefits. The **discount rate used is the same** as that used to calculate the net interest on the net defined benefit liability/(asset). The net defined benefit asset would be reduced to the asset ceiling threshold. Any related write down would be treated as a **remeasurement** and recognised in **other comprehensive income**.

6.4 Suggested approach and question

The suggested approach to defined benefit schemes is to deal with the change in the obligation and asset in the following order.

Step	Item	Recognition	
1	**Record opening figures:** • Asset • Obligation		
2	**Interest cost on plan liabilities** • Based on discount rate and PV obligation at start of period. • Should also reflect any changes in obligation during period.	DEBIT CREDIT	*Net interest cost (P/L)* *(x% × b/d liabilities)* *Plan liabilities (SOFP)*
3	**Interest on plan assets** • Based on discount rate and asset value at start of period. • Technically, this interest is also time apportioned on contributions less benefits paid in the period.	DEBIT CREDIT	*Plan assets (SOFP)* *Net interest cost (P/L)* *(x% × b/d assets)*
4	**Current service cost** • Increase in the present value of the obligation resulting from employee service in the current period.	DEBIT CREDIT	*Current service cost (P/L)* *Plan liabilities (SOFP)*
5	**Contributions** • As advised by actuary.	DEBIT CREDIT	*Plan assets (SOFP)* *Company cash*
6	**Benefits** • Actual pension payments made.	DEBIT CREDIT	*Plan liabilities (SOFP)* *Plan assets (SOFP)*
7	**Past service cost** • Change in pension liabilities for employee service in prior periods, resulting from a plan amendment or curtailment.	**Positive (increase in obligation):** DEBIT CREDIT **Negative (decrease in obligation):** DEBIT CREDIT	 *Past service cost (P/L)* *Plan liabilities (SOFP)* *Plan liabilities (SOFP)* *Past service cost (P/L)*

Step	Item	Recognition	
8	**Gains and losses on settlement** • Difference between the value of the obligation being settled and the settlement price.	**Gain** DEBIT	*Plan liabilities (SOFP)*
		CREDIT	*Plan assets*
		CREDIT	*Cash*
		Loss	
		DEBIT	*Service cost (P/L)*
		DEBIT	*Plan liabilities (SOFP)*
		CREDIT	*Plan assets*
		CREDIT	*Cash*
9	**Remeasurements: actuarial gains and losses** • Arising from annual valuations of liabilities. • On plan liabilities, differences between actuarial assumptions and actual experience during the period, or changes in actuarial assumptions.	**Gain** DEBIT	*Plan liabilities (SOFP)*
		CREDIT	*Other comprehensive income*
		Loss	
		DEBIT	*Other comprehensive income*
		CREDIT	*Plan liabilities(SOFP)*
10	**Remeasurements: return on assets less interest income** • Arising from annual valuations of plan assets	**Gain** DEBIT	*Plan assets (SOFP)*
		CREDIT	*Other comprehensive income*
		Loss	
		DEBIT	*Other comprehensive income*
		CREDIT	*Plan assets (SOFP)*
11	**Disclose in accordance with the standard**	See comprehensive question.	

Exam skills

It would be useful for you to do one last question on accounting for post-employment defined benefit schemes. Questions on these are likely in the exam.

Question 3.2 Comprehensive

Learning outcomes B1

For the sake of simplicity and clarity, all transactions are assumed to occur at the year end.

The following data applies to the post employment defined benefit compensation scheme of BCD Co.

Discount rate: 10% (each year)

Present value of plan liabilities at start of 20X2: $1,600,000

Market value of plan assets at start of 20X2: $1,402,000

The following figures are relevant.

	20X2 $'000
Current service cost	150
Benefits paid out	130
Contributions paid by entity	120
Present value of plan liabilities at year end	1,710
Fair value of plan assets at year end	1,610

At the end of 20X2, a decision was taken to make a one-off additional payment to former employees currently receiving pensions from the plan. This was announced to the former employees before the year end. This payment was not allowed for in the original terms of the scheme. The actuarial valuation of the obligation in the table above **includes** the additional liability of $40,000 relating to this additional payment.

Required

Show how the reporting entity should account for this defined benefit plan in 20X2.

Section summary

You should know how to deal with curtailments and settlements.

7 Other long term benefits

7.1 Definition

IAS 19 defines **other long-term employee benefits** as all employee benefits other than short-term employee benefits, post-employment benefits and termination benefits if not expected to be settled wholly before twelve months after the end of the annual reporting period in which the employees render the related service.

The types of benefits that might fall into this category include:

(a)   Long-term paid absences such as long-service or sabbatical leave
(b)   Jubilee or other long-service benefits
(c)   Long-term disability benefits; profit-sharing and bonuses
(d)   Deferred remuneration

7.2 Accounting treatment for other long-term benefits

There are many similarities between these types of benefits and defined benefit pensions. For example, in a long-term bonus scheme, the employees may provide service over a number of periods to earn their entitlement to a payment at a later date. In some case, the entity may put cash aside, or invest it in some way (perhaps by taking out an insurance policy) to meet the liabilities when they arise.

As there is normally far less uncertainty relating to the measurement of these benefits, IAS 19 requires a simpler method of accounting for them. Unlike the accounting method for post-employment benefits, this method does **not recognise remeasurements in other comprehensive income**.

The entity should recognise all of the following in **profit or loss**.

(a)   **Service cost**
(b)   **Net interest** on the defined benefit liability (asset)
(c)   **Remeasurement** of the defined benefit liability (asset)

8   Disclosures

8.1 Principles of disclosures required by IAS 19

The outline requirements are for the entity to disclose information that:

(a)   Explains the characteristics of its defined benefit plans and risks associated with them;

(b)   Identifies and explains the amounts in its financial statements arising from its defined benefit plans; and

(c)   Describes how its defined benefit plans may affect the amount, timing and uncertainty of the entity's future cash flows.

9   Other issues

This section is unlikely to be tested in detail, but it gives you some background knowledge in recent developments around pension reporting.

9.1 Revisions to IAS 19

In June 2011, the IASB issued a revised version of *IAS 19 Employee benefits*. It is the revised version that has been covered in this chapter. The purpose of the revision is to improve accounting in the short-term for employee benefits in the light of criticisms of the current IAS 19 by users and preparers of financial statements, including the US SEC and the EU's European Financial Reporting Advisory Group (that approves IFRS for use in the EU). In the long term, the IASB intends to produce a common IASB-FASB standard, but recognises that this will take many years to complete.

Accounting for employee benefits, particularly retirement benefits, had been seen as **problematic** in the following respects:

(a)   **Income statement (statement of profit or loss and other comprehensive income) treatment.** It has been argued that the complexity of the presentation makes the treatment hard to understand and the splitting up of the various components is arbitrary.

(b)   **Fair value and volatility.** The fair value of plan assets may be volatile, and values in the statement of financial position may fluctuate. However, not all those fluctuations are recognised in the statement of financial position.

(c)   **Fair value and economic reality.** Fair value, normally market value, is used to value plan assets. This may not reflect economic reality, because fair values fluctuate in the short term, while pension scheme assets and liabilities are held for the long term. It could be argued that plan assets should be valued on an actuarial basis instead.

(d)   **Problems in determining the discount rate used in measuring the defined benefit obligation.** Guidance is contradictory.

9.2 The main changes

9.2.1 Scope

Because the revised standard is a short-term measure, its **scope is limited to** the following areas.

(a)   Recognition of gains and losses arising from defined benefit plans

(b)   Presentation of changes in value of the defined benefit obligation and assets

However, the IASB recognises that the scope **could be expanded** to include items such as:

(a) **Recognition of the obligation based on the 'benefit' formula**. This current approach means that unvested benefits are recognised as a liability which is inconsistent with other IFRSs.

(b) **Measurement of the obligation**. The 'projected unit credit method' (as defined before) is used which is based on expected benefits (including salary increases). Alternative approaches include accumulated benefit, projected benefit, fair value and settlement value.

(c) **Presenting of a net defined benefit obligation**. Defined benefit plan assets and liabilities are currently presented net on the grounds that the fund is not controlled (which would require consolidation of the fund).

(d) **Multi-employer plans**. Current accounting is normally for the entity's proportionate share of the obligation, plan assets and costs as for a single-employer plan, but an exemption is currently provided where sufficient information is not available, and defined contribution accounting can be used instead. Should the exemption be removed?

(e) Accounting for **benefits that are based on contributions and a promised return**.

9.2.2 The main changes

(a) **Actuarial gains and losses**

   (i) The revised standard requires actuarial gains and losses to be **recognised in the period incurred**.

   (ii) The previous standard permitted a range of choices for the recognition of actuarial gains and losses:

   (1) Immediate recognition in other comprehensive income (as now) was permitted

   (2) Deferral of actuarial gains and losses was permitted through what was known as the 'corridor' method. The 'corridor' was defined as the higher of 10% of the opening plan assets or 10% of the opening plan obligation. If the accumulated actuarial gains and losses brought forward exceeded the corridor, the excess would then be divided by the average remaining service lives of employees in the scheme and this amount recognised in profit or loss. The balance of unrecognised gains and losses was carried on the statement of financial position.

   (3) Actuarial gains and losses could also be recognised in profit or loss on any other systematic basis, subject to the 'corridor' amount as a minimum.

   (iii) The changes will improve comparability between companies and will also eliminate some of the anomalies where the effect of unrecognised actuarial gains and losses (and unrecognised past service costs (see point (d) below) could turn a deficit into a surplus on the statement of financial position.

(b) **Remeasurements**

   (i) The revised standard introduced the term 'remeasurements'. This is made up of the actuarial gains and losses on the defined benefit obligation, the difference between actual investment returns and the return implied by the net interest cost and the effect of the asset ceiling. Remeasurements are recognised immediately in other comprehensive income and **not** reclassified to profit or loss.

   (ii) This reduces diversity of presentation that was possible under the previous standard.

(c) **Net interest cost**

   (i) The revised standard requires interest to be calculated on **both** the plan assets and plan obligation at the same rate and the **net** interest to be recognised in the statement of profit or loss and other comprehensive income. The rationale for this is the view that the **net**

defined benefit liability/(asset) is equivalent to an amount owed by the company to the plan.

(ii) The difference under the previous standard was that an 'Expected return on assets' was calculated, based on assumptions about the long term rates of return on the particular classes of asset held within the plan.

(d) **Past service costs**

(i) The revised standard requires all past service costs to be recognised in the period of plan amendment.

(ii) The previous standard made a distinction between past service costs that were **vested** (all past service costs related to former employees and those that related to current employees and not subject to any condition relating to further service) and those that were **not vested** (relating to current employees and where the entitlement was subject to further service). Only **vested** past service costs were recognised in profit or loss, and unvested benefits were deferred, and spread over remaining service lives.

Chapter Roundup

✓   **IAS 19** *Employee benefits* is a long and complex standard covering both short-term and long-term (post-employment) benefits. The complications arise when dealing with **post-employment benefits**.

✓   There are **no specific disclosure requirements for short-term employee benefits** in the Standard.

✓   There are **two types of post-employment benefit plan**:

    –   Defined contribution plans
    –   Defined benefit plans

✓   **Defined contribution plans** are simple to account for as the benefits are defined by the contributions made. The contributions for the year should be recognised as an expense in profit or loss and an accrual should be recognised for any unpaid amounts at the year end.

✓   **Defined benefit plans** are much more difficult to deal with as the benefits are promised, so they define the contributions to be made. The present value of plan liabilities and the fair value of the plan assets should be recognised as a net pension liability (asset) in the entity's statement of financial position.

✓   Future benefits are attributed to services performed by employees using **the projected unit credit method**. **Discount rates** used should be determined by reference to market yields on high-quality fixed-rate corporate bonds.

✓   **Net interest cost (income)** should be calculated on the opening plan assets and liabilities.

✓   **Actuarial assumptions** made should be unbiased and based on market expectations.

✓   **Remeasurement gains and losses** arise due to differences between **the year end valuation of the defined benefit obligation and plan assets** and their **accounting value**. They are to be recognised **other comprehensive income**.

✓   You should know how to deal with **past service costs** and **settlements**.

Quick Quiz

1   What are the four categories of employee benefits covered by IAS 19?

2   What is the difference between defined contribution and defined benefit plans?

3   What is a 'constructive obligation' compared to a legal obligation?

4   How should a defined benefit expense be recognised in the statement of profit or loss and other comprehensive income?

5   What causes remeasurements gains or losses?

Answers to Quick Quiz

1   • Short-term   • Other long-term
     • Post-employment   • Termination

2   Under a defined contribution plan, the employer engages to pay an agreed amount of contributions and undertakes no further liability. Under a defined benefit plan, the employer engages to pay an agreed level of benefits – if the plan assets are insufficient to meet the plan liabilities, the employer will have to make up the deficit.

3   A constructive obligation exists when the entity has no realistic alternative than to pay employee benefits.

4   P/L: Current service cost + net interest on net defined asset/liability + past service cost + cost of curtailments or settlements.

     OCI: Gains and losses on remeasurement of plan assets or obligation.

5   Remeasurement gains/losses arise as the result of actuarial assumptions about benefit payment options, salary and employee turnover estimates, and discount rates.

 # Answers to Questions

3.1   Sick leave

Plyman Co expects to pay an additional 12 days of sick pay as a result of the unused entitlement that has accumulated at 31 December 20X8, ie 1½ days × 8 employees. For the year ended 31 December 20X8, Plyman Co should recognise a liability and corresponding expense equal to 12 days of sick pay.

3.2 Comprehensive

The gain or loss on remeasurement is established as a balancing figure in the calculations, as follows.

It is always useful to set up a working reconciling the assets and obligation:

	Assets 20X2 $'000	Liabilities 20X2 $'000
Opening fair value/present value at 1/1/X2	1,402	1,600
Interest (10%)	140	160
Current service cost		150
Contributions received	120	
Benefits paid	(130)	(130)
Past service cost	-	40
	1,532	1,820
Remeasurement gain on plan assets through OCI (balancing figure)	78	–
Remeasurement gain on defined benefit obligation through OCI (balancing figure)	-	(110)
Closing fair value/present value at 31/1/X2	1,610	1,710

In the statement of financial position, the liability that is recognised is calculated as follows.

	20X2 $'000
Present value of plan liabilities	1,710
Market value of plan assets	(1,610)
Net pension liability/(asset) in statement of financial position	100

The following will be recognised in profit or loss for the year:

	20X2 $'000
Current service cost	150
Past service cost	40
Net interest on defined benefit liability (asset) (160 – 140)	20
Expense recognised in profit or loss	210

The following remeasurements will be recognised in other comprehensive income for the year:

	20X2 $'000
Remeasurement gain on plan liabilities	110
Remeasurement gain on plan assets	78
	188

Now try this question from the Exam Question Bank

Number	Level	Marks	Time
Q3	Examination	12	22 mins

SHARE-BASED PAYMENTS

 This chapter deals with IFRS 2 on share based payment, a controversial area.

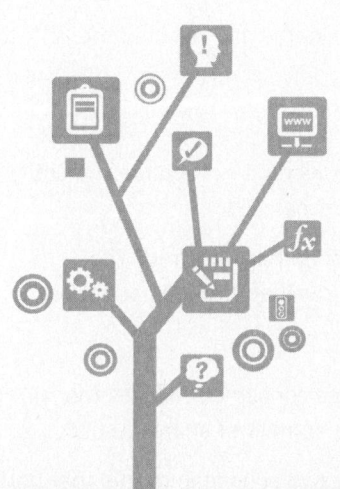

4

topic list	learning outcomes	syllabus references	ability required
1 IFRS 2 *Share based payment*	B1	B1 (vi)	Evaluation

1 IFRS 2 Share based payment   3/12, 5/12, 9/12

Introduction

Transactions whereby entities purchase goods or services from other parties, such as suppliers and employees, by **issuing shares or share options** to those other parties are **increasingly common**.

1.1 Background

Share schemes are a common feature of employee and executive remuneration. In some countries, tax incentives are offered to encourage the use of share-based payment. Companies whose shares or share options are regarded as a valuable 'currency' may also use share-based payment to obtain professional services.

The increasing use of share-based payment raised questions about the accounting treatment of such transactions in company financial statements. Because the granting of share options often involved no initial cost, no expense would be recorded. This led to an **anomaly:** if a company paid its employees in cash, an expense would be recognised in profit or loss, but if the payment took the form of share options, no expense would be recognised. The omission also gave rise to corporate governance concerns.

IFRS 2 Share-based payment was issued to deal with this.

1.1.1 Arguments against recognition of share-based payment in the financial statements

There were a number of arguments against recognition. The IASB has considered and rejected the arguments below.

(a) **No cost therefore no charge**

 There is no cost to the entity because the granting of shares or options does not require the entity to sacrifice cash or other assets. Therefore a charge should not be recognised.

 This argument is unsound because it ignores the fact that a transaction has occurred. The employees have provided valuable services to the entity in return for valuable shares or options.

(b) **Earnings per share is hit twice**

 It is argued that the charge to profit or loss for the employee services consumed reduces the entity's earnings, while at the same time there is an increase in the number of shares issued.

 However, the dual impact on earnings per share simply reflects the two economic events that have occurred.

 (i)   The entity has issued shares or options, thus increasing the denominator of the earnings per share calculation.

 (ii) It has also consumed the resources it received for those shares or options, thus reducing the numerator.

(c) **Adverse economic consequences**

 It could be argued that entities might be discouraged from introducing or continuing employee share plans if they were required to recognise them on the financial statements. However, if this happened, it might be because the requirement for entities to account properly for employee share plans had revealed the economic consequences of such plans.

 A situation where entities are able to obtain and consume resources by issuing valuable shares or options without having to account for such transactions could be perceived as a distortion.

1.2 Objective and scope

IFRS 2 requires an entity to **reflect the effects of share-based payment transactions** in its statement of profit or loss and statement of financial position.

The accounting requirements depend on how the share-based payment transaction is settled: by equity, by cash, or a choice between the two.

(a)   **Equity-settled**: The entity receives goods or services in exchange for equity instruments of the entity (including shares or share options)

(b)   **Cash-settled**: The entity receives goods or services in exchange for amounts of cash that are based on the price (or value) of the entity's shares or other equity instruments of the entity

(c)   **Equity or cash**: Either the entity or the supplier has a **choice** as to whether the entity settles the transaction in cash (or other assets) or by issuing equity instruments

Exam alert

For the purposes of your exam, you only need to know about (a) and (b).

IFRS 2 only applies to share-based transactions for the acquisition of goods and services. It does not apply to other transactions with holders of equity instruments, such as share dividends, purchase of treasury shares, or the issue of additional shares in a rights issue.

Certain transactions are **outside the scope** of the IFRS, such as the issue of equity instruments in exchange for control of another entity in a business combination.

KEY TERMS

SHARE-BASED PAYMENT TRANSACTION A transaction in which the entity receives or acquires goods or services either **as consideration** for its equity instruments or by **incurring liabilities** for amounts based on the price **of the entity's shares or other equity instruments** of the entity.

SHARE-BASED PAYMENT ARRANGEMENT An agreement between the entity and another party (including an employee) to enter into a share-based payment transaction, which thereby entitles the other party to receive cash or other assets of the entity for amounts that are based on the price of the entity's shares or other equity instruments of the entity, or to receive equity instruments of the entity, provided the specified vesting conditions, if any, are met.

EQUITY INSTRUMENT A contract that evidences a residual interest in the assets of an entity after deducting all of its liabilities.

EQUITY INSTRUMENT GRANTED The right (conditional or unconditional) to an equity instrument of the entity conferred by the entity on another party, under a share-based payment arrangement.

SHARE OPTION A contract that gives the holder the right, but not the obligation, to subscribe to the entity's shares at a fixed or determinable price for a specified period of time.

FAIR VALUE is the amount for which an asset could be exchanged, a liability settled, or an equity instrument granted could be exchanged, between knowledgeable, willing parties in an arm's length transaction. (Note that this definition is different from that in IFRS 13 *Fair value measurement,* but the IFRS 2 definition applies.)

INTRINSIC VALUE The difference between the fair value of the shares to which the counterparty has the (conditional or unconditional) right to subscribe or which it has the right to receive, and the price (if any) the other party is (or will be) required to pay for those shares. For example, a share option with an exercise price of $15 on a share with a fair value of $20, has an intrinsic value of $5.

MEASUREMENT DATE The date at which the fair value of the equity instruments granted is measured. For transactions with employees and others providing similar services, the measurement date is grant date.

For transactions with parties other than employees (and those providing similar services), the measurement date is the date the entity obtains the goods or the counterparty renders service.

To VEST means to become an entitlement. Under a share-based payment arrangement, a counterparty's right to receive cash, other assets, or equity instruments of the entity vests upon satisfaction of any specified vesting conditions.

VESTING CONDITIONS The conditions that must be satisfied for the counterparty to become entitled to receive cash, other assets or equity instruments of the entity, under a share-based payment arrangement. Vesting conditions include service conditions, which require the other party to complete a specified period of service, and performance conditions, which require specified performance targets to be met (such as a specified increase in the entity's profit over a specified period of time).

1.3 Recognition: the basic principle

An entity should **recognise goods or services received or acquired in a share-based payment transaction when it obtains the goods or as the services are received.** Goods or services received or acquired in a share-based payment transaction **should be recognised as expenses** unless they qualify for recognition as **assets**. For example, services are normally recognised as expenses (because they are normally rendered immediately), while goods are recognised as assets.

If the goods or services were received or acquired in an **equity-settled** share-based payment transaction the entity should recognise **a corresponding increase in equity** (reserves).

If the goods or services were received or acquired in a **cash-settled** share-based payment transaction the entity should recognise a **liability.**

For example, where an entity grants share options to its employees for their services, the transaction should be recorded as follows:

DEBIT Staff costs

CREDIT   Other reserves [within equity] (*if equity-settled*)/ Liability (*if cash-settled*).

Where performance by the counterparty is not immediate, the expense is **spread** over the period until the counterparty becomes entitled to receive the share-based payment (the **'vesting' period'**). For example, employee services where a minimum period of service must be completed before entitlement to the share-based payment.

VESTING PERIOD The period during which all the specified vesting conditions of a share-based payment arrangement are to be satisfied.

KEY TERM

Exam alert

Most share-based payment questions in past exams have focused on share-based payment transactions for employee services, rather than those for the purchase of goods.

1.4 Equity-settled share-based payment transactions
11/10, 3/11, 9/11

1.4.1 Measurement

The issue here is how to measure the 'cost' of the goods and services received and the equity instruments (eg the share options) granted in return.

The general principle in IFRS 2 is that when an entity recognises the goods or services received and the corresponding increase in equity, it should measure these at the **fair value of the goods or services**

received. Where the transaction is with **parties other than employees**, there is a rebuttable presumption that the fair value of the goods or services received can be estimated reliably.

In such cases, the entity should measure the share-based payment **expense using the fair value of the goods or services received**. This is called the **direct method**.

Where the direct method is used, fair value should be measured at the date the entity obtains the goods or the counterparty renders service.

If the fair value of the goods or services received cannot be measured reliably, the entity should measure their value by reference to the **fair value of the equity instruments granted.** This is called the **indirect method**, and is the method often adopted for employee services.

Where the indirect method is used, the fair value of those equity instruments should be measured at **grant date**.

KEY TERM

GRANT DATE The date at which the entity and another party (including an employee) agree to a share-based payment arrangement, being when the entity and the other party have a shared understanding of the terms and conditions of the arrangement. At grant date, the entity confers on the other party (the counterparty) the right to cash, other assets, or equity instruments of the entity, provided the specified vesting conditions, if any, are met. If that agreement is subject to an approval process (for example, by shareholders), grant date is the date when that approval is obtained.

1.4.2 Determining the fair value of equity instruments granted

Where the indirect method is used, the fair value of the equity instruments is based on **market prices** if available, taking into account the terms and conditions upon which those equity instruments were granted.

If market prices are not available, the entity should estimate the fair value of the equity instruments granted using a **valuation technique**. (These are beyond the scope of this exam.)

1.4.3 Transactions in which services are received

If the equity instruments granted **vest immediately** (ie the counterparty is not required to complete a specified period of service before becoming unconditionally entitled to the equity instruments), it is presumed that the services have already been received. The entity should **recognise the services received in full**, with a corresponding increase in equity, **on the grant date**.

If the equity instruments granted **do not vest until the counterparty completes a specified period of service**, the entity should account for those services **as they are rendered** by the counterparty during the vesting period.

For example, if an employee is granted share options on condition that he or she completes three years' service, then the fair value of the share-based payment, determined at the grant date, should be expensed over that three-year vesting period.

Where the share-based payment is equity-settled, the fair value of each equity instrument should be based on the fair value at the grant date. No adjustment should be made to this fair value in subsequent years.

The total fair value to be recognised should be based on the **best available estimate** of the **number of equity instruments expected to vest**. The entity should **revise** that estimate if subsequent information indicates that the number of equity instruments expected to vest differs from previous estimates. On **vesting date**, the entity should revise the estimate to **equal the number of equity instruments that actually vest**.

For example, for share options granted to employees, the entity will estimate the number of employees entitled to exercise their share options. Any changes in the number of employees expected to receive the share options is treated as a change in accounting estimate and is recognised in the period of the change.

Example: equity-settled share-based payment transaction

On 1 January 20X1, an entity grants 100 share options to each of its 400 employees. Each grant is conditional upon the employee working for the entity until 31 December 20X3. The fair value of each share option is $20.

During 20X1, 20 employees leave and the entity estimates that 20% of the employees (ie. 80 employees) will leave during the three year period.

During 20X2 a further 25 employees leave and the entity now estimates that 25% of its employees (ie. 100 employees) will leave during the three year period.

During 20X3 a further 10 employees leave. The share options granted to the remaining employees are vested at the end of 20X3.

Required

Calculate the remuneration expense that will be recognised in respect of the share-based payment transaction for each of the three years, and show the accounting entries required.

Solution

IFRS 2 requires the entity to recognise the remuneration expense, based on the fair value of the share options granted, as the services are received during the three year vesting period.

In 20X1 and 20X2, the entity estimates the number of options expected to vest (by estimating the number of employees likely to leave) and bases the amount that it recognises for the year on this estimate.

In 20X3, it recognises an amount based on the number of options that actually vest. A total of 55 employees left during the three year period and therefore 34,500 options (400 – 55 employees × 100 options) are vested.

The amount recognised as an expense for each of the three years is calculated as follows:

		Cumulative expense at year-end $	Expense for year $
20X1	(400 – 80) × 100 × $20 × 1/3	213,333	213,333
20X2	(400 – 100) × 100 × $20 × 2/3	400,000	186,667
20X3	345 × 100 × $20	690,000	290,000

20X1

DEBIT	Staff costs	$213,333	
CREDIT	Other reserves (within equity)		$213,333

20X2

DEBIT	Staff costs	$186,667	
CREDIT	Other reserves (within equity)		$186,667

20X3

DEBIT	Staff costs	$290,000	
CREDIT	Other reserves (within equity)		$290,000

Section summary

Share-based payment transactions should be recognised in the financial statements. You need to understand and be able to advise on:

- Recognition
- Measurement
- Disclosure

of both equity settled and cash settled transactions.

Chapter Roundup

✓ **Share-based payment** transactions should be recognised in the financial statements. You need to understand and be able to advise on:

- Recognition
- Measurement
- Disclosure

of both equity settled and cash settled transactions.

Quick Quiz

1 What is a cash-settled share based payment transaction?

2 What does grant date mean?

3 If an entity has entered into an equity settled share-based payment transaction, what should it recognise in its financial statements?

4 Where an entity has granted share options to its employees in return for services, how is the transaction measured?

Answers to Quick Quiz

1   A transaction in which the entity receives goods or services in exchange for amounts of cash that are based on the price (or value) of the entity's shares or other equity instruments of the entity.

2   The date at which the entity and another party (including an employee) agree to a share based payment arrangement, being when the entity and the other party have a shared understanding of the terms and conditions of the arrangement.

3   The goods or services received and a corresponding increase in equity.

4   By reference to the fair value of the equity instruments granted, measured at grant date.

Answers to Questions

4.1   Share based payment

			$
20X5			
Equity c/d and P/L expense ((500 − 75) × 100 × $15 × 1/3)			212,500

DEBIT	Staff costs	$212,500	
CREDIT	Other reserves (within equity)		$212,500

			$
20X6			
Equity b/d			212,500
∴ Profit or loss expense			227,500
Equity c/d ((500 − 60) × 100 × $15 × 2/3) =			440,000

DEBIT	Expenses	$227,500	
CREDIT	Other reserves (within equity)		$227,500

			$
20X7			
Equity b/d			440,000
∴ Profit or loss expense			224,500
Equity c/d (443 × 100 × $15) =			664,500

DEBIT	Expenses	$224,500	
CREDIT	Other reserves (within equity)		$224,500

Now try this question from the Exam Question Bank

Number	Level	Marks	Time
Q4	Introductory	10	18 mins

ASSET VALUATION AND CHANGING PRICES

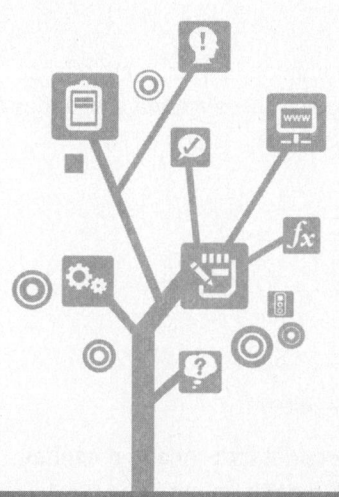

Some companies publish **current cost information** (particularly the utility companies). It is important, therefore to have a background knowledge of the way current cost information differs from historic cost.

5

topic list	learning outcomes	syllabus references	ability required
1 Profit, capital maintenance and asset valuation	B(1)	B(i)	Evaluation
2 Changes in price levels	B(1)	B(ii)	Evaluation
3 Hyperinflation	B(1)	B(ii)	Evaluation
4 Fair value measurement	B(1)	B(ii)	Evaluation

1   Profit, capital maintenance and asset valuation

Introduction

A useful starting point in the definition of profit is the work of economists, most notably Sir John Hicks, on the meaning of personal income.

1.1 Introduction

There are three main factors affecting any system of accounting.

(a)   **Asset valuation basis**: Historical cost or current cost (HCA)

(b)   **Capital maintenance concept**: Financial or operating

(c)   **Unit of measurement**: Nominal or current purchasing power (stabilised) (CPP)

These factors may be combined as follows:

	Assets valuation	Capital maintenance concept	Units of measurement	System of accounting
1	Historical cost	Financial	Nominal	HCA
2	Historical cost	Financial	CPP (stable monetary unit)	CPP
3	Current cost	Operating	Nominal	CCA
4	Current cost	Operating	CPP	'Real' CCA

In this chapter, we will discuss each of the different approaches to asset valuation, capital maintenance, and unit of measurement. Come back to the table above after you have studied these approaches and use it as a summary.

1.2 Capital maintenance

There are different views of capital.

1.2.1 Financial capital

In the financial capital view, capital is seen as a **fund attributable to shareholders**.

Focusing on the equity ownership of the entity is often referred to as the **proprietary concept of capital**. The objective of financial capital maintenance is to **maintain shareholders' wealth**, either in nominal terms or in real terms.

	$
Financial capital is represented by:	
Share capital	X
Reserves	X
	$\overline{\overline{X}}$

Does this look familiar? This is because this view of capital is adopted in IFRS financial statements.

1.2.2 Operating capital

Under this concept, capital is looked at as the capacity to maintain physical operating capital.

Alternatively referred to as the **physical capacity capital maintenance concept**, or the **entity concept**, the objective of operating capital maintenance is to maintain the **operating capacity of the business**. This requires specific price changes to be incorporated.

	$
Physical operating capital is represented by:	
Non-current assets	X
Inventories	X
Monetary working capital	X
	X̄

1.3 The meaning of profit

Hicks' conclusions on personal income can be adapted to the measurement of a company's profit. Note that in this chapter the term 'income' is used in preference to 'profit' in order to compare economic and accounting theories. 'Income' is not intended here to mean 'revenue'.

Hicks defined income (in *Value and capital*, 1946).

KEY TERM

INCOME: 'the maximum value which an individual can consume during a week and still expect to be as well off at the end of the week as he was at the beginning.'

When a UK committee (the Sandilands Committee) reported in 1975 on the problems of accounting during periods of inflation, they adapted Hicks' definition to provide a definition of accounting profit:

KEY TERM

'A company's PROFIT for the year is the maximum value which the company can distribute during the year, and still expect to be as well off at the end of the year as it was at the beginning.'

In other words, if an **entity** can **maintain its opening capital** (the measure of 'well-offness' in the definition above), any excess value created over and above this is profit. This means, assuming there is no new capital injection:

Profit	=	Capital at end of year	X
		Capital at beginning of year	(X)
			X

Needless to say, what 'profit' is exactly will vary depending on the capital maintenance concept adopted.

1.4 Statement of financial position view

This view of profit corresponds with a view of the **statement of financial position as the primary accounting statement**. This is because once the opening statement of financial position and the closing statement of financial position for a period have been drawn up, profit emerges as merely a balancing figure between the capital values shown by the two statements of financial position. (Of course, adjustments would need to be made for any capital injected or withdrawn during the period.)

1.5 Statement of profit or loss and other comprehensive income

Some regard the **statement of profit or loss and other comprehensive income as the primary accounting statement**. To them, **matching is the key**. In this view, it is the statement of financial position which is residual, in that it is merely a collection of unallocated debits and credits.

1.6 Inflation accounting   9/11

We can use historical cost maintenance concepts to show 'profits' and statement of financial position values, but if the 'profit' gained by holding assets over time is paid out by way of dividend, the company's operating capacity will decline.

To prevent this situation occurring we could:

(a)   Alter financial statements for the general rate of inflation to reflect the decreasing purchasing power of money

(b)   Alter the financial statements to reflect specific rates of inflation on the business assets: this is the operating capital maintenance concept.

We will look at inflation accounting in more detail in section 2.5 below.

Section summary

Profit can be viewed as a measure of the increase in an entity's capital over the duration of an accounting period.

The **measurement of profit** depends on the concept of **capital maintenance**.

2 Changes in price levels

Introduction

Historical cost accounting (HCA) is the traditional form of Western accounting, modified in some instances by revaluations of certain assets. It is objective, but it has its disadvantages.

2.1 Main characteristics of HCA

(a)   All transactions are recorded at their **historical cost**. When money is paid over, this money value will be recorded in the books of the business. The final financial statements (statement of financial position, statement of profit or loss and other comprehensive income, and statement of cash flows) will reflect the transactions at historical cost.

(b)   The transactions thus recorded are *matched*, so that the income generated by the company is 'matched' against the costs involved in getting that income.

There is a common **modification of HCA** in that some non-current assets can be **revalued** to a current cost figure. Any holding gain or loss (ie. the fact that something is worth more, or costs more, over time simply due to price increases) must be taken to a revaluation reserve. Once the asset is disposed of, this unrealised holding gain can be released.

We can now look at HCA in terms of **capital maintenance**, which allows us to break down HCA profits into different types of gains and losses.

Profit can be measured as the difference between how wealthy an entity is at the beginning and at the end of an accounting period. This wealth can be expressed in terms of the equity (capital and reserves) as shown in its opening and closing statements of financial position. A business which maintains its capital unchanged during an accounting period can be said to have 'broken even'. Once capital has been maintained, anything achieved in excess represents profit. This is known as **financial capital maintenance**.

For this analysis to be of any use, we must be able to draw up a statement of financial position at the beginning and at the end of a period, so as to place a value on the opening and closing capital. There are particular difficulties in doing this during a period of rising prices.

In conventional historical cost accounts, assets are stated in the statement of financial position at the amount it cost to acquire them (less any amounts written off in respect of depreciation or impairment). Capital is simply the difference between assets and liabilities. If prices are rising, it is possible for an entity to show a profit in its historical cost accounts despite having identical physical assets and owing identical liabilities at the beginning and end of its accounting period.

For example, consider the following opening and closing statements of financial position.

	Opening $	Closing $
Inventory (100 items at cost)	500	600
Other net assets	1,000	1,000
Capital	1,500	1,600

Assuming that no new capital has been introduced during the year, and no capital has been distributed as dividends, the profit shown in historical cost accounts would be $100, being the excess of closing capital

over opening capital. And yet, in physical terms, the entity is no better off: it still has 100 units of inventory (which cost $5 each at the beginning of the period, but $6 each at the end) and its other net assets are identical. The **'profit' earned has merely enabled the entity to keep pace with inflation**.

An alternative to the concept of capital maintenance based on historical costs is to express capital in **physical terms**. On this basis, no profit would be recognised in the example above because the physical substance of the entity is unchanged over the accounting period. The entity's **operating capacity** remains unchanged. Capital is maintained if at the end of the period the entity is in a position to achieve the **same physical output** as it was at the beginning of the period.

2.2 Criticisms of historical cost accounting

2.2.1 Overstatement of profit

HCA shows current revenues, but out of date costs (depreciation, cost of sales where the cost of products and materials are based on historical cost). This causes the profit reported to be overstated.

2.2.2 Non-current asset values are unrealistic

The most striking example here is **property**. If non-current assets are retained in the books at their historical cost, **unrealised holding gains** are not recognised. This means that the total holding gain, if any, will be brought into account during the year in which the asset is realised, rather than spread over the period during which it was owned.

2.2.3 Unreliable investors' ratios

Because of the two issues above, giving us distorted profits and asset values, the entity's return on assets and capital employed are also distorted. Based on this, there is a risk that the entity appears more attractive to investors than it would otherwise do.

2.2.4 Depreciation is inadequate to finance the replacement of non-current assets

This criticism is generally well understood and you will appreciate that what is important is not the replacement of one asset by an identical new one (something that rarely happens), but the replacement of the **operating capability** represented by the old asset.

2.2.5 Holding gains on inventories are not measured separately from operating profits

During a period of high inflation the **monetary value of inventories held may increase significantly** while they are being processed. The conventions of historical cost accounting lead to the **realised part of this holding gain** (known as *inventory appreciation*) being **included** in **profit** for the year.

This problem can be illustrated using a simple example. At the beginning of the year, an entity has 100 units of inventory and no other assets. Its trading account for the year is shown below.

TRADING ACCOUNT

	Units	$		Units	$
Opening inventory	100	200	Sales (made 31 December)	100	500
Purchases (made 31 December)	100	400			
	200	600			
Closing inventory (FIFO basis)	100	400			
	100	200			
Gross profit	–	300			
	100	500		100	500

Apparently, the entity has made a gross profit of $300. But, at the beginning of the year the entity owned 100 units of inventory and at the end of the year it owned 100 units of inventory and $100 (sales $500, purchases $400). From this it would seem that a profit of $100 is more reasonable. The remaining $200 is inventory appreciation arising as the purchase price increased from $2 to $4.

This criticism can be overcome by using a **capital maintenance** concept based on **physical units** rather than monetary values.

2.2.6 Gains/losses on holdings of net monetary items are not shown

In periods of inflation, the **purchasing power**, and thus the value, of money **falls**. As a result, gains and losses arise from the impact of inflation. Savers lose because the purchasing power of their savings is eroded, while borrowers gain because they still owe the same nominal amount while their earnings have risen due to inflation. This is not reflected in traditional HCA financial statements.

2.2.7 Comparisons over time are unrealistic

As comparative figures from prior years are not restated for the effects of inflation, this may tend to an **exaggeration of growth**. For example, if an entity's profit in 1995 was $100,000 and in 2013 $500,000, a shareholder's initial reaction might be that the entity had done rather well. If, however, he then realised that with $100,000 in 1995 he could buy exactly the same goods as with $500,000 in 2013, the apparent growth would seem less impressive.

2.2.8 Alternatives to HCA

The points mentioned above have demonstrated some of the accounting problems which arise in times of severe and prolonged inflation. Of the various possible systems of accounting for price changes, most fall into one of three categories as follows.

(a)   General price changes bases and in particular, **current purchasing power** (CPP).

(b)   **Current value bases**. The basic principles of all these are:

   (i)   To show statement of financial position items at some form of current value rather than historical cost

   (ii)   To compute profits by matching the current value of costs at the date of consumption against revenue

   The current value of an item will normally be based on replacement cost, net realisable value or economic value.

(c)   A **combination** of these two systems: suggestions of this type have been put forward by many writers.

2.3 Why modified historical cost accounting is still used

It must seem strange, given the criticisms levelled at it, that modified HCA is still in such widespread use. There are various reasons for this, not the least of which is **resistance to change** in the conservative accounting profession.

Modified historical cost financial statements are **easy** to prepare, easy to read and easy to understand. While they do not reflect current values, the revaluation of non current assets is seen as one of the most important items requiring such an adjustment, and therefore the value of the financial statements is improved enormously by such revaluations taking place.

In periods of **low inflation**, historical cost financial statements are seen as a reasonable reflection on the reality of the given situation.

Exam alert

A question could ask for a comparison between historical cost and current value accounting.

2.4 Current cost accounting (CCA)

The current value of an asset to a business can be measured in various ways. We look at two of them here: entry value, and exit value.

2.4.1 Entry values

Under this concept, **non-monetary assets** are converted to current replacement cost.

CIMA's Official Terminology defines **replacement cost** as 'the price at which identical goods or capital equipment could be purchased at the date of valuation'.

In times of rising prices, the increase in replacement cost over historical cost results in a 'holding gain', i.e. an asset is worth more simply because it would now cost more to replace.

Advantages	Disadvantages
It ensures operating capital maintenance by recognising operating profit.	It is based on the historical cost convention.
	Replacement costs may not always be available.
It separates operational gains from holding gains, so we can distinguish gains under the control of management.	It is subjective.
It produces a realistic value of capital employed.	

2.4.2 Exit values

Using exit values, income is determined as closing capital valued at exit price less opening capital at exit price. Exit prices are the amounts at which **non-monetary assets** could be sold in an orderly realisation.

Advantages	Disadvantages
It is based on the concept of **opportunity cost**.	It is not based upon the **going concern concept**.
Most people **understand** realisable values.	The valuation of assets is **subjective**.
It **shows creditors** the amounts available on a winding up.	The assumption of **orderly realisation** of assets in their existing state may be misleading.
	It **does not ensure operating capability**.

2.4.3 CCA concept

Current cost accounting (CCA) reflects an approach to capital maintenance based on maintaining the **operating capability** of a business, and takes into account entry and exit values.

The value of assets consumed or sold, and the value of assets in the statement of financial position should be stated at their **value to the business** (also known as 'deprival value').

Deprival value is an important concept, which you may find rather difficult to understand at first, and you should read the following explanation carefully.

KEY TERM

The DEPRIVAL VALUE 'of an asset is the loss which a business entity would suffer if it were deprived of the use of the asset.

(a)   A basic assumption in CCA is that 'capital maintenance' should mean maintenance of the 'business substance' or 'operating capability' of the business entity. As we have seen already, it is generally

BPP
LEARNING MEDIA

accepted that profit is earned only after a sufficient amount has been charged against sales to ensure that the capital of the business is maintained. In CCA, a **physical** rather than financial definition of capital is used: capital maintenance is measured by the ability of the business entity to keep up the same level of operating capability.

(b)　'Value to the business' is the required method of valuation in current cost accounting, because it reflects the extra funds which would be required to maintain the operating capability of the business entity if it suddenly lost the use of an asset.

Value to the business, or deprival value, can be any of the following values.

(a)　**Replacement cost** (RC): In the case of non-current assets, it is assumed that the replacement cost of an asset would be its net replacement cost (NRC), its gross replacement cost minus an appropriate provision for depreciation to reflect the amount of its life already 'used up'.

(b)　**Net realisable value** (NRV): What the asset could be sold for, net of any disposal costs.

(c)　**Value in use** (VIU) or economic value: What the existing asset will be worth to the company over the rest of its useful life.

The diagram below summarises how deprival value is normally determined.

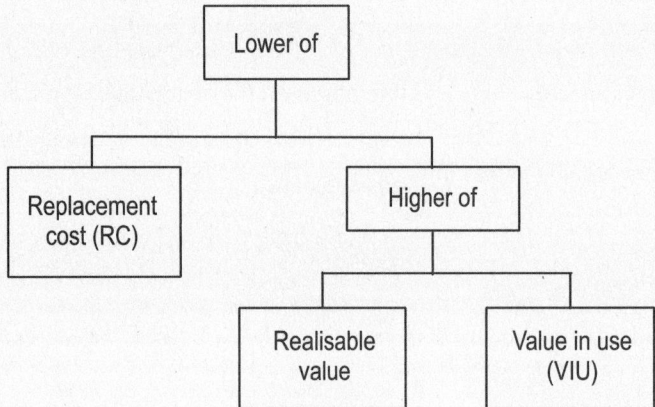

If the asset is worth replacing, its deprival value will always be net replacement cost.

If the asset is not worth replacing, it might have been disposed of straight away, or else it might have been kept in operation until the end of its useful life. Where the asset is not worth replacing, the deprival value will be NRV or EV.

However, there are many assets which will not be replaced either:

(a)　Because the asset is **technologically obsolete**, and has been (or will be) superseded by more modern equipment

(b)　Because the business is **changing the nature of its operations** and will not want to continue in the same line of business once the asset has been used up

Such assets, even though there are reasons not to replace them, would still be valued (usually) at net replacement cost, because this 'deprival value' still provides an estimate of the **operating capability** of the company.

2.4.4 CCA profits and deprival value

The deprival value of assets is reflected in the CCA statement of profit or loss and other comprehensive income by the following means.

(a)　**Depreciation** is charged on non-current assets on the basis of **gross replacement cost** of the asset (where RC is the deprival value).

(b)   Where **NRV or VIU** is the deprival value, the charge against CCA profits will be the **gain/loss in the value of the asset** during the accounting period; ie from its previous statement of financial position value to its current NRV or VIU.

(c)   **Cost of sales** are charged at the **replacement cost** of goods sold.
        Thus if an item of inventory cost $15 to produce, and sells for $20, by which time its replacement cost has risen to $17, the CCA profit would be $3.

	$
Sales	20
Less replacement cost of goods sold	17
Current cost profit	3

2.4.5 Current cost adjustments to historical cost profit

In current cost accounting, profit is calculated as follows

	$
Historical cost profit	X
Less: current cost operating adjustments	(X)
Current cost profit	X

The holding gains, both realised and unrealised, are excluded from current cost profit. The double entry for the debits in the current cost statement of profit or loss and other comprehensive income is to credit each operating adjustment to a non-distributable current cost reserve.

2.4.6 The current cost statement of profit or loss and other comprehensive income

The format of the current cost statement of profit or loss and other comprehensive income would show the following information, although not necessarily in the order given.

	$	$
Historical cost profit (before interest and taxation)		X
Current cost operating adjustments		
Cost of sales adjustment (COSA)	(X)	
Monetary working capital adjustment (loss or gain) (MWCA)	(X) or X	
Depreciation adjustment	(X)	
		(X)
Current cost operating profit (before interest and taxation)		X
Less interest payable and receivable		(X)
Add gearing adjustment		X
Current cost profit attributable to shareholders		X
Less taxation		(X)
Current cost profit for the year		X

2.4.7 Cost of sales adjustment (COSA)

The COSA is necessary to **eliminate realised holding gains** on inventory. It represents the difference between **the replacement cost and the historical cost of goods sold**.

The exclusion of holding gains from CC profit is a necessary consequence of the need to maintain operating capability. The COSA represents that portion of the HC profit which must be consumed in replacing the inventory item sold so that trading can continue. Where practical difficulties arise in estimating replacement cost, a simple indexing system can be used.

Thus, if an item of inventory cost $15 to produce, and sells for $20, by which time its replacement cost has risen to $17, the CCA adjustment would be $2.

	$
Sales	20
Historical cost of sales	(15)
Historical cost profit	5
Cost of sales adjustment (17 – 15)	(2)
Current cost profit	3

2.4.8 Depreciation adjustment

The depreciation adjustment is the **difference between the depreciation charge on the gross replacement cost of the assets and the historical cost depreciation**. This is (as with the COSA) a realised holding gain which is excluded from the CC profit. Where comparison is made with a different asset for the purposes of calculating replacement cost (because of the obsolescence of the old asset), then allowance must be made for different useful lives and different production capabilities.

2.4.9 Monetary working capital adjustment (MWCA)

Where a company gives or takes credit for the sale or purchase of goods, the goods are paid for at the **end** of the credit period, at the replacement cost as at the **beginning** of the credit period. If a company measures profit as the excess of revenue over cost:

(a)   **Outstanding payables** protect the company to some extent from **price changes** because the company lags behind current prices in its payment

(b)   **Outstanding receivables**, in contrast, would be a **burden on profits** in a period of rising prices because sales receipts will always relate to previous months' sales at a lower price/cost/profit level

The MWCA can therefore be either a gain or a loss. An adjustment would be required to record the effect of price changes on movement in monetary working capital (trade receivables less trade payables).

2.4.10 Gearing adjustment

If the operating net assets of the business (inventories, non-current assets and monetary working capital) are financed by **external creditors**, gearing adjustments to the other adjustments discussed above would be required.

The reason for the gearing adjustments is that since the amount owed to these creditors is fixed in monetary terms, and does not rise with inflation, it follows that they are **financing some part of the holding gains** represented by COSA, depreciation adjustment and MWCA. In calculating the amount of current cost profit earned by the shareholders, it is therefore inappropriate to deduct the *whole* of these adjustments from historical cost profit. The proportion of the COSA, depreciation and MWCA adjustments that are financed by debt rather than equity therefore should be added back to profit.

2.4.11 The current cost statement of financial position

In the current cost statement of financial position:

- **Assets** will be valued at their '**value to the business**'.
- **Liabilities** will be valued at their **monetary amount**.
- There will be a current cost reserve to reflect the revaluation surpluses.

2.4.12 Restatements in the statement of financial position

Non monetary items in the statement of financial position are restated to current cost.

Monetary items would already be stated at current cost. Therefore, they do not need to be restated.

Example: current cost accounts

At the beginning of a period, Arthur Smith Co has the following statement of financial position.

	$
Assets	
Non-current asset (newly acquired)	10,000
Inventories (newly acquired)	2,000
	12,000

Capital

Equity	8,000
Loan stock (10% interest)	4,000
	12,000

The company gearing is 33%, in terms of both HC and CCA. During the period, sales of goods amounted to $15,000, the replacement cost of sales was $13,200 and the historical cost of sales was $12,000. Closing inventories, at replacement cost, were $4,600 and at HC were $4,400. Depreciation is provided for at 10% straight line, and at the end of the period the non-current assets had a gross replacement cost of $11,000. The HC financial statements were as follows.

STATEMENT OF PROFIT OR LOSS AND OTHER COMPREHENSIVE INCOME

	$
Sales	15,000
Less cost of sales	12,000
	3,000
Depreciation	1,000
Profit before interest	2,000
Interest	400
Profit	1,600

CLOSING STATEMENT OF FINANCIAL POSITION

	$
Non-current asset at cost less depreciation	9,000
Inventories	4,400
Cash	200
	13,600
Equity	9,600
Loan stock	4,000
	13,600

Taxation is ignored.

Required

Prepare workings for the CCA financial statements. (Depreciation for the period will be based on the end of year value of the non-current asset. All sales and purchases were for cash.)

Solution

The COSA is ($13,200 – $12,000) = $1,200
The depreciation adjustment is (($11,000 × 10%) – $1,000) = $100

The MWCA is nil (there are no payables and receivables).

Note. The small cash balance in the closing statement of financial position might be regarded as necessary for business purposes and therefore taken up in the MWCA as monetary working capital. In this example, we will treat the $200 as a cash surplus.

	$	$
Historical cost profit (before interest)		2,000
Current cost adjustments		
COSA	1,200	
MWCA	0	
Depreciation	100	
		1,300
Current cost operating profit		700

The gearing adjustment is calculated by multiplying the three current cost adjustments (here $1,300) by the gearing proportion (by the proportion of the gains which is financed by borrowing and which therefore provides additional profits for equity, since the real value of the borrowing is declining in a period of rising prices).

The gearing proportion is the ratio:

$$\frac{\text{Long - term debt}}{\text{Long - term debt + equity}}$$

As you will see in more detail in Chapter 14, we can think of a company as consisting of non-current assets and net current assets (ie working capital, which is current assets minus current liabilities). These are financed partly by net borrowings and partly by equity.

Average figures are taken, as they are more representative than end of year figures.

	$
Opening figures	
Long-term debt (loan stock)	4,000
Equity	8,000
Equity plus long-term debt	12,000

Closing figures: since cash is here regarded as a surplus amount, the company is losing value during a period of inflation by holding cash – just as it is gaining by having fixed loans. If cash is not included in MWC, it is:

(a)   Deducted from long-term debt

(b)   Excluded from net operating assets

(Net operating assets consist of non-current assets, long-term trade investments, inventories and monetary working capital.)

The closing figures are therefore as follows.

	$	$
Non-current assets (at net replacement cost $11,000 – $1,100)		9,900
Inventories (at replacement cost)		4,600
Monetary working capital		0
Net operating assets (equals equity + long-term debt)		14,500
Less: Long-term debt	4,000	
Surplus cash	(200)	
		3,800
Therefore equity =		10,700

Average figures	Opening	Closing	Average
Long-term debt	$4,000	$3,800	$3,900
Net operating assets (equals equity + long-term debt)	$12,000	$14,500	$13,250

The gearing proportion is $\dfrac{3,900}{13,250} \times 100\% = 29.43\%$

Exam alert

The above example is more complicated than you would meet in the exam. The full workings are shown for illustrative purposes.

2.4.13 The advantages and disadvantages of current cost accounting

Advantages

(a)   By excluding holding gains from profit, CCA can be used to indicate whether the dividends paid to shareholders will **reduce the operating capability** of the business.

(b)   Assets are valued after management has considered the **opportunity cost** of holding them, and the expected benefits from their future use. CCA is therefore a useful guide for management in deciding whether to hold or sell assets.

(c)   It is **relevant** to the needs of information users in:

   (i)   Assessing the stability of the business entity

   (ii)   Assessing the vulnerability of the business (eg to a takeover), or the liquidity of the business

   (iii)   Evaluating the performance of management in maintaining and increasing the business substance

   (iv)   Judging future prospects

(d)   It can be **implemented fairly easily** in practice, by making simple adjustments to the historical cost accounting profits. A current cost statement of financial position can also be prepared with reasonable simplicity.

Disadvantages

(a)   Valuations of VIU or NRV are inherently **subjective**.

(b)   There are several problems to be overcome in deciding how to provide an **estimate of replacement** costs for non-current assets.

   (i)   While depreciation based on the historical cost of an asset can be viewed as a means of spreading the cost of the asset over its estimated life, depreciation based on replacement costs does not conform to this traditional accounting view.

   (ii)   Depreciation based on replacement costs would appear to be a means of providing that sufficient funds are set aside in the business to ensure that the asset can be replaced at the end of its life. But if it is not certain what technological advances might be in the next few years and how the type of assets required might change between the current time and the estimated time of replacement, it is difficult to argue that depreciation based on today's costs is a valid way of providing for the eventual physical replacement of the asset.

   (iii)   It may be argued that depreciation based on historical cost is more accurate than replacement cost depreciation, because the historical cost is known, whereas replacement cost is simply an estimate. However, replacement costs are re-assessed each year, so that inaccuracies in the estimates in one year can be rectified in the next year.

(c)   The mixed value approach to valuation means that some assets will be valued at replacement cost, but others will be valued at NRV or VIU. It is arguable that the **total assets** will, therefore, have an **aggregate value** which is **not particularly meaningful** because of this mixture of different concepts.

(d)   The **MWCA and GA calculations are demanding**, and people have different ideas of what belongs in them and the indices to use. So, there is a **lack of comparability** between different companies adopting current cost accounting.

2.5 Current purchasing power (CPP)

2.5.1 Capital maintenance in times of inflation

As we saw at the start of this chapter, **profit** can be measured as the **difference between how wealthy a company is at the beginning and at the end of an accounting period.**

For this analysis to be of any use, we must be able to draw up a company's statement of financial position at the beginning and at the end of a period, so as to place a value on the opening and closing capital. There are particular difficulties in doing this during a **period of changing prices**.

In conventional historical cost financial statements, assets are stated in the statement of financial position at the amount it cost to acquire them (less any amounts written off in respect of depreciation or impairment in value). Capital is simply the **difference between assets and liabilities**.

If prices are rising, it is possible for a company to show a profit in its historical cost accounts despite having identical physical assets and owing identical liabilities at the beginning and end of its accounting period.

For example, consider the following opening and closing statements of financial position of a company.

	Opening $	Closing $
Inventory (100 items at cost)	500	600
Other net assets	1,000	1,000
Capital	1,500	1,600

Assuming that no new capital has been introduced during the year, and no capital has been distributed as dividends, the profit shown in historical cost accounts would be $100, being the excess of closing capital over opening capital. And yet, in physical terms, the company is no better off: it still has 100 units of inventory (which cost $5 each at the beginning of the period, but $6 each at the end) and its other net assets are identical. The 'profit' earned has merely enabled the company to keep pace with inflation.

2.5.2 The unit of measurement

Another way to tackle the problems of capital maintenance in times of rising prices is to look at the **unit of measurement** in which accounting values are expressed.

It is an axiom of conventional accounting, as it has developed over the years, that value should be measured in terms of money. It is also **implicitly assumed** that **money values are stable**, so that $1 at the start of the financial year has the same value as $1 at the end of that year. But when **prices are rising**, this assumption is invalid: **$1 at the end of the year has less value (less purchasing power) than it had one year previously**.

This leads to problems when aggregating amounts which have arisen at different times. For example, a company's non current assets may include items bought at different times over a period of many years. They will each have been recorded in $CPP, but the value of $1 will have varied over the period. In effect, the **non current asset figure in a historical cost statement of financial position is an aggregate of a number of items expressed in different units**. It could be argued that such a figure is **meaningless**.

Faced with this argument, one possibility would be to re-state all accounts items in terms of a stable monetary unit. There would be difficulties in practice, but in theory there is no reason why a stable unit should not be devised. In this section, we will look at a system of accounting called **current purchasing power accounting** (CPP) based on precisely this idea.

2.5.3 The CPP concept

The idea behind CPP is that some or all of the accounts items are **restated** for changes in **current price level** in terms of a stable monetary unit – the $CPP.

Changes in purchasing power are based on the general level of inflation using the general prices index (GPI).

CPP measures profits as the **increase in the current purchasing power of equity**. Profits are therefore stated after allowing for the declining purchasing power of money due to price inflation.

2.5.4 Specific and general price changes

We can identify two different types of price inflation.

(a)   There is **specific price inflation**, which measures price changes over time for a specific asset or group of assets.

(b)   There is **general price inflation**, which is the average rate of inflation, which reduces the general purchasing power of money.

Specific price inflation is not always consistent with general price inflation. For example, if the replacement cost of a machine on 1 January 20X2 was $5,000, and the general rate of inflation in 20X2 was 8%, we would not necessarily expect the replacement cost of the machine at 31 December 20X2 to be $5,000 plus 8% = $5,400. In fact, it is conceivable that, in spite of general inflation, the replacement cost of the machinery might have gone down.

Current cost accounting can counter the problems of specific price inflation. However, the capital maintenance concepts that underlie current cost accounting do not allow for the maintenance of real value in money terms.

Current purchasing power (CPP) accounting is based on a different concept of capital maintenance.

KEY TERM

CPP measures profits as the **increase in the current purchasing power of equity**. Profits are therefore stated after allowing for the declining purchasing power of money due to price inflation.

When applied to historical cost accounting, CPP is a system of accounting which makes adjustments to income and capital values to allow for the **general rate of price inflation**.

2.5.5 The principles and procedures of CPP accounting

In CPP accounting, profit is measured after allowing for general price changes. It is a fundamental idea of CPP that capital should be maintained in terms of the **same monetary purchasing power**, so that:

$$P_{CPP} = D_{CPP} + (E_{t\,(CPP)} - E_{(t-1)CPP})$$

where P_{CPP} is the CPP accounting profit

D_{CPP} is distributions to shareholders, re-stated in current purchasing power terms

$E_{t(CPP)}$ is the total value of assets attributable to the owners of the business entity at the end of the accounting period, restated in current purchasing power terms

$E_{(t-1)CPP}$ is the total value of the owners' equity at the beginning of the accounting period, restated in current purchasing power terms at the end of the of the accounting period.

A CPP $ relates to the value of money on the last day of the accounting period.

Profit in CPP accounting is therefore measured after allowing for maintenance of equity capital. To the extent that a company is financed by loans, there is no requirement to allow for the maintenance of the purchasing power of the non current liabilities. Indeed, as we shall see, the equity of a business can profit from the loss in the purchasing power value of loans.

2.5.6 Monetary and non-monetary items

KEY TERM

A MONETARY ITEM is an asset or liability whose value is **fixed by contract or statute** in terms of $s, regardless of changes in general price levels and the purchasing power of the currency.

The main examples of monetary items are cash, receivables, payables and loan capital.

KEY TERM

A NON-MONETARY ITEM is an asset or liability whose value is **not fixed by contract or statute**.

These include property, plant and equipment and inventory.

In CPP accounting, the monetary items held must be looked at carefully.

(a)   If a company **borrows money in a period of inflation**, the amount of the debt will remain fixed (by law) so that when the debt is eventually paid, it will be paid in $s of a lower purchasing power.

    For example, suppose a company borrows $2,000 on 1 January 20X5 and repays the loan on 1 January 20X9. In a period of inflation, the purchasing power of the $2,000 repaid in 20X9 will be less than the value of $2,000 in 20X5. Since the company by law must repay only $2,000 of principal, it has gained by having the use of the money from the loan for 4 years. (The lender of the $2,000 will try to protect the value of his loan in a period of inflation by charging a higher rate of interest; however, this does not alter the fact that the loan remains fixed at $2,000 in money value.)

(b)   If a company **holds cash in a period of inflation**, its value in terms of current purchasing power will decline. The company will 'lose' by holding the cash instead of converting it into a non monetary asset.

    Similarly, if goods are sold on credit, the amount of the receivable is fixed by contract. In a period of inflation, the current purchasing power of the cash received from the credit sale will be less than the purchasing power of the receivable when it was first incurred.

In CPP accounting, it is therefore argued that there are **gains from having monetary liabilities**, and **losses from having monetary assets**.

(a)   In the case of **monetary assets**, a charge needs to be made against in profit or loss, for the loss in purchasing power. For example, if a company has a cash balance of $200, which is just sufficient to buy 100 new items of raw material inventory on 1 January 20X5, and if the rate of inflation during 20X5 is 10%, the company would need $220 to buy the same 100 items on 1 January 20X6 (assuming the items increase in value by the general rate of inflation). By holding the $200 as a monetary asset throughout 20X5, the company would need $20 more to buy the same goods and services on 1 January 20X6 that it could have obtained on 1 January 20X5. $20 would be a CPP loss on holding the monetary asset (cash) for a whole year.

(b)   In the case of **monetary liabilities**, the argument in favour of including a 'profit' in CPP accounting is not as strong. By incurring a debt, say, on 1 January 20X5, there will not be any eventual cash input to the business. The 'profit' from the monetary liabilities is a 'paper' profit, and T A Lee has argued against including it in the CPP statement of profit or loss and other comprehensive income.

2.5.7 Restatement in the statement of financial position

Non-monetary items

An asset or liability whose value is not fixed by contract or statute e.g. inventories, non-current assets. Their worth measured in $CPP therefore alters due to inflation.

They are restated to year end value using the GPI.

Monetary items

An asset or liability fixed in $ by contract or statute – e.g. cash, receivables, payables, loan capital. In CPP accounts these are therefore fixed in value – when paid the dollars are of lower purchasing power.

No adjustment necessary as they are already stated in the year end values.

2.5.8 Restatement in the statement of profit or loss

All items that are not already stated in year end values must be restated. Unless told otherwise, we assume that sales and purchases etc accrue evenly throughout the period and so an average GPI is used.

A holding gain/loss is calculated on monetary items.

For monetary items, there are real gains and losses made. These are not measured in HCA but are in CPP.

Example: CPP accounting

Seep Co had the following assets and liabilities at 31 December 20X4.

(a)   All non-current assets were purchased on 1 January 20X1 at a cost of $60,000, and they had an estimated life of six years. Straight line depreciation is used.

(b)   Closing inventories have a historical cost value of $7,900. They were bought in the period November-December 20X4.

(c)   Receivables amounted to $8,000, cash to $2,000 and short-term payables to $6,000.

(d)   There are non-current liabilities of $15,000.

(e)   The general price index includes the following information:

Year	Date	Price index
20X1	1 January	100
20X4	30 November	158
20X4	31 December	160
20X5	31 December	180

The historical cost statement of financial position of Seep Co at 31 December 20X4 was as follows.

	$	$
Assets		
Non-current assets at cost		60,000
Less depreciation		40,000
		20,000
Current assets		
Inventories	7,900	
Receivables	8,000	
Cash	2,000	
		17,900
Total assets		37,900
Equity and liabilities		
Capital		
Equity		16,900
Loan capital		15,000
		31,900
Current liabilities: payables		6,000
Total equity and liabilities		37,900

Required

(a)   Prepare a CPP statement of financial position as at 31 December 20X4.

(b)   What was the depreciation charge against CPP profits in 20X4?

(c)   What must be the value of equity at 31 December 20X5 if Seep Co is to 'break even' and make neither a profit nor a loss in 20X5?

Solution

(a)   CPP STATEMENT OF FINANCIAL POSITION AS AT 31 DECEMBER 20X4

	$CPP	$CPP
Assets		
Non-current assets, at cost (60,000 × 160/100)	96,000	
Less depreciation (40,000 × 160/100)	64,000	
		32,000
Inventory* (7,900 × 160/158)	8,000	
Receivables**	8,000	
Cash**	2,000	
		18,000
		50,000
Equity and liabilities		
Capital		
Loan capital**		15,000
Equity ***		29,000
		44,000
Current liabilities: payables**		6,000
		50,000

Notes

*Inventories purchased between 1 November and 31 December are assumed to have an average index value relating to the mid-point of their purchase period, at 30 November.

**Monetary assets and liabilities are not re-valued, because they are already stated in year end values.

***Equity is a mixture of monetary and non-monetary asset values, and is the balancing figure in this example.

(b)   Depreciation in 20X4 would be one sixth of the CPP value of the assets at the end of the year.

$1/6$ of $96,000 = $16,000. Alternatively, it is:

($1/6$ × $60,000) × 160/100 = $16,000

(c)   To maintain the capital value of equity in CPP terms during 20X5, the CPP value of equity on 31 December 20X5 will need to be:

$29,000 × 180/160 = $32,625

Question 5.1   CPP profits

Learning outcomes B1

Rice and Price set up in business on 1 January 20X5 with no non current assets, and cash of $5,000. On 1 January, they acquired inventories for the full $5,000, which they sold on 30 June 20X5 for $6,000. On 30 November they obtained a further $2,100 of inventory on credit. The index of the general price level gives the following index figures.

Date	Index
1 January 20X5	300
30 June 20X5	330
30 November 20X5	350
31 December 20X5	360

Calculate the CPP profits (or losses) of Rice and Price for the year to 31 December 20X5.

2.5.9 The advantages and disadvantages of CPP accounting

Advantages

(a)   The restatement of asset values in terms of a **stable money value** provides **a more meaningful basis of comparison** with other companies.

(b)   Similarly, provided that previous years' profits are revalued into CPP terms, year-by-year comparisons are also more valid.

(c)   **Profit** is measured in **'real' terms** and excludes 'inflationary value increments'. This enables better forecasts of future prospects to be made.

(d)   CPP **avoids the subjective valuations** of current value accounting, because a single price index is applied to all non-monetary assets.

(e)   CPP **highlights the gains/losses** arising as a result of inflation

(f)   Since it is based on historical cost accounting, **raw data is easily verified**, and inflation adjustments can also be readily audited.

Disadvantages

(a)   For the reader of the financial statements, it is **not clear what $CPP means**. 'Generalised purchasing power' as measured by a retail price index, or indeed any other general price index, has no obvious practical significance.

(b)   How meaningful is $CPP, or gains/ losses made on monetary items?

(c)   The use of indices inevitably involves **approximations** in the measurements of value.

(d)   CPP does not show whether the business has maintained its **operating capability**. Companies hold specific purchasing power, not general purchasing power.

(e)   Due to inflation eroding the real value of debt, highly geared companies will seem more successful under CPP financial statements. (High interest costs will to some extent reduce this difficulty.)

In this respect, a CPP statement of financial position has similar drawbacks to an historical cost statement of financial position.

2.5.10 Example: CCA v CPP

Suppose that Arthur Smith Co buys an asset on 1 January for $10,000. The estimated life of the asset is five years, and straight line depreciation is charged. At 31 December the gross replacement cost of the asset is $10,500 (5% higher than on 1 January) but general inflation during the year, as measured by the retail price index, has risen 20%.

(a)   In CPP, to maintain the value of the business against inflation, the asset should be revalued as follows.

	$
Gross ($10,000 × 120%)	12,000
Depreciation charge for the year (@ 20%)	2,400
Net value in the statement of financial position	9,600

(b)   In CCA, the business maintains its operating capability if we revalue the asset as follows.

	$
Gross replacement cost	10,500
Depreciation charge for the year (note)	2,100
NRC; statement of financial position value	8,400

Notes

	$
Historical cost depreciation	2,000
CCA depreciation adjustment (5%)	100
Total CCA depreciation cost	2,100

CCA preserves the operating capability of the company but does not necessarily preserve it against the declining value in the purchasing power of money (against inflation). As mentioned previously, CCA is a system which takes account of specific price inflation (changes in the prices of specific assets or groups of assets) but **not of general price inflation**.

A strict view of current cost accounting might suggest that a set of CCA accounts should be prepared from the outset on the basis of deprival values. In practice, current cost accounts are usually prepared by **starting from historical cost accounts and making appropriate adjustments**.

Example: Comparing HCA, CPP and CCA

Thunderkat Co commenced business on 1 January 20X9, financed by 300,000 $1 ordinary shares and $100,000 10% debentures, interest payable on 31 December each year. Thunderkat Co used the cash raised to buy 40,000 Transformers at $10 each.

The statement of financial position on 1.1.20X9 was as follows.

	$
Inventories	400,000
Share capital and reserves	300,000
10% debentures	100,000
	400,000

All the Transformers were sold on 31 December 20X9 for $500,000. On that date the replacement cost of a Transformer was $11.50. The general rate of inflation as measured by the general prices index was 12% during 20X9. All profit is to be distributed by way of dividend.

Required

Produce a statement of profit or loss for the year ended 31 December 20X9 and a statement of financial position at that date under the following approaches to inflation:

(a)   Historical cost accounting

(b)   Current purchasing power

(c)   Current cost accounting.

Solution

Thunderkat Co – Statement of profit or loss

	(a) HCA $	(b) CPP $	(c) CCA $
Revenue	500,000	500,000	500,000
Cost of sales	(400,000)	(448,000)	(460,000)
Gross profit	100,000	52,000	40,000
Interest	(10,000)	(10,000)	(10,000)
Gain on monetary item	–	12,000	–
Profit for the period	90,000	54,000	30,000
Appropriation of profit for the period:			
Dividend	(90,000)	(54,000)	(30,000)
Profit transferred to retained earnings	0	0	0

	(a) HCA $	(b) CPP $	(c) CCA $
Statement of financial position			
Cash	400,000	436,000	460,000
Share capital and reserves	300,000	336,000	360,000
Debentures	100,000	100,000	100,000
	400,000	436,000	460,000

2.6 'Real terms' system

The 'real terms' system is a combination of CPP and CCA approaches, adopting the best of both methods.

In the 'real terms' concept, assets are measured entirely on a CCA basis, since this reflects more meaningfully the specific purchasing power that they represent.

By contrast, shareholders' equity is measured in terms of the value of the shareholders' investment in purchasing power terms.

2.6.1 Restatement in the statement of financial position

As discussed above, assets are valued on a CCA basis in a 'real terms' system.

Equity is restated, using the General Price Index (GPI).

2.6.2 Restatement in the statement of profit or loss

The 'real terms' system incorporates some of the CCA adjustments we have looked at above:

(a)   Cost of sales adjustment (COSA)
(b)   Additional depreciation adjustment

In addition, holding gains on non-monetary items (non-current assets and inventories are recorded as **replacement cost less historical cost**, along with with an adjustment for **changes in the GPI**.

As seen above, there will also be an adjustment to opening equity for changes in the GPI.

2.6.3 Advantages and disadvantages of the 'real terms' system

Advantages

(a)   It combines best features of CPP and CCA.

(b)   It shows real asset values and the purchasing power of equity.

Disadvantages

(a)   Practically, it is difficult to obtain data and indices.

(b)   Accounting under the 'real terms' system involves complex calculations.

(c)   Understandability is impaired due to its complexity.

Section summary

CCA attempts to overcome the problem of accounting for **specific price inflation**. It is based on the concept of **physical capital maintenance**.

CPP accounting is a method of accounting for **general (not specific) inflation**. It does so by expressing asset values in a stable monetary unit, the $CPP or $ of current purchasing power.

'**Real terms**' accounting incorporates aspects of both CCA and CPP.

---

3 Hyperinflation

Introduction

In a hyperinflationary economy, **money loses its purchasing power very quickly**. Comparisons of transactions at different points in time, even within the same accounting period, are misleading. It is therefore considered inappropriate for entities to prepare financial statements without making adjustments for the **fall in the purchasing power of money over time.**.

IAS 29 *Financial reporting in hyperinflationary economies* applies to the **primary financial statements** of entities (including consolidated financial statements and statements of cash flows) whose functional currency is the currency of a hyperinflationary economy. In this section, we will identify the hyperinflationary currency as $H.

The standard does not define a **hyperinflationary economy** in exact terms, although it indicates the characteristics of such an economy, for example, where the cumulative inflation rate over three years approaches or exceeds 100%.

Question 5.2	Hyperinflation

Learning outcomes B1

What other factors might indicate a hyperinflationary economy?

The reported value of **non-monetary assets**, in terms of current measuring units, increases over time. For example, if a non-current asset is purchased for $H1,000 when the price index is 100, and the price index subsequently rises to 200, the value of the asset in terms of current measuring units (ignoring accumulated depreciation) will rise to $H2,000.

In contrast, the value of **monetary assets and liabilities**, such as a debt for 300 units, is unaffected by changes in the prices index, because it is an actual money amount payable or receivable. If a debtor owes $H300 when the price index is 100, and the debt is still unpaid when the price index has risen to 150,

the debtor still owes just $H300. The purchasing power of monetary assets, however, will decline over time as the general level of prices goes up.

3.1 Requirement to restate financial statements in terms of measuring units current at the year end

In most countries, financial statements are produced on the basis of either:

(a)   **historical cost**, except to the extent that some assets (eg property and investments) may be revalued, or

(b)   **current cost**, which reflects the changes in the values of specific assets held by the entity.

In a hyperinflationary economy, neither of these methods of financial reporting are meaningful unless adjustments are made for the fall in the purchasing power of money. IAS 29 therefore requires that the **primary financial statements** of entities in a hyperinflationary economy should be restated on a **current purchasing power (CPP)** basis. The value of the assets and liabilities are expressed in terms of **measuring unit current at the year end date**.

KEY TERM

MEASURING UNIT CURRENT AT THE YEAR END DATE. This is a unit of local currency with a purchasing power as at the date of the statement of financial position, in terms of a general prices index.

Financial statements that are not restated (ie that are prepared on a historical cost basis or current cost basis without adjustments) may be presented as **additional statements** by the entity, but this is discouraged. The primary financial statements are those that have been restated.

After the assets, liabilities, equity and statement of profit or loss and other comprehensive income of the entity have been restated, there will be a **net gain or loss on monetary assets and liabilities (the 'net monetary position')** and this should be recognised separately in profit or loss for the period.

3.2 Making the adjustments

IAS 29 recognises that the resulting financial statements, after restating all items in terms of measuring units current at the year end, will **lack precise accuracy**. However, it is more important that certain procedures and judgements should be applied consistently from year to year. The implementation guidelines to the Standard suggest what these procedures should be.

3.3 Statement of financial position: historical cost

Where the entity produces its financial statements on a historical cost basis, the following procedures should be applied.

(a)   Items that are not already expressed in terms of measuring units current at the year end should be restated, using a **general prices index**, so that they are valued in measuring units current at the year end.

(b)   **Monetary assets and liabilities** are not restated, because they are already expressed in terms of measuring units current at the year end.

(c)   Assets that are **already stated at market value or net realisable value** need not be restated, because they too are already valued in measuring units current at the year end.

(d)   Any assets or liabilities **linked by agreement to changes in the general level of prices**, such as indexed-linked loans or bonds, should be adjusted in accordance with the terms of the agreement to establish the amount outstanding as at the year end.

(e)   All **other non-monetary assets**, ie tangible long-term assets, intangible long-term assets (including accumulated depreciation/amortisation) investments and inventories, should be restated in terms of measuring units as at the year end, by applying a general prices index.

Similar to what we have already seen in CPP accounting, the **method of restating** these assets should normally be to multiply the original cost of the assets by a factor: [prices index at year end /prices index at date of acquisition of the asset].

For example, if an item of machinery was purchased for $H2,000 units when the prices index was 400 and the prices index at the year end is 1,000, the restated value of the long-term asset (before accumulated depreciation) would be:

$$\$H2,000 \times [1,000/400] = \$H5,000$$

If, in the above example, the non current asset has been held for half its useful life and has no residual value, the **accumulated depreciation** would be restated as $H2,500. (The depreciation charge for the year should be the amount of depreciation based on historical cost, multiplied by the same factor as above: 1,000/400.)

If an asset has been **revalued** since it was originally purchased (eg a property), it should be restated in measuring units at the year end date by applying a factor: (prices index at year end/prices index at revaluation date) to the revalued amount of the asset.

If the restated amount of a non monetary asset **exceeds its recoverable value** (ie its net realisable value or market value), its value should be reduced accordingly.

The **owners' equity** (all components) as at the start of the accounting period should be restated using a general prices index from the beginning of the period.

3.4 Statement of profit or loss and other comprehensive income: historical cost

In the statement of profit or loss and other comprehensive income, all amounts of income and expense should be **restated in terms of measuring units current at the year end**.

All amounts therefore need to be restated by a factor that allows for the change in the prices index since the item of income or expense was first recorded.

3.5 Gain or loss on net monetary position

In a period of inflation, , an entity that holds monetary assets (cash, receivables) will suffer a fall in the purchasing power of these assets. By the same token, in a period of inflation, the value of monetary liabilities, such as a bank overdraft or bank loan, declines in terms of current purchasing power.

(a) If an entity has an **excess of monetary assets over monetary liabilities**, it will suffer a loss over time on its net monetary position, in a period of inflation, in terms of measuring units as at 'today's date'.

(b) If an entity has an **excess of monetary liabilities over monetary assets**, it will make a gain on its net monetary position, in a period of inflation.

In the financial statements of an entity reporting in the currency of a hyperinflationary economy, the gain or loss on the net monetary position:

(a) may be derived as the **difference between total assets and total equity and liabilities**, after restating the non-monetary assets, owners' equity, statement of profit or loss and other comprehensive income items and index-linked items, *or*

(b) may be estimated by **applying the change in the general prices index** for the period to the weighted average of the net monetary position of the entity in the period.

The gain or loss on the net monetary position should be **included in profit or loss** and disclosed separately. (Any adjustment that was made to index-linked items can be set off against this net monetary gain or loss.)

Example: hyperinflationary financial statements

At 1 January 20X3, when the general prices index was 100, the statement of financial position of X Co was as follows.

	$H
Assets	
Non-monetary assets	2,000
Monetary assets	2,000
	4,000
Liabilities and equity	
Monetary liabilities	1,000
Equity	3,000
	4,000

Suppose that the general prices index rises to 150 at 31 December 20X3. X Co has acquired no additional assets, liabilities or equity during the year.

Required

Show the adjustments required in the statement of financial position.

Solution

Restating this statement of financial position in terms of measuring units when the prices index is 50% higher gives the following.

	$H
Assets	
Non-monetary assets ($\times$ 150/100)	3,000
Monetary assets	2,000
	5,000
Liabilities and equity	
Monetary liabilities	1,000
Equity ($\times$ 150/100)	4,500
	5,500

X Co has suffered a loss on its net monetary position of $H500, in terms of measuring units at the current date $H(5,500 − 5,000). This is because it has held net monetary assets of $H2,000 during the period.

3.6 Current cost financial statements: restating the financial statements

A similar procedure is required to restate the financial statements of an entity that prepares its financial statements a current cost basis.

(a)   Items stated in the **statement of financial position at current cost do not need to be restated**. Other items should be restated in the same way as for adjusting accounts prepared on a historical cost basis.

(b)   In the **statement of profit or loss and other comprehensive income**, cost of sales and depreciation are generally reported at current costs at the time of consumption and sales and other expenses at money amounts at the time they occurred. These items **will need to be restated** in terms of measuring units as at the year end by making a prices index adjustment.

(c)   There will be a **gain or loss on the net monetary position**, which will be established in the same way as for accounts based on historical cost.

3.7 Economies ceasing to be hyperinflation economies

When an economy ceases to be a hyperinflation economy, entities reporting in the currency of the economy should cease to comply with IAS 29.

Suppose, for example, that in 20X4 an entity reports in compliance with IAS 29, but in 20X5 it reverts to historical cost accounting because the economy is no longer a hyperinflation economy. It should then treat the amounts expressed in the measuring unit at the end of 20X4 as the basis for the carrying amounts in its financial statements for 20X5.

3.8 Disclosures

IAS 29 requires the following disclosures.

*   The fact that the **financial statements have been restated** for the changes in general purchasing power.

*   Whether the financial statements as shown are based on **historical cost or current cost**.

*   The **identity of the prices index** used to make the restatements, its level at the year end the movement in the index during the current and the previous reporting periods.

In financial statements prepared under IAS 29, corresponding figures for the previous year should be **restated using the general prices index**.

3.9 Hyperinflation and changes in foreign exchange rates

IAS 21 *The effects of changes in foreign exchange rates* will be covered in a later chapter. However, a parent may have a foreign operation whose functional currency is the currency of a hyperinflationary economy. When the parent prepares consolidated financial statements it should:

(a)   **restate the financial statements** of the foreign operation in accordance with IAS 29; **before**

(b)   **translating all amounts** from the foreign operation's functional currency to the presentation currency **at the closing rate**.

The following example is a simple illustration of the problems that can arise where a foreign subsidiary operates in a hyperinflationary economy.

Example: 'disappearing assets'

A company has a subsidiary in a country which suffers from hyperinflation. On 31 December 20X2, the subsidiary acquired freehold land for $H1,000,000. At that date the exchange rate was $H4 = $1 and the relevant price index was 100.

At 31 December 20X3 the exchange rate was $H10 = $1 and the price index was 300.

Required

Show the value at which the freehold land is included in the consolidated financial statements of the parent at 31 December 20X3 if the subsidiary's financial statements:

(a)   are not restated to reflect current price levels;
(b)   are restated to reflect current price levels.

Solution

(a)   Without restatement

Assuming that the subsidiary has a different functional currency ($H) from that of its parent ($) the statement of financial position is translated at the closing rate.

At 31 December 20X3 the land is included at $100,000 ($H1,000,000 @ 10).

At 31 December 20X2 (the date of purchase) its was stated at $250,000 ($H1,000,000 @ 4). Therefore there has been an exchange loss of $150,000 (which may significantly reduce equity) and the land appears to have fallen to only 40% of its original value.

(b)   With restatement

At 31 December 20X3 the land is included at $300,000 ($H1,000,000 × 300/100 @ 10).

The value of the land is now adjusted so that it reflects the effect of inflation over the year and the 'disappearing assets' problem is overcome.

Where the financial statements of an entity whose functional currency is that of a hyperinflationary economy are translated into a different presentation currency, **comparative amounts** should be those that were presented as current year amounts in the prior year financial statements (ie, **not adjusted** for subsequent changes in the price level or subsequent changes in exchange rates).

Section summary

IAS 29 requires financial statements of entities operating within a hyperinflationary economy to be restated in terms of measuring units current at the year end.

- IAS 29 does not define **hyperinflationary economies**, but economies where the inflation rate over three years has cumulatively exceeded 100% are seen to be hyperinflationary economies.

- Financial statements should be **restated on a CPP basis, based on a measuring unit current** at the year end

    - **Monetary assets/liabilities** do not need to be restated
    - **Non-monetary assets/liabilities** must be restated by applying a general prices index
    - Items of income/expense must be restated
    - **Gain/loss on net monetary items** must be reported in profit or loss for the year

4   Fair value measurement

Introduction

In May 2011 the IASB published IFRS 13 *Fair value measurement*. The project arose as a result of the Memorandum of Understanding between the IASB and FASB (February 2006) reaffirming their commitment to the convergence of IFRSs and US GAAP. With the publication of IFRS 13, IFRS and US GAAP now have the same definition of fair value and the measurement and disclosure requirements are now aligned. You will meet IFRS 13 in Chapter 6.

4.1 Objective

IFRS 13 sets out to:

(a)   Define fair value
(b)   Set out in a single IFRS a framework for measuring fair value
(c)   Require disclosure about fair value measurements

4.2 Definitions

IFRS 13 defines fair value as '**the price that would be received to sell an asset or paid to transfer a liability in an orderly transaction between market participants at the measurement date.**'

The price which would be received to sell the asset or paid to transfer (not settle) the liability is described as the 'exit price' and this is the definition used in US GAAP. Although the concept of the 'arm's length transaction' has now gone, the market-based current exit price retains the notion of an exchange between unrelated, knowledgeable and willing parties.

4.3 Scope

IFRS 13 applies when another IFRS requires or permits fair value measurements or disclosures. The measurement and disclosure requirements do not apply in the case of:

(a)   Share-based payment transactions within the scope of IFRS 2 *Share-based payment*
(b)   Leasing transactions within the scope of IAS 17 *Leases*; and
(c)   Net realisable value as in IAS 2 *Inventories* or value in use as in IAS 36 *Impairment of assets.*

Disclosures are not required for;

(a)   Plan assets measured at fair value in accordance with IAS 19 *Employee benefits*

(b)   Plan investments measured at fair value in accordance with IAS 26 *Accounting and reporting by retirement benefit plans*; and

(c)   Assets for which the recoverable amount is fair value less disposal costs under IAS 36 *Impairment of assets*

Fair value measurements are based on an asset or a liability's **unit of account**, which is specified by each IFRS where a fair value measurement is required. For most assets and liabilities, the unit of account is the individual asset or liability, but in some instances may be a group of assets or liabilities.

For example, a premium or discount on a large holding of the same shares (because the market's normal daily trading volume is not sufficient to absorb the quantity held by the entity) is not considered when measuring fair value: the quoted price per share in an active market is used.

4.4 Measurement

Fair value is a market-based measurement, not an entity-specific measurement. It focuses on assets and liabilities and on exit (selling) prices. It also takes into account market conditions at the measurement date. In other words, it looks at the amount for which the holder of an asset could sell it and the amount which the holder of a liability would have to pay to transfer it. It can also be used to value an entity's own equity instruments.

Because it is a market-based measurement, fair value is measured using the assumptions that market participants would use when pricing the asset, taking into account any relevant characteristics of the asset.

It is assumed that the transaction to sell the asset or transfer the liability takes place either:

(a)   In the *principal market* for the asset or liability; or
(b)   In the absence of a principle market, in the *most advantageous* market for the asset or liability.

The principal market is the market which is the most liquid (has the greatest volume and level of activity) for that asset or liability. In most cases the principal market and the most advantageous market will be the same.

IFRS 13 acknowledges that when market activity declines an entity must use a valuation technique to measure fair value. In this case the emphasis must be on whether a transaction price is based on an **orderly transaction**, rather than a forced sale.

4.5 Valuation techniques

IFRS 13 states that valuation techniques must be those which are appropriate and for which sufficient data are available. Entities should maximise the use of relevant **observable inputs** and minimise the use of **unobservable inputs**.

The standard establishes a three-level hierarchy for the inputs that valuation techniques use to measure fair value:

Level 1   Quoted prices (unadjusted) in active markets for identical assets or liabilities that the reporting entity can access at the measurement date

Level 2   Inputs other than quoted prices included within Level 1 that are observable for the asset or liability, either directly or indirectly, eg quoted prices for similar assets in active markets or for identical or similar assets in non active markets or use of quoted interest rates for valuation purposes

Level 3   Unobservable inputs for the asset or liability, ie using the entity's own assumptions about market exit value.

Level 3 inputs are only used where relevant observable inputs are not available or where the entity determines that transaction price or quote price does not represent fair value.

The measurement of the **fair value of a liability** assumes that the liability **remains outstanding** and the market participant transferee would be required to fulfil the obligation, rather than being extinguished. The fair value of a liability also reflects the effect of **non-performance risk** (the risk that an entity will not fulfil an obligation), which includes, but may not be limited to, an entity's own credit risk (ie risk of non-payment).

4.5.1 Non-financial assets

For **non-financial assets** the fair value measurement looks at the use to which the asset can be put. The fair value measurement is the value for using the asset in its **highest and best use**, or by selling it to another market participant that would use it in its highest and best use.

4.6 Disclosure

An entity must disclose information that helps users of its financial statements assess both of the following:

(a)   For assets and liabilities that are measured at fair value on a recurring or non-recurring basis, the **valuation techniques** and **inputs** used to develop those measurements.

(b)   For recurring fair value measurements using significant **unobservable inputs** (Level 3), the effect of the measurements on profit or loss or other comprehensive income for the period. Disclosure requirements will include:

- Reconciliation from opening to closing balances
- Quantitative information regarding the inputs used
- Valuation processes used by the entity
- Sensitivity to changes in inputs

4.7 Was the project necessary?

The IASB is already considering the matter of the measurement basis for assets and liabilities in financial reporting as part of its conceptual framework project. It could therefore be argued that it was not necessary to have a separate project on fair value. The conceptual framework might have been the more appropriate forum for discussing **when** fair value should be used **as well as how to define and measure it.**

However, it has been argued that a concise definition and clear measurement framework is needed because there is so much inconsistency in this area, and this may form the basis for discussions in the conceptual framework project.

The IASB has also pointed out that the global financial crisis has highlighted the need for:

- Clarifying how to measure fair value when the market for an asset becomes less active; and

- Improving the transparency of fair value measurements through disclosures about measurement uncertainty.

4.8 Advantages and disadvantages of fair value vs historical cost

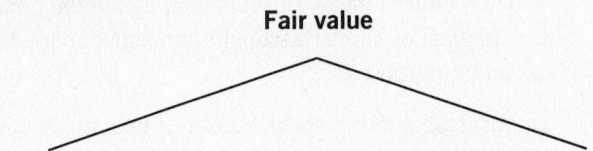

Fair value

Advantages

- Relevant to users' decisions
- Consistency between companies
- Predicts future cash flows

Disadvantages

- Subjective (not reliable)
- Hard to calculate if no active market
- Time and cost
- Lack of practical experience/familiarity
- Less useful for ratio analysis (bias)
- Misleading in a volatile market

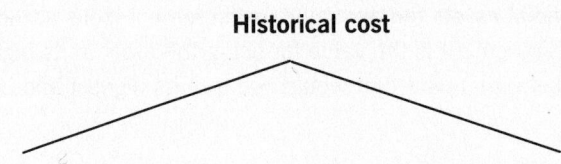

Historical cost

Advantages

- Reliable
- Less open to manipulation
- Quick and easy to ascertain
- Matching (cost and revenue)
- Practical experience & familiarity

Disadvantages

- Less relevant to users' decisions
- Need for additional measure of recoverable amounts (impairment test)
- Does not predict future cash flows

Section summary

IFRS 13 is an important recent standard giving guidance on fair value measurement.

Chapter Roundup

✓ **Profit** can be viewed as a measure of the increase in an entity's capital over the duration of an accounting period.

✓ The **measurement of profit** depends on the concept of **capital maintenance**.

✓ **CCA** attempts to overcome the problems of accounting for **specific price inflation.** It is based on a concept of **physical capital maintenance**.

✓ **CPP accounting** is a method of accounting for **general** (not specific) inflation. It does so by expressing asset values in a stable monetary unit, the **$CPP** or $ of current purchasing power.

✓ **IAS 29** requires financial statements of entities operating within a hyperinflationary economy to be restated in terms of measuring units current at the year end.

   • IAS 29 does not define **hyperinflationary economies**, but they have various characteristics

   • Financial statements should be **restated based on a measuring unit current** at the year end

     – **Monetary assets/liabilities** do not need to be restated

     – **Non-monetary assets/liabilities** must be restated by applying a general prices index

     – Items of income/expense must be restated

     – **Gain/loss on net monetary items** must be reported in profit or loss for the year

Quick Quiz

1   Under current cost accounting, capital is maintained if at the end of a period, the entity can achieve the same _____ as at the beginning of the period. *Complete the blank.*

2   Distinguish between specific price inflation and general price inflation.

Answers to Quick Quiz

1   Physical output

2   • Specific price inflation measures price changes over time for a specific asset or group of assets
    • General price inflation measures the continual reduction in the general purchasing power of money

Answers to Questions

5.1 CPP profits

The approach is to prepare a CPP statement of profit or loss and other comprehensive income.

	$CPP	$CPP
Sales ($6,000 × 360/330)		6,545
Less cost of goods sold ($5,000 × 360/300)		6,000
		545
Loss on holding cash for 6 months*	(545)	
Gain by owing payables for 1 month**	60	
		485
CPP profit		60

* ($6,000 × 360/330) – $6,000 = $CPP 545
**($2,100 × 360/350) – $2,100 = $CPP 60

5.2 Hyperinflation

These are examples, but the list is not exhaustive.

(a) The population prefers to retain its wealth in non-monetary assets or in a relatively stable foreign currency. Amounts of local currency held are immediately invested to maintain purchasing power.

(b) The population regards monetary amounts not in terms of the local currency but in terms of a relatively stable foreign currency. Prices may be quoted in that currency.

(c) Sales/purchases on credit take place at prices that compensate for the expected loss of purchasing power during the credit period, if that period is short.

(d) Interest rates, wages and prices are linked to a price index.

<table>
<tr><td rowspan="2">Now try this question from the Exam Question Bank</td><th>Number</th><th>Level</th><th>Marks</th><th>Time</th></tr>
<tr><td>Q5</td><td>Introductory</td><td>10</td><td>18 mins</td></tr>
</table>

GROUP FINANCIAL STATEMENTS

Part B

126

REVISION OF BASIC GROUPS

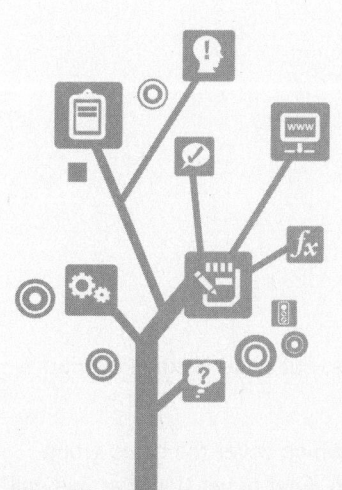

Consolidation is an extremely important area of your Paper F2 syllabus.

The key to consolidation questions in the examination is to adopt a logical approach and to practise as many questions as possible.

In this chapter we will revise the definitions and basic consolidation techniques that you met in Paper F1. We will also look at IFRS 10 (formerly IAS 27) in more detail. Make sure that you work through *all* the questions carefully.

topic list	learning outcomes	syllabus references	ability required
1 Group accounts	A1	A1(i)	Comprehension
2 IFRS 10 *Consolidated financial statements*	A1	A1(ii)	Comprehension
3 Consolidated statement of financial position	A1	A1(ii)	Application
4 Fair values in acquisition accounting	A1	A1(ii)	Application
5 Consolidated statement of profit or loss and other comprehensive income	A1	A1(ii)	Application

> ### Brought forward knowledge
>
> This chapter is mainly revision but pay particular attention to Section 4, which includes some material on IFRS 13. The rest may be skimmed to make sure you understand it.

1   Group accounts

> ### Introduction
>
> In this section we will deal with the concept of a group and start to see how groups are accounted for in accordance with IFRSs.

1.1 Why group accounts

There are many reasons for businesses to operate as groups; for the goodwill associated with the names of the subsidiaries, for tax or legal purposes and so forth. In many countries, company law requires that the results of a group should be presented as a whole. Unfortunately, it is not possible simply to add all the results together and this chapter will teach you how to **consolidate** all the results of companies within a group.

In traditional accounting terminology, a **group of companies** consists of a **parent company** and one or more **subsidiary companies** which are controlled by the parent company.

1.2 Accounting standards

We will be looking at five accounting standards in this and the next three chapters.

- IFRS 3 *Business combinations*
- IFRS 10 *Consolidated financial statements*
- IAS 28 *Investments in associates and joint ventures*
- IFRS 11 *Joint arrangements*
- IFRS 12 *Disclosure of interests in other entities*

These standards are all concerned with different aspects of group accounts, but there is some overlap between them, particularly between IFRS 3 and IFRS 10.

In this and the next chapter we will concentrate on IFRS 3 and IFRS 10, which cover the basic group definitions and consolidation procedures of a parent-subsidiary relationship. First of all, however, we will look at all the important definitions involved in group accounts, which **determine how to treat each particular type of investment** in group accounts.

1.3 Definitions   5/10

We will look at some of these definitions in more detail later, but they are useful here in that they give you an overview of all aspects of group accounts.

Exam skills

All the definitions relating to group accounts are extremely important. You must **learn them** and **understand** their meaning and application.

KEY TERMS

CONTROL. An investor controls an investee when the investor **is exposed**, or has **rights**, **to variable returns** from its involvement with the investee and has the **ability to affect those returns** through **power** over the investee.   *(IFRS 10)*

POWER. Existing rights that give the current ability to direct the relevant activities of the investee   *(IFRS 10)*

SUBSIDIARY. An entity that is **controlled** by another entity.   *(IFRS 10)*

PARENT. An entity that **controls** one or more subsidiaries.   *(IFRS 10)*

GROUP. A **parent** and all its **subsidiaries**.   *(IFRS 10)*

ASSOCIATE. An entity over which an investor has **significant influence**.   *(IAS 28)*

SIGNIFICANT INFLUENCE is the power to **participate in the financial and operating policy** decisions of an investee but is not control or joint control over those policies.   *(IAS 28)*

JOINT ARRANGEMENT. An arrangement of which two or more parties have **joint control**.   *(IAS 28)*

JOINT CONTROL. The **contractually agreed sharing of control** of an arrangement, which exists only when decisions about the relevant activities require the unanimous consent of the parties sharing control.
                                                                                                (IAS 28)

JOINT VENTURE. A joint arrangement whereby the parties that have joint control (the joint venturers) of the arrangement have rights to the net assets of the arrangement.   *(IAS 28, IFRS 11)*

We can summarise the different types of investment *and* the required accounting for them as follows.

Investment	Criteria	Required treatment in group accounts
Subsidiary	Control	Full consolidation
Associate	Significant influence	Equity accounting (see Chapter 9)
Joint venture	Joint control with rights to net assets	Equity accounting (see Chapter 9)
Joint operation	Joint control with rights to individual assets and obligations for individual liabilities	Line by line (see Chapter 9)
Investment which is none of the above	Asset held for accretion of wealth	As for single company accounts per IAS 39 (see Chapter 2)

1.4 Investments in subsidiaries

The important point here is **control**. In most cases, this will involve the holding company or parent owning a majority of the ordinary shares in the subsidiary (to which normal voting rights are attached). There are circumstances, however, when the parent may own only a minority of the voting power in the subsidiary, *but* the parent still has control.

IFRS 10 provides a definition of control and identifies three separate elements of control:

An investor controls an investee if and only if it has all of the following:

    (1)   Power over the investee

    (2)   Exposure to, or rights to, variable returns from its involvement with the investee; and

    (3)   The ability to use its power over the investee to affect the amount of the investor's returns

If there are changes to one or more of these three elements of control, then an investor should reassess whether it controls an investee.

BPP
LEARNING MEDIA

Power (as defined under Key Terms) can be obtained directly from ownership of the majority of voting rights or can be derived from other rights, such as:

- Rights to appoint, reassign or remove key management personnel who can direct the relevant activities

- Rights to appoint or remove another entity that directs the relevant activities

- Rights to direct the investee to enter into, or veto changes to, transactions for the benefit of the investor

- Other rights, such as those specified in a management contract

 Exam skills

You should learn the contents of the above paragraph as you may be asked to apply them in the exam, for example as at May 2010.

1.4.1 Accounting treatment in group accounts

IFRS 10 requires a parent to present consolidated financial statements, in which the accounts of the parent and subsidiary (or subsidiaries) are combined and presented **as a single entity**.

1.5 Investments in associates

This type of investment is something less than a subsidiary, but more than a simple investment. The key criterion here is **significant influence**. This is defined as the 'power to participate', but *not* to 'control' (which would make the investment a subsidiary).

Significant influence can be determined by the holding of voting rights (usually attached to shares) in the entity. IAS 28 states that if an investor holds **20% or more** of the voting power of the investee, it can be presumed that the investor has significant influence over the investee, *unless* it can be clearly shown that this is not the case.

Significant influence can be presumed *not* to exist if the investor holds **less than 20%** of the voting power of the investee, unless it can be demonstrated otherwise.

The **existence of significant influence** is evidenced in one or more of the following ways.

(a) Representation on the **board of directors** (or equivalent) of the investee
(b) Participation in the **policy making process**
(c) **Material transactions** between investor and investee
(d) Interchange of management personnel
(e) Provision of essential technical information

1.5.1 Accounting treatment in group accounts

IAS 28 requires the use of the **equity method** of accounting for investments in associates. This method will be explained in detail in Chapter 9.

1.6 Accounting for investments in joint arrangements

IFRS 11 classes joint arrangements as either **joint operations** or **joint ventures**. The classification of a joint arrangement as a joint operation or a joint venture depends upon the rights and obligations of the parties to the arrangement. The detail of how to distinguish between joint operations and joint ventures will be considered in Chapter 9.

1.6.1 Accounting treatment in group accounts

IFRS 11 requires that a joint operator recognises **line-by-line** the following in relation to its interest in a **joint operation**:

(a)   its assets, including its share of any jointly held assets
(b)   its liabilities, including its share of any jointly incurred liabilities
(c)   its revenue from the sale of its share of the output arising from the joint operation
(d)   its share of the revenue from the sale of the output by the joint operation, and
(e)   its expenses, including its share of any expenses incurred jointly.

This treatment is applicable in both the separate and consolidated financial statements of the joint operator.

In its consolidated financial statements, IFRS 11 requires that a joint venturer recognises its interest in a **joint venture** as an investment and accounts for that investment using the **equity method** in accordance with IAS 28 *Investments in associates and joint ventures* unless the entity is exempted from applying the equity method.

In its separate financial statements, a joint venturer should account for its interest in a joint venture in accordance with IAS 27 (2011) *Separate financial statements*, namely:

(a)   At cost, or
(b)   In accordance with IAS 39 *Financial instruments: recognition and measurement*

1.7 Other investments

Investments which do not meet the definitions of any of the above should be accounted for according to IAS 39 (see Chapter 2).

Section summary

Many large businesses consist of several companies controlled by one central or administrative company. Together these companies are called a **group**. The controlling company, called the **parent** or **holding company**, will own some or all of the shares in the other companies, called subsidiaries.

---

2   IFRS 10 *Consolidated financial statements*

Introduction

There are a number of regulations governing the preparation of group accounts.

2.1 Definitions

KEY TERM

CONSOLIDATED FINANCIAL STATEMENTS. The financial statements of a **group** presented as those of a **single** economic entity.   *(IFRS 10)*

When a parent issues consolidated financial statements, it should consolidate **all subsidiaries**, both foreign and domestic. The first step in any consolidation is to identify the subsidiaries using the definition as set out in Section 1.4 above.

2.2 Power

Power is defined as **existing rights that give the current ability to direct the relevant activities of the investee**. There is no requirement for that power to have been exercised.

Relevant activities may include:

(a)   Selling and purchasing goods or services
(b)   Managing financial assets
(c)   Selecting, acquiring and disposing of assets
(d)   Researching and developing new products and processes
(e)   Determining a funding structure or obtaining funding.

In some cases assessing power is straightforward, for example, where power is obtained directly and solely from having the majority of voting rights or potential voting rights, and as a result the ability to direct relevant activities.

In other cases, assessment is more complex and more than one factor must be considered. IFRS 10 gives the following examples of **rights**, other than voting or potential voting rights, which individually, or alone, can give an investor power.

(a)   Rights to appoint, reassign or remove key management personnel who can direct the relevant activities

(b)   Rights to appoint or remove another entity that directs the relevant activities

(c)   Rights to direct the investee to enter into, or veto changes to transactions for the benefit of the investor

(d)   Other rights, such as those specified in a management contract.

IFRS 10 suggests that the **ability** rather than contractual right to achieve the above may also indicate that an investor has power over an investee.

An investor can have power over an investee even where other entities have significant influence or other ability to participate in the direction of relevant activities.

2.2.1 Returns

An investor must have exposure, or rights, to **variable returns** from its involvement with the investee in order to establish control.

This is the case where the investor's returns from its involvement have the potential to vary as a result of the investee's performance.

Returns may include:

(a)   Dividends

(b)   Remuneration for servicing an investee's assets or liabilities

(c)   Fees and exposure to loss from providing credit support

(d)   Returns as a result of achieving synergies or economies of scale through an investor combining use of their assets with use of the investee's assets

2.2.2 Link between power and returns

In order to establish control, an investor must be able to use its power to affect its returns from its involvement with the investee. This is the case even where the investor delegates its decision making powers to an agent.

2.3 Exemption from preparing group accounts

A parent **need not present** consolidated financial statements if and only if all of the following hold:

(a)   The parent is itself a **wholly-owned subsidiary** or it is a **partially owned subsidiary** of another entity and its other owners, including those not otherwise entitled to vote, have been informed about, and do not object to, the parent not presenting consolidated financial statements

(b)   Its securities are **not publicly traded**

(c)   It is **not in the process of issuing securities** in public securities markets; and

(d)   The **ultimate or intermediate parent** publishes consolidated financial statements that comply with International Financial Reporting Standards

A parent that does not present consolidated financial statements must comply with the IAS 27 rules on separate financial statements (discussed later in this section).

2.4 Potential voting rights

An entity may own share warrants, share call options, or other similar instruments that are **convertible into ordinary shares** in another entity. If these are exercised or converted they may give the entity voting power or reduce another party's voting power over the financial and operating policies of the other entity (potential voting rights). The **existence and effect** of potential voting rights, including potential voting rights held by another entity, should be considered when assessing whether an entity has control over another entity (and therefore has a subsidiary). Potential voting rights are considered only if the rights are **substantive** (meaning that the holder must have the practical ability to exercise the right).

In assessing whether potential voting rights give rise to control, the investor should consider the **purpose and design of the instrument**. This includes an assessment of the various terms and conditions of the instrument as well as the investor's apparent expectations, motives and reasons for agreeing to those terms and conditions.

2.5 Exclusion of a subsidiary from consolidation   11/11

Where a parent controls one or more subsidiaries, IFRS 10 requires that consolidated financial statements are prepared to include **all subsidiaries, both foreign and domestic** other than:

- Those held for sale in accordance with IFRS 5 *Non-current assets held for sale and discontinued operations*

In this instance, the subsidiary will still be included in the consolidated financial statements but not on a line by line basis (see Chapter 7, Section 8 for more detail).

The rules on exclusion of subsidiaries from consolidation are necessarily strict, because this is a common method used by entities to manipulate their results. If a subsidiary which carries a large amount of debt can be excluded, then the gearing of the group as a whole will be improved. In other words, this is a way of taking debt **out of the consolidated statement of financial position**.

2.6 Different reporting dates

In most cases, all group companies will prepare accounts to the same reporting date. One or more subsidiaries may, however, prepare accounts to a different reporting date from the parent and the bulk of other subsidiaries in the group.

In such cases the subsidiary may prepare additional statements to the reporting date of the rest of the group, for consolidation purposes. If this is not possible, the subsidiary's accounts may still be used for the consolidation, *provided that* the gap between the reporting dates is **three months or less**.

Where a subsidiary's accounts are drawn up to a different accounting date, **adjustments should be made** for the effects of significant transactions or other events that occur between that date and the parent's reporting date.

2.7 Uniform accounting policies

Consolidated financial statements should be prepared using **the same accounting policies** for like transactions and other events in similar circumstances.

Adjustments must be made where members of a group use different accounting policies, so that their financial statements are suitable for consolidation.

2.8 Date of inclusion/exclusion

IFRS 10 requires the results of subsidiary undertakings to be included in the consolidated financial statements from:

(a)   the date of 'acquisition', ie the **date on which the investor obtains control of the investee**, to

(b)   the date of 'disposal', ie the **date the investor loses control of the investee**.

Once an investment is no longer a subsidiary, it should be treated as an associate under IAS 28 (if applicable) or as an investment under IAS 39 (see Chapter 2).

2.9 Accounting for subsidiaries, associates and joint ventures in the parent's separate financial statements

A parent company will usually produce its own single company financial statements. In these statements, investments in subsidiaries, associates and joint ventures included in the consolidated financial statements should be *either*:

(a)   Accounted for at **cost**, *or*

(b)   In accordance with **IAS 39**

Where subsidiaries are **classified as held for sale** in accordance with IFRS 5, the investment should be accounted for in accordance with IFRS 5 in the parent's separate financial statements. The treatment of the held for sale subsidiary in the group financial statements is covered in Chapter 7 (Section 8).

2.10 Disclosure

Disclosure is now regulated by a new standard IFRS 12 *Disclosure of interests in other entities* (see Chapter 9).

2.11 Attribution of losses

Under IFRS 10, non-controlling interests can be negative. This is consistent with the idea that non-controlling interests are part of the equity of the group.

2.12 Structured entities (special purpose entities)   11/11

These are dealt with here because they are another example of the exercise of power and control.

A structured entity is defined by IFRS 12 as 'an entity that has been designed so that voting or similar rights are not the dominant factor in deciding who controls the entity, such as when any voting rights related to administrative tasks only and the relevant activities are directed by means of contractual arrangements'.

A structured entity (sometimes referred to as a 'special purpose entity') may be created to accomplish a specific, defined objective. Examples include research and development, or securitisation of financial assets. Such special purpose entities (SPE) may be incorporated or unincorporated. Often there are strict and permanent limits on the decision-making powers of their governing board or other management. They operate on 'autopilot', ie the policy guiding their activities cannot be modified other than perhaps by their sponsor. The sponsor frequently transfers assets to the structured entity or performs services for it.

If the IFRS 10 **definition of control** is met (see Section 2.2), structured entities must be **consolidated**. If the definition of control is not met, the entity is not consolidated but significant disclosures are still required by IFRS 12.

Exam alert

This topic was examined as a 5 mark part question in the November 2011 paper (the example below is a simplified version of that question).

Example: Structured entities

A company, XY, operates a payroll services division for itself and a number of external customers. It decides to transfer the business of the division to a new entity ABC set up by XY. The sales director of ABC owns 100% of the share capital of ABC. The operating and financial policies of ABC will be decided by the board of XY under a signed contract. ABC's profits and losses will flow to XY and ABC has acquired a loan guaranteed by XY.

The directors of XY wish to avoid consolidating the results of ABC as the loan will adversely affect their gearing ratio.

Discuss how the relationship with ABC should be reflected in the financial statements of the XY group.

Solution

IFRS 10 *Consolidated financial statements* defines a **subsidiary** as **an entity that is controlled by another entity.** An investor controls an investee when the investor:

- Has power of over the investee to direct relevant activities;
- Is exposed, or has rights, to variable returns from its involvement with the investee; and
- Has the ability to use its power to affect those returns.

Whilst control is presumed to exist when the parent owns more than half of the voting power, **control may exist when a parent owns less than half the voting power but exercises control over the entity** under a statute or agreement.

Here, on the face of it, ABC does not look like a subsidiary of XY because XY does not own any of the shares (it is 100% owned by ABC's sales director). However, XY has **power** over ABC to direct its relevant activities through the **contractual agreement** between ABC and XY states that the board of XY is to make the operating and financial policies of ABC.

XY is also **exposed to the variable returns** of ABC as the **profits and losses of ABC flow to XY**. Further exposure comes from **XY acting as guarantor** for ABC's loan as XY would become liable on default.

Finally, DRT has the **ability to use their power** through the contractual agreement. Therefore, **the IFRS 10 definition of control has been met**.

DRT should consolidate 100 per cent of GHJ's assets and loan liability. Non-consolidation just to avoid increasing gearing would result in non-compliance with IFRS 10 and therefore is not permitted.

2.13 Main points

IFRS 10 covers the basic rules and definitions of the parent-subsidiary relationship. You should learn:

* **Definitions**
* Rules for **exemption** from preparing consolidated financial statements
* **Disclosure requirements**

Section summary

IFRS 10 requires a parent to present **consolidated** financial statements.

3 Consolidated statement of financial position   9/11, 3/12

Introduction

We will now consider how the consolidated financial statement of financial position is prepared.

3.1 Basic procedure

The preparation of a consolidated statement of financial position, in a very simple form, consists of two procedures.

(a)   Take the individual accounts of the parent company and each subsidiary and **cancel out items** which appear as an asset in one company and a liability in another.

(b)   Add together all the uncancelled assets and liabilities throughout the group.

Items requiring cancellation may include the following.

(a)   The asset **'shares in subsidiary companies'** which appears in the parent company's accounts will be matched with the 'share capital' in the subsidiaries' accounts.

(b)   There may be **intra-group trading** within the group. For example, S Co may sell goods on credit to P Co. P Co would then be a receivable in the accounts of S Co, while S Co would be a payable in the accounts of P Co. These need to be cancelled out, so that the consolidated statement of financial position shows amounts owing between the group as a single entity and the outside world, and **not** those due between members of the group.

Example: Cancellation

P Co regularly sells goods to its wholly owned subsidiary company, S Co, which it has owned since S Co's incorporation. The statements of financial position of the two companies on 31 December 20X6 are given below.

STATEMENT OF FINANCIAL POSITION AS AT 31 DECEMBER 20X6

	P Co $	S Co $
Assets		
Non-current assets		
Property, plant and equipment	35,000	45,000
Investment in 40,000 $1 shares in S Co at cost	40,000	
	75,000	
Current assets		
Inventories	16,000	12,000
Receivables: S Co	2,000	
Other	6,000	9,000
Cash at bank	1,000	
Total assets	100,000	66,000
Equity and liabilities		
Equity		
40,000 $1 ordinary shares		40,000
70,000 $1 ordinary shares	70,000	
Retained earnings	16,000	19,000
	86,000	59,000
Current liabilities		
Bank overdraft		3,000
Payables: P Co		2,000
Payables: Other	14,000	2,000
Total equity and liabilities	100,000	66,000

Required

Prepare the consolidated statement of financial position of P Co at 31 December 20X6.

Solution

The cancelling items are:

(a)   P Co's asset 'investment in shares of S Co' ($40,000) cancels with S Co's 'share capital' ($40,000);

(b)   P Co's asset 'receivables: S Co' ($2,000) cancels with S Co's liability 'payables: P Co' ($2,000).

The remaining assets and liabilities are added together to produce the following consolidated statement of financial position.

P CO

CONSOLIDATED STATEMENT OF FINANCIAL POSITION AS AT 31 DECEMBER 20X6

	$	$
Assets		
Non-current assets		
Property, plant and equipment (35,000 + 45,000)		80,000
Current assets		
Inventories (16,000 + 12,000)	28,000	
Receivables (6,000 + 9,000)	15,000	
Cash at bank	1,000	
		44,000
Total assets		124,000
Equity and liabilities		
Equity		
70,000 $1 ordinary shares	70,000	
Retained earnings (16,000 + 19,000)	35,000	
		105,000
Current liabilities		
Bank overdraft	3,000	
Payables (14,000 + 2,000)	16,000	
		19,000
Total equity and liabilities		124,000

(a) P Co's bank balance is **not netted off** with S Co's bank overdraft, as this would be less informative and would conflict with the principle that assets and liabilities should not be netted off.

(b) The share capital in the consolidated statement of financial position is the **share capital of the parent company alone**. This must *always* be the case, no matter how complex the consolidation, because the share capital of subsidiary companies must *always* be a wholly cancelling item.

(c) The **retained earnings of P and S are aggregated** because S was **acquired on incorporation** so all of S's retained earnings are post acquisition and have been generated under the control of P.

3.2 Complications with cancellation

An item may appear in the statements of financial position of a parent company and its subsidiary, but not at the same amounts.

(a) The parent company may have acquired **shares in the subsidiary** at a price **greater or less than their par value**. The asset will appear in the parent company's accounts at cost, while the share capital will appear in the subsidiary's accounts at par value. This raises the issue of **goodwill**, which is dealt with later in this chapter.

(b) The parent company **may not** have **acquired all the shares of the subsidiary** (so the subsidiary may be only partly owned). This raises the issue of **non-controlling interests**, which are dealt with in the next chapter.

(c) The intra-group trading balances may be out of step because of **goods or cash in transit**.

(d) One company may have **issued loan stock** of which a **proportion only** is taken up by the other company.

The following question illustrates the techniques needed to deal with items (c) and (d) above. The procedure is to **cancel as far as possible**.

(a) **Uncancelled loan stock** will appear as a **liability of the group**.

(b) **Differences in balances on intra-group accounts** represent **goods or cash in transit**, which will **need to be adjusted** so that they agree and can then be cancelled. The adjustment for goods or cash in transit is to **accelerate the transaction to its ultimate destination**.

Question 6.1	Cancellation

Learning outcomes A1

The statements of financial position of P Co and of its subsidiary S Co have been made up to 30 June. P Co has owned all the ordinary shares and 40% of the loan stock of S Co since its incorporation.

P CO
STATEMENT OF FINANCIAL POSITION AS AT 30 JUNE

	$	$
Assets		
Non-current assets		
Property, plant and equipment	120,000	
Investment in S Co, at cost		
80,000 ordinary shares of $1 each	80,000	
$20,000 of 12% loan stock in S Co	20,000	
		220,000
Current assets		
Inventories	50,000	
Receivables	40,000	
Current account with S Co	18,000	
Cash	4,000	
		112,000
Total assets		332,000
Equity and liabilities		
Equity		
Ordinary shares of $1 each, fully paid	100,000	
Retained earnings	95,000	
		195,000
Non-current liabilities		
10% loan stock		75,000
Current liabilities		
Payables	47,000	
Taxation	15,000	
		62,000
Total equity and liabilities		332,000

S CO
STATEMENT OF FINANCIAL POSITION AS AT 30 JUNE

	$	$
Assets		
Property, plant and equipment		100,000
Current assets		
Inventories	60,000	
Receivables	30,000	
Cash	6,000	
		96,000
Total assets		196,000
Equity and liabilities		
Equity		
80,000 ordinary shares of $1 each, fully paid	80,000	
Retained earnings	28,000	
		108,000
Non-current liabilities		
12% loan stock		50,000
Current liabilities		
Payables	16,000	
Taxation	10,000	
Current account with P Co	12,000	
		38,000
Total equity and liabilities		196,000

The difference on current account arises because of goods in transit.

Required

Prepare the consolidated statement of financial position of P Co.

3.3 Goodwill arising on consolidation   5/12

3.3.1 Accounting

To begin with, **we will examine the entries made by the parent company in its own statement of financial position when it acquires shares.**

When a company P Co wishes to **purchase shares** in a company S Co it must pay the previous owners of those shares. The most obvious form of payment would be in **cash**. Suppose P Co purchases all 40,000 $1 shares in S Co and pays $60,000 cash to the previous shareholders in consideration. The entries in P Co's books would be:

DEBIT   Investment in S Co at cost $60,000
CREDIT   Bank $60,000

However, the previous shareholders might be prepared to accept some other form of consideration. For example, they might accept an agreed number of **shares** in P Co. P Co would then issue new shares in the agreed number and allot them to the former shareholders of S Co. This kind of deal might be attractive to P Co since it avoids the need for a heavy cash outlay. The former shareholders of S Co would retain an indirect interest in that company's profitability via their new holding in its parent company.

Continuing the example, suppose the shareholders of S Co agreed to accept one $1 ordinary share in P Co for every two $1 ordinary shares in S Co. P Co would then need to issue and allot 20,000 new $1 shares. How would this transaction be recorded in the books of P Co?

The former shareholders of S Co have presumably agreed to accept 20,000 shares in P Co because they consider each of those shares to have a value of $3. This view of the matter suggests the following method of recording the transaction in P Co's books.

DEBIT   Investment in S Co $60,000
CREDIT   Share capital $20,000
                Share premium account $40,000

The issues relating to the measurement of consideration at **fair value** are covered in more detail in section 4 of this chapter.

The amount which P Co records in its books as the cost of its investment in S Co may be more or less than the book value of the assets it acquires. Suppose that S Co in the previous example has nil reserves and nil liabilities, so that its share capital of $40,000 is balanced by net assets with a book value of $40,000. For simplicity, assume for now that the book value of S Co's assets is the same as their market or fair value.

Now when the directors of P Co agree to pay $60,000 for a 100% investment in S Co they must believe that, in addition to its tangible assets of $40,000, S Co must also have say reputation or customer base worth $20,000. This amount of $20,000 paid over and above the value of the identifiable assets acquired is called **goodwill arising on consolidation** (sometimes **premium on acquisition**).

Following the normal cancellation procedure the $40,000 share capital in S Co's statement of financial position could be cancelled against $40,000 of the 'investment in S Co' in the statement of financial position of P Co. This would leave a $20,000 debit uncancelled in the parent company's accounts and this $20,000 would appear in the consolidated statement of financial position under the caption 'Intangible non-current assets: goodwill arising on consolidation'.

We will consider goodwill in more detail later in this chapter and in Chapter 7.

3.3.2 Goodwill and pre-acquisition profits

Up to now we have assumed that S Co had nil retained earnings when its shares were purchased by P Co. Assuming instead that S Co had earned profits of $8,000 in the period before acquisition, its statement of financial position just before the purchase would look as follows.

	$
Total assets	48,000
Share capital	40,000
Retained earnings	8,000
	48,000

If P Co now purchases all the shares in S Co it will acquire total assets worth $48,000 at a cost of $60,000. Clearly in this case S Co's intangible assets (goodwill) are being valued at $12,000. It should be apparent that any earnings retained by the subsidiary **prior to its acquisition** by the parent company must be **incorporated in the cancellation** process so as to arrive at a figure for goodwill arising on consolidation. In other words, not only S Co's share capital, but also its **pre-acquisition** retained earnings, must be cancelled against the asset 'investment in S Co' in the accounts of the parent company. The uncancelled balance of $12,000 appears in the consolidated statement of financial position.

The consequence of this is that **any pre-acquisition retained earnings of a subsidiary company are not aggregated with the parent company's retained earnings** in the consolidated statement of financial position. The figure of consolidated retained earnings comprises the retained earnings of the parent company plus the **post-acquisition retained earnings only of subsidiary companies**. The post-acquisition retained earnings are simply retained earnings now *less* retained earnings at acquisition (see question 6.2).

Example: Goodwill and pre-acquisition profits

Sing Co acquired the ordinary shares of Wing Co on 31 March when the draft statements of financial position of each company were as follows.

SING CO
STATEMENT OF FINANCIAL POSITION AS AT 31 MARCH

	$
Assets	
Non-current assets	
Investment in 50,000 shares of Wing Co at cost	80,000
Current assets	40,000
Total assets	120,000
Equity and liabilities	
Equity	
Ordinary shares	75,000
Retained earnings	45,000
Total equity and liabilities	120,000

WING CO
STATEMENT OF FINANCIAL POSITION AS AT 31 MARCH

	$
Current assets	60,000
Equity	
50,000 ordinary shares of $1 each	50,000
Retained earnings	10,000
	60,000

Prepare the consolidated statement of financial position as at 31 March.

Solution

The technique to adopt here is to produce a new working: 'Goodwill'. A proforma working is set out below. This working is just a tidier version of the cancellation seen earlier.

Goodwill

	$	$
Consideration transferred		X
Net assets at acquisition:		
Ordinary share capital	X	
Share premium	X	
Retained earnings on acquisition	X	
		(X)
Goodwill		X

Applying this to our example the working will look like this.

	$	$
Consideration transferred		80,000
Net assets at acquisition:		
Ordinary share capital	50,000	
Pre-acquisition retained earnings	10,000	
		(60,000)
Goodwill		20,000

SING CO
CONSOLIDATED STATEMENT OF FINANCIAL POSITION AS AT 31 MARCH

	$
Assets	
Non-current assets	
Goodwill arising on consolidation (40,000 + 60,000)	20,000
Current assets	100,000
	120,000
Equity	
Ordinary shares	75,000
Retained earnings (parent only – as no post-acquisition yet in subsidiary)	45,000
	120,000

3.4 Intra-group trading

3.4.1 Unrealised profit

Any receivable/payable balances outstanding between the companies are cancelled on consolidation. No further problem arises if all such intra-group transactions are **undertaken at cost**, without any mark-up for profit.

However, each company in a group is a separate trading entity and may wish to treat other group companies in the same way as any other customer. In this case, a company (say A Co) may buy goods at one price and sell them at a higher price to another group company (B Co). The accounts of A Co will quite properly include the profit earned on sales to B Co; and similarly B Co's statement of financial position will include inventories at their cost to B Co, ie at the amount at which they were purchased from A Co.

This gives rise to two problems.

(a) Although A Co makes a profit as soon as it sells goods to B Co, the group does not make a sale or achieve a profit until an outside customer buys the goods from B Co.

(b) Any purchases from A Co which remain unsold by B Co at the year end will be included in B Co's inventory. Their value in the statement of financial position will be their cost to B Co, which is not the same as their cost to the group.

The objective of consolidated accounts is to present the financial position of several connected companies as that of a single entity, the group. This means that **in a consolidated statement of financial position the only profits recognised should be those earned by the group** in providing goods or services to outsiders; and similarly, inventory in the consolidated statement of financial position should be valued at cost to the group.

Suppose that a parent company P Co buys goods for $1,600 and sells them to a wholly owned subsidiary S Co for $2,000. The goods are in S Co's inventory at the year end and appear in S Co's statement of financial position at $2,000. In this case, P Co will record a profit of $400 in its individual accounts, but from the group's point of view the figures are:

Cost	$1,600
External sales	nil
Closing inventory at cost	$1,600
Profit/loss	nil

If we add together the figures for retained earnings and inventory in the individual statements of financial position of P Co and S Co the resulting figures for consolidated retained earnings and consolidated inventory will each be overstated by $400. A **consolidation adjustment** is therefore necessary as follows.

DEBIT   Group retained earnings (adjust in the seller's column in the retained earnings working)
CREDIT   Group inventory (statement of financial position)

with the amount of **profit unrealised** by the group.

Question 6.2   Unrealised profit

Learning outcomes A1

P Co acquired all the shares in S Co one year ago when the reserves (retained earnings) of S Co stood at $10,000. Draft statements of financial position for each company are as follows.

	P Co $	P Co $	S Co $	S Co $
Assets				
Non-current assets				
Property, plant and equipment	80,000			40,000
Investment in S Co at cost	46,000			
		126,000		
Current assets		40,000		30,000
Total assets		166,000		70,000
Equity and liabilities				
Equity				
Ordinary shares of $1 each	100,000		30,000	
Retained earnings	45,000		22,000	
		145,000		52,000
Current liabilities		21,000		18,000
Total equity and liabilities		166,000		70,000

During the year S Co sold goods to P Co for $50,000, the profit to S Co being 20% of selling price. At the end of the reporting period, $15,000 of these goods remained unsold in the inventories of P Co.

At the same date, P Co owed S Co $12,000 for goods bought and this debt is included in the trade payables of P Co and the receivables of S Co.

The goodwill arising on consolidation has been impaired. The amount of the impairment is $1,500.

Required

Prepare a draft consolidated statement of financial position for P Co.

3.5 Intra-group sales of non-current assets

The transfer of property, plant and equipment at a profit within the group gives rise to the same kind of issues as the transfer of inventories, namely that the property, plant and equipment should be stated at cost to the group and the profit on the sale is unrealised.

An additional issue is that the items of property, plant and equipment will subsequently be depreciated based on the new carrying value. This means that the unrealised profit on sale becomes realised through use which therefore reduces the consolidation adjustment.

The adjustment should be made in the books of the company making the sale.

Method

(1)   Calculate the unrealised profit:

Unrealised profit on transfer	X
Less: proportion depreciated by year end	(X)
	X

(2)   Adjust in the books of the company making the sale:

DEBIT (↓) Retained earnings
CREDIT (↓) Property, plant and equipment

Example:

P owns 100% of S. On 1 January 20X3, P transfers a machine with a NBV of $20,000 to S for $25,000. At that date, the asset has a remaining useful life of 5 years.

Required

What is the adjustment required in the consolidated statement of financial position of the P group regarding the intra-group transfer of the machine for the year ended 31 December 20X3?

Solution

(1)   Calculate the unrealised profit:

	$
Unrealised profit on transfer ($25,000 - $20,000)	5,000
Less proportion depreciated by year end ($5,000/5 years)	(1,000)
	4,000

(2)   Adjust in the books of the company making the sale:

DEBIT (↓) Retained earnings of P	$4,000	
CREDIT (↓) Property, plant and equipment		$4,000

3.6 Pre-acquisition dividends

The syllabus mentions the treatment of pre-acquisition dividends, but the revisions made to IAS 27 *Consolidated and separate financial statements* in 2008 simplified this area. There is no longer any need to identify whether a subsidiary's dividends are paid from pre- or post-acquisition earnings. Any dividends received by a parent from a subsidiary, jointly controlled entity or associate are recognised as income in the parent's separate financial statements (and cancelled out as intra-group income in the consolidated statement of profit or loss and other comprehensive income).

Section summary

The steps to be used in preparing consolidated statements of financial position for a parent with fully owned subsidiaries are:

-   Aggregate assets and liabilities and cancel out intra-group balances
-   Calculate goodwill and consolidated retained earnings

4 Fair values in acquisition accounting   3/11

Introduction

The use of fair values is key in acquisition accounting. At the date of acquisition, both the consideration transferred and the assets and liabilities acquired must be measured at fair values.

4.1 Goodwill

To understand the importance of fair values in the acquisition of a subsidiary consider again what we mean by goodwill.

KEY TERM

GOODWILL. Any excess of the consideration transferred over the acquirer's interest in the fair value of the identifiable assets and liabilities acquired as at the date of the exchange transaction.

The **statement of financial position of a subsidiary company** at the date it is acquired may not be a guide to the fair value of its net assets. For example, the market value of a freehold building may have risen greatly since it was acquired, but it may appear in the statement of financial position at historical cost less accumulated depreciation.

4.1.1 What is fair value?

Fair value is defined as follows by IFRS 13 *Fair value measurement*. You have seen this several times now - it is an important definition.

KEY TERM

FAIR VALUE. The price that would be received to sell an asset or paid to transfer a liability in an orderly transaction between market at the measurement date.   *(IFRS 13)*

We will look at the requirements of IFRS 3 (revised) and IFRS 13 regarding fair value in more detail below. First, let us look at some practical matters.

4.2 Fair value adjustment calculations

Until now we have calculated goodwill as the difference between the cost of the investment and the **book value** of net assets acquired by the group. If this calculation is to comply with the definition above we must ensure that the book value of the subsidiary's net assets is the same as their **fair value**.

There are two possible ways of achieving this.

(a)   The **subsidiary company** might **incorporate any necessary revaluations** in its own books of account. In this case, we can proceed directly to the consolidation, taking asset values and reserves figures straight from the subsidiary company's statement of financial position.

(b)   The **revaluations** may be made as a **consolidation adjustment without being incorporated** in the subsidiary company's books. In this case, we must make the necessary adjustments to the subsidiary's statement of financial position as a working. Only then can we proceed to the consolidation.

Note. Remember that when depreciating assets are revalued there may be a corresponding alteration in the amount of depreciation charged and accumulated.

4.3 Example: Fair value adjustments

P Co acquired 100 per cent of the ordinary shares of S Co on 1 September 20X5. At that date the fair value of S Co's non-current assets was $23,000 greater than their net book value, and the balance of retained earnings was $21,000. The statements of financial position of both companies at 31 August 20X6 are given below. S Co has not incorporated any revaluation in its books of account.

P CO
STATEMENT OF FINANCIAL POSITION AS AT 31 AUGUST 20X6

	$	$
Assets		
Non-current assets		
Tangible assets	63,000	
Investment in S Co at cost	68,000	
		131,000
Current assets		66,000
Total assets		196,000
Equity and liabilities		
Equity		
Ordinary shares of $1 each	80,000	
Retained earnings	96,000	
		176,000
Current liabilities		20,000
Total equity and liabilities		196,000

S CO

STATEMENT OF FINANCIAL POSITION AS AT 31 AUGUST 20X6

	$	$
Assets		
Tangible non-current assets		28,000
Current assets		43,000
Total assets		71,000
Equity and liabilities		
Equity		
Ordinary shares of $1 each	20,000	
Retained earnings	41,000	
		61,000
Current liabilities		10,000
Total equity and liabilities		71,000

If S Co had revalued its non-current assets at 1 September 20X5, an addition of $3,000 would have been made to the depreciation charged to profit or loss for 20X5/X6.

Required

Prepare P Co's consolidated statement of financial position as at 31 August 20X6.

Solution

P CO CONSOLIDATED STATEMENT OF FINANCIAL POSITION AS AT 31 AUGUST 20X6

	$	$
Non-current assets		
Property, plant and equipment (63,000 + 28,000 + 20,000 (W4))	111,000	
Goodwill (W2)	4,000	
		115,000
Current assets (65,000 + 43,000)		108,000
		223,000
Equity and liabilities		
Equity		
Ordinary shares of $1 each	80,000	
Retained earnings (W3)	113,000	
		193,000
Current liabilities (20,000 + 10,000)		30,000
		223,000

Workings

1   *Group structure*

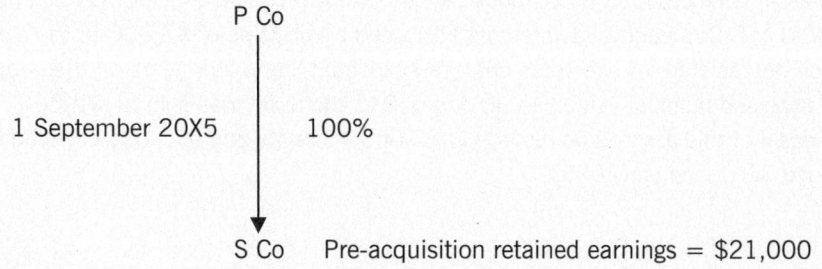

P Co

1 September 20X5   100%

S Co   Pre-acquisition retained earnings = $21,000

2   *Goodwill*

	$	$
Consideration transferred		68,000
Net assets at acquisition as represented by		
Ordinary share capital	20,000	
Retained earnings (W1)	21,000	
Fair value adjustment (W4)	23,000	
		(64,000)
Goodwill		4,000

3   *Retained earnings*

	P Co	S Co
	$	$
Per question	96,000	41,000
Depreciation adjustment (W4)		(3,000)
Pre acquisition retained earnings (W1)		(21,000)
Post acquisition S Co		17,000
Group share in S Co		
(17,000 × 100%)	17,000	
Group retained earnings	113,000	

4   *Fair value adjustments*

	At acq'n date	Movement	Year end
	$	$	$
Property plant and equipment	23,000	(3,000)	20,000
	23,000	(3,000)	20,000
	↓	↓	↓
	Goodwill	Ret'd earnings	SOFP

Note. S Co has not incorporated the revaluation in its draft statement of financial position. Before beginning the consolidation workings we must therefore adjust for the fair vaue uplift at the acquisition date, the additional depreciation charge that must be reflected in the subsidiary's post acquisition retained earnings and the remaining uplift that must be reflected in the consolidated statement of financial position. The 'fair value table' working is an efficient way of dealing with this, even where there are several fair value adjustments.

Question 6.3   Fair value

Learning outcomes A1

An asset is recorded in S Co's books at its historical cost of $4,000. On 1 January 20X5 P Co bought 100% of S Co's equity. Its directors attributed a fair value of $3,000 to the asset as at that date. It had been depreciated for two years out of an expected life of four years on the straight line basis. There was no expected residual value. On 30 June 20X5 the asset was sold for $2,600. What is the profit or loss on disposal of this asset to be recorded in S Co's accounts and in P Co's consolidated accounts for the year ended 31 December 20X5?

4.4 IFRS 3 (revised) and IFRS 13: Fair values

The general rule under the revised IFRS 3 (revised) is that the subsidiary's assets and liabilities **must be measured at fair value** except in **limited, stated cases**. The assets and liabilities must:

(a)   Meet the definitions of assets and liabilities in the *Framework*.

(b)   Be part of what the acquiree (or its former owners) exchanged in the business combination rather than the result of separate transactions

IFRS 13 *Fair value measurement* (see Chapter 7) provides extensive guidance on how the fair value of assets and liabilities should be established.

This standard requires that the following are considered in determining fair value:

(a)   The asset or liability being measured

(b)   The principal market (ie that where the most activity takes place) or where there is no principal market, the most advantageous market (ie that in which the best price could be achieved) in which an orderly transaction would take place for the asset or liability

(c)   The highest and best use of the asset or liability and whether it is used on a standalone basis or in conjunction with other assets or liabilities

(d)   Assumptions that market participants would use when pricing the asset or liability.

Having considered these factors, IFRS 13 provides a hierarchy of inputs for arriving at fair value. It requires that Level 1 inputs are used where possible:

Level 1   Quoted prices in active markets for identical assets that the entity can access at the measurement date.

Level 2   Inputs other than quoted prices that are directly or indirectly observable for the asset.

Level 3   Unobservable inputs for the asset.

4.4.1 Examples of fair value and business combinations

For non-financial assets, fair value is decided based on the highest and best use of the asset as determined by a market participant. The following examples, adapted from the illustrative examples to IFRS 13, demonstrate what is meant by this.

Example: Land

Anscome Co has acquired land in a business combination. The land is currently developed for industrial use as a site for a factory. The current use of land is presumed to be its highest and best use unless market or other factors suggest a different use. Nearby sites have recently been developed for residential use as sites for high-rise apartment buildings. On the basis of that development and recent zoning and other changes to facilitate that development, Anscome determines that the land currently used as a site for a factory could be developed as a site for residential use (ie for high-rise apartment buildings) because market participants would take into account the potential to develop the site for residential use when pricing the land.

How would the highest and best use of the land be determined?

Solution

The highest and best use of the land would be determined by comparing both of the following:

(a) The value of the land as currently developed for industrial use (ie the land would be used in combination with other assets, such as the factory, or with other assets and liabilities).

(b) The value of the land as a vacant site for residential use, taking into account the costs of demolishing the factory and other costs (including the uncertainty about whether the entity would be able to convert the asset to the alternative use) necessary to convert the land to a vacant site (ie the land is to be used by market participants on a stand-alone basis).

The highest and best use of the land would be determined on the basis of the higher of those values.

Example: Research and development project

Searcher acquires a research and development (R & D) project in a business combination. Searcher does not intend to complete the project. If completed, the project would compete with one of its own projects (to provide the next generation of the entity's commercialised technology). Instead, the entity intends to hold (ie lock up) the project to prevent its competitors from obtaining access to the technology. In doing this the project is expected to provide defensive value, principally by improving the prospects for the entity's own competing technology.

If it could purchase the R & D project, Developer Co would continue to develop the project and that use would maximise the value of the group of assets or of assets and liabilities in which the project would be used (ie the asset would be used in combination with other assets or with other assets and liabilities). Developer Co does not have similar technology.

How would the fair value of the project be measured?

Solution

The fair value of the project would be measured on the basis of the price that would be received in a current transaction to sell the project, assuming that the R & D would be used with its complementary assets and the associated liabilities and that those assets and liabilities would be available to Developer Co.

4.4.2 Restructuring and future losses

An acquirer **should not recognise liabilities for future losses** or other costs expected to be incurred as a result of the business combination.

IFRS 3 (revised) explains that a plan to restructure a subsidiary following an acquisition is not a present obligation of the acquiree at the acquisition date. Neither does it meet the definition of a contingent liability. Therefore, an acquirer **should not recognise a liability for** such **a restructuring plan** as part of allocating the cost of the combination unless the subsidiary was already committed to the plan before the acquisition.

This **prevents creative accounting**. An acquirer cannot set up a provision for restructuring or future losses of a subsidiary and then release this to profit or loss in subsequent periods in order to reduce losses or smooth profits.

4.4.3 Intangible assets

The acquiree may have **intangible assets**, such as development expenditure. These can be recognised separately from goodwill only if they are **identifiable**. An intangible asset is identifiable only if it:

(a)   Is **separable**, ie capable of being separated or divided from the entity and sold, transferred, or exchanged, either individually or together with a related contract, asset or liability, or

(b)   Arises from **contractual or other legal rights**.

4.4.4 Contingent liabilities

Contingent liabilities of the acquirer are **recognised** if their **fair value can be measured reliably**. A **contingent liability** must be recognised even if the outflow is not probable, provided there is a present obligation.

This is a departure from the normal rules in IAS 37 *Provisions, contingent liabilities and contingent assets*; contingent liabilities are not normally recognised, but only disclosed.

After their initial recognition, the acquirer should measure contingent liabilities that are recognised separately at the higher of:

(a)   The amount that would be recognised in accordance with IAS 37
(b)   The amount initially recognised

4.4.5 Other exceptions to the recognition or measurement principles

(a)   **Deferred tax:** use IAS 12 *Income taxes* values.

(b)   **Employee benefits:** use IAS 19 *Employee benefits* values.

(c)   **Indemnification assets:** measurement should be consistent with the measurement of the indemnified item, for example an employee benefit or a contingent liability.

(d)   **Reacquired rights**: value on the basis of the remaining contractual term of the related contract regardless of whether market participants would consider potential contractual renewals when measuring its fair value.

(e)   **Share-based payment**: use IFRS 2 *Share-based payment* values.

(f)   **Assets held for sale**: use IFRS 5 *Assets held for sale and discontinued operations* values.

Question 6.4	Fair values

Learning outcomes A1

AB acquired all of CD's 400,000 ordinary shares for $2,000,000 on 28 February 20X5. CD was purchased from its directors who will remain directors of the business. AB incurred legal and professional fees as a result of the acquisition of $75,000.

The book values of the assets and liabilities of CD acquired extracted from the general ledger were $1,300,000.

As at the date of acquisition:

*   CD had a customer list which it had not recognised as an asset because it was internally generated. However, on acquisition, as customer lists are often leased or exchanged, external experts managed to establish a fair value for the list of $100,000.

*   An item of equipment with a book value of $440,000, was found to have a market value of $660,000.

*   CD had a contingent liability in respect of a major warranty claim with a fair value of $30,000.

*   AB intended to reorganise CD's operations following the acquisition at an approximate cost of $150,000.

Required

Calculate goodwill on the acquisition of CD, in accordance with the requirements of IFRS 3 *Business combinations,* explaining your treatment of the legal fees, the customer list, the contingent liability and the reorganisation costs.

4.5 Goodwill arising on acquisition

Goodwill should be carried in the statement of financial position at **cost less any accumulated impairment losses**. The treatment of goodwill is covered in detail in Chapter 7.

4.6 Forms of consideration

The consideration paid by the parent for the shares in the subsidiary can take different forms. IFRS 3 requires this consideration to be measured at fair value. This will affect the calculation of goodwill. Here are some examples:

4.6.1 Contingent consideration

Contingent consideration is where the acquirer has an obligation to transfer additional assets (eg cash) or equity interests (shares) to the former owners of the subsidiary as part of the exchange for control of the subsidiary if **specified future events occur or conditions are met**.

The parent should **measure** this contingent consideration at its **acquisition date fair value** and record it as part of the consideration transferred in the goodwill working. It should be classified as either a liability or equity on the basis of the definitions of an equity instrument and a financial liability in IAS 32 *Financial instruments: presentation.*

Subsequently, for changes in the fair value due to additional information about facts and circumstances that **existed at the acquisition date, goodwill should be adjusted** as long as it is within one year of the acquisition date.

For all other changes (eg targets met), contingent consideration classified as **equity** should **not be remeasured**. Contingent consideration classified as a **liability** should be **remeasured** with the subsequent **gain or loss** being recorded in **profit or loss.**

4.6.2 Deferred consideration

An agreement may be made that part of the consideration for the combination will be paid at a future date. This consideration will therefore be discounted to its present value using the acquiring entity's cost of capital.

Example: Contingent and deferred consideration

P acquired 75% of S's 80 million $1 shares on 1 January 20X6. Scheduled payments comprised:

* $3.50 per share payable immediately in cash

* $108 million payable on 1 January 20X7

*   An amount equivalent to 3 times the profit after tax of S for the year ended 31 December 20X6, payable on 31 March 20X7.

*   New shares issued in P on a 1 for 3 basis (the nominal value of P's shares is $1 and the market value of P's shares at 1 January 20X6 was $4.50)

On 1 January 20X6, the fair value attributed to the consideration based on profit was $50 million. By 31 December 20X6, the fair value was considered to be $55 million. The change arose as a result of a change in expected profits.

P's cost of capital is 8%.

How should the consideration transferred be treated in the financial statements of the P group for the year ended 31 December 20X6?

Solution

As at 1 January 20X6, the consideration transferred will be recorded at:

	$m
Cash consideration (80m shares × 75% × $3.50)	210
Deferred consideration ($108m × 1/1.08)	100
Contingent consideration	50
Shares (1/3 × 75% × 80m × $4.50)	90
Total consideration	450

At 31 December 20X6 $8m ($100m x 10%) will be charged to finance costs, being the **unwinding of the discount** on the deferred consideration. The deferred consideration was discounted by $8m to allow for the time value of money. At 1 January 20X7 the full amount becomes payable.

The **liability** relating to the **contingent consideration** must be **remeasured** to its revised fair value of $55 million at 31 December 20X6 and the **loss** of $5 million should be **recorded in profit or loss**. Goodwill should not be revised because the change in fair value relates to a post acquisition event (change in expected profits) rather than additional information regarding facts at the acquisition date.

4.7 Adjustments after the initial accounting is complete

Sometimes the fair values of the acquiree's identifiable assets, liabilities or contingent liabilities or the consideration transferred can only be determined **provisionally** by the **end of the period in which the combination takes place**. In this situation, the acquirer **should account for the combination using those provisional values**. The acquirer should **recognise any adjustments** to those provisional values as a result of completing the initial accounting:

(a)   **Within twelve months** of the acquisition date, and

(b)   **From** the acquisition date (ie, retrospectively)

This means that:

(a)   The **carrying amount** of an item that is recognised or adjusted as a result of completing the initial accounting shall be calculated **as if its fair value** at the acquisition date **had been recognised from that date**.

(b)   **Goodwill should be adjusted** from the acquisition date by an amount equal to the adjustment to the fair value of the item being recognised or adjusted.

Any further adjustments after the initial accounting is complete should be **recognised only to correct an error** in accordance with IAS 8 *Accounting policies, changes in accounting estimates and errors*. Any subsequent changes in estimates are dealt with in accordance with IAS 8 (ie, the effect is recognised in the current and future periods). IAS 8 requires an entity to account for an error correction retrospectively, and to present financial statements as if the error had never occurred by restating the comparative information for the prior period(s) in which the error occurred.

4.7.1 Reverse acquisitions

IFRS 3 (revised) also addresses a certain type of acquisition, known as a **reverse acquisition or takeover**. This is where Company A acquires ownership of Company B through a share exchange. (For example, a private entity may arrange to have itself 'acquired' by a smaller public entity as a means of obtaining a stock exchange listing.) The number of shares issued by Company A as consideration to the shareholders of Company B is so great that control of the combined entity after the transaction is with the shareholders of Company B.

In legal terms Company A may be regarded as the parent or continuing entity, but IFRS 3 (revised) states that, as it is the Company B shareholders who control the combined entity, **Company B should be treated as the acquirer**. Company B should apply the acquisition (or purchase) method to the assets and liabilities of Company A.

Section summary

Goodwill is calculated by comparing the fair value of the consideration with the fair value of the identifiable assets and liabilities acquired.

The accounting requirements and disclosures of the **fair value exercise** are covered by **IFRS 3 (revised)**. **IFRS 13** *Fair value measurement* gives extensive guidance on how the fair value of assets and liabilities should be established.

IFRS 3 does not allow combinations to be accounted for as a **uniting of interests; all combinations must be treated as acquisitions**.

5   The consolidated statement of profit or loss and other comprehensive income

5.1 The consolidated statement of profit or loss

Introduction

The consolidated statement of profit or loss summarises the revenue and expenses of the group as a single entity.

5.1.1 Consolidation procedure

It is customary in practice to prepare a working paper (known as a **consolidation schedule**) on which the individual statements of profit or loss are set out side by side and totalled to form the basis of the consolidated statement of profit or loss.

Exam alert

In an examination it is very much quicker not to do this. Use workings to show the calculation of complex figures such as goodwill and show the derivation of others on the face of the statement of profit or loss, as shown in our examples.

Example: Consolidated statement of profit or loss

P Co acquired 100% of the ordinary shares of S Co on that company's incorporation in 20X3. The summarised statements of profit or loss of the two companies for the year ending 31 December 20X6 are set out below.

	P Co	S Co
	$	$
Sales revenue	75,000	38,000
Cost of sales	(30,000)	(20,000)
Gross profit	45,000	18,000
Administrative expenses	(14,000)	(8,000)
Profit before tax	31,000	10,000
Income tax expense	(10,000)	(2,000)
Profit for the year	21,000	8,000

Required

Prepare the consolidated statement of profit or loss for P Co and its subsidiary for the year ending 31 December 20X6.

Solution

P CO
CONSOLIDATED STATEMENT OF PROFIT OR LOSS
FOR THE YEAR ENDED 31 DECEMBER 20X6

	$
Sales revenue (75,000 + 38,000)	113,000
Cost of sales (30,000 + 20,000)	(50,000)
Gross profit	63,000
Administrative expenses (14,000 + 8,000)	(22,000)
Profit before tax	41,000
Income tax expense (10,000 + 2,000)	(12,000)
Profit for the year	29,000

We will now look at the complications introduced by **intra-group trading** and **intra-group dividends**.

5.1.2 Intra-group trading

Like the consolidated statement of financial position, the consolidated statement of profit or loss should deal with the results of the group as those of a single entity. When one company in a group sells goods to another an identical amount is included in the sales revenue of the first company and in the cost of sales of the second. Yet as far as the entity's dealings with outsiders are concerned no sale has taken place.

The consolidated figures for sales revenue and cost of sales should represent **sales to**, and **purchases from**, outsiders. An adjustment is therefore necessary to reduce the sales revenue and cost of sales figures by the value of intra-group sales during the year.

We have also seen earlier in this chapter that any unrealised profits on intra-group trading should be excluded from the figure for group profits. This will occur whenever goods sold at a profit within the group remain in the inventory of the purchasing company at the year end. The best way to deal with this is to **calculate the unrealised profit** on unsold inventories at the year end as we have already seen and **reduce profit by adding it to the cost of sales**.

Example: Intra-group trading

Suppose in our earlier example that S Co had recorded sales of $5,000 to P Co during 20X6. S Co had purchased these goods from outside suppliers at a cost of $3,000. One half of the goods remained in P Co's inventory at 31 December 20X6. Prepare the revised consolidated statement of profit or loss.

Solution

The consolidated statement of profit or loss for the year ended 31 December 20X6 would now be as follows.

	$
Sales revenue (75,000 + 38,000 – 5,000)	108,000
Cost of sales (30,000 + 20,000 – 5,000 + 1,000*)	(46,000)
Gross profit	62,000
Administrative expenses	(22,000)
Profit before taxation	40,000
Income tax expense	(12,000)
Profit for the year	28,000

*Unrealised profit: ½ × ($5,000 – $3,000). An adjustment will be made for the unrealised profit against the inventory figure in the consolidated statement of financial position.

5.1.3 Intra-group dividends

In our example so far we have assumed that S Co retains all of its after-tax profit. It may be, however, that S Co distributes some of its profits as dividends.

If the parent company has received dividends from the subsidiary during the year, these should be eliminated (cancelled) from the consolidated statement of profit or loss. The only investment income to appear in the consolidated statement of profit or loss is that received from outside the group.

5.1.4 Recap

The table below summarises the main points about the consolidated statement of profit or loss.

Purpose	To show the results of the group for an accounting period as if it were a single entity.
Sales revenue to profit for year	100% P + 100% S (excluding adjustments for intra-group transactions).
Reason	To show the results of the group which were controlled by the parent company.
Intra-group sales	Strip out intra-group activity from both sales revenue and cost of sales.
Unrealised profit on intra-group sales	Increase cost of sales by unrealised profit.
Depreciation	If the value of S's non-current assets have been subjected to a fair value uplift then any additional depreciation for the year must be charged in the consolidated statement of profit or loss.
Transfer of noncurrent assets	The profit on transfer must be eliminated and expenses must be reduced by any additional depreciation arising from the increased carrying value of the asset.

5.2 The consolidated statement of profit or loss and other comprehensive income

Introduction

A consolidated statement of profit or loss and other comprehensive income will be easy to produce once you have done the statement of profit or loss. In this section, we take the last question and add an item of other comprehensive income to illustrate this.

Example: consolidated statement of profit or loss and other comprehensive income

Using the answer to the previous example, show the consolidated statement of profit or loss and other comprehensive income if P Co and S Co made a revaluation gain on their properties during the year of $15,000 and $5,000 respectively.

Solution

	$
Sales revenue	108,000
Cost of sales	(46,000)
Gross profit	62,000
Administrative expenses	(22,000)
Profit before taxation	40,000
Income tax expense	(12,000)
Profit for the year	28,000
Other comprehensive income:	
Gain on property revaluation (15,000 + 5,000)	20,000
Total comprehensive income for the year	48,000

IAS 1 (revised) also allows a two-statement format, where we would produce a separate statement of profit or loss and statement of other comprehensive income. The separate consolidated statement of other comprehensive income would be as follows.

CONSOLIDATED STATEMENT OF OTHER COMPREHENSIVE INCOME

Profit for the year	28,000
Other comprehensive income	
Gain on property revaluation	20,000
Total comprehensive income for the year	48,000

5.3 Approach to answering exam questions

Introduction

A methodical approach to answering questions on consolidated statements of comprehensive income will help you in the exam. In this section we summarise our recommended approach.

Exam skills

This step-by-step approach will help you answer exam questions that ask you to prepare a consolidated statement of profit or loss and other comprehensive income.

 Read the question and draw up the group structure. Make a note of useful information such as the acquisition date and the pre-acquisition reserves.

 Draw up a proforma for the consolidated statement of profit or loss and other comprehensive income (or statement of profit or loss if there is no other comprehensive income). If the question includes an associate, leave a line space for 'share of profit of associate' before group profit before tax (associates are revised later in this Study Text).

 Work methodically down the statement of profit or loss and other comprehensive income, transferring figures to either the proforma or to workings as necessary:

put 100% of all income/expenses in brackets on the face of the proforma, ready for any adjustments you need to make exclude dividends received from subsidiaries.

 Read through the extra information provided in the question again and attempt the adjustments required, showing your workings for all calculations. Put the adjustments on to the statement of profit or loss and other comprehensive income as necessary.

 Finally, if the question contains an associate, calculate share of profit of associate (associates are revised later in this Study Text).

Section summary

Following our step-by-step approach to preparing a consolidated statement of profit or loss and other comprehensive income will help you in the exam.

Chapter Roundup

✓   Many large businesses consist of several companies controlled by one central or administrative company. Together these companies are called a **group**. The controlling company, called the **parent** or **holding company** will own some or all of the shares in the other companies, called **subsidiaries**.

✓   IFRS 10 requires a parent to present consolidated financial statements.

✓   The steps to be used in preparing consolidated statements of financial position for a parent with fully owned subsidiaries are:

     –   Aggregate the assets and liabilities and cancel out intra-group balances.
     –   Calculate goodwill/Calculate retained earnings.

✓   Goodwill is calculated by comparing the fair value of the consideration with the fair value of the identifiable assets and liabilities acquired

✓   The accounting requirements and disclosures of the **fair value exercise** are covered by **IFRS 3 (revised)**. **IFRS 13** *Fair value measurement* gives extensive guidance on how the fair value of assets and liabilities should be established.

✓   IFRS 3 does not allow combinations to be accounted for as a **uniting of interests; all combinations must be treated as acquisitions.**

✓   Following our step-by-step approach to preparing a consolidated statement of profit or loss and other comprehensive income will help you in the exam.

Quick Quiz

1   Define a 'subsidiary'.

2   What are the three criteria that need to be met under IFRS 10 to determine control?

3   What accounting treatment does IFRS 10 require of a parent company?

4   When is a parent exempted from preparing consolidated financial statements?

5   Under what circumstances should subsidiary undertakings be excluded from consolidation?

6   How should an investment in a subsidiary be accounted for in the separate financial statements of the parent?

7   Under IFRS 13 *Fair value measurement,* what is meant by Level 1 inputs?

8   Where does unrealised profit on intra-group trading appear in the statement of profit or loss?

Answers to Quick Quiz

1   An entity that is controlled by another entity.

2   An investor (the parent) controls an investee (the subsidiary) if all of the following IFRS 10 criteria are met:

   –   Power over the investee;

   –   Exposure or rights to variable returns from its involvement with the investee; and

   –   The ability to use its power over the investee to affect the amount of the investor's return.

3   The financial statements of parent and subsidiary are combined and presented as a single entity.

4   When the parent is itself a wholly owned subsidiary, or a partially owned subsidiary and the non-controlling interests do not object.

5   Very rarely, if at all. See Section 2.5.

6   (a)   At cost, or
       (b)   In accordance with IAS 39.

7   Quoted prices in active markets for identical assets or liabilities that the entity can access at the measurement date.

8   As an addition to cost of sales.

Answers to Questions

6.1 Cancellation

P CO
CONSOLIDATED STATEMENT OF FINANCIAL POSITION AS AT 30 JUNE

	$	$
Assets		
Non-current assets		
Property, plant and equipment (120,000 + 100,000)		220,000
Current assets		
Inventories (50,000 + 60,000 + 6,000)	116,000	
Receivables (40,000 + 30,000)	70,000	
Cash (4,000 + 6,000)	10,000	
		196,000
Total assets		416,000
Equity and liabilities		
Equity		
Ordinary shares of $1 each, fully paid (parent)	100,000	
Retained earnings (95,000 + 28,000)	123,000	
		223,000
Non-current liabilities		
10% loan stock	75,000	
12% loan stock (50,000 × 60%)	30,000	
		105,000
Current liabilities		
Payables (47,000 + 16,000)	63,000	
Taxation (15,000 + 10,000)	25,000	
		88,000
Total equity and liabilities		416,000

Note especially how:

(a)   The uncancelled loan stock in S Co becomes a liability of the group

(b)   The goods in transit is the difference between the current accounts ($18,000 – $12,000). The goods are in transit to S Co (as S's current account showing the amount payable to P co is $6,000 less than the corresponding receivable shown by P Co).This is adjusted in S's books as:

DEBIT: Inventories $6,000
CREDIT: Current account with P Co $6,000

The current accounts then agree and cancel.

(c)   The investment in S Co's shares is cancelled against S Co's share capital

6.2   Unrealised profit

P CO

CONSOLIDATED STATEMENT OF FINANCIAL POSITION

	$	$
Assets		
Non-current assets		
Property, plant and equipment (80,000 + 40,000)	120,000	
Goodwill (W2)	4,500	
		124,500
Current assets (W4)		55,000
Total assets		179,500
Equity and liabilities		
Equity		
Ordinary shares of $1 each	100,000	
Retained earnings (W3)	52,500	
		152,500
Current liabilities (W5)		27,000
Total equity and liabilities		179,500

Workings

1   *Group structure*

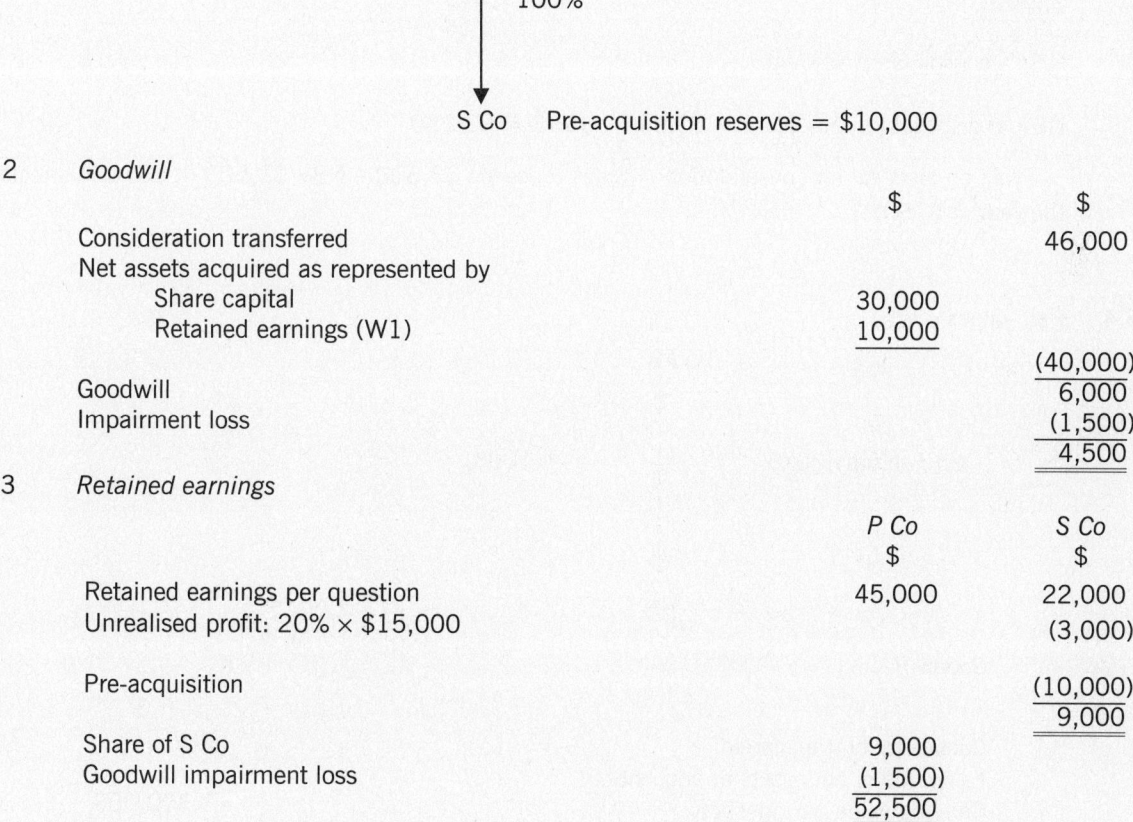

P Co

100%

S Co   Pre-acquisition reserves = $10,000

2   *Goodwill*

	$	$
Consideration transferred		46,000
Net assets acquired as represented by		
Share capital	30,000	
Retained earnings (W1)	10,000	
		(40,000)
Goodwill		6,000
Impairment loss		(1,500)
		4,500

3   *Retained earnings*

	P Co $	S Co $
Retained earnings per question	45,000	22,000
Unrealised profit: 20% × $15,000		(3,000)
Pre-acquisition		(10,000)
		9,000
Share of S Co	9,000	
Goodwill impairment loss	(1,500)	
	52,500	

4 *Current assets*

	$	$
In P Co's statement of financial position		40,000
In S Co's statement of financial position	30,000	
Less S Co's current account with P Co cancelled	(12,000)	
		18,000
		58,000
Less unrealised profit excluded from inventory valuation		(3,000)
		55,000

5 *Current liabilities*

	$
In P Co's statement of financial position	21,000
Less P Co's current account with S Co cancelled	(12,000)
	9,000
In S Co's statement of financial position	18,000
	27,000

6.3 Fair value

<u>S Co's financial statements:</u>

NBV at disposal (at historical cost) = $4,000 × 1½/4 = $1,500

*4- 2½

∴ Profit on disposal = Sales proceeds $2,600 – NBV $1,500 = $2,250 (depreciation for the year = $500)

<u>P Co's consolidated accounts:</u>

NBV at disposal (at fair value) = $3,000 × 1½/2 = $2,250

∴ Profit on disposal for consolidation = Sales proceeds $2,600 – NBV $1,500 = $350 (depreciation for the year = $750)

6.4 Fair values

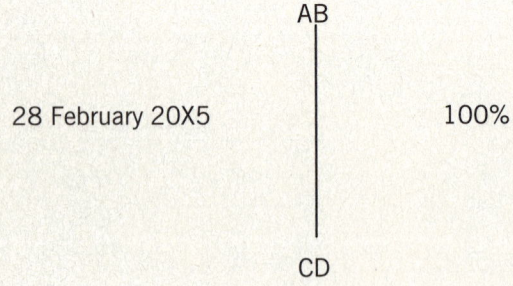

28 February 20X5   100%

Goodwill

	$	$
Consideration transferred		2,000,000
Fair value of net assets at acquisition:		
Carrying value per question	1,300,000	
Fair value adjustments:		
Intangible asset	100,000	
Property, plant and equipment (660,000 – 440,000))	220,000	
Contingent liability	(30,000)	
		(1,590,000)
		410,000

Explanation

- The legal and professional fees of $75,000 should be recognised as an expense as they relate to a benefit (service) immediately consumed.

- The customer list should be recognised as an intangible asset in the consolidated accounts as it is capable of being sold separately from the rest of the business ie identifiable.

- Even though contingent liabilities are normally only disclosed under IAS 37 *Provisions, contingent liabilities and contingent assets,* IFRS 3 makes an exception and states that it should be recognised at acquisition at its fair value of $30,000 as there is a present legal obligation (the warranty contract) and it can be measured reliably.

- The potential provision for reorganisation of $150,000 should not be recognised at acquisition because it is merely an intention not an obligation.

Now try this question from the Exam Question Bank	Number	Level	Marks	Time
	Q6	Introductory	10	18 mins

NON-CONTROLLING INTERESTS AND MID-YEAR ACQUISITIONS

 This chapter introduces the idea of subsidiaries that are not fully owned by the parent company. Instead there are (outside) shareholders called **non-controlling interests (NCI)**.

In this chapter, we will see the effect of NCI on goodwill, reserves, dividends, intra-group trading and fair values.

A new standard, IFRS 13, deals with fair value measurements.

We will also see consolidations where the acquisition takes place midway through the accounting year.

In the exam, any consolidation is highly likely to involve NCI. Therefore you need to practise these techniques thoroughly.

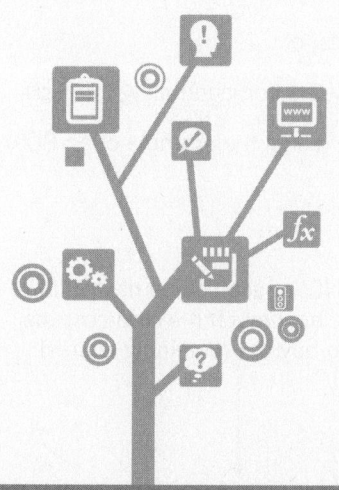

7

topic list	learning outcomes	syllabus references	ability required
1 Non-controlling interests in the statement of financial position	A1	A1(ii), (iii)	Application
2 Non-controlling interests and intra-group trading	A1	A1 (ii), (iii)	Application
3 Non-controlling interests and intra-group sales of non-current assets	A1	A1(ii), (iii)	Application
4 Non-controlling interests and fair values	A1	A1(ii), (iii)	Application
5 Fair value measurements	A1	A1(ii), (iii)	Application
6 Acquisition of a subsidiary during its accounting period	A1	A1(ii), (iii)	Application
7 Exam technique	A1	A1(ii), (iii)	Application
8 Subsidiaries acquired exclusively with a view to resale	A1	A1(ii), (iii)	Application

1 Non-controlling interests in the statement of financial position 5/10, 11/10, 3/11, 5/11, 5/12, 9/12, 11/12, 3/13

Introduction

The definition of a subsidiary that you saw in Chapter 6 makes it clear that a parent does not have to **own** 100% of a subsidiary in order to **control it. Usually a holding of** more than 50% of the voting shares gives **control.** In this chapter you will learn how to consolidate groups where some of the shares in subsidiaries are owned by outside shareholders, known as **non-controlling interests (NCI).**

1.1 Principles of the consolidated statement of financial position

It was mentioned in Chapter 6 that 100% of the assets and liabilities of subsidiary companies are included in the consolidated statement of financial position. This applies even in the case of subsidiaries which are only partly owned, as the consolidated statement of financial position shows all of the assets and liabilities that are **controlled** by the parent. However a proportion of the net assets of such subsidiaries in fact belongs to investors from outside the group (**non-controlling interests**, referred to as 'NCI' below). This figure must be shown within the equity section of the statement of financial position.

KEY TERM

NON-CONTROLLING INTEREST. The equity in a subsidiary not attributable, directly or indirectly, to a parent.   *(IFRS 3, IFRS 10)*

IFRS 3 allows two alternative ways of calculating non-controlling interest in the group statement of financial position. Non-controlling interest **at the acquisition date** can be valued at:

(a)   Its **proportionate share** of the fair value of the subsidiary's net assets; or

(b)   **Fair value** (usually based on the market value of the shares held by the non-controlling interest).

The diagram below summarises the differences between the two methods (using the example of an 80% subsidiary).

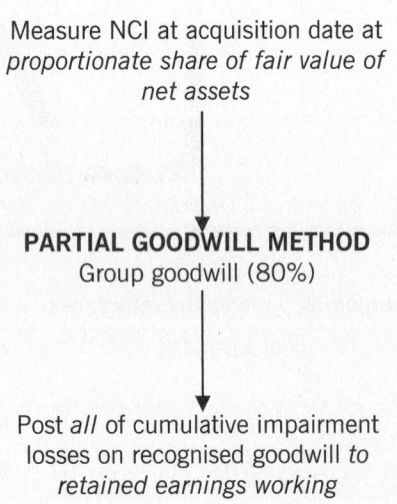

You are required to be able to apply both of these methods in F2. The option to value non-controlling interest at fair value at acquisition was introduced by the revised IFRS 3, but it is just an option. Companies can choose to adopt it or to continue to value non-controlling.

Exam skills

The exam question will tell you which method to use. If you are required to use the fair value method, then you will be given the share price or told what the fair value of the non-controlling interest is. In recent years, the fair value method has been more frequently examined in the F2 paper.

1.2 Non-controlling interest with pre-acquisition reserves

If the subsidiary is acquired on its **incorporation**, it will have no pre-acquisition reserves. However, you're likely to encounter scenarios where you will need to deal with pre-acquisition reserves. At each year end, the non-controlling interest will have increased by its share of the subsidiary's post-acquisition retained reserves.

1.3 Non-controlling interest at fair value

IFRS 3 (revised) gives entities the option of valuing non-controlling interests at acquisition at fair value. The thinking behind this is that the non-controlling interest, in purchasing their shares, also purchased goodwill in the subsidiary, and that the proportionate method does not show this goodwill.

IFRS 3 (revised) suggests that the closest approximation to fair value will be the market price of the shares held by non-controlling shareholders at the date of acquisition by the parent.

It is entirely possible that the prices paid for the shares by the parent and NCI will be different, due to the parent paying a **control premium**. In the exam, you will be told the fair value of the NCI shares if you are to use the fair value method.

The following example shows the two different methods for valuing the non-controlling interests.

Example: Non-controlling interest

P buys 75% of S for $60m on 1/1/X8. On 1/1/X8, the share capital of S was $15m and the retained earnings of S were $25m. The fair value of S's net assets were equivalent to their book values at acquisition.

Required

(a) Calculate goodwill on the assumption it is group policy to value non-controlling interest at the date of acquisition at the proportionate share of the fair value of the acquiree's identifiable assets acquired and liabilities assumed.

(b) Calculate goodwill on the assumption it is group policy to value non-controlling interest at fair value at the date of acquisition which was $16m.

(c) Demonstrate that the fair value goodwill method results in goodwill for the group and non-controlling interest.

Solution

(a) *Partial goodwill method*

	$m	$m
Consideration transferred		60
NCI (at % FV of net assets) (25% × 40)		10
Fair value of net assets at acquisition		
Share capital		
Retained earnings	15	
	25	
		(40)
		30

(b)   Fair value goodwill method

	$m	$m
Consideration transferred		60
NCI (at 'full' fair value)		16
Fair value of net assets at acquisition		
Share capital	15	
Retained earnings	25	
		(40)
		36

(c)   Proof that fair value goodwill method results in goodwill for group and NCI

	Group		NCI
	$m	$m	$m
Consideration transferred/FV of NCI		60	16
Fair value of net assets at acquisition			
Share capital	15		
Retained earnings	25		
	40		
Group share/NCI share	× 75%	(30)	× 25% (10)
		30	6

36

Below, the two methods are applied in an extended exam-standard example. The proportionate method and the fair value method are presented side by side for ease of comparison.

Note the example below covers the impairment of goodwill and fair value adjustments, two areas which we will look at later in this Chapter. As you go through the example, don't worry too much about these two areas – simply note how they are treated in the workings. After completing the chapter, revisit this lecture example to consolidate what you have learnt.

Example: Non-controlling interest

The statements of financial position for two entities for the year ended 31 December 20X9 are presented below:

STATEMENTS OF FINANCIAL POSITION AS AT 31 DECEMBER 20X9

	BC	HJ
	$'000	$'000
Non-current assets		
Property, plant and equipment	2,300	1,900
Available for sale investment (note 1)	920	-
	3,220	1,900
Current assets	3,340	1,790
	6,560	3,690
Equity		
Share capital	1,000	500
Retained earnings	3,430	1,800
Other components of equity	200	-
	4,630	2,300
Non-current liabilities	350	290
Current liabilities	1,580	1,100
	66,560	3,690

Additional information

(a)   BC acquired a 60% investment in HJ on 1 January 20X6 for $720,000 when the retained earnings of HJ were $300,000. The investment has been classified as available for sale in BC's individual financial statements with any associated gains or losses recorded within other components of equity.

(b)   As at 1 January 20X6, the fair value of the net assets acquired was the same as the book value with the exception of an item of property plant and equipment with a fair value of $800,000 and a carrying value of $600,000. This asset was assessed to have a remaining useful life of 10 years from the date of acquisition.

(c)   An impairment review was conducted at 31 December 20X9 and it was decided that the goodwill on acquisition of HJ was impaired by 10%.

Required

Prepare the consolidated statement of financial position for the BC group as at 31 December 20X9 under the following assumptions:

(a)   It is group policy to value non-controlling interest at fair value at the date of acquisition. The fair value of the non-controlling interest at 1 January 20X6 was $480,000.

(b)   It is group policy to value non-controlling interest at the proportionate share of the fair value of the net assets at acquisition.

Solution

BC GROUP
CONSOLIDATED STATEMENT OF FINANCIAL POSITION AS AT 31 DECEMBER 20X9

	(a)	(b)
	$'000	$'000
Non-current assets		
Property, plant and equipment (2,300 + 1,900 + 120 (W5))	4,320	4,320
Goodwill (W2)	180	108
	4,500	4,428
Current assets (3,340 + 1,790)	5,130	5,130
	9,630	9,558
Equity attributable to owners of the parent		
Share capital	1,000	1,000
Retained earnings (W3)	4,270	4,270
	5,270	5,270
Non-controlling interests (W4)	1,040	968
	6,310	6,238
Non-current liabilities (350 + 290)	640	640
Current liabilities (1,580 + 1,100)	2,680	2,680
	9,630	9,558

Tutorial note:

'Other components of equity' has been cancelled on consolidation as it relates to the revaluation gains on the investment in HJ (which has been treated as 'available for sale'). In order to cancel the cost of the investment of $720,000 in the goodwill working, both the investment at its fair value of $920,000 and the revaluation gains of $200,000 must be eliminated on consolidation.

Workings

1   *Group structure*

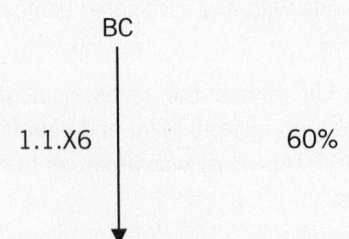

BC

1.1.X6   60%

HJ   Pre-acquisition retained earnings = $300,000

2   *Goodwill*

	Part (a)		Part (b)	
	$'000	$'000	$'000	$'000
Consideration transferred *		720		720
Non-controlling interests		480	(1,000 × 40%)	400
Fair value of net assets at acquisition:				
Share capital	500		500	
Retained earnings (W1)	300		300	
Fair value adjustment (W5)	200		200	
		(1,000)		(1,000)
		200		120
Less: impairment losses to date (10%)		(20)		(12)
		180		108

* This comprises the investment at its fair value of $920,000 less the revaluation gains of $200,000 in 'other components of equity'.

3   *Retained earnings*

	BC $'000	HJ $'000
Per question	3,430	1,800
Fair value adjustment – extra depreciation (W5)		(80)
Pre-acquisition (W1)		(300)
		1,420
Group share of HJ's post-acquisition reserves:		
(1,420 × 60%)	852	
Less: impairment loss on goodwill:		
Part (a) (20 (W2) × 60%)/**Part (b)** (12 (W2))	(12)	
	4,270	

4   *Non-controlling interests*

	Part (a) $'000	Part (b) $'000
NCI at acquisition (W2)	480	400
NCI share of post- acquisition reserves	568	568
(1,420 (W3) × 40%)		
NCI share of impairment losses (20 (W2) × 40%)	(8)	(-)
	1,040	968

5   *Fair value adjustment*

	At acquisition 1/1/X6 $'000	Movement X6, X7, X8, X9 $'000	Year end 31/12/X9 $'000
Property, plant and equipment (800 – 600)	200	(80)*	120
	↓	↓	↓
	Goodwill	Retained earnings	PPE

* extra depreciation = 200 × 1/10 = 20 annual deprecation × 4 years = 80

Exam skills

In the exam, the **consolidation question** will tell you which method to use. It will state either:

'It is the group policy to value the non-controlling interest at full (or fair) value;' or

'It is the group policy to value the non-controlling interest at its proportionate share of the (fair value of the) subsidiary's identifiable net assets'.

1.4 Impairment of goodwill

Goodwill arising on consolidation is subjected to an annual impairment review and impairment may be expressed as an amount or as a percentage. When non-controlling interest is measured using the **proportionate method**, the double entry to write off the impairment is:

DEBIT   Group retained earnings   CREDIT   Goodwill

However, when non-controlling interest is valued **at fair value**, the goodwill in the statement of financial position includes goodwill attributable to the non-controlling interest. In this case the double entry will reflect the non-controlling interest proportion based on their shareholding as follows:

DEBIT   Group retained earnings   CREDIT   Goodwill

DEBIT   Non-controlling interest   CREDIT   Goodwill

In our solution to the example in 1.1 above, the non-controlling interest holds 40%. The double entry for the 10% impairment of goodwill using the proportionate method would be:

		$		$
DEBIT	Retained earnings	12,000	CREDIT Goodwill	12,000

The double entry for the impairment of goodwill using the fair value method would be:

		$		$
DEBIT	Retained earnings	12,000	CREDIT Goodwill	20,000
DEBIT	Non-controlling interest	8,000		

1.5 Gain on a bargain purchase

Goodwill arising on consolidation is one form of **purchased goodwill**, and is governed by IFRS 3. IFRS 3 requires that goodwill arising on consolidation should **be capitalised in the consolidated statement of financial position** and **reviewed for impairment every year**.

Goodwill arising on consolidation is the difference between the cost of an acquisition and the value of the subsidiary's net assets acquired. This difference can be **negative**: the aggregate of the fair values of the separable net assets acquired may **exceed** what the parent company paid for them. IFRS 3 refers to this as a 'bargain purchase'. In this situation:

(a)   An entity should first **re-assess** the amounts at which it has measured both the cost of the combination and the acquiree's identifiable net assets. This exercise should identify any errors.

(b)   Any **excess remaining** should be recognised immediately in profit or loss.

Section summary

When there is a non-controlling interest in a subsidiary the consolidated statement of financial position will include 100% of the subsidiary's assets and liabilities. This shows the assets and liabilities under group **control**.

The **ownership** of the net assets is shown by including a **non-controlling interest** in the equity section of the statement of financial position.

There are **two methods** of calculating the non-controlling interest at acquisition:

(a) The NCI's proportionate share of the subsidiary's net assets (the partial goodwill method)
(b) Fair value (the full goodwill method)

2 Non-controlling interests and intra-group trading

Introduction

We have already seen the adjustments for intra-group trading with 100% subsidiaries. We now need to consider the effect on NCI.

2.1 Non-controlling interests and unrealised intra-group profits

A further problem occurs where a subsidiary company which is **not wholly owned is involved in intragroup trading** within the group. If a subsidiary S Co is 75% owned and sells goods to the parent company for $16,000 cost plus $4,000 profit, ie for $20,000 and if these items are unsold by P Co at the end of the reporting period, the 'unrealised' profit of $4,000 earned by S Co and charged to P Co will be partly owned by the non-controlling interest of S Co.

To do this, using the methods we have followed up to now, the adjustment is:

Entries to learn

DEBIT　　　　　Retained earnings (of the company who made the **sale**)
CREDIT　　　　Group inventories (statement of financial position)

The credit is made on the face of the group statement of financial position and the debit to the **appropriate column** of the retained reserves working. This will then split the unrealised profit between the group and the NCI if the subsidiary made the sale.

If the sale was made by the parent, there is no effect on the NCI.

Exam alert

The May 2012 exam included a 10 mark question asking for the SOFP workings for goodwill, reserves and NCI after adjusting for intra-group trading. You can expect to find non-controlling interests in every exam and intra-group trading in most sittings.

Example: non-controlling interests and intra-group profits (1)

P Co has owned 75% of the shares of S Co since the incorporation of that company. During the year to 31 December 20X2, S Co sold goods costing $16,000 to P Co at a price of $20,000 and these goods

were still unsold by P Co at the end of the year. Draft statements of financial position of each company at 31 December 20X2 were as follows.

	P Co		S Co	
	$	$	$	$
Assets				
Non-current assets				
Property, plant and equipment	125,000		120,000	
Investment: 75,000 shares in S Co at cost	75,000		–	
		200,000		120,000
Current assets				
Inventories	50,000		48,000	
Trade receivables	20,000		16,000	
		70,000		64,000
Total assets		270,000		184,000
Equity and liabilities				
Equity				
Ordinary shares of $1 each fully paid	80,000		100,000	
Retained earnings	150,000		60,000	
		230,000		160,000
Current liabilities		40,000		24,000
Total equity and liabilities		270,000		184,000

Required

Prepare the consolidated statement of financial position of P Co at 31 December 20X2. It is the group policy to value the non-controlling interest at acquisition at its proportionate share of the subsidiary's net assets.

Solution

P CO

CONSOLIDATED STATEMENT OF FINANCIAL POSITION AS AT 31 DECEMBER 20X2

	$	$
Assets		
Property, plant and equipment (125,000 + 120,000)		245,000
Current assets		
Inventories $(50,000 + 48,000 – 4,000 unrealised profit)	94,000	
Trade receivables (20,000 + 16,000)	36,000	
		130,000
Total assets		375,000
Equity and liabilities		
Equity		
Ordinary shares of $1 each	80,000	
Retained earnings (W2)	192,000	
		272,000
Non-controlling interest (W3)		39,000
		311,000
Current liabilities		64,000
Total equity and liabilities		375,000

Workings

1   *Group structure*

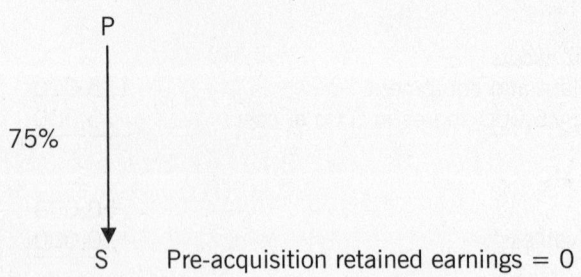

P

75%

S   Pre-acquisition retained earnings = 0

2   *Retained earnings*

	P Co $	S Co $
Per question	150,000	60,000
Less unrealised profit (20,000 – 16,000)		(4,000)
Pre-acquisition		–
		56,000
Share of S Co: $56,000 × 75%	42,000	
	192,000	

3   *Non-controlling interest*

	$
NCI at acquisition (25% × 100,000)	25,000
NCI share of post acquisition retained earnings (25% × 56,000)	14,000
	39,000

Note: No goodwill working is necessary as the acquisition was at the date of incorporation. The profit earned by S Co but unrealised by the group is $4,000 of which $3,000 (75%) is attributable to the group and $1,000 (25%) to the non-controlling interest. Remove the whole of the profit loading, charging the non-controlling interest with their proportion. This is done by making the adjustment to profit in S's column in the retained earnings working.

Example: non-controlling interests and intra-group profits (2)

Explain how the answer to the above example would change if the facts remained the same except that the goods were sold by P Co to S Co.

Solution

Note: As above, no goodwill working is necessary as the acquisition was at the date of incorporation. The full unrealised profit is always deducted from group inventories but this time, as P made the sale, the debit is made against P Co's retained earnings $4,000. The full amount is charged to consolidated retained earnings and none to the non-controlling interest.

BPP
LEARNING MEDIA

	P Co $	S Co $
Retained earnings		
Per question	150,000	60,000
Less unrealised profit	(4,000)	
Pre-acquisition		-
		60,000
Share of S Co: $60,000 × 75%	45,000	
	191,000	
Non-controlling interest		
NCI at acquisition (25% × 100,000)		25,000
NCI share of post acquisition retained earnings (25% × 60,000)		15,000
		40,000

Section summary

Unrealised profit must be removed from the consolidated financial statement of financial position charged against the retained earnings of the company that **made the sale**.

3 Non-controlling interest and intra-group sales of non-current assets

Introduction

We will now consider the effect of NCI on intra-group sales of non-current assets.

We have already dealt with this topic for 100% subsidiaries in Chapter 6. The principle is the same as when dealing with unrealised profits on intra-group trading, adjust the retained earnings of the company that made the sale. The effect of NCI is best dealt with by the following example.

Example: intra-group sale of non-current assets

P Co acquired 60% of S Co on incorporation. On 1 January 20X1 S Co sells plant with a net book value $10,000 to P Co for $12,500. At 1 January 20X1, the plant had a remaining useful life of ten years. The companies make up financial statements to 31 December 20X1 and the balances on their retained earnings at that date are:

P Co	After charging depreciation of 10% on plant	$27,000
S Co	Including profit on sale of plant	$18,000

Required

Show the working for consolidated retained earnings.

Solution

Retained earnings

	P Co $	S Co $
Per question	27,000	18,000
Unrealised profit on sale of plant (W1)		(2,250)
Pre-acquisition		-
		15,750
Share of S Co: $15,750 × 60%	9,450	
	36,450	

Workings

1 *Unrealised profit*

	$
Unrealised profit on transfer ($12,500 - $10,000)	2,500
Less: proportion depreciated by year end ($250/10 years)	(250)
	2,250

Notes

1 The non-controlling interest in the retained earnings of S Co is 40% × $15,750 = $6,300.

2 The asset is written down to cost and depreciation on the 'profit' element is removed. The group profit for the year is thus reduced by a net (($2,250) × 60%) = $1,350.

3 As shown above, the adjustment to retained earnings is made in the company that made the sale.

Section summary

The unrealised profits on the intra-group sale of non-current assets includes an adjustment for excess depreciation.

4 Non-controlling interests and fair values

Introduction

Fair value adjustments affect the assets of the subsidiary, so we need to look at how this will affect the NCI.

4.1 Fair value adjustments

There are two issues to consider.

(a) Part of the fair value uplift at acquisition belongs to the NCI (as they own a share of the assets and liabilities). No extra adjustment needs to be made as this will already be reflected in the figure used for 'NCI at acquisition' in the goodwill working irrespective of whether the NCI is valued at its proportionate share of net assets or at full fair value.

(b) Any movement in the fair value difference (such as additional depreciation charged on assets subject to fair value uplifts) is charged against the subsidiary's retained earnings in the consolidated retained earnings working. Then the adjusted retained earnings figure will be used in the calculation of NCI for the statement of financial position.

Example: non-controlling interests and fair value adjustments

P Co acquired 75% of the ordinary shares of S Co on 1 September 20X5. At that date the fair value of S Co's non-current assets was $23,000 greater than their net book value, and the balance of retained earnings was $21,000.

The statements of financial position of both companies at 31 August 20X6 are given below. S Co has not incorporated any revaluation in its books of account.

P CO

STATEMENT OF FINANCIAL POSITION AS AT 31 AUGUST 20X6

	$	$
Assets		
Non-current assets		
Property, plant and equipment	63,000	
Investment in S Co at cost	51,000	
		114,000
Current assets		82,000
Total assets		196,000
Equity and liabilities		
Equity		
Ordinary shares of $1 each	80,000	
Retained earnings	96,000	
		176,000
Current liabilities		20,000
Total equity and liabilities		196,000

S CO

STATEMENT OF FINANCIAL POSITION AS AT 31 AUGUST 20X6

	$	$
Assets		
Property, plant and equipment		28,000
Current assets		44,000
Total assets		72,000
Equity and liabilities		
Equity		
Ordinary shares of $1 each	20,000	
Retained earnings	42,000	
		62,000
Current liabilities		10,000
Total equity and liabilities		72,000

If S Co had revalued its non-current assets at 1 September 20X5, an addition of $3,000 would have been made to the depreciation charged for 20X5/X6.

It is group policy to measure non-controlling interest at acquisition at fair value. The fair value of the non-controlling interest in S Co at 1 September 20X5 was $17,000.

Required

Prepare P Co's consolidated statement of financial position as at 31 August 20X6.

Solution

P CO CONSOLIDATED STATEMENT OF FINANCIAL POSITION AS AT 31 AUGUST 20X6

	$	$
Non-current assets		
Property, plant and equipment (63,000 + 48,000*)	111,000	
Goodwill (W2)	4,000	
		115,000
Current assets (82,000 + 44,000)		126,000
		241,000
Equity and liabilities		
Equity		
Ordinary shares of $1 each	80,000	
Retained earnings (W3)	109,500	
		189,500
Non-controlling interest (W4)		21,500
		211,000
Current liabilities (20,000 + 10,000)		30,000
		241,000

* (28,000 + 23,000 – 3,000) = $48,000

Workings

1   *Group structure*

P

1 September 20X5   75%

S   Pre-acquisition retained earnings = $21,000

2   *Goodwill*

	$	$
Consideration transferred		51,000
Non-controlling interest (fair value)		17,000
		68,000
Net assets at acquisition:		
Ordinary share capital	20,000	
Retained earnings (W1)	21,000	
Fair value adjustment (W5)	23,000	
		(64,000)
Goodwill		4,000

3   *Retained earnings*

	P Co $	S Co $
Per question	96,000	42,000
Fair value depreciation adjustment (W5)		(3,000)
Pre acquisition (W1)		(21,000)
Post acquisition S Co		18,000
Group share in S Co		
($18,000 × 75%)	13,500	
Group retained earnings	109,500	

4   *Non-controlling interest at reporting date*

	$
NCI at acquisition (W2)	17,000
NCI share of S's post-acquisition retained earnings (25% × 18,000)	4,500
	21,500

5   *Fair value adjustments*

	At acq'n date	Movement	Year end
	$	$	$
Property plant and equipment	23,000	(3,000)	20,000
	23,000	(3,000)	20,000
	↓	↓	↓
	Goodwill	Ret'd earnings	SOFP

Section summary

Fair values are very important in the computation of goodwill.

---

5   Fair value measurements

IFRS 13 defines fair value as **'the price that would be received to sell an asset or paid to transfer a liability in an orderly transaction between market participants at the measurement date.'**

Please refer to Chapter 5, Section 4 for a full discussion of fair value measurements. You will need to apply the concept of fair value measurements in the context of group accounting.

6   Acquisition of a subsidiary during its accounting period

Introduction

In paper F1 all acquisitions of subsidiaries took place at the end of the accounting period. In paper F2 you may be asked to deal with examples where the parent acquires a subsidiary during its accounting period.

6.1 Accounting problem

As we have already seen, at the end of the accounting year it will be necessary to prepare consolidated accounts.

The subsidiary company's statement of financial position to be consolidated will show the subsidiary's retained earnings as at the end of the period. For consolidation purposes, however, it is necessary to distinguish between:

(a)   Profits earned before acquisition
(b)   Profits earned after acquisition

In practice, a subsidiary company's profit may not accrue evenly over the year; for example, the subsidiary might be engaged in a trade, such as toy sales, with marked seasonal fluctuations. Nevertheless, in the exam the assumption can be made that **profits accrue evenly** whenever it is impracticable to arrive at an accurate split of pre- and post-acquisition profits. Questions will normally say 'assume that profits accrue evenly over the period'.

Once the amount of pre-acquisition profit has been established the appropriate consolidation workings (goodwill, retained earnings) can be produced.

Question 7.1	Mid-year acquisition

Learning outcomes A1

Hinge Co acquired 80% of the ordinary shares of Singe Co on 1 April 20X5.

On 31 December 20X4, Singe Co's financial statements showed a share premium account of $4,000 and retained earnings of $15,000. The statements of financial position of the two companies at 31 December 20X5 are set out below. Neither company has paid any dividends during the year. Non-controlling interest at acquisition should be valued at fair value. The share price just prior to the acquisition was $3.10.

You are required to prepare the consolidated statement of financial position of Hinge Co at 31 December 20X5. You should assume that profits have accrued evenly over the year to 31 December 20X5. There has been no impairment of goodwill.

HINGE CO
STATEMENT OF FINANCIAL POSITION AS AT 31 DECEMBER 20X5

	$	$
Assets		
Non-current assets		
Property, plant and equipment	32,000	
16,000 ordinary shares of 50c each in Singe Co	50,000	
		82,000
Current assets		85,000
Total assets		167,000
Equity and liabilities		
Equity		
Ordinary shares capital ($1 shares)	100,000	
Share premium account	7,000	
Retained earnings	40,000	
		147,000
Current liabilities		20,000
Total equity and liabilities		167,000

SINGE CO
STATEMENT OF FINANCIAL POSITION AS AT 31 DECEMBER 20X5

	$	$
Assets		
Property, plant and equipment		30,000
Current assets		43,000
Total assets		73,000
Equity and liabilities		
Ordinary share capital (20,000 shares of 50c each)	10,000	
Share premium account	4,000	
Retained earnings	39,000	
		53,000
Current liabilities		20,000
Total equity and liabilities		73,000

Example: pre-acquisition losses of a subsidiary

As an illustration of the entries arising when a subsidiary has pre-acquisition *losses*, suppose P Co acquired all 50,000 $1 ordinary shares in S Co for $20,000 on 1 January 20X1 when there was a debit balance of $35,000 on S Co's retained earnings. In the years 20X1 to 20X4 S Co makes profits of $45,000 in total, leaving a credit balance of $10,000 on retained earnings at 31 December 20X4. P Co's retained earnings at the same date are $70,000.

Solution

The consolidation workings would appear as follows.

1   *Goodwill*

	$	$
Consideration transferred		20,000
Net assets at acquisition		
Ordinary share capital	50,000	
Retained earnings	(35,000)	
		(15,000)
Goodwill		5,000

2   *Retained earnings*

	P Co	S Co
	$	$
At the end of the reporting period	70,000	10,000
Pre-acquisition loss		35,000
		45,000
S Co – share of post-acquisition retained earnings		
(45,000 × 100%)	45,000	
	115,000	

Section summary

When a parent company acquires a subsidiary during its accounting period the profits for the period need to be apportioned between pre and post acquisition. **Only post-acquisition profits are included in group retained earnings.**

7 Exam technique

This is a useful point to summarise the method you should use when preparing the consolidated statement of financial position.

Read the question and draw up the group structure (W1), highlighting useful information:

- – the percentage owned
- – acquisition date
- – pre-acquisition reserves

Draw up a proforma taking into account the group structure identified:

- – leave out cost of investment
- – put in a line for goodwill
- – put in a line for investment in associate (where appropriate, see Chapter 9)
- – remember to include non-controlling interests
- – leave lines in case of any additions

 Work methodically down the statement of financial position, transferring:

– Figures to proforma or workings:

– 100% of all assets/liabilities controlled at the year end aggregated in brackets on face of proforma, ready for adjustments

– Cost of subsidiary/associate and reserves to group workings, setting them up as you work down the statement of financial position

– Share capital and share premium (parent only) to face of proforma answer

– Open up a (blank) working for non-controlling interests.

 Read through the additional notes and attempt the adjustments showing workings for all calculations.

Do the double entry for the adjustments onto your proforma answer and onto your group workings (where the group workings are affected by one side of the double entry).

Examples:

Cancel any intragroup items e.g. current account balances, loans

Adjust for unrealised profits:

Unrealised profit on intragroup sales	X
% held in inventories at year end	%
=Provision for unrealised profit (PUP)	X
(adjust in company **selling** goods)	

DR Retained earnings
CR Group inventories

Make fair value adjustments:

	Acq'n date	Movement	Year end
Inventories	X	(X)	X
Depreciable non-current assets	X	(X)	X
Non-depreciable non-current assets	X	(X)	X
Other fair value adjustments	X/(X)	(X)/X	X/(X)
	X	(X)	X

This total appears in the goodwill working	*This total is used to adjust the subsidiary 's reserves in the reserves working.*	*The individual figures here are used to adjust the relevant balances on the consolidated statement of financial position.*

STEP 5   Complete goodwill calculation

Consideration transferred		X
Non-controlling interests (at % FV of net assets or at fair value)		X
Less fair value of net assets at acquisition:		
Share capital	X	
Share premium	X	
Retained earnings at acquisition	X	
Other reserves at acquisition	X	
Fair value adjustments at acquisition	X̲	
		(X)̲
		X
Less: Impairment losses on goodwill to date		(X)̲
		X̲

STEP 6   Complete the consolidated retained earnings calculation:

	Parent	Subsidiary	Associate/ joint venture
Per question	X	X	X
Adjustments	X/(X)	X/(X)	X/(X)
Fair value adjustments movement		X/(X)	X/(X)
Pre-acquisition retained earnings		(X)̲	(X)̲
Group share of post acq'n ret'd earnings:		Y̲	Z̲
Subsidiary (Y × %)	X		
Associate/joint venture (Z × %)	X		
Less: group share of impairment losses to date	(X)̲		
	X̲		

Note: Other reserves are treated in a similar way.

STEP 7   Complete 'Investment in associate/joint venture' calculation (if appropriate, see Chapter 9):

Cost of associate/joint venture	X
Share of post-acquisition retained reserves (from reserves working Z × %)	X
Less group impairment losses on associate/joint venture to date	(X)̲
	X̲

STEP 8   Complete the non-controlling interests calculation:

NCI at acquisition (from goodwill working)	X
NCI share of post acq'n reserves (from reserves working Y × NCI %)	X
Less NCI share of impairment losses (only if NCI at 'full' FV at acq'n)	(X)̲
	X̲

8   Subsidiaries acquired exclusively with a view to resale

Under IFRS 5 *Non-current assets held for sale and discontinued operations,* a subsidiary acquired exclusively with the intention of reselling it, is likely to qualify as:

- A disposal group 'held for sale' in the statement of financial position and
- A 'discontinued operation' in the statement of profit or loss and other comprehensive income

if the 'held for sale' criteria are met.

Let's first look at what the key terms mean.

8.1 Criteria for subsidiaries held for sale

KEY TERM

DISCONTINUED OPERATION. A component of an entity that either has been disposed of or is classified as held for sale and:

(a)   represents a separate major line of business or geographical area of operations, *or*

(b)   is part of a single coordinated plan to dispose of a separate major line of business or geographical area of operations, *or*

(c)   is a subsidiary acquired exclusively with a view to resale.   *(IFRS 5)*

A **component** of an entity is one that has operations and cash flows that can be clearly distinguished, operationally and for financial reporting purposes, from the rest of the entity. at fair value.

To be classified as **'held for sale'**, all of the following criteria must be met:

(a)   The disposal group (ie the subsidiary) must be **available for immediate sale** in its present condition and

(b)   The sale must be **highly probable**. This means:

–   **P**rice at which the disposal group (i.e. the subsidiary) is actively marketed for sale must be reasonable in relation to its current fair value

–   **U**nlikely that significant changes will be made to the plan or the plan withdrawn (indicated by actions required to complete the plan)

–   **M**anagement (at the appropriate level) must be committed to a plan to sell

–   **A**ctive programme to locate a buyer and complete the plan must have been initiated

–   **S**ale expected to qualify for recognition as a completed sale within one year from the date of classification as held for sale (subject to limited specified exceptions). 8.1.1 Statement of financial position

If the 'held for sale' criteria are met, the disposal group (i.e. the subsidiary classified as held for sale) is measured at the lower of:

•   Carrying amount, and
•   Fair value less costs to sell

Additionally, instead of consolidating the subsidiary's assets and liabilities line by line in the consolidated statement of financial position, its assets and liabilities should be disclosed:

•   As single amounts (of assets and liabilities)

•   On the face of the statement of financial position

•   Separately from other assets and liabilities, and

•   Normally as current assets and liabilities (individually, not offset against each other as a net amount).

8.2 Statement of profit or loss and other comprehensive income

A subsidiary acquired exclusively with a view to resale is likely to meet the **'discontinued operation'** criteria and should be presented separately as follows in the consolidated statement of profit or loss and other comprehensive income:

On the face of the statement of profit or loss and other comprehensive income:

- **Single amount** comprising the total of:

    (i)   The **post-tax profit or loss** of discontinued operations, and

    (ii)   The **post-tax gain or loss recognised on the remeasurement to fair value** less costs to sell or on the disposal of assets/disposal groups comprising the discontinued operation.

On the face of the statement of profit or loss and other comprehensive income or in the notes:

- Revenue

- Expenses

- Profit before tax

- Income tax expense

- Post-tax gain or loss on disposal of assets/disposal groups or on remeasurement to fair value less costs to sell.

Chapter Roundup

✓   When there is a non-controlling interest in a subsidiary the consolidated statement of financial position will include 100% of the subsidiary's assets and liabilities. This shows the assets and liabilities under group **control**.

     The **ownership** of the net assets is shown by including a **non-controlling interest** in the equity section of the statement of financial position.

     There are **two methods** of calculating the non-controlling interest at acquisition:

     (a) The NCI's proportionate share of the subsidiary's net assets

     (b) Fair value

✓   Unrealised profit must be removed from the consolidated financial statement of financial position, charged against the retained earnings of the company that **made the sale**.

✓   The unrealised profit on the intra-group sale of non-current assets includes an adjustment for excess depreciation.

✓   Fair values are very important in the computation of goodwill.

✓   When a parent company acquires a subsidiary during its accounting period the profits for the period need to be apportioned between pre and post acquisition. **Only post acquisition profits are included in group retained earnings.**

Quick Quiz

1   What is a non-controlling interest?

2   Chicken Co owns 80% of Egg Co. Egg Co sells goods to Chicken Co at cost plus 50%. The total invoiced sales to Chicken Co by Egg Co in the year ended 31 December 20X9 were $900,000 and, of these sales, goods which had been invoiced at $60,000 were held in inventory by Chicken Co at 31 December 20X9. What is the reduction in aggregate group gross profit?

3   Major Co, which makes up its accounts to 31 December, has an 80% owned subsidiary Minor Co. Minor Co sells goods to Major Co at a mark-up on cost of 33.33%. At 31 December 20X8, Major had $12,000 of such goods in its inventory and at 31 December 20X9 had $15,000 of such goods in its inventory.

     What is the amount by which the consolidated profit attributable to Major Co's shareholders should be adjusted in respect of the above?

     Ignore taxation

     A $1,000 Debit

     B $800 Credit

     C $750 Credit

     D $600 Debit

4   What are the components making up the figure of non-controlling interest in a consolidated statement of financial position?

Answers to Quick Quiz

1   The equity in a subsidiary not attributable, directly or indirectly, to a parent.

2    $\dfrac{\$60,000 \times 50}{150} = \$20,000$

3   D $600 Debit

      $(15,000 - 12,000) \times 33.3/133.3 \times 80\%$

4   The non-controlling interests at acquisition (measured either at their proportionate share of the subsidiary's net assets or at fair value) plus their share of the subsidiary's post acquisition retained reserves, less impairment of goodwill (if NCI measured at fair value at the date of acquisition)

Answers to Questions

7.1   Mid-year acquisition

HINGE CO
CONSOLIDATED STATEMENT OF FINANCIAL POSITION AS AT 31 DECEMBER 20X5

	$	$
Assets		
Property, plant and equipment (32,000 + 30,000)		62,000
Goodwill (W2)		27,400
Current assets (85,000 + 43,000)		128,000
Total assets		217,400
Equity and liabilities		
Ordinary share capital	100,000	
Share premium account	7,000	
Retained earnings (W3)	54,400	
		161,400
Non-controlling interest (W4)		16,000
		177,400
Current liabilities (20,000 + 20,000)		40,000
Total equity and liabilities		217,400

Workings

1   *Group structure*

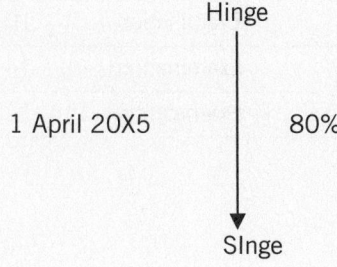

1 April 20X5   80%

Pre-acquisition retained earnings of Singe Co:

	$
Balance at 31 December 20X4	15,000
Profit for three months to 31 March 20X5 ($\frac{3}{12} \times 24{,}000^*$)	6,000
Pre-acquisition retained earnings	21,000

Singe Co has made a profit of $24,000 ($39,000 – $15,000) for the year. This is assumed to have arisen evenly over the year; $6,000 in the three months to 31 March and $18,000 in the nine months after acquisition.

The balance of $4,000 on share premium account is all pre-acquisition.
The consolidation workings can now be drawn up.

2   *Goodwill*

	$	$
Consideration transferred		50,000
Non-controlling interest (20% × 20,000 shares × $3.10)		12,400
		62,400
Net assets at acquisition:		
Ordinary share capital	10,000	
Retained earnings (pre-acquisition) (W1)	21,000	
Share premium	4,000	
		(35,000)
Goodwill		27,400

3   *Retained earnings*

	Hinge Co $	Singe Co $
Per question	40,000	39,000
Pre-acquisition (W2)		(21,000)
		18,000
Share of Singe: $18,000 × 80%	14,400	
	54,400	

4   *Non-controlling interest at reporting date*

	$
NCI at acquisition (W1)	12,400
NCI share of Singe's post acquisition retained earnings (20% × 18,000 (W2))	3,600
	16,000

Now try these questions from the Exam Question Bank

Number	Level	Marks	Time
Q7	Examination	10	18 mins
Q8	Examination	10	18 mins
Q9	Examination	14	25 mins
Q10	Examination	12	22 mins

THE CONSOLIDATED STATEMENT OF PROFIT OR LOSS AND OTHER COMPREHENSIVE INCOME AND THE STATEMENT OF CHANGES IN EQUITY

 This chapter deals with the consolidated statement of profit or loss and other comprehensive income, a topic that is examined frequently.

In addition, you need to be able to prepare the consolidated statement of changes in equity.

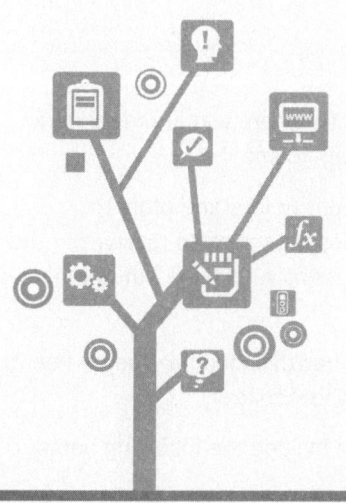

topic list	learning outcomes	syllabus references	ability required
1 Non-controlling interests and the consolidated statement of profit or loss and other comprehensive income	A1	A1(ii)	Application
2 The consolidated statement of changes in equity	A1	A1(ii)	Application

1 Non-controlling interests and the consolidated statement of profit or loss and other comprehensive income

Introduction

The statement of profit or loss and other comprehensive income must show the profit or loss and other comprehensive income **controlled** by the group. It must also identify the **ownership** of the profit and total comprehensive income, splitting these amounts into the portions owned by the parent and the non-controlling interest.

We will now look at the effect of non-controlling interests on the statement of profit or loss and other comprehensive income. You will recognise that this section applies the same principles that we have already covered in relation to the statement of financial position.

1.1 Other comprehensive income

Exam alert

The May 2010 exam included a 25 mark question on the preparation of the consolidated statement of profit or loss and other comprehensive income.

At F2, items of 'other comprehensive income' are more likely to be tested in a consolidation question than at F1. This is because new accounting standards are examinable at F2 which result in items being recorded in 'other comprehensive income' (such as revaluation gains on available for sale financial assets and remeasurement gains or losses on defined benefit pension plans).

We will now consider how to deal with non-controlling interests in questions where you are required to prepare a consolidated statement of profit or loss and other comprehensive income.

The difference between a statement of profit or loss and a statement of profit or loss and other comprehensive income (SPLOCI) is 'other comprehensive income' (gains/losses posted to reserves in the year) which is included in the statement of profit or loss and other comprehensive income but not in statement of profit or loss.

We add across the parent's and 100% of the subsidiary's 'other comprehensive income' line by line (in the same way as we add across revenue to profit for year line by line) to show control.

As well as revaluation gains, the elements of other comprehensive income include the following items, taken from IAS 1 (revised).

Other comprehensive income	Chapter	20X7	20X6
Exchange differences on translating foreign operations (may be reclassified to P/L)	12	X	X
Available-for-sale financial assets (may be reclassified to P/L)	2	X	X
Cash flow hedges (may be reclassified to P/L)	2	(X)	(X)
Gains on property revaluation (not reclassified)	–	X	X
Gains (losses) on remeasurement of defined benefit pension plans (not reclassified)	3	(X)	X
Share of other comprehensive income of associates (not reclassified)	9	X	(X)
Income tax relating to components of other comprehensive income	8	X	(X)
		X	X

The chapter reference given above shows the chapter in this Study Text where you will find further information on these elements. Gains on property revaluation were dealt with at F1 and should be revision. IAS 1 was revised in 2011 and these changes are dealt with in Chapter 17.

Exam alert

Exam questions often cover a wide range of topics from across the syllabus, so you should be prepared to encounter issues like accounting for pensions or financial instruments within consolidation questions. The treatment of any type of other comprehensive income in a consolidation follows the procedure set out in the question in the previous section.

1.2 Preparing the consolidated statement of profit or loss and other comprehensive income 11/10, 3/11, 11/11, 3/12, 5/12

Adding the parent's and 100% of the subsidiary's income, expenses and other comprehensive income line by line denotes **control**. However, we also need to reflect **ownership** in the consolidated statement of profit or loss and other comprehensive income. This is reflected in a new reconciliation presented at the foot of the consolidated statement of profit and loss and other comprehensive income which shows ownership of the profit and total comprehensive income for the year.

The diagram below illustrates the method to be followed.

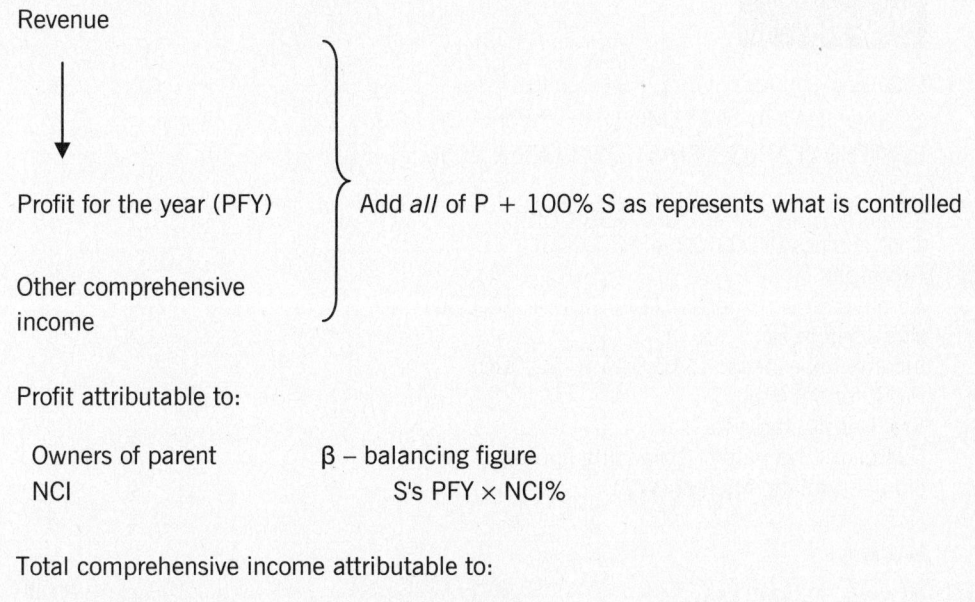

Revenue

Profit for the year (PFY)

Other comprehensive income

Add *all* of P + 100% S as represents what is controlled

Profit attributable to:

| Owners of parent | β – balancing figure |
| NCI | S's PFY × NCI% |

Total comprehensive income attributable to:

| Owners of parent | β – balancing figure |
| NCI | S's TCI × NCI% |

Note. You should always add **all** of the impairment loss on recognised goodwill for the year to expenses (regardless of whether the full or partial goodwill method is used).

The following example will introduce the most important point about consolidating a subsidiary with a non-controlling interest in the statement of profit or loss. We will still consolidate 100% of the subsidiary's results to show the results arising under group control, but we also need to show how much is owned by the non-controlling interest.

Example

P Co acquired 75% of the ordinary shares of S Co on that company's incorporation in 1 January 20X3. The summarised statements of profit or loss of the two companies for the year ending 31 December 20X6 are set out below.

	P Co $	S Co $
Revenue	75,000	38,000
Cost of sales	(30,000)	(20,000)
Gross profit	45,000	18,000
Distribution and administrative expenses	(14,000)	(8,000)
Profit before tax	31,000	10,000
Income tax expense	(10,000)	(2,000)
Profit for the year	21,000	8,000

Required

Prepare the consolidated statement of profit or loss for the year ending 31 December 20X6.

Solution

P CO
CONSOLIDATED STATEMENT OF PROFIT OR LOSS
FOR THE YEAR ENDED 31 DECEMBER 20X6

	$
Sales revenue ($75,000 + $38,000)	113,000
Cost of sales ($30,000 + $20,000)	(50,000)
Gross profit	63,000
Administrative expenses ($14,000 + $8,000)	(22,000)
Profit before tax	41,000
Income tax expense ($10,000 + $2,000)	(12,000)
Profit for the year	29,000
Profit attributable to:	
Owners of the parent (balancing figure)	27,000
Non-controlling interest (W2)	2,000
	29,000

Workings

1   Group structure

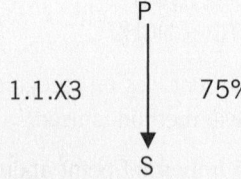

1.1.X3   75%

2   *Non-controlling interests*

	$
Profit for the year - per question	8,000
NCI share	× 25%
	= 2,000

Notice how the non-controlling interest is dealt with.

(a)   Down to the line **'Profit for the year,'** the **whole** of S Co's results is included without reference to group share or non-controlling share. A **reconciliation** is then inserted to show the ownership of the profits.

(b)   Complete the reconciliation in this order:

   (i)   Fill in the total profit for the year

(ii)   Calculate the NCI share of profit (NCI % × Subsidiary's profit after tax)

(iii)   Deduce the amount attributable to the members of the parent as a balancing figure

We will now look at the complications introduced by **intra-group trading, intra-group dividends** and **mid-year acquisitions** of subsidiaries.

1.2.1 Non-controlling interests and intra-group trading

In Chapter 6, we revised the basic issues relating to intra-group trading.

The consolidated figures for sales revenue and cost of sales should represent **sales to, and purchases from, outsiders**. An adjustment is therefore necessary to reduce the sales revenue and cost of sales figures by the value of **intra-group sales** during the year.

We have also seen that any **unrealised profits** on intra group trading should be excluded from the figure for group profits. This will occur whenever goods sold at a profit within the group remain in the inventory of the purchasing company at the year end.

If there is a non-controlling interest in the subsidiary, the impact of intra-group trading on the non-controlling interest depends on whether the parent, or the subsidiary, made the sale:

(a)   If the **parent** is the seller, there will be no **effect on the non-controlling interests**

(b)   If the **subsidiary** is the seller, then any adjustment that results in a change to the subsidiary's profit in the consolidated financial statements will require an adjustment to non-controlling interests.

    (i)   The **intra-group sale** will be eliminated in full – no further effect on non-controlling interest.

    (ii)   Any **unrealised profit** will be eliminated.

    (iii)   The figure for the subsidiary's **profit after tax** used to calculate the **non-controlling interest** must be adjusted for the unrealised profit.

    (iv)   **Fair value adjustments** for intra-group sales of non-current assets.

    (v)   **Impairment of goodwill** for the year (only if using the full goodwill method).

Example: intra-group trading

Suppose in our earlier example that S Co had recorded sales of $5,000 to P Co during 20X6. S Co had purchased these goods from outside suppliers at a cost of $3,000. One half of the goods remained in P Co's inventory at 31 December 20X6. Prepare the revised consolidated statement of profit or loss.

Solution

The consolidated statement of profit or loss for the year ended 31 December 20X6 would now be as follows.

	$
Sales revenue ($75,000 + $ 38,000 − $5,000 (W3))	108,000
Cost of sales ($30,000 + $20,000 − $5,000 + $1,000(W3))	(46,000)
Gross profit	62,000
Administrative expenses	(22,000)
Profit before taxation	40,000
Income tax expense	(12,000)
Profit for the year	28,000
Profit attributable to:	
Owners of the parent	26,250
Non-controlling interest (W2)	1,750
	28,000

Workings

1   *Group structure*

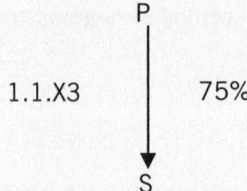

P

1.1.X3   75%

S

2   *Non-controlling interests*

	$
Profit for the year - per question	8,000
PUP	(1,000)
	7,000
NCI share	× 25%
	= 1,750

3   *Intra-group trading*

S → P

- Intra –group revenue and cost of sales:
  Cancel $5,000 out of revenue and cost of sales

- PUP = 1/2 in inventories × ($5,000 - $3,000) mark up = $1,000
  Increase cost of sales by $1,000 and reduce profit for the year in non-controlling interest working (as subsidiary is the seller)

Note. In this example, the unrealised profit arose on sales made by the subsidiary. This means that it has to be eliminated from the subsidiary's profit before the non-controlling interest is calculated.

Question 8.1	Non-controlling interests

Learning outcomes A1

The statements of profit or loss and other comprehensive income for two entities for the year ended 30 September 20X5 are presented below:

STATEMENTS OF PROFIT OR LOSS AND OTHER COMPREHENSIVE INCOME
FOR THE YEAR ENDED 30 SEPTEMBER 20X5

	CV $'000	SG $'000
Revenue	5,000	4,200
Cost of sales	(4,100)	(3,500)
Gross profit	900	700
Distribution and administrative expenses	(320)	(180)
Investment income	50	-
Profit before tax	630	520
Income tax expense	(240)	(170)
PROFIT FOR THE YEAR	390	350
Other comprehensive income:		
Gain on revaluation of property (net of deferred tax)	60	20
TOTAL COMPREHENSIVE INCOME FOR THE YEAR	450	370

Additional information:

1   CV acquired a 75% investment in SG on 1 October 20X2. It is group policy to measure non-controlling interests at fair value at acquisition. Goodwill of $250,000 arose on acquisition. The fair value of the net assets was deemed to be the same as the carrying value of net assets.

2   No impairment of goodwill had been necessary up to 1 October 20X4. However, the directors conducted an impairment review at 30 September 20X5 and decided that goodwill on acquisition was impaired by 20%.

3   During the year ended 30 September 20X5, SG sold goods to CV for $300,000. Two thirds of these goods remain in CV's inventories at the year end. SG charges a mark-up of 25% on cost.

4   SG paid a dividend of $60,000 to its equity shareholders on 30 September 20X5. CV includes its share of the dividend in investment income.

Requirement

(a)   Prepare the consolidated statement of profit or loss and other comprehensive income for the CV group for the year ended 30 September 20X5.

(b)   How would non-controlling interests differ if non-controlling interests at acquisition had been measured at the proportionate share of the net assets and if CV had sold the goods to SG in note (3)?

1.2.2 Mid-year acquisitions

We have seen in the previous chapters that retained earnings in the consolidated statement of financial position include the group's share of the **post acquisition** retained earnings of the subsidiary. We only consolidate what the subsidiary has earned since it came under the parent's control.

A **similar principle** is followed in the **consolidated statement of profit or loss/consolidated statement of profit or loss and other comprehensive income**.

If the subsidiary is **acquired during the accounting year**, only the post acquisition results are included in the consolidated statement of profit or loss. In exam, you may have to **time-apportion** the income and expenses of the subsidiary to calculate the post acquisition elements. You may find it helpful to draw a timeline. Assume revenue, expenses and other comprehensive income accrue evenly, unless told otherwise.

1.2.3 Intra-group dividends

If the subsidiary has paid a dividend during the year, the parent will have recognised their share of this in profit or loss. In the consolidated statement of profit or loss and other comprehensive income, this must be cancelled out.

This follows the same principle that we saw in connection with the statement of financial position. In the statement of financial position, the investment that appears in the parent's separate financial statements is cancelled out and the subsidiary's assets and liabilities are included instead. In the consolidated statement of profit or loss and other comprehensive income, the dividend income recognised by the parent is **cancelled out** and we show the subsidiary's income and expenses instead.

196 | 8: The consolidated statement of profit or loss and other comprehensive income and the statement of changes in equity

PART B GROUP FINANCIAL STATEMENTS

Question 8.2

Mid year acquisition

Learning outcomes A1

JT acquired 90% of the issued share capital of MB on 1 April 20X7.

At the year end 31 December 20X7 the two companies have the following statements of financial position:

	JT		MB	
	$'000	$'000	$'000	$'000
Investment in MB		4,000		–
Other assets		10,500		6,000
		14,500		6,000
Share capital ($1 shares)		6,000		1,000
Share premium		–		500
Retained earnings				
1 Jan 20X7	4,000		1,500	
Profit for 20X7	2,000		1,000	
		6,000		2,500
		12,000		4,000
Liabilities		2,500		2,000
		14,500		6,000

The statements of profit or loss for the two companies for the year ended 31 December 20X7 are as follows.

	JT	MB
	$'000	$'000
Revenue	10,000	4,000
Cost of sales and expenses	(6,000)	(2,100)
Profit before tax	4,000	1,900
Income tax expense	(1,400)	(900)
Profit for the year	2,600	1,000

Notes

(i)   On 14 November 20X7, JT sold inventories to MB at a transfer price of $200,000, which included a profit on transfer of $30,000. Half of these inventories had been sold by MB by the year end.

(ii)   An impairment test carried out at the year end revealed impairment losses of $20,000 relating to recognised goodwill. The group measures non-controlling interests at fair value at the date of acquisition. The share price just prior to the acquisition was $4.50

(iii) On 1 April 20X7 MB owned some items of equipment with a fair value that was $100,000 in excess of its book value. Additional depreciation on fair value adjustments amounted to $10,000 in the post-acquisition period.

Required

(a)   Calculate the goodwill figure that would appear in the consolidated statement of financial position as at 31 December 20X7.

(b)   Prepare the consolidated statement of profit or loss for JT Group for the year ended 31 December 20X7.

1.3 Income tax relating to components of other comprehensive income

You will not be expected to calculate the income tax effects. In the pilot paper, you were given the figures for tax effects and asked to prepare a consolidated statement of profit or loss and other comprehensive income. All that was needed was to include the figure in other comprehensive income, as shown above.

1.4 Technique summary

Purpose	To show the results of the group for an accounting period as if it were a single entity.
Sales revenue to profit for year, and other comprehensive income	100% P + 100% S (excluding adjustments for inter-company transactions). Time-apportioned to include only **post-acquisition** results if subsidiary was acquired part way through the year.
Reason	To show the results of the group which were controlled by the parent company.
Intra-group sales	Strip out inter-company activity from both sales revenue and cost of sales.
Unrealised profit on intra-group sales	(a) Goods sold by parent: Increase cost of sales by unrealised profit. (b) Goods sold by subsidiary: Increase cost of sales by full amount of unrealised profit and decrease non-controlling interest by their share of unrealised profit.
Depreciation	If the value of subsidiary's non-current assets have been subjected to a fair value uplift then any additional depreciation must be charged in the consolidated statement of profit or loss (see Chapter 6). The non-controlling interests will need to be adjusted for their share.
Transfer of non-current assets	The profit on transfer must be eliminated and expenses must be reduced by any additional depreciation arising from the increased carrying value of the asset (see Chapter 6). The non-controlling interest is adjusted if the asset was sold by the subsidiary.
Non-controlling interests in profit	Subsidiary's profit after tax (PAT) X Less: Impairment loss for the year (X) * unrealised profit (X) additional depreciation following FV uplift (X) Less: ** unrealised profit net of additional depreciation following disposal of non-current assets (X) Y × NCI% X NCI profit X * Only applicable if sales of goods made by subsidiary. ** Only applicable if sale of non-current assets made by subsidiary.
Non-controlling interests in total comprehensive income	Apply adjustments to total comprehensive income, as applied above to PAT
Reason	To show the extent to which income generated through parent's control is in fact owned by other parties.

Section summary

The consolidated statement of profit or loss and other comprehensive income is produced using the same principles as the consolidated statement of profit or loss.

198 | 8: The consolidated statement of profit or loss and other comprehensive income and the statement of changes in equity

PART B GROUP FINANCIAL STATEMENTS

2 The consolidated statement of changes in equity   5/11, 5/12

Introduction

The deals with movements in equity. In a consolidated statement of changes in equity this means share capital, plus reserves and non-controlling interests.

2.1 Purpose of the consolidated statement of changes in equity

The statement of changes in equity simply reconciles the movement in equity in the consolidated statement of financial position at the beginning and end of the period.

The calculation of the component figures is therefore the same as for the consolidated statement of financial position.

2.2 Consolidated statement of changes in equity

The IAS 1 (revised) proforma is as follows:

	Share capital	Retained earnings	Translation of foreign operations	Available-for-sale financial assets	Re-valuation surplus	Total	NCI	Total
Bal at 1 Jan 20X6	X	X	X	X	X	X	X	X
Issue of share cap	X	–	–	–	–	X	–	X
Dividends	–	(X)	–	–	–	(X)	(X)	(X)
Total comprehensive income for year	–	X	X	X	X	X	X	X
Transfer to retained earnings	=	X	=	=	(X)	X	=	X
Bal at 31 Dec 20X6	X	X	X	X	X	X	X	X

Exam alert

In the F2 exam, you will not be expected to prepare such a detailed statement as the example above.

You could be expected to prepare a more summarised version, where share capital and reserves are combined into one column, headed **Equity attributable to owners of the parent**.

The exam question in May 2011 combined this topic with a step acquisition (covered in Chapter 11).

A consolidated statement of changes in equity in the F2 exam would look like this:

	Equity attributable to owners of the parent $'000	Non-controlling interest $'000	Total $'000	
Balance at 31/12X1	X	X	X	(P SC/SP + Group reserves)/ NCI
Share issue	X	-	X	Given in question *
Total comprehensive income for the year	X	X	X	From SPLOCI
Dividends	(X)	(X)	(X)	P/(S × NCI%)
Adjustment to equity	X/(X)	X/(X)	X/(X)	See later in Ch 11
Balance at 31/12/X2	X	X	X	(P SC/SP + Group reserves)/ NCI

* no balance in NCI column as share issue by subsidiary in the year not examinable in F2

The figures in the statement involve no new calculations. They are worked out as follows:

 Read the question and draw up the group structure (W1), highlighting useful information:

- The % owned
- Acquisition date
- Pre-acquisition reserves.

 Draw up a proforma

 Complete the dividends line:

- parent's dividend in 'equity attributable to owners of the parent' column
- subsidiary's dividend multiplied by NCI % in 'non-controlling interest' column

 Copy total comprehensive income attributable to owners of parent and to NCI from consolidated SPLOCI if given. If not given, calculate as follows:

- Work out consolidated TCI by adding the parent's TCI, the subsidiary's TCI, the group share of the associate's TCI and deducting any intra-group adjustments that affect profit (eg PUP, fair value adjustments)

- Calculate NCI in total comprehensive income as per standard consolidated SPLOCI working and post to NCI column in the consolidated SOCIE:

	$
Subsidiary's TCI	X
Adjustments that affect sub's profit/OCI (eg PUP, FV adj, impairment if full goodwill method)	(X)
	X
NCI share	×%
	= X

- Calculate TCI attributable to the owners of the parent as consolidated TCI less NCI (as if preparing the ownership reconciliation at the foot of the consolidated SPLOCI). Post this figure to the 'attributable to the owners of the parent' column in the consolidated SOCIE.

STEP 5   Calculate equity and NCI at the end of the period as follows:

- Equity = parent's share capital + consolidated reserves (from standard reserves working from consolidated SOFP – see below)

	Parent	Subsidiary	Assoc/JV
Per question	X	X	X
Adjustments	X(X)	X(X)	X(X)
Fair value adjustments movement		X/(X)	X/(X)
Pre-acquisition retained earnings		(X)	(X)
		A	B

Group share of post acq'n ret'd earnings:	
Subsidiary (A × %)	X
Associate/Joint venture (B × %)	X
Less: group share of impairment losses to date	(X)
	X

- NCI – complete standard NCI working for consolidated SOFP:

NCI at acquisition (NCI % of net assets OR fair value)	X
NCI share of post acquisition reserves	X
NCI share of impairment losses *(only if using full goodwill method)*	(X)
	X

STEP 6   Find equity and NCI at beginning of the period as a balancing figure.

Example: Consolidated statement of changes in equity

The summarised consolidated financial statements of the P Group for the year ended 31 December 20X4 are as follows:

CONSOLIDATED STATEMENT OF FINANCIAL POSITION AS AT 31 DECEMBER 20X4

	$'000
Non-current assets	36,900
Current assets	28,200
	65,100
Equity attributable to owners of the parent	
Share capital	12,300
Share premium	5,800
Revaluation surplus	350
Retained earnings	32,100
	50,550
Non-controlling interests	1,750
	52,300
Non-current liabilities	5,200
Current liabilities	7,600
	65,100

CONSOLIDATED STATEMENT OF PROFIT OR LOSS AND OTHER COMPREHENSIVE INCOME
FOR THE YEAR ENDED 31 DECEMBER 20X4

	$'000
Profit before tax	16,500
Income tax expense	(5,200)
Profit for the year	11,300
Other comprehensive income	500
Total comprehensive income for the year	11,800
Profit attributable to:	
Owners of the parent	11,100
Non-controlling interests	200
	11,300
Total comprehensive income for the year attributable to	
Owners of the parent	11,450
Non-controlling interests	350
	11,800

Additional information

The P group is made up of the parent P and a 70% owned subsidiary S. The dividends paid for the year ended 31 December 20X4 by P and S were $800,000 and $500,000 respectively.

Required

Prepare the consolidated statement of changes in equity for the P group for the year ended 31 December 20X4.

Solution

P GROUP – CONSOLIDATED STATEMENT OF CHANGES IN EQUITY

	Equity attributable to owners of the parent	Non-controlling interest	Total
	$'000	$'000	$'000
Balance at 1 January 20X4 *(balancing figure)*	39,900	1,550	41,450
Total comprehensive income for the year *(consol SPLOCI)*	11,450	350	11,800
Dividends			
(Parent)/(NCI % of subsidiary's i.e. 30% × $500,000)	(800)	(150)	(950)
Balance at 31 December 20X4 *(consol SOFP)*	50,550	1,750	52,300

Workings

1   *Group structure*

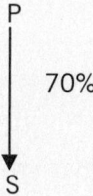

P

70%

S

2.2.1 Intra-group dividends

If a consolidated statement of financial position and consolidated statement of profit or loss and other comprehensive income are not given in the question, the figures needed for the consolidated statement of changes in equity must be recreated with a series of workings:

- Cancellation of intra-group items affecting profit

- Ownership reconciliation from consolidated statement of profit or loss and other comprehensive income

- Equity carried forward (similar to retained earnings working for consolidated statement of financial position)

- Non-controlling interests carried forward (same as non-controlling interests working for consolidated statement of financial position)

Question 8.3	Consolidated statement of changes in equity

Learning outcomes A1

Summarised statements of changes in equity for the year ended 30 June 20X5 for SM and its only subsidiary CE, are shown below:

STATEMENTS OF CHANGES IN EQUITY FOR THE YEAR ENDED 30 JUNE 20X5

	SM	CE
	$'000	$'000
Balance at 1 July 20X4	500,000	130,000
Issue of shares	25,000	-
Total comprehensive income for the year	75,000	40,000
Dividends	(16,000)	(10,000)
Balance at 30 June 20X5	584,000	160,000

Notes

1   SM acquired 37.5m of CE's 50m $1 ordinary shares on 1 July 20X2, when CE's total equity was $80m. The first dividend CE has paid since acquisition is the amount of $10m shown in the summarised statement above. The total comprehensive income for the year in SM's summarised statement of changes in equity includes its share of the dividend paid by CE.

2   During the year ended 30 June 20X5, CE sold some goods to SM for $15m at a mark up of 25% on cost. At the year end, two thirds of these goods had been sold on to third parties.

3   It is group accounting policy to measure non-controlling interest at acquisition at the proportionate share of the fair value of net assets. There has been no impairment of recognised goodwill in CE to date.

Required

Prepare the consolidated statement of changes in equity for the year ended 30 June 20X5.

Section summary

The consolidated statement of changes in equity reconciles the movement on equity over the year with the results recognised in the consolidated statement of profit or loss and other comprehensive income and dividends paid out of the group. It links the consolidated statement of financial position with the consolidated statement of profit or loss and other comprehensive income.

Chapter Roundup

✓   The consolidated statement of profit or loss and other comprehensive income is produced using the same principles as the consolidated statement of profit or loss.

✓   The consolidated statement of changes in equity reconciles the movement on equity over the year with the results recognised in the consolidated statement of profit or loss and other comprehensive income and dividends paid out of the group. It links the consolidated statement of financial position with the consolidated statement of profit or loss and other comprehensive income.

Quick Quiz

1   Where does unrealised profit on intra-group trading appear in the consolidated statement of profit or loss and other comprehensive income?

2   At the beginning of the year a 75% subsidiary transfers a non-current asset to the parent for $500,000. Its carrying value was $400,000 and it has 4 years of useful life left. How is this accounted for at the end of the year in the consolidated statement of profit or loss and other comprehensive income? (See coverage of this type of transaction in Chapter 6).

204 8: The consolidated statement of profit or loss and other
comprehensive income and the statement of changes in equity

PART B GROUP FINANCIAL STATEMENTS

Answers to Quick Quiz

1   As an addition to consolidated cost of sales (reducing the group profit).

2

	$
Unrealised profit	100,000
Additional depreciation (100 ÷ 4)	(25,000)
Net charge to statement of profit or loss	75,000

	DR $	CR $
Non-current asset		100,000
Additional depreciation	25,000	
Group profit (75%)	56,250	
Non-controlling interest (25%)	18,750	
	100,000	100,000

Answers to Questions

8.1   Non-controlling interests

(a)   CV GROUP
CONSOLIDATED STATEMENT OF PROFIT OR LOSS AND OTHER COMPREHENSIVE INCOME FOR THE
YEAR ENDED 31 DECEMBER 20X9

	$'000
Revenue (5,000 + 4,200 – 300 (W4))	8,900
Cost of sales (4,100 + 3,500 – 300 (W4) + 40 (W4))	(7,340)
Gross profit	1,560
Distribution and administration expenses (320 + 180 + 50 (W2))	(550)
Investment income (50 – 45 (W5))	5
Profit before tax	1,015
Income tax expense (240 + 170)	(410)
Profit for the year	605
Other comprehensive income:	
Gains on property revaluation (net of tax) (60 + 20)	80
Total comprehensive income for the year	685
Profit attributable to:	
Owners of the parent (615 – 65)	540
Non-controlling interests (W2)	65
	605
Total comprehensive income attributable to:	
Owners of the parent (695 – 70)	615
Non-controlling interests (W2)	70
	685

Workings

1   *Group structure*

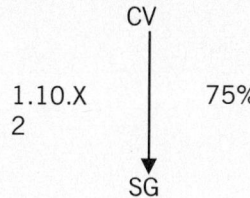

CV

1.10.X
2   75%

SG

2   *Non-controlling interests*

	PFY $000	TCI $000
Per question	350	370
Impairment loss for year (W3)	(50)	(50)
PUP (W4)	(40)	(40)
	260	280
NCI share	× 25%	× 25%
	= 65	= 70

3   *Impairment of goodwill*

Impairment of goodwill for the year = $250,000 goodwill × 20% impairment = $50,000

Add $50,000 to 'administration expenses' and deduct from PFY/TCI in NCI working (as full goodwill method adopted here)

4   *Intra-group trading*

SG → CV

- Intra –group revenue and cost of sales:
  Cancel $300,000 out of revenue and cost of sales

- PUP = $300,000 × 2/3 in inventories × 25/125 mark up = $40,000
  Increase cost of sales by $40,000 and reduce PFY/TCI in NCI working (as subsidiary is the seller)

5   *Intra-group dividend*

CV's share of SG's dividend = $60,000 x 75% = $45,000

Cancel $45,000 out of 'Investment income'

(b)   **Non-controlling interests (under partial goodwill method and if parent sells to subsidiary for intra-group trading)**

Non-controlling interests

	PFY $'000	TCI $'000
Per question	350	370
NCI share	× 25%	× 25%
	= 87.5	= 92.5

Tutorial note: PUP is only deducted when the subsidiary is the seller and the parent is the seller here. Impairment loss for the year is only deducted under the full goodwill method and the partial goodwill method is used in part (b).

8.2   Mid year acquisition

(a) **Goodwill**

	$'000	$'000
Consideration transferred		4,000
Non-controlling interests (1,000 × 10% × $4.50)		450
Net assets at acquisition as represented by::		
Share capital	1,000	
Share premium	500	
Retained earnings (W1)	1,750	
Fair value adjustment	100	
		(3,350)
		1,100
Impairment losses to date		(20)
Goodwill at 31 December 20X7		1,080

Workings

1   *Group structure*

JT

1.4.X7 | 90%

MB

1.1.X7   1.4.X7

Acquisition   ——— Consolidate 9/12 ———→

SOFP: Consolid

MB – PAR (1.4.X7)

	$'000
Retained earnings at 1.1.X7	1,500
For the 3 months to 1.4.X7 (1000 x 3/12)	250
Retained earnings at 1.4.X7	1,750

(b) JT GROUP – CONSOLIDATED STATEMENT OF PROFIT OR LOSS
FOR THE YEAR ENDED 31 DECEMBER 20X7

	$'000
Revenue $(10,000 + (4,000 \times \frac{9}{12}) - 200)$	12,800
Cost of sales and expenses $(6,000 + (2,100 \times \frac{9}{12}) - 200 + 15 + 20 + 10))$	(7,420)
Profit before tax	5,380
Income tax expense $(1,400 + (900 \times \frac{9}{12}))$	(2,075)
Profit for the year	3,305
Attributable to:	
Equity holders of the parent	3,233
Non-controlling interest $[((1,000 \times \frac{9}{12}) - 20 - 10) \times 10\%]$	72
	3,305

8.3   Exam standard practice

SM GROUP – CONSOLIDATED STATEMENT OF CHANGES IN EQUITY

	Equity attributable to owners of the parent $'000	Non-controlling interest $'000	Total $'000
Balance at 1 July 20X4 (balancing figure)	537,500	32,500	570,000
Issue of shares	25,000	-	25,000
Total comprehensive income for the year (W4)	96,750	9,750	106,500
Dividends (25% × $10m)	(16,000)	(2,500)	(18,500)
Balance at 30 June 20X5 (W5)/(W6)	643,250	39,750	683,000

Workings

1   *Group structure*

SM

1.7.X2   37.5m/50m = 75%

↓

CE

PAR = $80m – $50m = $30m

2   *Unrealised profit*

CE →SM

PUP = $15m × 1/3 in inventory x 25/125 mark up = $1m
Dr CE's cost of sales (& CE's retained earnings) $1m
Cr Inventories $1m

3   *Intragroup dividend*

Intragroup dividend income = 75% × $10m = $7.5m → Cancel out of SM's profit/total comprehensive income

4   *Consolidated total comprehensive income for the year*

	$'000
Consolidated TCI [($75m – $7.5m (W3)] + [$40m – $1m (W2))]	106,500
Total comprehensive income attributable to:	
Owners of parent (balancing figure)	96,750
Non-controlling interest ($40m – $1m (W2)) × 25%	9,750
	106,500

5   *Consolidated equity at 30 June 20X5*

	SM $'000	CE $'000
Per question	584,000	160,000
PUP (W2)		(1,000)
Pre-acquisition equity		(80,000)
		79,000
Share CE post acquisition (75% × $79m)	59,250	
	643,250	

208 | 8: The consolidated statement of profit or loss and other comprehensive income and the statement of changes in equity

PART B GROUP FINANCIAL STATEMENTS

6   *Non-controlling interest at 30 June 20X5*

	$'000
NCI at acquisition (25% × $80m)	20,000
NCI share of post acquisition reserves ($79m (W5) × 25%)	19,750
	39,750

7   *Proof of consolidated equity at 1 July 20X4*

	SM $'000	*CE* $'000
Per question	500,000	130,000
Pre-acquisition equity		(80,000)
		50,000
Share CE post acquisition (75% × $50m)	37,500	
	537,500	

8   *Proof of non-controlling interest at 1 July 20X4*

	$'000
NCI at acquisition (W6)	20,000
NCI share of post acquisition reserves ($50m (W7) x 25%)	12,500
	32,500

Now try this question from the Exam Question Bank

Number	Level	Marks	Time
Q11	Examination	15	27 mins

ASSOCIATES AND JOINT ARRANGEMENTS

Some investments are not subsidiaries but they may be much more than simple trade investments. The most important of these are associates and joint arrangements, which are the subject of this chapter.

Associates and joint ventures have to be included in consolidated financial statements, according to the revised IAS 28, under the **equity method.** Section 1

shows how to do this. You have already studied associates in paper F1.

Joint arrangements can take a number of forms and section 2 will look at the IFRS 11 provisions and the different forms of joint arrangement.

Section 3 deals with a new standard, IFRS 12, on the disclosures about interests in other entities needed in the financial statements.

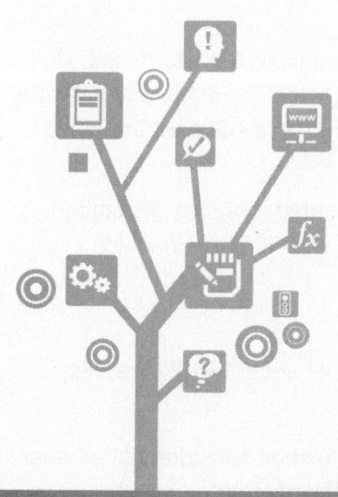

topic list	learning outcomes	syllabus references	ability required
1 IAS 28 *Investments in associates and joint ventures*	A1	A1(iv)	Application
2 IFRS 11 *Joint arrangements*	A1	A1(iv)	Application
3 IFRS 12 *Disclosure of interests in other entities*	A1	A1(iv)	Application

1 IAS 28 *Investments in associates and joint ventures*

11/10, 9/12

Introduction

We looked at investments in associates and joint ventures briefly in Chapter 6. IAS 28 Investments in associates and joint ventures covers this type of investment.

Students who studied F1 will find that most of this is revision.

1.1 Definitions

In this section we will focus on **associates.** The criteria that exist to identify a **joint venture** will be covered in Section 2, although the method for accounting for a joint venture is identical to that used for associates.

Some of the important definitions in Chapter 6 are repeated here, with some additional important terms.

KEY TERMS

ASSOCIATE An entity over which an investor has significant influence.

SIGNIFICANT INFLUENCE is the power to participate in the financial and operating policy decisions of an economic activity but is not control or joint control over those policies.

JOINT CONTROL is the contractually agreed sharing of control over an economic activity.

EQUITY METHOD. A method of accounting whereby the investment is initially recorded at cost and adjusted thereafter for the post acquisition change in the investor's share of investee's net assets. The investor's profit or loss includes its share of the investee's profit or loss and the investor's other comprehensive income includes its share of the investee's other comprehensive income.

We have already looked at how the **status** of an investment in an associate should be determined. Go back to Chapter 6 to revise it if necessary. (Note that, as for an investment in a subsidiary, any **potential voting rights** should be taken into account in assessing whether the investor has **significant influence** over the investee.)

IAS 28 requires all investments in associates and joint ventures to be accounted for using the equity method, *unless* the investment is classified as 'held for sale' in accordance with IFRS 5, in which case it should be accounted for under IFRS 5.

An investor is exempt from applying the equity method if:

(a)   It is a parent exempt from preparing consolidated financial statements under IAS 27 (revised) or

(b)   All of the following apply:

    (i)   The investor is a **wholly-owned subsidiary** or it is a **partially owned subsidiary** of another entity and its other owners, including those not otherwise entitled to vote, have been informed about, and do not object to, the investor not applying the equity method;

    (ii)   Its securities are **not publicly traded**;

    (iii)   It is **not in the process of issuing securities** in public securities markets; and

    (iv)   The **ultimate or intermediate parent** publishes consolidated financial statements that comply with International Financial Reporting Standards.

IAS 28 **does not allow** an investment in an associate to be excluded from equity accounting when an investee operates under severe long-term restrictions that significantly impair its ability to transfer funds to the investor. Significant influence must be lost before the equity method ceases to be applicable.

The use of the equity method should be **discontinued** from the date that the investor **ceases to have significant influence**.

From that date, the investor shall account for the investment in accordance with IAS 39 *Financial instruments: recognition and measurement*. The fair value of the retained interest must be regarded as its fair value on initial recognition as a financial asset under IAS 39.

1.2 Separate financial statements of the investor

Note that in the separate financial statements of the investor, an interest in an associate is accounted for either:

(a)   At **cost**, *or*

(b)   In accordance with **IAS 39.**

1.3 Application of the equity method: consolidated accounts

KEY POINT

The **equity method** should be applied in the consolidated accounts:

- **Statement of financial position:** investment in associate at cost plus (or minus) the group's share of the associate's post-acquisition profits (or losses) less impairment losses on the investment in associate to date.

- **Profit or loss (statement of profit or loss and other comprehensive income):** group share of associate's profit after tax.

- **Other comprehensive income (statement of profit or loss and other comprehensive income):** group share of associate's other comprehensive income after tax.

Many of the procedures required to apply the equity method are the same as are required for full consolidation. In particular, **fair value adjustments** are required and the group share of **intra-group unrealised profits** must be excluded.

1.3.1 Consolidated statement of profit or loss and other comprehensive income

The basic principle is that the investing company (X Co) should take account of its **share of the earnings** of the associate, Y Co, whether or not Y Co distributes the earnings as dividends. X Co achieves this by adding to consolidated profit the group's share of Y Co's profit after tax.

Notice the difference between this treatment and the **consolidation** of a subsidiary company's results. If Y Co were a subsidiary X Co would take credit for the whole of its sales revenue, cost of sales etc and would then prepare a reconciliation at the end of the statement showing how much of the group profit and total comprehensive income is owned by non-controlling interests.

Under equity accounting, the associate's sales revenue, cost of sales and so on are *not* **amalgamated** with those of the group. Instead the **group share** only of the associate's **profit after tax** and **other comprehensive income** for the year is included in the relevant sections of the statement of profit or loss and other comprehensive income.

1.3.2 Consolidated statement of financial position

A figure for **investment in associates** is shown which at the time of the acquisition must be stated at cost. This amount will increase (decrease) each year by the amount of the group's share of the associate's total comprehensive income retained for the year. Any impairments to date of the investment in the associate are then deducted from both the investment and consolidated reserves.

The group share of the associate's reserves are also included within the group reserves figure in the equity section of the consolidated statement of financial position.

Example: Associate

P Co, a company with subsidiaries, acquires 25,000 of the 100,000 $1 ordinary shares in A Co for $60,000 on 1 January 20X8. In the year to 31 December 20X8, A Co earns a profit for the year of $24,000, from which it declares a dividend of $6,000.

How will A Co's results be accounted for in the individual and consolidated accounts of P Co for the year ended 31 December 20X8?

Solution

In the **individual accounts** of P Co, the investment will be recorded on 1 January 20X8 at cost. Unless there is an impairment in the value of the investment (see below), this amount will remain in the individual statement of financial position of P Co permanently. The only entry in P Co's statement of profit or loss and other comprehensive income will be to record dividends received (25% x $6,000 = $1,500). For the year ended 31 December 20X8, P Co will:

DEBIT	Cash	$1,500	
CREDIT	Income from shares in associates		$1,500

In the **consolidated accounts** of P Co equity accounting principles will be used to account for the investment in A Co. Consolidated profit for the year will include the group's share of A Co's profit after tax (25% × $24,000 = $6,000).

To the extent that this has been distributed as dividend, it is already included in P Co's individual accounts and will automatically be brought into the consolidated results. That part of the group's profit share which has not been distributed as dividend ($4,500) will be brought into consolidation by the following adjustment.

DEBIT	Investment in associates	$4,500	
CREDIT	Income from shares in associates		$4,500

The asset 'Investment in associates' is then stated at $64,500, being cost plus the group share of post-acquisition retained profits.

1.4 Consolidated statement of profit or loss and other comprehensive income

The treatment of associates' profits in the following proforma should be studied carefully.

1.4.1 Pro-forma consolidated statement of profit or loss and other comprehensive income

The following is a **suggested layout** (for a statement of profit or loss and other comprehensive income) for a company having subsidiaries as well as associates.

	$'000
Revenue	1,400
Cost of sales	(770)
Gross profit	630
Distribution costs and administrative expenses	(290)
	340
Interest and similar income receivable	30
	370
Finance costs	(20)
	350
Share of profit (after tax) of associate	17
Profit before taxation	367
Income tax expense (parent company and subsidiaries)	(145)
Profit for the year	222
Profit attributable to:	
Owners of the parent	200
Non-controlling interest	22
	222

1.5 Consolidated statement of financial position

As explained earlier, the consolidated statement of financial position will contain an **asset 'Investment in associates'**. The amount at which this asset is stated will be its original cost plus the **group's share** of the associate's **total comprehensive income earned since acquisition** which has not been distributed as dividends. Any **impairments** of the investment in associate to date must be **deducted**.

1.6 Other accounting considerations

The following points are also relevant and are similar to a parent-subsidiary consolidation situation.

(a)   Use financial statements drawn up to the **same reporting date.**

(b)   If this is impracticable, adjust the financial statements for **significant transactions/ events** in the intervening period. The difference between the reporting date of the associate and that of the investor must be no more than three months.

(c)   Use **uniform accounting policies** for like transactions and events in similar circumstances, adjusting the associate's statements to reflect group policies if necessary.

(d)   If an associate has **cumulative preference shares** held by outside interests, calculate the share of the investor's profits/losses after adjusting for the preference dividends (whether or not declared).

1.7 'Upstream' and 'downstream' transactions

A group (made up of a parent and its consolidated subsidiaries) may trade with its associates. This introduces the possibility of unrealised profits if goods sold within the group are still in inventories at the year end. This is similar to unrealised profits arising on trading between a parent and a subsidiary. The important thing to remember is that when an **associate** is involved, **only the group's share is eliminated**.

The precise accounting entries depend on the direction of the transaction. 'Upstream' transactions are sales from an associate to the investor. 'Downstream' transactions are sales of assets from the investor to an associate.

The double entry in the consolidated statement of financial position is as follows, where A% is the parent's holding in the associate, and PUP is the provision for unrealised profit.

DEBIT	Retained earnings of parent	PUP × A%
CREDIT	Group inventories	PUP × A%

For upstream transactions (associate sells to parent/subsidiary) where the parent holds the inventories.

OR

DEBIT	Retained earnings of parent /subsidiary	PUP × A%
CREDIT	Investment in associate	PUP × A%

For downstream transactions, (parent/subsidiary sells to associate) where the associate holds the inventory.

In the consolidated statement of profit or loss and other comprehensive income, for upstream transactions (associate sells to parent/subsidiary), the 'share of associate's profit' is reduced by the group share of the unrealised profit (resulting in the above debit to retained earnings). For downstream transactions (parent/subsidiary sells to associate), 'cost of sales' is increased by the group share of the unrealised profit (resulting in the above debit to retained earnings).

Example: Downstream transaction

A Co, a parent with subsidiaries, holds 25% of the equity shares in B Co. During the year, A Co makes sales of $1,000,000 to B Co at cost plus a 25% mark-up. At the year-end, B Co has all these goods still in inventories.

Solution

A Co has made an unrealised profit of $200,000 (1,000,000 × 25/125) on its sales to the associate (B Co). The group's share of this is 25%, ie $50,000. This must be eliminated.

The double entry is:

DEBIT	A: Retained earnings	$50,000	
CREDIT	Investment in associate (B)		$50,000

Because the sale was made to the associate, the group's share of the unsold inventories forms part of the investment in associate at the year end.

In the consolidated statement of profit or loss, the 'share of the profit of the associate' would also be reduced by $50,000.

If the sale had been from the associate B to A, ie an upstream transaction, the double entry would have been.

DEBIT	A: Retained earnings	$50,000	
CREDIT	A: Inventories		$50,000

If preparing the consolidated statement of profit or loss and other comprehensive income, you would add the $50,000 to cost of sales, as the **parent** made the sales in this example.

1.8 Associate's losses

When the equity method is being used and the investor's share of losses of the associate equals or exceeds its interest in the associate, the investor should **discontinue** including its share of further losses. The investment is reported at nil value. The interest in the associate is normally the carrying amount of the investment in the associate, but it also includes any other long-term interests, for example, preference shares or long term receivables or loans.

After the investor's interest is reduced to nil, **additional losses** should only be recognised where the investor has incurred obligations or made payments on behalf of the associate (for example, if it has guaranteed amounts owed to third parties by the associate).

Should the associate return to profit, the parent may resume recognising its share of profits only after they equal the share of losses not recognised.

1.9 Impairment losses

IAS 39 sets out a list of indications that a financial asset (including an associate) may have become impaired. Any impairment loss is recognised in accordance with IAS 36 *Impairment of assets* for each associate as a single asset. There is no separate testing for impairment of goodwill, as the goodwill that forms part of the carrying amount of an investment in an associate is not separately recognised. An impairment loss is not allocated to any asset, including goodwill, that forms part of the carrying amount of the investment in associate. Accordingly any reversal of that impairment loss is recognised in accordance with IAS 36 to the extent that the recoverable amount of the investment subsequently increases.

Exam alert

In the exam, impairment losses on the associate for the current year should be deducted from the 'share of the associate's profits'.

1.10 Non-controlling interest/associate held by a subsidiary

Where the investment in an associate is held by a subsidiary in which there are non-controlling interests, the non-controlling interest shown in the consolidated financial statements of the group should include the **non-controlling interest of the subsidiary's interest** in the results and post-acquisition reserves of the associate.

This means that the group accounts must include the 'gross' share of post-acquisition reserves and post-tax profits and the **non-controlling interest** should be accounted **for separately**. For example, we will suppose that P Co owns 60% of S Co which owns 25% of A Co. A Co is then an indirect associate (or sub-associate) of P Co. The relevant amounts for inclusion in the consolidated financial statements of the P Co group would be as follows.

CONSOLIDATED STATEMENT OF PROFIT OR LOSS AND OTHER COMPREHENSIVE INCOME

Profit before interest and tax (P 100% + S 100%)
Share of profit after tax of associate (A 25%)
Tax (P 100% + S 100%)
Profit for the year attributable to:
Owners of the parent (P 100% + S 60% + A 15%*)
Non-controlling interest (S 40% + A 10%**)

CONSOLIDATED STATEMENT OF FINANCIAL POSITION
Investment in associate (figures based on 25% holding)
Non-controlling interest (NCI at acq'n + (40% × post-acq'n reserves of S) + (10%** × post-acq'n reserves of A))
Group reserves ((100% × P) + (60% × post-acquisition of S) + (15% * × post-acquisition of A))

Notes
* Share of A attributable to owners of the parent = 60% × 25% = 15%
** Share of A attributable to non-controlling interests of S = 40% × 25% = 10%

1.11 Comprehensive question

The following question provides comprehensive revision of the topics covered up to this point in the chapter. It is written in the style of a F2 question, but only includes issues that you should remember from your earlier studies. It is important that you are confident about these techniques before moving on to the new and more complicated group accounting topics that are tested in paper F2.

Question 9.1	Basic group accounting techniques

Learning outcomes A1

Otway, a public limited company, acquired a subsidiary, Holgarth, on 1 July 20X2 and an associate, Batterbee, on 1 July 20X5. The details of the acquisitions at the respective dates are as follows:

Investee	Ordinary share capital of $1		Reserves		Fair value of net assets at acquisition	Cost of investment	Ordinary share capital acquired
		Share premium	Retained earnings	Revaluation surplus			
	$m	$m	$m	$m	$m	$m	$m
Holgarth	400	140	120	40	800	765	320
Batterbee	220	83	195	54	652	203	55

The draft financial statements for the year ended 30 June 20X6 are as follows.

STATEMENTS OF FINANCIAL POSITION AS AT 30 JUNE 20X6

	Otway $m	Holgarth $m	Batterbee $m
Non-current assets			
Property, plant and equipment	1,012	920	442
Intangible assets	–	350	27
Investment in Holgarth	765	–	–
Investment in Batterbee	203	–	–
	1,980	1,270	469
Current assets			
Inventories	620	1,460	214
Trade receivables	950	529	330
Cash and cash equivalents	900	510	45
	2,470	2,499	589
	4,450	3,769	1,058
Equity			
Share capital	1,000	400	220
Share premium	200	140	83
Retained earnings	1,128	809	263
Revaluation surplus	142	70	62
	2,470	1,419	628
Non-current liabilities			
Deferred tax liability	100	50	36
Current liabilities			
Trade and other payables	1,880	2,300	394
	4,450	3,769	1,058

STATEMENTS OF PROFIT OR LOSS AND OTHER COMPREHENSIVE INCOME
FOR THE YEAR ENDED 30 JUNE 20X6

	Otway $m	Holgarth $m	Batterbee $m
Revenue	4,480	4,200	1,460
Cost of sales	(2,690)	(2,940)	(1,020)
Gross profit	1,790	1,260	440
Distribution costs and administrative expenses	(620)	(290)	(196)
Finance costs	(50)	(80)	(24)
Dividend income (from Holgarth and Batterbee)	260	-	-
Profit before tax	1,380	890	220
Income tax expense	(330)	(274)	(72)
Profit for the year	1,050	616	148
Other comprehensive income that will not be reclassified to profit or loss			
Gain on revaluation of property	30	7	12
Income tax expense relating to other comp income	(9)	(2)	(4)
Other comprehensive income, net of tax	21	5	8
Total comprehensive income for the year	1,071	621	156
Dividends paid in the year	250	300	80
Retained earnings brought forward	328	493	195

Additional information:

(a) Neither Holgarth nor Batterbee had any reserves other than retained earnings and share premium at the date of acquisition. Neither issued new shares since acquisition.

(b) The fair value difference on the subsidiary relates to property, plant and equipment being depreciated through cost of sales over a remaining useful life of 10 years from the acquisition date. The fair value difference on the associate relates to a piece of land (which has not been sold since acquisition).

(c) Group policy is to measure non-controlling interests at acquisition at fair value. The fair value of the non-controlling interests on 1 July 20X2 was calculated as $188m.

(d)   During the year ended 30 June 20X6 Holgarth sold goods to Otway for $1,300 million. The company makes a profit of 30% on the selling price. $140 million of these goods were held by Otway on 30 June 20X6.

(e)   Annual impairment tests have indicated impairment losses of $100m relating to the recognised goodwill of Holgarth including $25m in the current year. The Otway Group recognises impairment losses on goodwill in administrative expenses. No impairment losses to date have been necessary for the investment in Batterbee.

Required

Prepare the statement of profit or loss and other comprehensive income for the year ended 30 June 20X6 for the Otway Group and a statement of financial position at that date.

Exam alert

It is not unusual in the exam to have both an associate and a subsidiary to account for in a consolidation.

1.12 Summary of entries

Consolidated statement of profit or loss and other comprehensive income	Profit after tax	Include group share of associate, disclosed separately.	
	Other comprehensive income	Include group share of associate, disclosed separately.	
Consolidated statement of financial position	Interests in associated companies should be stated at:		$
	(a) Cost		X
	(b) Share of post-acquisition retained earnings		X
	(c) Less: Impairment losses to date		(X)
			X
	Also disclose group's share of post-acquisition reserves of associates and movements therein.		

Section summary

IAS 28 deals with accounting for associates. The definitions are important as they govern the accounting treatment, particularly 'significant influence'

The **equity method** should be applied in the consolidated accounts:

*   **Statement of financial position:** investment in associate at cost plus (or minus) the group's share of the associate's post-acquisition profits (or losses) less impairment losses to date.

*   **Statement of profit or loss and other comprehensive income:**

    –   group share of profits of the associate (profit after tax)
    –   group share of other comprehensive income of the associate

2 IFRS 11 *Joint arrangements*

Introduction

IFRS 11 classes joint arrangements as either **joint operations** or **joint ventures**.

The classification of a joint arrangement as a joint operation or a joint venture depends upon the **rights and obligations** of the parties to the arrangement.

Joint arrangements are often found when each party can **contribute in different ways** to the activity. For example, one party may provide finance, another purchases or manufactures goods, while a third offers his marketing skills.

IFRS 11 *Joint arrangements* covers all types of joint arrangements. It is not concerned with the accounts of the joint arrangement itself (if separate accounts are maintained), but rather **how the interest in a joint arrangement is accounted for by each party.**

2.1 Definitions

The IFRS begins by listing some important definitions.

KEY TERMS

JOINT ARRANGEMENT An arrangement of which two or more parties have **joint control**.

JOINT CONTROL. The contractually agreed sharing of control of an arrangement, which exists only when decisions about the relevant activities require the **unanimous consent** of the parties sharing control.

JOINT OPERATION. A joint arrangement whereby the parties that have joint control of the arrangement have **rights to the assets and obligations for the liabilities** relating to the arrangement.

JOINT VENTURE. A joint arrangement whereby the parties that have joint control of the arrangement have **rights to the net assets** of the arrangement.

(IFRS 11)

2.2 Forms of joint arrangement

IFRS 11 classes joint arrangements as either joint operations or joint ventures. The classification of a joint arrangement as a joint operation or a joint venture depends upon the rights and obligations of the parties to the arrangement.

A **joint operation** is a joint arrangement whereby the parties that have joint control (the joint operators) have rights to the assets, and obligations for the liabilities, of that joint arrangement. A joint arrangement that is **not structured through a separate entity** is always a joint operation.

A **joint venture** is a joint arrangement whereby the parties that have **joint control** (the joint venturers) of the arrangement have **rights to the net assets** of the arrangement.

A **joint arrangement** that is structured through a **separate entity** may be either a joint operation or a joint venture. In order to ascertain the classification, the parties to the arrangement should assess the terms of the contractual arrangement together with any other facts or circumstances to assess whether they have:

(a)   Rights to the assets, and obligations for the liabilities, in relation to the arrangement (indicating a joint operation)

(b)   Rights to the net assets of the arrangement (indicating a joint venture)

Detailed guidance is provided in the appendices to IFRS 11 in order to help this assessment, giving consideration to, for example, the wording contained within contractual arrangements.

IFRS 11 summarises the basic issues that underlie the classifications in the following diagram:

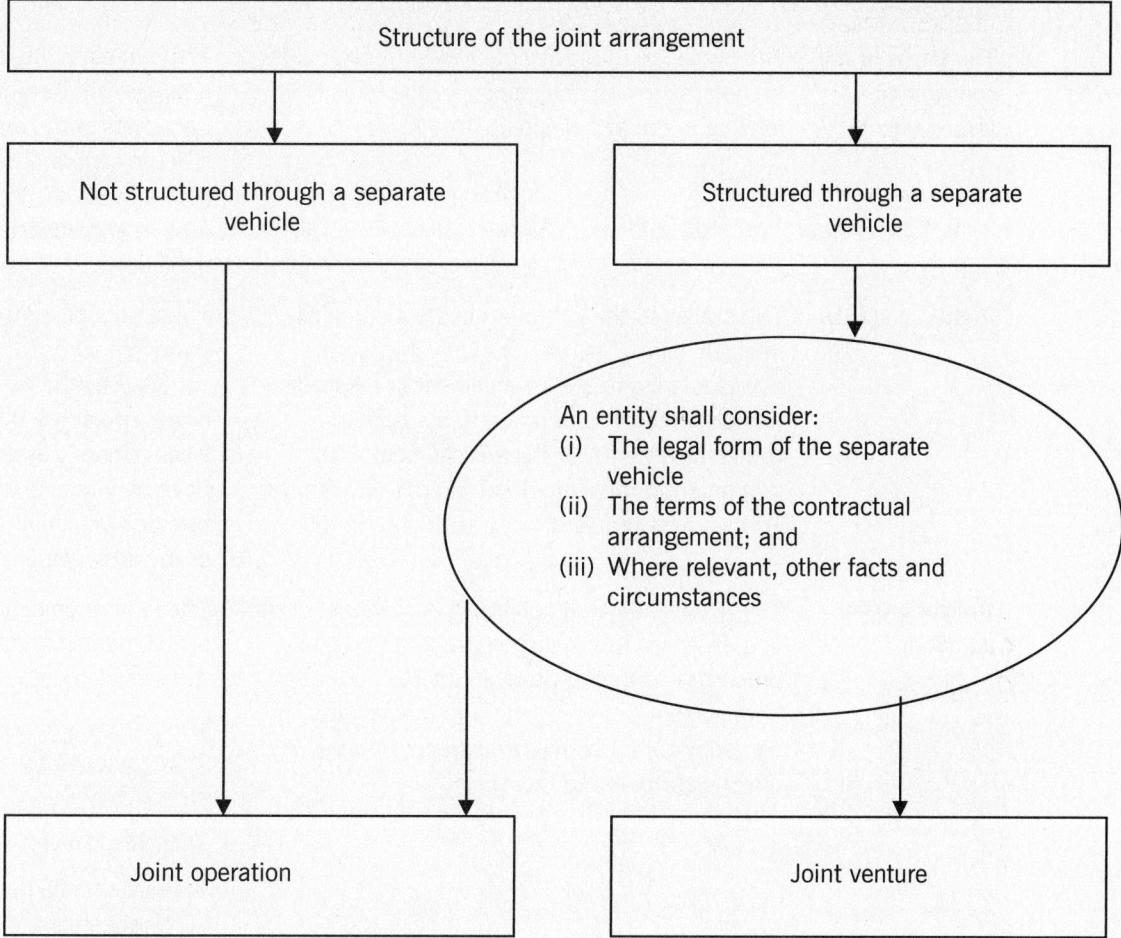

2.2.1 Contractual arrangement

The existence of a contractual agreement distinguishes a joint arrangement from an investment in an associate. **If there is no contractual arrangement, then a joint arrangement does not exist**.

Evidence of a contractual arrangement could be in one of several forms.

(a)   **Contract** between the parties
(b)   **Minutes** of discussion between the parties
(c)   Incorporation in the **articles or by-laws** of the joint venture

The contractual arrangement is usually **in writing**, whatever its form, and it will deal with the following issues surrounding the joint venture.

(a)   **Its purpose, activity and duration**
(b)   The appointment of its **board of directors** (or equivalent) and the **voting rights** of the parties
(c)   **Capital contributions** to it by the parties
(d)   How its output, income, expenses or results are **shared** between the parties

It is the contractual arrangement which establishes **joint control** over the joint venture, so that no single party can control the activity of the joint venture on its own.

The terms of the contractual arrangement are key to deciding whether the arrangement is a joint venture or joint operation. IFRS 11 includes a table of issues to consider and explains the influence of a range of points that could be included in the contract . The table is summarised below:

	Joint operation	Joint venture
The terms of the contractual arrangement	The parties to the joint arrangement have rights to the assets, and obligations for the liabilities, relating to the arrangement.	The parties to the joint arrangement have rights to the net assets of the arrangement (ie it is the separate vehicle, not the parties, that has rights to the assets, and obligations for the liabilities).
Rights to assets	The parties to the joint arrangement share all interests (eg rights, title or ownership) in the assets relating to the arrangement in a specified proportion (eg in proportion to the parties' ownership interest in the arrangement or in proportion to the activity carried out through the arrangement that is directly attributed to them).	The assets brought into the arrangement or subsequently acquired by the joint arrangement are the arrangement's assets. The parties have no interests (ie no rights, title or ownership) in the assets of the arrangement.
Obligations for liabilities	The parties share all liabilities, obligations, costs and expenses in a specified proportion (eg in proportion to their ownership interest in the arrangement or in proportion to the activity carried out through the arrangement that is directly attributed to them). The parties to the joint arrangement are liable for claims by third parties.	The joint arrangement is liable for the debts and obligations of the arrangement. The parties are liable to the arrangement only to the extent of: Their respective: • Investments in the arrangement, or • Obligations to contribute any unpaid or additional capital to the arrangement, or • Both Creditors of the joint arrangement do not have rights of recourse against any party.
Revenues, expenses, profit or loss	The contractual arrangement establishes the allocation of revenues and expenses on the basis of the relative performance of each party to the joint arrangement. For example, the contractual arrangement might establish that revenues and expenses are allocated on the basis of the capacity that each party uses in a plant operated jointly.	The contractual arrangement establishes each party's share in the profit or loss relating to the activities of the arrangement.
Guarantees	The provision of guarantees to third parties, or the commitment by the parties to provide them, does not, by itself, determine that the joint arrangement is a joint operation.	

Question 9.2   Joint arrangement

Learning outcomes A1

This question is based on illustrative example 2 from IFRS 11.

Two real estate companies (the parties) set up a separate vehicle (Supermall) for the purpose of acquiring and operating a shopping centre. The contractual arrangement between the parties establishes joint control of the activities that are conducted in Supermall. The main feature of Supermall's legal form is that the entity, not the parties, has rights to the assets, and obligations for the liabilities, relating to the arrangement. These activities include the rental of the retail units, managing the car park, maintaining the centre and its equipment, such as lifts, and building the reputation and customer base for the centre as a whole.

The terms of the contractual arrangement are such that:

(a)   Supermall owns the shopping centre. The contractual arrangement does not specify that the parties have rights to the shopping centre.

(b)   The parties are not liable in respect of the debts, liabilities or obligations of Supermall. If Supermall is unable to pay any of its debts or other liabilities or to discharge its obligations to third parties, the liability of each party to any third party will be limited to the unpaid amount of that party's capital contribution.

(c)   The parties have the right to sell or pledge their interests in Supermall.

(d)   Each party receives a share of the income from operating the shopping centre (which is the rental income net of the operating costs) in accordance with its interest in Supermall.

Required

Explain how Supermall should be classified in accordance with IFRS 11 *Joint arrangement*.

2.3 Accounting treatment

KEY POINT

> The accounting treatment of joint arrangements depends on whether the arrangement is a joint venture or joint operation.

2.3.1 Accounting for joint operations

IFRS 11 requires that a joint operator recognises line-by-line the following in relation to its interest in a joint operation:

(a)   Its assets, including its share of any jointly held assets
(b)   Its liabilities, including its share of any jointly incurred liabilities
(c)   Its revenue from the sale of its share of the output arising from the joint operation
(d)   Its share of the revenue from the sale of the output by the joint operation, and
(e)   Its expenses, including its share of any expenses incurred jointly.

This treatment is applicable in both the separate and consolidated financial statements of the joint operator.

Question 9.3   Joint operations

Learning outcomes A1

Can you think of examples of situations where this type of joint venture might take place?

2.3.2 Joint ventures

KEY POINT

> **IFRS 11** and **IAS 28** require **joint ventures** to be accounted for using **the equity method**.

Prior to the new group accounting standards issued in 2011, the old standard on joint ventures (IAS 31) permitted either equity accounting or proportionate consolidation to be used for joint ventures. The choice has now been removed. (Proportionate consolidation meant including the investor's share of the assets, liabilities, income and expenses of the joint venture, line by line).

The rules for equity accounting are included in IAS 28 *Associates and joint ventures.* These have been covered in detail in section 1 above.

2.3.3 Application of IAS 28 (2011) to joint ventures

The consolidated statement of financial position is prepared by:

(a)   Including the interest in the joint venture at cost plus share of post-acquisition reserves less impairment losses to date

(b)   Including the group share of the post-acquisition total comprehensive income in group reserves

The consolidated statement of profit or loss and other comprehensive income will include:

(a)   The group share of the joint venture's profit or loss
(b)   The group share of the joint venture's other comprehensive income.

The use of the equity method should be **discontinued** from the date on which the joint venturer ceases to have joint control over, or have significant influence on, a joint venture.

2.3.4 Transactions between a joint venturer and a joint venture

Upstream transactions

When a joint venture sells assets to the joint venturer, the joint venturer should not recognise its share of the profit made by the joint venture on the transaction in question until it resells the assets to an independent third party, ie until the profit is realised.

Therefore, as for an associate, the **group share of the unrealised profit or loss** in year end inventory or non-current assets must be **eliminated**.

Downstream transactions

When the joint venturer sells assets to the joint venture, as above, the group **share of the unrealised profit or loss** in year end inventory or non-current assets must be **eliminated** unless:

(a)   There is a loss; and

(b)   The transaction provides evidence of a reduction in the net realisable value of the asset or of an impairment loss.

In this instance, the **loss should be reocognised in full** by the joint venturer.

Section summary

- There are two types of joint arrangement: joint operations and joint ventures

- A contractual arrangement must exist which establishes joint control

- Joint control is important: unanimous consent of the parties sharing control is required

- Joint operations are accounted for by including the investor's share of assets, liabilities, income and expenses as per the contractual arrangement

- Joint ventures are accounted for using the equity method as under IAS 28

3 IFRS 12 *Disclosure of interests in other entities*

IFRS 12 *Disclosure of interests in other entities* was issued in May 2011 as part of the 'package of five standards' relating to consolidation. It removes all disclosure requirements from other standards relating to group accounting and provides guidance applicable to consolidated financial statements.

The standard requires disclosure of:

(a)   The significant judgments and assumptions made in determining the nature of an interest in another entity or arrangement, and in determining the type of joint arrangement in which an interest is held.

(b)   Information about interests in subsidiaries, associates, joint arrangements and structured entities that are not controlled by an investor.

3.1 Disclosure for subsidiaries

The following disclosures are required in respect of subsidiaries:

(a)   The interest that non-controlling interests have in the group's activities and cash flows, including the name of relevant subsidiaries, their principal place of business, and the interest and voting rights of the non-controlling interests

(b)   Nature and extent of significant restrictions on an investor's ability to use group assets and liabilities

(c)   Nature of the risks associated with an entity's interests in consolidated structured entities, such as the provision of financial support

(d)   Consequences of changes in ownership interest in subsidiary (whether control is lost or not)

3.2 Disclosure for associates and joint arrangements

The following disclosures are required in respect of associates and joint arrangements:

(a)   Nature, extent and financial effects of an entity's interests in associates or joint arrangements, including name of the investee, principal place of business, the investor's interest in the investee, method of accounting for the investee and restrictions on the investee's ability to transfer funds to the investor

(b)   Risks associated with an interest in an associate or joint venture

(c)   Summarised financial information, with more detail required for joint ventures than for associates.

3.3 Disclosure for unconsolidated structured entities

IFRS 12 defines a structured entity as 'an entity that has been designed so that voting or similar rights are not the dominant factor in deciding who controls the entity, such as when any voting rights relate to administrative tasks only and the relevant activities are directed by means of contractual arrangements'.

If these structured entities are not consolidated in the group accounts, the following disclosures are required:

(a)   Nature and extent of interests in unconsolidated structure entities including nature, purpose, size and activities of the structured entity and how the structured entity is financed.

(b)   Risks associated with the unconsolidated structured entity including the assets and liabilities in its financial statements relating to unconsolidated structured entities, the entity's maximum exposure to loss from its interest in unconsolidated structured entities and details of any financial support the entity has provided or intends to provide to unconsolidated structured entities.

Section summary

IFRS 12 deals with the disclosures required for each type of investment.

Chapter Roundup

- ✓ **IAS 28** deals with accounting for associates. The definitions are important as they govern the accounting treatment, particularly **'significant influence'**.

- ✓ The equity method should be applied in the consolidated accounts:

  - • **Statement of financial position:** investment in associate at cost plus (or minus) the group's share of the associate's post-acquisition profits (or losses) less impairment losses to date

  - • **Statement of profit or loss and other comprehensive income:**

    - – group share of profits of the associate (profit after tax)
    - – group share of other comprehensive income of the associate

- ✓ There are two **types of joint arrangement**: joint ventures and jointly controlled operations

- ✓ A **contractual arrangement** must exist which establishes joint control

- ✓ **Joint control** is important: **unanimous consent** of the parties sharing joint control is required

- ✓ **Joint operations** are accounted for by including the investor's share of assets, liabilities, income and expenses as per the contractual arrangement

- ✓ **Joint ventures** are accounted for using the **equity method** as under IAS 28

- ✓ IFRS 12 deals with the disclosures required for each type of investment.

Quick Quiz

1   An associate is an _____ over which the investor has _____ . *Complete the blanks*.

2   If a company holds 20% or more of the shares of another company, it is presumed that the company has significant influence (unless it can be clearly demonstrated that this is not the case). True or false?

3   What is significant influence?

4   What is the effect of the equity method on the statement of profit or loss and other comprehensive income and the statement of financial position?

5   A joint venture is a joint arrangement whereby the parties that have_____ of the arrangement have rights to the_____of the arrangement. *Complete the blanks.*

6   What forms of evidence of a contractual agreement might exist?

7   How should a venturer account for its share of a joint operation?

8   How should a venturer account for its share of a joint venture?

9   A joint arrangement that is structured through a separate vehicle will always be a joint venture. True or false?

Answers to Quick Quiz

1   An associate is an **entity** over which the investor has a **significant influence**.

2   True.

3   The power to participate in the financial and operating decisions of the investee but not control or joint control.

4   (a)   *Statement of profit or loss and other comprehensive income.* Investing entity includes its share of the profit for the year of the associate or joint venture.

    (b)   *Statement of financial position.* The investment in associates or joint ventures is initially recorded at cost. This will then increase each year by the group share of the associate/joint venture's post acquisition reserves. Any impairment losses in the investment in associate to date should be deducted.

5   A joint venture is a joint arrangement whereby the parties that have **joint control** of the arrangement have rights to the **net assets** of the arrangement.

6   **Evidence** of a contractual arrangement could be in one of several forms.

    •   **Contract** between the parties
    •   **Minutes** of discussion between the parties
    •   Incorporation in the **articles or by-laws** of the joint venture

7   IFRS 11 requires that a joint operator recognises line-by-line the following in relation to its interest in a joint operation:

    (a)   Its assets, including its share of any jointly held assets
    (b)   Its liabilities, including its share of any jointly incurred liabilities
    (c)   Its revenue from the sale of its share of the output arising from the joint operation
    (d)   Its share of the revenue from the sale of the output by the joint operation, and
    (e)   Its expenses, including its share of any expenses incurred jointly.

8   A joint venture is accounted for using the equity method as required by IAS 28 *Associates and joint ventures.*

9   False. Joint arrangements that are structured through a separate vehicle may be either joint ventures or joint operations. The classification will depend on whether the venturer has **rights to the net assets** of the arrangement (joint venture) or **rights to the assets and obligations for the liabilities** (joint operation). This will depend on the terms of the contractual arrangement.

Answers to Questions

9.1   Basic group accounting techniques

OTWAY GROUP
CONSOLIDATED STATEMENT OF FINANCIAL POSITION AS AT 30 JUNE 20X6

	$m
Non-current assets	
Property, plant and equipment (1,012 + 920 + (W9) 60)	1,992
Goodwill (W2)	53
Other intangible assets	350
Investment in associate (W3)	222
	2,617
Current assets	
Inventories (620 + 1,460 – (W8) 42)	2,038
Trade receivables (950 + 529)	1,479
Cash and cash equivalents (900 + 510)	1,410
	4,927
	7,544
Equity attributable to owners of the parent	
Share capital	1,000
Share premium	200
Retained earnings (W4)	1,551
Revaluation surplus (W5)	168
	2,919
Non-controlling interests (W6)	295
	3,214
Non-current liabilities	
Deferred tax liability (100 + 50)	150
Current liabilities	
Trade and other payables (1,880 + 2,300)	4,180
	7,544

OTWAY GROUP
CONSOLIDATED STATEMENT OF PROFIT OR LOSS OR OTHER COMPREHENSIVE INCOME
FOR THE YEAR ENDED 30 JUNE 20X6

	$m
Revenue (4,480 + 4,200 – (W8) 1,300)	7,380
Cost of sales (2,690 + 2,940 – (W8) 1,300 + (W8) 42 + (W9) 10)	(4,382)
Gross profit	2,998
Distribution costs and administrative expenses (620 + 290 + 25 impairment)	(935)
Finance costs (50 + 80)	(130)
Share of profit of associate (148 × 25%)	37
Profit before tax	1,970
Income tax expense (330 + 274)	(604)
Profit for the year	1,366
Other comprehensive income that will not be reclassified to profit or loss:	
Gain on revaluation of property (30 + 7)	37
Share of other comprehensive income of associate (8 × 25%)	2
Income tax expense relating to other comprehensive income (9 + 2)	(11)
Other comprehensive income for the year, net of tax	28
Total comprehensive for the year	1,394
Profit attributable to:	
Owners of the parent (1,297 – 94)	1,258
Non-controlling interests (W7)	108
	1,366
Total comprehensive income attributable to:	
Owners of the parent (1,325 – 95)	1,285
Non-controlling interests (W7)	109
	1,394

Workings

1   *Group structure*

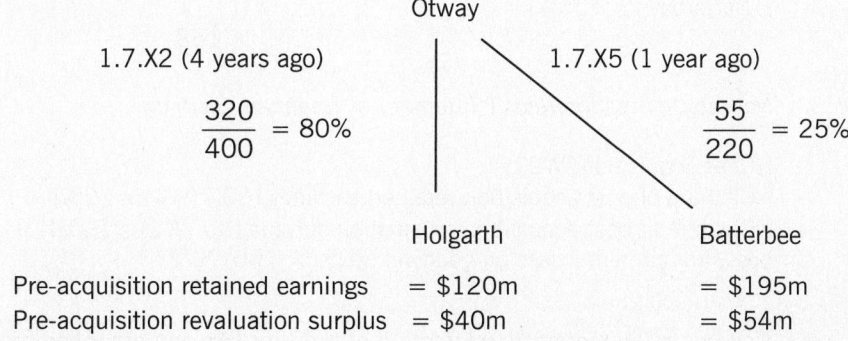

Otway

1.7.X2 (4 years ago)		1.7.X5 (1 year ago)
$\frac{320}{400}$ = 80%		$\frac{55}{220}$ = 25%

	Holgarth	Batterbee
Pre-acquisition retained earnings	= $120m	= $195m
Pre-acquisition revaluation surplus	= $40m	= $54m

2   *Goodwill*

	Holgarth	
	$m	$m
Consideration transferred		765
Non-controlling interests (fair value)		188
Fair value of net assets acquired:		
Share capital	400	
Share premium	140	
Retained earnings at acq'n (W1)	120	
Revaluation surplus at acq'n (W1)	40	
∴ fair value adjustment	100	
Total FV of net assets		(800)
		153
Less: cumulative impairment losses		(100)
		53

3   *Investment in associate*

	$m
Cost of associate	203
Share of post acquisition retained earnings (W4)	17
Share of post acquisition revaluation surplus (W5)	2
Less: impairment losses on associate to date	(0)
	222

4   *Consolidated retained earnings c/f*

	Otway $m	Holgarth $m	Batterbee $m
Per question	1,128	809	263
PUP (W8)		(42)	
Depreciation on FV adjustment (W9)		(40)	(0)
Less: Pre-acquisition (W1)		(120)	(195)
		607	68
Group share:			
Holgarth [607 × 80%]	486		
Batterbee [68 × 25%]	17		
Less: impairment losses on goodwill:			
Holgarth [80% × 100] (W2)	(80)		
Less: impairment losses on associate			
Batterbee	(0)		
	1,551		

5   *Consolidated revaluation surplus c/f*

	Otway $m	Holgarth $m	Batterbee $m
Per question	142	70	62
Less: Pre-acquisition		(40)	(54)
		30	8
Group share:			
Holgarth [30 × 80%]	24		
Batterbee [8 × 25%]	2		
	168		

6   *Non-controlling interests (statement of financial position)*

	$m
NCI at acquisition (W2)	188
NCI share of post acquisition retained earnings [607 (W4) × 20%]	121
NCI share of post acquisition revaluation surplus [30 (W5) × 20%]	6
Less: impairment losses on goodwill [20% × 100] (W2)	(20)
	295

7   *Non-controlling interests (statement of profit or loss and other comprehensive income)*

	PFY $m	TCI $m
Holgarth's PFY/TCI per question	616	621
Less: impairment losses	(25)	(25)
Less: PUP (W8)	(42)	(42)
Less: FV depreciation (W9)	(10)	(10)
	539	544
× NCI share 20% =	108	109

8   *Intragroup trading*

Cancel intragroup sales and purchases:

DEBIT   Revenue $1,300 million
CREDIT   Cost of sales $1,300 million

Unrealised profit (Holgarth to Otway):
= $140 million in inventories x 30/100 margin = $42 million

DEBIT   Cost of sales/Retained earnings of Holgarth $42 million
CREDIT   Inventories $42 million

9   *Fair value adjustment – Holgarth*

	At acquisition	Additional depreciation*	At year end
	$m	$m	$m
Property, plant and equipment (800 – 400 – 140 –120 – 40)	100	(40)	60
	100	(40)	60

* Additional depreciation = $^{100}/_{10}$ = 10 per annum to cost of sales × 4 years = 40

9.2   Joint arrangement

Supermall has been set up as a **separate vehicle**. As such, it could be either a joint operation or joint venture, so other facts must be considered.

There are no facts that suggest that the two real estate companies have rights to substantially all the benefits of the assets of Supermall nor an obligation for its liabilities. Therefore, it appears that Supermall (the joint arrangement) rather than the two real estate companies has rights to the assets and obligations for the liabilities of the joint arrangement.

The real estate companies' liability is limited to any unpaid capital contribution.

As a result, each party has an interest in the **net assets** of Supermall and should account for it as a **joint venture** using the **equity method.**

IFRS 11 contains many examples illustrating the principles of how to classify joint arrangements, You can find them at: www.iasb.org.

9.3   Joint operations

IFRS 11 gives examples in the oil, gas and mineral extraction industries. In such industries companies may, say, jointly control and operate on oil or gas pipeline. Each company transports its own products down the pipeline and pays an agreed proportion of the expenses of operating the pipeline (perhaps based on volume). In this case the parties have rights to assets (such as exploration permits and the oil or gas produced by the activities).

A further example is a property which is jointly controlled, each venturer taking a share of the rental income and bearing a portion of the expense.

Now try this question from the Exam Question Bank	Number	Level	Marks	Time
	Q12	Examination	20	36 mins

MORE COMPLEX GROUP TOPICS

Part C

MORE COMPLEX GROUP STRUCTURES

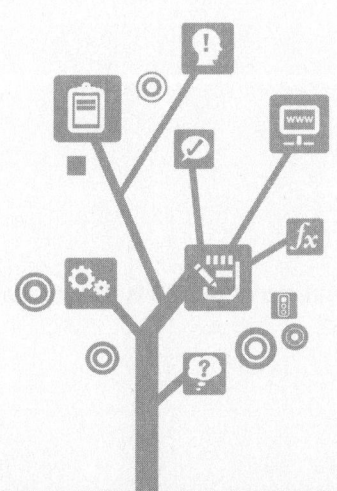

This chapter introduces the second of several more complicated consolidation topics. The best way to tackle these questions is to be logical and to carry out the consolidation on a **step by step** basis.

In questions of this nature, it is very helpful to sketch a **diagram of the group structure**, as we have done. This clarifies the situation and it should point you in the right direction: always sketch the group structure as your first working and double check it against the information in the question.

topic list	learning outcomes	syllabus references	ability required
1 Complex groups	A1, A2	A2 (i)	Application
2 Consolidating sub-subsidiaries	A1, A2	A2 (i)	Application
3 Direct holdings in sub-subsidiaries	A1, A2	A2 (i)	Application
4 Indirect associates	A1, A2	A2 (i)	Application

1 Complex groups

Introduction

In this section we shall consider how the principles of statement of financial position consolidation may be applied to more complex structures of companies within a group.

1.1 Types of complex group

(a) **Several subsidiary companies**

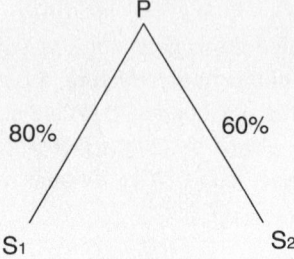

You have already seen this type of structure in your previous studies.

(b) **Sub-subsidiaries**

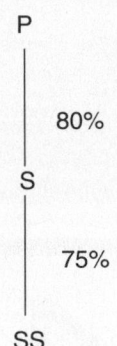

P holds a controlling interest in S which in turn holds a controlling interest in SS. SS is therefore a subsidiary of a subsidiary of P, in other words, a *sub-subsidiary* of P.

(c) **Direct holdings in sub-subsidiaries: 'D' shaped groups**

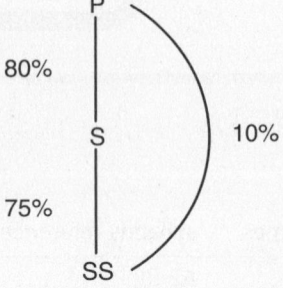

In this example, SS is a sub-subsidiary of P with additional shares held directly by P.

In practice, groups are usually larger, and therefore more complex, but the procedures for consolidation of large groups will not differ from those we shall now describe for smaller ones.

1.2 A parent company which has several subsidiaries

Where a company P has several subsidiaries S_1, S_2, S_3 and so on, the technique for consolidation is exactly as previously described. **Cancellation** is from the parent company, which has assets of investments in subsidiaries S_1, S_2, S_3, to each of the several subsidiaries.

The consolidated statement of financial position will show:

(a)   A single figure for **non-controlling interest**, and
(b)   A single figure for **goodwill** arising.

A single working should be used for each of the constituents of the consolidated statement of financial position: one working for goodwill, one for non-controlling interest, one for retained earnings (reserves), and so on.

1.3 Sub-subsidiaries

A slightly different problem arises when there are sub-subsidiaries in the group, which is how should we **identify the non-controlling interest** in the retained earnings of the group? Suppose P owns 80% of the equity of S, and that S in turn owns 60% of the equity of SS.

It would appear that in this situation:

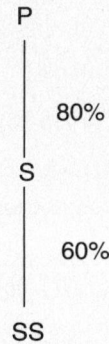

P

80%

S

60%

SS

(a)   P owns 80% of 60% = 48% of SS
(b)   The non-controlling interest in S owns 20% of 60% = 12% of SS
(c)   The non-controlling interest in SS itself owns the remaining 40% of the SS equity

SS is nevertheless a **sub-subsidiary** of P, because it is a subsidiary of S which in turn is a subsidiary of P. The chain of control thus makes SS a sub-subsidiary of P which owns only 48% of its equity.

The total non-controlling interest in SS may be checked by considering a **dividend** of $100 paid by SS where S then distributes its share of this dividend in full to its own shareholders.

		$
S will receive	$60	
P will receive	80% × $60 =	48
Leaving for the total NCI in SS		52
		100

Question 10.1	Effective interest

Learning outcomes A2

Top owns 60% of the equity of Middle Co, which owns 75% of the equity of Bottom Co. What is Top Co's effective holding in Bottom Co?

1.4 Date of effective control

The date the sub-subsidiary comes under the **control of the parent company** is either:

(a)   The date P acquired S if S already holds shares in SS, or
(b)   If S acquires shares in SS later, then that later date.

You need to think about the dates of acquisition and the order in which the group is built up when you identify which balances to select as the **pre-acquisition** reserves of the sub-subsidiary.

Section summary

When a parent company has **several subsidiaries**, the consolidated statement of financial position shows a single figure for non-controlling interests and for goodwill arising on consolidation. Analysing the group structure, calculating the effective ownership and identifying the dates of control are the key issues in questions on this area.

2 Consolidating sub-subsidiaries

2.1 Consolidated statement of financial position

Introduction

The basic consolidation method in the statement of financial position is as follows.

(a) **Net assets**: show what the group controls (P + 100% S + 100% SS).

(b) **Equity (capital and reserves)**: show who owns the net assets included elsewhere in the statement of financial position. Reserves (retained earnings), therefore, are based on **effective holdings**.

The basic steps are exactly as you have seen in simpler group structures. As you will see in the examples in this chapter, there are some new complications to be aware of in the workings for **goodwill** and **non-controlling interests**.

Exam alert

Don't panic when a question seems very complicated – sketch the group structure and analyse the information in the question methodically.

Example: subsidiary acquired first

The draft statements of financial position of P Co, S Co and SS Co on 30 June 20X7 were as follows.

	P Co $	S Co $	SS Co $
Assets			
Non-current assets			
Tangible assets	105,000	125,000	180,000
Investments, at cost			
80,000 shares in S Co	120,000	–	–
60,000 shares in SS Co	–	110,000	–
Current assets	80,000	70,000	60,000
	305,000	305,000	240,000
Equity and liabilities			
Equity			
Ordinary shares of $1 each	80,000	100,000	100,000
Retained earnings	195,000	170,000	115,000
	275,000	270,000	215,000
Payables	30,000	35,000	25,000
	305,000	305,000	240,000

P Co acquired its shares in S Co on 1 July 20X4 when the reserves of S Co stood at $40,000.

S Co acquired its shares in SS Co on 1 July 20X5 when the reserves of SS Co stood at $50,000.

It is the group's policy to measure the non-controlling interest at acquisition at its proportionate share of the fair value of the subsidiary's net assets.

Required

Prepare the draft consolidated statement of financial position of the subsidiary's net assets at 30 June 20X7.

Note. Assume no impairment of goodwill.

Solution

This is **two acquisitions** from the point of view of the P group. In 20X4, the group buys 80% of S. Then in 20X5 S (which is now part of the P group) buys 60% of SS.

P buys 80% of S, then S (80% of S from the group's point of view) buys 60% of SS.

Having calculated the non-controlling interest and the P group interest (see working 1 below), the workings can be constructed. You should, however, note the following.

(a)   Group structure working (see working 1)

(b)   **Goodwill working**: compare the costs of investments and the non-controlling interests (at proportionate share of net assets, based on effective interest for SS) with the net assets. You should set this out in two columns. In SS Co's goodwill working, as the investment in SS Co is in S Co's books, you need to multiply the investment by P Co's share in S Co. The share of the investment in SS Co belonging to the non-controlling interests of S Co is cancelled in the non-controlling interest working for S Co.

(c)   **Retained earnings working**: bring in the share of S Co's and SS Co's post-acquisition retained earnings in the normal way (using the effective % for SS).

(d)   **Non-controlling interest working**: calculate non-controlling interests in the usual way, using a 20% NCI in S Co's post acquisition retained earnings and a 52% non-controlling interests in SS Co's post acquisition retained earnings. In S Co's NCI working, you will need to deduct the NCI's share of the investment in SS Co – this is because we always cancel 100% of the investment on consolidation and P Co's share is cancelled in the goodwill working so we need to cancel the NCI in S Co's share in S Co's NCI working.

1   *Group structure*

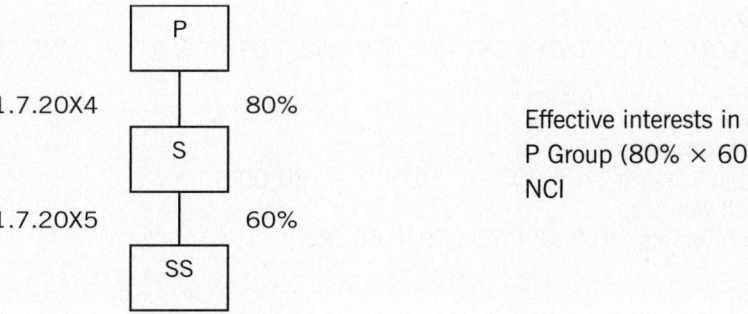

Effective interests in SS:
P Group (80% × 60%)   = 48%
NCI   = 52%

2   *Goodwill*

	S		SS	
	$	$	$	$
Consideration transferred		120,000	(80% × 110,000)	88,000
Non-controlling interests	(20% × 140,000)	28,000	(52% × 150,000)	78,000
Fair value of identifiable NA acquired:				
Share capital	100,000		100,000	
Retained earnings	40,000		50,000	
		(140,000)		(150,000)
		8,000		16,000

24,000

3   *Retained earnings*

	P Co	S Co	SS Co
	$	$	$
Per question	195,000	170,000	115,000
Pre-acquisition		(40,000)	(50,000)
Post-acquisition		130,000	65,000
Group share:			
In S Co ($130,000 × 80%)	104,000		
In SS Co ($65,000 × 48%)	31,200		
Group retained earnings	330,200		

4   *Non-controlling interests*

	S	SS
	$	$
NCI at acquisition (W2)	28,000	78,000
NCI share of post acquisition retained earnings ($130,000(W3) × 20%)/($65,000(W3) × 52%)	26,000	33,800
Less NCI in investment in SS ($110,000 × 20%)	(22,000)	–
	32,000	111,800

$ 143,800

P CO
CONSOLIDATED STATEMENT OF FINANCIAL POSITION AT 30 JUNE 20X7

	$
Assets	
Non-current assets	
Tangible assets (105,000 + 125,000 + 180,000)	410,000
Goodwill (W2)	24,000
Current assets (80,000 + 70,000 + 60,000)	210,000
	644,000
Equity	
Ordinary shares of $1 each fully paid	80,000
Retained earnings	330,200
	410,200
Non-controlling interest (W4)	143,800
	554,000
Payables (30,000 + 35,000 + 25,000)	90,000
	644,000

2.2 Date of acquisition

Care must be taken when consolidating sub-subsidiaries, because (usually) either:

(a)   The parent company acquired the subsidiary **before** the subsidiary bought the sub-subsidiary (as in the example above); *OR*

(b)   The parent company acquired the subsidiary **after** the subsidiary bought the sub-subsidiary

Depending on whether (a) or (b) is the case, the retained earnings of the sub-subsidiary held at acquisition will be different.

The rule to remember here, when considering pre- and post-acquisition profits, is that we are only interested in the consolidated results of the **parent company**. We will use the example above to demonstrate the required approach. Therefore the pre-acquisition reserves should be at the date the **parent** obtains control of the sub-subsidiary. If the parent company acquires the subsidiary before the subsidiary acquires the sub-subsidiary, this will be the date that the subsidiary acquires the subsidiary. However, if the parent company acquires the subsidiary after the subsidiary has acquired the sub-subsidiary, this will be the date the parent buys the subsidiary (rather than when the subsidiary acquired the sub-subsidiary).

Example: sub-subsidiary acquired first

Again using the figures in Example: subsidiary acquired first, assume that:

(a)   S Co purchased its holding in SS Co on 1 July 20X4
(b)   P Co purchased its holding in S Co on 1 July 20X5

The retained earnings figures on the respective dates of acquisition are the same, but on 1 July 20X5 when P Co purchased its holding in S Co, the retained earnings of SS Co were $60,000.

It is the group's policy to measure the non-controlling interest at its **proportionate share of the fair value of the subsidiary's net assets.**

Solution

The point here is that SS Co only became part of the P group on 1 July 20X5, *not* on 1 July 20X4. This means that only the retained earnings of SS Co arising *after* 1 July 20X5 can be included in the post-acquisition reserves of P Co group. Goodwill arising on the acquisition will be calculated by comparing P's share of cost of SS investment by S in SS and the non-controlling interest in SS (using the effective %) to the net assets at acquisition represented by the share capital of SS and its retained earnings **at the date P acquired S** (here $60,000).

P CO
CONSOLIDATED STATEMENT OF FINANCIAL POSITION AS AT 30 JUNE 20X7

	$
Non-current assets	
Tangible (105,000 + 125,000 + 180,000)	410,000
Goodwill (W2)	19,200
	429,200
Current assets (80,000 + 70,000 + 60,000)	210,000
	639,200
Equity and liabilities	
Ordinary shares $1 each, fully paid	80,000
Retained earnings (W3)	325,400
	405,400
Non-controlling interest (W4)	143,800
	549,200
Payables	90,000
	639,200

Workings

1   *Group structure*

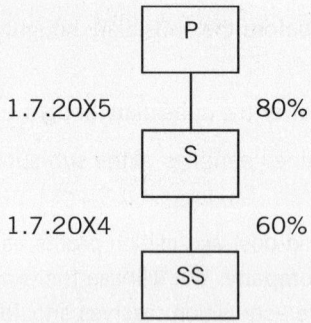

1.7.20X5   80%

1.7.20X4   60%

P owns an effective interest of 48% in SS. NCI in SS is 52%.

2   *Goodwill*

The working should be set out as:

	S		SS	
	$	$	$	$
Consideration transferred		120,000	(80% × 110,000)	88,000
Non-controlling interests	(20% × 140,000)	28,000	(52% × 160,000)	83,200
Fair value of net assets at acquisition:				
Share capital	100,000		100,000	
Retained earnings	40,000		60,000	
		(140,000)		(160,000)
		8,000		11,200

19,200

Note. retained earnings of SS are as at 1 July 20X5 when P got control of S.

3   *Retained earnings*

	P Co	S Co	SS Co
	$	$	$
Per question		170,000	115,000
Pre-acquisition		(40,000)	(60,000)
Post-acquisition		130,000	55,000
Group share:			
In S Co ($130,000 × 80%)	104,000		
In SS Co ($55,000 × 48%)	26,400		
Group retained earnings	325,400		

4   *Non-controlling interests*

The cost of investment in SS is again deducted as 100% of the investment in SS must be cancelled and only 80% was cancelled in SS's goodwill working.

	S	SS
	$	$
NCI at acquisition (W2)	28,000	83,200
NCI share of post acquisition retained earnings	26,000	28,600
($130,000 (W3) ×20%)/($55,000 (W3) × 52%)		
Less NCI in investment in SS ($110,000 × 20%)	(22,000)	–
	32,000	111,800

$ 143,800

Example: subsidiary acquired first: non-controlling interest at fair value

The draft statements of financial position of P Co, S Co and SS Co on 30 June 20X7 were as follows.

	P Co $	S Co $	SS Co $
Assets			
Non-current assets			
Tangible assets	105,000	125,000	180,000
Investments, at cost			
80,000 shares in S Co	120,000	–	–
60,000 shares in SS Co	–	110,000	–
Current assets	80,000	70,000	60,000
	305,000	305,000	240,000

	P Co $	S Co $	SS Co $
Equity and liabilities			
Equity			
Ordinary shares of $1 each	80,000	100,000	100,000
Retained earnings	195,000	170,000	115,000
	275,000	270,000	215,000
Payables	30,000	35,000	25,000
	305,000	305,000	240,000

P Co acquired its shares in S Co on 1 July 20X4 when the reserves of S Co stood at $40,000; and

S Co acquired its shares in SS Co on 1 July 20X5 when the reserves of SS Co stood at $50,000.

It is the group's policy to measure the non-controlling interest at **fair value** at the date of acquisition. The fair value of the non-controlling interests in S on 1 July 20X4 was $30,000. The fair value of the 52% non-controlling interest on 1 July 20X5 was $95,160.

Required

Prepare the draft consolidated statement of financial position of P Group at 30 June 20X7.

Note. Assume no impairment of goodwill.

Solution

As we have seen in earlier chapters, the group's policy on measurement of the non-controlling interest at acquisition does not change the steps we follow in the consolidation.

P CO
CONSOLIDATED STATEMENT OF FINANCIAL POSITION AT 30 JUNE 20X7

	$
Assets	
Non-current assets	
Tangible assets	410,000
Goodwill (W2)	43,160
Current assets	210,000
	663,160
Equity	
Ordinary shares of $1 each fully paid	80,000
Retained earnings (W3)	330,200
	410,200
Non-controlling interest (W4)	162,960
	573,160
Payables	90,000
	663,160

Workings

1   *Group structure*

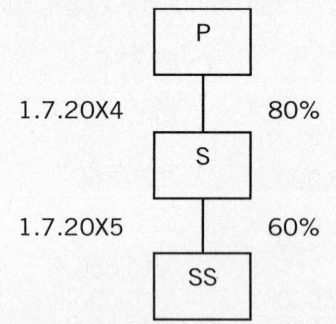

Effective interests in SS:
P Group (80% × 60%)   = 48%
NCI   = 52%

2   *Goodwill*

		S		SS	
	$	$		$	$
Consideration transferred		120,000	($110,000 × 80%)	88,000	
Non-controlling interests (at FV)		30,000		95,160	
Fair value of identifiable net assets acquired					
Share capital	100,000		100,000		
Retained earnings	40,000		50,000		
		(140,000)		(150,000)	
		10,000		33,160	

$43,160

3   *Retained earnings*

	P Co	S Co	SS Co
	$	$	$
Per question	195,000	170,000	115,000
Pre-acquisition		(40,000)	(50,000)
Post-acquisition		130,000	65,000
Group share:			
In S Co ($130,000 × 80%)	104,000		
In SS Co ($65,000 × 48%)	31,200		
Group retained earnings	330,200		

4   *Non-controlling interests*

	S	SS
	$	$
NCI at acquisition (W2)	30,000	95,160
NCI share of post acquisition retained earnings ($130,000(W3)× 20%)/($65,000(W3) × 52%)	26,000	33,800
Less NCI in investment in SS ($110,000 × 20%)	(22,000)	–
	34,000	128,960

$ 162,960

Question 10.2				Sub-subsidiary

Learning outcomes A2

The statements of financial position of Antelope Co, Yak Co and Zebra Co at 31 March 20X4 are summarised as follows.

	Antelope Co		Yak Co		Zebra Co	
	$	$	$	$	$	$
Assets						
Non-current assets						
Freehold property		100,000		100,000		–
Plant and machinery		210,000		80,000		3,000
		310,000		180,000		3,000
Investments in subsidiaries						
Shares, at cost	110,000		6,200		–	
Loan account	–		13,200		–	
		110,000		19,400		3,000
Current assets						
Inventories	170,000		20,500		15,000	
Receivables	140,000		50,000		1,000	
Due from Yak Co	10,000		–			
Cash at bank	60,000		16,500		4,000	
		380,000		87,000		20,000
		800,000		286,400		23,000
Equity and liabilities						
Equity						
Ordinary share capital	200,000		100,000		10,000	
Retained earnings	379,600		129,200		(1,000)	
		579,600		229,200		9,000
Non-current liabilities						
Loan from Yak Co		–		–		13,200
Current liabilities						
Trade payables	160,400		40,200		800	
Due to Yak Co	–		10,000		–	
Taxation	60,000		7,000		–	
				–		–
		220,400		57,200		800
		800,000		286,400		23,000

Notes

1   Antelope Co acquired 75% of the shares of Yak Co on 1 April 20X1 when the credit balance on the retained earnings of that company was $40,000. No dividends have been paid since that date.

2   Yak Co acquired 80% of the shares in Zebra Co on 1 January 20X3 when there was a debit balance on the retained earnings of that company of $3,000.

3   During the year to 31 March 20X4 Antelope Co sold inventory at to Yak Co for $20,000. At 31 March 20X4 one half of this amount was still held in the inventories of Yak Co. Antelope earns a mark up of 25% on all sales.

4   It is the group's policy to measure the non-controlling interest at fair value at the date of acquisition. The fair value of the non-controlling interest in Yak Co at 1 April 20X1 was $36,000. The fair value of the 40% non-controlling interest in Antelope Co at 1 January 20X3 was $3,100.

Required

Prepare the draft consolidated statement of financial position of Antelope Co at 31 March 20X4. (Assume no impairment of goodwill.)

2.3 Consolidated statement of profit or loss and other comprehensive income

The basic consolidation method in the statement of profit or loss and other comprehensive income is as follows.

(a)   **Income, expenses, other comprehensive income**: show what the group controls line by line (P + 100% S + 100% SS).

(b)   **Non-controlling interest**: show the non-controlling interest's share of S and SS's profit and total comprehensive income. The NCI in SS should be based on the **effective holding**.

The basic steps are exactly as you have seen in simpler group structures.

Example: consolidated statement of profit or loss and other comprehensive income

The statements of profit or loss and other comprehensive income of A, B and C for the year ended 31 December 20X2 are provided below:

	A $m	B $m	C $m
Revenue	2,000	1,200	800
Cost of sales	(1,400)	(800)	(400)
Gross profit	600	400	400
Operating expenses	(240)	(160)	(200)
	360	240	200
Investment income (Note 3)	100	30	–
Profit before tax	460	270	200
Income tax expense	(140)	(90)	(60)
Profit for the year	320	180	140
Other comprehensive income	80	50	10
Total comprehensive income for the year	400	230	150

Notes:

1   A acquired 80% of the ordinary share capital of B on 1 January 20X0 and B acquired 75% of the ordinary share capital of C on 1 January 20X1.

2   There has been no impairment to goodwill since the acquisition date.

3   In the year ended 31 December 20X2 all three entities paid a dividend to their ordinary shareholders. A paid a dividend of $160 million, B paid a dividend of $100 million and C paid a dividend of $40 million.

Required

Prepare the consolidated statement of profit or loss and other comprehensive income for the A Group for the year ended 31 December 20X2.

Solution

As we have seen in earlier chapters, the group's policy on measurement of the non-controlling interest at acquisition does not change the steps we follow in the consolidation.

	$m
Revenue (2,000 + 1,200 + 800)	4,000
Cost of sales (1,400 + 800 + 400)	(2,600)
Gross profit	1,400
Operating expenses (240 + 160 + 200)	(600)
	800
Investment income (100 + 30 – 80 (W3) – 30 (W3))	20
Profit before tax	820
Income tax expense (140 + 90 + 60)	(290)
Profit for the year	530
Other comprehensive income (80 + 50 + 10)	140
Total comprehensive income for the year	670
Profit attributable to:	
Owners of the parent (530 – 92)	438
Non-controlling interest (W2)	92
	530
Total comprehensive income attributable to:	
Owners of the parent (670 – 106)	564
Non-controlling interest (W2)	106
	670

1   *Group structure*

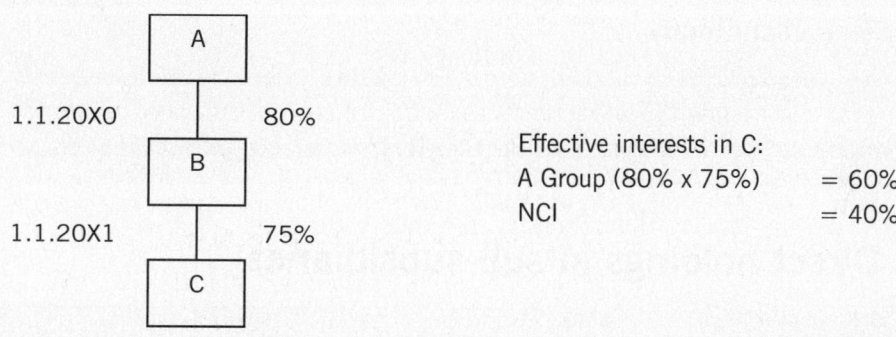

Effective interests in C:
A Group (80% x 75%)   = 60%
NCI   = 40%

2   *Non-controlling interests*

	$m
In profit for the year:	
B (180 × 20%)	36
C (140 × 40%)	56
	92
In total comprehensive income:	
B (230 × 20%)	46
C (150 × 40%)	60
Group retained earnings	106

3   *Intra-group dividend income*

Dividends paid by B to A = $100m x 80% = $80m (cancel out of investment income)
Dividends paid by C to B = $40m x 75% = $30m (cancel out of investment income)

You should follow this **step by step approach** in all questions. This applies to Section 3 below as well.

 Sketch the **group structure** and check it to the question

 **Add details** to the sketch of dates of acquisition, holdings acquired (percentage and nominal values) and cost.

 Draw up a pro-forma for the statement of financial position.

 Work methodically down the statements of financial position, transferring figures to proforma or workings.

 Use the notes in the question to make adjustments such as eliminating intra-group balances and unrealised profits.

 **Goodwill working**: compare costs of investment with the **effective** group interests acquired.

 **Reserves working**: include the group share of subsidiary and sub-subsidiary post-acquisition retained earnings (effective holdings again).

 **Non-controlling interest working**: total NCI in subsidiary plus total NCI in sub-subsidiary.

 Prepare the **consolidated statement of financial position** (and statement of profit or loss and other comprehensive income if required).

Section summary

When dealing with **sub-subsidiaries,** you will need to calculate the effective interests owned by the group and by the non-controlling interest. The date of acquisition is important when dealing with sub-subsidiaries. Remember that it is the post-acquisition reserves from a group perspective which are important.

3 Direct holdings in sub-subsidiaries

Introduction

Consider the following structure, sometimes called a **'D-shaped' group**.

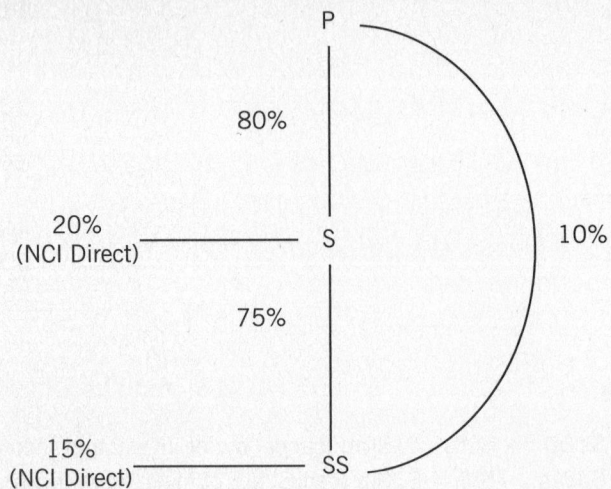

In the structure above, there is:

(a)	A **direct** non-controlling share in S of		20%
(b)	A **direct** non-controlling share in SS of	15%	
(c)	An **indirect** non-controlling share in SS of 20% × 75% =	15%	
			30%

The effective interest in SS is:

Indirect group interest 80% × 75%	=	60% interest	
Direct group interest		10%	
		70%	
∴ NCI		30%	
		100%	

Having ascertained the structure and non-controlling interests, proceed as for a typical sub-subsidiary situation.

Question 10.3   'D' shaped group

Learning outcome: A2

The draft statements of financial position of Hulk Co, Molehill Co and Pimple Co as at 31 May 20X5 are as follows.

	Hulk Co		Molehill Co		Pimple Co	
	$	$	$	$	$	$
Assets						
Non-current assets						
Tangible assets		90,000		60,000		60,000
Investments in subsidiaries(cost)						
Shares in Molehill Co	90,000		–		–	
Shares in Pimple Co	25,000		42,000		–	
		115,000		42,000		–
		205,000		102,000		60,000
Current assets		40,000		50,000		40,000
		245,000		152,000		100,000
Equity and liabilities						
Equity						
Ordinary shares $1	100,000		50,000		50,000	
Revaluation surplus	50,000		20,000		–	
Retained earnings	45,000		32,000		25,000	
		195,000		102,000		75,000
Non-current liabilities						
12% loan		–		10,000		–
		195,000		112,000		75,000
Current liabilities						
Payables		50,000		40,000		25,000
		245,000		152,000		100,000

(a) Hulk Co acquired 60% of the shares in Molehill on 1 January 20X3 when the balance on that company's retained earnings was $8,000 (credit) and there was no revaluation surplus.

(b) Hulk acquired 20% of the shares of Pimple Co and Molehill acquired 60% of the shares of Pimple Co on 1 January 20X4 when that company's retained earnings stood at $15,000.

(c) There has been no payment of dividends by either Molehill or Pimple since they became subsidiaries.

(d) There was no impairment of goodwill.

(e) It is the group's policy to measure the non-controlling interest at acquisition at its proportionate share of the fair value of the subsidiary's net assets.

Required

Prepare the consolidated statement of financial position of Hulk Co as at 31 May 20X5.

Section summary

'D shaped' groups are consolidated in the same way as a typical sub-subsidiary situation. It is the structure and non-controlling interest calculations that are important.

4 Indirect associates

A group may have an indirect associate as illustrated in the following diagram.

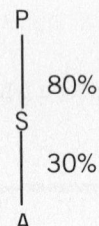

```
P
|
|  80%
S
|
|  30%
A
```

Points to note:

- P **controls** a 30% investment in A, so A is an associate. This is the % we use for the 'investment in associate working' in the consolidated statement of financial position and for the 'share of the associate's profit and other comprehensive income' in the consolidated statement of profit or loss and other comprehensive income.
- P **owns** 80% × 30% = 24% in A. This is the % we use in the consolidated retained earnings working.
- The **non-controlling interests in S** own 20% × 30% = 6% in A.

4.1 Treatment in the consolidated financial statements

The principles are very similar to those seen earlier in the context of indirect subsidiaries:

- in the statement of financial position, the investment is based on **control**, while retained earnings and non-controlling interests are based on **ownership**.

- in the statement of profit or loss and other comprehensive income, the profit/other comprehensive income is based on **control**, with **ownership** being shown in the analysis of profits/total comprehensive income at the end of the statement.

STATEMENT OF FINANCIAL POSITION

Investment in associate			
Cost of investment (per S's SOFP)			X
S's share (**30%**) of A's post-acquisition earnings			X
			$\overline{X}$

Retained earnings	P	S	A
Per question	X	X	X
Less: pre-acq'n		(X)	(X)
		$\underline{Y}$	$\underline{Z}$
P's share of S's post-acq'n earnings (Y x 80%)	X		
P's share of A's post-acqn earnings (Z x **24%**)	X		
	$\overline{X}$		

Non-controlling interest			
NCI at acq'n		X	
Add: NCI in S's post acq'n earnings (Y x 20%)		X	
Add: NCI in A's post acq'n earnings (Z x **6%**)			
		$\underline{X}$	

STATEMENT OF PROFIT OR LOSS AND OTHER COMPREHENSIVE INCOME

Share of associate's profit for the year	30% × A's PFY
Share of associate's other comprehensive income for the year	30% × A's OCI

Profit attributable to:
Owners of the parent   X
Non-controlling interest [(20% × S's PFY) + (**6%** × A's PFY)]   X
                                                                                                X

Total comprehensive income attributable to:
Owners of the parent   X
Non-controlling interest [(20% × S's TCI) + (**6%** × A's TCI)]   X
                                                                                                X

Section summary

- A group may have an indirect associate

- The equity accounted investment in the statement of financial position and the share of the associate's profit in the statement of profit or loss and other comprehensive income should be based on the proportion **owned by the subsidiary** (and **controlled by the group**)

- Effective ownership percentages are used to calculate group retained earnings and the NCI in the indirect associate.

Chapter Roundup

✓ When a parent company has **several subsidiaries**, the consolidated statement of financial position shows a single figure for non-controlling interests and for goodwill arising on consolidation. Analysing the group structure, calculating the effective ownership and identifying the dates of control are the key issues in questions on this area.

✓ When dealing with **sub-subsidiaries,** you will need to calculate effective interest. The date of acquisition is important when dealing with sub-subsidiaries – it should be the date that the **parent** gains control of the sub-subsidiary. Remember that it is the post-acquisition reserves from a group perspective which are important.

✓ 'D shaped' groups are consolidated in the same way as a typical sub-subsidiary situation. It is the structure and non-controlling interest calculations that are important.

✓ A group may have an **indirect associate**

- The equity accounted investment in the statement of financial position and the share of the associate's profit in the statement of profit or loss and other comprehensive income should be based on the proportion **owned by the subsidiary** (and **controlled by the group**)

- Effective ownership percentages are used to calculate group retained earnings and the NCI in the indirect associate.

Quick Quiz

1 B Co owns 60% of the equity of C Co which owns 75% of the equity of D Co. What is the total non-controlling interest percentage ownership in D Co?

2 What is the basic consolidation method for sub-subsidiaries in the consolidated statement of financial position?

3 P Co owns 25% of R Co's equity and 75% of Q Co's equity. Q Co owns 40% of R Co's equity. What is the total non-controlling interest percentage ownership in R Co?

Answers to Quick Quiz

1   B

| 60%

C

| 75%

D

Effective interest in D = 60% x 75% = 45%
Therefore, non-controlling interest   = <u>55%</u>
                                  100%

(Alternatively could calculate as 25% + (40% of 75%) = 55%)

2   •   Net assets: show what the group controls
    •   Equity (capital and reserves): show who owns the net assets

3

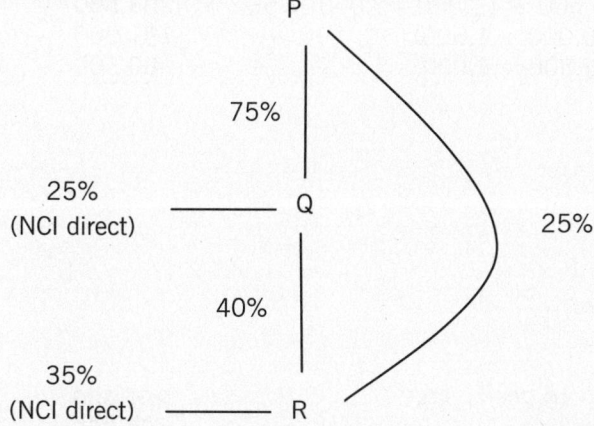

Effective interest in R: Direct   25%
                               Indirect (75% x 40%)   <u>30%</u>
                                             55%

                              Non-controlling interest <u>45%</u>
                                             100%

(Alternatively, could calculate non-controlling interest as 35% + (25% × 40%) = 45%)

Answers to Questions

10.1 Effective interest

Top owns 60% of 75% of Bottom Co = 45%.

10.2 Sub-subsidiary

ANTELOPE CO
CONSOLIDATED STATEMENT OF FINANCIAL POSITION AS AT 31 MARCH 20X4

	$	$
Assets		
Non-current assets		
Freehold property (100,000 + 100,000)		200,000
Plant and machinery (210,000 + 80,000 + 3,000)		293,000
		493,000
Goodwill (W2)		6,750
		499,750
Current assets		
Inventories (170,000 + 20,500 + 15,000 – 2,000 (W5))	203,500	
Receivables (140,000 + 50,000 + 1,000)	191,000	
Cash at bank (60,000 + 16,500 + 4,000)	80,500	
		475,000
		974,750
Equity and liabilities		
Equity		
Ordinary share capital		200,000
Retained earnings (W3)		445,700
		645,700
Non-controlling interests (W4)		60,450
		706,350
Current liabilities		
Trade payables (160,400 + 40,200 + 800)	201,400	
Taxation (60,000 + 7,000)	67,000	
		268,400
		974,750

Workings

1 *Group structure*

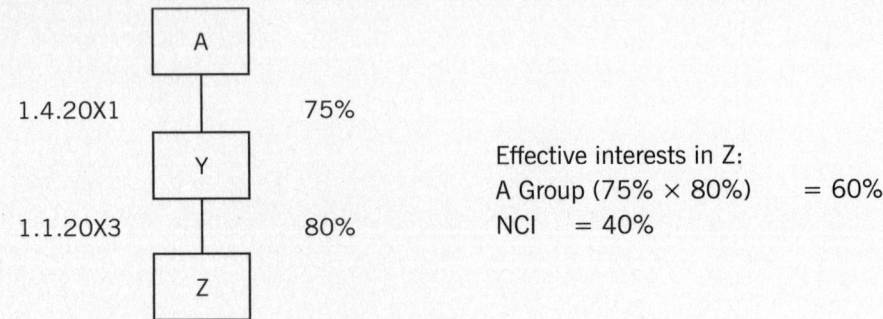

Effective interests in Z:
A Group (75% × 80%)   = 60%
NCI   = 40%

2   *Goodwill*

	Y		Z	
	$	$	$	$
Consideration transferred		110,000	(75% × 6,200)	4,650
Non-controlling interests (at fair value)		36,000		3,100
Fair value of identifiable NA acquired:				
Share capital	100,000		10,000	
Retained earnings	40,000		(3,000)	
		(140,000)		(7,000)
		6,000		750

$6,750

3   *Retained earnings*

	Antelope	Yak	Zebra
	$	$	$
Per question	379,600	129,200	(1,000)
Unrealised profit in inventories (W5)	(2,000)		
Pre-acquisition profit/losses		(40,000)	3,000
Post-acquisition profits		89,200	2,000
Group share			
In Yak ($89,200 × 75%)	66,900		
In Zebra ($2,000 × 60%)	1,200		
Group retained earnings	445,700		

4   *Non-controlling interests*

	Yak	Zebra
	$	$
NCI at acquisition (W1)	36,000	3,100
NCI in post acquisition retained earnings	22,300	800
($89,200 (W3) × 25%)/($2,000 (W3) × 40%)		
Less NCI share of investment in Zebra ($6,200 × 25%)	(1,550)	–
	56,750	3,900

60,650

5   *Unrealised profit*

Antelope (parent) sells to Yak (subsidiary)

PUP = $20,000 × ½ in inventory × 25/125 mark up = $2,000

DEBIT	Retained earnings of Antelope	$2,000	
CREDIT	Inventories		$2,000

6   *Intra-group balances*

The intra-group receivable of $10,000 in Antelope's books cancels with the intra-group payable of $10,000 in Yak's books.

The intra-group loan receivable of $13,200 in Yak's books cancels with the intra-group loan payable in Zebra's books of $13,200.

The end result is that all intra-group payables and receivables are eliminated in the consolidated statement of financial position.

10.3 'D' shaped group

HULK CO
CONSOLIDATED STATEMENT OF FINANCIAL POSITION AS AT 31 MAY 20X8

	$	$
Assets		
Non-current assets		
Tangible assets (90,000 + 60,000 + 60,000)	210,000	
Goodwill (W2)	69,000	
		279,000
Current assets (40,000 + 50,000 + 40,000)		130,000
		409,000
Equity and liabilities		
Equity		
Ordinary shares $1	100,000	
Revaluation surplus (W4)	62,000	
Retained earnings (W3)	65,000	
	227,000	
Non-controlling interests (W5)	57,000	
		284,000
Non-current liabilities		
12% loan		10,000
		294,000
Current liabilities		
Payables (50,000 + 40,000 + 25,000)		115,000
		409,000

Workings

1 *Group structure*

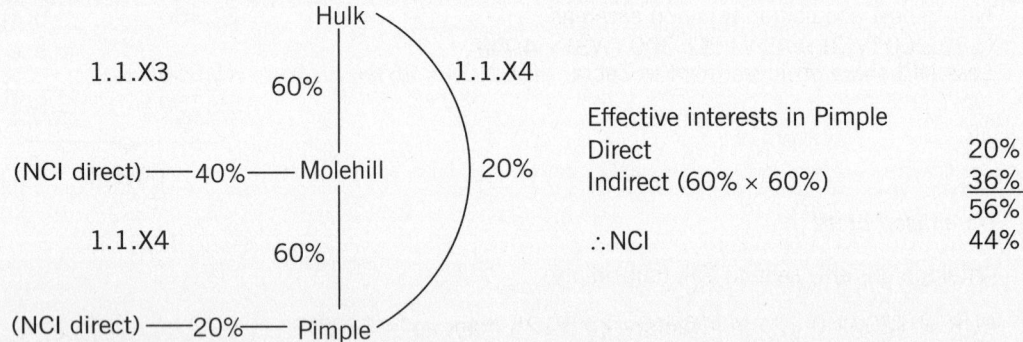

Effective interests in Pimple

Direct	20%
Indirect (60% × 60%)	36%
	56%
∴NCI	44%

Note. Pimple comes into Hulk's control on 1 January 20X4. As the investments in Pimple by Hulk and Molehill both happened on the same date, only one goodwill calculation is needed in respect of Pimple.

The direct non-controlling interest in Molehill Co is		40%
The direct non-controlling interest in Pimple Co is	20%	
The indirect non-controlling interest in Pimple Co is (40% of 60%)	24%	
The total non-controlling interest in Pimple Co is		44%
The group share of Molehill Co is 60% and of Pimple Co is 56%		

2   *Goodwill*

	Hulk in Molehill		Hulk and Molehill in Pimple	
	$	$	$	$
Consideration transferred - direct		90,000		25,000
- indirect			(60% × 42,000)	25,200
Non-controlling interests		23,200		28,600
($58,000 × 40%)/($65,000 × 44%)				
Fair value at net assets at acquisition:				
Share capital	50,000		50,000	
Retained earnings	8,000		15,000	
		(58,000)		(65,000)
		55,200		13,800

$69,000

3   *Retained earnings*

	Hulk	Molehill	Pimple
	$	$	$
Per question	45,000	32,000	25,000
Pre-acquisition profits		(8,000)	(15,000)
Post-acquisition retained earnings		24,000	10,000
Group share:			
In Molehill ($24,000 × 60%)	14,400		
In Pimple ($10,000 × 56%)	5,600		
Group retained earnings	65,000		

4   *Revaluation surplus*

	$
Hulk Co	50,000
Molehill Co: all post-acquisition ($20,000 × 60%)	12,000
	62,000

Note. Pimple does not have any revaluation surplus.

5   *Non-controlling interests*

	Molehill	Pimple
	$	$
NCI at acquisition (W2)	23,200	28,600
NCI share of post acquisition retained earnings		
($24,000 (W3) × 40%)/($10,000 (W3) × 44%)	9,600	4,400
NCI share of post acquisition revaluation surplus		
($20,000 (W4) × 40%)	8,000	–
Less: NCI share of investment in Pimple ($42,000 × 40%)	(16,800)	–
	24,000	33,000

$57,000

Now try these questions from the Exam Question Bank

Number	Level	Marks	Time
Q13	Examination	10	18 mins
Q14	Examination	18	32 mins

CHANGES IN GROUP STRUCTURES

 Changes in group structures appear regularly in consolidation questions in both sections of the F2 exam paper. Your approach should be the same as for more simple consolidation questions: *methodical and logical*. As long as you can identify the basic elements of the consolidation there will be plenty of marks available even if you cannot deal with the more complicated aspects.

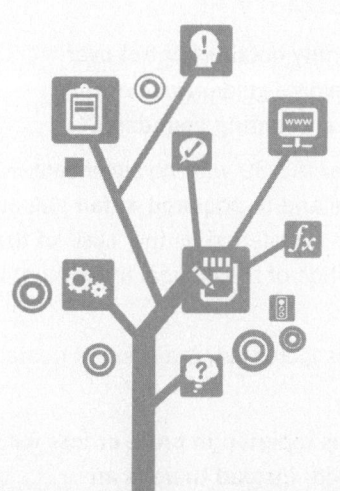

topic list	learning outcomes	syllabus references	ability required
1 Business combinations achieved in stages	A1	A1 (ii),(iii)	Application
2 Disposals when control is retained	A1	A1 (ii),(iii)	Application
3 Disposals where control/significant influence is lost	A1	A1 (ii),(iii)	Application
4 Business reorganisations	A2	A2 (i),(ii)	Application

1 Business combinations achieved in stages 11/10, 5/12

Introduction

A parent company may acquire a controlling interest in the shares of a subsidiary as a result of **several successive share purchases**, rather than by purchasing the shares all on the same day. Business combinations achieved in stages may also be known as 'step acquisitions' or 'piecemeal acquisitions'. We will use this term 'step acquisitions' throughout this Chapter.

1.1 Types of step acquisitions

Step acquisitions can lead to a holding in another entity progressing from an investment to an associate to a subsidiary.

There are three possible types of step acquisitions:

(a) A previously held **interest**, say 10%, with **no significant influence** (accounted for under IAS 39) is **increased to a controlling interest** of 50% or more.

(b) A **previously held equity interest**, say 35%, accounted for as an **associate** under IAS 28, is increased to a controlling interest of 50% or more.

(c) A **controlling interest** in a subsidiary is **increased**, say from 60% to 80%.

The first two transactions are treated in the same way, but the third is not. There is a reason for this.

1.2 General principle: 'crossing an accounting boundary'

Under the revised IFRS 3 a business combination occurs only when one entity **obtains control over another**, which is generally when 50% or more has been acquired. The Deloitte guide: *Business Combinations and Changes in Ownership interests* calls this '**crossing an accounting boundary**'.

When this happens, the original investment – whether an investment under IAS 39 with no significant influence, or an associate – is treated as if it were **disposed of at fair value and re-acquired at fair value**. This **previously held interest** at fair value, together with any consideration transferred, is the **'cost' of the combination** used in calculating the goodwill. A gain or loss on de-recognition of the original investment is recognised in profit or loss.

If the 50% **boundary is not crossed**, as when the interest in a subsidiary is increased, the event is treated as a **transaction between owners**.

Whenever you cross the 50% boundary, you revalue, and a gain or loss is reported in profit or loss for the year. If you do not cross the 50% boundary, no gain or loss is reported; instead there is an adjustment to the parent's equity.

The following diagram, from the *Deloitte* guide may help you visualise the boundary:

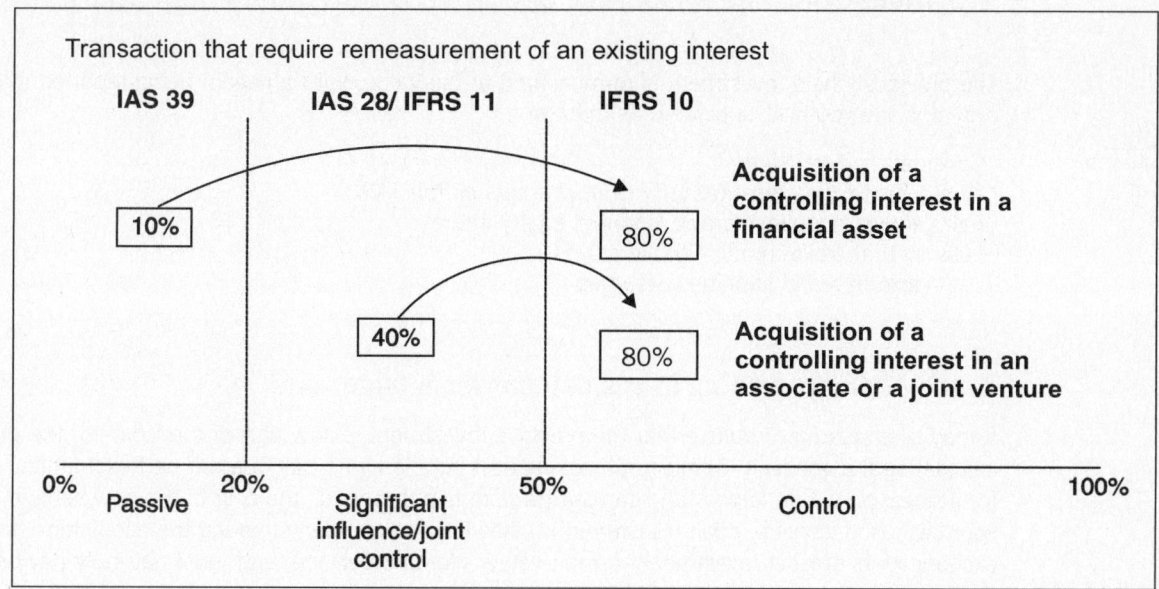

As you will see from the diagram, the third situation in paragraph 1.1, where an interest in a subsidiary is increased from, say, 60% to 80%, does not involve crossing that all-important 50% threshold. Likewise, purchases of stakes of up to 50% do not involve crossing the control boundary, and therefore do not trigger a calculation of goodwill.

In the first example above, in substance, the parent has:

- 'Sold' a 10% investment – so we need to remeausure the investment to fair value and record a gain or loss on de-recognition in profit or loss

- 'Purchased' an 80% subsidiary – so we need to calculate goodwill including the consideration transferred for the 70% acquired and the fair value of the previously held 10% at the date control is achieved.

In the second example, in substance, the parent has:

- 'Sold' a 40% associate – so we need to remeasure the investment in associate to fair value and record a gain or loss on de-recognition in profit or loss.

- 'Purchased' an 80% subsidiary – so we need to calculate goodwill including the consideration transferred for the 40% acquired and the fair value of the previously held 40% at the date control is achieved.

Exam alert

In an exam, if the control boundary is crossed, this triggers two events:

- Revalue the previously held investment to fair value and recognise a gain or loss on de-recognition
- Calculate goodwill on the whole shareholding (including the previously held investment at fair value).

Remember that the examiner may include a consolidated statement of changes in equity as well as a statement of profit or loss and other comprehensive income or a statement of financial position.

1.3 Investment or associate becomes a subsidiary: calculation of goodwill

The previously held investment is re-measured to fair value, with any gain being reported in profit and loss, and the goodwill calculated as follows:

Consideration transferred	X
Non-controlling interest (at %FV of new assets or 'full' FV)	X
Fair value of acquirer's previously held equity interest	X
Less net fair value of identifiable assets	
acquired and liabilities assumed	(X)
	XI

1.3.1 Analogy: trading in a small car for a larger one

It may seem counter-intuitive that the previous investment is now part of the 'cost' for the purposes of calculating the goodwill. One way of looking at it is to imagine that you are part-exchanging a small car for a larger one. The value of the car you trade in is put towards the cost of the new vehicle, together with your cash (the 'consideration transferred'). Likewise, the company making the acquisition has part-exchanged its smaller investment – at fair value – for a larger one, and must naturally pay on top of that to obtain the larger investment.

This analogy is not exact, but may help.

Try the following question to get the hang of the calculation of goodwill and profit on de-recognition of the investment.

Question 11.1	Step acquisition

Learning outcomes A1

Good, whose year end is 30 June 20X9 has a subsidiary, Will, which it acquired in stages. The details of the acquisition are as follows:

Date of acquisition	Holding acquired %	Retained earnings at acquisition $m	Purchase consideration $m
1 July 20X7	20	270	120
1 July 20X8	60	400	480

The share capital of Will has remained unchanged since its incorporation at $300m. The fair values of the net assets of Will were the same as their carrying amounts at the date of the acquisition. Good did not have significant influence over Will at any time before gaining control of Will. At 1 July 20X8, the fair value of Good's 20% holding in Will was $160m. The group policy is to measure non-controlling interests at acquisition at their proportionate share of the fair value of the subsidiary's identifiable net assets.

Required

(a) Calculate the goodwill on the acquisition of Will that will appear in the consolidated statement of financial position at 30 June 20X9.

(b) Calculate the profit on the de-recognition of any previously held investment in Will to be reported in group profit or loss for the year ended 30 June 20X9.

1.4 Increase in previously held controlling interest: adjustment to parent's equity   5/11

An example of this would be where an investment goes from a 60% subsidiary to an 80% subsidiary. In substance, there has been no acquisition as the entity is still a subsidiary. The 50% threshold has not been crossed, so there is no re-measurement to fair value and no gain or loss to profit or loss for the year. Instead, in substance, there has been a **transaction between owners** ie the parent has purchased a 20% shareholding from the non-controlling interest. This should be recorded in the equity section of the consolidated statement of financial position as follows:

(a)   A decrease in non-controlling interests (in the above example from 40% to 20%)

(b)   An adjustment to the parent's equity (the consideration paid less the decrease in NCI.

Both of these movements in equity need to be recorded in a separate line in the consolidated statement of changes in equity.

The proforma for **the calculation of the adjustment to the parent's equity** is as follows:

	$
Fair value of consideration paid	(X)
Decrease in NCI in net assets and goodwill* at date of transaction	X
Adjustment to parent's equity	$(\overline{X})$

*Note. There will only be a decrease in the NCI share in goodwill where non-controlling interests are measured at fair value at the date of acquisition. If non-controlling interests are measured at the proportionate share of the net assets at acquisition, there is no goodwill for NCI.

If you are wondering why the increase in shareholding is treated as a transaction between owners, the revised IFRS 3 views **the group as an economic entity,** and **views all providers of equity**, including non-controlling interests, as **owners of the group.**

You can practise this adjustment in the example below.

Example: step or piecemeal acquisition of a subsidiary

Peace acquired 25% of Miel on 1.1.20X1 for $2,020,000 (equivalent to the fair value of $10.10 per share acquired on that date) when Miel's reserves were standing at $5,800,000. The fair value of Miel's identifiable assets and liabilities at that date was $7,200,000. Both Peace and Miel are stock market listed entities.

A further 35% stake in Miel was acquired on 30 September 20X2 for $4,200,000 (paying a premium over Miel's market share price to achieve control). The fair value of Miel's identifiable assets and liabilities at that date was $9,200,000, and Miel's reserves stood at $7,800,000.

At 30 September 20X2, Miel's share price was $14.50.

Summarised statements of financial position of the two companies at that date show:

	Peace $'000	Miel $'000
Non-current assets		
Property, plant and equipment	38,650	7,600
Investment in Miel (cost)	6,220	–
	44,870	7,600
Current assets	12,700	2,200
	57,570	9,800
Equity		
Share capital ($1 shares)	10,200	800
Reserves	39,920	7,900
	50,120	8,700
Liabilities	7,450	1,100
	57,570	9,800

SUMMARISED STATEMENTS OF PROFIT OR LOSS AND OTHER COMPREHENSIVE INCOME
FOR THE YEAR TO 31 DECEMBER 20X2

	Peace $'000	Miel $'000
Revenue	10,200	4,000
Cost of sales and expenses	(9,000)	(3,600)
Profit before tax	1,200	400
Income tax expense	(360)	(80)
Profit for the year	840	320
Other comprehensive income:		
Gain on property valuation, net of tax	240	80
Other comprehensive income for the year, net of tax	240	80
Total comprehensive income for the year	1,080	400

The difference between the fair value of the identifiable assets and liabilities of Miel and their book value relates to the value of a plot of land. The land had not been sold by 31 December 20X2.

Group policy is to measure non-controlling interests at the date of acquisition at fair value.

No impairment losses on recognised goodwill have been necessary to date.

Required

(a) Prepare the consolidated statement of financial position of Peace Group as at 31 December 20X2 and the consolidated statement or profit or loss and other comprehensive income in the following circumstances:

  (i) The 25% interest in Miel allowed Peace significant influence over the financial and operating policy decisions of Miel.

  (ii) The 25% interest in Miel has not constituted significant influence and the investment had been revalued at 31 December 20X1 to its stock market value of $2,440,000.

(b) Show the consolidated current assets, non-controlling interests and reserves figures if Peace acquired an *additional* 10% interest in Miel on 1 January 20X3 for $1,200,000.

Solution

Parts (a)(i) and (a)(ii) to the example would generate the same overall answer for the consolidated statement of financial position.

(a) PEACE GROUP
CONSOLIDATED STATEMENT OF FINANCIAL POSITION AS AT 31 DECEMBER 20X2

	$'000
Non-current assets	
Property, plant and equipment (38,650 + 7,600 + (W2) 600)	46,850
Goodwill (W2)	2,540
	49,390
Current assets (12,700 + 2,200)	14,900
	64,290
Equity attributable to owners of the parent	
Share capital	10,200
Reserves (W3)/(W4)	40,860
	51,060
Non-controlling interests (W5)	4,680
	55,740
Liabilities (7,450 + 1,100)	8,550
	64,290

(i) CONSOLIDATED STATEMENT OF PROFIT OR LOSS AND OTHER COMPREHENSIVE INCOME FOR THE YEAR ENDED 31 DECEMBER 20X2

	$'000
Revenue (10,200 + (4,000 × 3/12))	11,200
Cost of sales and expenses (9,000 + (3,600 × 3/12))	(9,900)
Profit on de-recognition of associate (W3)	380
Share of profit of associate (320 × 9/12 × 25%)	60
Profit before tax	1,740
Income tax expense (360 + (80 × 3/12))	(380)
Profit for the year	1,360
Other comprehensive income:	
Gains on property revaluation, net of tax (240 + (80 × 3/12))	260
Share of gain on property revaluation of associate (80 × 9/12 × 25%)	15
Other comprehensive income for the year, net of tax	275
Total comprehensive income for the year	1,635
Profit attributable to:	
Owners of parent	1,328
Non-controlling interests ((320 × 3/12) × 40%)	32
	1,360
Total comprehensive income attributable to:	
Owners of parent	1,595
Non-controlling interests ((400 × 3/12) × 40%)	40
	1,635

Tutorial note: Miel was a 25% associate for the first 3 months of the year (1.1.X2 – 31.3.X2) so has been equity accounted for 3/12 of the year. Miel was a 60% subsidiary for the last 9 months of the year (1.4.X2 – 31.12.X2) so has been consolidated line by line for 9/12 of the year.

(ii) CONSOLIDATED STATEMENT OF PROFIT OR LOSS AND OTHER COMPREHENSIVE INCOME FOR THE YEAR ENDED 31 DECEMBER 20X2

	$'000
Revenue (10,200 + (4,000 × 3/12))	11,200
Cost of sales and expenses (9,000 + (3,600 × 3/12))	(9,900)
Profit on de-recognition of investment (W3)	880
Profit before tax	2,180
Income tax expense (360 + (80 × 3/12))	(380)
Profit for the year	1,800
Other comprehensive income:	
Gains on property revaluation, net of tax (240 + (80 × 3/12))	260
Reclassification of revaluation gains on available for sale investment (W3)	(420)
Other comprehensive income for the year, net of tax	(160)
Total comprehensive income for the year	1,640
Profit attributable to:	
Owners of parent (balancing figure)	1,766
Non-controlling interests ((320 × 3/12) × 40%)	32
	1,800
Total comprehensive income attributable to:	
Owners of parent (balancing figure)	1,600
Non-controlling interests ((400 × 3/12) × 40%)	40
	1,640

Tutorial note: Miel was a 60% subsidiary for the last 9 months of the year (1.4.X2 – 31.12.X2) so has been consolidated line by line for 9/12 of the year.

Workings

1   *Group structure*

Peace

| 1.1.X1 | 30.9.X2 |
| | |

25% + 35% =   60%

∴ Non-controlling interests = 40%

Miel   Reserves (1.1.X1) = $5,800,000

Reserves (30.9.X2) = $7,800,000

2   *Goodwill*

	$'000	$'000
Consideration transferred		4,200
Non-controlling interests (800 × 40% × $14.50)		4,640
FV of P's previously held equity interest (800 × 25% × $14.50)		2,900
Fair value of identifiable assets acq'd & liabilities assumed:		
Share capital	800	
Reserves	7,800	
Fair value adjustments (W6)	600	
		(9,200)
		2,540

3   *Consolidated reserves (if previously held as an associate) (a)(i)*

	$'000 Peace	$'000 Miel 25%	$'000 Miel 60%
Per question	39,920	7,800	7,900
Profit on derecognition of investment *	380		
Fair value movement (W6)			(0)
Reserves at acquisition		(5,800)	(7,800)
		2,000	100
Share of post acquisition reserves			
Miel 25% (2,000 × 25%)	500		
Miel 60% (100 × 60%)	60		
	40,860		

* Profit on derecognition of 25% associate

	$'000
Fair value at date control obtained (800 × 25% × $14.50)	2,900
P's share of carrying value (2,020 + [(7,800 – 5,800) × 25%])	(2,520)
	380

4   *Consolidated reserves (if previously held as an AFSFA) (a)(ii)*

	$'000 Peace	$'000 Miel
Per question	39,920	7,900
Profit on de-recognition of investment*	880	
Fair value movement (W6)		(0)
Reserves at acquisition		(7,800)
		100
Miel - Share of post acquisition reserves		
(100 × 60%)	60	
	40,860	

* Profit on derecognition of 25% investment

	$'000
Fair value at date control obtained	2,900
Cost	(2,020)
	880

Previous revaluation gains of $420,000 on the available for sale investment (fair value at 31.12.X1 of $2,440,000 less cost of $2,020,000) must be reclassified from other comprehensive income to profit or loss (as part of the $880,000 profit on derecognition above).

5   *Non-controlling interests*

	$'000
NCI at acquisition (W2)	4,640
NCI share of reserves since *control*(100 (W3/4) × 40%)	40
	4,680

6   *Fair value adjustments*

Measured at date control achieved (only)

	At acquisition 30.9.X2 $'000	Movement $'000	At year end 31.12.X2 $'000
Land (9,200 – (800 + 7,800))	600	–	600

(b)   *Current assets* (14,900 – 1,200)   13,700

Non-controlling interests

	$'000
NCI at acquisition (part (a) (W2))	4,640
NCI share of retained earnings since *control* (part (a) (W3/4) × 40%)	40
	4,680
Decrease in NCI (4,680 × 10%/40%)	(1,170)
	3,510

Consolidated reserves

	$'000
Per part (a)	40,860
Adjustment to parent's equity on acq'n of 10% (W)	(30)
	40,830

Note. no other figures in the statement of financial position are affected.

Working: Adjustment to parent's equity on acquisition of additional 10% of Miel

	$'000
Fair value of consideration paid	(1,200)
Decrease in NCI in net assets at acq'n (from NCI working)	1,170
	(30)

A journal entry may help you to understand the effect of this adjustment:

		$'000	$'000
DEBIT	Consolidated reserves	30	
DEBIT	NCI	1,170	
CREDIT	Cash (consideration paid)		1,200

Section summary

Transactions of the type described in this chapter can be very complicated and certainly look rather daunting. Remember and apply the **basic techniques** and you should find such questions easier than you expected.

Step acquisitions (piecemeal acquisitions) can lead to a company becoming an investment, an associate and then a subsidiary over time. Make sure you can deal with each of these situations.

Where control is achieved in stages:

- Remeasure any previously held equity interest to fair value at the date control is achieved (and include this amount in the goodwill calculation)
- Report any gain or loss on derecognition in profit or loss
- Where a controlling interest is increased, treat as a transaction between owners by decreasing non-controlling interests and recording an adjustment in the parent's equity

2 Disposals where control is retained

3/12

Introduction

Disposals of shares in a subsidiary may or may not result in a loss of control. In this section we will consider what happens when control is retained.

KEY POINT

Disposals are in many ways a mirror image of step acquisitions. The same principles underly both.

2.1 Types of disposal

2.1.1 Disposals where control is lost

There are three main kinds of disposals in which control is lost:

(a) Full disposal: all the holding is sold (say, 80% to nil)
(b) Subsidiary to associate (say, 80% to 30%)
(c) Subsidiary to trade investment (say, 80% to 10%)

In your exam, you are most likely to meet a partial disposal, either subsidiary to associate or subsidiary to trade investment.

2.1.2 Disposals where control is retained

There is only one kind of disposal where control is retained: **subsidiary to subsidiary**, for example an 80% holding to a 60% holding.

Disposals where control is lost are treated differently from disposals where control is retained. There is a reason for this.

2.2 General principle: 'crossing an accounting boundary'

Under the revised IFRS 3 disposal occurs only when one entity loses control over another, which is generally when its holding is decreased to less than 50%. The Deloitte guide: *Business Combinations and Changes in Ownership Interests* calls this 'crossing an accounting boundary'.

On disposal of a controlling interest, any retained interest (an associate or trade investment) is measured at fair value on the date that control is lost. This fair value is used in the calculation of the gain or loss on disposal, and also becomes the carrying amount for subsequent accounting for the retained interest.

If the **50%** boundary is **not crossed**, as when the interest in a subsidiary is reduced, the event is treated as a **transaction between owners**.

Whenever you cross the 50% boundary, you revalue the remaining shareholding, and a gain or loss is reported in profit or loss for the year. If you do not cross the 50% boundary, no gain or loss is reported; instead there is an adjustment to the parent's equity.

The following diagram, from the *Deloittes* guide may help you visualise the boundary:

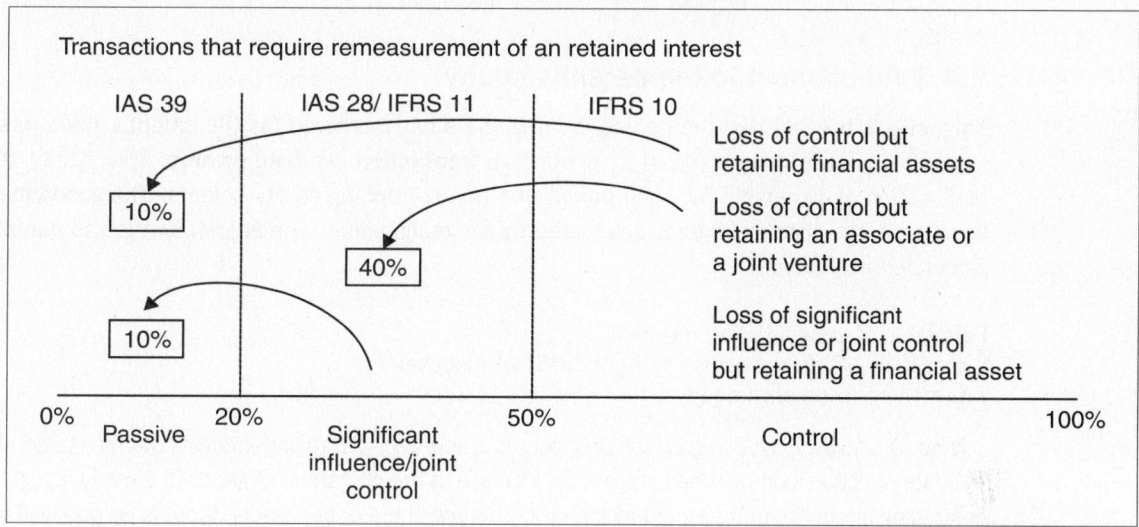

As you will see from the diagram, the situation in paragraph 2.1.2, where an interest in a subsidiary is reduced from say 80% to 60%, would not involve crossing that all-important 50% threshold.

2.3 Effective date of disposal

The effective date of disposal is **when control passes**: the date for accounting for an undertaking ceasing to be a subsidiary undertaking is the date on which its former parent undertaking relinquishes its control over that undertaking. The consolidated statement of profit or loss (statement of profit or loss and other comprehensive income) should include the results of a subsidiary undertaking up to the date of its disposal. IAS 37 on provisions and IFRS 5 on disclosure of discontinued operations will have an impact here.

2.4 Disposals where control is retained

Control is retained where the disposal is from **subsidiary to subsidiary.** In substance there has been no disposal as the entity is still a subsidiary. Instead, it is treated as a transaction been group shareholders ie the parent is selling shares to the non-controlling interest. Therefore, the following two steps must be taken:

• Record an increase in non-controlling interests in the NCI working for the consolidated statement of financial position; and

• Record an adjustment to the parent's equity (consideration received less increase in NCI).

The detail of the accounting treatment in the consolidated financial statements is shown below.

2.4.1 Statement of profit or loss and other comprehensive income

(a) The subsidiary is **consolidated in full** for the whole period.

(b) The **non-controlling interest in the statement of profit or loss** will be based on percentage before and after disposal, ie time apportion.

(c) There is no profit or loss on disposal.

2.4.2 Statement of financial position

(a)   The increase in the non-controlling interest on disposal must be shown in the non-controlling interest working (the end result being year end NCI based on year end percentage).

(b)   The consideration received less the increase in non-controlling interests is shown as an adjustment to the parent's equity.

(c)   Goodwill on acquisition is unchanged in the consolidated statement of financial position.

2.4.3 Adjustment to the parent's equity

This reflects the fact that the non-controlling share has increased (as the parent's share has reduced). A subsidiary to subsidiary disposal is, in effect, **a transaction between owners.** Specifically, it is a reallocation of ownership between parent and non-controlling equity holders. **The goodwill is unchanged,** because it is a historical figure, unaffected by the reallocation. The adjustment to the parent's equity is calculated as follows:

	$
Fair value of consideration received	X
Increase in NCI in net assets and goodwill* at disposal	(X)
Adjustment to parent's equity	X

* **Note.** A change in NCI in goodwill only occurs where non-controlling interests are measured at fair value at the date of acquisition (ie when there is an increase in the NCI share of goodwill already recognised). If non-controlling interests are measured at the proportionate share of net assets, there is no goodwill for NCI.

If you are wondering why the decrease in shareholding is treated as a transaction between owners, the revised IFRS 3 views **the group as an economic entity**, and views **all providers of equity**, including non-controlling interests, as **owners of the group**. Non-controlling shareholders are not outsiders, they are owners of the group just like the parent.

You can practise the adjustment to parent's equity in the example and in requirement (b) of Question 11.2 later in this chapter.

Exam alert

Exam questions with a disposal where control is not lost could require a statement of changes in equity to be prepared as this is where the increase in non-controlling interest and the adjustment to parent's equity will be shown in a separate line.

2.4.4 Gain in the parent's separate financial statements

This calculation is more straightforward: the proceeds are compared with the carrying value of the investment sold. The investment will be held at cost or at fair value if held as an available-for-sale financial asset:

	$
Fair value of consideration received	X
Less carrying value of investment disposed	(X)
Profit/(loss) on disposal	X/(X)

The profit on disposal is generally taxable, and the **tax based on the parent's gain** rather than the group's will also need to be recognised in the consolidated financial statements.

Section summary

Disposals do not always result in a loss of control. Remember particularly how to deal with **goodwill**.

3 Disposals where control/significant influence is lost   3/12

> **Introduction**
>
> Disposals of shares in a subsidiary may or may not result in a loss of control. If control is lost, then any remaining investment will need to be recategorised as an associate or a trade investment.

3.1 Control lost: calculation of group gain on disposal

A proforma calculation is shown below. This needs to be adapted for the circumstances in the question, in particular whether it is a full or partial disposal:

	$	$
Fair value of consideration received		X
Fair value of any investment retained		X
Less share of consolidated carrying amount at date control lost		(X)
Net assets	X	
Goodwill	X	(X)
Less non-controlling interests	(X)	
		(X)
Group profit/(loss)		X/(X)

Following IAS 1, this gain may need to be disclosed separately if it is material.

3.1.1 Analogy: trading in a large car for a smaller one

It may seem counter-intuitive that the investment retained is now part of the 'proceeds' for the purposes of calculating the gain. One way of looking at it is to imagine that you are selling a larger car and putting part of the proceeds towards a smaller one. If the larger car you are selling cost you less than the smaller car and cash combined, you have made a profit. Likewise, the company making the disposal sold a larger stake to gain, at fair value, a smaller stake and some cash on top, which is the 'consideration received'.

This analogy is not exact, but may help.

3.2 Control lost: calculation of gain in parent's separate financial statements

This is calculated as for disposals where control is retained: see Paragraph 2.4.4 above.

3.3 Disposals where control is lost: accounting treatment

For a **full disposal**, apply the following treatment.

(a) **Statement of profit or loss and other comprehensive income**

    (i) Consolidate results and non-controlling interest to the date of disposal.

    (ii) Show the group profit or loss on disposal.

(b) **Statement of financial position**

There will be no non-controlling interest and no consolidation as there is no subsidiary at the date the statement of financial position is being prepared.

A full disposal is illustrated in requirement (a) of Question 11.2 later in this chapter.

For **partial disposals**, use the following treatments.

(a) **Subsidiary to associate**

    (i) **Statement of profit or loss and other comprehensive income**

(1)   Treat the undertaking as a subsidiary up to the date of disposal, ie consolidate for the correct number of months and show the non-controlling interest in that amount.

(2)   Show the profit or loss on disposal.

(3)   Treat as an associate thereafter, ie equity account by including the group share of the associate's profit and the group share of the associate's other comprehensive income pro-rated for the number of months the investment was an associate.

(ii)   **Statement of financial position**

(1)   The investment remaining is at its fair value at the date of disposal (to calculate the gain)

(2)   Equity account (as an associate) thereafter, using the fair value as the new 'cost'. (Post 'acquisition' retained earnings are added to this cost in future years to arrive at the carrying value of the investment in the associate in the statement of financial position.)

A part disposal where a subsidiary becomes an associate is illustrated in the next example and in requirement (c) of Question 11.2 later in this chapter.

(b)   **Subsidiary to trade investment**

(i)   **Statement of profit or loss and other comprehensive income)**

(1)   Treat the undertaking as a subsidiary up to the date of disposal, ie consolidate.
(2)   Show profit or loss on disposal.
(3)   Show dividend income and revaluation gains/losses on the investment only thereafter.

(ii)   **Statement of financial position**

(1)   The investment remaining is at its fair value at the date of disposal (to calculate the gain).

(2)   Thereafter, treat as an available-for-sale financial asset under IAS 39.

A part disposal where a subsidiary becomes an available-for-sale financial asset is illustrated in requirement (d) of Question 11.2 later in this chapter.

Example: partial disposals

Chalk Co bought 100% of the voting share capital of Cheese Co on its incorporation on 1 January 20X2 for $160,000. Cheese Co earned and retained $240,000 from that date until 31 December 20X7. At that date the statements of financial position of the company and the group were as follows.

	Chalk Co $'000	Cheese Co $'000	Consolidated $'000
Investment in Cheese	160	–	–
Other assets	1,000	500	1,500
	1,160	500	1,500
Share capital	400	160	400
Retained earnings	560	240	800
	960	400	1,200
Current liabilities	200	100	300
	1,160	500	1,500

It is the group's policy to value the non-controlling interest at its proportionate share of the fair value of the subsidiary's identifiable net assets.

On 1 January 20X8 Chalk Co sold 40% of its shareholding in Cheese Co for $280,000. The profit on disposal (ignoring tax) in the financial statements of the parent company is calculated as follows.

	Chalk $'000
Fair value of consideration received	280
Carrying value of investment (40% × 160)	(64)
Profit on sale	216

We now move on to calculate the adjustment to equity for the group financial statements.

Because only 40% of the 100% subsidiary has been sold, leaving a 60% subsidiary, **control is retained**. This means that there is **no group profit on disposal in profit or loss for the year**. Instead, there is an **adjustment to the parent's equity**, which affects group retained earnings.

KEY POINT

Remember that, when control is retained, the disposal is just a transaction between owners. The non-controlling shareholders are owners of the group, just like the parent.

The adjustment to parent's equity is calculated as follows:

	$'000
Fair value of consideration received	280
Increase in non-controlling interest in net assets at the date of disposal (40% × 400)	(160)
Adjustment to parent's equity	120

This increases group retained earnings and does not go through group profit or loss for the year. (Note that there is no goodwill in this example, as the subsidiary was acquired on incorporation.)

Solution

Subsidiary status

The statements of financial position immediately after the sale will appear as follows.

	Chalk Co $'000	Cheese Co $'000	Consolidated $'000
Investment in Cheese (160-64)	96	–	–
Other assets	1,280	5500	1,780
	1,376	500	1,780
Share capital	400	160	400
Retained earnings*	776	240	920
Current liabilities	200	100	300
	1,376	500	1,620
Non-controlling interest			160
			1,780

*Chalk's retained earnings are $560,000 + $216,000 profit on disposal. Group retained earnings are increased by the adjustment above: $800,000 + $120,000 = $920,000. Non-controlling interest is measured at the proportionate share of the net assets ie $400,000 × 40% = $160,000.

Solution

Associate status

Using the above example, assume that Chalk Co sold 60% of its holding in Cheese Co for $440,000. The fair value of the 40% holding retained was $200,000. The gain or loss on disposal in the books of the parent company would be calculated as follows.

	Parent company $'000
Fair value of consideration received	440
Carrying value of investment (60% × 160)	(96)
Profit on sale	344

This time control is lost, so there will be a gain in group profit or loss, calculated as follows:

	$'000
Fair value of consideration received	440
Fair value of investment retained	200
Less Chalk's share of consolidated carrying value at date control lost (100% × 400)	(400)
Group profit on sale	240

Note that there was no goodwill arising on the acquisition of Cheese (as Cheese was acquired on incorporation), otherwise this too would be deducted in the calculation.

The statements of financial position would now appear as follows.

	Chalk Co $'000	Cheese Co $'000	Consolidated $'000
Investment in Cheese (Note 1)	64		200
Other assets	1,440	500	1,440
	1,504	500	1,640
Share capital	400	160	400
Retained earnings (Note 2)	904	240	1,040
Current liabilities	200	100	200
	1,504	500	1,640

Notes

1   The investment in Cheese is at fair value in the group SOFP. In fact it is equity accounted at fair value at date control lost plus share of post-'acquisition' retained earnings. But there are no retained earnings yet because control has only just been lost.

2   Chalk's retained earnings are $560,000 (per question) plus the parent's profit on disposal of $344,000. Group retained earnings are $800,000 (per the original consolidated statement of financial position in the question) plus group profit on the sale of $240,000, ie $1,040,000.

The following comprehensive question should help you get to grips with disposal problems. **Give yourself at least two hours**. This is a very difficult question.

Exam alert

Questions may involve part-disposals leaving investments with both subsidiary and associate status. Disposals are likely to come up regularly at F2, since you have not covered them before.

Question 11.2 Disposal

Learning outcomes A1

Smith Co bought 80% of the share capital of Jones Co for $324,000 on 1 October 20X5. At that date Jones Co's retained earnings balance stood at $180,000. The statements of financial position at 30 September 20X8 and the summarised statements of profit or loss and other comprehensive income to that date are given below.

	Smith Co $'000	Jones Co $'000
Non-current assets	360	270
Investment in Jones Co	324	–
Current assets	370	370
	1,054	640
Equity		
$1 ordinary shares	540	180
Retained earnings	414	360
	954	540
Current liabilities	100	100
	1,054	640
Profit before tax	153	126
Tax	(45)	(36)
Profit for the year	108	90

No entries have been made in the financial statements for any of the following transactions.

Assume that profits accrue evenly throughout the year. Neither entity has any other comprehensive income.

It is the group's policy to value the non-controlling interest at fair value at the date of acquisition. The fair value of the non-controlling interest in Jones Co on 1 October 20X5 was $81,000.

Ignore taxation.

Required

Prepare the consolidated statement of financial position and statement of profit or loss at 30 September 20X8 in each of the following circumstances. (Assume no impairment of goodwill.)

(a)   Smith Co sells its entire holding in Jones Co for $650,000 on 30 September 20X8.

(b)   Smith Co sells one quarter of its holding in Jones Co for $162,500 on 30 June 20X8. For part (b) only, prepare the consolidated statement of changes in equity, as well as the statement of financial position and statement of profit or loss. The total group equity as at 30 September 20X7 was $1,017,000, which included $99,000 attributable to the non-controlling interests.

(c)   Smith Co sells one half of its holding in Jones Co for $325,000 on 30 June 20X8, and the remaining holding (fair value $325,000) is to be dealt with as an associate.

(d)   Smith Co sells one half of its holding in Jones Co for $325,000 on 30 June 20X8, and the remaining holding (fair value $325,000) is to be dealt with as an available-for-sale financial asset. There was no increase in the fair value of the remaining holding between 30 June 20X8 and 30 September 20X8.

Section summary

Disposals may occur in consolidation questions.

- The effective date of disposal is when **control passes**.
- Treatment of **goodwill** is according to IFRS 3.
- Disposals may be **full** or **partial**, to subsidiary, associate or investment status.
  - if control is lost, the interest retained is **fair valued** and becomes part of the calculation of the gain on disposal.
  - if control is retained, the change in non-controlling interests is shown as **an adjustment to parent's equity.**
- **Gain or loss** on disposal is calculated for the parent company and the group.

4 Business reorganisations

Introduction

Business reorganisations (ie internal group reorganisations) can take many forms. Apart from divisionalisation, all other internal reorganisations will not affect the consolidated financial statements, but they will affect the accounts of individual companies within the group.

Groups will reorganise on occasions for a variety of reasons.

(a)   A group may want to **float** a business to **reduce the gearing** of the group. The holding company will initially transfer the business into a separate company.

(b)   Companies may be transferred to another business during a **divisionalisation** process.

(c)   The group may 'reverse' into another company to obtain a **stock exchange quotation**.

(d)   Internal reorganisations may create efficiencies of group structure for **tax purposes**.

Such reorganisations involve a restructuring of the relationships within a group. Companies may be transferred to another business during a divisionalisation process. There is generally no effect on the consolidated financial statements, provided that no non-controlling interests are affected, because such reorganisations are only internal. The impact on the individual companies within the group, however, can be substantial. A variety of different transactions are described here, **only involving 100% subsidiaries**.

4.1 New top parent company

A new top holding company might be needed as a vehicle for flotation or to improve the co-ordination of a diverse business. The new company, P, will issue its own shares to the holders of the shares in S.

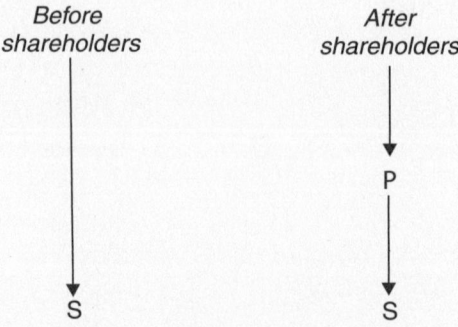

4.2 Subsidiary moved up

This transaction is shown in the diagram below. It might be carried out to allow S_1 to be **sold** while S_2 is retained, or to **split diverse businesses**.

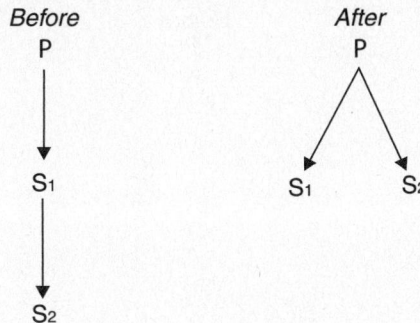

S_1 could transfer its investment in S_2 to P as a dividend *in specie* or by P paying cash. A share for share exchange is not possible because an allotment by P to S_1 is void. A **dividend in specie** is simply a dividend paid other than in cash.

S_1 must have sufficient **distributable profits** for a dividend *in specie*. If the investment in S_2 has been revalued then that can be treated as a realised profit for the purposes of determining the legality of the distribution. For example, suppose the statement of financial position of S_1 is as follows.

	$m
Investment in S_2 (cost $100m)	900
Other net assets	100
	1,000
Share capital	100
Revaluation surplus	800
Retained earnings	100
	1,000

It appears that S_1 cannot make a distribution of more than $100m. If, however, S_1 makes a distribution in kind of its investment in S_2, then the **revaluation surplus** can be treated as realised.

It is not clear how P should account for the transaction. The carrying value of S_2 might be used, but there may be **no legal rule**. P will need to write down its investment in S_1 at the same time. A transfer for cash is probably easiest, but there are still legal pitfalls as to what is distributable, depending on how the transfer is recorded.

There will be **no effect** on the group financial statements as the group has stayed the same: it has made no acquisitions or disposals.

4.3 Subsidiary moved along

This is a transaction which is treated in a very similar manner to that described above.

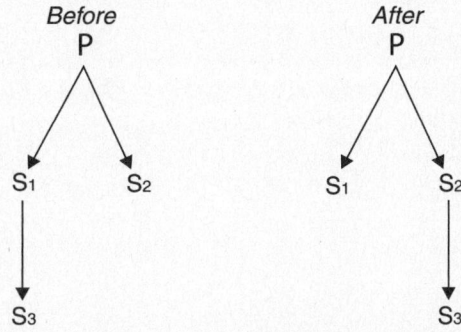

The problem of an effective distribution does not arise here because the holding company did not buy the subsidiary. There may be problems with **financial assistance** if S_2 pays less than the fair value to purchase S_3 as a prelude to S_1 leaving the group.

4.4 Subsidiary moved down

This situation could arise if P is in one country and S_1 and S_2 are in another. A **tax group** can be formed out of such a restructuring.

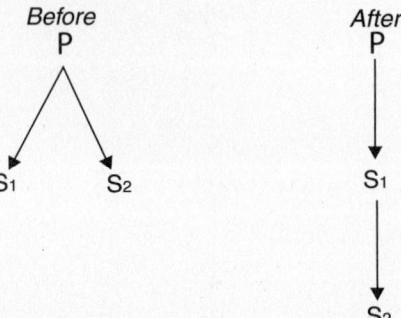

If S_1 paid cash for S_2, the transaction would be straightforward (as described above). It is unclear whether P should recognise a gain or loss on the sale if S_2 is sold for more or less than carrying value. S_1 would only be deemed to have made a distribution (avoiding any advance tax payable) only if the **price was excessive**.

Section summary

Reasons for business reorganisations include:

- Stock exchange floatation
- Divisionalisation
- Potential tax advantages

There is usually no effect on the consolidated financial statements provided the non-controlling interests are unchanged. However, a gain or loss may arise in the individual financial statements of the subsidiaries, which will need to be eliminated in the consolidated financial statements.

Chapter Roundup

✓   Transactions of the type described in this chapter can be very complicated and certainly look rather daunting. Remember and apply the **basic techniques** and you should find such questions easier than you expected.

✓   **Step acquisitions (piecemeal acquisitions)** can lead to a company becoming a trade investment, an associate and then a subsidiary over time. Make sure you can deal with each of these situations.

✓   Where control is achieved in stages:

   •   Remeasure any previously held equity interest to fair value at the date control is achieved.

   •   Report any gain in profit or loss

   •   Where a controlling interest is increased, * particularly how to deal with **goodwill**.

✓   Disposals may occur in consolidation questions.

   •   The effective date of disposal is when **control passes**.

   •   Treatment of **goodwill** is according to IFRS 3.

   •   Disposals may be **full** or **partial**, to subsidiary, associate or investment status.

      –   **if control is lost,** the interest retained is **fair valued** and becomes part of the calculation of the gain on disposal.

      –   **if control is retained**, treat as a transaction between owners by **increasing non-controlling interest** and **adjusting parent's equity** (by consideration received less increase in NCI).

   •   **Gain or loss** on disposal is calculated for the parent company and the group.

✓   Business reorganisations can take many forms. Apart from divisionalisation, all other internal reorganisations will not affect the consolidated financial statements, but they will affect the financial statements of individual companies within the group.

Quick Quiz

1   Control is always lost when there is a disposal. True or false?

2   Why is the fair value of the interest retained used in the calculation of a gain on disposal where control is lost?

3   When is the effective date of disposal of shares in an investment?

4   Subside owns 60% of Diary at 31 December 20X8. On 1 July 20X9, it buys a further 20% of Diary. How should this transaction be treated in the group financial statements at 31 December 20X9.

5   Ditch had a 75% subsidiary, Dodge, at 30 June 20X8. On 1 January 20X9, it sold two-thirds of this investment, leaving it with a 25% holding, over which it retained significant influence. How will the remaining investment in Dodge appear in the group financial statements for the year ended 30 June 20X9?

Answers to Quick Quiz

1   False. Control may be retained if the disposal is from subsidiary to subsidiary, even though the parent owns less and the non-controlling interest owns more.

2   It may be viewed as part of the consideration received.

3   When control passes.

4   As a transaction between owners, with a decrease in non-controlling interest (from 40% to 20%) and an adjustment to the parent's equity to reflect the difference between the consideration paid and the decrease in non-controlling interest.

5   It will be equity accounted as an associate. In the consolidated statement of financial position, an investment in associate will be recorded taking its fair value at the date of disposal plus a 25% share of the profits accrued between the date of disposal and the year end, less any impairment at the year end. In the consolidated statement of profit or loss and other comprehensive income, Dodge will be consolidated for the first six months and equity accounted for the remaining six months.

Answers to Questions

11.1   Step acquisition

(a)   *Goodwill (at date control obtained)*

	$m	$m
Consideration transferred		480
NCI (20% × 700)		140
Fair value of previously held equity interest		160
Fair value of identifiable assets acquired and liabilities assumed		
Share capital	300	
Retained earnings	400	
		(700)
		80

(b)   *Profit on derecognition of investment*

	$m
Fair value at date control obtained (see part (a))	160
Cost	(120)
	40

11.2   Disposal

(a)   *Complete disposal at year end (80% to 0%)*

CONSOLIDATED STATEMENT OF FINANCIAL POSITION AS AT 30 SEPTEMBER 20X8

	$'000
Non-current assets	360
Current assets (370 + 650)	1,020
	1,380
Equity	
$1 ordinary shares	540
Retained earnings (W3)	740
Current liabilities	100
	1,380

CONSOLIDATED STATEMENT OF PROFIT OR LOSS FOR THE YEAR ENDED 30 SEPTEMBER 20X8

	$'000
Profit before tax (153 + 126)	279
Profit on disposal (W4)	182
Tax (45 + 36)	(81)
Profit for the year	380
Profit attributable to:	
Owners of the parent	362
Non-controlling interest (20% × 90)	18
	380

Workings

1   *Group structure and timeline*

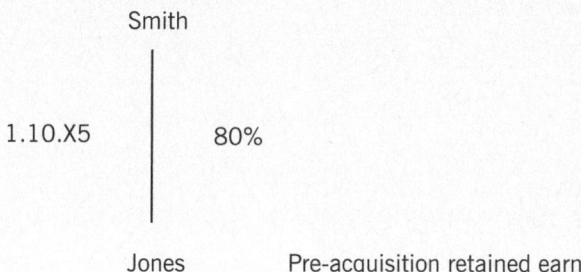

Smith

1.10.X5   80%

Jones   Pre-acquisition retained earnings = $180,000

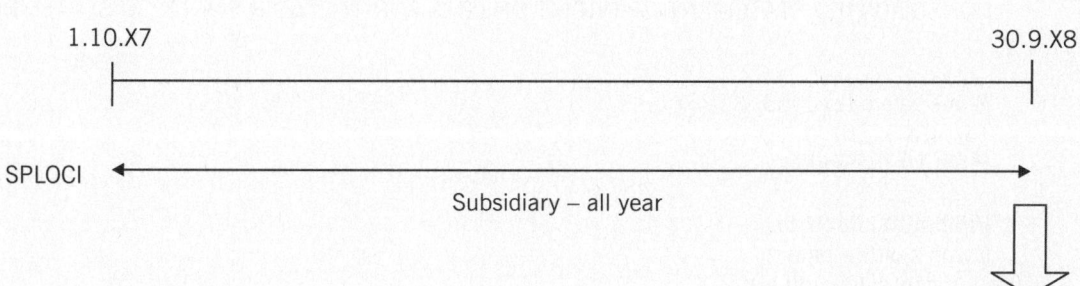

1.10.X7   30.9.X8

SPLOCI   Subsidiary – all year

Group gain on disposal *not* sub at y/e

2   *Goodwill (for group profit on disposal calculation)*

	$'000	$'000
Consideration transferred		324
Non-controlling interest		81
Less net assets at acquisition		
Share capital	180	
Retained earnings (W1)	180	
		(360)
		45

3   *Retained earnings carried forward*

	Smith	Jones
	$'000	$'000
Per question/date of disposal	414	360
Add: group gain on disposal (W4)	182	–
Pre-acquisition (W1)	–	(180)
		180
Share of post-acquisition reserves up to the disposal (80% × 180)	144	
	740	

4   *Profit on disposal of Jones Co*

	$'000	$'000
Fair value of consideration received		650
Less share of consolidated carrying value when control lost:		
Net assets (540 × 80%)	432	
Goodwill (45 (W2) × 80%)	36	
		(468)
		182

(b)   *Partial disposal: subsidiary to subsidiary (80% to 60%)*

CONSOLIDATED STATEMENT OF FINANCIAL POSITION AS AT 30 SEPTEMBER 20X8

	$'000
Non-current assets (360 + 270)	630.0
Goodwill (part (a))	45.0
Current assets (370 + 370 + 162.5)	902.5
	1,577.5
Equity	
$1 ordinary shares	540.0
Retained earnings (W2)	603.5
	1,143.5
Non-controlling interest (W3)	234.0
Current liabilities (100 + 100)	200.0
	1,577.5

CONSOLIDATED STATEMENT OF PROFIT OR LOSS FOR THE YEAR ENDED 30 SEPTEMBER 20X8

	$'000	$'000
Profit before tax (153 + 126)		279
Tax (45 + 36)		(81)
Profit for the period		198
Profit attributable to:		
Owners of the parent		175.5
Non-controlling interest		
20% × 90 × 9/12	13.5	
40% × 90 × 3/12	9.0	
		22.5
		198.0

CONSOLIDATED STATEMENT OF CHANGES IN EQUITY
FOR THE YEAR TO 30 SEPTEMBER 20X8

	Equity attributable to owners of the parent	Non-controlling interest	Total
	$'000	$'000	$'000
Balance at 1 October 20X7 (per question)	918.0	99.0	1,017.0
Total comprehensive income for the year (per SPL)	175.5	22.5	198.0
Adjustment to parent's equity (W4)	50.0	112.5	162.5
Balance at 30 September 20X8 (per SOFP)	1,143.5	234.0	1,377.5

Workings

1   *Timeline*

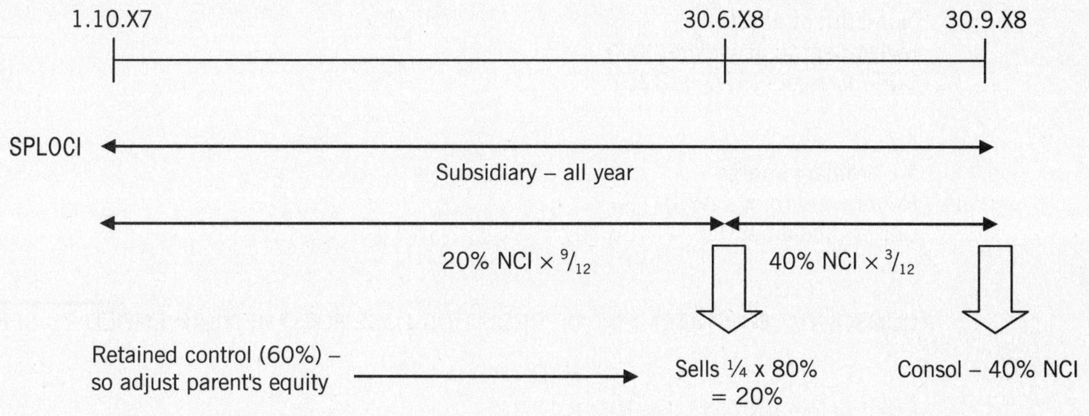

| 1.10.X7 | 30.6.X8 | 30.9.X8 |

SPLOCI ⟷

Subsidiary – all year

⟷

20% NCI × $^9/_{12}$ 40% NCI × $^3/_{12}$

Retained control (60%) –   Sells ¼ × 80%   Consol – 40% NCI
so adjust parent's equity   = 20%

2   *Group retained earnings*

	Smith	Jones 80%	Jones 60% retained
	$'000	$'000	$'000
Per question/at date of disposal			
$(360 - (90 \times \frac{3}{12}))$	414.0	337.5	360.0
Adjustment to parent's equity on disposal (W4)	50.0		
Retained earnings at acquisition		(180.0)	(337.5)
		157.5	22.5
Jones: share of post acqn. earnings			
(157.5 × 80%)	126.0		
Jones: share of post acqn. earnings			
(22.5 × 60%)	13.5		
	603.5		

3   *Non-controlling interests (SOFP)*

	$'000
NCI at acquisition (part a – goodwill)	81.0
NCI share of post acq'n reserves to disposal (W2) (157.5 × 20%)	31.5
NCI at disposal	112.5
Increase in NCI on disposal (112.5 × 20%/20%)	112.5
NCI share of post acq'n reserves to year end (W2) (22.5 × 40%)	9.0
	234.0

4   *Adjustment to parent's equity on disposal of 20% of Jones*

	$'000
Fair value of consideration received	162.5
Less increase in NCI in net assets and goodwill at disposal (W3)	(112.5)
	50.0

Note. A journal entry will explain how this is treated in the consolidated financial statements:

	$'000	$'000
DEBIT Cash (added to Smith's current assets on SOFP)	160.0	
CREDIT NCI		112.5
CREDIT Equity attributable to owners of the parent		47.5

(c)   *Partial disposal: subsidiary to associate (80% to 40%)*

CONSOLIDATED STATEMENT OF FINANCIAL POSITION AS AT 30 SEPTEMBER 20X8

	$'000
Non-current assets	360
Investment in associate (W2)	334
Current assets (370 + 325)	695
	1,389
Equity	
$1 ordinary shares	540
Retained earnings (W3)	749
Current liabilities	100
	1,389

CONSOLIDATED STATEMENT OF PROFIT OR LOSS FOR THE YEAR ENDED 30 SEPTEMBER 20X8

	$'000
Profit before tax (153 + (9/12 × 126))	247.5
Profit on disposal (W4)	200.0
Share of profit of associate (90 × 3/12× 40%)	9.0
Tax (45 + (9/12 × 36))	(72.0)
Profit for the period	384.5
Profit attributable to:	
Owners of the parent	371.0
Non-controlling interest (20% × 90 × 9/12)	13.5
	384.5

Workings

1   *Timeline*

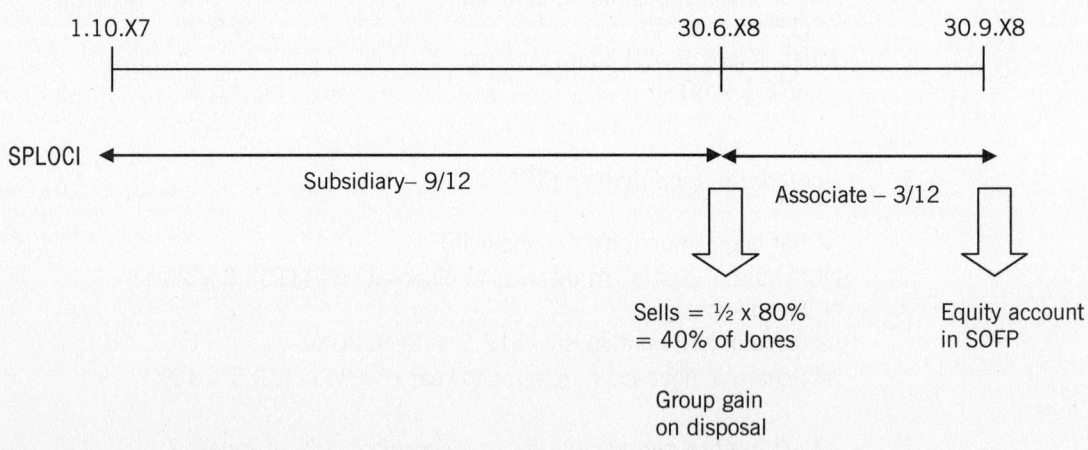

2   *Investment in associate*

	$'000
Fair value at date control lost (new 'cost')	325
Share of post 'acq'n' retained reserves (90 × 3/12 × 40%) (or from W3)	9
	334

3   *Group retained earnings*

	Smith	Jones 80%(sub)	Jones 40% retained (assoc.)
	$'000	$'000	$'000
Per question/at date of disposal			
(360 – (90 × 3/12))	414	337.5	360
Group profit on disposal (W2)	200		
Retained earnings at acquisition/date control lost		(180)	(337.5)
		157.5	22.5
Jones: share of post acqn. earnings			
(157.5 × 80%)	126		
Jones: share of post acqn. earnings			
(22.5 × 40%)	9		
	749		

4   *Profit on disposal in Smith Co*

	$'000	$'000
Fair value of consideration received		325
Fair value of 40% investment retained		325
Less share of consolidated carrying value when control lost		
Net assets: 540 – (90 × 3/12)	517.5	
Goodwill (Part (a))	45.0	
Less non-controlling interests (W5)	(112.5)	
		(450)
		200

5   *Non-controlling interests*

	$'000
Non-controlling interest at acquisition	81.0
NCI share of post-acquisition retained earnings to date of disposal: 20% × 157.5	31.5
	112.5
Decrease in NCI on loss of control	(112.5)
	0.0

(d)   *Partial disposal: subsidiary to available-for-sale financial asset (80% to 40%)*

CONSOLIDATED STATEMENT OF FINANCIAL POSITION AS AT 30 SEPTEMBER 20X8

	$'000
Non-current assets	360
Investment	325
Current assets (370 + 325)	695
	1,380
Equity	
$1 ordinary shares	540
Retained earnings (W2)	740
Current liabilities	100
	1,380

CONSOLIDATED STATEMENT OF PROFIT OR LOSS FOR THE YEAR ENDED 30 SEPTEMBER 20X8

	$'000
Profit before tax (153 + (9/12 × 126))	247.5
Profit on disposal (See (c) above)	200.0
Tax (45 + (9/12 × 36))	(72.0)
Profit for the period	375.5

Profit attributable to:
Owners of the parent

Non-controlling interest (20% × 90 × 9/12)

	362.0
	13.5
	375.5

Workings

1   *Timeline*

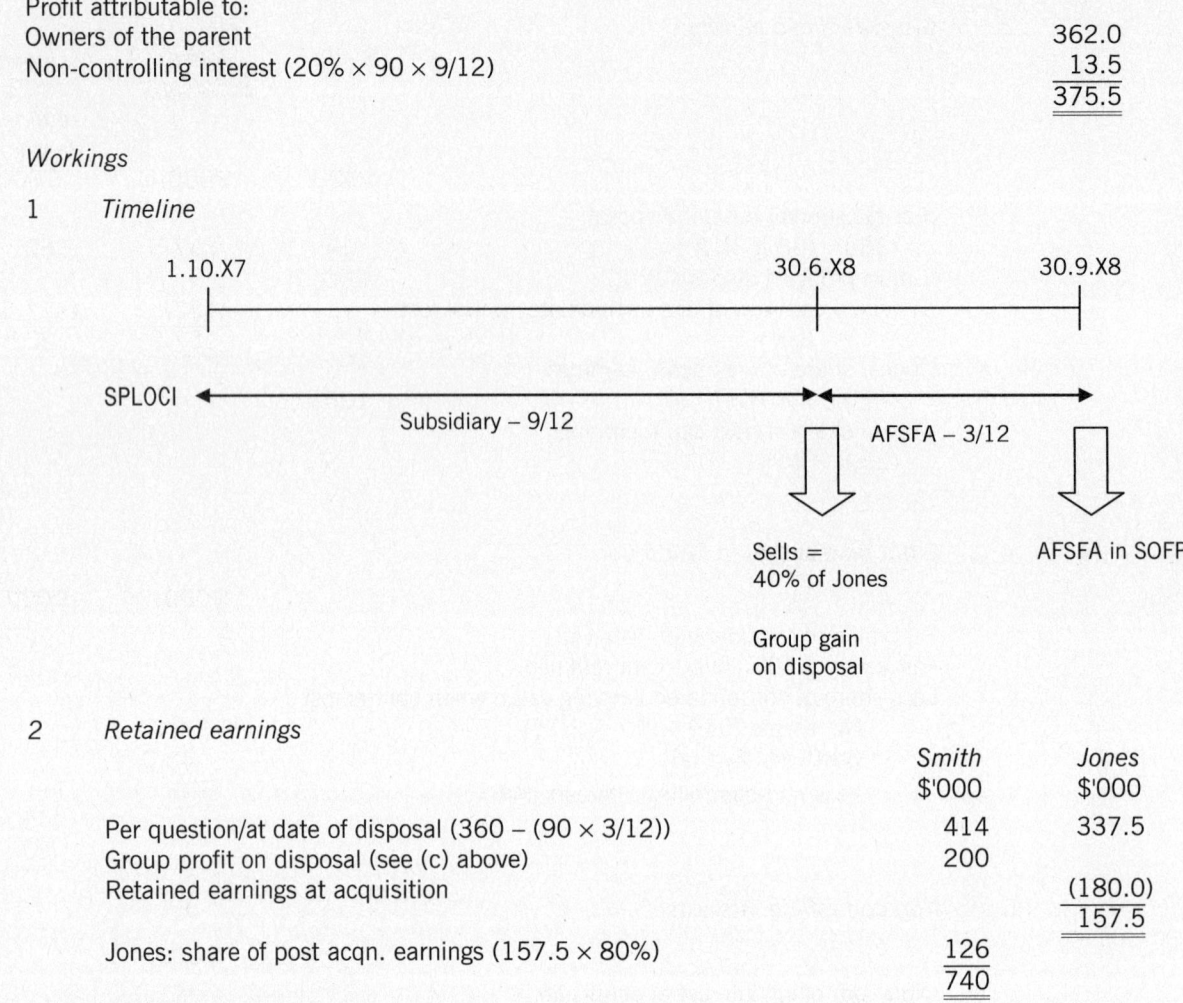

2   *Retained earnings*

	Smith $'000	Jones $'000
Per question/at date of disposal (360 − (90 × 3/12))	414	337.5
Group profit on disposal (see (c) above)	200	
Retained earnings at acquisition		(180.0)
		157.5
Jones: share of post acqn. earnings (157.5 × 80%)	126	
	740	

Now try this question from the Exam Question Bank

Number	Level	Marks	Time
Q15	Examination	25	45 mins
Q16	Examination	17	31 mins

FOREIGN CURRENCY TRANSLATION

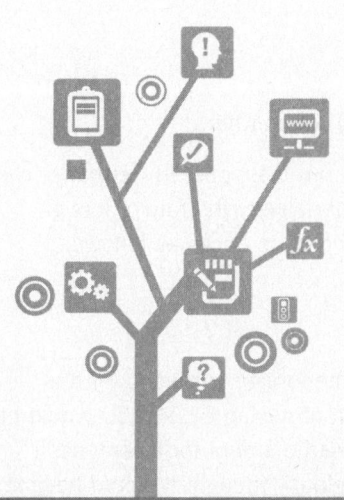

Many of the largest companies in any country, while based there, have subsidiaries and other interests all over the world: they are truly **global companies** and so foreign currency consolidations take place frequently in practice.

topic list	learning outcomes	syllabus references	ability required
1 Foreign currency translation	A2	A2 (ii)	Application
2 IAS 21: *Individual company stage*	A2	A2 (ii)	Application
3 IAS 21: *Consolidated financial statements stage*	A2	A2 (ii)	Application

1 Foreign currency translation

Introduction

If a company trades overseas, it will buy or sell assets in foreign currencies. For example, an Indian company might buy materials from Canada, and pay for them in US dollars, and then sell its finished goods in Germany, receiving payment in euros. The purchase and sale must be translated into the company's local currency (here the Indian rupee) to record the double entry in the nominal ledger. If the company owes money in a foreign currency at the end of the accounting year, or holds monetary assets which were bought in a foreign currency, those liabilities or assets must be also translated into the local currency.

A company might have a subsidiary abroad (ie a foreign entity that it owns), and the subsidiary will trade in its own local currency. The subsidiary will keep its nominal ledger and prepare its annual financial statements in its own currency. However, at the year end, the parent company must consolidate the results of the overseas subsidiary into its group financial statements, so that the assets and liabilities and the annual profits of the subsidiary are translated into the parent company's currency.

If foreign currency exchange rates remained constant, there would be no accounting problem. As you will be aware, however, foreign exchange rates are continually changing. It is not inconceivable, for example, that the rate of exchange between the Polish zlotych and British sterling might be Z6.2 to £1 at the start of the accounting year, and Z5.6 to £1 at the end of the year (in this example, a 10% increase in the relative strength of the zlotych).

There are two distinct types of foreign currency transaction, conversion and translation.

1.1 Conversion gains and losses   3/12

Conversion is the process of exchanging amounts of one foreign currency for another.

For example, suppose a US company buys a large consignment of goods from a supplier in Germany. The order is placed on 1 May and the agreed price is €124,250. At the time of delivery the rate of foreign exchange was €2 to $1. The local company would record the amount owed in its books as follows.

DEBIT	Purchases (124,250 ÷ 2)	$62,125	
CREDIT	Payables		$62,125

When the local company comes to pay the supplier, it needs to obtain some foreign currency. By this time, however, if the rate of exchange has altered to €2.05 to $1, the cost of raising €124,250 would be (÷ 2.05) $60,610. The company would need to spend only $60,610 to settle a debt for inventories 'costing' $62,125. As the payable is settled for less than the company originally thought it would have to pay, a profit on conversion or exchange gain of $1,515 ($62,125 - $60,610) has arisen.

DEBIT	Payables account	$62,125	
CREDIT	Cash		$60,610
CREDIT	Profit on conversion (exchange gain)		$1,515

Profits (or losses) on conversion would be included in profit or loss for the year in which conversion (whether payment or receipt) takes place.

Suppose that another US company sells goods to a Chinese company, and it is agreed that payment should be made in Chinese Yuan at a price of Y116,000. We will further assume that the exchange rate at the time of sale is Y10.75 to $1, but when the debt is eventually paid, the rate has altered to Y10.8 to $1. The company would record the sale as follows.

DEBIT	Receivables (116,000 ÷ 10.75)	$10,791	
CREDIT	Revenue		$10,791

When the Y116,000 are paid, the local company will convert them into $, to obtain (÷ 10.8) $10,741. In this example, there has been a loss on conversion of $50 which will be written off to profit or loss for the year:

DEBIT	Cash	$10,741	
DEBIT	Loss on conversion (exchange loss)	$50	
CREDIT	Receivables account		$10,791

There are **no accounting difficulties** concerned with foreign currency conversion gains or losses, and the procedures described above are uncontroversial.

1.2 Translation

Foreign currency translation, as distinct from conversion, does not involve the act of exchanging one currency for another. **Translation is required at the end of an accounting period when a company still holds assets or liabilities in its statement of financial position which were obtained or incurred in a foreign currency.**

These assets or liabilities might consist of any of the following.

(a)   An individual home company holding individual **assets** or **liabilities** originating in a foreign currency 'deal'.

(b)   An individual home company with a separate **branch** of the business operating abroad which keeps its own books of account in the local currency.

(c)   A home company which wishes to consolidate the **results of a foreign subsidiary**.

There has been great **uncertainty** about the method which should be used to translate the following.

- Value of assets and liabilities from a foreign currency into $ for the year end statement of financial position

- Profits of an independent foreign branch or subsidiary into $ for the annual statement of profit or loss and other comprehensive income

Suppose, for example, that an Indian subsidiary purchases a piece of property for 2,100,000 rupees on 31 December 20X7. The rate of exchange at this time was 70 rupees to $1. During 20X8, the subsidiary charged depreciation on the building of 16,800 rupees, so that at 31 December 20X8, the subsidiary recorded the asset as follows.

	Rupees
Property at cost	2,100,000
Less accumulated depreciation	16,800
Net book value	2,083,200

At this date, the rate of exchange has changed to 60 rupees to $1.

The parent company must translate the subsidiary and this particular asset's value into $, but there is a **choice of exchange rates**.

(a)   Should the rate of exchange for translation be the rate which existed at the date of purchase, which would give a net book value of 2,083,200 ÷ 70 = $29,760?

(b)   Should the rate of exchange for translation be the rate existing at the end of 20X8 (the closing rate of 60 rupees to $1)? This would give a net book value of $34,720.

Similarly, should depreciation be charged to group profit or loss at the rate of 70 rupees to $1 (the historical rate), 60 rupees to $1 (the closing rate), or at an average rate for the year (say, 64 rupees to $1)?

1.3 Consolidated financial statements

If a parent has a subsidiary whose financial statements are presented in a foreign currency, those financial statements must be translated into the local currency before they can be included in the consolidated financial statements.

The **closing rate** is used for most items in the **statement of financial position** and the statement of financial position is prepared as at the year end. The **statement of profit or loss and other comprehensive income** is translated at the actual rate or **average rate** if a close approximation. **Exchange differences** are recognised in **other comprehensive income**.

We will look at the consolidation of foreign subsidiaries in much more detail in Section 3 of this chapter.

Section summary

Questions on foreign currency translation have always been popular with examiners. In general you are required to prepare **consolidated financial statements** for a group which includes a foreign subsidiary.

2 IAS 21: *Individual company stage*

Introduction

The questions discussed above are addressed by IAS 21 *The effects of changes in foreign exchange rates*. We will examine those matters which affect single company accounts here.

2.1 Definitions

These are some of the definitions given by IAS 21.

KEY TERMS

FOREIGN CURRENCY. A currency other than the functional currency of the entity.

FUNCTIONAL CURRENCY. The currency of the primary economic environment in which the entity operates.

PRESENTATION CURRENCY. The currency in which the financial statements are presented.

EXCHANGE RATE. The ratio of exchange for two currencies.

EXCHANGE DIFFERENCE. The difference resulting from translating a given number of units of one currency into another currency at different exchange rates.

CLOSING RATE. The spot exchange rate at the year end date.

SPOT EXCHANGE RATE. The exchange rate for immediate delivery.

MONETARY ITEMS. Units of currency held and assets and liabilities to be received or paid in a fixed or determinable number of units of currency. *(IAS 21)*

Each entity – whether an individual company, a parent of a group, or an operation within a group (such as a subsidiary, associate or branch) – should determine its **functional currency** and **measure its results and financial position in that currency**.

For most individual companies the functional currency will be the currency of the country in which they are located and in which they carry out most of their transactions. Determining the functional currency is much more likely to be an issue where an entity operates as part of a group. IAS 21 contains detailed guidance on how to determine an entity's functional currency and we will look at this in more detail in Section 3.

An entity can **present** its financial statements in any currency (or currencies) it chooses: in other words, it can have a **presentation currency** that is different from its functional currency. IAS 21 deals with the situation in which financial statements are presented in a currency other than the functional currency.

Again, this is unlikely to be an issue for most individual companies. Their presentation currency will normally be the same as their functional currency (the currency of the country in which they operate).

A company's presentation currency may be different from its functional currency if it is listed on a foreign stock exchange or operates within a group and we will look at this in Section 3.

2.2 Determining functional currency

IAS 21 states that an entity should consider the following factors in determining its functional currency:

(a)   The currency that mainly **influences sales prices** for goods and services (often the currency in which prices are denominated and settled)

(b)   The currency of the **country whose competitive forces and regulations** mainly determine the sales prices of its goods and services

(c)   The currency that mainly **influences labour, material and other costs** of providing goods or services (often the currency in which prices are denominated and settled)

Sometimes the functional currency of an entity is not immediately obvious. Management must then exercise judgement and may also need to consider:

(a)   The currency in which **funds from financing activities** (raising loans and issuing equity) are generated

(b)   The currency in which **receipts from operating activities** are usually retained

2.3 Foreign currency transactions: initial recognition

IAS 21 states that a foreign currency transaction should be recorded, on initial recognition in the functional currency, by applying the exchange rate between the reporting currency and the foreign currency **at the date of the transaction** to the foreign currency amount.

An **average rate** for a period may be used if exchange rates do not fluctuate significantly.

2.4 Reporting at subsequent year ends

The following rules apply at each subsequent year end.

(a)   Report foreign currency **monetary items** (eg receivables, payables, cash, loans) using the **closing rate**

(b)   Report **non-monetary items** (eg non-current assets, inventories) which are carried at **historical cost** in a foreign currency using the **exchange rate at the date of the transaction** (historical rate)

(c)   Report **non-monetary items** which are carried at **fair value** in a foreign currency using the exchange rates that existed **when the values were measured.**

2.5 Recognition of exchange differences

Exchange differences occur when there is a **change in the exchange rate** between the transaction date and the date of settlement of monetary items arising from a foreign currency transaction.

Exchange differences arising on the settlement of monetary items (receivables, payables, loans, cash in a foreign currency) or on translating an entity's monetary items at rates different from those at which they were translated initially, or reported in previous financial statements, should be **recognised in profit or loss** in the period in which they arise.

There are two situations to consider.

(a) The transaction is **settled in the same period** as that in which it occurred: all the exchange difference is recognised in that period.

(b) The transaction is **settled in a subsequent accounting period**: the exchange difference recognised in each intervening period up to the period of settlement is determined by the change in exchange rates during that period.

In other words, where a monetary item has not been settled at the end of a period, it should be **restated using the closing exchange rate** and any gain or loss taken to the statement of profit or loss.

For **non-monetary items carried at fair value** which are retranslated at the date of remeausurement, exchange differences should be **recognised in the same place as the revaluation gain or loss**. If a gain or loss on a non-monetary item is recognised in other comprehensive income (eg revaluation of a property), any exchange component of that gain or loss shall be recognised in other comprehensive income. Where a gain or loss is recognised in profit or loss, any exchange component of that gain or loss shall be recognised in profit or loss.

Question 12.1

Entries

Learning outcomes A2

White Cliffs Co, whose year end is 31 December, buys some goods from Rinka SA of France on 30 September. The invoice value is €40,000 and is due for settlement in equal instalments on 30 November and 31 January. The exchange rate moved as follows.

	€= $1
30 September	1.60
30 November	1.80
31 December	1.90
31 January	1.85

Required

State the accounting entries in the books of White Cliffs Co.

Section summary

Foreign transactions are initially translated at the **exchange rate at the date of the transaction**. At the year end, **monetary** assets and liabilities are translated at the **closing rate**. **Exchange differences** are recognised in **profit or loss**.

Non-monetary assets and liabilities are only **retranslated if they are carried at fair value**. The exchange gain or loss is recognised in the same place as the revaluation gain or loss (either profit or loss or other comprehensive income).

3 IAS 21: *Consolidated financial statements* stage 5/11,11/11

Introduction

We will now look at the effect on consolidated financial statements.

3.1 Definitions

The following definitions are relevant here.

KEY TERMS

FOREIGN OPERATION. A subsidiary, associate, joint arrangement or branch of a reporting entity, the activities of which are based or conducted in a country or currency other than those of the reporting entity.

NET INVESTMENT IN A FOREIGN OPERATION. The amount of the reporting entity's interest in the net assets of that operation.   *(IAS 21)*

In consolidated financial statements, **the presentation currency used is the functional currency of the parent company.**

Therefore, a holding or parent company with foreign operations must translate the financial statements of those operations into its own reporting currency before they can be consolidated into the group financial statements. Whether or not the subsidiary needs translating depends on whether the functional currency of the subsidiary is the same as or different to the parent's functional currency. If the subsidiary's functional currency is the same as the parent's, it won't need translating for the group financial statements. However, if the subsidiary's functional currency is different to the parent's, it will need translation for the group financial statements.

To determine the functional currency of the foreign operation, the indicators in Section 2.2 must be considered but in addition, the following factors should be considered in determining whether its functional currency is the same as that of the reporting entity:

(a)   Whether the activities of the foreign operation are carried out as an **extension of the parent**, rather than being carried out with a **significant degree of autonomy**.

(b)   Whether **transactions with the parent** are a high or a low proportion of the foreign operation's activities.

(c)   Whether **cash flows** from the activities of the foreign operation **directly affect the cash flows of the parent** and are readily available for remittance to it.

(d)   Whether **cash flows** from the activities of the foreign operation are **sufficient to service** existing and normally expected **debt** obligations without funds being made available by the reporting entity.

Exam alert

A question involving foreign currency is almost certain to consist of a foreign operation consolidation.

The question in May 2011 required the preparation of the consolidated statement of profit or loss and other comprehensive income and consolidated statement of financial position for a group with a foreign subsidiary.

To sum up: in order to determine the functional currency of a foreign operation it is necessary to consider the **relationship** between the foreign operation and its parent:

•   If the foreign operation carries out its business as though it were an **extension of the parent's operations**, it almost certainly has the **same functional currency** as the parent.

•   If the foreign operation is **semi-autonomous** it almost certainly has **a different functional currency** from the parent.

The translation method used has to reflect the economic reality of the relationship between the reporting entity (the parent) and the foreign operation.

3.1.1 Same functional currency as the reporting entity

In this situation, the foreign operation normally carries on its business as though it were an **extension of the reporting entity's operations.** For example, it may only sell goods imported from, and remit the proceeds directly to, the reporting entity.

Any **movement in the exchange rate** between the reporting currency and the foreign operation's currency will have an **immediate impact** on the reporting entity's cash flows from the foreign operations. In other words, changes in the exchange rate affect the **individual monetary items** held by the foreign operation, *not* the reporting entity's net investment in that operation.

In this instance, the foreign operation will maintain its nominal ledger in the parent's currency, so there will be **no need to translate** the subsidiary's financial statements for consolidation purposes.

3.1.2 Different functional currency from the reporting entity

In this situation, although the reporting entity may be able to exercise control, the foreign operation normally operates in a **semi-autonomous** way. It accumulates cash and other monetary items, generates income and incurs expenses, and may also arrange borrowings, all **in its own local currency**.

A change in the exchange rate will produce **little or no direct effect on the present and future cash flows** from operations of either the foreign operation or the reporting entity. Rather, the change in exchange rate affects the reporting entity's **net investment** in the foreign operation, not the individual monetary and non-monetary items held by the foreign operation.

In this instance, the foreign operation will maintain its nominal ledger in its own local currency, so its financial statements will **need to be translated** into the parent's currency for consolidation purposes.

Exam alert

Where the foreign operation's functional currency is different from the parent's, the financial statements need to be translated before consolidation.

3.2 Accounting treatment: different functional currency from the reporting entity

The financial statements of the foreign operation must be translated to the functional currency of the parent. Different procedures must be followed here, because the functional currency of the parent is the **presentation currency** of the foreign operation.

(a)   The **assets and liabilities** shown in the foreign operation's statement of financial position are translated at the **closing rate** at the year end, regardless of the date on which those items originated.

(b)   Amounts in the **statement of profit or loss and other comprehensive income** should be translated at the rate ruling at the date of the transaction (an **average rate** will usually be used for practical purposes if exchange rates do not fluctuate significantly).

(c)   **Exchange differences** arising from the re-translation at the end of each year of the parent's net investment should be **recognised in other comprehensive income**, not through the profit or loss for the year, until the disposal of the net investment. On disposal, the gains or losses recognised to date will be reclassified to profit or loss.

Any **goodwill and fair value adjustments** are treated as assets and liabilities of the foreign operation and are translated at the **closing rate**.

3.3 Practical approach in the exam

You will find it helpful to adopt the following approach when translating the functional currency of foreign operations in the exam:

(a)   **Statement of financial position**

        All assets and liabilities – at the closing rate

Share capital and pre-acquisition reserves – at the rate at date of acquisition of the subsidiary

Post-acquisition reserves – balancing figure

(b)   **Statement of profit or loss and other comprehensive income**

All items – at the actual rate or average rate (AR) as an approximation

Example: different functional currency from the reporting entity

A dollar-based company, Stone Co, set up a foreign subsidiary on 30 June 20X7. Stone subscribed €24,000 for share capital when the exchange rate was €2 = $1. The subsidiary, Brick Inc, borrowed €72,000 and bought a non-monetary asset for €96,000. Stone Co prepared its accounts on 31 December 20X7 and by that time the exchange rate had moved to €3 = $1. As a result of highly unusual circumstances, Brick Inc sold its asset early in 20X8 for €96,000. It repaid its loan and was liquidated. Stone's capital of €24,000 was repaid in February 20X8 when the exchange rate was €3 = $1.

Required

Account for the above transactions as if the entity has a different functional currency from the parent.

Solution

From the above it can be seen that Stone Co will record its initial investment at $12,000 (€24,000/2) which is the starting cost of its shares. The statement of financial position of Brick Inc at 31 December 20X7 is summarised below.

	€'000
Non-monetary asset	96
Share capital	24
Loan	72
	96

This may be translated as follows.

	$'000
Non-monetary asset (€96,000/3)	32
Share capital and reserves (retained earnings) (balancing figure)	8
Loan (€72,000/3)	24
	32
Exchange gain/(loss) for 20X7	(4)

The exchange gain and loss are the differences between the value of the original investment ($12,000) and the total of share capital and reserves (retained earnings) as disclosed by the above statement of financial position.

On liquidation, Stone Co will receive $8,000 (€24,000 converted at €3 = $1). No gain or loss will arise in 20X8.

3.4 Some practical points

The following points apply.

(a)   For consolidation purposes calculations are simpler if a subsidiary's share capital and pre-acquisition reserves are translated at the **historical rate** (the rate when the investing company acquired its interest) and post-acquisition reserves are found as a balancing figure.

(b)   IAS 21 requires that the accumulated exchange differences should be shown as a separate component of equity but for exam purposes these can be merged with retained earnings.

3.5 Summary of method

A summary of the translation method is given below, which shows the main steps to follow in the consolidation process.

Step	Method
 Translate the **closing statement of financial position** and use this for preparing the consolidated statement of financial position in the normal way.	Use the following rates: • Assets and liabilities at closing rate • Share capital + pre-acquisition reserves at historical rate (at date of acquisition of subsidiary) • Post-acquisition reserves as a balancing figure (includes exchange differences)
 Translate the **statement of profit or loss/statement of profit or loss and other comprehensive income**. (In all cases, dividends should be translated at the rate ruling when the dividend was paid).	Use the **average rate** for the year for all items (but see comment on dividends). The figures obtained can then be used in preparing the consolidated statement of profit or loss but the statement of profit or loss and other comprehensive income cannot be completed until the exchange difference has been calculated.
 Translate **net assets** (equity) at the **beginning of the year**. (Only do this if you are preparing a consolidated statement of profit or loss and other comprehensive income and need to find exchange differences for the year.)	Calculate opening net assets (equity) in the foreign currency as: Closing net assets (equity) X Less total comprehensive income for yr (X) Opening net assets (equity) X Then divide opening net assets by the opening rate (ie the exchange rate as at the previous year end).
 Calculate the **total exchange difference** for the year as follows. $ Closing net assets at closing rate (Step 1) X Less opening net assets at opening rate (Step 3) (X) X Less retained profit as translated (Step 2 less any dividends) (X) Exchange differences on net assets X It may be necessary to adjust for any profits or losses taken direct to reserves during the year. You will also need to add on any exchange differences arising on goodwill in the year (see Section 3.2).	This stage will be **unnecessary** if you are only required to prepare the statement of financial position. If you are asked to state the total exchange differences or are asked to prepare a statement of profit or loss and other comprehensive income, where the exchange difference will be shown. For **exam purposes** you can translate the closing shareholders' funds as follows. (a) Share capital + pre-acquisition reserves at historical rate. (b) Post-acquisition reserves as a balancing figure.

Exam alert

You should learn this summary.

Question 12.2	Consolidated financial statements

Learning outcomes A2

The abridged statements of financial position and statements of profit or loss of Darius Co and its foreign subsidiary, Xerxes Inc, appear below.

DRAFT STATEMENT OF FINANCIAL POSITION AS AT 31 DECEMBER 20X9

	Darius Co		Xerxes Inc	
	$000	$000	€000	€000
Assets				
Non-current assets				
Plant at cost	600		500	
Less depreciation	(250)		(200)	
		350		300
Investment in Xerxes (100,000 €1 shares)		25		–
		375		300
Current assets				
Inventories	225		200	
Receivables	150		100	
		375		300
		750		600
Equity and liabilities				
Equity				
Ordinary $1/€1 shares	300		100	
Retained earnings	300		280	
		600		380
Loans		50		110
Current liabilities		100		110
		750		600

STATEMENTS OF PROFIT OR LOSS AND COMPREHENSIVE INCOME
FOR THE YEAR ENDED 31 DECEMBER 20X9

	Darius Co	Xerxes Inc
	$000	€000
Profit before tax	200	160
Tax	100	80
Profit for the year, retained	100	80

The following further information is given.

(a) Darius Co has had its interest in Xerxes Inc since the incorporation of the company. Neither company paid dividends during the year to 31 December 20X9 and neither company had any other comprehensive income in their separate financial statements.

(b) Depreciation is 8% per annum on cost.

(c) There have been no loan repayments or movements in non-current assets during the year. The opening inventory of Xerxes Inc was €120,000. Assume that inventory turnover times are very short. Opening receivables were $80,000 and opening current liabilities $130,000.

(d) Exchange rates: € 4 to $1 when Xerxes Inc was incorporated
€ 2 to $1 on 31 December 20X8
€ 1.6 to $1 average rate of exchange year ending 31 December 20X9
€ 1 to $1 on 31 December 20X9.

Required

Prepare the summarised consolidated financial statements of Darius Co for the year ended 31 December 20X9.

3.6 Analysis of exchange differences

The exchange differences in the above exercise could be reconciled by splitting them into their component parts.

Exam alert

Such a split is not required by IAS 21, nor is it required in your exam, but it may help your understanding of the subject.

The exchange difference consists of those exchange gains/losses arising from:

- Translating **income/expense items** at the exchange rates at the date of transactions (or **average rate** as a close approximation), whereas **assets/liabilities** are translated at the **closing rate**.

- Translating the **opening net investment** (opening net assets) in the foreign entity at a closing rate different from the closing rate at which it was previously reported.

This can be demonstrated using the above question.

The opening statement of financial position of Xerxes Inc in € is:

	$000
Non-current assets (300 NBV c/f – [500 x 8%] depreciation for year)	340
Inventories (given in question)	120
Receivables (given in question)	80
	540
Equity (380 c/f – 80 profit for year)	300
Loans (question says no repayments)	110
Current liabilities (given in question)	130
	540

Using the opening statement of financial position and translating at €2 = $1 (the opening rate) and €1 = $1 (the closing rate) gives the following.

	€2 = $1 $000	€1 = $1 $000	Difference $000
Non-current assets	170	340	170
Inventories	60	120	60
Receivables	40	80	40
	270	540	270
Shareholders' funds	150	300	150
Loans	55	110	55
	205	410	205
Current liabilities	65	130	65
	270	540	270

Translating the statement of profit or loss using €1.60 = $1 and €1 = $1 gives the following results.

	€1.60 = $1 $000	€1 = $1 $000	Difference $000
Profit before tax, depreciation and increase in inventory values (balancing figure)	75	120	45
Increase in inventory values (200 – 120)	50	80	30
	125	200	75
Depreciation (500 x 8%)	(25)	(40)	(15)
	100	160	60
Tax	(50)	(80)	(30)
Profit for the year, retained	50	80	30

The overall position is then:

	$000	$000
Gain on non-current assets (170 – 15)		155
Loss on loan		(55)
Gain on inventories (60 + 30)	90	
Loss on net monetary current assets/liabilities (all other differences) (40 receivables – 65 current liabilities + 45 profit - 30 tax)	(10)	
		80
Net exchange gain (as above)		180

3.7 Non-controlling interest

In problems involving non-controlling interest the following points should be noted.

(a)   The figure for **non-controlling interest in the statement of financial position** will be calculated in $ using the method seen in earlier chapters:

	$
NCI at acquisition (either at fair value or NCI % of net assets) [from goodwill working]	X
NCI share of post acquisition reserves	X
Less: Impairment losses to date	(X)
	X

(b)   The **non-controlling interest in the reconciliation following the statement of profit or loss/statement of profit or loss and other comprehensive income** will be the appropriate proportion of dollar profits and other comprehensive income. The non-controlling interest in other comprehensive income will include their share of exchange differences on translating the subsidiary but will exclude exchange differences arising on retranslating goodwill (see below) if the group measures non-controlling interests at acquisition using the proportionate method.

3.8 Goodwill and fair value adjustments

Goodwill and fair value adjustments arising on the acquisition of a foreign operation should be treated as assets and liabilities of the acquired entity. This means that they should be expressed in the functional currency of the foreign operation and translated at the **closing rate**.

First goodwill needs to be calculated using the foreign currency, then translated using each year end's closing rate. IAS 21 allows impairment losses to either be translated at the average or closing rate. As the examiner uses the average rate in her answers, the average rate should be used.

Here is a layout for calculating goodwill and the exchange gain or loss. 'FC' stands for foreign currency.

Goodwill

	FC'000	FC'000	Rate	$'000
Consideration transferred		X	HR	
Non-controlling interests		X	HR	
Share capital	X			
Retained earnings	X			
		(X)	HR	
At acquisition (1.1.X1)		X	HR	X
Impairment losses 20X1		(X)	OR	(X)
Exchange differences 20X1		-	-	β
At 31.12.20X1		X	OR	X
Impairment losses 20X2		(X)	CR	(X)
Exchange differences 20X2 *(to OCI)*		-	-	β
At 31.12.20X2		X	CR	X

Cumulative FX differences (post to reserves & NCI working *[if NCI at FV at acq'n]*)

Exchange differences for the year calculated for the consolidated statement of profit or loss will now need to include the exchange differences arising on goodwill in the current year. The complete proforma for the exchange differences arising in the year is shown below:

	$'000
On translation of financial statements	
Closing net assets as translated	X
Less: opening net assets as translated at the time	(X)
	X
Less: retained profit as translated at the time	(X)
	X/(X)
On goodwill (see above)	X/(X)
	X/(X)

Example: including goodwill and non-controlling interests

Bennie, a public limited company, acquired 80% of Jennie, a limited company, for $993,000 on 1 January 20X1. Jennie is a foreign operation whose functional currency is the Jen.

STATEMENTS OF FINANCIAL POSITION AT 31 DECEMBER 20X2

	Bennie $'000	Jennie J'000
Property, plant and equipment	5,705	7,280
Cost of investment in Jennie	993	–
	6,698	7,280
Current assets	2,222	5,600
	8,920	12,880
Share capital	1,700	1,200
Pre-acquisition reserves		5,280
Post-acquisition reserves	5,185	2,400
	6,885	8,880
Current liabilities	2,035	4,000
	8,920	12,880

STATEMENTS OF PROFIT OR LOSS AND OTHER COMPREHENSIVE INCOME
FOR THE YEAR ENDED 31 DECEMBER 20X2

	Bennie $'000	Jennie J'000
Revenue	9,840	14,620
Cost of sales	(5,870)	(8,160)
Gross profit	3,970	6,460
Operating expenses	(2,380)	(3,570)
Dividend from Jennie	112	
Profit before tax	1,702	2,890
Income tax expense	(530)	(850)
Profit/total comprehensive income for the year	1,172	2,040

STATEMENTS OF CHANGES IN EQUITY FOR THE YEAR (EXTRACT FOR RETAINED RESERVES)

	Bennie $'000	Jennie J'000
Balance at 1 January 20X2	4,623	6,760
Dividends paid	(610)	(1,120)
Total profit/comprehensive income for the year	1,172	2,040
Balance at 31 December 20X2	5,185	7,680

Jennie pays its dividends on 31 December. A dividend of 1,160,000 Jens was paid on 31 December 20X1.

Jennie's statements of financial position at acquisition and at 31 December 20X1 were as follows:

	1.1.X1 J'000	31.12.X1 J'000
Property, plant and equipment	5,710	6,800
Current assets	3,360	5,040
	9,070	11,840
Share capital	1,200	1,200
Retained reserves	5,280	6,760
	6,480	7,960
Current liabilities	2,590	3,880
	9,070	11,840

Exchange rates were as follows

1 January 20X1	$1: 12 Jens
31 December 20X1	$1: 10 Jens
31 December 20X2	$1: 8 Jens
Weighted average rate for 20X1	$1: 11 Jens
Weighted average rate for 20X2	$1: 8.5 Jens

The fair value of the identifiable net assets of Jennie were equivalent to their book values at the acquisition date. Bennie chose to measure the non-controlling interests in Jennie at fair value at the date of acquisition. The fair value of the non-controlling interests in Jennie was measured at 2,676,000 Jens on 1 January 20X1.

An impairment test conducted at the year end revealed impairment losses of 1,870,000 Jens on recognised goodwill. No impairment losses were necessary in the year ended 31 December 20X1.

Required

Prepare the consolidated statement of financial position as at 31 December 20X2 and consolidated statement of profit or loss and other comprehensive income for the Bennie Group for the year then ended. (Round to nearest $'000.)

Solution

BENNIE GROUP CONSOLIDATED STATEMENT OF FINANCIAL POSITION AT 31 DECEMBER 20X2

	$'000
Property, plant and equipment (5,705 + (W2) 910)	6,615
Goodwill (W4)	780
	7,395
Current assets (2,222 + (W2) 700)	2,922
	10,317
Share capital	1,700
Retained reserves (W5)	5,724
	7,424
Non-controlling interests (W6)	358
	7,782
Current liabilities (2,035 + (W2) 500)	2,535
	10,317

CONSOLIDATED STATEMENT OF PROFIT OR LOSS AND OTHER COMPREHENSIVE INCOME
FOR YEAR ENDED 31 DECEMBER 20X2

	$'000
Revenue (9,840 + (W3) 1,720)	11,560
Cost of sales (5,870 + (W3) 960)	(6,830)
Gross profit	4,730
Operating expenses (2,380 + (W3) 420)	(2,800)
Goodwill impairment loss (W4)	(220)
Profit before tax	1,710
Income tax expense (530 + (W3) 100)	(630)
Profit for the year	1,080
Other comprehensive income	
Items that may subsequently be reclassified to profit or loss	
Exchange differences on translating foreign operations (W8)	403
Total comprehensive income for the year	1,483
Profit attributable to:	
Owners of the parent (balancing figure)	1,076
Non-controlling interests (W6)	4
	1,080
Total comprehensive income attributable to:	
Owners of the parent (balancing figure)	1,398
Non-controlling interests (W6)	85
	1,483

Workings

1   *Group structure*

Bennie

1.1.X1 | 80%

Jennie   Pre-acquisition ret'd reserves 5,280,000 Jens

2   *Translation of Jennie – Statement of financial position*

	J'000	@	$'000
Property, plant and equipment	7,280	8	910
Current assets	5,600	8	700
	12,880		1,610
Share capital	1,200	12	100
Pre-acquisition reserves	5,280	12	440 ⎫
Post-acquisition reserves	2,400	Bal	570 ⎬ 1,010
	8,880		1,110
Current liabilities	4,000	8	500
	12,880		1,610

3   *Translation of Jennie – Statement of profit or loss and other comprehensive income*

	J'000	@	$'000
Revenue	14,620	8.5	1,720
Cost of sales	(8,160)	8.5	(960)
Gross profit	6,460		760
Operating expenses	(3,570)	8.5	(420)
Profit before tax	2,890		340
Income tax expense	(850)	8.5	(100)
Profit for the year	2,040		240

4   *Goodwill*

	J'000	J'000	Rate	$'000
Consideration transferred (993 × 12)		11,916	12	993
Non-controlling interests (at fair value)		2,676	12	223
Less: Fair value of net assets at acquisition				
Share capital	1,200			
Retained reserves	5,280			
		(6,480)	12	(540)
Goodwill at acquisition		8,112	12	676
Impairment losses 20X1		(0)		(0)
Exchange gain/(loss) 20X1		-	Bal	135
Goodwill at 31 December 20X1		8,112	10	811
Impairment losses 20X2		(1,870)	8.5	(220)
Exchange gain/(loss) 20X2		-	Bal	189
Goodwill at year end		6,242	8	780

Note. Goodwill is initially measured in the **subsidiary's currency**, then retranslated at each year end so that we can identify the cumulative exchange differences. In the consolidated statement of financial position these are taken to reserves and non-controlling interests as NCI is measured at fair value at acquisition (see workings 5 and 6)

5   *Consolidated retained reserves carried forward*

	Bennie	Jennie
	$'000	$'000
Per question/(W2)	5,185	1,010
Reserves at acquisition (W2)		(440)
		570
Group share of post acquisition retained reserves:		
Jennie (570 × 80%)	456	
Less: group share of impairment losses to date (W4)	(176)	
((W4) 220 x 80%)		
Group share of exchange differences on goodwill		
[((W4) 135 + 189) × 80%]	259	
	5,724	

6   *Non-controlling interests (SOFP)*

	$'000
NCI at acquisition (W4)	223
Add: NCI share of post-acquisition retained reserves of Jennie ((W2) 570 × 20%)	114
Less: NCI share of impairment losses (W4) (220 × 20%)	(44)
NCI share of exchange differences on goodwill [((W4) 135 + 189) × 20%]	65
	358

Note: NCI are only given their share of the impairment losses and exchange differences on goodwill because NCI is measured at fair value at acquisition (full goodwill method). If NCI had been measured at the proportionate share of net assets at acquisition, the NCI would not be allocated any impairment losses or exchange differences on goodwill (they would have been posted to reserves in full).

7   *Non-controlling interests (SPLOCI)*

	PFY	TCI
	$'000	$'000
Profit for the year (W3)	240	240
Impairment losses (W4)	(220)	(220)
Other comprehensive income: exchange differences (W8)	-	403
	20	423
× 20%	4	85

Note: NCI are only given their share of impairment losses because NCI is measured at fair value at acquisition (full goodwill method).

8   *Exchange differences arising during the year*

	SPLOCI
	$'000
On translation of net assets of Jennie:	
Closing NA at CR (W2)	1,110
Opening NA @ OR (7,960/10)	(796)
	314
Less: retained profit as translated ((W3) 240 − J1,120/8)	(100)
	214
On goodwill (W4)	189
	403

Note: To arrive at retained profit, dividends must be deducted (copied from Jennie's statement of changes in equity given in the question) translated at the exchange rate at the date they were paid (here at the year end date). These exchange differences only need to be calculated if you are preparing a consolidated statement of profit or loss and other comprehensive income.

3.9 Further matters relating to foreign operations

3.9.1 Consolidation procedures

Follow normal consolidation procedures, except that where an exchange difference arises on **long- or short-term intra-group monetary items**, these cannot be offset against other intra-group balances. This is because these are commitments to convert one currency into another, thus exposing the reporting entity to a gain or loss through currency fluctuations. This type of exchange difference should be recognised in profit or loss unless relates to a long-term receivable or loan for which settlement is neither planned nor likely to occur in the foreseeable future. This is because, in substance, it is part of the entity's net investment in the foreign operation. In this case, in the consolidated financial statements, these exchange

differences should be initially recognised in other comprehensive income and reclassified to profit or loss on disposal of the net investment.

If the foreign operation's **reporting date** is different from that of the parent, it is acceptable to use the accounts made up to that date for consolidation, as long as adjustments are made for any significant changes in rates in the interim.

3.9.2 Hyperinflationary economies

We looked at IAS 29 *Financial reporting in hyperinflationary economies* in Chapter 5. The financial statements of a foreign operation operating in a hyperinflationary economy must be adjusted under IAS 29 before they are translated into the parent's reporting currency and then consolidated. When the economy **ceases to be hyperinflationary**, and the foreign operation ceases to apply IAS 29, the amounts restated to the price level at the date the entity ceased to restate its financial statements should be used as the historical costs for translation purposes.

3.9.3 Disposal of foreign entity

When a parent disposes of a foreign entity, the cumulative amount of deemed exchange differences relating to that foreign entity should be **recognised as an income or expense** in the same period in which the gain or loss on disposal is recognised. Effectively, this means that these exchange differences are recognised once by taking them to other comprehensive income and reserves and then are recognised for a second time ('recycled' or 'reclassified') by transferring them from other comprehensive income and reserves to the statement of profit or loss and other comprehensive income on disposal of the foreign operation.

3.9.4 In the parent's financial statements

In the parent company's own financial statements, exchange differences arising on a **monetary item** that is effectively part of the parent's net investment in the foreign entity should be recognised **in profit or loss** in the separate financial statements of the reporting entity or the individual financial statements of the foreign operation, as appropriate.

3.10 Change in functional currency

The functional currency of an entity can be changed only if there is a change to the underlying transactions, events and conditions that are relevant to the entity. For example, an entity's functional currency may change if there is a change in the currency that mainly influences the sales price of goods and services.

Where there is a change in an entity's functional currency, the entity translates all items into the new functional currency **prospectively** (ie, from the date of the change) using the exchange rate at the date of the change.

3.11 Tax effects of exchange differences

IAS 12 *Income taxes* should be applied when there are tax effects arising from gains or losses on foreign currency transactions and exchange differences arising on the translation of the financial statements of foreign operations.

Section summary

You may have to make the decision yourself as to whether the subsidiary has the same functional currency as the parent or a different functional currency from the parent. This determines whether you need to translate the subsidiary for consolidation purposes.

You must be able to calculate **exchange differences**. These are posted to **other comprehensive income**,

Practising examination questions is the best way of learning this topic.

Where the functional currency of a foreign operation is **different** from that of the parent/reporting entity, they need to be translated before consolidation

-     Operation is semi-autonomous

-     Translate assets and liabilities at closing rate

-     Translate share capital and pre-acquisition reserves at acquisition date rate

-     Find post acquisition reserves as a balancing figure

-     Translate statement of profit or loss and other comprehensive income at average rate

-     Exchange differences through other comprehensive income

Chapter Roundup

✓ Questions on foreign currency translation have always been popular with examiners. In general you are required to prepare consolidated financial statements for a group which includes a foreign subsidiary.

✓ Foreign transactions are initially translated at the **exchange rate at the date of the transaction**. At the year end, **monetary** assets and liabilities are translated at the **closing rate**. **Exchange differences** are recognised in **profit or loss**.

✓ **Non-monetary** assets and liabilities are only **retranslated if they are carried at fair value**. The exchange gain or loss is recognised in the same place as the revaluation gain or loss (either profit or loss or other comprehensive income.

✓ You may have to make the decision yourself as to whether the subsidiary has the same functional currency as the parent or a different functional currency from the parent. This determines whether the subsidiary has to be translated for consolidation purposes.

✓ You must be able to calculate **exchange differences**.

✓ **Practising** examination questions is the best way of learning this topic.

✓ Where the functional currency of a foreign operation is **different** from that of the parent/reporting entity, they need to be translated before consolidation

  – Operation is semi-autonomous
  – Translate assets and liabilities at **closing rate**
  – Translate share capital and pre-acquisition reserves at the **acquisition date** rate
  – Find post acquisition reserves as a **balancing figure**
  – Translate statement of profit or loss and other comprehensive income at **average rate**
  – Exchange differences through **other comprehensive income**

Quick Quiz

1   What is the difference between conversion and translation?

2   Define 'monetary' items according to IAS 21.

3   How should foreign currency transactions be recognised initially in an individual enterprise's accounts?

4   What factors must management take into account when determining the functional currency of a foreign operation?

5   How should goodwill and fair value adjustments be treated on consolidation of a foreign operation?

6   When can an entity's functional currency be changed?

Answers to Quick Quiz

1   (a)   Conversion is the process of exchanging one currency for another.

    (b)   Translation is the restatement of the value of one currency in another currency.

2   Units of currency held and assets and liabilities to be received or paid in a fixed or determinable number of units of currency (eg cash, receivables, payables, loans).

3   Use the exchange rate at the date of the transaction. An average rate for a period can be used if the exchange rates did not fluctuate significantly.

4   See Section 3.1

5   Treat as assets/liabilities of the foreign operation and translate at the closing rate.

6   Only if there is a change to the underlying transactions relevant to the entity.

Answers to Questions

12.1   Entries

The purchase will be recorded in the books of White Cliffs Co using the rate of exchange ruling on 30 September.

DEBIT	Purchases	$25,000	
CREDIT	Trade payables		$25,000

Being the $ cost of goods purchased for €40,000 (€40,000 ÷ €1.60)

On 30 November, White Cliffs must pay €20,000. This will cost €20,000 ÷ €1.80= $11,111 and the company has therefore made an exchange gain of $12,500 – $11,111 = $1,389.

DEBIT	Trade payables	$12,500	
CREDIT	Exchange gains: Profit or loss		$1,389
CREDIT	Cash		$11,111

On 31 December, the year end, the outstanding liability will be recalculated using the rate applicable to that date: €20,000 ÷ €1.90= $10,526. A further exchange gain of $1,974 has been made and will be recorded as follows.

DEBIT	Trade payables	$1,974	
CREDIT	Exchange gains: Profit or loss		$1,974

The total exchange gain of $3,363 will be included in the operating profit for the year ending 31 December.

On 31 January, White Cliffs must pay the second instalment of €20,000. This will cost them $10,811 (€20,000 ÷ €1.85).

DEBIT	Trade payables	$10,526	
DEBIT	Exchange losses: Profit or loss	$285	
CREDIT	Cash		$10,811

12.2 Consolidated financial statements

 The statement of financial position of Xerxes Inc at 31 December 20X9 should be translated – the assets and liabilities at the closing rate of €1 = $1; the share capital and pre-acquisition reserves at the historic rate at the date of acquisition of the subsidiary of €4 = $1; pre-acquisition reserves should be found as a balancing figure (as they will include exchange differences).

SUMMARISED TRANSLATED STATEMENT OF FINANCIAL POSITION OF XERXES INC AT 31 DECEMBER 20X9

	$000	$000
Non-current assets (NBV) (€300,000/1 CR)		300
Current assets		
Inventories (€200,000/1 CR)	200	
Receivables (€100,000/1 CR)	100	
		300
		600
Equity		
Share capital (€100,000/4 HR)		25
Pre-acquisition retained earnings (nil as acquired on incorporation)		-
Post-acquisition retained earnings (balancing figure – includes exchange differences)		355
		380
Non-current liabilities (€110,000/1 CR)		110
Current liabilities (€110,000/1 CR)		110
		600

SUMMARISED CONSOLIDATED STATEMENT OF FINANCIAL POSITION AS AT 31 DECEMBER 20X9

		$000	$000
Assets			
Non-current assets (NBV)	(350 + 300)		650
Current assets			
Inventories	(225 + 200)	425	
Receivables	(150 + 100)	250	
			675
			1,325
Equity and liabilities			
Equity			
Ordinary $1 shares (Darius only)			300
Retained earnings	(300 + 355)		655
			955
Non-current liabilities: loans	(50 + 110)		160
Current liabilities	(100 + 110)		210
			1,325

Note. It is quite unnecessary to know the amount of the exchange differences when preparing the consolidated statement of financial position.

 The statement of profit or loss and other comprehensive income should be translated at average rate (€1.6 = $1).

SUMMARISED TRANSLATED STATEMENT OF PROFIT OR LOSS AND OTHER COMPREHENSIVE INCOME OF XERXES INC FOR THE YEAR ENDED 31 DECEMBER 20X9

	$000
Profit before tax (€160,000/1.6 AR)	100
Tax (€80,000/1.6 AR)	(50)
Profit for the year	50

SUMMARISED CONSOLIDATED STATEMENT OF PROFIT OR LOSS AND OTHER COMPREHENSIVE INCOME FOR THE YEAR ENDED 31 DECEMBER 20X9

		$000
Profit before tax	(200 + 100)	300
Tax	(100 + 50)	(150)
Profit for the year	(100 + 50)	150

The statement of profit or loss and other comprehensive income cannot be completed until the exchange difference has been calculated.

 Net assets (equity) at the beginning of the year can be found as follows.

	€000
Net assets (equity) at 31 December 20X9	380
Retained profit for year	(80)
Net assets (equity) at 31 December 20X8	300

Translated at €2 = $1, this gives $150,000

 The exchange difference can now be calculated and the statement of profit or loss and other comprehensive income completed.

	$000
Closing net assets at closing rate (stage 1)	380
Opening net assets at opening rate (stage 3)	(150)
	230
Less retained profit (stage 2)	(50)
Exchange gain	180

SUMMARISED CONSOLIDATED STATEMENT OF PROFIT OR LOSS AND OTHER COMPREHENSIVE INCOME FOR THE YEAR ENDED 31 DECEMBER 20X9

		$000
Profit before tax	(200 + 100)	300
Tax	(100 + 50)	150
Profit for the year	(100 + 50)	150
Other comprehensive income		
Exchange difference on translating foreign operations		180
Total comprehensive income		330

CONSOLIDATED STATEMENT OF CHANGES IN EQUITY (EXTRACT FOR RESERVES) FOR THE YEAR ENDED 31 DECEMBER 20X9

	$
Consolidated reserves at 31 December 20X8	325
Total comprehensive income	330
Consolidated reserves at 31 December 20X9	655

(*Note*. The post-acquisition reserves of Xerxes Inc at the beginning of the year must have been $150,000 opening net assets – $25,000 share capital = $125,000 and the reserves of Darius Co must have been $300,000 reserves at 31.12.X9 – $100,000 profit for the year = $200,000. The consolidated reserves must therefore have been $325,000.)

Now try this question from the Exam Question Bank

Number	Level	Marks	Time
Q17	Examination	18	32 mins

GROUP STATEMENTS OF CASH FLOWS

 A statement of cash flows is an additional primary statement of **great value** to users of financial statements for the extra information it provides.

You should be familiar with the basic principles, techniques and definitions relating to statements of cash flows from your earlier studies. This chapter develops the principles and preparation techniques to include **consolidated financial statements**.

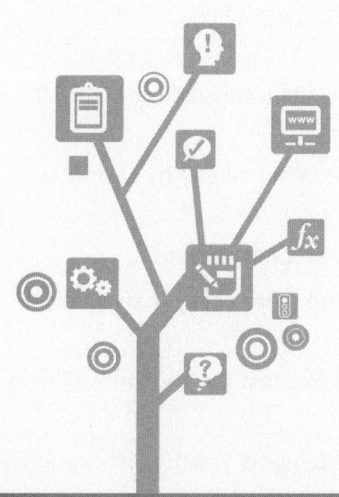

topic list	learning outcomes	syllabus references	ability required
1 Cash flows	A1	A1 (ii)	Application
2 IAS 7 Statement of cash flows: single company	A1	A1 (ii)	Application
3 Consolidated statements of cash flows	A1	A1 (ii)	Application
4 Foreign exchange and statements of cash flows	A1	A1 (ii)	Application

1 Cash flows

Introduction

Cash flows are much easier than profit to understand as a concept.

1.1 Cash flows: advantages

The main advantages of using cash flow accounting (including both historical and forecast cash flows) are as follows.

(a) The **survival** of a company depends on its ability to generate cash. Cash flow accounting directs attention towards this critical issue.

(b) Cash flow is more **comprehensive** than 'profit' which is dependent on accounting conventions and concepts.

(c) Creditors (long– and short-term) are more interested in an entity's **ability to repay** them than in its profitability. While 'profits' might indicate that cash is likely to be available, cash flow accounting is more direct with its message.

(d) Cash flow reporting provides a better means of **comparing** the results of different companies than traditional profit reporting.

(e) Cash flow reporting satisfies the **needs of all users** better.

    (i) For **management**. It provides the sort of information on which decisions should be taken (in management accounting, 'relevant costs' to a decision are future cash flows). Traditional profit accounting does not help with decision-making.

    (ii) For **shareholders and auditors**. Cash flow accounting can provide a satisfactory basis for stewardship accounting.

    (iii) For **creditors and employees**. Their information needs will be better served by cash flow accounting.

(f) **Cash flow forecasts** are easier to prepare, as well as more useful, than profit forecasts.

(g) Cash flow statements are more easily understood, and can be **audited more easily** than financial statements based on the accruals concept.

(h) Cash flow accounting can be both **retrospective**, and also include a **forecast** for the future. This is of great information value to all users of accounting information.

(i) Forecasts can subsequently be monitored by the use of **variance statements** which compare actual cash flows against the forecast.

Looking at the same question from a different angle, readers of financial statements can be **misled** by the profit figure.

(a) Shareholders might believe that if a company makes a profit after tax of, say $100,000, then this is the amount which it could afford to pay as a **dividend**. Unless the company has sufficient cash available to stay in business and also to pay a dividend, the shareholders' expectations would be wrong.

(b) Employees might believe that if a company makes profits, it can afford to pay **higher wages** next year. This opinion may not be correct: the ability to pay wages depends on the availability of cash.

(c) Creditors might consider that a profitable company is a **going concern**.

    (i) If a company builds up large amounts of **unsold inventories** of goods, their cost would not be chargeable against profits, but cash would have been used up in making them, thus weakening the company's liquid resources.

(ii)   A company might **capitalise** large development costs, having spent considerable amounts of money on R & D, but only charge small amounts against current profits. As a result, the company might show reasonable profits, but get into severe difficulties with its liquidity position.

(d)   Management might suppose that if their company makes a historical cost profit, and reinvests some of those profits, then the company must be **expanding**. This is not the case: in a period of inflation, a company might have a historical cost profit but a current cost accounting loss, which means that the operating capability of the firm will be declining.

(e)   The **survival** of a business entity depends not so much on profits as on its ability to pay its debts when they fall due. Such payments might include 'SPLOCI' items such as material purchases, wages, interest and taxation etc, but also capital payments for new fixed assets and the repayment of loan capital when this falls due (eg on the redemption of debentures).

Exam alert

The March 2011 resit paper included a question where a statement of cash flows had to be **analysed**, rather than prepared.

Section summary

Statements of cash flows are a useful addition to the financial statements of companies because it is recognised that accounting profit is not the only indicator of a company's performance.

Statements of cash flows concentrate on the sources and uses of cash and are a useful indicator of a company's **liquidity and solvency**.

2   IAS 7 Statement of cash flows: single company

Introduction

The aim of IAS 7 is to provide information to users of financial statements about the cash flows of an entity's **ability to generate cash and cash equivalents**, as well as indicating the cash needs of the entity. The statement of cash flows provides *historical* information about cash and cash equivalents, classifying cash flows between operating, investing and financing activities. It is worth revising the basic principles in the context of a single company before moving on to the extra considerations when preparing the statement of cash flows for a group.

2.1 Scope

A statement of cash flows should be presented as an **integral part** of an entity's financial statements. All types of entity can provide useful information about cash flows as the need for cash is universal, whatever the nature of their revenue-producing activities. Therefore **all entities are required by the standard to produce a statement of cash flows**.

2.2 Benefits of cash flow information

The use of statements of cash flows is very much **in conjunction** with the rest of the financial statements. Users can gain further appreciation of the change in net assets, of the entity's financial position (liquidity and solvency) and the entity's ability to adapt to changing circumstances by affecting the amount and timing of cash flows. Statements of cash flows **enhance comparability** as they are not affected by differing accounting policies used for the same type of transactions or events.

Cash flow information of a historical nature can be used as an indicator of the amount, timing and certainty of **future cash flows**. Past forecast cash flow information can be **checked for accuracy** as actual figures emerge. The relationship between profit and cash flows can be analysed as can changes in prices over time.

2.3 Definitions

The standard gives the following definitions, the most important of which are **cash** and **cash equivalents**.

KEY TERMS

CASH comprises cash on hand and demand deposits.

CASH EQUIVALENTS are short-term, highly liquid investments that are readily convertible to known amounts of cash and which are subject to an insignificant risk of changes in value.

CASH FLOWS are inflows and outflows of cash and cash equivalents.

OPERATING ACTIVITIES are the principal revenue-producing activities of the entity and other activities that are not investing or financing activities.

INVESTING ACTIVITIES are the acquisition and disposal of long-term assets and other investments not included in cash equivalents.

FINANCING ACTIVITIES are activities that result in changes in the size and composition of the contributed equity and borrowings of the entity.   *(IAS 7)*

2.4 Cash and cash equivalents

The standard expands on the definition of cash equivalents: they are not held for investment or other long-term purposes, but rather to meet short-term cash commitments. To fulfil the above definition, an investment's **maturity date should normally be three months from its acquisition date**. It would usually be the case then that equity investments (ie shares in other companies) are *not* cash equivalents. An exception would be where preferred shares were acquired with a very close maturity date.

Loans and other borrowings from banks are classified as investing activities. In some countries, however, **bank overdrafts** are repayable on demand and are treated as part of an entity's total cash management system. In these circumstances, an overdrawn balance will be included in cash and cash equivalents. Such banking arrangements are characterised by a balance which fluctuates between overdrawn and credit.

Movements between different types of cash and cash equivalent are not included in cash flows. The investment of surplus cash in cash equivalents is part of cash management, not part of operating, investing or financing activities.

2.5 Presentation of a statement of cash flows

IAS 7 requires statements of cash flows to report cash flows during the period classified by **operating, investing** and **financing activities.**

The manner of presentation of cash flows from operating, investing and financing activities **depends on the nature of the entity**. By classifying cash flows between different activities in this way, users can see the impact on cash and cash equivalents of each one, and their relationships with each other. We can look at each in more detail.

2.5.1 Operating activities

This is perhaps the key part of the statement of cash flows, because it shows whether, and to what extent, companies can **generate cash from their operations**. It is these operating cash flows which must,

in the end pay for all cash outflows relating to other activities, ie paying loan interest, dividends and so on. Most of the components of cash flows from operating activities will be those items which **determine the net profit or loss of the entity**, ie they relate to the main revenue-producing activities of the entity. The standard gives the following as examples of cash flows from operating activities.

- Cash receipts from the sale of goods and the rendering of services
- Cash receipts from royalties, fees, commissions and other revenue
- Cash payments to suppliers for goods and services
- Cash payments to and on behalf of employees
- Cash payments/refunds of income taxes unless they can be specifically identified with financing or investing activities
- Cash receipts and payments from contracts held for dealing or trading purposes

Certain items may be included in the net profit or loss for the period which do *not* relate to operational cash flows, for example the profit or loss on the sale of a piece of plant will be included in net profit or loss, but the cash flows will be classed as **financing**.

2.5.2 Investing activities

The cash flows classified under this heading show the extent of new investment in **assets which will generate future profit and cash flows**. Only expenditures which result in a recognised asset in the statement of financial position should be classified as investing activities. The standard gives the following examples of cash flows arising from investing activities.

- Cash payments to acquire property, plant and equipment, intangibles and other long-term assets, including those relating to capitalised development costs and self-constructed property, plant and equipment
- Cash receipts from sales of property, plant and equipment, intangibles and other long-term assets
- Cash payments to acquire equity or debt instruments in other entities, and interests in joint ventures
- Cash receipts from sales of equity or debt instruments in other entities, and interests in joint ventures
- Cash advances and loans made to other parties
- Cash receipts from the repayment of advances and loans made to other parties
- Cash payments for, or receipts from, futures/forward/option/swap contracts except where the contracts are held for dealing purposes, or the payments/receipts are classified as financing activities

2.5.3 Financing activities

This section of the statement of cash flows shows the share of cash which the entity's capital providers have claimed during the period. This is an indicator of the likely **claims on future cash flows** from the providers of capital (ie. interest and dividend payments). The standard gives the following examples of cash flows which might arise under these headings.

- Cash proceeds from issuing shares
- Cash payments to owners to acquire or redeem the entity's shares
- Cash proceeds from issuing debentures, loans, notes, bonds, mortgages and other short or long-term borrowings
- Cash repayments of amounts borrowed
- Cash payments by a lessee for the reduction of the outstanding liability relating to a finance lease

2.6 Reporting cash flows from operating activities

The standard offers a choice of method for this part of the statement of cash flows.

(a)   **Direct method:** disclose major classes of gross cash receipts and gross cash payments

(b)   **Indirect method:** net profit or loss is adjusted for:

   (i)   changes during the period in inventories and operating payables and receivables

   (ii)   non-cash items (such as depreciation, provisions, deferred taxes, unrealised foreign exchanges gains and losses, and undistributed profits of associates)

   (iii)   all other items for which the cash effects are investing or financing cash flows

Pro formas of both methods are shown in Section 2.11.

2.6.1 Using the direct method

There are different ways in which the **information about gross cash receipts and payments** can be obtained. The most obvious way is simply to extract the information from the accounting records. This may be a laborious task, however, and the indirect method below may be easier.

2.6.2 Using the indirect method

This method is undoubtedly **easier** from the point of view of the preparer of the statement of cash flows. As we have mentioned above, the net profit or loss for the period is adjusted for the following.

(a)   Changes during the period in inventories, operating receivables and payables

(b)   Non-cash items, as discussed in section 2.6 above, and

(c)   Other items, the cash flows from which should be classified under investing or financing activities.

It is important to understand why **certain items are added and others subtracted**. Note the following points.

(a)   Depreciation is not a cash expense, but is deducted in arriving at the profit figure in the statement of profit or loss and other comprehensive income. It makes sense, therefore, to eliminate it by adding it back.

(b)   By the same logic, a loss on a disposal of a non-current asset (arising through underprovision of depreciation) needs to be added back and a profit deducted.

(c)   An increase in inventories means less cash – you have spent cash on buying inventory.

(d)   An increase in receivables means the company's debtors have not paid as much, and therefore there is less cash.

(e)   If we pay off payables, causing the figure to decrease, again we have less cash.

2.6.3 Indirect versus direct

The direct method is encouraged where the necessary information is not too costly to obtain, but IAS 7 does not require it. The reason why the direct method is preferred is that it provides information not available elsewhere in the financial statements.

Exam alert

For the purposes of your F2 exam, the indirect method is more often used.

2.7 Interest and dividends

Cash flows from interest and dividends received and paid should each be **disclosed separately**. Each should be classified in a consistent manner from period to period as either operating, investing or financing activities.

Dividends paid by the entity can be classified in **one of two ways**.

(a)   As a **financing cash flow**, showing the cost of obtaining financial resources.

(b)   As a component of **cash flows from operating activities** so that users can assess the entity's ability to pay dividends out of operating cash flows.

2.8 Taxes on income

Cash flows arising from taxes on income should be **separately disclosed** and should be classified as cash flows from operating activities *unless* they can be specifically identified with financing and investing activities.

Taxation cash flows are often **difficult to match** to the originating underlying transaction, so most of the time all tax cash flows are classified as arising from operating activities.

2.9 Components of cash and cash equivalents

The components of cash and cash equivalents should be disclosed and a **reconciliation** should be presented, showing the amounts in the statement of cash flows reconciled with the equivalent items reported in the statement of financial position.

It is also necessary to disclose the **accounting policy** used in deciding the items included in cash and cash equivalents, in accordance with IAS 1, but also because of the wide range of cash management practices worldwide.

2.10 Other disclosures

All entities should disclose, together with a **commentary by management**, the amount of cash or cash equivalent balances held by the entity that are not available for use by the group.

IAS 7 encourages the disclosure of other information relevant to users in understanding the financial position and liquidity of the entity, including:

(a)   The amount of undrawn borrowing facilities which are available, and any restrictions on the use of these facilities.

(b)   The aggregate amount of cash flows that represent **increases in operating capacity**, separately from cash flows that are required to maintain operating capacity.

(c)   The amount of cash flows arising from the operating, investing and financing activities of each reporting **segment**

2.11 Pro forma statements of cash flows

In the next section we will look at the procedures for preparing a statement of cash flows. First, the example below, adapted from the example given in the standard, shows pro forma statements of cash flows under the direct and indirect methods.

2.11.1 Direct method

STATEMENT OF CASH FLOWS (DIRECT METHOD)
YEAR ENDED 20X7

	$m	$m
Cash flows from operating activities		
Cash receipts from customers	30,150	
Cash paid to suppliers and employees	(27,600)	
Cash generated from operations	2,550	
Interest paid	(270)	
Income taxes paid	(900)	
Net cash from operating activities		1,380
Cash flows from investing activities		
Acquisition of subsidiary net of cash acquired (see note below)		
Purchase of property, plant and equipment	(350)	
Proceeds from sale of equipment	20	
Interest received	200	
Dividends received	200	
Net cash used in investing activities		(480)
Cash flows from financing activities		
Proceeds from issuance of share capital	250	
Proceeds from long-term borrowings	250	
Payment of finance lease liabilities	(90)	
Dividends paid*	(1,200)	
Net cash used in financing activities		(790)
Net increase in cash and cash equivalents		110
Cash and cash equivalents at beginning of period (Note A)		120
Cash and cash equivalents at end of period (Note A)		230

* This could also be shown as an operating cash flow

2.11.2 Indirect method

STATEMENT OF CASH FLOWS (INDIRECT METHOD)
YEAR ENDED 20X7

	$m	$m
Cash flows from operating activities		
Profit before taxation	3,350	
Adjustments for:		
Depreciation	450	
Foreign exchange loss (see note below)	40	
Investment income	(500)	
Interest expense	400	
	3,740	
Increase in trade and other receivables	(500)	
Decrease in inventories	1,050	
Decrease in trade payables	(1,740)	
Cash generated from operations	2,550	
Interest paid	(270)	
Income taxes paid	(900)	
Net cash from operating activities		1,380

	$m	$m
Cash flows from investing activities		
Acquisition of subsidiary net of cash acquired (see note below)		
Purchase of property, plant and equipment	(350)	
Proceeds from sale of equipment	20	
Interest received	200	
Dividends received	200	
Net cash used in investing activities		(480)
Cash flows from financing activities		
Proceeds from issue of share capital	250	
Proceeds from long-term borrowings	250	
Payment of finance lease liabilities	(90)	
Dividends paid*	(1,200)	
Net cash used in financing activities		(790)
Net increase in cash and cash equivalents		110
Cash and cash equivalents at beginning of period (Note A)		120
Cash and cash equivalents at end of period (Note A)		230

* This could also be shown as an operating cash flow

Note A

Cash and cash equivalents

	20X7 $m	20X6 $m
Cash on hand and balances with banks	40	25
Short-term investments	190	135
Cash and cash equivalents as previously reported	230	160
Effect of exchange rate changes	-	(40)
Cash and cash equivalents as restated	230	120

Note. While foreign losses and the acquisition of subsidiaries are less relevant to single company statements of cash flows, they are likely to appear in group consolidated statements of cash flows, which we will look at later in this chapter. They have therefore been included here for completeness.

2.12 Step procedure

Remember the steps involved in the preparation of a statement of cash flows.

 Read the question and set up a proforma statement of cash flows .

 Transfer the statement of financial position figures to the face of the statement of cash flows or workings. Work methodically, line by line down the statement of financial position.

 Transfer the statement of profit or loss and other comprehensive income figures to the face of the statement of cash flows or workings.

 Deal with additional information.

 Finish off workings and transfer figures to answer.

STEP 6   Do additional workings for the direct method (if required).

STEP 7   Finish off statement of cash flows.

Question 13.1	Single company

Learning outcomes A1

Kane Co's statement of profit or loss for the year ended 31 December 20X8 and statements of financial position at 31 December 20X7 and 31 December 20X8 were as follows.

KANE CO
STATEMENT OF PROFIT OR LOSS FOR THE YEAR ENDED 31 DECEMBER 20X8

	$'000	$'000
Sales		720
Raw materials consumed	70	
Staff costs	94	
Depreciation	118	
Loss on disposal of long-term asset	18	
		300
		420
Interest payable		28
Profit before tax		392
Income tax expense		124
Profit for the year		268

KANE CO
STATEMENT OF FINANCIAL POSITION AS AT 31 DECEMBER

	20X8		20X7	
	$'000	$'000	$'000	$'000
Assets				
Non-current assets				
Cost	1,596		1,560	
Depreciation	318		224	
		1,278		1,336
Current assets				
Inventory	24		20	
Trade receivables	76		58	
Bank	48		56	
		148		134
Total assets		1,426		1,470
Equity and liabilities				
Equity				
Share capital	360		340	
Share premium	36		24	
Retained earnings	686		490	
		1,082		854
Non-current liabilities				
Long-term loans		200		500
Current liabilities				
Trade payables	42		30	
Taxation	102		86	
		144		116
		1,426		1,470

During the year, the company paid $90,000 for a new piece of machinery.

Required

Prepare a statement of cash flows for Kane Co for the year ended 31 December 20X8 in accordance with the requirements of IAS 7, using the indirect method.

Section summary

Remember the **step-by-step preparation procedure** and use it for all the questions you practise.

You need to be aware of the **format** of the statement as laid out in **IAS 7**. Setting out the format is an essential first stage in preparing the statement, so this format must be learnt.

3 Consolidated statements of cash flows   11/11, 5/12

Introduction

Consolidated statements of cash flows follow the same principles as for single company statements, with some additional complications.

A group's statement of cash flows should only show flows of cash **external** to the group. This follows the same principle that you have already met in the context of the group statement of financial position and statement of profit or loss and other comprehensive income.

Exam questions usually provide the opening and closing **consolidated statement of financial position** and the **consolidated statement of profit or loss and other comprehensive income** for the year. This means that you can apply the same techniques that you have used for single company statements of cash flows, without the need to eliminate intra-group items, as the intra-group transactions and balances will have been eliminated already in the consolidated financial statements given in the question.

The extra issues that you will have to deal with in consolidated statements of cash flows are:

(a)   Cash paid to non-controlling interests
(b)   Cash received from associates
(c)   Payments to acquire subsidiaries
(d)   Receipts from sales of subsidiaries.

3.1 Non-controlling interests

The group statement of cash flows shows movements in 'group cash'. In earlier chapters you have seen that the cash shown on the consolidated statement of financial position includes 100% of the cash balance of any subsidiaries, irrespective of whether there are non-controlling interests in the subsidiaries.

The only item you will have to calculate is the actual amount of cash paid out by the group to the non-controlling interests, ie any dividends paid to the non-controlling interests. **Dividends paid to non-controlling interest** should be included under the heading 'cash flow from financing' and disclosed separately.

You will need to set up a working, in the same style as the earlier examples in this chapter. This will reconcile the opening and closing balances on the non-controlling interest account from the consolidated statement of financial position, and the amount of **total comprehensive income** attributed to the non-controlling interest, to identify the cash paid out as dividends as a balancing item.

Example: non-controlling interest

The following are extracts of the consolidated results for Jarvis Co for the year ended 31 December 20X8.

CONSOLIDATED STATEMENT OF PROFIT OR LOSS (EXTRACT)

	$'000
Group profit before tax	90
Income tax expense	(30)
Profit for the year	60
Profit attributable to:	
Owners of the parent	45
Non-controlling interest	15
	60

CONSOLIDATED STATEMENT OF FINANCIAL POSITION (EXTRACT)

	20X1 $'000	20X2 $'000
Non-controlling interest	300	306

Required

Calculate the dividends paid to the non-controlling interest during the year

Solution

Dividends paid to non-controlling interests

	$'000
B/d	300
TCI attributable to NCI	15
	315
Dividends paid to NCI (balancing figure)	(9)
C/d	306

Points to note:

(1)   In this example, there is no 'other comprehensive income' so the total comprehensive income (TCI) here is equal to the profit for the year.

(2)   On the statement of financial position, the NCI balance includes the NCI share of **retained earnings** (ie **after** deduction of dividends). Dividends are not deducted in the statement of profit or loss and other comprehensive income so the NCI share of total comprehensive income is stated **before** deduction of dividends. Therefore the balancing figure in this working must be the dividends paid to the NCI.

3.2 Associates and joint ventures

An entity which reports its interest in an associate or a joint venture using the equity method, includes in its statement of cash flows the cash flows in respect of its investments in the associate or joint venture, and distributions and other payments or receipts between it and the associate or joint venture.

Dividends from associates are normally included as a separate item in '**cash flows from investing activities.**'

In the following example, you will see that the method used to calculate the dividend received from an associate is very similar to the method used to calculate the dividend paid to the non-controlling interest.

Example: Associate

CONSOLIDATED STATEMENT OF PROFIT OR LOSS AND OTHER COMPREHENSIVE INCOME FOR THE YEAR ENDED 31 DECEMBER 20X2

	$'000
Profit before interest and tax	60
Share of profit of associates	9
Profit before tax	69
Income tax expense	(20)
Profit for the year	49
Other comprehensive income:	
Gains on property revaluation	15
Share of other comprehensive income of associates	3
Exchange loss on translating foreign associate	(2)
Income tax relating to components of other comprehensive income	(5)
Other comprehensive income for the year, net of tax	11
Total comprehensive income for the year	60

CONSOLIDATED STATEMENTS OF FINANCIAL POSITION AS AT 31 DECEMBER

	20X2	20X1
	$'000	$'000
Investment in associates	94	88

Required

Calculate the dividend received from associates.

Solution

Investment in associate

	$000
B/d	88
SPLOCI – share of profit	9
SPLOCI – share of OCI	3
Exchange loss on translating foreign associate	(2)
	98
Dividends received from associate (balancing figure)	(4)
C/d	94

Note. In the statement of financial position, the investment in associate balance includes the group share of the associate's **retained earnings** (ie **after** deduction of dividends). Dividends are not deducted in the statement of comprehensive income so the group share of the associate's profit and other comprehensive income (if any) is stated **before** deduction of dividends. Therefore the balancing figure in this working must be the dividends received from the associate.

3.3 Acquisitions and disposals of subsidiaries and other business units

An entity should present separately the aggregate cash flows arising from acquisitions and from disposals of subsidiaries or other business units and classify them as **investing activities**.

When a group **acquires** a new subsidiary, there are **two** effects on group cash:

(a) A **decrease in group cash** to the extent that **consideration is paid in cash** by the parent, and

(b) An **increase** in group cash as the cash held by the new subsidiary at acquisition will be consolidated within group cash from that date.

When a group **disposes of** a subsidiary, the **two** effects are

(a) An **increase** in group cash if cash proceeds are received by the parent, and

(b) A **decrease** in group cash as the cash held by the subsidiary at the dates of its disposal will cease to be consolidated from that date.

Disclosure is required of the following, in aggregate, in respect of both acquisitions and disposals of subsidiaries or other business units during the period.

(a) Total purchase/disposal consideration

(b) Portion of purchase/disposal consideration discharged by means of cash/cash equivalents

(c) Amount of cash/cash equivalents in the subsidiary or business unit disposed of

(d) Amount of assets and liabilities other than cash/cash equivalents in the subsidiary or business unit acquired or disposed of, summarised by major category

The acquisition or disposal of a subsidiary should be included under the heading '**cash flows from investing activities**' and show the cash flow **net** of cash/cash equivalents acquired or disposed of.

3.4 Finance lease transactions

When rentals under a finance lease are paid, the **interest and capital elements are split out** and included under the net cash from 'operations (interest paid)' and ' financing activities' headings respectively.

3.5 Recap

The preparation of consolidated statements of cash flows will, in many respects, be the same as those for single companies, with the following **additional complications**.

- Acquisitions and disposals of subsidiary undertaking
- Cancellation of intra-group transactions
- Non-controlling interest
- Associates and joint ventures
- Finance leases

Exam alert

Various complications may arise in a consolidated statement of cash flows in the exam, the most important of which are covered above. Question 13.2, given below, is comprehensive. The Pilot Paper

asked for the preparation of a consolidated statement of cash flows and a report on the usefulness of group statements of cash flows, generally and specifically to the entity in the question.

Exam skills

Your priority must be to **show the cash flow** relating to an acquisition or disposal on the statement of cash flows. This is straightforward as you simply need to identify the relevant cash inflows and outflows.

On the group statement of cash flows, the acquisition or disposal is shown as a one-line item. The complication is that you will be working from consolidated statements of financial position where the subsidiary' assets and liabilities will have been added in line by line. You must **adjust for the assets and liabilities acquired (or disposed of)** in the relevant workings, otherwise you will double-count the acquisition or disposal.

Question 13.2	Consolidated cash flow

Learning outcomes A1

Topiary Co is a 40 year old company producing garden statues carved from marble. Twenty two years ago it acquired a 100% interest in a marble importing company, Hardstuff Co. In 20W9 it acquired a 40% interest in a competitor, Landscapes Co and on 1 January 20X7 it acquired a 75% interest in Garden Furniture Designs. The draft consolidated financial statements for the Topiary Group are as follows.

DRAFT CONSOLIDATED STATEMENT OF PROFIT OR LOSS
FOR THE YEAR ENDED 31 DECEMBER 20X7

	$'000	$'000
Operating profit		4,455
Share of profits after tax of associates		1,050
Income from long-term investment		465
Interest payable		(450)
Profit before taxation		5,520
Tax on profit		
Income tax	1,173	
Deferred taxation	312	
		(1,485)
Profit for the year		4,035
Attributable to: owners of the parent		3,735
non-controlling interest		300
		4,035

DRAFT CONSOLIDATED STATEMENT OF FINANCIAL POSITION
AS AT 31 DECEMBER

	20X6		20X7	
	$'000	$'000	$'000	$'000
Non-current assets				
Tangible assets				
Buildings at net book value		6,600		6,225
Plant and machinery at cost	4,200		9,000	
Aggregate depreciation	(3,300)		(3,600)	
Net book value		900		5,400
		7,500		11,625
Goodwill				300
Investments in associates		3,000		3,300
Long-term investments		1,230		1,230
		11,730		16,455
Current assets				
Inventories	3,000		5,925	
Receivables	3,825		5,550	
Cash	5,460		13,545	
		12,285		25,020
		24,015		41,475
Equity attributable to owners of the parent				
Share capital (25c shares)	6,000		11,820	
Share premium account	6,285		8,649	
Retained earnings	7,500		10,335	
	19,785		30,804	
Non-controlling interest	–		345	
		19,785		31,149
Non-current liabilities				
Obligations under finance leases	510		2,130	
Loans	1,500		4,380	
Deferred tax	39		90	
		2,049		6,600
Current liabilities				
Trade payables	840		1,500	
Obligations under finance leases	600		720	
Income tax	651		1,386	
Accrued interest and finance charges	90		120	
		2,181		3,726
		24,015		41,475

Notes

1   There had been no acquisitions or disposals of buildings during the year.

Machinery costing $1.5m was sold for $1.5m resulting in a profit of $300,000. New machinery was acquired in 20X7 including additions of $2.55m acquired under finance leases.

2   *Information relating to the acquisition of Garden Furniture Designs*

	$'000
Machinery	495
Inventories	96
Trade receivables	84
Cash	336
Trade payables	(204)
Income tax	(51)
	756
Non-controlling interest	(189)
	567
Goodwill	300
	867
2,640,000 shares issued as part consideration	825
Balance of consideration paid in cash	42
	867

3   Loans were issued at a discount in 20X7 and the carrying amount of the loans at 31 December 20X7 included $120,000 representing the finance cost attributable to the discount and allocated in respect of the current reporting period.

Required

Prepare a consolidated statement of cash flows for the Topiary Group for the year ended 31 December 20X7 as required by IAS 7, using the indirect method. There is no need to provide notes to the statement of cash flows.

Section summary

Consolidated cash flows should not present a great problem if you understand how to deal with acquisitions and disposals of subsidiaries, non-controlling interest and dividends.

4 Foreign exchange and statements of cash flows

Introduction

An additional complication would involve translating foreign currencies prior to preparing a statement of cash flows.

Exam alert

Complications like foreign currencies in cash flow are unlikely to come up, so skim read this section if you're in a hurry.

4.1 Individual companies

Receipts and payments should be translated into the reporting currency at the **rate ruling** at the date on which the receipt or payment is made.

Exchange differences **do not give rise to cash flows** and therefore they would not be reflected in the statement of cash flows.

4.2 Group companies

The main problems relating to foreign exchange differences are when dealing with the cash flows of an overseas subsidiary. IAS 7 requires that all cash flows relating to an overseas subsidiary be translated at the exchange rates between the functional currency and the foreign currency at the date of the cash flows. Where the presentation currency method has been used to consolidate the subsidiary's results (as will be the case most of the time) then the subsidiary's cash flows will be translated using the average rate (because this is the rate used to translate the subsidiary's statement of comprehensive income).

If the **average rate** is used, then merely using the statements of financial position to derive the figures would not be appropriate as the resulting statement of cash flows would not comply with IAS 7, some items being translated at the closing rate. The practical answer to this problem is to use the following method (which would be time consuming in practice).

 Produce a statement of cash flows for each subsidiary.

 Translate each into dollars using the average rate.

 Consolidate them into the group statement of cash flows (after eliminating intra-group items).

The other main point to note is that the exchange differences on translation must be **analysed into their constituent parts**, namely long-term assets, receivables, cash, payables and non-controlling interests and so forth. You may be asked to perform this exercise in the examination although, in the example shown below, the split is given.

Example: foreign currency translation

Acquisitions

On 1 October 20X8, P, a public limited company, acquired 90% of S, a limited company, by issuing 100,000 shares at an agreed value of $1.60 per share and $140,000 in cash.

At that time the statement of financial position of S, a public limited company, (equivalent to the fair value of the assets and liabilities) was as follows:

	$'000
Property, plant and equipment	190
Inventories	70
Trade receivables	30
Cash and cash equivalents	10
Trade payables	(40)
	260

Group policy is to value non-controlling interests at the date of acquisition at the proportionate share of the fair value of the acquiree's identifiable assets acquired and liabilities assumed.

The consolidated statements of financial position of P as at 31 December were as follows:

	20X8 $'000	20X7 $'000
Non-current assets		
Property, plant and equipment	2,642	2,300
Goodwill	66	–
	2,708	2,300
Current assets		
Inventories	1,450	1,200
Trade receivables	1,370	1,100
Cash and cash equivalents	2	50
	2,822	2,350
	5,530	4,650
Equity attributable to owners of the parent		
Share capital ($1 ordinary shares)	1,150	1,000
Share premium account	590	500
Retained earnings	1,784	1,530
Revaluation surplus	74	–
	3,598	3,030
Non-controlling interests	32	–
	3,630	3,030
Non-current liabilities		
Deferred tax	80	40
Current liabilities		
Trade payables	1,710	1,520
Current tax	110	60
	1,820	1,580
	5,530	4,650

The consolidated statement of profit or loss and other comprehensive income for the year ended 31 December 20X8 was as follows:

	$'000
Revenue	10,000
Cost of sales	(7,500)
Gross profit	2,500
Administrative expenses	(2,077)
Profit before tax	423
Income tax expense	(150)
Profit for the year	273
Other comprehensive income:	
Items that will not be reclassified to profit or loss	
Gains on property revaluation	115
Income tax relating to items that will not be reclassified	(40)
Other comprehensive income for the year, net of tax	75
Total comprehensive income for the year	348

Profit attributable to:	
Owners of the parent	264
Non-controlling interests	9
	273
Total comprehensive income attributable to:	
Owners of the parent	338
Non-controlling interests	10
	348

You are also given the following information:

1   All other subsidiaries are wholly owned.

2   Depreciation charged to the consolidated profit or loss amounted to $210,000.

3   Part of the additions to property, plant and equipment during the year were imports made by P, a public limited company, from a foreign supplier on 30 September 20X8 for 108,000 corona. This was paid in full on 30 November 20X8.

Exchange gains and losses are included in administrative expenses. Relevant exchange rates were as follows:

	Corona to $1
30 September 20X8	4.0
30 November 20X8	4.5

4   There were no disposals of property, plant and equipment during the year.

Required

Prepare a consolidated statement of cash flows for the year ended 31 December 20X8 under the indirect method in accordance with IAS 7.

Solution

P Group
STATEMENT OF CASH FLOWS FOR THE YEAR ENDED 31 DECEMBER 20X8

	$'000	$'000
Cash flows from operating activities		
Profit before taxation	423	
Adjustments for:		
Depreciation	210	
Foreign exchange gain (W8)	(3)	
	630	
Increase in trade receivables (W3)	(240)	
Increase in inventories (W3)	(180)	
Increase in trade payables (W3)	150	
Cash generated from operations	360	
Income taxes paid (W7)	(100)	
Net cash from operating activities		260
Cash flows from investing activities		
Acquisition of subsidiary net of cash acquired (140 – 10)	(130)	
Foreign purchase of property, plant and equipment (W8)	(24)	
Purchase of property, plant and equipment (W1)	(220)	
Net cash used in investing activities		(374)
Cash flows from financing activities		
Proceeds from issuance of share capital (W4)	80	
Dividends paid to owners of the parent (W5)	(10)	
Dividends paid to non-controlling interests (W6)	(4)	
Net cash from financing activities		66
Net decrease in cash and cash equivalents		(48)
Cash and cash equivalents at the beginning of the year		50
Cash and cash equivalents at the end of the year		2

Workings

1   *Property, plant and equipment*

	$000
B/d	2,300
Revaluation	115
Depreciation	(210)
Foreign purchase (W87)	27
Acquisition of subsidiary	190
	2,422
Additions (in $) (balancing figure)	220
C/d	2,642

2   *Goodwill*

	$000
B/d	-
Acquisition of subsidiary *	66
	66
Impairment loss (balancing figure)	(-)
C/d	66

* Goodwill on acquisition of subsidiary:

	$000
Consideration transferred (140 + (100 × $1.60))	300
NCI (260 × 10%)	26
Less: Net assets at acquisition	(260)
	66

3   *Inventories, trade receivables and trade payables*

	Inventories	Trade receivables	Trade payables
	$'000	$'000	$'000
B/d	1,200	1,100	1,520
Acquisition of subsidiary	70	30	40
	1,270	1,130	1,560
Increase (balancing figure)	180	240	150
C/d	1,450	1,370	1,710

4   *Share capital and share premium*

	$'000
B/d (1,000 + 500)	1,500
Acquisition of subsidiary (100 × $1.60)	160
	1,660
Issue for cash (balancing figure)	80
C/d (1,150 + 590)	1,740

5   *Retained earnings (to find dividends paid to owners of the parent)*

	$000
B/d	1,530
SPLOCI – profit attributable to owners of parent	264
	1,794
Dividends paid to owners of the parent (balancing figure)	(10)
C/d	1,784

6   *Non-controlling interests*

	$000
B/d	-
SPLOCI – TCI	10
Acquisition of subsidiary (W2)	26
	36
Dividends paid (balancing figure)	(4)
C/d	32

7   *Current and deferred tax*

	$000
B/d (40 + 60)	100
SPLOCI – P/L	150
SPLOCI - OCI	40
	290
Tax paid (balancing figure)	(100)
C/d (80 + 110)	190

8   *Foreign transaction*

Transactions recorded on: $'000

(1)	30 Sep	DR Property, plant & equipment (108/4)	27 (to (W1))	
		CR Payables		27
(2)	30 Nov	DR Payables (to clear)	27	
		CR Cash (108/4.5)		24 (to CF 'investing')
		CR P/L (Admin expenses)		3 (to CF 'operating (adj)')

Section summary

A **foreign exchange difference** in a group statement of cash flows must be analysed into its constituent parts.

Chapter Roundup

✓   **Statements of cash flows** are a useful addition to the financial statements of companies because it is recognised that accounting profit is not the only indicator of a company's performance.

✓   Statements of cash flows concentrate on the sources and uses of cash and are a useful indicator of a company's **liquidity and solvency**.

✓   Remember the **step-by-step preparation procedure** and use it for all the questions you practise.

✓   You need to be aware of the **format** of the statement as laid out in **IAS 7**. Setting out the format is an essential first stage in preparing the statement, so this format must be learnt.

✓   **Consolidated cash flows** should not present a great problem if you understand how to deal with acquisitions and disposals of subsidiaries, non-controlling interest and dividends.

✓   A **foreign exchange difference** in a group statement of cash flows must be analysed into its constituent parts.

Quick Quiz

1   What is the objective of IAS 7?

2   What are the benefits of cash flow information according to IAS 7?

3   What are the standard headings required by IAS 7 to be included in a statement of cash flows?

4   What is the 'indirect method' of preparing a statement of cash flows?

5   How should an acquisition or disposal of a subsidiary be shown in the statement of cash flows?

Answers to Quick Quiz

1   To provide users of financial statements with information about the entity's ability to generate cash and cash equivalents, and the entity's cash needs.

2   See Paragraph 2.2.

3   Operating, investing and financing activities.

4   The net profit or loss for the period is adjusted for non-cash items; changes in inventories, receivables and payables from operations; and other items resulting from investing or financing activities.

5   Cash flows from acquisitions and disposal are disclosed separately under investing activities.

Answers to Questions

13.1   Single company

KANE CO

STATEMENT OF CASH FLOWS FOR THE YEAR ENDED 31 DECEMBER 20X8

	$'000	$'000
Net cash flow from operating activities		
Operating profit	420	
Depreciation charges	118	
Loss on sale of tangible non-current assets	18	
Increase in inventories	(4)	
Increase in receivables	(18)	
Increase in payables	12	
Cash generated from operations	546	
Interest paid	(28)	
Dividends paid (W2)	(72)	
Tax paid (W3)	(108)	
Net cash flow from operating activities		338
Cash flows from investing activities		
Payments to acquire tangible non-current assets	(90)	
Receipts from sales of tangible non-current assets (W1)	12	
Net cash outflow from investing activities		(78)
Cash flows from financing activities		
Issues of share capital (W4)	32	
Long-term loans repaid (500 – 200)	(300)	
Net cash flows from financing		(268)
Decrease in cash and cash equivalents		(8)
Cash and cash equivalents at 1.1.X8		56
Cash and cash equivalents at 31.12.X8		48

Note. The workings in this example have been set out as T-accounts (as you may have seen in your earlier studies) and also as simple schedules. As the other areas of the F2 syllabus do not require the use of T-accounts, we will use the simpler working format in the later examples in this chapter. Of course, you only need to produce one version of each working in exam questions.

Workings

1   *Non-current asset disposals*

COST

	$'000		$'000
At 1.1.X8	1,560	At 31.12.X8	1,596
Purchases	90	Disposals (balance)	54
	1,650		1,650

	$'000
Non-current asset cost c/d	1,560
Purchases	90
Disposals (balancing figure)	(54)
Non-current asset cost c/d	1,596

ACCUMULATED DEPRECIATION

	$'000		$'000
At 31.12.X8	318	At 1.1.X8	224
Depreciation on disposals (balance)	24	Charge for year	118
	342		342

	$'000
Non-current asset depreciation b/d	224
Depreciation charge for year	118
Depreciation on disposals (balancing figure)	(24)
Non-current asset depreciation c/d	318
NBV of disposals (54 – 24)	30
Net loss reported	(18)
Proceeds of disposals	12

2   *Dividends paid to owners of the parent*

RETAINED EARNINGS

	$'000		$'000
At 31.12.X8	686	At 1.1.X8	490
Dividends paid (balance)	72	Profit for the year	268
	758		758

	$'000
Retained earnings b/d	490
Profit for the year	268
Dividends paid (balance)	(72)
Retained earnings c/d	686

3   *Tax paid*

TAXATION LIABILITY

	$'000		$'000
At 31.12.X8	102	At 1.1.X8	86
Tax paid (balance)	108	Income tax expense	124
	210		210

	$'000
B/d	86
Income tax expense	124
Tax paid (balance)	(108)
C/d	102

4   *Proceeds of issues of shares*

SHARE CAPITAL (INCLUDING SHARE PREMIUM)

	$'000		$'000
		At 1.1.X8 share capital	340
At 31.12.X8 share capital	360	At 1.1.X8 share premium	24
At 31.12.X8 share premium	36	Cash received (balance)	32
	396		396

	$'000
B/d (340 + 24)	364
Cash received (balance)	32
C/d (360 + 36)	396

13.2 Consolidated cash flow

TOPIARY CO
CONSOLIDATED STATEMENT OF CASH FLOWS
FOR THE YEAR ENDED 31 DECEMBER 20X7

	$'000	$'000
Cash flows from operating activities		
Profit before taxation	5,520	
Adjustments for:		
Depreciation (W3)	975	
Profit on sale of plant	(300)	
Share of associate's profits (see note on (W5))	(1,050)	
Investment income	(465)	
Interest payable	450	
Operating profit before working capital changes	5,130	
Increase in trade and other receivables (W6)	(1,641)	
Increase in inventories (W6)	(2,829)	
Increase in trade payables (W6)	456	
Cash generated from operations	1,116	
Interest paid (W13)	(300)	
Income taxes paid (W12)	(750)	
Net cash from operating activities		66
Cash flows from investing activities		
Acquisition of subsidiary net of cash required (W14)	294	
Purchase of property, plant and equipment (W2)	(3,255)	
Proceeds from sale of plant	1,500	
Dividends from investment	465	
Dividends from associate (W5)	750	
Dividends paid to non-controlling interests (W9)	(144)	
Net cash used in investing activities		(390)
Cash flows from financing activities		
Issue of ordinary share capital (W7)	7,359	
Issue of loan notes (W11)	2,760	
Capital payments under finance leases (W10)	(810)	
Dividends paid (W8)	(900)	
Net cash flows from financing activities		8,409
Net increase in cash and cash equivalents		8,085
Cash and cash equivalents at 1.1.X7		5,460
Cash and cash equivalents at 31.12.X7		13,545

Workings

1   *Buildings*

	$'000
Net book value b/d	6,600
Depreciation charge (balancing figure)	(375)
Net book value c/d	6,225

2   *Purchase of plant and machinery*

	$'000
Cost b/d	4,200
Disposal	(1,500)
Additions under finance leases	2,550
Acquisition of subsidiary	495
	5,745
Additions (balancing figure)	3,255
Cost c/d	9,000

3   *Depreciation charges*

	$'000
Accumulated depreciation b/d	3,300
Depreciation on disposal (1,500 – 1,200*)	(300)
Depreciation charge (balancing figure)	600
Accumulated depreciation c/d	3,600

	$'000
*Disposal	
Proceeds	1,500
Net book value (balancing figure)	(1,200)
Profit on disposal	300

Freehold

Total depreciation charge: ($375,000 (W1) + $600,000) = $975,000

4   *Goodwill*

	$'000
Balance b/d	–
Impairment in year	–
Acquisition of subsidiary	300
Balance c/d	300

Note. This working shows that there has been no impairment of goodwill in the year.

5   *Dividends from associate*

Investment in associate

	$'000
Balance b/d	3,000
SLOCI - share of profit after tax	1,050
Dividends received from associate (balancing figure)	(750)
Balance c/d	3,300

Note. The share of the associate's profit, recognised in the consolidated statement of profit or loss and other comprehensive income, is not a cash item so is added back on the face of the statement of cash flows in the section that calculates the cash generated from operations. The **dividend received** from the associate is the cash item and appears in the investing activities section.

6   *Inventories, trade receivables and trade payables*

	Inventories	Receivables	Payables
	$'000	$'000	$'000
Balance b/d	3,000	3,825	840
Acquisition of subsidiary	96	84	204
	3,096	3,909	1,044
Increase/(decrease) (balancing figure)	2,829	1,641	456
Balance c/d	5,925	5,550	1,500

7   *Issue of ordinary share capital*

Share capital (including share premium)

	$'000
Balance b/d (6,000 + 6,285)	12,285
Acquisition of subsidiary	825
Issue for cash (balancing figure)	7,359
Balance c/d (11,820 + 8,649)	20,469

8   *Dividends paid to owners of the parent*

	$'000
Retained earnings b/d	7,500
Profit attributable to owners of the parent	3,735
Dividends paid (balancing figure)	(900)
Retained earnings c/d	10,335

9   *Dividends paid to non-controlling interests*

	$'000
Non-controlling interest b/d	–
Acquisition of subsidiary	189
Profit attributable to NCI	300
Dividends paid (balancing figure)	(144)
Non-controlling interest c/d	345

10   *Capital payments under leases*

	$'000	$'000
Balance b/d		
Current	600	
Long-term	510	
		1,110
New lease commitment (machinery)		2,550
Cash outflow (balancing figure)		(810)
Balance c/d		
Current	720	
Long-term	2,130	
		2,850

11   *Issue of loan notes*

	$'000
Balance b/d	1,500
Finance cost	120
Cash inflow (balancing figure)	2,760
Balance c/d	4,380

12   *Taxation*

	$'000	$'000
Balance b/d		
Income tax	651	
Deferred tax	39	
		690
SPLOCI – P/L (1,173 + 312)		1,485
On acquisition of subsidiary		51
Tax paid (balancing figure)		(750)
Balance c/d		
Income tax	1,386	
Deferred tax	90	
		1,476

13   *Interest*

	$'000
Balance b/d	90
SPLOCI (450 – 120) (excluding the discount credited to the carrying value of loans)	330
Interest paid in cash (balancing figure)	(300)
Balance c/d	120

Note. The finance cost shown in the statement of profit or loss is net of the gain on the held for trading investment. On the statement of cash flows these have been dealt with separately.

14   *Purchase of subsidiary*

	$'000
Cash received on acquisition of subsidiary	336
Less cash consideration	(42)
Cash inflow	294

Note. Only the **cash** consideration is included in the figure reported in the statement of cash flows. The **shares** issued as part of the consideration are reflected in the share capital working (W7) above.

Now try this question from the Exam Question Bank	Number	Level	Marks	Time
	Q18	Examination	25	45 mins

ANALYSIS AND INTERPRETATION OF FINANCIAL ACCOUNTS

Part D

RATIO AND TREND ANALYSIS

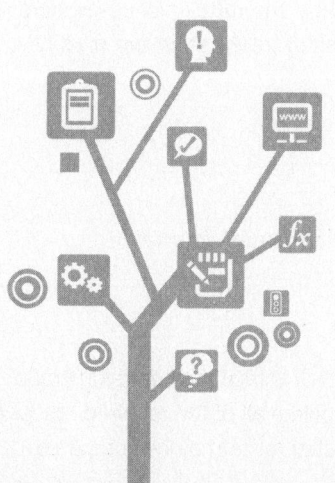

You must be able to **comment** on the ratios as well as calculate them and give suggested reasons for trends and differences. Pay close attention to Section 8 on report writing, as this will help you to improve your exam technique.

CIMA have stated that this syllabus places considerable emphasis on interpretation.

topic list	learning outcomes	syllabus references	ability required
1 Sources of information and the role of regulation	C1	C1(i)	Application
2 The broad categories of ratios	C1	C1(i)	Application
3 Profitability and return on capital	C1	C1(i)	Application
4 Liquidity, gearing/leverage and working capital	C1	C1(i),(iii)	Application
5 Investment ratios	C1	C1(i)	Application
6 The nature of profit	C1	C1(i)	Application
7 Other problems with financial analysis	C1	C1(i),(iv)	Application
8 Presentation of reports	C1	C1(i)	Application

1 Sources of information and the role of regulation   11/12

Introduction

The accounts of a business are designed to provide users with information about its performance and financial position. The bare figures, however, are not particularly useful and it is only through **comparisons** (usually in ratios) that their significance can be established. Comparisons may be made with previous financial periods, with other similar businesses or with averages for the particular industry. The choice will depend on the purpose for which the comparison is being made and the information that is available.

1.1 User groups

Various groups are interested in the performance and financial position of a company.

(a)   **Management** will use comparisons to ensure that the business is performing efficiently and according to plan

(b)   **Employees**, trade unions and so on, as a basis of wage negotiation for example

(c)   **Government** may use financial statements to prepare statistics or for assessing the worthiness of a government grant

(d)   Present and potential **investors** will assess the company with a view to judging whether it is a sound investment

(e)   **Lenders** and **suppliers** will want to judge its creditworthiness

This text is concerned with financial rather than management accounting and the ratios discussed here are therefore likely to be calculated by external users. The following sources of information are readily available to external users.

- Published financial statements and interim financial statements
- Documents filed as required by company legislation
- Statistics published by the government
- Other published sources eg *Investor's Chronicle*, *The Economist*, *Wall Street Journal*

1.2 Financial analysis

The **lack of detailed information** available to the outsider is a considerable disadvantage in undertaking ratio analysis. The first difficulty is that there may simply be insufficient data to calculate all of the required ratios. A second concerns the availability of a suitable 'yardstick' with which the calculated ratios may be compared.

1.2.1 Inter-temporal analysis

Looking first at inter-temporal or trend analysis (comparisons for the same business over time), some of the **problems** include the following.

- Changes in the nature of the business
- Unrealistic depreciation rates under historical cost accounting
- The changing value of the currency unit being reported
- Changes in accounting policies

Other factors will include changes in government incentive packages, changes from purchasing equipment to leasing and so on.

1.2.2 Cross-sectional analysis

When undertaking 'cross-sectional' analysis (making comparisons with other companies) the position is even more difficult because of the problem of identifying companies that are comparable. **Comparability** between companies may be impaired due to the following reasons.

(a)   Different degrees of diversification

(b)   Different production and purchasing policies (if an investor was analysing the smaller car manufacturers, he would find that some of them buy in engines from one of the 'majors' whilst others develop and manufacture their own)

(c)   Different financing policies (eg leasing as opposed to buying)

(d)   Different accounting policies (one of the most serious problems particularly in relation to non-current assets and inventory valuation)

(e)   Different effects of government incentives

The major **intra-group comparison organisations** (whose results are intended for the use of participating companies and are not generally available) go to considerable length to adjust accounts to comparable bases. The external user will rarely be in a position to make such adjustments. Although the position is improved by increases in disclosure requirements direct comparisons between companies will inevitably, on occasion, continue to give rise to misleading results.

1.3 Social and political considerations

In recent years, the **social aspect** much in evidence has been that of **environmental issues**. Presenting a sustainable, environmentally-responsible image is now increasingly important for a company's reputation. Sometimes, the public perception of how well a company is doing in environmental terms can even affect the company's financial profits (for example, increased margins on organic foods, or fines for environmental breaches).

Political considerations may also be far reaching. The regulatory regime may be instituted by statutes, but often self-regulation is encouraged through bodies such as the stock exchange.

1.4 Multinational companies

Multinational companies have great difficulties sometimes because of the need to comply with **legislation** in a large number of countries. As well as different reporting requirements, different rules of incorporation exist, as well as different directors' rules, tax legislation and so on. Sometimes the local rules can be so harsh that companies will avoid them altogether.

Different local reporting requirements will also make **consolidation** more difficult. The results of subsidiaries must be translated, not only to the company's base currency, but also using the accounting rules used by head office. This is a requirement of IFRSs as 'uniform accounting policies' are called for.

1.5 The efficient market hypothesis and stock exchanges

It has been argued that stock markets in the most sophisticated economies, eg the USA, are **efficient capital markets**.

(a)   The prices of securities bought and sold reflect all the relevant information which is available to the buyers and sellers. In other words, share prices change quickly to reflect all new information about future prospects.

(b)   No individual dominates the market.

(c)   Transaction costs are not so high as to discourage trading significantly.

If the stock market is efficient, share prices should vary in a **rational way**, ie reflecting the known profits or losses of a company and the rate of return required based on interest rates.

Research in both Britain and the USA has suggested that market prices anticipate mergers several months before they are formally announced, and the conclusion drawn is that the stock markets in these countries *do* exhibit **semi-strong efficiency**. It has also been argued that the market displays sufficient efficiency for investors to see through 'window dressing' of accounts by companies which use accounting conventions to overstate profits (ie creative accounting).

Evidence suggests that stock markets show efficiency that is **at least weak form**, but tending more towards a semi-strong form. In other words, current share prices reflect all or most publicly available information about companies and their securities. However, it is very difficult to assess the market's efficiency in relation to shares which are not usually actively traded.

Fundamental analysis and **technical analysis** carried out by analysts and investment managers play an important role in creating an efficient stock market. This is because an efficient market depends on the widespread availability of cheap information about companies, their shares and market conditions, and this is what the firms of market makers and other financial institutions *do* provide for their clients and for the general investing public. In a market which demonstrates strong-form efficiency, such analysis would not identify profitable opportunities, ie where shares are undervalued, because such information would already be known and reflected in the share price.

On the other hand stock market crashes raise serious questions about the validity of the **fundamental theory of share values** and the efficient market hypothesis. If these theories are correct, how can shares that were valued at one level on one day suddenly be worth 40% less the next day, without any change in expectations of corporate profits and dividends? On the other hand, a widely feared crash may fail to happen, suggesting that stock markets may not be altogether out of touch with the underlying values of companies.

Section summary

Keep the various **sources of financial information** in mind and the effects of insider dealing, the efficient market hypothesis and Stock Exchange regulations.

2 The broad categories of ratios 11/10, 3/11, 11/11, 9/12

Introduction

If you were to look at a statement of financial position or statement of profit or loss and other comprehensive income, how would you decide whether the company was doing well or badly? Or whether it was financially strong or financially vulnerable? And what would you be looking at in the figures to help you to make your judgement?

Ratio analysis involves **comparing one figure against another** to produce a ratio, and assessing whether the ratio indicates a weakness or strength in the company's affairs.

2.1 The broad categories of ratios

Broadly speaking, basic ratios can be grouped into five categories.

- Profitability and return
- Long-term solvency and stability
- Short-term solvency and liquidity
- Efficiency (turnover ratios)
- Investor ratios

Within each heading we will identify a number of standard measures or ratios that are normally calculated and generally accepted as meaningful indicators. One must stress, however, that each individual business must be considered separately, and a ratio that is meaningful for a manufacturing company may be completely meaningless for a financial institution. When working out ratios, you should constantly think about what you are trying to achieve.

The key to obtaining meaningful information from ratio analysis is **comparison**. This may involve comparing ratios over time within the same business to establish whether things are improving or declining, and comparing ratios between similar businesses to see whether the company you are analysing is better or worse than average within its specific business sector.

It must be stressed that ratio analysis on its own is not sufficient for interpreting company accounts, and that there are **other items of information** which should be looked at, for example:

(a)   The content of any **accompanying commentary** on the accounts and other statements

(b)   The age and nature of the **company's assets**

(c)   **Current and future developments** in the company's markets, at home and overseas, recent acquisitions or disposals of a subsidiary by the company

(d)   **Unusual** items separately disclosed in the statement of profit or loss and other comprehensive income

(e)   Any other **noticeable features** of the report and accounts, such as events after the reporting date, contingent liabilities, a qualified auditors' report, the company's taxation position, and so on.

Further reading

The March edition of the Financial Management magazine contains an article by Jayne Howson, a marker for this paper, about how ratio analysis is tested in the CIMA F2 exams. Make sure you read this article, as it contains some very helpful explanations about how you should calculate and analyse ratios in the exam.

The article can be accessed via this link: http://www.fm-magazine.com/study-centre/course-notes/financial-management-3 (Valid as of 18 April 2013).

Exam skills

In the exam, you must relate the analysis to the scenario given in the question.

Make sure that you use the formulae provided below when you calculate your ratios. If you do not use the exam-specified formula, you will not get any marks. Be warned!

Example: calculating ratios

To illustrate the calculation of ratios, the following **draft** statement of financial position and statement of profit or loss figures will be used.

FURLONG CO
STATEMENT OF PROFIT OR LOSS FOR THE YEAR ENDED 31 DECEMBER 20X8

	Notes	20X8 $	20X7 $
Revenue		3,095,576	1,909,051
Cost of sales		(2,402,609)	(1,441,950)
Gross profit		692,967	467,101
Administrative expenses		(333,466)	(222,872)
Share of profit of associate		10,000	8,500
Interest	1	(17,371)	(19,127)
Profit before taxation		352,130	233,602
Taxation		(74,200)	(31,272)
Profit for the year		277,930	202,330
Dividend		(41,000)	(16,800)
Earnings per share		13.2c	9.6c

FURLONG CO
STATEMENT OF FINANCIAL POSITION AS AT 31 DECEMBER 20X8

	Notes	20X8 $	20X8 $	20X7 $	20X7 $
Assets					
Non-current assets					
Property, plant and equipment		712,180		576,071	
Investment in associate		90,000		80,000	
			802,180		656,071
Current assets					
Inventory		64,422		86,550	
Receivables	2	1,002,701		853,441	
Cash at and cash equivalents		1,327		68,363	
			1,068,450		1,008,354
Total assets			1,870,630		1,664,425
Equity and liabilities					
Equity					
Ordinary shares 10c each	4	210,000		210,000	
Share premium account		48,178		48,178	
Retained earnings		630,721		393,791	
			888,899		651,969
Non-current liabilities					
10% loan stock 20X4/20Y0			100,000		100,000
Current liabilities	3		881,731		912,456
Total equity and liabilities			1,870,630		1,664,425

Notes

		20X8 $	20X7 $
1	*Interest*		
	Payable on bank overdrafts and other loans	8,115	11,909
	Payable on loan stock	10,000	10,000
		18,115	21,909
	Receivable on short-term deposits	(744)	(2,782)
	Net payable	17,371	19,127
2	*Receivables*		
	Amounts falling due within one year		
	Trade receivables	884,559	760,252
	Prepayments and accrued income	97,022	45,729
		981,581	805,981
	Amounts falling due after more than one year		
	Trade receivables	21,120	47,460
	Total receivables	1,002,701	853,441
3	*Current liabilities*		
	Trade payables	627,018	545,340
	Accruals and deferred income	81,279	280,464
	Corporate taxes	108,000	37,200
	Other taxes	44,434	32,652
	Dividend	21,000	16,800
		881,731	912,456
4	*Called-up share capital*		
	Authorised ordinary shares of 10c each	1,000,000	1,000,000
	Issued and fully paid ordinary shares of 10c each	210,000	210,000

Section summary

Your syllabus requires you to **appraise and communicate** the position and prospects of a business based on given and prepared statements and ratios.

Much of the material here on **basic ratios** should be revision for you.

Make sure that you can **define** all the ratios. Look out for variations in definitions of ratios which might appear in questions.

3 Profitability and return on capital

Introduction

In our example, the company made a profit in both 20X8 and 20X7, and there was an increase in profit between one year and the next:

(a)   Of 51% before taxation   (b)   Of 37% after taxation

Profit before taxation is generally thought to be a better figure to use than profit after taxation, because there might be unusual variations in the tax charge from year to year which would not affect the underlying profitability of the company's operations

Another profit figure that should be calculated is PBIT, **profit before interest and tax**. This is the amount of profit which the company earned before having to pay interest to the providers of loan capital. By providers of loan capital, we usually mean longer-term loan capital, such as debentures and medium-term bank loans, which will be shown in the statement of financial position as non-current liabilities.

> **Profit before interest and tax** is therefore:
>
> (a) the profit on ordinary activities before taxation; **plus**
> (b) interest payable shown in the statement of profit or loss.
>
> The PBIT **must not** include any profits or losses from **investments in associate**.

PBIT in our example is therefore:

	20X8	20X7
	$	$
Profit before tax	352,130	233,602
Less share of profit of associate	(10,000)	(8,500)
Add back interest payable	18,115	21,909
PBIT	360,245	247,011

This shows a 45% growth between 20X7 and 20X8.

3.1 Return on capital employed (ROCE)

It is impossible to assess profits or profit growth properly without relating them to the **amount of funds (capital) that were employed in making the profits**. The most important profitability ratio is therefore return on capital employed (ROCE), which states the profit as a percentage of the amount of capital employed.

> $$\text{ROCE} = \frac{\text{Profit before interest and taxation}}{\text{Capital employed}} \times 100\%$$
>
> Capital employed = Shareholders' equity plus non-current liabilities* less investments in associates
>
> * Also include overdraft if the company is using it as a long-term source of finance

The underlying principle is that we must **compare like with like**, and so if capital means share capital and reserves plus non-current liabilities less investments in associates, profit must also exclude the associate (share of associate's profit or loss) and mean the profit earned by all this capital together.

In our example, capital employed = 20X8 $888,899 + $100,000 - $90,000= $898,899
20X7 $651,959 + $100,000 - $80,000= $671,969

These total figures are the total assets less current liabilities figures for 20X8 and 20X7 in the statement of financial position.

	20X8	20X7
ROCE =	$\dfrac{\$360,245}{\$898,899}$	$\dfrac{\$247,011}{\$671,969}$
=	40.1%	36.8%

What does a company's ROCE tell us? What should we be looking for? There are three comparisons that can be made.

(a) The **change in ROCE from one year to the next** can be examined. In this example, there has been an increase in ROCE by just over 3 percentage points from its 20X7 level.

(b) The **ROCE being earned by other companies**, if this information is available, can be compared with the ROCE of this company. Here the information is not available.

(c) A comparison of the ROCE with **current market borrowing rates** may be made.

    (i) What would be the cost of extra borrowing to the company if it needed more loans, and is it earning a ROCE that suggests it could make profits to make such borrowing worthwhile?

(ii)   Is the company making a ROCE which suggests that it is getting value for money from its current borrowing?

(iii)   Companies are in a risk business and commercial borrowing rates are a good independent yardstick against which company performance can be judged.

In this example, if we suppose that current market interest rates, say, for medium-term borrowing from banks, are around 10%, then the company's actual ROCE of 40.1% in 20X8 would not seem low. On the contrary, it might seem high.

However, it is easier to spot a low ROCE than a high one, because there is always a chance that the company's non-current assets, especially property, are **undervalued** in its statement of financial position, and so the capital employed figure might be unrealistically low. If the company had earned a ROCE, not of 40.1%, but of, say only 6%, then its return would have been below current borrowing rates and so disappointingly low.

3.2 Return on equity (ROE)

Return on equity gives a more restricted view of capital than ROCE, but it is based on the same principles.

$$ROE = \frac{\text{Profit after tax and preferred dividend}}{\text{Ordinary share capital and other equity}} \times 100\%$$

In our example, ROE is calculated as follows.

$$ROE = \quad \overset{\textit{20X8}}{\frac{\$267,930}{\$888,899}} = 31.2\% \qquad \overset{\textit{20X7}}{\frac{\$193,830}{\$651,969}} = 31.0\%$$

ROE is **not a widely-used ratio**, however, because there are more useful ratios that give an indication of the return to shareholders, such as earnings per share, dividend per share, dividend yield and earnings yield, which are described later.

3.3 Analysing profitability and return in more detail: the secondary ratios

We often sub-analyse ROCE, to find out more about why the ROCE is high or low, or better or worse than last year. There are two factors that contribute towards a return on capital employed, both related to revenue.

(a)   **Operating profit margin.** A company might make a high or low operating profit margin on its sales. For example, a company that makes a profit of 25c per $1 of sales is making a bigger return on its revenue than another company making a profit of only 10c per $1 of sales.

(b)   **Asset turnover**. Asset turnover is a measure of how well the assets of a business are being used to generate sales. For example, if two companies each have capital employed of $100,000 and Company A makes sales of $400,000 per annum whereas Company B makes sales of only $200,000 per annum, Company A is making a higher revenue from the same amount of assets (twice as much asset turnover as Company B) and this will help A to make a higher return on capital employed than B. Asset turnover is expressed as 'x times' so that assets generate x times their value in annual sales. Here, Company A's asset turnover is 4 times and B's is 2 times.

Operating profit margin and asset turnover together explain the ROCE and if the ROCE is the primary profitability ratio, these other two are the secondary ratios. The relationship between the three ratios can be shown mathematically.

Operating profit margin × Asset turnover = ROCE

$$\therefore \quad \frac{PBIT}{Revenue} \quad \times \quad \frac{Revenue}{Capital\ employed} \quad = \quad \frac{PBIT}{Capital\ employed}$$

where capital employed is as defined for ROCE

In our example:

		Operating profit margin		Asset turnover		ROCE
(a)	20X8	$\dfrac{\$360,245}{\$3,095,576}$	×	$\dfrac{\$3,095,576}{\$898,899}$	=	$\dfrac{\$360,245}{\$898,899}$
		11.64%	×	3.44 times	=	40.1%
(b)	20X7	$\dfrac{\$247,011}{\$1,909,051}$	×	$\dfrac{\$1,909,051}{\$671,969}$	=	$\dfrac{\$247,011}{\$671,969}$
		12.94%	×	2.84 times	=	36.8%

In this example, the company's improvement in ROCE between 20X7 and 20X8 is attributable to a higher asset turnover. Indeed the operating profit margin has fallen a little, but the higher asset turnover has more than compensated for this.

It is also worth commenting on the change in revenue from one year to the next. You may already have noticed that Furlong achieved sales growth of over 60% from $1.9 million to $3.1 million between 20X7 and 20X8. This is very strong growth, and this is certainly one of the most significant items in the statement of profit or loss and other comprehensive income.

There are two other asset turnover ratios that you may meet in the exam. Again, remember that your total assets and non-current assets figures must exclude any investments in associate as the revenue figure does not incorporate the associate and you need to compare like with like.

Total asset turnover = Revenue/Total assets

Non-current asset turnover = Revenue/ Non-current assets

3.3.1 A warning about comments on profit margin and asset turnover

It might be tempting to think that a high profit margin is good, and a low asset turnover means sluggish trading. In broad terms, this is so. But there is a trade-off between operating profit margin and asset turnover, and you cannot look at one without allowing for the other.

(a) A **high operating profit margin** means a high profit per $1 of sales, but if this also means that sales prices are high, there is a strong possibility that sales revenue will be depressed, and so asset turnover lower.

(b) A **high asset turnover** means that the company is generating a lot of sales, but to do this it might have to keep its prices down and so accept a low profit margin per $1 of sales.

Consider the following.

Company A		Company B	
Revenue	$1,000,000	Revenue	$4,000,000
Capital employed	$1,000,000	Capital employed	$1,000,000
PBIT	$200,000	PBIT	$200,000

These figures would give the following ratios.

$$ROCE = \frac{\$200,000}{\$1,000,000} = 20\% \qquad ROCE = \frac{\$200,000}{\$1,000,000} = 20\%$$

$$Profit\ margin = \frac{\$200,000}{\$1,000,000} = 20\% \qquad Profit\ margin = \frac{\$200,000}{\$4,000,000} = 5\%$$

$$Asset\ turnover = \frac{\$1,000,000}{\$1,000,000} = 1 \qquad Asset\ turnover = \frac{\$4,000,000}{\$1,000,000} = 4$$

The companies have the same ROCE, but it is arrived at in a very different fashion. Company A operates with a low asset turnover and a comparatively high profit margin whereas company B carries out much more business, but on a lower profit margin. Company A could be operating at the luxury end of the market, whilst company B is operating at the popular end of the market.

3.4 Gross profit margin, operating profit margin, net profit margin and profit analysis

There are three possible profit margin figures that you can calculate:

$$Gross\ profit\ margin = \frac{Gross\ profit}{Revenue} \times 100\%$$

The gross profit margin measures how well a company is running its core operations.

$$Operating\ profit\ margin = \frac{Profit\ before\ interest\ and\ tax}{Revenue} \times 100\%$$

Profit before interest and taxation (PBIT) is used because it avoids distortion when comparisons are made between two different companies where one is heavily financed by means of loans, and the other is financed entirely by ordinary share capital. The extra consideration for the operating margin over the gross margin is how well the company is controlling its overheads.

$$Net\ profit\ margin = \frac{Profit\ for\ year}{Revenue} \times 100\%$$

The extra considerations for the net margin over the operating margin are interest and tax.

Looking at the three together can be quite informative.

For example, suppose that a company has the following summarised statement of profit or loss for two consecutive years.

	Year 1	Year 2
	$	$
Revenue	70,000	100,000
Cost of sales	(42,000)	(55,000)
Gross profit	28,000	45,000
Distribution and administrative expenses	(16,000)	(29,000)
Finance costs	(2,000)	(2,000)
Profit before tax	10,000	14,000
Income tax expense	(3,000)	(4,000)
Profit for the year	7,000	10,000

Although the net profit margin is the same for both years at 10%, the gross profit margin is not.

In Year 1 it is: $\dfrac{\$28,000}{\$70,000}$ =   40%

and in Year 2 it is: $\dfrac{\$45,000}{\$100,000}$ =   45%

The improved gross profit margin has not led to an improvement in the net profit margin. We can see that this is largely due to poor cost control of operating overheads since the operating margin has deteriorated despite the improvement in the gross margin:

In Year 1 it is: $\dfrac{\$10,000 + \$2,000}{\$70,000}$ =   17%

In Year 2 it is: $\dfrac{\$14,000 + \$2,000}{\$100,000}$ =   16%

Finance costs and presumably borrowings and the rate of interest have remained constant so this is not the reason for the difference in gross and net margins.

Section summary

Make sure you learn the ratios given.

4 Liquidity, gearing/leverage and working capital   11/12

Introduction

Debt ratios are concerned with **how much the company owes in relation to its size**, whether it is getting into heavier debt or improving its situation, and whether its debt burden seems heavy or light.

(a)   When a company is heavily in debt banks and other potential lenders may be unwilling to advance further funds.

(b)   When a company is earning only a modest profit before interest and tax, and has a heavy debt burden, there will be very little profit left over for shareholders after the interest charges have been paid. And so if interest rates were to go up (on bank overdrafts and so on) or the company were to borrow even more, it might soon be incurring interest charges in excess of PBIT. This might eventually lead to the liquidation of the company.

4.1 Long-term solvency: gearing and interest cover ratios

These are two big reasons why companies should keep their debt burden under control. There are two ratios that are particularly worth looking at: the gearing ratio and interest cover.

4.2 Gearing

Gearing is concerned with a company's **long-term capital structure**. We can think of a company as consisting of non-current assets and net current assets (ie working capital, which is current assets minus current liabilities). These assets must be financed by long-term capital of the company, which is one of two things.

(a)   Equity which can be divided into:

(i)   Ordinary share capital and share premium

(ii)   Cumulative irredeemable preference share capital and share premium (see Chapter 2)

(iii)   Reserves (eg retained earnings, revaluation reserve)

(b)   Long-term debt, including:

   (i)   Pension liabilities
   (ii)   Overdraft, only if it is used as a **long-term source of finance**
   (iii) Redeemable or cumulative irredeemable preference shares (see Chapter 2)

There are two ways of calculating the capital gearing ratio, one giving a percentage and the other a number, as follows.

$$\text{Gearing} = \frac{\text{Long}-\text{term debt}}{\text{Long}-\text{term debt}+\text{Equity}} \times 100\%$$

$$\text{Gearing} = \frac{\text{Long}-\text{term debt}}{\text{Equity}} \times 100\%$$

Exam alert

Unless specified in the question, you can use either method in the exam, as long as you are consistent and set out the basis of your workings accordingly.

If you are not certain whether or not an overdraft should be included as prior charge capital, set out your reasons for including or excluding it in your answer.

There is **no absolute limit** to what a gearing ratio ought to be. A company with a gearing ratio of more than 50% is said to be highly geared (whereas low gearing means a gearing ratio of less than 50%). Many companies are highly geared, but if a highly geared company is becoming increasingly highly geared, it is likely to have difficulty in the future when it wants to borrow even more, unless it can also boost its shareholders' capital, either with retained profits or by a new share issue.

4.3 The implications of high or low gearing

We mentioned earlier that **gearing or leverage** is, amongst other things, an attempt to **quantify the degree of risk involved in holding equity shares in a company**, risk both in terms of the company's ability to remain in business and in terms of expected ordinary dividends from the company. The problem with a highly geared company is that by definition there is a lot of debt. Debt generally carries a fixed rate of interest (or fixed rate of dividend if in the form of preferred shares), hence there is a given (and large) amount to be paid out from profits to holders of debt before arriving at a residue available for distribution to the holders of equity. The level of risk will perhaps become clearer with the aid of an example.

	Company A $'000	Company B $'000	Company C $'000
Ordinary shares	600	400	300
Retained earnings	200	200	200
Revaluation reserve	100	100	100
	900	700	600
5% cumulative redeemable preference shares	-	-	100
10% loan stock	100	300	300
Capital employed	1,000	1,000	1,000
Gearing ratio	10%	30%	40%
Equity to assets ratio	90%	70%	60%

Now suppose that each company makes a profit before interest and tax of $50,000, and the rate of tax on company profits is 30%. Amounts available for distribution to equity shareholders will be as follows.

	Company A $'000	Company B $'000	Company C $'000
Profit before interest and tax	50	50	50
Interest	(10)	(30)	(35)
Taxable profit	40	20	15
Taxation at 30%	(12)	(6)	(4.5)
Profit after tax available for ordinary shareholders	28	14	10.5

If in the subsequent year profit before interest and tax falls to $40,000, the amounts available to ordinary shareholders will become as follows.

	Company A $'000	Company B $'000	Company C $'000
Profit before interest and tax	40	40	40
Interest	(10)	(30)	(35)
Taxable profit	30	10	5
Taxation at 30%	(9)	(3)	(1.5)
Profit after tax available for ordinary shareholders	21	7	3.5

Note the following (assuming that all profit is paid out as dividends so equity is unchanged).

Gearing ratio	10%	30%	40%
Equity to assets ratio	90%	70%	60%
Change in PBIT	– 20%	– 20%	– 20%
Change in profit available for ordinary shareholders	– 25%	– 50%	– 67%

The more highly geared the company, the greater the risk that little (if anything) will be available to distribute by way of dividend to the ordinary shareholders. The example clearly displays this fact in so far as the more highly geared the company, the greater the percentage change in profit available for ordinary shareholders for any given percentage change in profit before interest and tax. The relationship similarly holds when profits increase, and if PBIT had risen by 20% rather than fallen, you would find that once again the largest percentage change in profit available for ordinary shareholders (this means an increase) will be for the highly geared company. This means that there will be greater *volatility* of amounts available for ordinary shareholders, and presumably therefore greater volatility in dividends paid to those shareholders, where a company is highly geared. That is the risk: you may do extremely well or extremely badly without a particularly large movement in the PBIT of the company.

The risk of a company's ability to remain in business was referred to earlier. Gearing is relevant to this. A highly geared company has a large amount of interest to pay annually. If those borrowings are '**secured**' in any way (and debentures in particular are secured), then the **holders of the debt are perfectly entitled to force the company** to **realise assets to pay their interest** if funds are not available from other sources. Clearly the more highly geared a company the more likely this is to occur when and if profits fall.

4.4 Interest cover

The interest cover ratio shows whether a company is earning enough profits before interest and tax to pay its interest costs comfortably, or whether its interest costs are high in relation to the size of its profits, so that a fall in PBIT would then have a significant effect on profits available for ordinary shareholders.

LEARN

$$\text{Interest cover} = \frac{\text{Profit before interest and tax}}{\text{Interest charges}}$$

Ideally interest cover should be at least one. Some consider an interest cover of 2 times or less to be low, and believe that it should really exceed 3 times before the company's interest costs are to be considered within acceptable limits. However, the level of acceptable interest cover varies depending on the industry in which the company operates.

Exam alert

As mentioned above, make sure you exclude any profit or loss from investments in associate when calculating the profit before interest and tax figure.

Returning first to the example of Companies A, B and C, the interest cover was as follows.

		Company A	Company B	Company C
(a)	When PBIT was $50,000 =	$\dfrac{\$50,000}{\$10,000}$	$\dfrac{\$50,000}{\$30,000}$	$\dfrac{\$50,000}{\$35,000}$
		5 times	1.67 times	1.43 times
(b)	When PBIT was $40,000 =	$\dfrac{\$40,000}{\$10,000}$	$\dfrac{\$40,000}{\$30,000}$	$\dfrac{\$40,000}{\$35,000}$
		4 times	1.33 times	1.14 times

Note. We look at all interest payments, even interest charges on short-term debt, and so interest cover and gearing do not quite look at the same thing.

Both B and C have a low interest cover, which is a warning to ordinary shareholders that their profits are highly vulnerable, in percentage terms, to even small changes in PBIT.

Question 14.1	Interest cover

Learning outcomes C1

Returning to the example of Furlong in Paragraph 2.1, what is the company's interest cover?

4.5 Short-term solvency and liquidity

Profitability is of course an important aspect of a company's performance and gearing or leverage is another. Neither, however, addresses directly the key issue of *liquidity*.

KEY TERM

LIQUIDITY is the amount of cash a company can put its hands on quickly to settle its debts (and possibly to meet other unforeseen demands for cash payments too).

Liquid funds consist of:

(a)   Cash

(b)   Short-term investments for which there is a ready market

(c)   Fixed-term deposits with a bank or other financial institution, for example, a six month high-interest deposit with a bank

(d)   Trade receivables (because they will pay what they owe within a reasonably short period of time)

(e)   Bills of exchange receivable (because like ordinary trade receivables, these represent amounts of cash due to be received within a relatively short period of time)

In summary, **liquid assets are current asset items that will or could soon be converted into cash, and cash itself.** Two common definitions of liquid assets are:

- All current assets without exception
- All current assets with the exception of inventories

A company can obtain liquid assets from sources other than sales of goods and services, such as the issue of shares for cash, a new loan or the sale of non-current assets. But a company cannot rely on these at all times, and in general, obtaining liquid funds depends on making sales revenue and profits. Even so, profits do not always lead to increases in liquidity. This is mainly because funds generated from trading may be immediately invested in non-current assets or paid out as dividends. You should refer back to the chapter on statements of cash flows to examine this issue.

The reason why a company needs liquid assets is so that it can meet its debts when they fall due. Payments are continually made for operating expenses and other costs, and so there is a **cash cycle** from trading activities of cash coming in from sales and cash going out for expenses.

4.6 The cash cycle

To help you to understand liquidity ratios, it is useful to begin with a brief explanation of the cash cycle or working capital cycle. The cash cycle describes **the flow of cash out of a business and back into it again as a result of normal trading operations.**

Cash goes out to pay for supplies, wages and salaries and other expenses, although payments can be delayed by taking some credit. A business might hold inventory for a while and then sell it. Cash will come back into the business from the sales, although customers might delay payment by themselves taking some credit.

The main points about the cash cycle are as follows.

(a) The timing of cash flows in and out of a business does not coincide with the time when sales and costs of sales occur. **Cash flows out can be postponed by taking credit. Cash flows in can be delayed by having receivables.**

(b) **The time between making a purchase and making a sale also affects cash flows**. If inventories are held for a long time, the delay between the cash payment for inventory and cash receipts from selling it will also be a long one.

(c) **Holding inventories and having receivables can therefore be seen as two reasons why cash receipts are delayed.** Another way of saying this is that if a company invests in working capital, its cash position will show a corresponding decrease.

(d) Similarly, **taking credit from creditors can be seen as a reason why cash payments are delayed**. The company's liquidity position will worsen when it has to pay the suppliers, unless it can get more cash in from sales and receivables in the meantime.

The liquidity ratios and working capital turnover ratios are used to test a company's liquidity, length of cash cycle, and investment in working capital.

4.7 Liquidity ratios: current ratio and quick ratio

The 'standard' test of liquidity is the **current ratio**. It can be obtained from the statement of financial position.

$$\text{Current ratio} = \frac{\text{Current assets}}{\text{Current liabilities}}$$

The idea behind this is that a company should have enough current assets that give a promise of 'cash to come' to meet its future commitments to pay off its current liabilities. Obviously, a **ratio in excess of 1 should be expected**. Otherwise, there would be the prospect that the company might be unable to pay its debts on time. In practice, a ratio comfortably in excess of 1 should be expected, but what is 'comfortable' varies between different types of businesses.

Companies are not able to convert all their current assets into cash very quickly. In particular, some manufacturing companies might hold large quantities of raw material inventories, which must be used in production to create finished goods inventory. These might be warehoused for a long time, or sold on lengthy credit. In such businesses, where inventory turnover is slow, most inventories are not very 'liquid' assets, because the cash cycle is so long. For these reasons, we calculate an additional liquidity ratio, known as the quick ratio or acid test ratio.

The **quick ratio**, or **acid test ratio**, is calculated as follows.

$$\text{Quick ratio} = \frac{\text{Current assets less inventory}}{\text{Current liabilities}}$$

This ratio should ideally be **at least 1** for companies with a slow inventory turnover. For companies with a fast inventory turnover, a quick ratio can be comfortably less than 1 without suggesting that the company could be in cash flow trouble.

Both the current ratio and the quick ratio offer an indication of the company's liquidity position, but the absolute figures **should not be interpreted too literally**. It is often theorised that an acceptable current ratio is 1.5 and an acceptable quick ratio is 0.8, but these should only be used as a guide. Different businesses operate in very different ways. A supermarket group for example might have a current ratio of 0.52 and a quick ratio of 0.17. Supermarkets have low receivables (people do not buy groceries on credit), low cash (good cash management), medium inventories (high inventories but quick turnover, particularly in view of perishability) and very high payables.

Compare this with a manufacturing and retail organisation, with a current ratio of 1.44 and a quick ratio of 1.03. Such businesses operate with liquidity ratios closer to the standard.

What is important is the **trend** of these ratios. From this, one can easily ascertain whether liquidity is improving or deteriorating. If a supermarket has traded for the last 10 years (very successfully) with current ratios of 0.52 and quick ratios of 0.17 then it should be supposed that the company can continue in business with those levels of liquidity. If in the following year the current ratio were to fall to 0.38 and the quick ratio to 0.09, then further investigation into the liquidity situation would be appropriate. It is the relative position that is far more important than the absolute figures.

Don't forget the other side of the coin either. A current ratio and a quick ratio can get **bigger than they need to be**. A company that has large volumes of inventories and receivables might be over-investing in working capital, and so tying up more funds in the business than it needs to. This would suggest poor management of receivables (credit) or inventories by the company.

4.8 Efficiency ratios: control of receivables and inventories

A rough measure of the average length of time it takes for a company's customers to pay what they owe is the accounts receivable collection period, known as receivables days.

The estimated average receivables days is calculated as:

$$\frac{\text{Trade receivables}}{\text{Revenue}} \times 365 \text{ days}$$

The figure for sales should be taken as the sales revenue figure in the statement of profit or loss and other comprehensive income. The trade receivables are not the total figure for receivables in the statement of

financial position, which includes prepayments and non-trade receivables. The trade receivables figure will be itemised in an analysis of the receivable total, in a note to the accounts.

The estimate of the receivables days is **only approximate**.

(a) The statement of financial position value of receivables might be abnormally high or low compared with the 'normal' level the company usually has.

(b) Revenue in the statement of profit or loss and other comprehensive income is exclusive of sales taxes, but receivables in the statement of financial position are inclusive of sales tax. We are not strictly comparing like with like.

Sales are usually made on 'normal credit terms' of payment within 30 days. A collection period significantly in excess of this might be representative of poor management of funds of a business. However, some companies must allow generous credit terms to win customers. Exporting companies in particular may have to carry large amounts of receivables, and so their average collection period might be well in excess of 30 days. Equally, if the majority of an entity's sales are cash sales (eg for a retailer), receivables days will be very low.

The **trend of the collection period over time** is probably the best guide. If the collection period is increasing year on year, this is indicative of a poorly managed credit control function (and potentially therefore a poorly managed company).

Examples: receivables days

Using the same types of company as examples, the collection period for each of the companies was as follows.

Company	Trade receivables sales	Receivables days (× 365)	Previous year	Receivables days (× 365)
Supermarket	$\dfrac{\$5,016,000}{\$284,986,000} =$	6.4 days	$\dfrac{\$3,977,000}{\$290,668,000} =$	5.0 days
Manufacturer	$\dfrac{\$458.3m}{\$2,059.5m} =$	81.2 days	$\dfrac{\$272.4m}{\$1,274.2m} =$	78.0 days
Sugar refiner and seller	$\dfrac{\$304.4m}{\$3,817.3m} =$	29.3 days	$\dfrac{\$287.0m}{\$3,366.3m} =$	31.1 days

The differences in collection period reflect the differences between the types of business. Supermarkets have hardly any trade receivables at all, whereas the manufacturing companies have far more. The collection periods are fairly constant from the previous year for all three companies.

4.9 Inventory days

Another ratio worth calculating is the inventory turnover period or inventory days. This is another estimated figure, obtainable from published accounts, which indicates the average number of days that items of inventory are held for. As with receivables days, however, it is only an approximate estimated figure, but one which should be reliable enough for comparing changes year on year.

LEARN

The inventory days is calculated as:

$$\frac{\text{Inventory}}{\text{Cost of sales}} \times 365 \text{ days}$$

This is another measure of how vigorously a business is trading. Increasing inventory days from one year to the next indicates:

(a)   a slowdown in trading; or

(b)   a build-up in inventory levels, perhaps suggesting that the investment in inventories is becoming excessive.

Generally the **lower the inventory days the better**, but several aspects of inventory holding policy have to be balanced.

(a)   Lead times
(b)   Seasonal fluctuations in orders
(c)   Alternative uses of warehouse space
(d)   Bulk buying discounts
(e)   Likelihood of inventory perishing or becoming obsolete

Presumably if we add together the inventory days and receivables days, this should give us an indication of how soon inventory is converted into cash. Both receivables days and inventory days therefore give us a further indication of the company's liquidity.

Example: inventory days

The estimated inventory days for a supermarket are as follows.

Company	$\dfrac{\text{Inventory}}{\text{Cost of sales}}$	Inventory days $(days \times 365)$	Previous year
Supermarket	$\dfrac{\$15,554,000}{\$254,571,000}$	22.3 days	$\dfrac{\$14,094,000}{\$261,368,000} \times 365 = 19.7$ days

4.10 Payables days

LEARN

Payables days is ideally calculated by the formula:

$$\frac{\text{Trade accounts payable}}{\text{Purchases}} \times 365 \text{ days}$$

It is rare to find purchases disclosed in published accounts and so **cost of sales serves as an approximation**. Payable days often help to assess a company's liquidity; an increase is often a sign of lack of long-term finance or poor management of current assets, resulting in the use of extended credit from suppliers, increased bank overdraft and so on.

Question 14.2   Liquidity and working capital

Learning outcomes C1

Calculate liquidity and working capital ratios from the accounts of TEB Co, a business which provides service support (cleaning etc) to customers worldwide. Comment on the results of your calculations.

	20X7 $m	20X6 $m
Revenue	2,176.2	2,344.8
Cost of sales	(1,659.0)	(1,731.5)
Gross profit	517.2	613.3
Current assets		
Inventories	42.7	78.0
Receivables (note 1)	378.9	431.4
Cash and cash equivalents	205.2	145.0
	626.8	654.4

Current liabilities

Loans and overdrafts	32.4	81.1
Tax payable	67.8	76.7
Dividend	11.7	17.2
Payables (note 2)	487.2	467.2
	599.1	642.2
Net current assets	27.7	12.2

Notes

1	Trade receivables	295.2	335.5
2	Trade payables	190.8	188.1

The company in the exercise is a service company and hence it would be expected to have very low inventory and a very short inventory days. The similarity of receivables days and payables days means that the company is passing on most of the delay in receiving payment to its suppliers.

Question 14.3	Operating cycle

Learning outcomes C1

(a)   Calculate the operating cycle for Moribund plc for 20X2 on the basis of the following information.

		$
Inventory:	raw materials	150,000
	work in progress	60,000
	finished goods	200,000
Purchases		500,000
Trade receivables		230,000
Trade payables		120,000
Revenue		900,000
Cost of sales		750,000

Tutorial note. You will need to calculate inventory days, receivables days and payables days.

(b)   List the steps which might be taken in order to improve the operating cycle.

Section summary

Make sure you understand and can define the ratios given.

---

5   Investor ratios

9/12

Introduction

The value of an investment in ordinary shares in a company **listed on a stock exchange** is its market value, and so investor ratios must have regard not only to information in the company's published financial statements, but also to the current price, and the fourth and fifth ratios involve using the share price.

5.1 Earnings per share

It is possible to calculate the return on each ordinary share in the year. This is the earnings per share (EPS). Earnings per share is the amount of net profit for the period that is attributable to each ordinary share which is outstanding during all or part of the period.

> **Earnings per share:** $\dfrac{\text{Profit available to ordinary shareholders}}{\text{Number of ordinary shares}}$
>
> **Profit available to ordinary shareholders** = Profit after tax and preference dividends

We will look at earnings per share in more detail in Chapter 15.

5.2 Dividend per share and dividend cover

The **dividend per share** in cents is self-explanatory, and clearly an item of some interest to shareholders.

> **Dividend cover** is a ratio of: $\dfrac{\text{Earnings per share}}{\text{Dividend per (ordinary) share}}$

It shows the **proportion of profit for the year that is available for distribution to shareholders that has been paid (or proposed) and what proportion will be retained in the business to finance future growth.** A dividend cover of 2 times would indicate that the company had paid 50% of its distributable profits as dividends, and retained 50% in the business to help to finance future operations. Retained profits are an important source of funds for most companies, and so the dividend cover can in some cases be quite high.

A **significant change** in the dividend cover from one year to the next would be worth looking at closely. For example, if a company's dividend cover were to fall sharply between one year and the next, it could be that its profits had fallen, but the directors wished to pay at least the same amount as in the previous year, so as to keep shareholder expectations satisfied.

5.3 P/E ratio

> The **Price/Earnings (P/E) ratio** is the ratio of a company's current share price to the earnings per share.

A high P/E ratio indicates strong shareholder **confidence** in the company and its future, eg in profit growth, and a lower P/E ratio indicates lower confidence.

The P/E ratio of one company can be compared with the P/E ratios of:

- Other companies in the same business sector
- Other companies generally

It is often used in **stock exchange reporting** where prices are readily available.

5.4 Profit retention ratio

> **Profit retention ratio** = Profit after dividends/Profit before dividends x 100%.

As you know, shareholders invest in companies for their ability to generate future wealth. Some shareholders seek high capital growth, while others prefer the lower-risk dividend income.

The profit retention ratio it shows the portion of the profit to be reinvested into the business for future growth (rather than being paid out as dividends). Whether a high profit retention ratio is favourable, therefore, depends on which form of future wealth the shareholder prefers.

5.5 Dividend yield

Dividend yield is the return a shareholder is currently expecting on the shares of a company.

$$\text{Dividend yield} = \frac{\text{Dividend on the share for the year}}{\text{Current market value of the share (ex - div)}} \times 100\%$$

(a)   The dividend per share is taken as the dividend for the previous year.

(b)   Ex-div means that the share price does *not* include the right to the most recent dividend.

Shareholders look for **both dividend yield and capital growth**. Obviously, dividend yield is therefore an important aspect of a share's performance.

Question 14.4	Dividend yield

Learning outcomes C1

In the year to 30 September 20X8, an advertising agency declares an interim ordinary dividend of 7.4c per share and a final ordinary dividend of 8.6c per share. Assuming an ex-div share price of 315 cents, what is the dividend yield?

Question 14.5	Ratio analysis report: 1

Learning outcomes C1

RST Co is considering purchasing an interest in its competitor XYZ Co. Both RST Co and XYZ Co operate in the clothes manufacturing industry. The managing director of RST Co has obtained the three most recent statements of profit or loss and statements of financial position of XYZ Co as shown below.

XYZ CO
STATEMENTS OF PROFIT OR LOSS FOR YEARS ENDED 31 DECEMBER

	20X6 $'000	20X7 $'000	20X8 $'000
Revenue	18,000	18,900	19,845
Cost of sales	(10,440)	(10,340)	(11,890)
Gross profit	7,560	8,560	7,955
Distribution costs	(1,565)	(1,670)	(1,405)
Administrative expenses	(1,409)	(1,503)	(1,591)
Operating profit	4,586	5,387	4,959
Interest payable on bank overdraft	(104)	(215)	(450)
Interest payable on 12% debentures	(600)	(600)	(600)
Profit before taxation	3,882	4,572	3,909
Income tax	(1,380)	(2,000)	(1,838)
Profit for the year	2,502	2,572	2,071

XYZ CO
STATEMENTS OF FINANCIAL POSITION AS AT 31 DECEMBER

	20X6 $'000	20X6 $'000	20X7 $'000	20X7 $'000	20X8 $'000	20X8 $'000
Assets						
Non-current assets						
Land and buildings	11,460		12,121		11,081	
Plant and machinery	8,896		9,020		9,130	
		20,356		21,141		20,211
Current assets						
Inventory	1,775		2,663		3,995	
Trade receivables	1,440		2,260		3,164	
Cash	50		53		55	
		3,265		4,976		7,214
		23,621		26,117		27,425

	20X6		20X7		20X8	
	$'000	$'000	$'000	$'000	$'000	$'000
Equity and liabilities						
Equity						
Share capital	8,000		8,000		8,000	
Retained earnings	6,434		7,313		7,584	
		14,434		15,313		15,584
Non-current liabilities						
12% debentures 20Y1 –						
20Y4		5,000		5,000		5,000
Current liabilities						
Trade payables	1,990		2,254		2,246	
Bank	1,300		2,300		3,400	
Taxation	897		1,250		1,195	
		4,187		5,804		6,841
		23,621		26,117		27,425

XYZ Co paid dividends of $1.6m, $1.693m and $1.8m in the years ended 31 December 20X6, 20X7 and 20X8 respectively.

During 20X7, XYZ Co managed to negotiate a bulk buying discount with its suppliers. However, in 20X8, due to XYZ regularly exceeding agreed credit terms, the suppliers withdrew the discount.

Required

Prepare a report for the managing director of RST Co commenting on the financial performance and position of XYZ Co and highlighting any areas that require further investigation.

(Include ratios and other financial statistics where appropriate.)

Question 14.6	Ratio analysis report: 2

Learning outcomes C1

GD is an entity that operates in the packaging industry across a number of different markets and activities. GD has applied to the financial institution where you are employed, for a long term loan of $150 million. Your immediate supervisor was working on the report and recommendation in response to GD's request, but has fallen ill and you have been asked to complete the analysis and prepare the supporting documentation for the next management meeting to discuss applications for lending.

Extracts from the consolidated financial statements of GD are provided below:

STATEMENT OF FINANCIAL POSITION AS AT 30 JUNE

	20X8 $m	20X7 $m
Assets		
Non-current assets		
Property, plant and equipment	548	465
Goodwill	29	24
	577	489
Current assets		
Inventories	146	120
Receivables	115	125
Held for trading investments	31	18
Cash and cash equivalents	-	41
	292	304
Total assets	869	793
Equity and liabilities		
Equity attributable to owners of the parent		
Share capital ($1 shares)	120	120
Revaluation reserve	18	-
Retained earnings	293	183
	431	303
Non-controlling interest	65	61
Total equity	496	364

	20X8 $m	20X7 $m
Non-current liabilities		
Long term loans	90	180
Current liabilities		
Payables	185	160
Bank overdraft	50	-
Income tax payable	48	89
	283	249
Total liabilities	373	429
Total equity and liabilities	869	793

STATEMENT OF COMPREHENSIVE INCOME FOR THE YEAR ENDED 30 JUNE

	20X8 $m	20X7 $m
Revenue	1,200	1,400
Cost of sales	(840)	(930)
Gross profit	360	470
Distribution costs	(40)	(45)
Administrative expenses	(130)	(120)
Finance costs	(11)	(15)
Profit before tax	179	290
Income tax expense	(50)	(85)
Profit for the year	129	205
Other comprehensive income		
Revaluation of property	18	-
Total comprehensive income (net of tax)	147	205
Profit for the year attributable to:		
Owners of the parent	121	195
Non-controlling interest	8	10
	129	205
Total comprehensive income attributable to:		
Owners of the parent	139	195
Non-controlling interest	8	10
	147	205

Additional information

1   In August 20X7, a new competitor entered one of GD's markets and pursued an aggressive strategy of increasing market share by undercutting GD's prices and prioritising volume sales. The directors had not anticipated this as GD had been the market leader in this area for the past few years.

2   The minutes from the most recent meeting of the Board of Directors state that the directors believe they can implement a new strategy to regain GD's market position in this segment, providing long term funding can be secured. GD acquired a subsidiary during the year as part of the new strategy and revenue is forecast to increase by the second quarter of 20X9.

3   A meeting is scheduled with GD's main suppliers to discuss a reduction in costs for bulk orders.

4   The existing long-term loan is due to be repaid on 1 August 20X9.

5   Gains of $9 million generated by the held for trading investments have been offset against administrative expenses.

Required

(a)   **Analyse** the financial performance and financial position of GD and recommend whether or not GD's application for borrowing should be considered further
      Note. *8 marks are available for the calculation of relevant ratios.*   **(21 marks)**

(b)   **Explain** what further information might be useful in assessing the future prospects of GD and its ability to service a new long term loan.   **(4 marks)**

                                                                                        (Total = 25 marks)

Section summary

The ratios which help equity shareholders and other investors to assess the value and quality of an investment in the ordinary shares of a company are:

- Earnings per share
- Dividend per share
- Dividend cover

- P/E ratio
- Dividend yield
- Profit retention ratio

6   The nature of profit

Introduction

We have seen throughout this text that accounting 'profit' is an arbitrary figure, subject to the whims and biases of accountants and the variety of treatments in accounting standards. Go back to the contents page and pick out all the topics which demonstrate or indicate how company results are manipulated. Isn't it nearly all of them? Let us briefly mention some of them again.

6.1 IAS 20 *Accounting for government grants*

IAS 20 allows capital grants to be credited to revenue over the expected life of the asset in two ways.

(a)   By reducing the acquisition cost of the non-current asset by the amount of the grant and charging depreciation on the reduced amount

(b)   By treating the amount of the grant as a deferred credit and transferring a portion of it to revenue annually

The final profit figure is the same under both methods but the depreciation charge disclosed will be different, as will the carrying value of the asset.

6.2 IAS 2 *Inventories*

Entities are allowed to use different methods of valuing inventory under IAS 2, which means that the final inventory figure in the statement of financial position will be different under each method. Profit will be affected by the closing inventory valuation, particularly where the level of inventory fluctuates to a great extent.

6.3 IAS 16 *Property, plant and equipment*

As with IAS 2, IAS 16 allows different accounting bases for depreciation. Choosing to use the reducing balance method rather than the straight line method can front-load the depreciation charge for assets. It is also the case that the subjectivity surrounding the estimated economic lives of assets can lead to manipulation of profits. (*Note*. Remember that some entities refuse to depreciate some assets at all – mainly freehold property.)

6.4 IAS 38 *Intangible assets*

Development costs must be capitalised under IAS 38 if certain criteria are met, whereas all research costs should be written off. Although the criteria for capitalisation are quite strict, there is room for manipulation.

Section summary

You should note that the IASB is trying to stop abuses such as those described here by forcing entities to follow general tenets (*Framework*) and also by restricting abusive practice.

7   Other problems with financial analysis   11/10, 3/11, 5/12

Introduction

Two frequent problems affecting financial analysis are discussed here.

- **Seasonal fluctuations**   •   **Window dressing**

7.1 Seasonal fluctuations

Many entities are located in industries where trade is **seasonal**. For example:

- Firework manufacturers
- Swimwear manufacturers
- Ice cream makers
- Umbrella manufacturers

- Gas utilities
- Travel agents
- Flower suppliers and deliverers
- Football clubs

Year on year the seasonal fluctuations affecting such entities does not matter; a year end has to be chosen and as long as the fluctuations are at roughly the same time every year, then there should be no problem. Occasionally a perverse sense of humour will cause an entity to choose an accounting period ending in the middle of the busy season: this may affect the cut off because the busy season might be slightly early or late.

A **major difficulty** can arise if entities affected by seasonal fluctuations **change their accounting date**. A shorter period (normally) may encompass part, all or none of the busy season. Whatever happens, the figures will be distorted and the comparatives will be meaningless. Analysts would not know how to

extrapolate the figures from the shorter period to produce a comparison for the previous year. Weightings could be used, but these are likely to be inaccurate.

CASE STUDY

Case Study

An example of the problems this can cause occurred when British Gas plc changed its accounting period to 31 December from 31 March. The entity published two sets of figures:

- For the year to 31 March 1991
- For the year to 31 December 1991

Thus including the first three months of the calendar year in both reports. As a note to the later accounts, the entity produced a statement of profit or loss and other comprehensive income for the last nine months of the calendar year.

Although the British Gas auditors did not qualify the audit report, the Review Panel was not very happy about this double counting of results. The nine-month profit and loss account did not meet the legal provisions of CA 1985 'either as to its location or its contents, nor did it contain the relevant earnings per share figure'. British Gas had to promise that, in their 1992 results, the 1991 comparative would be for the nine months period only.

The effect here is obvious. The first three months of the calendar year are when British Gas earns a high proportion of its profits (winter!). If the 1991 results had covered the period from 1 April only, then the profits would have been reduced by more than an average loss of three months' profit. By using a 12-month period, British Gas avoided the risk of the period's results looking too bad.

7.2 Creative accounting

Whilst still following international financial reporting standards, there is scope for a company to manipulate its accounting policy to its advantage, so that the financial statements are presented in the best light.

- **Timing** of transactions may be delayed/speeded up to improve results
- **Profit smoothing** through choice of accounting policy e.g. inventory valuation
- **Distortion** when using **year-end figures**, particularly in seasonal industries or two entities with different year ends
- **Classification** of items e.g. expenses versus non-current assets
- **Off balance sheet financing** to improve gearing and return on capital employed e.g. operating lease
- **Revenue recognition policies** e.g. through adopting an aggressive accounting policy of early recognition.

IAS 10 *Events after the reporting date* targets creative accounting policies focussed around the timing of transactions and cut-off. IAS 10 require companies to disclose the reversal or maturity after the reporting date of transactions, the substance of which was primarily to alter the appearance of the statement of financial position. Note that creative accounting was not outlawed, but full disclosure would render such transactions useless.

In the exam, you should be aware of accounts and circumstances which may provide opportunities for creative accounting.

7.3 Other useful information

The information provided by the statements of financial position and profit or loss and other comprehensive income is limited. This restricts the conclusions that can be made. Useful information can be drawn from other sources as follows:

Financial

- Statement of cash flows
- Notes to the financial statements eg segment reporting
- Budgeted figures and forecasts
- Management accounts
- Industry averages
- Figures for a competitor
- Figures over a longer period eg five years

Non-financial

- Management commentary
- Market share
- Key employee information
- Sales mix
- Product range
- Pricing information
- State of order book
- Long term plans of management

7.4 Summary of limitations of ratio analysis   11/11

Besides calculating and interpreting the ratios, you may be asked in the F2 exam to discuss the limitations of ratio analysis. Some of these limitations are summarised below.

(a) **Limitations of financial reporting information**

    (i)   The base information is often out of date since the financial statements are filed months after the reporting date. This lack of timely information leads to problems of interpretation.

    (ii)   Historic cost information may not be the most appropriate information for the decision for which the analysis is being undertaken.

    (iii)   Information in published financial statements is generally summarised information and detailed information may be needed.

    (iv)   Analysis of accounting information only identifies symptoms, not causes, and thus is of limited use.

    (v)   Year-end figures are not representative, because they include year end accounting adjustments

(b) **Comparison problems: inter-temporal**

    (i)   Effects of price changes make comparisons difficult unless adjustments are made.

    (ii)   Impacts of changes in technology on the price of assets, the likely return and the future markets.

    (iii)   Impacts of a changing environment on the results are reflected in the accounting information.

    (iv)   Potential effects of changes in accounting policies on the reported results.

    (v)   Problems associated with establishing a normal base year to compare other years with.

    (vi)   New companies do not have prior year comparatives.

(c)   **Comparison problems: inter-firm**

(i)   Selection of industry norms and the usefulness of norms based on averages.

(ii)   Different firms having different financial and business risk profiles and the impact on analysis.

(iii)   Different firms using different accounting policies.

(iv)   Impacts of the size of the business and its comparators on risk, structure and returns.

(v)   Impacts of different environments on results, for example different countries or home-based versus multinational firms.

(vi)   Companies within the same industry may still engage in different business activities.

(vii)   Related party transactions make the ratios incomparable, because these transactions may not have been at arm's length.

(viii) Firms operating in different countries are subject to different legislations, taxation, regulations, economies and currencies.

You should use this summary as a type of checklist.

Exam alert

The 25 mark analysis question in Section B of the exam often has a part (b) asking for limitations of analysis or additional information required. The key is to tailor your answer to the specific requirement and scenario.

Section summary

Financial analysis is a vital tool for **many users of the financial statements**, especially investors.

Financial analysis is not a precise science. The nature of accounting information means that distortions and differences will always exist between sets of accounts not only from entity to entity but also over time.

Always remember that 'profit' and 'net assets' are fairly **arbitrary figures**, affected by different accounting policies and manipulation.

Seasonal fluctuations and window dressing arise quite often in practice. You must be on your guard to spot them.

8 Presentation of reports   5/10, 5/11, 9/11, 11/11, 3/12, 5/12

Introduction

You may have experience already in writing reports within your organisation. Accountants are called upon to write reports for many different purposes. These range from very formal reports, such as those addressed to the board of directors or the audit committee, to one-off reports of a more informal nature. You should appreciate the following general points about report writing.

8.1 Checklist for report writing

The following check list for report writing indicates many of the factors that should be considered.

(a) **Purpose or terms of reference**

    (i)   What is the report being written about?

    (ii)   Why is it needed?

    (iii)   What effect might the report have if its findings or recommendations are acted upon?

    (iv)   Who are the report users? How much do they know already?

    (v)   What is wanted – a definite recommendation or less specific advice?

    (vi)   What previous reports have there been on the subject, what did they find or recommend, and what action was taken on these findings, or recommendations?

(b) **Information in the report**

    (i)   What is the source of each item of information in the report?

    (ii)   How old is the information?

    (iii)   What period does the report cover - a month, a year?

    (iv)   How can the accuracy of the information be checked and verified? To what extent might it be subject to error?

(c) **Preparing the report**

    (i)   Who is responsible for preparing the report?

    (ii)   How long will it take to prepare?

    (iii)   How is the information in the report put together (for numerical information, what computations are carried out on the source data to arrive at the figures in the report?)

    (iv)   How many copies of the report should be prepared and to whom should they be sent?

(d) **Usefulness of the report**

    (i)   What use will the report be in its present form? What action is it intended to trigger?

    (ii)   How will each recipient of the report use it for his or her own purposes?

    (iii)   Does the report meet the requirements of the terms of reference?

Further reading

The March 2013 edition of Financial Management contains a useful article by Sally Baker on writing reports in the CIMA F2 exam. This article can be accessed via the link: http://www.fm-magazine.com/study-centre/course-notes/financial-management-4 (Valid as of 18 April 2013).

8.2 Format of reports in the examination

In an examination your time is limited and you are under pressure. To make life a little easier, we suggest that you adopt the following format for any report you are requested to write.

REPORT [OR MEMORANDUM]

To: Board of Directors [or Chief Accountant, etc]
From: Management Accountant   **Date:**
Subject: Report Format

                           Body of report

Signed: Management Accountant

If you adopt this style in your practice questions, you should end up producing it automatically. This should ensure that you do not lose any presentation marks.

Note that the date is always set to the right in CIMA solutions and is always left blank. The word 'Re' is sometimes used in place of 'Subject'. CIMA model solutions often include 'Signed' at the bottom, and although you might think this is superfluous (you have already said who the report is from) we recommend that you follow this style. Do not sign your own name, however! Do not draw a box round your report: we have only done this to make our example stand out. You may like to use underlining to distinguish headings. If so, use a ruler and stick to your normal colour ink (*not* a colour that the marker of your script might be using).

Exam alert

The May 2010 exam included a 25 mark question asking for a report on expansion plans.

Section summary

You must be able to draw conclusions when writing reports. Support these with ratio calculations given in an appendix.

Chapter Roundup

✓   Keep the various **sources of financial information** in mind and the effects of insider dealing, the efficient market hypothesis and Stock Exchange regulations.

✓   Your syllabus requires you to **appraise and communicate** the position and prospects of a business based on given and prepared statements and ratios.

✓   Much of the material here on **basic ratios** should have been revision for you.

✓   Make sure that you can **define** all the ratios. Look out for variations in definitions of ratios which might appear in questions.

✓   Make sure that you learn the ratios given.

✓   Make sure you understand and can define the ratios given.

✓   The ratios which help equity shareholders and other investor to assess the value and quality of an investment in the ordinary shares of a company are:

- Earnings per share
- Dividends per share
- Dividends cover

- P/E ratio
- Dividend yield
- Profit retention ratio

✓   You should note that the IASB is trying to stop abuses such as those described in Section 6 by forcing entities to follow general tenets (*Framework*) and also by restricting abusive practice.

✓   Financial analysis is a vital tool for **users of financial statements**.

✓   Financial analysis is not a precise science. The nature of accounting information means that distortions and differences will always exist between sets of accounts not only from entity to entity but also over time.

✓   Always remember that 'profit' and 'net assets' are fairly **arbitrary figures**, affected by different accounting policies and manipulation.

✓   Seasonal fluctuations and window dressing arise quite often in practice. You must be on your guard to spot them.

✓   You must be able to draw conclusions when writing reports. Support these with ratio calculations given in an appendix.

Quick Quiz

1   What are the main sources of financial information available to the external users?

2   What is the efficient market hypothesis?

3   Apart from ratio analysis, what other information might be helpful in interpreting a company's accounts?

4   In a period when profits are fluctuating, what effect does a company's level of gearing have on the profits available for ordinary shareholders?

5   Name some accounting standards which allow a choice of accounting policies.

6   The acid test or quick ratio should include:

A	Inventory of finished goods	C	Long-term loans
B	Raw materials and consumables	D	Trade receivables

7   The asset turnover of Taplow Co is 110% that of Stoke Co.

The return on capital of Taplow Co is 80% of that of Stoke Co.

Calculate Taplow Co's operating profit margin expressed as a percentage of Stoke Co's.

8   Deal Co has the following capital structure:

	$'000
$1 ordinary shares	55,000
Retained earnings	12,000
	67,000
6% $1 cumulative redeemable preference shares	15,000
8% loan notes	30,000
	112,000

What is the most appropriate measure of the debt/equity ratio for a potential equity investor?

Answers to Quick Quiz

1 Published interim financial statements, filed documents, government statistics.

2 See Section 1.5

3 • Other comments in the accounts eg Directors' Report
   • Age and nature of the assets
   • Current and future market developments
   • Recent acquisition or disposal of subsidiaries
   • Notes to the accounts, auditors' report, post reporting date events, etc.

4 Profits available for the shareholders will be highly volatile and some years there may not be an ordinary dividend paid.

5 IAS 2, 16, 20 and 38

6 D   Acid test ratio $= \dfrac{CA - Inventory}{CL}$

7 $\dfrac{80}{110} = 73\%$

8 Debt =   15 + 30 = 45
   Equity =   55 + 12 = 67
   ∴ 45/67 × 100 = 67.2%

 ## Answers to Questions

14.1 Interest cover

Interest payments should be taken gross, from the note to the accounts, and not net of interest receipts as shown in the statement of profit or loss and other comprehensive income.

	20X8	20X7
PBIT	360,245	247,011
Interest payable	18,115	21,909
	= 20 times	= 11 times

Furlong has more than sufficient interest cover. In view of the company's low gearing, this is not too surprising and so we finally obtain a picture of Furlong as a company that does not seem to have a debt problem, in spite of its high (although declining) debt ratio.

14.2   Liquidity and working capital

	20X7	*20X6*
Current ratio	$\dfrac{626.8}{599.1} = 1.05$	$\dfrac{654.4}{642.2} = 1.02$
Quick ratio	$\dfrac{584.1}{599.1} = 0.97$	$\dfrac{576.4}{642.2} = 0.90$
Receivables days	$\dfrac{295.2}{2,176.2} \times 365 = 49.5$ days	$\dfrac{335.5}{2,344.8} \times 365 = 52.2$ days
Inventory days	$\dfrac{42.7}{1,659.0} \times 365 = 9.4$ days	$\dfrac{78.0}{1,731.5} \times 365 = 16.4$ days
Payables days	$\dfrac{190.8}{1,659.0} \times 365 = 42.0$ days	$\dfrac{188.1}{1,731.5} \times 365 = 40.0$ days

Both the current and quick ratios have improved year on year. This is because TEB is collecting its debts more quickly from its customers (evidenced by a decrease in receivables days from 52.2 days to 49.5 days) and selling its inventory more quickly (evidenced by a decrease in inventory days from 16.4 days to 9.4 days). Paying its suppliers more slowly (taking an average of 42 days as opposed to 40 days in the prior year) has also improved short term liquidity. However, payables are being paid more quickly than money is collected from customers which is not a good strategy from a cash flow perspective.

The reason for inventory days being so low is because TEB is a services company and therefore holds very low levels of inventories.

14.3   Operating cycle

(a)   The operating cycle can be found as follows.

Inventory days: $\dfrac{\text{Total closing inventory} \times 365}{\text{Cost of goods sold}}$ x 365

plus

Receivables days: $\dfrac{\text{Closing trade receivables} \times 365}{\text{Sales}}$

less

Payables days: $\dfrac{\text{Closing trade payables} \times 365}{\text{Purchases}}$ x 365

	20X2
Total closing inventory ($)	410,000
Cost of goods sold ($)	750,000
Inventory days (410,000/750,000 x 365)	199.5 days
Closing receivables ($)	230,000
Sales ($)	900,000
Receivables days (230,000/900,000 x 365)	93.3 days
Closing payables ($)	120,000
Purchases ($)	500,000
Payables days (120,000/500,000 x 365)	(87.6 days)
Length of operating cycle (199.5 + 93.3 – 87.6)	205.2 days

BPP
LEARNING MEDIA

(b) The steps that could be taken to reduce the operating cycle include the following.

     (i)   Reducing the raw material inventory days by using inventory more quickly in the production process.

     (ii)   Reducing the time taken to produce goods. However, the company must ensure that quality is not sacrificed as a result of speeding up the production process.

     (iii)   Increasing the period of credit taken from suppliers. The credit period already seems very long – if the company is allowed three months' credit by its suppliers, this could probably not be increased. If the credit period is extended then the company may lose discounts for prompt payment.

     (iv)   Reducing the finished goods inventory days by holding lower levels of finished goods.

     (v)   Reducing the receivables days. The administrative costs of speeding up debt collection and the effect on sales of reducing the credit period allowed must be evaluated. However, the credit period does already seem very long by the standards of most industries. It may be that generous terms have been allowed to secure large contracts and little will be able to be done about this in the short term.

14.4 Dividend yield

The total dividend per share is (7.4 + 8.6) = 16 cents

$$\frac{16}{315} \times 100 = 5.1\%$$

14.5 Ratio analysis report: 1

REPORT

To: MD of RST Co
From: An Accountant   Date:
Subject: Financial performance and position of XYZ Co

Introduction

This report analyses the financial performance and position of a key competitor XYZ Co as a potential acquisition target.

Financial performance

Revenue has increased at a steady 5% per annum over the three-year period, showing a healthy growth.

In contrast, the gross profit margin has increased from 42% in 20X6 to 45% in 20X7 before dropping back to 40% in 20X8. The improvement in gross margin in 20X7 appears to be due to cheaper purchasing prices of raw materials from suppliers as a result of the negotiation of a new bulk discount. However, due to consistently exceeding credit terms, this bulk discount was lost in 20X8 which would have resulted in a return to the original higher purchasing price and partly explain the fall in gross margin. The fall in 20X8 below the 20X6 level suggests that there might also have been some manufacturing inefficiencies.

Similarly, the operating profit margin followed a similar trend moving from 26% in 20X6 to 28.5% in 20X7 and 25% in 20X8. Operating margin did not improve as much as the gross margin in 20X7 suggesting some cost inefficiencies. However, this trend was reversed in 20X8 where operating margin did not fall as much as gross margin and in fact, distribution costs fell by almost 16% showing improved cost control in this area.

Growing interest on an increasing overdraft has had an adverse impact on net profit. Relying on an overdraft as a long term source of finance is both expensive and risky as the bank could withdraw the facility at any time. Investment by RST Co would help with the long term financing of XYZ Co and potentially allow the overdraft to be repaid. However, XYZ Co would need to improve their working capital management (see below) to avoid returning to an overdraft.

Return on capital employed, as one would expect, has shown a similar pattern with an increase in 20X7 with a subsequent fall in 20X8 to a level below that of 20X6. The overdraft has been treated as debt when calculating ROCE as XYZ Co appears to be using the overdraft as a long term source of finance given that the overdraft balance is significant and increasing year on year.

Financial position

Solvency

Gearing has increased year on year (20X6: 43.6%; 20X7: 47.7%; 20X8: 53.9%). The overdraft has been included as debt since XYZ Co seem to be using it as a source of long term finance. The reason for the increase in gearing is the growing overdraft rather than the debentures which have remained stable. Refinancing will be necessary to replace the overdraft with long term finance. Also the debentures will need repaying in the next three to five years. As the overall gearing level is not excessive, XYZ Co may be able to raise further debt. If RST Co were to invest in debt or equity, it would help the long term funding of XYZ Co.

Liquidity

At a first glance it appears that XYZ Co's liquidity the situation has improved over the period as the current ratio has increased from 0.78 in 20X6 to 0.86 in 20X7 and 1.05 in 20X8. However, the current ratio measures a company's ability to meet its current liabilities out of current assets. In most industries, a ratio of at least 1 would be idea but XYZ Co did not meet this expectation in 20X6 and 20X7. Furthermore, this ratio is misleading as the largest asset in the form of inventory is the least liquid asset. This is especially the case for XYZ Co, a clothes manufacturer as fashions change rapidly and inventory can easily become obsolete.

Therefore, the quick ratio which excludes inventory should be considered. XYZ Co's quick ratio, although improving, is low and this shows that current liabilities cannot be met from current assets if inventory is excluded. The only reason that the quick ratio has improved is because the overdraft has increased at a faster rate than inventory. As a major part of current liabilities is the bank overdraft, the company is obviously relying on the overdraft as a long term source of finance. It would be useful to find out the terms of the bank funding and the projected cash flow requirements for future funding.

Working capital management

Inventory days have increased year on year (62 days in 20X6, 94 days in 20X7 and 123 days in 20X8). The increase in 20X7 can partly be explained by bulk buying to take advantage of the discount negotiated with suppliers. However, as the discount was lost in 20X8, this does not explain the further increase in 20X8. Given that XYZ Co operates in the fast-moving fashion industry, there is a high risk of inventory obsolescence.

As can be seen from the appendix the receivables days have increased over the three years from 29 days to 58 days. This appears to be an indication of poor credit control or perhaps XYZ Co has given increased credit terms to some or all of its customers.

The increase in payable days in from 70 days in 20X6 to 80 days in 20X7 has led to the suppliers withdrawing their bulk discount. This in turn has had an adverse effect on profitability. Payable days did fall again in 20X8 back down to 79 days so it is possible that XYZ Co may be able to renegotiate the discount again in the future. Whilst taking advantage of free credit from suppliers helps improve liquidity, XYZ Co need to be careful not to exceed the credit terms too much as there is a risk of withdrawal of credit or even supplies.

Conclusion

XYZ Co is growing steadily and is profitable although profitability has been fluctuating. If working capital management could be improved, on initial analysis, it appears that it is worth considering the possibility of investing in XYZ Co further.

Signed:

Management Accountant

APPENDIX TO REPORT

	20X6	20X7	20X8
% sales increase		5%	5%

Gross profit margin

$$= \frac{\text{Gross profit}}{\text{Revenue}}$$

	20X6	20X7	20X8
	$\frac{7{,}560}{18{,}000}$	$\frac{8{,}560}{18{,}900}$	$\frac{7{,}955}{19{,}845}$
	= 42%	= 45%	= 40%

Operating profit margin

$$= \frac{\text{Profit before interest and tax}}{\text{Revenue}}$$

	20X6	20X7	20X8
	$\frac{4{,}586}{18{,}000}$	$\frac{5{,}387}{18{,}900}$	$\frac{4{,}959}{19{,}845}$
	= 25.5%	= 28.5%	= 25%

Return on capital employed

$$= \frac{\text{Profit before interest and tax}}{\text{Capital employed}} \times 100\%$$

	20X6	20X7	20X8
	$\frac{4{,}586}{14{,}434+6{,}300}$	$\frac{5{,}387}{15{,}313+7{,}300}$	$\frac{4{,}959}{15{,}584+8{,}400}$
	= 22.1%	= 23.8%	= 20.7%

Gearing ratio

$$= \frac{\text{Debt}}{\text{Equity}} \times 100\%$$

	20X6	20X7	20X8
	$\frac{5{,}000+1{,}300}{14{,}434}$	$\frac{5{,}000+2{,}300}{15{,}313}$	$\frac{5{,}000+3{,}400}{15{,}584}$
	= 43.6%	= 47.7%	= 53.9%

Current ratio

$$= \frac{\text{Current assets}}{\text{Current liabilities}}$$

	20X6	20X7	20X8
	$\frac{3{,}265}{4{,}187}$	$\frac{4{,}976}{5{,}804}$	$\frac{7{,}214}{6{,}841}$
	= 0.78	= 0.86	= 1.05

Quick ratio

$$= \frac{\text{Current assets}-\text{inventory}}{\text{Current liabilities}}$$

	20X6	20X7	20X8
	$\frac{3{,}265-1{,}775}{4{,}187}$	$\frac{4{,}976-2{,}663}{5{,}804}$	$\frac{7{,}214-3{,}995}{6{,}841}$
	= 0.36	= 0.40	= 0.47

Receivables days

$$= \frac{\text{Trade receivables}}{\text{Revenue}} \times 365 \text{ days}$$

	20X6	20X7	20X8
	$\frac{1{,}440}{18{,}000}$	$\frac{2{,}260}{18{,}900}$	$\frac{3{,}164}{19{,}845}$
	= 29 days	= 44 days	= 58. days

Inventory days

$$= \frac{\text{Inventory}}{\text{Cost of sales}} \times 365 \text{ days}$$

	20X6	20X7	20X8
	$\frac{1{,}775}{10{,}440}$	$\frac{2{,}663}{10{,}340}$	$\frac{3{,}995}{11{,}890}$
	= 62 days	= 94 days	= 123 days

Payable days

$$= \frac{\text{Trade payables}}{\text{Cost of sales}}$$

	20X6	20X7	20X8
	$\frac{1{,}990}{10{,}440}$	$\frac{2{,}254}{10{,}340}$	$\frac{2{,}246}{11{,}890}$
	= 70 days	= 80 days	= 69 days

14.6 Ratio analysis report: 2

(a)   Analysis

Financial performance

<u>Revenue trend</u>

The new competitor in one of GD's markets appears to have stolen market share from GD with its aggressive pricing strategy. This has resulted in a year on year reduction in revenue of 14%.

Even the acquisition of a new subsidiary during the year has not been enough to counteract this effect. If it was acquired towards the end of the year the full impact of the acquisition may not yet have been seen and the subsidiary may contribute more to group revenue in future years.

Profitability

GD's gross profit margin has **deteriorated**, so as well as a decline in volume, there has been a decline in the profitability.

This could be due to increases in the purchase prices of inventories and profitability may improve in future if GD is successful in its negotiations over bulk buying discounts with its suppliers. Although this may improve the gross margin, there is a risk that carrying excessive levels of inventory could place further stress on GD's cashflow and incur increased holding costs.

The **operating margin has also decreased** mainly due to an 8% increase in administration costs (a 15% increase if the gains on held for trading investments are ignored) despite the 14% decline in sales.

This may indicate that GD is not controlling costs effectively, but part of the increase may be due to higher depreciation charges as a result of the revaluation during the year.

Financial position

Liquidity

GD's liquidity has deteriorated during the year, as illustrated by the current ratio falling from 1.22 to 1.03 and the quick ratio falling from 0.74 to 0.52.

GD's cash position has deteriorated, going from a cash balance of $41 million in 20X7 to an overdraft of $50 million in 20X8. An overdraft is an expensive and risky form of finance as it can be recalled at any time.

The reasons for the decline in liquidity are:

- Purchases of property, plant and equipment during the year

- Acquisition of a subsidiary during the year

- Repayment of long-term loans

- Poor working capital management (see below).

Working capital management

There has been a **significant increase in inventory days** (from 47 to 63) which is tying up cash. This may be a result of GD selling lower volumes as a result of the competition in one its markets. This could mean that they are holding unsaleable inventories, although this is likely to be a major risk with non-perishable packaging products.

Part of GD's new strategy is to negotiate discount for bulk buying but this could result in even longer holding periods with the related adverse effect on liquidity.

GD appears to **have reasonably efficient credit control** procedures as there is only a slight increase in receivables days from 33 to 35.

However, there has been a worrying increase in the time taken to settle payables. Payables days have increased from 63 to 80 days. Along with the overdraft, this suggests that GD **is struggling to pay its liabilities as they fall due**. This may put the company at a disadvantage in its negotiations for discounts from these suppliers and could result in the suppliers withdrawing credit or even refusing to supply GD.

GD also appears to be **trading in investments**. This has generated some gains in the current year but is a risky activity and in the company's current situation the $31 million could be more effectively applied to the overdue payables or to reducing the overdraft.

Solvency

The low levels of the gearing ratio and the substantial margin of safety shown by the interest cover ratio (17.2 in 20X8 and 20.3 in 20X7) would appear to indicate that GD can easily afford to pay its interest as it falls due.

However, this does not allow us to conclude that GD's solvency is not at risk. As at the date of its last statement of financial position, if the overdraft were to be called in and suppliers to demand payment of all overdue balances, it looks as if GD would not be in a position to pay this.

Recommendation

The financial institution should have **serious reservations** about granting GD a loan because:

(i)   The company has been losing market share to the new competitor.

(ii)   There has been a decline in profit margins.

(iii) GD's poor working capital management has led to deteriorating liquidity.

(iv)   It appears that the loan of $150 million would have to be applied to clearing the overdraft, the existing loan due for repayment in 20X9 and paying overdue trade payables accounts rather than in investing in new assets or further acquisitions that would improve the company's future trading prospects.

Lending to GD **should not ruled out entirely** because:

(i)   GD is still profitable.

(ii)   GD has low gearing and can easily afford to pay increased amounts of interest.

(iii) GD has significant assets to offer as security for loans.

(iv)   GD has a new subsidiary that may well contribute increasing revenue and profits in future.

Ratios

Note. Only 8 ratios would be required to achieve 8 marks. Any 8 from the following would be relevant to the analysis in this question.

		20X8	20X7
ROCE $= \dfrac{\text{PBIT}}{\text{Equity}+\text{Debt}}$		$= \dfrac{179+11}{496+90}$	$= \dfrac{290+15}{364+180}$
		$= 32.4\%$	$= 56\%$
Gross Margin $= \dfrac{\text{Gross, Profit}}{\text{Revenue}}$		$= \dfrac{360}{1200}$	$= \dfrac{470}{1400}$
		$= 30\%$	$= 33.6\%$
		20X8	20X7
Operating Margin $= \dfrac{\text{PBIT}}{\text{Revenue}}$		$= \dfrac{179+11}{1200}$	$= \dfrac{290-15}{1400}$
		$= 15.8\%$	$= 21.81\%$

Current Ratio $= \dfrac{\text{Profit on ordinary activities before interest and taxation (PBIT)}}{\text{Capital employed}}$ $\dfrac{\text{CA}}{\text{CL}}$ $=$

		20X8	20X7
$\dfrac{292}{283}$	$=$	$\dfrac{304}{249}$	
		$= 1.03$	$= 1.22$
Quick Ratio $= \dfrac{\text{CA - Inventories}}{\text{CL}}$	$=$	$\dfrac{292-146}{283}$	$= \dfrac{304-120}{249}$
		$= 0.52$	$= 0.74$

$$\text{Inventory Days} = \frac{\text{Inventory}}{\text{Cost of sales}} \times 365 = \frac{146}{840} \times 365 = \frac{120}{930} \times 365$$

$$= \text{63 Days} \qquad = \text{47 Days}$$

$$\text{Receivable Days} = \frac{\text{Receivables}}{\text{Revenue}} \times 365 = \frac{115}{1200} \times 365 = \frac{125}{1400} \times 365$$

$$= \text{35 Days} \qquad = \text{33 Days}$$

$$\text{Payable Days} = \frac{\text{Payables}}{\text{Cost of sales}} \times 365 = \frac{185}{840} \times 365 = \frac{160}{930} \times 365$$

$$= \text{80 Days} \qquad = \text{63 Days}$$

$$\text{Gearing} = \frac{\text{Debt}}{\text{Equity}} = \frac{90}{496} = \frac{180}{364}$$

$$= 18\% \qquad = 49\%$$

$$\text{Interest cover} = \frac{\text{PBIT}}{\text{Interest}} = \frac{179 + 11}{11} = \frac{290 + 15}{15}$$

$$= 17.2 \qquad = 20.3$$

(b)   Further information required

(**Note.** Four points would be sufficient here, our answer shows a wider range of points that would be relevant)

(i)   Details about when the new subsidiary was acquired and forecasts of how much revenue and profit it is likely to contribute to the group in future years.

(ii)   Details of any security over the existing loans and which assets are involved.

(iii)   The limit of the overdraft facility and when it is due for renegotiation.

(iv)   A consolidated statement of cash flows for the year.

(v)   Profit and loss and cash flow forecasts indicating how GD intends to repay the loan due in August 20X9.

(vi)   Segmental information allowing analysis of trends in GD's different markets and activities

(vii)   More details of the directors' new strategy to assess the reasonableness of any estimates and assumptions.

	Number	Level	Marks	Time
Now try this question from the Exam Question Bank	Q19	Examination	25	45 mins

EARNINGS PER SHARE

 Earnings per share is important: it is used internationally as a comparative performance figure.

As a result, there is an accounting standard that sets out detailed rules on how it must be calculated.

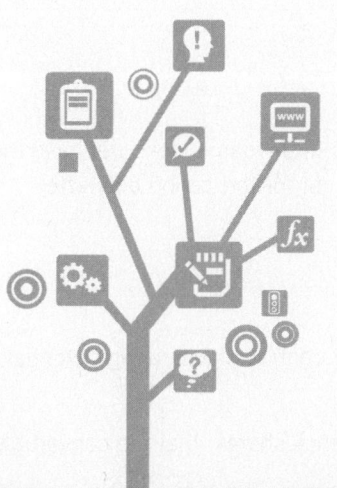

topic list	learning outcomes	syllabus references	ability required
1 IAS 33 *Earnings per share*	C1	C1 (ii)	Application

1   IAS 33 *Earnings per share* (EPS)

Introduction

The objective of IAS 33 is to improve the comparability of the performance of different entities in the same period and of the same entity in different accounting periods.

1.1 Definitions

The following definitions are given in IAS 33.

KEY TERMS

ORDINARY SHARE: an equity instrument that is subordinate to all other classes of equity instruments.

POTENTIAL ORDINARY SHARE: a financial instrument or other contract that may entitle its holder to ordinary shares.

OPTIONS, WARRANTS AND THEIR EQUIVALENTS: financial instruments that give the holder the right to purchase ordinary shares.

DILUTION is a reduction in earnings per share or an increase in loss per share resulting from the assumption that convertible instruments are converted, that options or warrants are exercised, or that ordinary shares are issued upon the satisfaction of certain conditions.

ANTIDILUTION is an increase in earnings per share or a reduction in loss per share resulting from the assumption that convertible instruments are converted, that options or warrants are exercised, or that ordinary shares are issued upon the satisfaction of certain conditions.   *(IAS 33)*

1.1.1 Ordinary shares

There may be more than one class of ordinary shares, but ordinary shares of the same class will have the same rights to receive dividends. Ordinary shares participate in the net profit for the period **only after other types of shares**, eg preference shares.

1.1.2 Potential ordinary shares

IAS 33 identifies the following examples of financial instrument and other contracts generating potential ordinary shares.

(a)   **Debts** (financial liabilities) **or equity instruments**, including preference shares, that are convertible into ordinary shares

(b)   **Share warrants and options**

(c)   Shares that would be issued upon the satisfaction of **certain conditions** resulting from contractual arrangements, such as the purchase of a business or other assets

1.2 Scope

IAS 33 has the following **scope restrictions**.

(a)   Only companies with (potential) ordinary shares which are **publicly traded** need to present EPS (including companies in the process of being listed).

(b)   EPS need only be presented on the basis of **consolidated results** where the parent's results are shown as well.

(c)   Where companies **choose** to present EPS, even when they have no (potential) ordinary shares which are traded, they must do so according to IAS 33.

Exam alert

The May 2010 exam included a 10 mark question on EPS, including basic and diluted EPS with an issue of shares at full market price and a bonus issue during the year.

1.3 Basic EPS   9/11, 11/11

Basic EPS should be calculated for **profit or loss attributable to ordinary equity holders** of the parent entity and **profit or loss from continuing operations** attributable to those equity holders (if this is presented).

Basic EPS should be calculated by dividing the **net profit** or loss for the period attributable to ordinary equity holders by the **weighted average number of ordinary shares** outstanding during the period.

$$\frac{\text{Net profit/(loss) attributable to ordinary shareholders}}{\text{Weighted average number of ordinary shares outstanding during the period}}$$

1.3.1 Earnings

Earnings includes **all items of income and expense** (including tax) attributable to ordinary equity holders of the parent that are recognised in the period, including tax expense and dividends on preference shares classified as liabilities. Preference dividends on preference shares classified as equity should also be deducted.

In **group** financial statements, the earnings figure used to calculate earnings per share is the **profit attributable to the owners of the parent**, ie the profit or loss of the consolidated entity after adjusting for non-controlling interests.

1.3.2 Per share

The number of ordinary shares used should be the weighted average number of ordinary shares during the period. This figure (for all periods presented) should be **adjusted for events**, other than the conversion of potential ordinary shares, that have changed the number of shares outstanding without a corresponding change in resources.

The **time-weighting factor** is the number of days the shares were outstanding compared with the total number of days in the period. A reasonable approximation is usually adequate. In the exam, time weighting can normally be performed based on the number of months the shares were in issue.

Shares are usually included in the weighted average number of shares from the **date consideration is receivable** which is usually the date of issue. In other cases consider the specific terms attached to their issue (consider the substance of any contract). Ordinary shares issued as **purchase consideration** in an acquisition should be included as of the date of acquisition because the acquired entity's results will also be included from that date.

Ordinary shares that will be issued on the **conversion** of a mandatorily convertible instrument are included in the calculation from the **date the contract is entered into**.

If ordinary shares are **partly paid**, they are treated as a fraction of an ordinary share to the extent they are entitled to dividends relative to fully paid ordinary shares.

1.4 Effect on basic EPS of changes in capital structure   5/10

1.4.1 New issues/buy backs

When there has been an issue of new shares or a buy-back of shares at full market price, the corresponding figures for EPS for the previous year will be comparable with the current year because, as the weighted average of shares has risen or fallen, there has been a **corresponding increase or decrease in resources**. Nothing has affected the value or the earnings capacity of the remaining shares.

If the issue occurred part way through the year, this needs to be **time-apportioned** to reflect the fact that the extra funds could only be employed by the company to generate extra earnings for part of the year.

There are other events, however, which change the number of shares outstanding, **without a corresponding change in resources**. In these circumstances (four of which are considered by IAS 33) it is necessary to make adjustments so that the current and prior period EPS figures are comparable.

Example

Alpha Co has earnings of $300,000 for the year ended of 31 December 20X7. The company had 3 million shares in issue on 1 January 20X7.On 1 September 20X7 the company issued 900,000 shares at full market price.

The weighted average number of shares to use in the EPS calculation can be worked out as follows, keeping track of the number of shares in issue over the year, and working out the appropriate time fractions:

Date	Narrative	No. of shares	Time period	Weighted average
1.1X7	B/d	3,000,000	$\times \dfrac{8}{12}$	2,000,000
1.9.X7	Issue at FMP	900,000	$\times \dfrac{4}{12}$	1,300,000
		3,900,000		3,300,000

The EPS for the year would be:

$$\$\frac{300,000}{3,300,000} = 9.1 \text{ c}$$

1.4.2 Capitalisation/bonus issue

In a capitalisation or bonus issue, ordinary shares are issued to existing shareholders for **no additional consideration**. The number of ordinary shares has increased without an increase in resources, so the company cannot be expected to generate the same return after a bonus issue.

This problem is solved by **adjusting the number of ordinary shares outstanding before the event** for the proportionate change in the number of shares outstanding as if the event had occurred at the beginning of the earliest period reported. This is referred to as applying the bonus fraction **retrospectively**. The **prior year's EPS**, shown as a comparative in the financial statements must also be restated for the effect of the bonus issue, otherwise the year on year comparison would be misleading.

Example

Following on from the previous example, Alpha Co has earnings of $300,000 for the year ended of 31 December 20X8. On 1 June 20X8 the company has a bonus issue of 1 share for every 3 shares held.

In the calculation of EPS for the year ended 31 December 20X8, the bonus issue is treated as if it had taken place on the first day of the year.

	20X8	20X7 (as previously stated)
Earnings	$300,000	$300,000
Shares ($3,300,000 \times \dfrac{4}{3}$)	4,400,000	3,300,000
EPS	6.8 c	9.1 c

Retrospective application of the effect of the bonus issue means that the 20X7 figure must be restated as if the bonus issue had taken place at the start of that year. This could be done by re-calculating the number of shares used in the EPS calculation:

$$\$\frac{300,000}{3,300,000\,(4/3)} = 6.8\,c$$

The number of shares has been increased by the **bonus fraction** (which puts the number of shares after the bonus issue over the number of shares before the bonus issue).

There is an alternative and simpler way to do the restatement. Rather than re-working the EPS calculation with a changed number of shares, multiply the prior year EPS figure by the **reciprocal** of the bonus fraction ie:

$$9.1\,c \times \frac{3}{4} = 6.8c$$

1.4.3 Rights issue

A rights issue of shares is an issue of new shares to existing shareholders **at a price below the current market value**. The offer of new shares is made on the basis of x new shares for every y shares currently held, eg a 1 for 3 rights issue is an offer of 1 new share at the offer price for every 3 shares currently held.

In this situation, the company does receive new funds to invest, and to this extent, the issue is similar to an issue at full market price so the shares must be **time-weighted**. The new resources received for each new share are less than the value of each existing share, so there is also a **bonus element** included in a rights issue.

A bonus fraction must be calculated as follows:

$$\frac{\text{Fair value per share immediately before the exercise of rights}}{\text{Theoretical ex - rights price}}$$

Exam questions normally state the market value of the shares before the rights issue. The calculation of the theoretical ex rights price (TERP) and the bonus fraction can be illustrated as follows:

- Assume a rights issue on the basis of 1 for 5.
- The share price immediately before the rights issue was $4.00
- The rights price was $3.40

	$
5 shares @ $4	20.00
1 share @ $3.40	3.40
6 shares	23.40

TERP = $23.40 ÷ 6 = $3.90

The bonus fraction is $\dfrac{4}{3.9}$

Once the bonus element of the rights issue has been calculated, it is used in exactly the same way as the bonus fraction in a bonus issue:

(a)   In the weighted average number of shares calculation, apply the fraction to all periods (ie months) prior to the issue

(b)   Restate the prior year comparative EPS by the reciprocal of the fraction

This technique will be illustrated in the numerical question below.

Question 15.1

Learning outcomes C1

Give the formula for the 'bonus element' of a rights issue.

Question 15.2

Learning outcomes C1

Macarone Co prepares financial statements to 31 December. It has produced the following net profit figures.

	$m
20X6	1.1
20X7	1.5

On 1 January 20X7 the number of shares outstanding was 500,000. During 20X7 the company announced a rights issue with the following details.

Rights:	1 new share for each 5 outstanding (100,000 new shares in total)
Exercise price:	$5.00
Last date to exercise rights:	1 March 20X7

The market (fair) value of one share in Macarone immediately prior to exercise on 1 March 20X7 = $11.00.

Required

Calculate the EPS for 20X6 and 20X7.

Question 15.3

On 1 January 20X1 Smith Co had 4,000,000 ordinary shares in issue.

On 30 April 20X1 the company issued at full market price, 540,000 ordinary shares.

On 31 July 20X1 the company made a rights issue of 1 for 10 @ $4.00. The fair value of the shares on the last day before the issue of shares from the rights issue was $6.20.

Finally, on 30 September 20X1 the company made a 1 for 20 bonus issue.

Profit for the period was $800,000.

The reported EPS for year ended 31 December 20X0 was 18.6c.

Required

Calculate the EPS for year ended 31 December 20X1 and the restated EPS for year ended 31 December 20X0.

1.5 Diluted EPS   11/11

At the end of an accounting period, a company may have in issue some **securities** which do not (at present) have any 'claim' to a share of equity earnings, but **may give rise to such a claim in the future**. These are the 'potential ordinary shares' that were mentioned earlier in the chapter. Examples include:

(a)   **Debts** (financial liabilities) **or equity instruments**, including preference **shares**, that are **convertible** into ordinary shares

(b)   **Share warrants and options**

(c)   Shares that would be issued upon the satisfaction of **certain conditions** resulting from contractual arrangements, such as the purchase of a business or other assets

In such circumstances, the future number of equity shares in issue might increase, which in turn results in a fall in the EPS. In other words, a **future increase** in the **number of equity shares will cause a dilution or 'watering down' of equity**, and it is possible to calculate a **diluted earnings per share** (ie the EPS that would have been obtained during the financial period if the dilution had already taken place).

This will indicate to investors the possible effects of a future dilution.

1.5.1 Earnings

The earnings calculated for basic EPS should be adjusted by the **post-tax** (including deferred tax) effect of the following.

(a)   Any **dividends** on dilutive potential ordinary shares that were deducted to arrive at earnings for basic EPS.

(b)   **Interest recognised** in the period for the dilutive potential ordinary shares.

(c)   Any **other changes in income or expenses** (fees and discount, premium accounted for as yield adjustments) that would result from the conversion of the dilutive potential ordinary shares.

The conversion of some potential ordinary shares may lead to changes in **other income or expenses**. For example, the reduction of interest expense related to potential ordinary shares and the resulting increase in net profit for the period may lead to an increase in the expense relating to a non-discretionary employee profit-sharing plan. When calculating diluted EPS, the net profit or loss for the period is adjusted for any such consequential changes in income or expense.

1.5.2 Per share

The number of ordinary shares is the weighted average number of ordinary shares calculated for basic EPS plus the weighted average number of ordinary shares that would be issued on the conversion of **all** the **dilutive potential ordinary shares** into ordinary shares.

It should be assumed that dilutive ordinary shares were converted into ordinary shares at the **beginning of the period** or, if later, at the actual date of issue. There are two other points.

(a)   The computation assumes the most **advantageous conversion rate** or exercise rate from the standpoint of the holder of the potential ordinary shares.

(b)   A **subsidiary, joint venture or associate** may issue potential ordinary shares that are convertible into either ordinary shares of the subsidiary, joint venture or associate, or ordinary shares of the reporting entity. If these potential ordinary shares have a dilutive effect on the consolidated basic EPS of the reporting entity, they are included in the calculation of diluted EPS.

Example: diluted EPS

For the year ended 31 December 20X7 Farrah Co had a basic EPS of 105c based on earnings of $105,000 and 100,000 ordinary $1 shares. On 1 January 20X7, Farrah Co issued convertible loan stock. Assuming the conversion is fully subscribed, there would be an increase of 32,000 shares. The liability element of the loan stock at 1 January 20X7 is $50,000 and the effective interest is 6%. The rate of tax is 30%.

Required

Calculate the diluted EPS.

Solution

Diluted EPS is calculated as follows.

 **Number of shares**: add the additional shares that would be issued on conversion of the loan stock to the weighted average number used in the basic EPS calculation.

	No of shares
Basic weighted average	100,000
Add: additional shares on conversion	32,000
Diluted number	132,000

 **Earnings**: Farrah Co will save effective interest on the liability component of $3,000 ($50,000 × 6%) but this increase in profits will be taxed. Hence the earnings figure may be recalculated:

Earnings	$
Basic earnings	105,000
Add back loan stock interest net of tax 'saved' ($3,000 × 70%)	2,100
	107,100

 **Calculation**: Diluted EPS

$107,100/132,000 = 81.1 c

1.5.3 Treatment of options

It should be assumed that options are exercised and that the assumed proceeds would have been received from the issue of shares at **fair value**. Fair value for this purpose is calculated on the basis of the average price of the ordinary shares during the period.

Options and other share purchase arrangements are dilutive when they would result in the issue of ordinary shares for **less than fair value**. In order to calculate diluted EPS, each transaction of this type is treated as consisting of two parts.

(a)   A contract to issue a certain number of ordinary shares at their **average market price** during the period. These shares are fairly priced and are assumed to be neither dilutive nor antidilutive. They are ignored in the computation of diluted earnings per share.

(b)   A contract to issue the remaining ordinary shares for **no consideration**. Such ordinary shares generate no proceeds and have no effect on the net profit attributable to ordinary shares outstanding. Therefore such shares are dilutive and they are added to the number of ordinary shares outstanding in the computation of diluted EPS.

Proforma calculation

Number of shares under option	X
Number that would have been issued at average market price (AMP) [(no. of options × exercise price)/AMP]	(X)
→No. shares treated as issued for nil consideration	X

Question 15.4 EPS 1

Learning outcomes C1

Brand Co has the following results for the year ended 31 December 20X7.

Net profit for year	$1,200,000
Weighted average number of ordinary shares outstanding during year	500,000 shares
Average fair value of one ordinary share during year	$20.00
Weighted average number of shares under option during year	100,000 shares
Exercise price for shares under option during year	$15.00

Required

Calculate both basic and diluted earnings per share.

1.6 Presentation

A entity should present on the **face of the statement of profit or loss and other comprehensive income** basic and diluted EPS for:

(a)   profit or loss from continuing operations; and

(b)   profit or loss for the period

For each class of ordinary share that has a different right to share in the net profit for the period.

The basic and diluted EPS should be presented with **equal prominence** for all periods presented.

Basic and diluted EPS for any **discontinuing operations** must also be presented.

Disclosure must still be made where the EPS figures (basic and/or diluted) are **negative** (ie a loss per share).

1.7 Disclosure

An entity should disclose the following.

(a)   The amounts used as the **numerators** in calculating basic and diluted EPS, and a **reconciliation** of those amounts to the profit or loss attributable to the parent entity for the period.

(b)   The weighted average number of ordinary shares used as the **denominator** in calculating basic and diluted EPS, and a **reconciliation** of these denominators to each other.

(c)   Instruments that could potentially dilute basic EPS but which were **not included** in the calculation because they were **antidilutive** for the period presented.

An entity should also disclose a description of ordinary share transactions or potential ordinary share transactions, other than capitalisation or bonus issues and share splits, which occur **after the reporting date** when they are of such importance that non-disclosure would affect the ability of the users of the financial statements to make proper evaluations and decisions (see IAS 10). Examples of such transactions include the following.

* Issue of shares for cash

* Issue of shares when the proceeds are used to repay debt or preferred shares outstanding at the reporting date

* Redemption of ordinary shares outstanding

* Conversion or exercise of potential ordinary shares, outstanding at the reporting date, into ordinary shares

* Issue of warrants, options or convertible securities

* Achievement of conditions that would result in the issue of contingently issuable shares

EPS amounts are not adjusted for such transactions occurring after the reporting date because such transactions **do not affect the amount of capital used** to produce the net profit or loss for the period.

1.8 Alternative EPS figures

An entity may present **alternative EPS figures if it wishes**. However, IAS 33 lays out certain rules where this takes place.

(a)   The weighted average number of shares as calculated under IAS 33 **must** be used.

(b)   A **reconciliation** must be given between the component of profit used in the alternative EPS (if it is not a line item in the statement of profit or loss and other comprehensive income) and the line item for profit reported in the statement of profit or loss and other comprehensive income.

(c)   The entity must indicate the basis on which the **numerator** is determined.

(d)   Basic and diluted EPS must be shown with **equal prominence**.

1.9 Significance of earnings per share

Earnings per share (EPS) is one of the most frequently quoted statistics in financial analysis. Because of the widespread use of the price earnings **(P/E) ratio** as a yardstick for investment decisions, it became increasingly important.

It seems that reported and forecast EPS can, through the P/E ratio, have a **significant effect on a company's share price**. Thus, a share price might fall if it looks as if EPS is going to be low. This is not very rational, as EPS can depend on many, often subjective, assumptions used in preparing a historical statement, namely the statement of profit or loss and other comprehensive income. It does not necessarily bear any relation to the value of a company, and of its shares. Nevertheless, the market is sensitive to EPS.

EPS has also served as a means of assessing the **stewardship and management** role performed by company directors and managers. Remuneration packages might be linked to EPS growth, thereby increasing the pressure on management to improve EPS. The danger of this, however, is that management effort may go into distorting results to produce a favourable EPS.

Section summary

Earnings per share is a measure of the amount of profits earned by a company for each ordinary share. Earnings are profits after tax, preference dividends and non-controlling interest.

Basic EPS is calculated by dividing the net profit or loss for the period attributable to ordinary shareholders by the weighted average number of ordinary shares outstanding during the period.

You should know how to calculate **basic EPS** and how to deal with related complications (issue of shares for cash, bonus issue, rights issues).

Diluted EPS is calculated by adjusting the net profit attributable to ordinary shareholders and the weighted average number of shares outstanding for the effects of all dilutive potential ordinary shares.

You must be able to deal with **convertible debt** and **options**.

EPS is an important measure for investors.

Chapter Roundup

✓   **Earnings per share** is a measure of the amount of profits earned by a company for each ordinary share. Earnings are profits after tax and preference dividends.

✓   **Basic EPS** is calculated by dividing the net profit or loss for the period attributable to ordinary shareholders by the weighted average number of ordinary shares outstanding during the period.

✓   You should know how to calculate **basic EPS** and how to deal with related complications (issue of shares for cash, bonus issue, rights issues).

✓   **Diluted EPS** is calculated by adjusting the net profit attributable to ordinary shareholders and the weighted average number of shares outstanding for the effects of all dilutive potential ordinary shares.

✓   You must be able to deal with **convertible debt** and **options**.

✓   EPS is an important measure for investors.

Quick Quiz

1   All entities must disclose earnings per share. True or false?

2   Why is the numerator adjusted for convertible bonds when calculating diluted EPS?

Answers to Quick Quiz

1   False. Only entities whose ordinary shares are publicly traded need to disclose EPS.

2   Because the conversion of bonds into shares will affect earnings by the interest saving (net of tax).

 ## Answers to Questions

15.1   Were you awake?

$$\frac{\text{Fair value per share immediately before exercise of rights}}{\text{Theoretical ex - rights price}}$$

15.2   Basic EPS

Computation of EPS

		20X6 $	20X7 $
20X6	EPS as originally reported $\dfrac{\$1,100,000}{500,000}$	2.20	
20X6	EPS restated for rights issue = $2.2 \times \dfrac{10}{11}$ (W2)	2.00	
20X7	EPS $\dfrac{\$1,500,000}{591,666\,(W1)}$		2.53

Workings

1   <u>Weighted average number of shares</u>

Date	Narrative	No. of shares	Time period	Bonus fraction	Weighted average
1.1.X7	b/d	500,000	$\times \dfrac{2}{12}$	$\times \dfrac{11}{10}$	91,666
1.3.X7	Rights issue 1 for 5	$\underline{100,000}$			
		600,000	$\times \dfrac{10}{12}$		$\underline{500,000}$
					$\underline{591,666}$

2   <u>Bonus element of rights issue</u>

	$
5 shares @ $11	55
<u>1</u> share @ $5	<u>5</u>
<u>6</u> shares	<u>60</u>

TERP = 60 ÷ 6 = $10

The bonus fraction is 11/10

15.3 Smith Co

EPS for year ended 31.12.X1 $\dfrac{\$800,000}{4,860,767(\text{W1})} = 16.5c$

Restated EPS for year ended 31.12.X0

$18.6c \times \dfrac{6.00}{6.20} \times 20/21 = 17.1c$

Workings

1   *Weighted average number of shares*

Date	Narrative	Shares	Time	Bonus fraction	Weighted average
1.1.X1		4,000,000	$\times \dfrac{4}{12}$	$\times \dfrac{6.20}{6.00\,(\text{W2})} \times \dfrac{21}{20}$	1,446,667
30.4.X1	Full market price	540,000			
		4,540,000	$\times \dfrac{3}{12}$	$\times \dfrac{6.20}{6.00\,(\text{W2})} \times \dfrac{21}{20}$	1,231,475
31.7.X1	Rights issue (1/10)	454,000			
		4,994,000	$\times \dfrac{2}{12}$	$\times \dfrac{21}{20}$	873,950
30.9.X1	Bonus issue (1/20)	249,700			
		5,234,700	$\times \dfrac{3}{12}$		1,308,675
					4,860,767

2   *TERP*

	$
10 shares @ $6.20	62.00
1 share @ $4.00	4.00
11 shares	66.00

∴ TERP = $66/11 shares = $6.00

15.4 EPS 1

Basic EPS $= \dfrac{\$1,200,000}{500,000} = \$2.40$

Diluted EPS $= \dfrac{\$1,200,000\,*}{500,000 + 25,000\,(\text{W1})} = \$2.29$

Workings

1   *Number of shares issued for nil consideration*

Number of shares under option	100,000
Number that would have been issued at average market price (AMP)	
[(100,000 x $15)/$20]	(75,000)
→No. shares treated as issued for nil consideration	25,000

*   The earnings have not been increased as the total number of shares has been increased only by the number of shares (25,000) deemed for the purpose of the computation to have been issued for no consideration.

Now try this question from the Exam Question Bank

Number	Level	Marks	Time
Q20	Examination	14	25 mins

SEGMENT REPORTING

 IFRS 8 *Operating segments* was published in 2006 and is covered in some detail here.

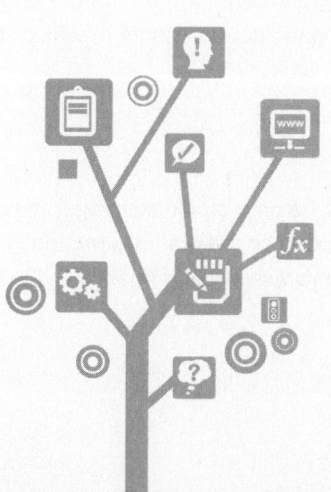

topic list	learning outcomes	syllabus references	ability required
1 IFRS 8 *Operating segments*	C2	C2	Application

1   IFRS 8 *Operating segments*   5/11, 3/12

Introduction

Large entities produce a wide range of products and services, often in several different countries. Further information on how the overall results of entities are made up from each of these product or geographical areas will help the users of the financial statements. This is the reason for **segment reporting**.

- The entity's **past performance** will be better understood
- The entity's **risks and returns** may be better assessed
- More **informed judgements** may be made about the entity as a whole

1.1 Introduction

The performance of a **diversified, multi-national company** can only be assessed by looking at the individual risks and rewards attached to groups of products or services or in different groups of products or services or in different geographical areas. These are subject to differing rates of profitability, opportunities for growth, future prospects and risks.

Segment reporting is covered by IFRS 8 *Operating segments*, which replaced IAS 14 *Segment reporting* in November 2006.

1.2 Objective

An entity must disclose information to enable users of its financial statements to evaluate the nature and financial effects of the business activities in which it engages and the economic environments in which it operates.

1.3 Scope

Only entities whose equity or debt securities are **traded in a public market** (ie on a stock exchange) need disclose segment information. In group financial statements, only **consolidated** segmental information needs to be shown. (The statement also applies to entities filing or in the process of filing financial statements for the purpose of issuing instruments.)

1.4 Definition of operating segment

You need to learn this definition, as it is crucial to the standard.

KEY TERM

OPERATING SEGMENT is a component of an entity:

(a)   That engages in business activities from which it may earn revenues and incur expenses (including revenues and expenses relating to transactions with other components of the same entity)

(b)   Whose operating results are regularly reviewed by the entity's chief operating decision maker to make decisions about resources to be allocated to the segment and assess its performance, and

(c)   For which discrete financial information is available.

(IFRS 8)

The term 'chief operating decision maker' identifies a function, not necessarily a manager with a specific title. That function is to allocate resources and to assess the performance of the entity's operating segments.

1.5 Determining reportable segments

An entity must report separate information about **each operating segment**:

(a)   That has been identified as meeting the **definition of an operating segment**; and

(b)　　　Whose segment total is **10% or more of total**:

　　(i)　　**Revenue** (internal and external), or

　　(ii)　　All **segments not reporting a loss** (or all segments in loss if greater), or

　　(iii)　　**Assets**

The criteria set out in (b) above are referred to as the **quantitative thresholds** in IFRS 8.

At least **75% of total external revenue** must be reported by operating segments. Where this is not the case, additional segments must be identified (even if they do not meet the 10% thresholds).

Two or more operating segments **below** the thresholds may be aggregated to produce a reportable segment if the segments have similar economic characteristics, and the segments are similar in a **majority** of the aggregation criteria above.

Operating segments that do not meet **any of the quantitative thresholds** may be reported separately if management believes that information about the segment would be useful to users of the financial statements.

1.6 Aggregation

Two or more operating segments may be **aggregated** if the segments have **similar economic characteristics**, and the segments are similar in *each* of the following respects:

* The nature of the products or services
* The nature of the production process
* The type or class of customer for their products or services
* The methods used to distribute their products or provide their services, and
* If applicable, the nature of the regulatory environment

1.6.1 Decision tree to assist in identifying reportable segments

The following decision tree will assist in identifying reportable segments.

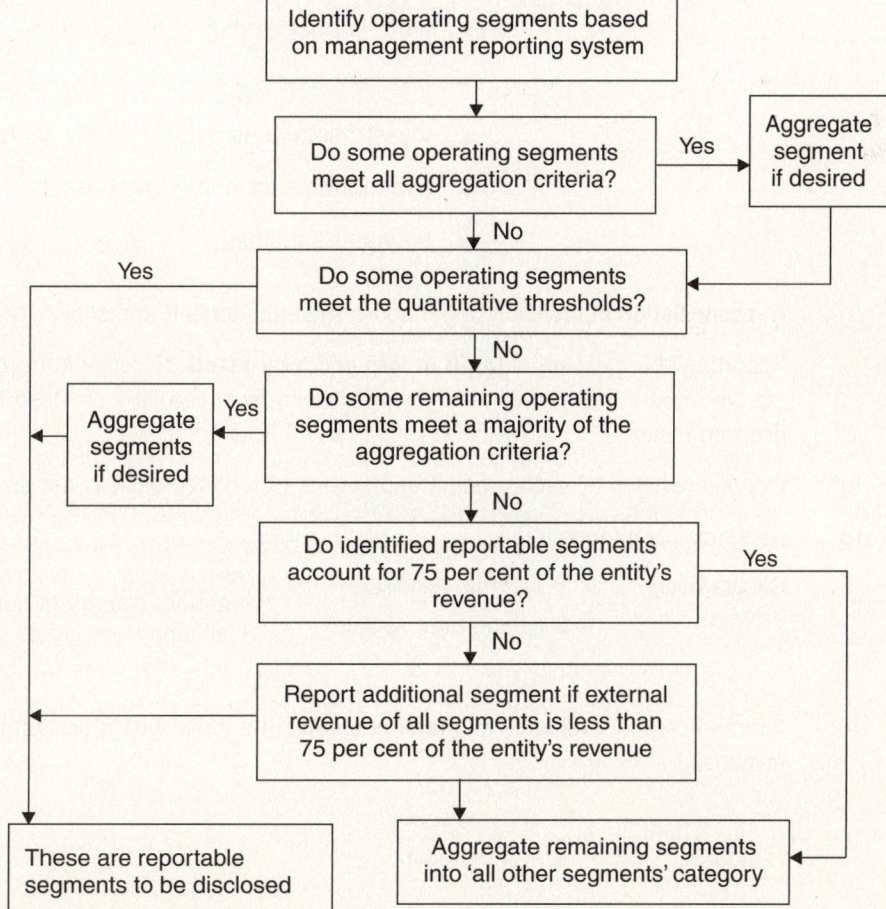

Exam alert

You may well be given a segment report and asked to interpret it, or to comment generally on the need for this kind of report and its limitations.

1.7 Disclosures

Disclosures required by the IFRS are extensive, and best learned by looking at the example and pro forma, which follow the list.

(a)   Factors used to identify the entity's reportable segments

(b)   **Types of products and services** from which each reportable segment derives its revenues

(c)   Reportable segment revenues, profit or loss, assets, liabilities and other material items:

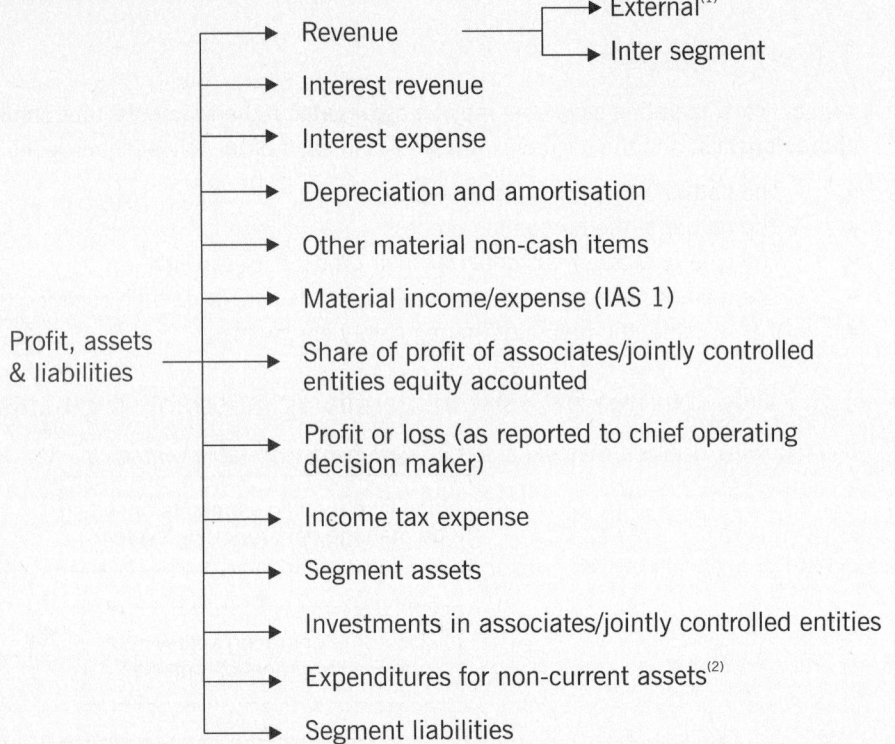

Revenue → External[1] / Inter segment

Interest revenue

Interest expense

Depreciation and amortisation

Other material non-cash items

Material income/expense (IAS 1)

Profit, assets & liabilities →

Share of profit of associates/jointly controlled entities equity accounted

Profit or loss (as reported to chief operating decision maker)

Income tax expense

Segment assets

Investments in associates/jointly controlled entities

Expenditures for non-current assets[2]

Segment liabilities

A **reconciliation** of the each of the above material items to the entity's reported figures is required.

Reporting of a measure of **profit or loss** and **total assets** by segment is compulsory. Other items are disclosed if included in the figures reviewed by or regularly provided to the chief operating decision maker.

(d)   External revenue by each product and service (if reported basis is not products and services)

(e)   Geographical information:

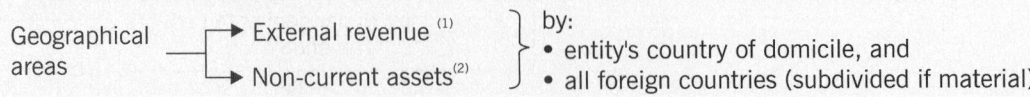

Geographical areas → External revenue [1] / Non-current assets[2] } by:
• entity's country of domicile, and
• all foreign countries (subdivided if material)

(f)   Information about **reliance on major customers** (ie those who represent more than 10% of external revenue)

Notes

(1)   External revenue is allocated based on the customer's location.

(2)   Non-current assets excludes financial instruments, deferred tax assets, post-employment benefit assets, and rights under insurance contracts.

1.7.1 Disclosure example from IFRS 8

The following example is adapted from the IFRS 8 Implementation Guidance. The guidance emphasises that this is for illustrative purposes only and that the information must be presented in the most understandable manner in the specific circumstances.

The hypothetical company does not allocate tax expense (tax income) or non-recurring gains and losses to reportable segments. In addition, not all reportable segments have material non-cash items other than depreciation and amortisation in profit or loss. The amounts in this illustration, denominated as dollars, are assumed to be the amounts in reports used by the chief operating decision maker.

	Car parts $	Motor vessel $	Software $	Electronics $	Finance $	All other $	Totals $
Revenues from external customers	3,000	5,000	9,500	12,000	5,000	1,000[a]	35,500
Intersegment revenues	–	–	3,000	1,500	–	–	4,500
Interest revenue	450	800	1,000	1,500	–	–	3,750
Interest expense	350	600	700	1,100	–	–	2,750
Net interest revenue[b]	–	–	–	–	1,000	–	1,000
Depreciation and amortisation	200	100	50	1,500	1,100	–	2,950
Reportable segment profit	200	70	900	2,300	500	100	4,070
Other material non-cash items:							
Impairment of assets	–	200	–	–	–	–	200
Reportable segment assets	2,000	5,000	3,000	12,000	57,000	2,000	81,000
Expenditure for reportable segment non-current assets	300	700	500	800	600	–	2,900
Reportable segment liabilities	1,050	3,000	1,800	8,000	30,000	–	43,850

(a)   Revenues from segments below the quantitative thresholds are attributable to four operating segments of the company. Those segments include a small property business, an electronics equipment rental business, a software consulting practice and a warehouse leasing operation. None of those segments has ever met any of the quantitative thresholds for determining reportable segments.

(b)   The finance segment derives a majority of its revenue from interest. Management primarily relies on net interest revenue, not the gross revenue and expense amounts, in managing that segment. Therefore, as permitted by IFRS 8, only the net amount is disclosed.

1.7.2 Suggested pro forma

Information about profit or loss, assets and liabilities

	Segment A	Segment B	Segment C	All other segments	Inter segment	Entity total
Revenue – external customers	X	X	X	X	–	X
Revenue – inter segment	<u>X</u>	<u>X</u>	<u>X</u>	<u>X</u>	<u>X</u>	<u>=</u>
	X	X	X	X	(X)	X
Interest revenue	X	X	X	X	(X)	X
Interest expense	(X)	(X)	(X)	(X)	X	(X)
Depreciation and amortisation	(X)	(X)	(X)	(X)	–	(X)
Other material non-cash items	X/(X)	X/(X)	X/(X)	X/(X)	X/(X)	X/(X)
Material income/expense (IAS 1)	X/(X)	X/(X)	X/(X)	X/(X)	X/(X)	X/(X)
Share of profit of associate/JVs	<u>X</u>	<u>X</u>	<u>X</u>	<u>X</u>	<u>=</u>	<u>X</u>
Segment profit before tax	X	X	X	X	(X)	X
Income tax expense	(X)	(X)	(X)	(X)	–	(X)
Unallocated items						<u>X/(X)</u>
Profit for the period						<u>X</u>
Segment assets	X	X	X	X	(X)	X
Investments in associate/JVs	X	X	X	X	–	X
Unallocated assets						<u>X</u>
Entity's assets						<u>X</u>
Expenditures for reportable assets	X	X	X	X	(X)	X
Segment liabilities	X	X	X	X	(X)	<u>X</u>
Unallocated liabilities						<u>X</u>
Entity's liabilities						<u>X</u>

Information about geographical areas

	Country of domicile	Foreign countries	Total
Revenue – external customers	X	X	X
Non-current assets	X	X	X

1.8 Key changes from IAS 14 *Segment reporting*

(a) IFRS 8 **converges with US GAAP** by adopting SFAS 131 Disclosures about segments of an enterprise and related information.

(b) The FASB managerial approach to identifying segments based on an internal organisation structure is used rather than the IAS 14 risk and returns approach.

(c) There is **no primary and secondary** (either business or geographical) **segment disclosure** hierarchy.

(d) There is no longer a requirement for more than 50% of revenue to be external for a segment to be reported separately.

(e) **Revenue, profit and assets** for reportable segment testing are **no longer defined**. The basis used depends on the information reported to the chief operating decision maker.

(f) The **level of compulsory segment disclosure** is **lower**, as only profit or loss and total assets are required figures. Other items are only disclosed if included in the figures reviewed by or regularly provided to the chief operating decision maker.

(g) The **scope of disclosure is widened** to include finance income, finance cost and income tax expense (if the specified amounts are included in the measure of segment profit or loss reviewed by the chief operating decision maker).

(h)   New disclosures are required on **factors used to determine reportable segments** and types of products and services.

(i)   **Geographical disclosures** are required on a **country by country** basis if material.

(j)   There is no requirement to disclose capital expenditure on a geographical basis.

1.9 Advantages and disadvantages of the old and new segment definition approaches

	Advantages	Disadvantages
'Risks and Returns' approach (IAS 14)	• The information can be reconciled to the financial statements • It is a consistent method • The method helps to highlight the profitability, risks and returns of an identifiable segment	• Segment determination is the responsibility of directors and is subjective • Management may report segments which are not consistent for internal reporting and control purposes making its usefulness questionable
'Managerial' approach (IFRS 8)	• It is cost effective because the marginal cost of reporting segmental data will be low • Users can be sure that the segment data reflects the operational strategy of the business	• The information may be commercially sensitive • The segments may include operations with different risks and returns

1.10 Analysing segment reporting

You may need to identify the following when analysing segment data. Remember, the ratio and trend analysis that we looked at in Chapter 14 may very well be relevant here.

•   Growing segments versus declining segments
•   Segments in loss
•   Return (and other key indicators) analysed by segment
•   The proportion of costs or assets etc that have remained unallocated
•   Any additional segment information required.

A good structure to the analysis would be to comment on the movement first for the whole entity, and then by segment.

When commenting on each segment, you may wish to organise your analysis under the following headings:

•   Growth (in revenue)
•   Margins (segment result/segment revenue)
•   Return on net assets (segment result/[segment assets – segment liabilities])
•   Return on associates (share of associate's profit/investment in associate)

1.11 Benefits and limitations of segment reporting

You may be asked to discuss the usefulness and limitations of segment reporting in the exam.

The benefits and limitations of segment reporting include the following:

Benefits	Limitations
• Different segments have **different risks, returns, rates of growth and future prospects**. Without information on these segments, the users would be unable to identify these differences and it would be impossible to properly assess the performance and position of the entity	• As the segments are determined by an entity's internal reporting, no two entities are likely to divide their business into segments in the same way causing **problems with comparability**
• The segment report reflects the information used by the chief operating decision maker of the entity to **make economic decisions** about the business	• The 'management' approach of segment identification is **subjective** and therefore, open to manipulation
• Users will be able to view what the decision makers believe to be important and **evaluate the decisions** made	• The minimum disclosure is of the segment's profit or loss which is very restricted
• IFRS 8 requires **information on major customers and a geographical split** of results and resources – this provides detail that is not evident in the main financial statements but is helpful for making decisions	• **Limited geographical information** is disclosed, breaking the link between the company and its stakeholders
• **As at least 75% of external revenue** must be reported, the information will be highly relevant as it covers the majority of the business	• There is **no defined measure** of segment profit or loss
	• Certain expenses, assets and liabilities **cannot be allocated** to segments, reducing the usefulness of the segment analysis

Section summary

An important aspect of reporting financial performance is **segment reporting**. This is covered by IFRS 8 *Operating segments,* which was published in 2006.

Reportable segments are **operating segments** or aggregation of operating segments that meet specified criteria.

- IFRS 8 disclosures are of:
    - Operating segment profit or loss   – Segment liabilities
    - Segment assets   – Certain income and expense items

- Disclosures are also required about the revenues derived from products or services and about the countries in which revenues are earned or assets held, even if that information is not used by management in making decisions.

IFRS 8 is a **disclosure standard**.
- **Segment reporting** is necessary for a better understanding and assessment of:
    - Past performance   – Informed judgements
    - Risks and returns

- IFRS 8 adopts the **managerial approach** to identifying segments

- The standard gives guidance on how segments should be identified and what information should be disclosed for each

It also sets out **requirements for related disclosures** about products and services, geographical areas and major customers.

Chapter Roundup

✓   An important aspect of reporting financial performance is **segment reporting**. This is covered by IFRS 8 *Operating segments,* which was published in 2006.

✓   **Reportable segments** are operating segments or aggregation of operating segments that meet specified criteria.

✓   IFRS 8 **disclosures** are of:

– Operating segment profit or loss	– Segment liabilities
– Segment assets	– Certain income and expense items

✓   Disclosures are also required about the **revenues derived from products or services** and about the **countries** in which revenues are earned or assets held, even if that information is not used by management in making decisions.

✓   IFRS 8 is a **disclosure standard.**

   •   **Segment reporting** is necessary for a better understanding and assessment of:

– Past performance	– Informed judgements
– Risks and returns	

   •   IFRS 8 adopts the **managerial approach** to identifying segments

   •   The standard gives guidance on how segments should be identified and what information should be disclosed for each.

✓   It also sets out **requirements for related disclosures** about products and services, geographical areas and major customers.

Quick Quiz

1   All entities must disclose segment information. True or false?

2   Geographical and segment information is no longer required. True or false?

Answers to Quick Quiz

1   False. Only entities whose equity or debt securities are publicly traded need disclose segment information.

2   False. Information about revenues from different countries must be disclosed unless it is not available and the cost to develop it would be excessive. It should always be disclosed if it is used by management in making operating decisions.

Now try this question from the Exam Question Bank

Number	Level	Marks	Time
Q21	Examination	25	45 mins

DEVELOPMENTS IN EXTERNAL REPORTING

Part E

DEVELOPMENTS IN FINANCIAL REPORTING

As business expands on an **international scale** so financial reporting must be viewed as it operates on an international rather than a national level. In studying the impact of the international environment we will look at the influences on accounting in a number of countries. These influences vary from country to country and include legal, political, socio-cultural and economic conditions prevailing at any time.

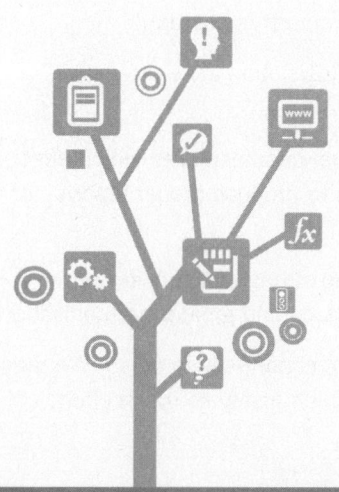

topic list	learning outcomes	syllabus references	ability required
1 International harmonisation	D1	D1	Evaluation
2 Financial reporting in the USA	D1	D1	Evaluation
3 IFRS vs US GAAP	D1	D1	Evaluation
4 Conceptual Framework	D1	D1	Evaluation
5 Amendments to IAS 1	D1	D1	Evaluation

1   International harmonisation   11/11, 11/12

Introduction

We must consider what barriers there are to international harmonisation and why harmonisation is considered so desirable, before looking at comparative accounting systems.

1.1 Barriers to harmonisation

There are undoubtedly many barriers to international harmonisation: if there were not then greater progress would probably have been made by now. The main problems are as follows.

(a)   **Different purposes of financial reporting**. In some countries the purpose is solely for tax assessment, while in others it is for investor decision-making.

(b)   **Different legal systems**. These prevent the development of certain accounting practices and restrict the options available.

(c)   **Different user groups**. Countries have different ideas about who the relevant user groups are and their respective importance. In the USA investor and creditor groups are given prominence, while in Europe employees enjoy a higher profile.

(d)   **Needs of developing countries**. Developing countries are obviously behind in the standard setting process and they need to develop the basic standards and principles already in place in most developed countries.

(e)   **Nationalism** is demonstrated in an unwillingness to accept another country's standard.

(f)   **Language**. The fact that financial reporting standards and national legislation are written in different languages adds further challenges around translation.

(g)   **Unique circumstances**. Some countries may be experiencing unusual circumstances which affect all aspects of everyday life and impinge on the ability of companies to produce proper reports, for example hyperinflation, civil war, currency restriction and so on.

(h)   **The lack of strong accountancy bodies**. Many countries do not have strong independent accountancy or business bodies which would press for better standards and greater harmonisation.

These are difficult problems to overcome, and yet attempts are being made continually to do so. We must therefore consider what the perceived advantages of harmonisation are, which justify so much effort.

1.2 Advantages of global harmonisation

The advantages of harmonisation will be based on the benefits to users and preparers of financial statements, as follows.

(a)   **Investors**, both individual and corporate, would like to be able to compare the financial results of different companies internationally as well as nationally in making investment decisions. Differences in accounting practice and reporting can prove to be a barrier to such cross-border analysis. There is a growing amount of investment across borders and there are few financial analysts able to follow shares in international markets. For example, it is not easy for an analyst familiar with UK accounting principles to analyse the financial statements of a Japanese or Indonesian company.

(b)   **Multinational companies** would benefit from harmonisation for many reasons including the following.

      (i)   Better access would be gained to foreign investor funds.

      (ii)   Management control would be improved, because harmonisation would aid internal communication of financial information.

      (iii)   Appraisal of foreign entities for take-overs and mergers would be more straightforward.

      (iv)   It would be easier to comply with the reporting requirements of overseas stock exchanges.

      (v)   Consolidation of foreign subsidiaries and associates would be easier.

      (vi)   A reduction in audit costs might be achieved.

      (vii)   Transfer of accounting staff across national borders would be easier.

(c)   **Governments** would save time and money if they could adopt international standards. This would also enable governments to better regulate the activities of foreign multinational companies in their own country. These companies could not 'hide' behind foreign accounting practices which are difficult to understand.

(d)   **Large international accounting firms** would benefit as accounting and auditing staff could be trained in accordance with the same standards, enabling them to work across national borders.

(e)   **Tax authorities**. It will be easier to calculate the tax liability of investors, including multinationals who receive income from overseas sources.

(f)   **Accounting students** will benefit because once converged, they will only need to learn one set of financial reporting standards! International employment opportunities will also increase.

1.3 Progress with harmonisation to date

The barriers to harmonisation may be daunting but some progress has been made. There are various bodies which are working on different aspects of harmonisation and these are discussed below. The most important of these bodies, in the light of recent developments, are the IASB and the US FASB.

In the following sections, we will consider the role of various international bodies in the harmonisation project.

1.4 The United Nations

The United Nations does not issue accounting standards, but contributes to research through the annual International Standards of Accounting and Reporting (ISAR) discussion forum. It also provides assistance to developing and other countries through the Conference on Trade and Development (UNCTAD), promoting transparent harmonised reporting.

1.5 Organisation for Economic Cooperation and Development ('OECD')

The OECD is an international forum where the governments of over 30 market democracies work together to address the economic, social, environmental and governance challenges of the globalising world economy, developing policies and guidance to foster growth, stability and cross-border investment.

While also not a standard setter, the OECD's work encourages the development of global reporting standards.

1.6 European Union

The European Union controls financial reporting in member states by issuing Directives that must be enacted into national legislation. The Fourth and Seventh Accounting Directives enforced harmonisation on certain key accounting treatments.

The EU has required since 1 January 2005 that **consolidated financial statements of EU companies listed on a regulated market must comply with international accounting standards**. The implications of this regulations are far reaching.

1.7 International Accounting Standards Board ('IASB')

The IASB was established in 2001 as part of a restructuring process of its forerunner, the International Accounting Standards Committee (IASC) which was established in 1973. Its stated formal objectives are:

(a)   To develop, in the public interest, a **single set** of high quality, understandable and enforceable global Accounting Standards that require high quality, transparent and comparable information in the financial statements and other financial reporting to help participants in the world's capital markets and other users make economic decisions;

(b)   To **promote the use** and rigorous application of those Standards; and

(c)   To bring about **convergence** of national Accounting Standards and International Accounting Standards to high quality solutions.

Before disbanding, the IASC achieved agreements (in 2000) with both the International Organisation of Securities Commissions (IOSCO) and the US Securities and Exchange Commission (SEC) allowing multinational companies to list on member exchanges using international standards rather than national ones for cross-border listings.

The regulation passed by the EU and the agreement with the US Financial Accounting Standards Board (see below) represent significant further progress towards convergence by the IASB.

1.8 US Financial Accounting Standards Board ('FASB')

FASB is the standard setter for US generally accepted accounting practice (US GAAP). Until the emergence of the IASB as the frontrunner in the development of 'global' GAAP, following corporate scandals involving entities reporting under US GAAP, it was seen as the *de facto* international GAAP.

As we'll see in the next section, the FASB now works in close partnership with the IASB.

1.9 The situation today and in the future

Many organisations committed to global harmonisation have done a great deal of work towards this goal. Challenges still exist, of course, as there are disagreements between countries and organisations about the way forward. One of the major gulfs is between the reporting requirements in developed countries and those in developing countries. It will be some time before these difficulties can be overcome. The **IASB** is likely to be the lead body in attempting to do so, as discussed above.

Section summary

Harmonisation in accounting is likely to come from international accounting standards, but not in the near future. There are enormous difficulties to overcome, both technical and political.

You should be able to discuss the **barriers to harmonisation** and the advantages of and **progress towards harmonisation**.

The EC has required **since 2005** that consolidated financial statements of all European listed companies should **comply with IFRS**.

2   Financial reporting in the USA

Introduction

Standard setting in the USA is characterised by a **plethora of highly detailed legislative rules**. These have largely obscured the concept of 'fair presentation', despite the development of a conceptual framework as discussed below. The Financial Accounting Standards Board (FASB) has produced well over 100 Statements of Financial Accounting Standards (SFASs). However the FASB and IASB are now jointly revisiting the *Framework*.

2.1 A conceptual framework in the USA

The FASB has been developing a conceptual framework since 1973. According to the FASB, the conceptual framework was expected to:

(a)   **Guide the body** responsible for establishing standards

(b)   Provide a **frame of reference** for resolving accounting questions in the absence of a specific promulgated standard

(c)   Determine **bounds for judgement** in preparing financial statements

(d)   Increase financial statement **users' understanding** of and confidence in financial statements

2.2 IFRS convergence with US GAAP 5/10

2.2.1 Norwalk agreement

In October 2002, the IASB reached an agreement with the FASB (the **'Norwalk' agreement**) to undertake a short-term convergence project aimed at removing a variety of individual differences between US GAAP and International standards. The first standard resulting from this project was IFRS 5 *Non-current assets held for sale and discontinued operations* (published March 2004).

2.2.2 Principles-based approach

In March 2003, an 'identical style and wording' approach was agreed for standards issued by FASB and the IASB on joint projects. Revised business combinations standards were issued as a result of this approach in January 2008.

FASB also recognised the need to follow a **'principles-based' approach** to standard-setting (as the IASB has always done) in the light of recent corporate failures and scandals which have led to criticism of the 'rules-based' approach.

2.2.3 Common conceptual framework

In October 2004 the IASB and FASB agreed to develop a **common conceptual framework** which would be a significant step towards harmonisation of future standards. The project has been divided into two stages:

(a)   The initial focus is on particular aspects of the frameworks dealing with objectives, qualitative characteristics, elements, recognition, and measurement, giving priority to issues affecting projects for new/ revised Standards.

(b)   Later, they will consider the applicability of those concepts to other sectors, beginning with not-for-profit entities in the private sector.

This common conceptual framework is covered in more detail in Section 4 below.

2.2.4 Memorandum of understanding

In February 2006, the two Boards signed a **'Memorandum of Understanding'**. This laid down a 'roadmap of convergence' between IFRSs and US GAAP in the period 2006-2008.

The aim was to remove by 2009 the requirement for foreign companies reporting under IFRSs listed on a US stock exchange to have to prepare a reconciliation to US GAAP.

Events moved faster than expected, and in November 2007 the **US Securities and Exchange Commission (SEC)** decided to allow non-US filers to report under IFRSs for years ended after 15 November 2007 with no reconciliation to US GAAP.

Consultation is also underway on the possibility of the use of IFRSs by US filers. In November 2008, the SEC published a proposal, titled *Roadmap for the Potential Use of Financial Statements Prepared in accordance with International Financial Reporting Standards by U.S. Issuers*. The proposed roadmap sets out milestones that, if achieved, could lead to the adoption of IFRSs in the US in 2016.

In August 2011, the American Institute of Certified Public Accountants (AICPA) recommended that the SEC allow optional adoption of IFRSs by US public companies whether or not the SEC decides to incorporate IFRSs into the US financial reporting system.

In October 2011, the FASB stated it favours an approach proposed in a May 2011 SEC staff paper of 'condorsement', a combination of continued convergence with IFRSs and endorsement of IFRSs on a standard by standard basis. FASB also defended its authority over standard setting for private companies in the US.

2.2.5 More recent developments

In April 2012, the IASB and FASB published a joint progress report in which they concluded that they were close to completing their Memorandum of Understanding convergence programme and remained committed to complete the three remaining outstanding areas – financial instruments, revenue recognition and leases.

In July 2012, the SEC published a long awaited report. It was entitled *Work Plan for the Consideration of Incorporating International Financial Reporting Standards into the Financial Reporting System for U.S. Issuers*. It discussed barriers to adoption, but did not draw any specific conclusions on adoption or endorsement of IFRSs, and was considered a disappointment in the IFRS world.

2.2.6 FASB/IASB projects

Some of the main results of the convergence project between FASB and the IASB have been:

(a)   The issue of IFRS 5 *Non-current assets held for sale and discontinued operations*

(b)   The issue of IFRS 8 *Operating segments*

(c)   Revision of IAS 23 *Borrowing costs*, to align with US GAAP (IAS 23 permitted borrowing costs on construction of assets to be capitalised or written off; revised to required capitalisation in line with US GAAP)

(d)   Revision of IAS 1 *Presentation of financial statements* and an agreement on common wording to be used in accounting standards

(e)   Revision of IFRS 3 *Business combinations* and IAS 27 Consolidated and separate financial statements (brought in full goodwill method and changed accounting treatment for disposals and step acquisitions)

(f)   The issue of IFRS 9 *Financial instruments* simplifying the categories and subsequent measurement of financial assets and liabilities (work on impairments is still ongoing)

(g)   The issue of IFRS *13 Fair value measurements* with the aim of providing a single definition of fair value; setting out a framework for measuring fair value and requiring disclosures about fair value measurements.

More recent developments include the issue of the 'pack of five' new or revised reporting standards in May 2011:

(a)   IFRS 10 *Consolidated financial statements* – IAS 27 used to cover separate and consolidated financial statements but now split into two; IFRS 10 covers consolidated financial statements (defining control and detailing accounting requirements for consolidated financial statements) and IAS 27 covers separate financial statements

(b)   IFRS 11 *Joint arrangements* – replaces IAS 31 Interests in Joint Ventures – the choice of proportionate consolidation or equity accounting for a jointly controlled entity has been removed; only equity accounting is permitted.

(c)   IFRS 12 *Disclosures of interests in other entities* – integrates and makes consistent the disclosure requirements of IAS 27 Separate and Consolidated Financial Statements, IAS 28 Investments in Associates and IAS 31 Joint Ventures

(d)   IAS 27 (revised) *Separate financial statements* – see IFRS 10

(e)   IAS 28 (revised) *Investments in associates and joint ventures* – now proportionate consolidation is no longer allowed for joint ventures, treatment for joint ventures is the same as for associates i.e. equity accounting so combined into one standard (IAS 28 previously only covered associates).

Revision of IAS 19 *Employee benefits* requiring actuarial gains/losses on defined benefit schemes to be recognised immediately in other comprehensive income (i.e 10% corridor and immediate recognition in profit or loss options removed) The revised IAS 19 is covered in Chapter 3.

The issue Presentation of Items of Other Comprehensive Income (Amendments to IAS 1) to improve presentation of items of other comprehensive income (OCI) in financial statements prepared in accordance with IFRS and those prepared in accordance with US GAAP. This amendment resulted in the 'statement of other comprehensive income' becoming the 'statement of profit or loss and other comprehensive income' and OCI being split into two categories:

•   Items that will not be reclassified to profit or loss
•   Items that may be reclassified subsequently to profit or loss.

There are also Exposure Drafts on the following topics:

(a)   Leases
(b)   Revenue Recognition

Exam alert

The progress being made towards convergence between IFRS and US GAAP is frequently tested in written questions in the F2 exam.

Section summary

Financial reporting in the USA is being reviewed with a view to convergence with IFRS.

3 IFRS vs US GAAP   5/10

Introduction

Your syllabus requires you to identify **major differences** between IFRS and US GAAP. An **overview** is given in the table below.

Exam alert

A **detailed knowledge of US GAAP is not necessary**. Such questions tend to be both interesting and relatively straightforward, requiring only a general overview of US GAAP.

	IFRS	US GAAP
Approach	• Principles-based	• Rules-based (but is changing)
Inventories	• Lower of cost and NRV	• Lower of cost and market (market = lower of RC and NRV – profit margin)
Inventories	• LIFO prohibited	• LIFO allowed (and widely used)
Separate component depreciation	• Separate significant components of PPE with different economic lives should be recorded & depreciated separately	• Separate component depreciation not required
Revaluations of PPE and intangible assets	• Allowed	• Generally prohibited
Development costs	• Capitalised where certain criteria met	• Expensed
Impairment losses	• Based on recoverable amount • Can be reversed (except goodwill)	• Based on fair value • Cannot be reversed
NCI share of acquired subsidiary	• Measured as a proportionate share of identifiable net assets acquired or at fair value	• Measured at fair value

Exam alert

The May 2010 exam included a 10 mark question on convergence between IFRS and US GAAP. Unusually it asked for examples of four areas where convergence had already occurred.

Knowing the areas where there are major differences, it should be quite straightforward to find examples where the treatment is the same, eg non-current assets, financial instruments, deferred tax and employee benefits.

Question 17.1
LIFO method

Learning outcomes D1

The LIFO method of inventory valuation is not permitted under .... LIFO is permitted under ....

(Fill in the blanks)

Section summary

You need to know the differences between IFRS and US GAAP.

4 Conceptual Framework

Introduction

The 1989 *Framework for the Preparation and Presentation of Financial Statements* was partially replaced in 2010 by the *Conceptual Framework for Financial Reporting*. This is the result of a joint project with the FASB. The *Conceptual Framework* is a work-in-progress.

Exam alert

You should familiarise yourself with the *Conceptual Framework*, as it may be tested as part of the convergence project and its progress.

4.1 The search for a conceptual framework

KEY TERM

A CONCEPTUAL FRAMEWORK, in the field we are concerned with, is a statement of generally accepted theoretical principles which form the frame of reference for financial reporting. These theoretical principles provide the basis for the development of new accounting standards and the evaluation of those already in existence.

The financial reporting process is concerned with providing information that is useful in the business and economic decision-making process. Therefore a conceptual framework will form the theoretical basis for determining which events should be accounted for, how they should be measured and how they should be communicated to the user.

BPP
LEARNING MEDIA

Although it is theoretical in nature, a conceptual framework for financial reporting has highly practical final aims.

The **danger of not having a conceptual framework** is demonstrated in the way some countries' standards have developed over recent years; standards tend to be produced in a **haphazard and fire-fighting approach**. Where an agreed framework exists, the standard-setting body acts as an architect or designer, rather than a fire-fighter, building accounting rules on the foundation of sound, agreed basic principles.

The lack of a conceptual framework also means that fundamental principles are tackled more than once in different standards, thereby producing contradictions and inconsistencies in basic concepts, such as those of prudence and matching. This leads to ambiguity and it affects the true and fair concept of financial reporting.

Another problem with the lack of a conceptual framework has become apparent in the USA. The large number of highly detailed standards produced by the Financial Accounting Standards Board (FASB) has created a financial reporting environment governed by specific rules rather than general principles. This would be avoided if a cohesive set of principles were in place.

A conceptual framework can also bolster standard setters against political pressure from various 'lobby groups' and interested parties. Such pressure would only prevail if it was acceptable under the conceptual framework.

4.2 Advantages of a conceptual framework

The **advantages** arising from using a conceptual framework may be summarised as follows.

(a)   The situation is **avoided** whereby standards are being developed on a **patchwork** basis, where a particular accounting problem is recognised as having emerged, and resources were then channelled into standardising accounting practice in that area, without regard to whether that particular issue was necessarily the most important issue remaining at that time without standardisation.

(b)   As stated above, the development of certain standards (particularly national standards) have been subject to considerable political interference from interested parties. Where there is a conflict of interest between user groups on which policies to choose, policies deriving from a conceptual framework will be **less open** to criticism that the standard-setter buckled to **external pressure**.

(c)   Some standards may concentrate on the statement of profit or loss and other comprehensive income (formerly statement of comprehensive income, see Chapter 18 for the details of the change of name) whereas some may concentrate on the valuation of net assets (statement of financial position).

4.3 Counter-argument

A counter-argument might be as follows.

(a)   Financial statements are intended for a variety of users, and it is not certain that a single conceptual framework can be devised which will suit all users.

(b)   Given the diversity of user requirements, there may be a need for a variety of accounting standards, each produced for a different purpose (and with different concepts as a basis).

(c)   It is not clear that a conceptual framework makes the task of preparing and then implementing standards any easier than without a framework.

Before we look at the IASB's attempt to produce a conceptual framework, we need to consider another term of importance to this debate: generally accepted accounting practice; or GAAP.

4.4 Generally Accepted Accounting Practice (GAAP)

This term has sprung up in recent years and its signifies all the rules, from whatever source, which govern accounting. In individual countries this is seen primarily as a combination of:

- National corporate law
- National accounting standards
- Local stock exchange requirements

Although those sources are the basis for the GAAP of individual countries, the concept also includes the effects of non-mandatory sources such as:

- International financial reporting standards
- Statutory requirements in other countries

In many countries, like the UK, GAAP does not have any statutory or regulatory authority or definition, unlike other countries, such as the USA. The term is mentioned rarely in legislation, and only then in fairly limited terms.

4.5 GAAP and a conceptual framework

A conceptual framework for financial reporting can be defined as an attempt to codify existing GAAP in order to reappraise current accounting standards and to produce new standards.

4.6 The IASB Conceptual Framework

The IASB *Framework for the Preparation and Presentation of Financial Statements* was produced in 1989 and is gradually being replaced by the new *Conceptual Framework for Financial Reporting*. This is the result of an IASB/FASB joint project and is being carried out in phases. The first phase, comprising Chapters 1 and 3, was published in September 2010. Chapter 2 entitled 'The reporting entity' has not yet been published. The current version of the *Conceptual Framework* includes the remaining chapters of the 1989 Framework as Chapter 4.

The *Conceptual Framework for Financial Reporting* is currently as follows:

Chapter 1: The objective of general purpose financial reporting

Chapter 2: The reporting entity (to be issued)

Chapter 3: Qualitative characteristics of useful financial information

Chapter 4: Remaining text of the 1989 Framework:

- Underlying assumption
- The elements of financial statements
- Recognition of the elements of financial statements
- Measurement of the elements of financial statements
- Concepts of capital and capital maintenance

You have studied the 1989 Framework in your earlier studies. We will now look at some of these sections in more detail.

4.7 Introduction to the Conceptual Framework

The Introduction provides a list of the purposes of the *Conceptual Framework*:

(a)   to assist the Board in the **development of future IFRSs** and in its review of existing IFRSs.

(b)   to assist the Board in **promoting harmonisation** of regulations, accounting standards and procedures relating to the presentation of financial statements by providing a basis for reducing the number of alternative accounting treatments permitted by IFRSs.

(c)   to assist **national standard-setting bodies** in developing national standards.

(d)   to assist **preparers of financial statements** in applying IFRSs and in dealing with topics that have yet to form the subject of an IFRS.

(e)   to assist **auditors** in forming an opinion as to whether financial statements comply with IFRSs.

(f)   to assist **users of financial statements** in interpreting the information contained in financial statements prepared in compliance with IFRSs.

(g)   to provide those who are interested in the work of the IASB with **information** about its approach to the formulation of IFRSs.

The *Conceptual Framework* is not an IFRS and so does not overrule any individual IFRS. In the (rare) case of conflict between an IFRS and the *Conceptual Framework*, the **IFRS will prevail**.

4.8 Chapter 1: The objective of general purpose financial reporting

The *Conceptual Framework* states that:

'The objective of general purpose financial reporting is to provide information about the reporting entity that is useful to existing and potential investors, lenders and other creditors in making decisions about providing resources to the entity.'

These users need information about:

*   the **economic resources of the entity**;
*   the **claims against the entity**; and
*   changes in the entity's **economic resources and claims**

Information about the entity's **economic resources and the claims against it** helps users to assess the entity's liquidity and solvency and its likely needs for additional financing.

Information about a reporting entity's financial performance (the **changes in its economic resources and claims**) helps users to understand the return that the entity has produced on its economic resources. This is an indicator of how efficiently and effectively management has used the resources of the entity and is helpful in predicting future returns.

The *Conceptual Framework* makes it clear that this information should be prepared on an **accruals basis**.

Information about a reporting entity's cash flows during a period also helps users assess the entity's ability to generate future net cash inflows and gives users a better understanding of its operations .

4.9 Chapter 3: Qualitative characteristics of useful financial information

Qualitative characteristics are attributes that make financial information useful to users.

Chapter 3 distinguishes between **fundamental** and **enhancing** qualitative characteristics, for analysis purposes. Fundamental qualitative characteristics distinguish useful financial reporting information from information that is not useful or misleading. Enhancing qualitative characteristics distinguish more useful information from less useful information.

The two fundamental qualitative characteristics are:

(a)   **Relevance**: relevant information has predictive value or confirmatory value, or both. It is capable of making a difference in the decisions made by users.

The relevance of information is affected by its **nature** and its **materiality**.

(b)   **Faithful representation**: information must be **complete, neutral** and **free from error** (replacing 'reliability').

Financial reports represent **economic phenomena** in words and numbers. To be useful, financial information must not only represent relevant phenomena but must **faithfully represent** the phenomena that it purports to represent.

A **complete** depiction includes all information necessary for a user to understand the phenomenon being depicted, including all necessary descriptions and explanations.

A **neutral** depiction is without bias in the selection or presentation of financial information. This means that information must not be manipulated in any way in order to influence the decisions of users.

Free from error means there are no errors or omissions in the description of the phenomenon and no errors made in the process by which the financial information was produced. It does not mean that no inaccuracies can arise, particularly where estimates have to be made.

Substance over form

This is **not a separate qualitative characteristic** under the *Conceptual Framework*. The IASB says that to do so would be redundant because it is **implied in faithful representation**. Faithful representation of a transaction is only possible if it is accounted for according to its **substance and economic reality**.

4.9.1 Enhancing qualitative characteristics

Comparability

Comparability is the qualitative characteristic that enables users to identify and understand similarities in, and differences among, items. Information about a reporting entity is more useful if it can be compared with similar information about other entities and with similar information about the same entity for another period or another date.

Consistency, although related to comparability, **is not the same**. It refers to the use of the same methods for the same items (i.e. consistency of treatment) either from period to period within a reporting entity or in a single period across entities.

The **disclosure of accounting policies** is particularly important here. Users must be able to distinguish between different accounting policies in order to be able to make a valid comparison of similar items in the accounts of different entities.

Comparability is **not the same as uniformity**. Entities should change accounting policies if those policies become inappropriate.

Corresponding information for preceding periods should be shown to enable comparison over time.

Verifiability

Verifiability helps assure users that information faithfully represents the economic phenomena it purports to represent. It means that different knowledgeable and independent observers could reach consensus that a particular depiction is a faithful representation.

Verification can be **direct** or **indirect**. Direct verification means verifying an amount or other representation through direct observation, for example, by counting cash. Indirect verification means checking the inputs to a model, formula or other technique and recalculating the outputs using the same methodology. An example is verifying the carrying amount of inventory by checking the inputs (quantities and costs) and recalculating the ending inventory using the same cost flow assumption (for example, using first-in, first-out method).

Timeliness

Information may become less useful if there is a delay in reporting it. There is a **balance between timeliness and the provision of reliable information**.

If information is reported on a timely basis when not all aspects of the transaction are known, it may not be complete or free from error.

Conversely, if every detail of a transaction is known, it may be too late to publish the information because it has become irrelevant. The overriding consideration is how best to satisfy the economic decision-making needs of the users.

Understandability

Financial reports are prepared for users who have a **reasonable knowledge of business and economic activities** and who review and analyse the information diligently. Some phenomena are inherently complex and cannot be made easy to understand. Excluding information on those phenomena might make the information easier to understand, but without it those reports would be incomplete and therefore misleading. Therefore matters should not be left out of financial statements simply due to their difficulty as even well-informed and diligent users may sometimes need the aid of an advisor to understand information about complex economic phenomena.

The cost constraint on useful financial reporting

This is a pervasive constraint, not a qualitative characteristic. When information is provided, its benefits must exceed the costs of obtaining and presenting it. This is a **subjective area** and there are other difficulties: others, not the intended users, may gain a benefit; also the cost may be paid by someone other than the users. It is therefore difficult to apply a cost-benefit analysis, but preparers and users should be aware of the constraint.

4.9.2 Underlying assumption

The 1989 Framework identified two underlying assumptions – **accruals** and **going concern**. The Conceptual Framework makes it clear that financial information should be prepared on an accruals basis but only identifies one underlying assumption – **going concern.**

4.10 Exposure Draft: Chapter 2: The Reporting Entity

This ED was issued in March 2010. It presents the IASB's consideration of issues in the development of a reporting entity concept for inclusion in the *Conceptual Framework for Financial Reporting.* There are four sections.

4.10.1 The reporting entity concept

This deals with general issues relating to the reporting entity concept. For example, it considers whether a precise definition of a reporting entity is necessary and whether a reporting entity must be a legal entity.

The Board's conclusion at this stage is that the conceptual framework should broadly describe rather than precisely define a reporting entity **as a circumscribed area of business activity of interest to present and potential equity investors, lenders and other creditors who cannot directly obtain the information they need** in making decisions about providing resources to the entity and in assessing whether management and the governing board of the entity have made efficient and effective use of the resources provided.

Examples of reporting entities include a sole trader, corporation, trust, partnership, association and group.

4.10.2 When does an entity control another entity?

Consolidated financial statements are presented **when control exists.** Control exists where an entity has the power to direct the activities of another entity to generate benefits or limit losses to itself.

If control is shared, no consolidated financial statements need be presented.

4.10.3 Portion of an entity

A portion of an entity could qualify as a reporting entity if the economic activities of that portion can be distinguished objectively from the rest of the entity and financial information about that portion of the entity has the potential to be useful in making decisions about providing resources to that portion of the entity.

4.10.4 Financial statements other than consolidated financial statements

This section considers two issues:

(a)   **Parent-only financial statements**

(b)   **Combined financial statements.** These would include information about two or more commonly controlled entities.

The IASB's preliminary conclusion is that (a) **parent-only financial statements may be presented** provided they are included in the same financial report as consolidated financial statements and (b) **combined financial statements** might provide useful information about **commonly controlled entities** as a group.

4.11 Potential problems

The UK's Financial Reporting Council (FRC) has highlighted a number of potential objections that may be made to the proposals.

(a)   **Users.** The FRC is concerned about the proposal that the objective of financial reporting should focus only on decision-usefulness, with stewardship being subsumed within this rather than being referred to as a specific part of the objective, or a separate objective. The FRC believes that stewardship should be a separate objective. The FRC is also concerned that the shareholder user perspective is being downplayed.

(b)   **Qualitative characteristics: what happens to reliability?** The DP proposes replacing the qualitative characteristic of 'reliability' in the current Framework with 'faithful representation'. The FRC believes that faithful representation is a softer notion which, when combined with a lack of specific identification of substance over form as a principle, could lead to a number of problems.

(c)   **Financial reporting or financial statements.** The FRC believes the boundary between financial statements and financial reporting has not been properly considered.

(d)   **Limited in scope.** The Discussion Paper is limited to private enterprises, rather than, as the FRC believes it should be, encompassing the not-for profit sector.

(e)   **Too theoretical.** This may alienate preparers and auditors of financial statements.

(f)   **Too piecemeal.** This is likely to lead to internal inconsistency

(g)   The **entity perspective is adopted without an in-depth comparison** with other possible perspectives (such as the proprietary perspective, the parent shareholder perspective and other hybrid models).

(h)   The differentiation between fundamental and enhancing qualitative characteristics is **artificial.**

(i)   The qualitative characteristic of **'verifiability'** is problematic.

(j)   In the proposed 'Reporting Entity' chapter, the **entity perspective and the definitions of control have been insufficiently thought through.** In addition, the 'risks and rewards' model is not adopted, thereby losing a useful concept.

4.12 Recent developments

So far the other parts of the *Framework* are still at the **discussion stage.** Below is a **summary of progress** so far:

(a)   **Objectives and qualitative characteristics** – see above.

(b)   **Elements and recognition.** The Board agreed that the focus of the definition of an asset should be on a present economic resource rather than on future economic benefits and an assessment of likelihood should be remove from the definition of an asset. The definition should focus on the present rather than on past transactions or events. No definition of a liability has been agreed.

(c)   **Measurement.** Various measurement bases have been discussed. They are divided into past present and future. Past bases are:

          (i)   Past entry price

          (ii)   Modified past entry amount

          (iii)   Past exit price

         Present bases are:

          (i)   Current entry price

          (ii)   Current exit price

          (iii)   Current equilibrium price

          (iv)   Value in use

         Future bases are:

          (i)   Future entry price

          (ii)   Future exit price

(d)   **Reporting entity** – see above

(f)   **Purpose and status** – Proposal that the primary purpose of the Conceptual Framework was to assist the IASB in the development of future IFRS and in its review of existing IFRS. The Conceptual Framework may also assist preparers of financial statements in developing accounting policies for transactions or events not covered by existing standards. In rare cases, the IASB might need to issue a new or revised IFRS that conflicts with some aspects of the Conceptual Framework. If so, the IASB would describe and explain that departure from the Framework in the basis for conclusions on the IFRS.

(g)   **Application to not for profit entities** – discussions pending

(h)   **Remaining issues** – discussions pending

Section summary

You need to know the new qualitative characteristics from the Conceptual Framework.

---

5   Amendments to IAS 1

Introduction

IAS 1 was amended in 2011. Part of this amendment was to change the name of the statement of comprehensive inome to the statement of profit or loss and other comprehensive income.

5.1 Amendment: Presentation of items of other comprehensive income

In June 2011, the IASB published an amendment to IAS 1 called *Presentation of items of other comprehensive income,* changing the presentation of items contained in Other Comprehensive Income (OCI) and their classification within OCI.

5.1.1 Background

The **blurring of distinctions** between different items in OCI is the result of an underlying **general lack of agreement** among users and preparers about **which items should be presented in OCI** and which should be part of the profit or loss section. For instance, a common misunderstanding is that the split between profit or loss and OCI is on the basis of realised versus unrealised gains. This is not, and has never been, the case.

This lack of a consistent basis for determining how items should be presented has led to the somewhat inconsistent use of OCI in financial statements.

5.1.2 Change

Entities are required to group items presented in other comprehensive income (OCI) on the basis of **whether they would be reclassified** to (recycled through) profit or loss at a later date, when specified conditions are met.

The amendment does not address which items are presented in other comprehensive income or which items need to be reclassified.

Section summary

IAS 1 was amended in 2011, make sure you know the changes.

Chapter Roundup

✓   **Harmonisation** in accounting is likely to come from international accounting standards, but not in the near future. There are enormous difficulties to overcome, both technical and political.

✓   You should be able to discuss the **barriers to harmonisation** and the advantages of and **progress towards harmonisation**.

✓   Financial reporting in the USA is being reviewed with a view to convergence with IFRS.

✓   You need to know the differences between the IFRS and US GAAP.

✓   You need to know the new qualitative characteristics from the Conceptual Framework.

✓   IAS 1 was amended in 2011, make sure you know the changes.

Quick Quiz

1   Which preparers and users of accounts can be expected to benefit from global harmonisation of accounting?

2   How many IFRS are in existence at the moment?

3   Give 5 examples of areas of accounting where convergence between IFRS and US GAAP has been achieved.

4   US GAAP permits but does not require capitalisation of development expenditure. True or false?

5   What other areas of difference are there between US GAAP and IFRS/IAS?

Answers to Quick Quiz

1   Investors, multinational companies, governments of developing countries, the authorities (overseas income), regional economic groups, large international accounting firms.

2   Thirteen (when this book was prepared)

3   Any of: IFRS 5, IFRS 8, IFRS 9, IFRS 10 – 13, revision of IAS 23, revision of IAS 1, revisions of IFRS 3 and IAS 27, joint Conceptual Framework, IFRS 10 – IFRS 13, revision of IAS 19.

4   False. Under US GAAP, development expenditure must be written off to the statement of profit or loss under all circumstances.

5   Measurement of inventory, separate component depreciation, revaluations, impairments and measurement of non-controlling interest at acquisition.

Answers to Questions

17.1   LIFO method

Not permitted under **IFRS**. Permitted under **US GAAP**.

DEVELOPMENTS IN NON-FINANCIAL REPORTING

 Environmental issues are very topical. Just because these topics are discursive does not mean that you can 'waffle'. Social responsibility and ethical issues relate to many aspects of the firm: its environment, its culture and management practice. However, it is the nature of ethics to deny easy answers; furthermore, in the context of business, ethical prescriptions have to be practical to be of any use.

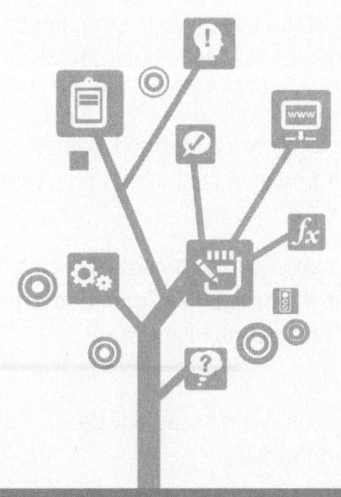

topic list	learning outcomes	syllabus references	ability required
1 Management commentary	D1	D1	Evaluation
2 Sustainability	D1	D1	Evaluation
3 Environmental reporting	D1	D1	Evaluation
4 The social and ethical environment	D1	D1	Evaluation
5 Social responsibility	D1	D1	Evaluation
6 Human resource accounting	D1	D1	Evaluation

1   Management commentary

Introduction

Recent proposals have been put forward for a **management commentary** to supplement and complement the financial statements.

1.1 Need for management commentary

Financial statements alone are not considered sufficient without an **accompanying explanation of the performance**, eg highlighting a restructuring that has reduced profits or the cost of developing a new business channel in the current period which will generate profits in the future.

The *Conceptual Framework* acknowledges that 'general purpose financial reports do not and cannot provide all of the information that existing and potential investors, lenders and other creditors need. Those users need to consider pertinent information from other sources, for example, general economic conditions and expectations, political events and political climate, and industry and company outlooks.' (para OB6)

Perhaps more importantly, good management commentary not only talks about the past position and performance, but how this will translate **into future financial position** and performance.

In the UK, companies have been encouraged to produce an Operating and Financial Review ('OFR'), as management commentary had been known in the UK, explaining the main factors underlying a company's financial position and performance, and analysing the main trends affecting this.

A Reporting Statement on the OFR was issued in January 2006 by the UK Financial Reporting Council (FRC), setting out a framework of the information that should be disclosed in the OFR. While compliance is not compulsory, the Reporting Statement is still widely used as an example of best practice both in the UK and across the world.

In December 2010, the IASB published a practice statement *Management Commentary* which gives a non-binding framework for the presentation of management commentary in financial statements prepared in accordance with IFRS.

Typically, larger companies are already making disclosures similar to a management commentary, eg as a 'Director's Report', but the aim of the IASB is **to define internationally what a management commentary** should contain. For example, a good commentary should be balanced and not just highlight the company's successes.

A management commentary would also address **risks and issues** facing the entity that may not be apparent from a review of the financial statements, and how they will be addressed

1.2 IFRS Practice Statement

The main objective of the Statement is to **improve the quality of financial reports** by providing **guidance** 'for all jurisdictions, on order to promote comparability across entities that present management commentary and to improve entities' communications with their stakeholders'. In preparing this guidance, the team reviewed existing requirements around the world, such as the OFR, Management's Discussion and Analysis (MD&A) in the USA and Canada, and the German accounting standard on Management Reporting.

1.2.1 Scope

The IASB has published a **Practice Statement rather than an IFRS** on management commentary.

This guidance is designed for publicly traded entities, but it would **be left to regulators to decide** who would be required to publish management commentary.

This approach avoids the **adoption hurdle**, ie that the perceived cost of applying IFRSs might increase, which could otherwise dissuade jurisdictions/ countries not having adopted IFRSs from requiring its adoption, especially where requirements differ significantly from existing national requirements.

1.2.2 Definition of management commentary

The following preliminary definition is given in the Practice Statement:

KEY TERM

MANAGEMENT COMMENTARY is 'a **narrative report** that relates to financial statements that have been prepared in accordance with IFRSs.

Management commentary provides users with **historical explanations** of the amounts presented in the financial statements, specifically the entity's **financial position**, **financial performance** and **cash flows**.

It also provides commentary on an entity's **prospects** and other information not presented in the financial statements. Management commentary also serves as a basis for understanding **management's objectives and its strategies** for achieving those objectives'.

1.2.3 Principles for the preparation of a management commentary

When a management commentary relates to financial statements, then those financial statements should either be provided with the commentary or the commentary should clearly identify the financial statements to which it relates. The management commentary must be clearly distinguished from other information and must state to what extent it has followed the Practice Statement.

Management commentary should follow these principles:

(a)   To provide **management's view** of the entity's performance, position and progress;

(b)   To **supplement and complement** information presented in the financial statements;

(c)   To include **forward-looking information**; and

(d)   To include information that possesses the **qualitative characteristics** described in the *Framework* (see Chapters 1 and 17).

1.2.4 Elements of management commentary

The Practice Statement says that to meet the objective of management commentary, an entity should include information that is essential to an understanding of:

(a)   The **nature of the business**

(b)   Management's **objectives and its strategies** for meeting those objectives

(c)   The entity's most significant **resources, risks and relationships**

(d)   The **results** of operations and **prospects**

(e)   The critical **performance measures and indicators** that management uses to evaluate the entity's performance against stated objectives

The Practice Statement does not propose a fixed format as the nature of management commentary would vary between entities. It does not provide application guidance or illustrative examples, as this could be interpreted as a floor or ceiling for disclosures. Instead, the IASB anticipates that other parties will produce guidance.

However, the IASB has provided a table relating the five elements listed above to its assessments of the needs of the primary users of a management commentary (existing and potential investors, lenders and creditors).

Element	User needs
Nature of the business	The knowledge of the business in which an entity is engaged and the external environment in which it operates.
Objectives and strategies	To assess the strategies adopted by the entity and the likelihood that those strategies will be successful in meeting management's stated objectives.
Resources, risks and relationships	A basis for determining the resources available to the entity as well as obligations to transfer resources to others; the ability of the entity to generate long-term sustainable net inflows of resources; and the risks to which those resource-generating activities are exposed, both in the near term and in the long term.
Results and prospects	The ability to understand whether an entity has delivered results in line with expectations and, implicitly, how well management has understood the entity's market, executed its strategy and managed the entity's resources, risks and relationships.
Performance measures and indicators	The ability to focus on the critical performance measures and indicators that management uses to assess and manage the entity's performance against stated objectives and strategies.

1.2.5 Advantages and disadvantages of management commentary

Advantages	Disadvantages
Entity	**Entity**
• Promotes the entity, ie attracts investors, lenders, customers & suppliers	• Costs may outweigh benefits
• Creates an image of transparency and accountability to stakeholders	• If compulsory, could encourage companies to de-list to avoid requirement to produce MC
• Communicates management plans & outlook	• Risk that investors may ignore the financial statements
• Provides an opportunity to explain financial trends and results which might be perceived negatively	
Users	**Users**
• Enables users to make more informed decisions based on a fuller understanding of financial and non-financial information	• Subjective, potential for management to be selective about the information they present
• Provides forward-looking information as well as historical information	• Not normally audited
• Highlights risks	• The lack of specific disclosure requirements reduces comparability with other entities
• Useful for making comparisons with other entities	• Risk of over-reliance on management commentary, to the exclusion of a closer analysis of the financial statements
• Can offer a concise summary of complex information	

Section summary

The **management commentary** supplements the financial statements with forward-looking information about the entity's prospects and risks.

2 Sustainability

Introduction

Pressure is mounting for companies to **widen** their **scope for corporate public accountability**. Many companies are responding by measuring and disclosing their social impacts.

2.1 What is sustainability?

Examples of social measures include: philanthropic donations, employee satisfaction levels and remuneration issues, community support, and stakeholder consultation information.

The next step beyond environmental and social reporting is sustainability reporting which includes the economic element of sustainability (such as wages, taxes and core financial statistics) and involves integrating environmental, social and economic performance data and measures.

2.2 The Global Reporting initiative (GRI)   3/12

The Global Reporting Initiative arose from the need to **address the failure of the current governance structures to respond to changes in the global economy**.

It is 'a long-term, multi-stakeholder, international undertaking whose mission is to develop and disseminate globally applicable Sustainability Reporting Guidelines for voluntary use by organisations reporting on the economic, environmental and social dimensions of their activities, products and services'.

2.3 GRI Guidelines

The GRI published revised guidelines (G3) in 2006. In 2011 the GRI launched G3.1, an update with expanded guidance for reporting on human rights (application of risk assessments, grievance remediation), local community impacts and gender (return and retention rates after employee leave, equal remuneration). The new revision of guidelines is currently underway: G4 will be published in May 2013.

The guidelines are available at the GRI website, www.globalreporting.org.

The main section of the Guidelines sets out the framework of a sustainability report. It consists of five sections.

(a)   **Strategy and analysis.** A statement from the CEO setting out the reporting organisation's strategy with regard to sustainability in the short, medium and long terms. Discussion of the organisation's key impacts on sustainability and effects on shareholders.

(b)   **Organisational profile.** Overview of the nature, size and structure of the reporting organisation's business.

(c)   **Report parameters.** The reporting period, the scope and boundary of the report, the basis of reporting on joint ventures and subsidiaries, and the location where the Standard Disclosures in the report can be found.

(d)   **Governance, commitment and engagement.** The governance structure of the organisation, the organisation's commitment to external initiatives and approaches to stakeholder engagement.

(e)   **Management approach and performance indicators.** Explanation of management's approach to managing sustainability. Disclosure of key performance indicators on the reporting organisation's economic, environmental, and social impact.

2.4 Indicators in the GRI framework

GRI structures performance indicators according to a hierarchy of category, aspect and indicator. As you have seen in the section above, the indicators are grouped in terms of the three dimensions of the conventional definition of sustainability – economic, environmental, and social.

	Category	Aspect
ECONOMIC	**Economic impacts**	Economic performance – direct economic value generated, government funding, pension provisions
		Market presence – wages, supplier relations
		Indirect economic impacts – pro bono work, infrastructure investments
ENVIRONMENTAL	**Environmental**	Materials
		Energy
		Water
		Biodiversity
		Emissions, effluents, and waste
		Suppliers
		Products and services
		Compliance
		Transport
		Overall – total environmental expenditures and investments by type
SOCIAL	**Labour practices and decent work**	Employment
		Labour/management relations
		Occupational health and safety
		Training and education
		Diversity and opportunity
		Equal remuneration for men and women
	Human rights	Investment and procurement practices
		Non-discrimination
		Freedom of association and collective bargaining
		Child labour
		Forced and compulsory labour
		Security practices
		Assessment
		Remediation
		Indigenous rights
	Society	Local communities
		Corruption
		Public policy
		Anti-competitive behaviour
		Compliance
	Product responsibility	Customer health and safety
		Products and service labelling
		Market communications – advertising, promotion, sponsorship
		Customer privacyCompliance

2.5 Influence of GRI

There is a trend to report on broader sustainability issues and to include **social and economic information** alongside environmental disclosures.

An increasing number of companies are following the GRI guidelines to some extent in their reporting. The companies' reports are featured on the GRI website.

Example: SAP

SAP, the German IT company, has been adopting GRI guidelines for a number of years. In 2012, it decided to publish an integrated report for the first time – combining the Annual Report and the Sustainability Report in one.

SAP gave its reasons for adopting integrated reporting on its annual report website (www.sapintegratedreport.com, valid as of 12 April 2013).

Have a look at the company's explanation of integrated reporting, and discuss the advantages that integrated reporting has brought SAP. Might there be any disadvantages to consider?

Section summary

Make sure you understand the influence of the GRI guidelines.

3 Environmental reporting   9/11, 3/13

Introduction

Environmental reporting aims to disclose an organisation's **corporate environmental responsibilities** and the **effects of its activities on its environment**. Although there is no requirement for environmental reporting in IFRS, the growing awareness of environmental issues among the global population means that there is now an expectation for quoted companies to make environmental disclosures. This section looks at environmental reporting mainly under three headings:

- The effect of environmental matters on management information and accounting
- External reporting and auditing
- Possible future developments

3.1 Background

Let us consider the major areas of impact on (any) accountant's job caused by consideration of environmental matters.

(a) **Management accountant**

   (i)   Investment appraisal: evaluation of environmental costs and benefits.
   (ii) Incorporating new costs, capital expenditure and so on, into budgets and business plans.
   (iii) Undertake cost/benefit analysis of any environmental improvements.

(b) **Financial accountant**

   (i)   The effect of revenue costs: site clean up costs, waste disposal or waste treatment costs and so on, which will affect the statement of profit or loss and other comprehensive income.

   (ii) Gauging statement of financial position impacts, particularly liabilities, contingencies, provisions and valuation of assets.

   (iii) The effect of environmental matters, and particularly potential liabilities, on a company's relationship with bankers, insurers and major shareholders (institutional shareholders).

   (iv) Environmental performance evaluation in annual reports.

(c)   **Project accountant**

     (i)   Environmental audit of proposed takeovers, mergers and other planning matters.

     (ii)   Investment appraisal.

(d)   **Internal auditor**: environmental audit.

(e)   **Systems accountant**: effect on, and required changes to management and financial information systems.

3.2 What is environmental accounting?

Environmental reports are either be published as part of a company's annual report, or as a separate document (now often on the company website).

The IASB encourages the environmental reporting if management believe this would assist users in making economic decisions. There is, however, no requirement to adopt environmental reporting.

The following list encompasses the major aspects of environmental accounting.

(a)   Recognising and seeking to mitigate the negative environmental effects of conventional accounting practice.

(b)   Separately identifying environmentally related costs and revenues within the conventional accounting systems.

(c)   Devising new forms of financial and non-financial accounting systems, information systems and control systems to encourage more environmentally benign management decisions.

(d)   Developing new forms of performance measurement, reporting and appraisal for both internal and external purposes.

(e)   Identifying, examining and seeking to rectify areas in which conventional (financial) criteria and environmental criteria are in conflict.

(f)   Experimenting with ways in which sustainability may be assessed and incorporated into organisational orthodoxy.'

                            Accounting for the Environment Rob Gray (with Jan Bebbington and Diane Walters)

The whole environmental agenda is **constantly changing** and businesses therefore need to monitor the situation closely.

3.3 Management information and accounting

The means of codifying a company's attitude towards the environment is often the creation of a published **environmental policy document** or charter. This may be internally generated or it may be adopted from a standard environmental charter, such as the **CERES Principles** (updated in 2010 as The CERES Roadmap to Sustainability).

The problem here, as with other similar principles or charters, is that the commitment required from companies is generally too high and the fear exists that the principles may have legal status which could have a severe effect on a company's liability. The Global Reporting Initiative ('GRI') which we looked at in the last section is similar to the *Ceres Principles* provides similar guidelines.

3.4 Environmental audit

Environmental auditing is exactly what is says: auditing a business to assess its impact on the environment, or as the CBI expressed it 'the systematic examination of the interactions between any business operation and its surroundings'.

The audit will cover a range of areas and will involve the performance of different types of testing. The scope of the audit must be determined and this will depend on each individual organisation.

3.5 Financial reporting

There are **no disclosure requirements relating to environmental matters under IFRSs**, so any disclosures tend to be **voluntary** unless environmental matters happen to fall under standard accounting principles (eg recognising liabilities).

(a)   In most cases, disclosure is descriptive and unquantified.

(b)   There is little motivation to produce environmental information and many reasons for not doing so, including secrecy.

(c)   The main factor seems to be apathy on the part of businesses but more particularly on the part of shareholders and investors. The information is not demanded, so it is not provided.

Environmental matters may be reported in the financial statements of companies in the following areas.

- Contingent liabilities
- Exceptional charges
- Management Commentary or Operating and Financial Review comments
- Profit and capital expenditure forecasts

The voluntary approach contrasts with the position in the United States, where the SEC/FASB accounting standards are obligatory.

You have met IAS 37 *Provisions, contingent liabilities and contingent assets* in your earlier studies. In case you have forgotten, the flow chart below summarises the Standard.

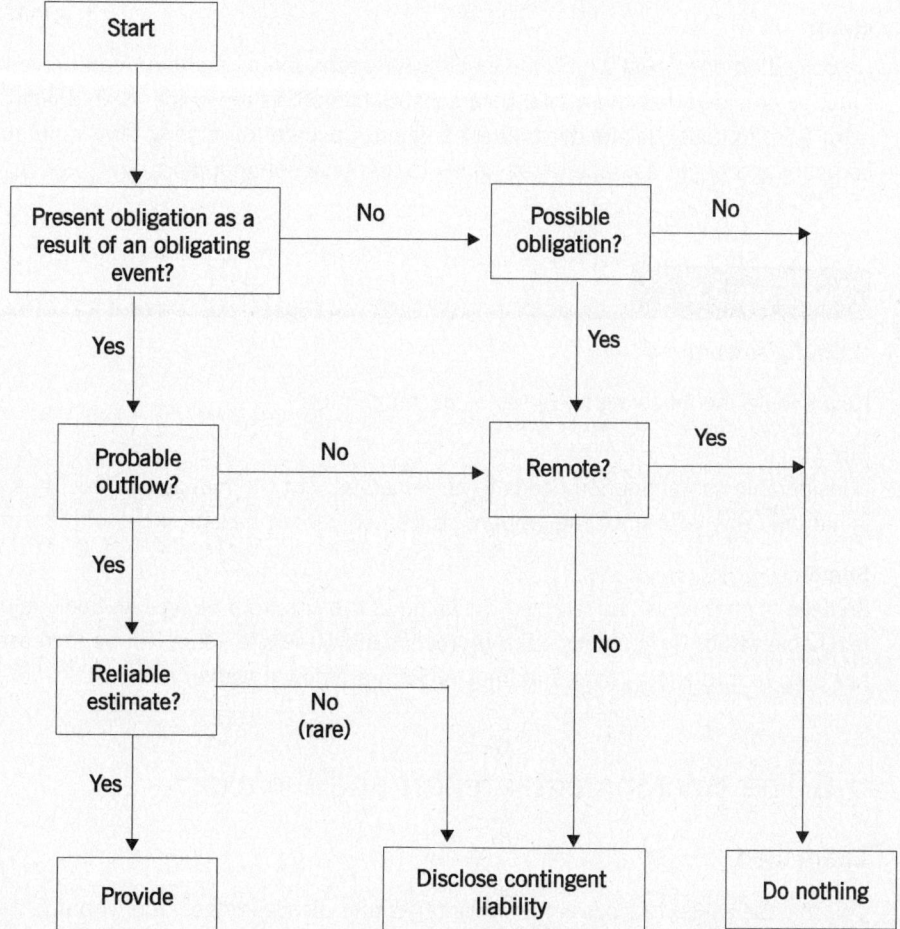

IAS 37 deals with the issue of whether environmental liabilities should be provided for. The example below is taken from an article by Alan Pizzey which appeared in *CIMA Student*. Study the example and attempt the question which follows it.

Example: environmental liabilities

MegaBux Co is a multinational parent company. During the year a number of situations have arisen and the board is to meet soon to determine an appropriate treatment.

Site A

This site is occupied by a small refinery. The site and some adjacent land has been contaminated by chemical spillages. The cost of remedying the contamination is $20m, but under local laws there is no requirement to clean up the site.

Site B

Similar contamination has arisen but the local government, and a neighbouring land owner, require the contamination to be remedied soon. The cost of cleaning up the site is $15m, but an extra $5m could be spent to raise the standard of the operation in line with undertakings given to the local community ten years ago.

How should these matters be accounted for?

Solution

Site A

The mere existence of contamination does not establish an obligation on the part of the company and without an obligation there is no need for a provision.

Site B

An obligation does exist which the local government and a neighbour can prove in court. At least $15m must be provided, but there may be a constructive obligation, wider than a legal obligation, to spend an extra $5m to raise the standard of rectification. Concern for its long term reputation may influence the company to honour its undertaking given to the local community.

Question 18.1
Contamination

Learning outcomes D1

How should the following two sites be accounted for?

Site C

Considerable contamination needs to be remedied, but the managing director is arguing that no provision is required this year since the amount concerned cannot be estimated with accuracy.

Site D

Spillage of chemicals has reduced the value of the site from $25m, its book value, to $10m, its current realisable value. By spending $5m on rectification, the site value will be increased to $20m. The spillage has seeped into a local river and fines of $3m are now payable.

3.6 The environmental report and the exam

Exam alert

You may be asked to discuss the advantages and disadvantages of environmental reporting, either from the point of view of the company or from the point of view of users of the financial statements.

The May 2012 edition of the CIMA Student contains an article titled 'Environmental Reporting'. This very useful article discusses what environmental reporting entails, and also, crucially, how you can ensure you do well on an environmental reporting question in the exam.

Your report should distinguish between:

(a)   Transactions that affect the financial statements, for example provisions that need to be made under IAS 37

(b)   Information to be disclosed elsewhere, for example in the operating and financial review, or in a separate environmental report.

Case Study: BP

BP adopted the GRI guidelines early on, and has been publishing sustainability reports since 2005. Its sustainability reporting was held up as a model for the industry.

In 2010, an explosion occurred on a BP oil platform, killing 11 employees and resulting in one of the largest environmental disasters in US history. The incident highlighted many serious deficiencies in BP's safety procedures. It was found that shortly before the explosion, BP made 'a series of blunders and money-saving shortcuts that dramatically increased the danger of a destructive oil spill.' BP officials reportedly ignored the advice of subcontractors to install 21 centralisers to secure the casing around the well, opting instead for 6 centralisers. One official recognised the risks that this would involve, but concluded: 'Who cares, it's done, end of story, will probably be fine.' (Associated Press, "Documents: BP cut corners in days before blowout," June 15, 2010.)

What happened in 2010 begs the question: to what extent does sustainability reporting reflect the reality of a company's impact on society and on the environment? To what extent is it just 'integrated spin'?

BP's 2012 Sustainability Report can be found online at: http://www.bp.com/liveassets/bp_internet/globalbp/STAGING/global_assets/downloads/S/BP_Sustainability _Review_2012.pdf (accessed 29 April 2013). From page 28 of the report, BP addresses some of the safety concerns raised by the Gulf of Mexico oil spill.

Read the Safety section of BP's Sustainability Report, and discuss whether you think it provides an adequate response to the Gulf of Mexico oil spill. What other questions remain unanswered?

Section summary

Although not compulsory, **environmental reports** are becoming increasingly important. You should distinguish

*   Items that affect the financial statements (eg IAS 37)
*   Items that affect the environmental report

4   The social and ethical environment

Introduction

Whereas the political environment in which an organisation operates consists of laws, regulations and government agencies, the social environment consists of the customs, attitudes, beliefs and education of society as a whole, or of different groups in society; and the ethical environment consists of a set (or sets) of well-established rules of personal and organisational behaviour.

4.1 What are ethics?

ETHICS: a set of moral principles to guide behaviour.

KEY TERM

Social attitudes, such as a belief in the merits of education, progress through science and technology, and fair competition, are significant for the management of a business organisation. Other beliefs have either gained strength or been eroded in recent years:

(a)   There is a growing belief in preserving and improving the quality of life by reducing working hours, reversing the spread of pollution, developing leisure activities and so on.

(b)   Many pressure groups have been organised in recent years to protect social minorities and under-privileged groups. Legislation has been passed in an attempt to prevent racial discrimination and discrimination against women and disabled people.

(c)   Issues relating to the environmental consequences of corporate activities are currently debated, and respect for the environment has come to be regarded as an unquestionable good.

The ethical environment refers to justice, respect for the law and a moral code. The conduct of an organisation, its management and employees will be measured against ethical standards by the customers, suppliers and other members of the public with whom they deal.

4.2 Ethical problems facing managers

Managers have a duty (in most entities) to aim for profit. At the same time, modern ethical standards impose a duty to guard, preserve and enhance the value of the entity for the good of all touched by it, including the general public. Large organisations tend to be more often held to account over this than small ones.

In the area of **products and production**, managers have responsibility to ensure that the public and their own employees are protected from danger. Attempts to increase profitability by cutting costs may lead to dangerous working conditions or to inadequate safety standards in products. In the United States, product liability litigation is so common that this legal threat may be a more effective deterrent than general ethical standards. The Consumer Protection Act 1987 and EU legislation generally is ensuring that ethical standards are similarly enforced in the UK.

Another ethical problem concerns **payments by companies to government or municipal officials** who have power to help or hinder the payers' operations. In *The Ethics of Corporate Conduct, Clarence Walton* refers to the fine distinctions which exist in this area.

(a)   **Extortion**. Foreign officials have been known to threaten companies with the complete closure of their local operations unless suitable payments are made.

(b)   **Bribery**. This refers to payments for services to which a company is not legally entitled. There are some fine distinctions to be drawn; for example, some managers regard political contributions as bribery.

(c)   **Grease money**. Multinational companies are sometimes unable to obtain services to which they are legally entitled because of deliberate stalling by local officials. Cash payments to the right people may then be enough to oil the machinery of bureaucracy.

(d)   **Gifts**. In some cultures, gifts are regarded as an essential part of civilised negotiation, even in circumstances where to Western eyes they might appear ethically dubious. Managers operating in such a culture may feel at liberty to adopt the local customs.

Business ethics are also relevant to competitive behaviour. This is because a market can only be free if competition is, in some basic respects, fair. There is a distinction between competing aggressively and competing unethically.

Example: social and ethical objectives

Companies are not passive in the social and ethical environment. Many organisations pursue a variety of social and ethical objectives.

Employees

(a)   A minimum wage, perhaps with adequate differentials for skilled labour
(b)   Job security (over and above the protection afforded to employees by government legislation)
(c)   Good conditions of work (above the legal minima)
(d)   Job satisfaction

Customers may be regarded as entitled to receive a produce of good quality at a reasonable price.

Suppliers may be offered regular orders and timely payment in return for reliable delivery and good service.

Society as a whole

(a)   Control of pollution
(b)   Provision of financial assistance to charities, sports and community activities
(c)   Co-operation with government authorities in identifying and preventing health hazards in the products sold

As far as it is possible, social and ethical objectives should be expressed quantitatively, so that actual results can be monitored to ensure that the targets are achieved. This is often easier said than done – more often, they are expressed in the organisation's mission statement which can rarely be reduced to a quantified amount.

Many of the above objectives are commercial ones – for example satisfying customers is necessary to stay in business. The question as to whether it is the role of businesses to be concerned about wider issues of social responsibility is discussed shortly.

Section summary

Ethical problems continue to arise in accountancy and the profession seeks to counter this by issuing ethical guidelines.

5 Social responsibility

Introduction

Not only does the environment have a significant influence on the structure and behaviour of organisations, but also organisations have some influence on their environment.

5.1 Background

Since organisations have an effect on their environment, it is arguable that they should act in a way which shows **social awareness and responsibility**.

'A society, awakened and vocal with respect to the urgency of social problems, is asking the managers of all kinds of organisations, particularly those at the top, what they are doing to discharge their social responsibilities and why they are not doing more.'   *Koontz, O'Donnell and Weihrich*

Social responsibility is expected from all types of organisation.

(a)   **Local government** is expected to provide services to the local community, and to preserve or improve the character of that community, but at an acceptable cost to the ratepayers.

(b)   **Businesses** are expected to provide goods and services, which reflect the needs of users and society as a whole. These needs may not be in harmony - for example, while an airline facilitates intercontinental travel, it also contributes to air and noise pollution.

(c) **Pollution control** is a particularly important example of social responsibility by industrial organisations, and some progress has been made in the development of commercial processes for re-cycling waste material. Green energy, such as wind farms, are becoming a more important part of the energy market.

(d) **Universities and schools** are expected to produce students whose abilities and qualifications will prove beneficial to society. A currently popular view of education is that greater emphasis should be placed on vocational training for students.

(e) In some cases, **legislation** may be required to enforce social need, for example to regulate the materials used to make crash helmets for motor cyclists, or to regulate safety standards in motor cars and furniture. Ideally, however, organisations should avoid the need for legislation by taking **earlier self-regulating action**.

5.2 Social responsibility and businesses

How far is it reasonable, or even appropriate, for businesses to exercise 'social responsibility' by giving to charities, voluntarily imposing strict environmental objectives on themselves and so forth?

One school of thought would argue that **the management of a business has only one social responsibility, which is to maximise wealth for its shareholders**. There are two reasons to support this argument.

(a) If the business is owned by the shareholders the assets of the company are, ultimately, the shareholders' property. Management has no moral right to dispose of business assets (like cash) on non-business objectives, as this has the effect of reducing the return available to shareholders.

(b) A second justification for this view is that management's job is to maximise wealth, as this is the best way that society can benefit from a business's activities.

 (i)   Maximising wealth has the effect of increasing the tax revenues available to the state to disburse on socially desirable objectives.

 (ii) Maximising wealth for the few is sometimes held to have a 'trickle down' effect on the disadvantaged members of society.

 (iii) Many company shares are owned by pension funds, whose ultimate beneficiaries may not be the wealthy anyway.

This argument rests on certain assumptions.

(a) The first assumption is, in effect, the opposite of the **stakeholder view**. It assumes that the *rights* of legal ownership are paramount over all other *interests* in a business.

(b) The second assumption is that a business's *only* relationship with the wider social environment is an economic one. After all, that is what businesses exist for, and any other activities are the role of the state.

(c) The defining purpose of business organisations is the maximisation of the wealth of their owners.

Henry Mintzberg (in *Power In and Around Organisations*) suggests that simply viewing organisations as vehicles for shareholder investment is inadequate.

(a) In practice, he says, organisations are rarely controlled effectively by shareholders. Most shareholders are passive investors.

(b) Large corporations can manipulate markets. Social responsibility, forced or voluntary, is a way of recognising this.

(c) Moreover, businesses do receive a lot of government support. The public pays for roads, infrastructure, education and health, all of which benefits businesses. Although businesses pay tax, the public ultimately pays, perhaps through higher prices.

(d) Strategic decisions by businesses always have wider social consequences. In other words, says Mintzberg, the firm produces two outputs: **goods and services** and the **social consequences of its activities** (eg pollution).

5.3 Corporate responsibility: a commercial necessity?

The arguments for and against corporate responsibility in business are complex, and the debate about whether a company owes any social duty towards its wider stakeholders and the environment is still ongoing today.

There is undeniably a growing public awareness of environmental and social issues around the globe. In China, local residents affected by industrial waste and pollution are becoming increasingly vocal, staging 'not in my backyard' protests that put direct pressure on companies to consider their impact on the local community and environment. At the same time, all companies want to avoid risk suffering the financial and reputational costs of serious environmental disasters, such as the BP oil spill.

For the large majority of listed companies, corporate responsibility is above all a public relations exercise. Most listed companies now show off their environmental credentials in order to win over investors and consumers. Notice, next time you go to the supermarket, how many times the words 'natural' and 'organic' appear prominently on the packaging of products on the shelves, and you will get an idea of how much social responsibility now forms part of corporate PR and marketing.

However, corporate responsibility will not become central to corporate strategy, until managers perceive a direct link between it and profitability. The trading of carbon credits under the Kyoto Protocol (where governments and companies buy and sell the right to emit units of carbon dioxide on markets similar to stock exchanges) is a move towards linking one form of social responsibility to financial performance.

A small number of companies are now taking social responsibility one step further. Faced with diminishing raw materials and increasing demand for products, some businesses have started to develop ways to recycle waste back into the supply chain. Their CEOs argue that the ability to reuse industrial by-products and generate profits from them will be crucial to the long-term sustainability of businesses.

Google, Ikea and Lego now all invest in wind farms, although they have no intention of entering into the power utility industry.

MacDonald's has responded to pressure from environmental groups by promising to not use chicken fed on soybeans – a crop which led to the deforestation in the Amazon.

Unilever is actively promoting a number of initiatives, including the development of concentrated detergents which uses less water, and educating farmers to use less pesticides. Unilever CEO, Paul Polman, famously told investors who disagreed with the company's green strategy, 'don't put your money in our company.'

John Elkington, a leading figure in the social responsibility movement, tells the *Financial Times*: 'There is this new breed of CEOs who are not in this simply to feel comfortable as they swim up and down the club swimming pool, so they can say: 'I've got a report, have you got a report?' They are saying: 'This is fundamentally about the future of capitalism and we're going to have to get this right.' (Source: 'Capitalist conservationalists', Pilita Clark, *Financial Times*, 5 June 2012).

Whether corporate responsibility will ever become 'mainstream', however, remains to be seen.

Section summary

The **stakeholder** view holds that there are many groups in society with an interest in the organisation's activities. Some firms have objectives for these issues. Some argue, however, that a business's only objective should be to make money: the state, representing the public interest, can levy taxes to spend on socially desirable projects or can regulate organisational activities.

Firms have to ensure they obey the law: but they also face **ethical concerns**, because their reputations depend on a good image.

6 Human resource accounting 11/10, 3/11, 5/12, 9/12

Introduction

Human resource accounting has at its core the principle that **employees are assets**. Competitive advantage is largely gained by **effective use of people**.

6.1 Implications of regarding people as organisational assets

(a) **People are a resource** which needs to be carefully and efficiently managed with overriding concern for organisational objectives.

(b) The organisation needs to **protect its investment** by retaining, safeguarding and developing its human assets.

(c) **Deterioration in the attitudes and motivation** of employees, increases in labour turnover (followed by costs of hiring and training replacements) are **costs to the company** – even though a 'liquidation' of human assets, brought about by certain managerial styles, may produce short-term increases in profit.

(d) A concept developed some time ago was that of **human asset accounting** (the inclusion of human assets in the financial reporting system of the organisation).

CASE STUDY

Case Study

There are difficulties in isolating and measuring human resources, and it is also hard to forecast the time period (and area of business) over which benefits will be received from expenditure on human assets. *Texas Instruments* uses a system which identifies potential replacement costs for groups of people, taking into account the learning time required by the replacement, and the individual's salary during that period.

6.2 Intellectual assets

Because of the difficulties found in both theory and practice, the concept of **human assets was broadened and became intellectual assets.** Intellectual assets, or 'intellectual capital' as they are sometimes called can be divided into three main types.

(a) **External assets.** These include the reputation of brands and franchises and the strength of customer relationships.

(b) **Internal assets.** These include patents, trademarks and information held in customer databases.

(c) **Competencies.** These reflect the capabilities and skills of individuals.

'Intellectual assets' thus includes 'human assets'.

The value of intellectual assets will continue to rise and will represent an increasing proportion of the value of most companies. Whether or not traditional accounting will be able to measure them, remains to be seen. Indeed it is difficult to see how a monetary value could be placed on human assets, as they do not meet the definition of assets according to either the current version of the IASB *Framework* (see Chapter 1) or the revised *Conceptual Framework* (see Chapter 17).

6.3 IASB Framework and human resource accounting

Under IFRS, the skills, knowledge and resources of employees ('human assets') may not be capitalised in the statement of financial position. This is because they fail to meet the IASB *Framework's* definition of an asset and recognition criteria.

An asset is defined as 'a resource controlled by an entity as a result of past events from which future economic benefits are expected to flow'.

- There is a past event – the employee starts work under an employment contract

- Future economic benefits – the employer has the ability to earn future profits and obtain future cash inflows as a result of the employee's services to the entity

- Control – this is hard to prove as it implies the ability to obtain economic benefits that arise or to restrict access of others to those benefits. An employee's contract will normally require them to work a minimum number of hours and there is usually an expectation that they will not provide services to anybody else. However, employees are free to leave the employer if they wish to – this implies that the employer does not control the rights to future benefits.

As the IASB *Framework's* definition of an asset is not met (failing on the control criteria), staff skills may not be recognised as an asset.

The IASB *Framework* requires two criteria to be met before recognising an element in the financial statements:

- Probable future economic benefits *and*

- Cost can be measured reliably – in practice, this second criteria is likely to cause problems. In theory, a human resource asset can be valued at historic cost, at current value (value to the business) or at fair value:

  - Historic cost: this would be the actual cost of recruiting, employing and training an employee

  - Value to the business: this is the lower of replacement cost (the cost of recruiting and developing another employee to the same level of competence as present staff) and recoverable amount (present value of future cash flows)

  - Fair value: this is an employee's 'market value' (in practice, probably the cost of recruiting and developing another employee to the same level of competence)

In practice, human resources would almost certainly have to be valued at historic cost as it is doubtful that any other basis would be sufficiently reliable. There would remain the problem of deciding which costs to capitalise and of selecting an amortisation period.

IAS 38 *Intangible assets* specifically lists training costs as an example of an item which must be expensed rather than capitalised.

Under current international GAAP (specifically the IASB *Framework* and IAS 38), human resource assets cannot be capitalised in the statement of financial position.

6.4 Advantages and disadvantages of human resource accounting

Advantages

- Under conventional accounting, SOFP doesn't show true value of business as intellectual capital not recognised

If we recognise intellectual capital, this would:

- Improve information to investors and potential investors encouraging them to keep their investment/invest

- Improve profitability through better identification of hidden resources

- Provide useful information to employees and future employees (i.e. recruit and retain motivated staff)

- Provide useful information to the local community

Disadvantages

- Defining and measuring intellectual capital is very difficult and subjective

- The majority of intellectual assets are not recognised by IFRS

- Intellectual assets don't meet framework or IAS 38 definition of an asset (ie uncertainty over whether the entity can control the benefits – the employer cannot normally prevent the employee from changing employment)

Section summary

Human resource accounting is an approach which regards **people as assets**.
There are **problems in putting a value on people** which traditional accounting has yet to overcome.

Chapter Roundup

✓   The **management commentary** supplements the financial statements with forward-looking information about the entity's prospects and risks.

✓   Although not compulsory, **sustainability reports** are becoming increasingly important. You should distinguish

  –   Items that affect the financial statements (eg IAS 37)
  –   Items that affect the sustainability report

✓   Make sure you understand the influence of the GRI guidelines.

✓   Ethical problems continue to arise in accountancy and the profession seeks to counter this by issuing ethical guidelines.

✓   The **stakeholder** view holds that there are many groups in society with an interest in the organisation's activities. Some firms have objectives for these issues. Some argue, however, that a business's only objective should be to make money: the state, representing the public interest, can levy taxes to spend on socially desirable projects or can regulate organisational activities.

✓   Firms have to ensure they obey the law: but they also face **ethical concerns**, because their reputations depend on a good image.

✓   **Human resource accounting** is an approach which regards **people as assets**.

✓   There are **problems in putting a value on people** which traditional accounting has yet to overcome.

Quick Quiz

1   Name four areas of company financial statements where environmental matters may be reported.

2   If a site is contaminated, a provision must be made.

    True ☐   False ☐

3   What ethical problems face management?

4   What objectives might a company have in relation to wider society?

5   To whom might management have responsibilities, and what are some of these responsibilities?

6   What is the basic principle of human resource accounting?

7   Give three examples of intellectual assets.

Answers to Quick Quiz

1   Contingent liabilities   Management commentary/Operating and financial review comments
     Exceptional charges   Profit and capital expenditure forecasts

2   False; an **obligation** must be established before a provision can be made.

3   There is a constant tension between the need to achieve current profitability, the need to safeguard the stakeholders' long term investment and the expectations of wider society.

4   Protection of the environment, support for good causes, a responsible attitude to product safety.

5   Managers of businesses are responsible to the owners for economic performance and to wider society for the externalities related to their business operations.

6   Employees are assets.

7   External assets, internal assets and competencies

Answers to Questions

18.1 Contamination

Site C

Whilst the exact amount of the expenditure may not be known with certainty, it should be possible to arrive at a realistic and prudent estimate. It is not acceptable to omit a liability on the grounds that its amount is not known with certainty – this would be a distortion.

Site D

The fines of $3m are a current cost to be charged to the statement of profit or loss and other comprehensive income. The spillage has impaired the value of the site, which must be written down to its new market value of $20m after rectification. The cost of the write-down ($5m) and the cost of the rectification ($5m) are charged to the statement of profit or loss and other comprehensive income. The site is now carried in the books at its recoverable amount.

Now try this question from the Exam Question Bank	Number	Level	Marks	Time
	Q22	Examination	20	36 mins

MATHEMATICAL TABLES & EXAM FORMULAE

Present value table

Present value of £1 = $(1+r)^{-n}$ where r = interest rate, n = number of periods until payment or receipt.

Periods	Discount rates (r)									
(n)	1%	2%	3%	4%	5%	6%	7%	8%	9%	10%
1	0.990	0.980	0.971	0.962	0.952	0.943	0.935	0.926	0.917	0.909
2	0.980	0.961	0.943	0.925	0.907	0.890	0.873	0.857	0.842	0.826
3	0.971	0.942	0.915	0.889	0.864	0.840	0.816	0.794	0.772	0.751
4	0.961	0.924	0.888	0.855	0.823	0.792	0.763	0.735	0.708	0.683
5	0.951	0.906	0.863	0.822	0.784	0.747	0.713	0.681	0.650	0.621
6	0.942	0.888	0.837	0.790	0.746	0.705	0.666	0.630	0.596	0.564
7	0.933	0.871	0.813	0.760	0.711	0.665	0.623	0.583	0.547	0.513
8	0.923	0.853	0.789	0.731	0.677	0.627	0.582	0.540	0.502	0.467
9	0.914	0.837	0.766	0.703	0.645	0.592	0.544	0.500	0.460	0.424
10	0.905	0.820	0.744	0.676	0.614	0.558	0.508	0.463	0.422	0.386
11	0.896	0.804	0.722	0.650	0.585	0.527	0.475	0.429	0.388	0.350
12	0.887	0.788	0.701	0.625	0.557	0.497	0.444	0.397	0.356	0.319
13	0.879	0.773	0.681	0.601	0.530	0.469	0.415	0.368	0.326	0.290
14	0.870	0.758	0.661	0.577	0.505	0.442	0.388	0.340	0.299	0.263
15	0.861	0.743	0.642	0.555	0.481	0.417	0.362	0.315	0.275	0.239
16	0.853	0.728	0.623	0.534	0.458	0.394	0.339	0.292	0.252	0.218
17	0.844	0.714	0.605	0.513	0.436	0.371	0.317	0.270	0.231	0.198
18	0.836	0.700	0.587	0.494	0.416	0.350	0.296	0.250	0.212	0.180
19	0.828	0.686	0.570	0.475	0.396	0.331	0.277	0.232	0.194	0.164
20	0.820	0.673	0.554	0.456	0.377	0.312	0.258	0.215	0.178	0.149

Periods	Discount rates (r)									
(n)	11%	12%	13%	14%	15%	16%	17%	18%	19%	20%
1	0.901	0.893	0.885	0.877	0.870	0.862	0.855	0.847	0.840	0.833
2	0.812	0.797	0.783	0.769	0.756	0.743	0.731	0.718	0.706	0.694
3	0.731	0.712	0.693	0.675	0.658	0.641	0.624	0.609	0.593	0.579
4	0.659	0.636	0.613	0.592	0.572	0.552	0.534	0.516	0.499	0.482
5	0.593	0.567	0.543	0.519	0.497	0.476	0.456	0.437	0.419	0.402
6	0.535	0.507	0.480	0.456	0.432	0.410	0.390	0.370	0.352	0.335
7	0.482	0.452	0.425	0.400	0.376	0.354	0.333	0.314	0.296	0.279
8	0.434	0.404	0.376	0.351	0.327	0.305	0.285	0.266	0.249	0.233
9	0.391	0.361	0.333	0.308	0.284	0.263	0.243	0.225	0.209	0.194
10	0.352	0.322	0.295	0.270	0.247	0.227	0.208	0.191	0.176	0.162
11	0.317	0.287	0.261	0.237	0.215	0.195	0.178	0.162	0.148	0.135
12	0.286	0.257	0.231	0.208	0.187	0.168	0.152	0.137	0.124	0.112
13	0.258	0.229	0.204	0.182	0.163	0.145	0.130	0.116	0.104	0.093
14	0.232	0.205	0.181	0.160	0.141	0.125	0.111	0.099	0.088	0.078
15	0.209	0.183	0.160	0.140	0.123	0.108	0.095	0.084	0.074	0.065
16	0.188	0.163	0.141	0.123	0.107	0.093	0.081	0.071	0.062	0.054
17	0.170	0.146	0.125	0.108	0.093	0.080	0.069	0.060	0.052	0.045
18	0.153	0.130	0.111	0.095	0.081	0.069	0.059	0.051	0.044	0.038
19	0.138	0.116	0.098	0.083	0.070	0.060	0.051	0.043	0.037	0.031
20	0.124	0.104	0.087	0.073	0.061	0.051	0.043	0.037	0.031	0.026

Cumulative present value table

This table shows the present value of £1 per annum, receivable or payable at the end of each year for *n* years.

Periods (n)	Discount rates (r)									
	1%	2%	3%	4%	5%	6%	7%	8%	9%	10%
1	0.990	0.980	0.971	0.962	0.952	0.943	0.935	0.926	0.917	0.909
2	1.970	1.942	1.913	1.886	1.859	1.833	1.808	1.783	1.759	1.736
3	2.941	2.884	2.829	2.775	2.723	2.673	2.624	2.577	2.531	2.487
4	3.902	3.808	3.717	3.630	3.546	3.465	3.387	3.312	3.240	3.170
5	4.853	4.713	4.580	4.452	4.329	4.212	4.100	3.993	3.890	3.791
6	5.795	5.601	5.417	5.242	5.076	4.917	4.767	4.623	4.486	4.355
7	6.728	6.472	6.230	6.002	5.786	5.582	5.389	5.206	5.033	4.868
8	7.652	7.325	7.020	6.733	6.463	6.210	5.971	5.747	5.535	5.335
9	8.566	8.162	7.786	7.435	7.108	6.802	6.515	6.247	5.995	5.759
10	9.471	8.983	8.530	8.111	7.722	7.360	7.024	6.710	6.418	6.145
11	10.37	9.787	9.253	8.760	8.306	7.887	7.499	7.139	6.805	6.495
12	11.26	10.58	9.954	9.385	8.863	8.384	7.943	7.536	7.161	6.814
13	12.13	11.35	10.63	9.986	9.394	8.853	8.358	7.904	7.487	7.103
14	13.00	12.11	11.30	10.56	9.899	9.295	8.745	8.244	7.786	7.367
15	13.87	12.85	11.94	11.12	10.38	9.712	9.108	8.559	8.061	7.606
16	14.718	13.578	12.561	11.652	10.838	10.106	9.447	8.851	8.313	7.824
17	15.562	14.292	13.166	12.166	11.274	10.477	9.763	9.122	8.544	8.022
18	16.398	14.992	13.754	12.659	11.690	10.828	10.059	9.372	8.756	8.201
19	17.226	15.678	14.324	13.134	12.085	11.158	10.336	9.604	8.950	8.365
20	18.046	16.351	14.877	13.590	12.462	11.470	10.594	9.818	9.129	8.514

Periods (n)	Discount rates (r)									
	11%	12%	13%	14%	15%	16%	17%	18%	19%	20%
1	0.901	0.893	0.885	0.877	0.870	0.862	0.855	0.847	0.840	0.833
2	1.713	1.690	1.668	1.647	1.626	1.605	1.585	1.566	1.547	1.528
3	2.444	2.402	2.361	2.322	2.283	2.246	2.210	2.174	2.140	2.106
4	3.102	3.037	2.974	2.914	2.855	2.798	2.743	2.690	2.639	2.589
5	3.696	3.605	3.517	3.433	3.352	3.274	3.199	3.127	3.058	2.991
6	4.231	4.111	3.998	3.889	3.784	3.685	3.589	3.498	3.410	3.326
7	4.712	4.564	4.423	4.288	4.160	4.039	3.922	3.812	3.706	3.605
8	5.146	4.968	4.799	4.639	4.487	4.344	4.207	4.078	3.954	3.837
9	5.537	5.328	5.132	4.946	4.772	4.607	4.451	4.303	4.163	4.031
10	5.889	5.650	5.426	5.216	5.019	4.833	4.659	4.494	4.339	4.192
11	6.207	5.938	5.687	5.453	5.234	5.029	4.836	4.656	4.486	4.327
12	6.492	6.194	5.918	5.660	5.421	5.197	4.988	4.793	4.611	4.439
13	6.750	6.424	6.122	5.842	5.583	5.342	5.118	4.910	4.715	4.533
14	6.982	6.628	6.302	6.002	5.724	5.468	5.229	5.008	4.802	4.611
15	7.191	6.811	6.462	6.142	5.847	5.575	5.324	5.092	4.876	4.675
16	7.379	6.974	6.604	6.265	5.954	5.668	5.405	5.162	4.938	4.730
17	7.549	7.120	6.729	6.373	6.047	5.749	5.475	5.222	4.990	4.775
18	7.702	7.250	6.840	6.467	6.128	5.818	5.534	5.273	5.033	4.812
19	7.839	7.366	6.938	6.550	6.198	5.877	5.584	5.316	5.070	4.843
20	7.963	7.469	7.025	6.623	6.259	5.929	5.628	5.353	5.101	4.870

Formulae

Annuity

Present value of an annuity of $1 per annum receivable or payable for *n* years, commencing in one year, discounted at *r*% per annum:

$$PV = \frac{1}{r}\left[1 - \frac{1}{[1+r]^n}\right]$$

Perpetuity

Present value of $1 per annum receivable or payable in perpetuity, commencing in one year, discounted at r% per annum:

$$PV = \frac{1}{r}$$

Growing perpetuity

Present value of $1 per annum, receivable or payable, commencing in one year, growing in perpetuity at a constant rate of *g*% per annum, discounted at *r*% per annum:

$$PV = \frac{1}{r - g}$$

EXAM QUESTION AND ANSWER BANK

What the examiner means

The very important table below has been prepared by CIMA to help you interpret exam questions.

Learning objectives	Verbs used	Definition
1 Knowledge What are you expected to know	• List • State • Define	• Make a list of • Express, fully or clearly, the details of/facts of • Give the exact meaning of
2 Comprehension What you are expected to understand	• Describe • Distinguish • Explain • Identify • Illustrate	• Communicate the key features of • Highlight the differences between • Make clear or intelligible/state the meaning of • Recognise, establish or select after consideration • Use an example to describe or explain something
3 Application How you are expected to apply your knowledge	• Apply • Calculate/compute • Demonstrate • Prepare • Reconcile • Solve • Tabulate	• Put to practical use • Ascertain or reckon mathematically • Prove with certainty or to exhibit by practical means • Make or get ready for use • Make or prove consistent/compatible • Find an answer to • Arrange in a table
4 Analysis How you are expected to analyse the detail of what you have learned	• Analyse • Categorise • Compare and contrast • Construct • Discuss • Interpret • Prioritise • Produce	• Examine in detail the structure of • Place into a defined class or division • Show the similarities and/or differences between • Build up or compile • Examine in detail by argument • Translate into intelligible or familiar terms • Place in order of priority or sequence for action • Create or bring into existence
5 Evaluation How you are expected to use your learning to evaluate, make decisions or recommendations	• Advise • Evaluate • Recommend	• Counsel, inform or notify • Appraise or assess the value of • Propose a course of action

Guidance in our Practice and Revision Kit focuses on how the verbs are used in questions.

1 JKA   18 mins

Learning outcome: B1

JKA entered into the following transactions in the year ended 31 May 20X3:

1   JKA held a portfolio of trade receivables with a carrying amount of $4 million at 31 May 20X3. At that date, the entity entered into a factoring agreement with a bank, whereby it transfers the receivables in exchange for $3.6 million in cash. JKA has agreed to reimburse the factor for any shortfall between the amount collected and $3.6 million. Once the receivables have been collected, any amounts above $3.6 million, less interest on this amount, will be repaid to JKA. JKA has derecognised the receivables and charged $0.4 million as a loss to profit or loss.

2   On 31 May 20X3, JKA sold a piece of land to DEX Finance for $500,000 when the carrying value of the land was $520,000 (the original cost of the asset). Under the terms of the sale agreement JKA has the option to repurchase the land within the next three years for between $560,000 and $600,000 depending on the date of the repurchase. The land must be repurchased for $600,000 at the end of the three year period if the option is not exercised before that time. JKA has derecognised the land and recorded the subsequent loss within profit for the year ended 31 May 20X3.

Required

(a)   **Explain** how the transfer of the receivables and the sale of the land should be accounted for in accordance with principles of the *Framework for Preparation and Presentation of Financial Statements*.   **(6 marks)**

(b)   **Prepare** any journal entries required to correct the accounting treatment for the year to 31 May 20X3.   **(4 marks)**

(Total: 10 marks)

2 Amps   18 mins

Learning outcome: B1

Amps is a highly acquisitive company operating in the leisure industry. In order to finance acquisitions, the company has issued a number of financial instruments, both debt and equity, the details of which are given below.

(a) $1 million redeemable bonds were issued on 1 January 20X0, redeemable ten years later for the same amount. The interest rate attached to the bonds is 4% for years 1 to 3, 7% for years 4 to 7 and 10% for the final period. This gives a constant rate of return of 7½%.

Amps has accounted for 20X0 interest by charging $40,000 to the statement of profit or loss and other comprehensive income.

(b)   Also during 20X0, the company issued $2m convertible debentures carrying interest at 7%. The debentures are convertible into ordinary shares in December 20X1 at the option of the holders.

Amps believe the conversion rights will be exercised and as a result has treated the debentures as part of equity. The annual return to the holders has been treated as a distribution.

Required

Explain how the above matters should be dealt with in the financial statements of Amps for the year ending 31 December 20X0.   **(10 marks)**

3 Radost

22 mins

Learning outcome: B1

Radost Co is a company employing 2,500 staff.

Radost has a defined benefit pension plan for its staff. Staff are eligible for an annual pension between the date of their retirement and the date of their death equal to:

$$\text{Annual pension} = \frac{\text{Final salary pe year}}{50} \times \text{years' service}$$

You are given the following data relating to the year ended 31 December 20X3:

(a)   Yield on high quality corporate bonds: 10% pa.

(b)   Contributions paid by Radost to pension plan: $12 million

(c)   Pensions paid to former employees: $8 million

(d)   Current service cost was $3.75 million

(e)   After consultation with employees, an amendment was agreed to the terms of the plan, reducing the benefits payable. The amendment takes effect from 31 December 20X3 and the actuary has calculated that the resulting reduction in the pension obligation is $6 million.

(f)   NPV of the pension obligation at:

1.1.X3 – $45 million

31.12.X3 – $44 million (as given by the actuary, after adjusting for the plan amendment)

(g)   Fair value of the plan assets, as valued by the actuary:

1.1.X3 – $52 million

31.12.X3 – $64.17 million

Required

(a)   **Prepare** the notes to the statement of financial position and statement of profit or loss and other comprehensive income in accordance with IAS 19.   **(8 marks)**

(b)   **Explain** why the pension plan assets are recognised in the financial statements of Radost, even though they are held in a separate legal trust for Radost's employees.   **(4 marks)**

(Total: 12 marks)

Notes.

(i)   Work to the nearest $1,000 throughout.

(ii)   You should assume contributions and benefits were paid on the last day of the accounting period.

4 Share-based payment   18 mins

Learning outcome: A1

J&B granted 200 options on its $1 ordinary shares to each of its 800 employees on 1 January 20X1. Each grant is conditional upon the employee being employed by J&B until 31 December 20X3.

J&B estimated at 1 January 20X1 that:

(i)   The fair value of each option was $4 (before adjustment for the possibility of forfeiture).

(ii)   Approximately 50 employees would leave during 20X1, 40 during 20X2 and 30 during 20X3 thereby forfeiting their rights to receive the options. The departures were expected to be evenly spread within each year.

The exercise price of the options was $1.50 and the market value of a J&B share on 1 January 20X1 was $3.

In the event, only 40 employees left during 20X1 (and the estimate of total departures was revised down to 95 at 31 December 20X1), 20 during 20X2 (and the estimate of total departures was revised to 70 at 31 December 20X2) and none during 20X3, spread evenly during each year.

Required

The directors of J&B have asked you to illustrate how the scheme is accounted for under IFRS 2 *Share-based Payment*.

(a)   **Prepare** the double entries for the charge to profit or loss for employee services over the three years and for the share issue, assuming all employees entitled to benefit from the scheme exercised their rights and the shares were issued on 31 December 20X3.   **(7 marks)**

(b)   **Explain** how your solution would differ had J&B offered its employees cash based options on the share value rather than share options.   **(3 marks)**

                                                                                        (Total: 10 marks)

5 KPG Bank   18 mins

Learning outcome: B1

KPG Bank is assessing the loan application of a foreign entity, ABC. ABC operates in a country which suffers from high inflation. KPG Bank is worried that the historic cost financial statements do not give a true reflection of ABC's financial performance and position in times of rising prices. The credit department of KPG Bank has heard of the term 'current purchasing power' and is aware that if adopted, non-monetary items will have to be restated in the statement of financial position using the General Prices Index, monetary items will not have to be adjusted but a holding gain or loss is calculated on these monetary items. However, they are unsure what this means exactly and why it is necessary.

Required

(a)   **Explain** why non-monetary items are restated and monetary items are not restated under the current purchasing power method of accounting and what is meant by 'holding gain or loss on monetary items'.   **(4 marks)**

(b)   **Identify** two advantages of adopting the current purchasing power method of accounting compared to historic cost accounting in times of rising prices.   **(2 marks)**

(c)   **Describe** an alternative method of accounting that could be adopted in times of rising prices.
                                                                                        (4 marks)

                                                                                        (Total: 10 marks)

6 Group financial statements   18 mins

Learning outcome: A1

In many countries, companies with subsidiaries have been required to publish group financial statements, usually in the form of consolidated financial statements. You are required to **state** why you feel the preparation of group financial statements is necessary and to **outline** their limitations, if any.

(10 marks)

7 Putney and Wandsworth   18 mins

Learning outcome: A1

Putney acquired 90% of the share capital of Wandsworth on 1 January 20X1 when Wandsworth's retained earnings stood at $10,000 and there was no balance on the revaluation surplus.

Their respective statements of financial position as at 31 December 20X5 are as follows.

	Putney $	Wandsworth $
Non-current assets		
Property, plant & equipment	135,000	60,000
Investment in Wandsworth	25,000	–
	160,000	60,000
Current assets	62,000	46,000
	222,000	106,000
Equity		
Share capital ($1 ordinary shares)	50,000	15,000
Revaluation surplus	50,000	15,000
Retained earnings	90,000	50,000
	190,000	80,000
Non-current liabilities	14,000	12,000
Current liabilities	18,000	14,000
	222,000	106,000

The group policy is to measure non-controlling interests at acquisition at their proportionate share of the fair value of the identifiable net assets. Impairment losses on goodwill to date have amounted to $1,250.

Required

Prepare the consolidated statement of financial position of Putney and its subsidiary as at 31 December 20X5.

(10 marks)

8 Balmes and Aribau   **18 mins**

Learning outcome: A1

Balmes Balmes acquired 80% of Aribau's ordinary share capital on 1 July 20X1 for $28.5 million. The balance on Aribau's retained earnings at that date was $24m and $2m on the general reserve.

Their respective statements of financial position as at 30 June 20X3 are as follows.

	Balmes	*Aribau*
	$'000	*$'000*
Non-current assets		
Property, plant & equipment	97,300	34,400
Intangible assets	5,100	1,200
Investment in Aribau (note 1)	35,500	–
	137,900	35,600
Current assets		
Inventories	43,400	14,300
Trade and other receivables	36,800	17,400
Cash and cash equivalents	700	-
	80,900	31,700
	218,800	67,300
Equity		
Share capital ($1 ordinary shares)	50,000	5,000
General reserve	4,300	3,000
Retained earnings	118,800	37,100
	173,100	45,100
Non-current liabilities		
Loan notes	10,000	4,000
Current liabilities		
Trade payables	28,400	15,700
Income tax payable	7,300	2,400
Bank overdraft	-	100
	35,700	18,200
	218,800	67,300

Additional information

(a)   Balmes' investment in Aribau has been classified as available for sale and is held at fair value. The gains earned on it have been recorded within the retained earnings of Balmes.

(b)   At the date of acquisition, Aribau's property, plant and equipment included land and buildings at a carrying value of $12.5m (of which $4.5m related to the land). The fair value of the land and buildings was $14m (of which $5m related to the land). The buildings had an average remaining useful life of 20 years at that date.

(c)   The group policy is to value non-controlling interests at acquisition at fair value. The fair value of the non-controlling interests in Aribau on 1 July 20X1 was $7 million.

(d)   During June 20X3, Balmes conducted an impairment review of its investment in Aribau in the consolidated financial statements. This revealed impairment losses relating to recognised goodwill of $200,000. No impairment losses had previously been recognised.

Required

Prepare the consolidated statement of financial position for the Balmes Group as at 30 June 20X3.

(10 marks)

9 Reprise   25 mins

Learning outcome: A1

Reprise purchased 75% of Encore for $2,000,000 10 years ago when the balance on its retained earnings was $1,044,000. The statements of financial position of the two companies as at 31 March 20X4 are as follows:

	Reprise $'000	Encore $'000
Non-current assets		
Investment in Encore	2,000	–
Land and buildings	3,350	–
Plant and equipment	1,010	2,210
Motor vehicles	510	345
	6,870	2,555
Current assets		
Inventories	890	352
Trade receivables	1,372	514
Cash and cash equivalents	89	51
	2,351	917
	9,221	3,472
Equity		
Share capital - $1 ordinary shares	1,000	500
Retained earnings	4,225	2,610
Revaluation surplus	2,500	–
	7,725	3,110
Non-current liabilities		
10% debentures	500	–
Current liabilities		
Trade payables	996	362
	9,221	3,472

The following additional information is available:

(a)   Included in trade receivables of Reprise are amounts owed by Encore of $75,000. The current accounts do not at present balance due to a payment for $39,000 being in transit at the year end from Encore.

(b)   Included in the inventories of Encore are items purchased from Reprise during the year for $31,200. Reprise marks up its goods by 30% to achieve its selling price.

(c) $180,000 of the recognised goodwill arising is to be written off due to impairment losses.

(d)   Encore shares were trading at $4.40 just prior to acquisition by Reprise.

Required

Prepare the consolidated statement of financial position for the Reprise group of companies as at 31 March 20X4. It is the group policy to value the non-controlling interests at fair value at acquisition.

(14 marks)

10 Fallowfield and Rusholme   22 mins

Learning outcome: A1

Fallowfield acquired a 60% holding in Rusholme three years ago when Rusholme's equity was $56,000 (share capital $40,000 plus reserves $16,000). Both businesses have been very successful since the acquisition and their respective statements of profit or loss and other comprehensive income for the year ended 30 June 20X8 and extracts from their statements of changes in equity are shown below.

	Fallowfield $	Rusholme $
Revenue	403,400	193,000
Cost of sales	(201,400)	(92,600)
Gross profit	202,000	100,400
Distribution costs	(16,000)	(14,600)
Administrative expenses	(24,250)	(17,800)
Dividends from Rusholme	15,000	
Profit before tax	176,750	68,000
Income tax expense	(61,750)	(22,000)
Profit for the year	115,000	46,000
Other comprehensive income (net of tax)	20,000	5,000
Total comprehensive income	135,000	51,000

STATEMENT OF CHANGES IN EQUITY (EXTRACT)

	Fallowfield Total equity $	Rusholme Total equity $
Balance at 30 June 20X7	243,000	101,000
Total comprehensive income for the year	135,000	51,000
Dividends	(40,000)	(25,000)
Balance at 30 June 20X8	338,000	127,000

Additional information

(a)   During the year Rusholme sold some goods to Fallowfield for $40,000, including 25% mark-up. Half of these items were still in inventories at the year-end.

(b)   Group policy is to measure non-controlling interests at acquisition at fair value. The fair value of Rusholme's non-controlling interest at acquisition was $30,000. There has been no impairment in goodwill since acquisition.

Required

Prepare the consolidated statement of profit or loss and other comprehensive income and statement of changes in equity (showing parent and non-controlling interest shares) of Fallowfield Co and its subsidiary for the year ended 30 June 20X8.   **(12 marks)**

11 Panther Group **27 mins**

Learning outcome: A1

Panther operated as a single company, but in 20X4 decided to expand its operations. On 1 July 20X4, Panther paid $2,000,000 to acquire a 60% interest in Sabre, a company to which Panther had advanced a loan of $800,000 at an interest rate of 5% on 1 January 20X4.

The statements of profit or loss and other comprehensive income of Panther and Sabre for the year ended 31 December 20X4 are as follows:

	Panther	Sabre
	$'000	$'000
Revenue	22,800	4,300
Cost of sales	(13,600)	(2,600)
Gross profit	9,200	1,700
Distribution costs	(2,900)	(500)
Administrative expenses	(1,800)	(300)
Finance costs	(200)	(40)
Finance income	50	–
Profit before tax	4,350	860
Income tax expense	(1,300)	(220)
Profit for the year	3,050	640
Other comprehensive income for the year, net of tax	1,600	180
Total comprehensive income for the year	4,650	820

Since acquisition, Sabre purchased $320,000 of goods from Panther. Of these, $60,000 remained in inventories at the year end. Sabre makes a mark-up on cost of 20% under the transfer pricing agreement between the two companies. The fair value of the identifiable net assets of Sabre on purchase were $200,000 greater than their book value. The difference relates to properties with a remaining useful life of 20 years.

Statement of changes in equity (extracts) for the two companies:

	Panther Reserves	Sabre Reserves
	$'000	$'000
Balance at 1 January 20X4	12,750	2,480
Dividend paid	(900)	–
Total comprehensive income for the year	4,650	820
Balance at 31 December 20X4	16,500	3,300

Panther and Sabre had $400,000 and $150,000 of share capital in issue throughout the period respectively.

Required

Prepare the consolidated statement of profit or loss and other comprehensive income and statement of changes in equity (extract for reserves) for the Panther Group for the year ended 31 December 20X4.

No adjustments for impairment losses were necessary in the group financial statements.

Assume income and expenses (other than intragroup items) accrue evenly. **(15 marks)**

12 Hever   **36 mins**

Learning outcome: A1

Hever has held shares in two companies, Spiro and Aldridge, for a number of years. As at 31 December 20X4 they have the following statements of financial position:

	Hever $'000	Spiro $'000	Aldridge $'000
Non-current assets			
Property, plant & equipment	370	190	260
Investments	218	–	–
	588	190	260
Current assets			
Inventories	160	100	180
Trade receivables	170	90	100
Cash	50	40	10
	380	230	290
	968	420	550
Equity			
Share capital ($1 ords)	200	80	50
Share premium	100	80	30
Retained earnings	568	200	400
	868	360	480
Current liabilities			
Trade payables	100	60	70
	968	420	550

You ascertain the following additional information:

(a)   The 'investments' in the statement of financial position comprise solely Hever's investment in Spiro ($128,000) and in Aldridge ($90,000).

(b)   The 48,000 shares in Spiro were acquired when Spiro's retained earnings balance stood at $20,000.

The 15,000 shares in Aldridge were acquired when that company had a retained earnings balance of $150,000.

(c)   When Hever acquired its shares in Spiro the fair value of Spiro's net assets equalled their book values with the following exceptions:

	$'000
Property, plant and equipment	50 higher
Inventories	20 lower (sold during 20X4)

Depreciation arising on the fair value adjustment to non-current assets since this date is $5,000.

(d)   During the year, Hever sold inventories to Spiro for $16,000, which originally cost Hever $10,000. Three-quarters of these inventories have subsequently been sold by Spiro.

(e)   No impairment losses on goodwill had been necessary by 31 December 20X4.

(f)   It is group policy to value non-controlling interests at fair value. The fair value of the non-controlling interests at acquisition was $90,000.

Required

Prepare the consolidated statement of financial position for the Hever group (incorporating the associate).

(20 marks)

13 Armoury

18 mins

Learning outcome: A1

Bayonet, a public limited company, purchased 6m shares in Rifle, a public limited company, on 1 January 20X5 for $10m. Rifle had purchased 4m shares in Pistol, a public limited company for $9m on 31 December 20X2 when its retained earnings stood at $5m. The balances on retained earnings of the acquired companies were $8m and $6.5m respectively at 1 January 20X5. The fair value of the identifiable assets and liabilities of Rifle and Pistol was equivalent to their book values at the acquisition dates.

The statements of financial position of the three companies as at 31 December 20X9 are as follows:

	Bayonet $'000	Rifle $'000	Pistol $'000
Non-current assets			
Property, plant and equipment	14,500	12,140	17,500
Investment in Rifle	10,000		
Investment in Pistol	–	9,000	–
	24,500	21,140	17,500
Current assets			
Inventories	6,300	2,100	450
Trade receivables	4,900	2,000	2,320
Cash	500	1,440	515
	11,700	5,540	3,285
	36,200	26,680	20,785
Equity			
50c ordinary shares	5,000	4,000	2,500
Retained earnings	25,500	20,400	16,300
	30,500	24,400	18,800
Current liabilities	5,700	2,280	1,985
	36,200	26,680	20,785

Group policy is to value non-controlling interests at fair value at acquisition. The fair value of the non-controlling interests in Rifle was calculated as $3,230,000 on 1 January 20X5. The fair value of the 40% non-controlling interests in Pistol on 1 January 20X5 was $4.6m.

Impairment tests in current and previous years did not reveal any impairment losses.

Required

Prepare the consolidated statement of financial position of Bayonet as at 31 December 20X9.

(10 marks)

14 Murder, Mystery and Suspense

32 mins

Learning outcome: A1

On 1 January 20X3 Murder, a public limited company acquired 60% of Mystery, a public limited company.

On 30 July 20X1 Murder acquired 10% of Suspense, a public limited company, and on the same day Mystery acquired 80% of Suspense.

The statements of financial position of the three companies as at 31 December 20X7 are as follows:

	Murder $'m	Mystery $'m	Suspense $'m
Non-current assets			
Property, plant and equipment	2,458	1,410	870
Investment in Mystery	900		
Investment in Suspense	27	240	–
	3,385	1,650	870
Current assets			
Inventories	450	200	260
Trade receivables	610	365	139
Cash	240	95	116
	1,300	660	515
	4,685	2,310	1,385
Equity			
Ordinary share capital	500	200	100
Share premium	250	120	50
Retained earnings	2,805	1,572	850
	3,555	1,892	1,000
Current liabilities			
Trade payables	1,130	418	385
	4,685	2,310	1,385

During the year, Mystery sold goods to Suspense of $260m including a mark-up of 25%. All of these goods remain in inventories at the year end.

The retained earnings of the three companies at the acquisition dates was:

	30.7.X1 $'m	1.1.X3 $'m
Murder	1,610	1,860
Mystery	700	950
Suspense	40	100

The book values of the identifiable net assets at the acquisition date are equivalent to their fair values. The fair value of Murder's 10% holding in Suspense on 1 January 20X3 was $50m.

Murder and Mystery hold their investments in subsidiaries at cost in their separate financial statements. It is group policy to value the non-controlling interests at fair value at acquisition. The directors valued the non-controlling interests in Mystery at $536m and Suspense at $210m on 1 January 20X3.

No impairment losses have been necessary in the consolidated financial statements to date.

Required

Prepare the consolidated statement of financial position of Murder group as at 31 December 20X7.

(18 marks)

15 CVB

45 mins

The statements of financial position for CVB and FG as at 30 September 20X5 are provided below:

	CVB $'000	FG $'000
Non-current assets		
Property, plant and equipment	22,000	5,000
Available for sale investment (note 1)	4,000	–
	26,000	5,000
Current assets		
Inventories	6,200	800
Trade receivables	6,600	1,900
Cash and cash equivalents	1,200	300
	14,000	3,000
Total assets	40,000	8,000
Equity		
Share capital - $1 ordinary shares	20,000	1,000
Retained earnings	7,500	5,000
Other components of equity	500	–
	28,000	6,000
Non-current liabilities		
5% bonds 2013 (note 2)	3,900	–
Current liabilities	8,100	2,000
Total liabilities	12,000	2,000
	40,000	8,000

Additional information

(a) CVB acquired a 15% investment in FG on 1 May 20X3 for $600,000. The investment was classified as available for sale and the gains earned on it have been recorded within 'other components of equity' in CVB's individual financial statements. The fair value of the 15% investment at 1 April 20X5 was $800,000. On 1 April 20X5, CVB acquired an additional 60% of the equity share capital of FG at a cost of $2,900,000. In its own financial statements, CVB has kept its investment in FG as an available for sale financial asset recorded at its fair value of $4,000,000 as at 30 September 20X5.

(b) CVB issued 4 million $1 5% redeemable bonds on 1 October 20X4 at par. The associated costs of issue were $100,000 and the net proceeds of $3.9 million have been recorded within non-current liabilities. The bonds are redeemable at $4.5 million on 30 September 20X8 and the effective interest associated with them is approximately 8.5%. The interest on the bonds is payable annually in arrears. The amount due has been paid in the year to 30 September 20X5 and charged to profit or loss.

(c) An impairment review was conducted at the year end and it was decided that the goodwill on acquisition of FG was impaired by 10%.

(d) It is the group policy to value non-controlling interest at fair value at the date of acquisition. The fair value of the non-controlling interest at 1 April 20X5 was $1.25 million.

(e) The profit of FG for the year was $3 million, and the profits were assumed to accrue evenly throughout the year.

(f) FG sold goods to CVB for $400,000. Half of these goods remained in inventories at 30 September 20X5. FG makes a 20% margin on all sales.

(g) No dividends were paid by either entity in the year to 30 September 20X5.

Required

(a)   **Explain** how the investment in FG should be accounted for in the consolidated financial statements of CVB following the acquisition of the additional 60%.   **(5 marks)**

(b)   **Prepare** the consolidated statement of financial position as at 30 September 20X5 for the CVB Group.   **(20 marks)**

(Total: 25 marks)

16   Holmes and Deakin   31 mins

Learning outcome: A1

Holmes Co has owned 85% of the ordinary share capital of Deakin Co for some years. The shares were bought for $255,000 and Deakin Co's reserves at the time of purchase were $20,000. The group policy is to value non-controlling interests at fair value at the date of acquisition. The fair value of the non-controlling interests in Deakin at acquisition was $45,000.

On 28.2.X3 Holmes Co sold 40,000 of the Deakin shares for $160,000. The only entry made in respect of this transaction has been the receipt of the cash, which was credited to the 'investment in subsidiary' account. No dividends were paid by either entity in the period.

The following draft summarised financial statements are available.

STATEMENTS OF PROFIT OR LOSS AND OTHER COMPREHENSIVE INCOME FOR THE YEAR TO 31 MAY 20X3

	Holmes Co $'000	Deakin Co $'000
Revenue	1,000	540
Cost of sales and operating expenses	(800)	(430)
Profit before tax	200	110
Income tax expense	(90)	(60)
Profit for the year	110	50
Other comprehensive income (net of tax)	20	10
Total comprehensive income for the year	130	60

STATEMENTS OF FINANCIAL POSITION AS AT 31 May 20X3

	$'000	$'000
Non-current assets		
Property, plant and equipment (NBV)	535	178
Investment in Deakin Co	95	–
	630	178
Current assets		
Inventories	320	190
Trade receivables	250	175
Cash	80	89
	650	454
	1,280	632
Equity		
Share capital ($1 ordinary shares)	500	200
Reserves	310	170
	810	370

Current liabilities

Trade payables	295	171
Income tax payable	80	60
Provisions	95	31
	470	262
	1,280	632

No impairment losses have been necessary in the group financial statements to date.

Assume that the capital gain will be subject to corporate income tax at 30%.

Required

Prepare:

(a)   The consolidated statement of profit or loss and other comprehensive income for Holmes for the year to 31 May 20X3   **(6 marks)**

(b)   A consolidated statement of financial position as at 31 May 20X3; and   **(9 marks)**

(c)   A consolidated statement of changes in equity extract (attributable to owners of the parent *only*) for the year ended 31 May 20X3.   **(2 marks)**

(Total: 17 marks)

17   Harvard   32 mins

Learning outcome: A1

The draft financial statements of Harvard and its subsidiary, Krakow sp. z o.o. are set out below.

STATEMENTS OF FINANCIAL POSITION AT 31 DECEMBER 20X5	Harvard $ '000	Krakow PLN '000
Non-current assets		
Property, plant and equipment	2,870	4,860
Investment in Krakow	840	–
	3,710	4,860
Current assets		
Inventories	1,990	8,316
Trade receivables	1,630	4,572
Cash	240	2,016
	3,860	14,904
	7,570	19,764
Equity		
Share capital ($1/PLN1)	118	1,348
Retained reserves	502	14,060
	620	15,408
Non-current liabilities		
Loans	1,920	–
Current liabilities		
Trade payables	5,030	4,356
	7,570	19,764

STATEMENTS OF PROFIT OR LOSS AND OTHER COMPREHENSIVE INCOME FOR THE YEAR
ENDED 31 DECEMBER 20X5

Revenue	40,425	97,125
Cost of sales	(35,500)	(77,550)
Gross profit	4,925	19,575
Distribution and administrative expenses	(4,400)	(5,850)
Investment income	720	–
Profit before tax	1,245	13,725
Income tax expense	(300)	(4,725)
Profit/total comprehensive income for the year	945	9,000
Dividends paid during the period	700	3,744

The following additional information is given:

(a)   Exchange rates

	Zloty (PLN) to *$*
31 December 20X2	4.40
31 December 20X3	4.16
31 December 20X4	4.00
15 May 20X5	3.90
31 December 20X5	3.60
Average for 20X5	3.75

(b)   Harvard acquired 1,011,000 shares in Krakow for $840,000 on 31 December 20X2 when
Krakow's retained earnings stood at PLN 2,876,000. Krakow operates as an autonomous
subsidiary. Its functional currency is the Polish zloty.

The fair value of the identifiable net assets of Krakow were equivalent to their book values at the
acquisition date. Group policy is to measure non-controlling interests at acquisition at their
proportionate share of the fair value of the identifiable net assets.

(c)   Krakow paid an interim dividend of PLN 3,744,000 on 15 May 20X5. No other dividends were
paid or declared by Krakow in the period.

(d)   No impairment losses were necessary in the consolidated financial statements by 31 December
20X5.

Required

(a)   **Prepare** the consolidated statement of financial position at 31 December 20X5.   **(6 marks)**

(b)   **Prepare** the consolidated statement of profit or loss and other comprehensive income and
statement of changes in equity (attributable to owners of the parent *only*) for the year ended 31
December 20X5.   **(12 marks)**

(Total = 18 marks)

18 AH Group   45 mins

Learning outcome: A1

Extracts from the consolidated financial statements of the AH group for the year ended 30 June 20X5 are given below.

AH GROUP CONSOLIDATED STATEMENT OF PROFIT OR LOSS FOR THE YEAR
ENDED 30 JUNE 20X5

	20X5
	$'000
Revenue	85,000
Cost of sales	59,750
Gross profit	25,250
Operating expenses	5,650
Finance cost	1,400
Disposal of property (note 2)	1,250
Profit before tax	19,450
Income tax	6,250
Profit/total comprehensive income for the year for the year	13,200
Profit/total comprehensive income attributable to:	
Owners of the parent	12,545
Non-controlling interest	655
	13,200

AH GROUP: EXTRACTS FROM STATEMENT OF CHANGES IN EQUITY FOR THE YEAR
ENDED 30 JUNE 20X5

	Share capital $'000	Share premium $'000	Consolidated retained earnings $'000
Opening balance	18,000	10,000	18,340
Issue of share capital	2,000	2,000	
Profit for year			12,545
Dividends			(6,000)
Closing balance	20,000	12,000	24,885

AH GROUP STATEMENT OF FINANCIAL POSITION AT 30 JUNE 20X5

	20X5 $'000	20X5 $'000	20X4 $'000	20X4 $'000
ASSETS				
Non current assets				
Property, plant and equipment	50,600		44,050	
Intangible assets (note 3)	6,410		4,160	
		57,010		48,210
Current assets				
Inventories	33,500		28,750	
Trade receivables	27,130		26,300	
Cash	1,870		3,900	
		62,500		58,950
		119,510		107,160
EQUITY AND LIABILITIES				
Equity				
Share capital	20,000		18,000	
Share premium	12,000		10,000	
Consolidated retained earnings	24,885		18,340	
		56,885		46,340
Non-controlling interest		3,625		1,920
Non current liabilities				
Interest-bearing borrowings		18,200		19,200

	20X5		20X4	
	$'000	$'000	$'000	$'000
Current liabilities				
Trade payables	33,340		32,810	
Interest payable	1,360		1,440	
Tax	6,100		5,450	
		40,800		39,700
		119,510		107,160

Notes

(a) Several years ago, AH acquired 80% of the issued ordinary shares of its subsidiary, BI. On 1 January 20X5, AH acquired 75% of the issued ordinary shares of CJ in exchange for a fresh issue of 2 million of its own $1 ordinary shares (issued at a premium of $1 each) and $2 million in cash. The net assets of CJ at the date of acquisition were assessed as having the following fair values.

	$'000
Property, plant and equipment	4,200
Inventories	1,650
Receivables	1,300
Cash	50
Trade payables	(1,950)
Tax	(250)
	5,000

(b) During the year, AH disposed of a non-current asset of property for proceeds of $2,250,000. The carrying value of the asset at the date of disposal was $1,000,000. There were no other disposals of non-current assets. Depreciation of $7,950,000 was charged against consolidated profits for the year.

(c) Intangible assets comprise goodwill on acquisition of BI and CJ (20X4: BI only). Goodwill has remained unimpaired since acquisition. Group policy is to measure non-controlling interests at acquisition at their proportionate share of the fair value of the identifiable net assets.

Required

Prepare the consolidated statement of cash flows of the AH Group for the financial year ended 30 June 20X5 in the form required by IAS 7 *Statement of cash flows*, and using the indirect method. Notes to the statement of cash flows are **not** required, but full workings should be shown.

(25 marks)

19 DM   **45 mins**

DM, a listed entity, has just published its financial statements for the year ended 31 December 20X4. DM operates a chain of 42 supermarkets in one of the six major provinces of its country of operation. During 20X4, there has been speculation in the financial press that the entity was likely to be a takeover target for one of the larger national chains of supermarkets that is currently under-represented in DM's province. A recent newspaper report has suggested that DM's directors are unlikely to resist a takeover. The six board members are all nearing retirement, and all own significant non-controlling shareholdings in the business.

You have been approached by a private shareholder in DM. She is concerned that the directors have a conflict of interests and that the financial statements for 20X4 may have been manipulated.

The statement of profit or loss and other comprehensive income and summarised statement of changes in equity of DM, with comparatives, for the year ended 31 December 20X4, and a statement of financial position with comparatives at that date are as follows:

DM STATEMENT OF PROFIT OR LOSS AND OTHER COMPREHENSIVE INCOME FOR THE YEAR ENDED 31 DECEMBER 20X4

	20X4 $m	20X3 $m
Revenue, net of sales tax	1,255	1,220
Cost of sales	(1,177)	(1,145)
Gross profit	78	75
Operating expenses	(21)	(29)
Finance cost	(10)	(10)
Profit before tax	47	36
Income tax expense	(14)	(13)
Profit/total comprehensive income for the year	33	23

DM SUMMARISED STATEMENT OF CHANGES IN EQUITY FOR THE YEAR ENDED 31 DECEMBER 20X4

	20X4 $m	20X3 $m
Opening balance	276	261
Profit/total comprehensive income for the year	33	23
Dividends	(8)	(8)
Closing balance	301	276

DM STATEMENT OF FINANCIAL POSITION AT 31 DECEMBER 20X4

	20X4 $m	20X4 $m	20X3 $m	20X3 $m
Non-current assets				
Property, plant and equipment	580		575	
Goodwill	100		100	
		680		675
Current assets				
Inventories	47		46	
Trade receivables	12		13	
Cash	46		12	
		105		71
		785		746
Equity				
Share capital	150		150	
Retained earnings	151		126	
		301		276
Non-current liabilities				
Interest-bearing borrowings	142		140	
Deferred tax	25		21	
		167		161
Current liabilities				
Trade and other payables	297		273	
Short-term borrowings	20		36	
		317		309
		785		746

Notes

(a) DM's directors have undertaken a reassessment of the useful lives of property, plant and equipment during the year. In most cases, they estimate that the useful lives have increased and the depreciation charges in 20X4 have been adjusted accordingly.

(b) Six new stores have been opened during 20X4, bringing the total to 42.

(c) Four key ratios for the supermarket sector (based on the latest available financial statements of twelve listed entities in the sector) are as follows:

    (i) Annual sales per store: $27.6m

    (ii) Gross profit margin: 5.9%

        (iii)   Net profit margin: 3.9%

        (iv)   Non-current asset turnover (including both tangible and intangible non-current assets): 1.93

Required

(a)   **Prepare** a report, addressed to the investor, analysing the performance and position of DM based on the financial statements and supplementary information provided above. The report should also include comparisons with the key sector ratios, and it should address the investor's concerns about the possible manipulation of the 20X4 financial statements.   **(20 marks)**

(b)   **Explain** the limitations of the use of sector comparatives in financial analysis.   **(5 marks)**

                                                                            (Total: 25 marks)

20   Pilum   25 mins

Learning outcome: C1

A statement showing the retained profit of Pilum Co for the year ended 31 December 20X4 is set out below.

	$	$
Profit before tax		2,530,000
Income tax expense		(1,127,000)
		1,403,000
Transfer to reserves		(230,000)
Dividends paid in the period:		
Preference share dividends	276,000	
Ordinary share dividends	414,000	
		(690,000)
Retained profit		483,000

On 1 January 20X4 the issued share capital of Pilum Co was 4,600,000 6% irredeemable non-cumulative preference shares of $1 each and 4,120,000 ordinary shares of $1 each.

Required

Calculate the earnings per share (on basic and diluted basis) in respect of the year ended 31 December 20X4 for each of the following circumstances. (Each of the three circumstances (a) to (c) is to be dealt with separately.)

(a)   On the basis that there was no change in the issued share capital of the company during the year ended 31 December 20X4.   **(3 marks)**

(b)   On the basis that the company made a rights issue of $1 ordinary shares on 1 October 20X4 in the proportion of 1 for every 5 shares held, at a price of $1.20. The market price for the shares at close of trade on the last day of quotation cum rights was $1.78 per share.   **(5 marks)**

(c)   On the basis that the company made no new issue of shares during the year ended 31 December 20X4 but on 1 January 20X4 issued $1,500,000 5% convertible loan stock with a five year term. The liability component of the loan stock at 1 January 20X4 was calculated as $1,320,975 using an effective interest rate of 8%. The loan stock may be converted into $1 ordinary shares as follows:

    20X5 90 $1 shares for $100 nominal value loan stock

    20X6 85 $1 shares for $100 nominal value loan stock

    20X7 80 $1 shares for $100 nominal value loan stock

    20X8 75 $1 shares for $100 nominal value loan stock   **(6 marks)**

Assume where appropriate that the income tax rate is 30%.

                                                                            (Total = 14 marks)

21 STV

45 mins

Learning outcome: C1

One of your colleagues has recently inherited investments in several listed entities and she frequently asks for your advice on accounting issues. She has recently received the consolidated financial statements of STV, an entity that provides haulage and freight services in several countries. She has noticed that note 3 to the financial statements is headed 'Segment information'.

Note 3 explains that STV's primary segment reporting format is business segments of which there are three: in addition to road and air freight, the entity provides secure transportation services for smaller items of high value. STV's *Operating and Financial Review* provides further background information: the secure transport services segment was established only three years ago. This new operation required a sizeable investment in infrastructure which was principally funded through borrowing. However, the segment has experienced rapid revenue growth in that time, and has become a significant competitor in the industry sector.

Extracts from STV's segment report for the year ended 31 August 20X5 are as follows.

	Road haulage		Air freight		Secure transport		Group	
	20X5	20X4	20X5	20X4	20X5	20X4	20X5	20X4
	$m	$m	$m	$m	$m	$m	$m	$m
Revenue	653	642	208	199	98	63	959	904
Segment result	169	168	68	62	6	(16)	243	214
Unallocated corporate expenses							(35)	(37)
Operating profit							208	177
Interest expense							(22)	(21)
Share of profits of associates	16	12					16	12
Profit before tax							202	168
Income tax							(65)	(49)
Profit							137	119
Other information								
Segment assets	805	796	306	287	437	422	1,548	1,505
Investment in equity method associates	85	84					85	84
Unallocated corporate assets							573	522
Consolidated total assets							2,206	2,111
Segment liabilities	345	349	176	178	197	184	718	711
Unallocated corporate liabilities							37	12
Consolidated total liabilities							755	723

Your colleague finds several aspects of this note confusing:

'I thought I'd understood what you told me about consolidated financial statements; the idea of aggregating several pieces of information to provide an overall view of the activities of the group makes sense. But the segment report seems to be trying to disaggregate the information all over again. What is the point of doing this? Does this information actually tell me anything useful about STV? I know from talking to you previously that financial information does not always tell us everything we need to know. So, what are the limitations in this statement?'

Required

(a) **Explain** the reasons for including disaggregated information about business segments in the notes to the consolidated financial statements. **(5 marks)**

(b) **Analyse** and **interpret** STV's segment disclosures for the benefit of your colleague, explaining findings in a brief report. **(12 marks)**

(c) **Explain** the general limitations of segment reporting, illustrating your answer where applicable with references to STV's segment report. **(8 marks)**

(Total = 25 marks)

22 Current Issues   36 mins

Learning outcome: D1

You are the management accountant of Clean, an entity listed in a country that permits enterprises to publish financial statements in accordance with International Financial Reporting Standards. Clean is considering seeking a listing on a US stock exchange in the near future. Your chief executive officer takes a keen interest in financial reporting but he is not a professionally-qualified accountant. He has recently sent you a memorandum that contains three issues relating to current financial reporting practice.

Issue (a)

I am concerned that Clean's financial statements will have to be converted from IFRS to US GAAP for the purposes of consolidation if Clean is acquired by the US quoted entity.   However, I have heard that a convergence process between IFRS and US GAAP is underway. Please could you outline the progress of this convergence to date and give some examples of remaining differences between IFRS and US GAAP.

Issue (b)

My political contacts tell me that government ministers are very interested in extending the practice of environment reporting. What exactly does 'environmental reporting' mean and to what extent is it mandatory? Why does there seem to be a trend towards greater environmental reporting? You don't need to go into massive detail, just give me an outline of what is involved.

Issue (c)

One of the phrases I often hear is 'our employees are our most important asset'. I largely agree with this sentiment, but if it is true, then surely this should be reflected in some way on the statement of financial position. I do not recall seeing such an asset in previous statements of financial position and would be most grateful for your advice.

Required

Draft a memorandum in response to the issues the Chief Executive Officer has raised. You should refer to the provisions of International Financial Reporting Standards and any other relevant guidance that you consider to be of assistance in supporting your reply.

The allocation of marks is: (a)   **(8 marks)**
                            (b)   **(6 marks)**
                            (c)   **(6 marks)**

                                                                     (Total = 20 marks)

1 JKA

(a) **Factoring of receivables**

The *Framework* principles include a requirement that financial statements should reflect the substance of transactions. To determine whether the trade receivables should be recognised in JKA's or the factor's financial statements, it needs to be established which entity has the risks and benefits associated with the receivables, ie. which can demonstrate that they meet the *Framework*'s definition of an asset.

JKA retains the bad debt risk of the receivables because JKA has to reimburse the factor for any shortfall between the amounts collected and the $3.6 million transferred by the factor to JKA. JKA also has slow movement risk as under the terms of the agreement, JKA pays interest to the factor on outstanding balances.

JKA also retains some of the benefits associated with the $4 million receivables as the factor has to pay JKA any amounts received in excess of $3.6 million less any interest.

Therefore, JKA should not have derecognised the $4 million receivables and recorded a loss of $0.4 million in profit or loss. As they retain the most significant risks and benefits associated with the trade receivables, they need to reinstate the $4 million receivables in their statement of financial position, reverse the $0.4 million loss and record the proceeds of $3.6 million from the factor as a liability. In substance, JKA has received a loan, secured on its trade receivables.

Sale of land

There are features of this sale of land that suggest that its true substance is not a sale. The land is being sold to a finance company (DEX Finance), at less than its carrying value in JKA's statement of financial position. There is also an agreement giving JKA an option to repurchase the land within three years and requiring the entity to repurchase the land by the end of that period. This means that if the land increases in value, JKA can repurchase it at the agreed price and benefit from the increase in value but if the value of the land decreases, JKA will still be obliged to repurchase it and will suffer a loss.

The risks and benefit of owning the land remain with JKA, so in substance the transaction is a refinancing exercise. The land should be reinstated in the statement of financial position, the "loss" on the disposal should be reversed and the proceeds of the sale should be treated as a loan.

As the repurchase price is higher than the sales proceeds (from $60,000 to $100,000 higher depending on the price at the date of repurchase), in substance the excess represents interest payable on the loan. However, as the sale took place on the final day of the accounting period, no interest should be recognised in the current year.

(b) **Factoring of receivables**

DEBIT	Trade receivables	$4,000,000	
CREDIT	Liabilities		$3,600,000
CREDIT	Profit or loss		$400,000

Being correction of accounting treatment for factored receivables.

Sale of land

DEBIT	Property, plant and equipment	$520,000	
CREDIT	Liabilities		$500,000
CREDIT	Profit or loss		$20,000

Being correction of accounting treatment for sale of land.

2 Amps

(a)   **Redeemable bonds**

The current treatment accounts for interest on a cash basis. IAS 32 classifies these bonds as financial liabilities since they are not derivatives and they are not held for trading purposes. IAS 39 states that they should be held at amortised cost using their effective interest rate which means that the finance charge in any one year is equal to a constant rate based on the carrying amount. This applies the matching concept. Based upon an effective constant rate of interest of 7½% the charge in 20X0 should be $75,000. The difference between the revised charge of $75,000 and the amount paid to debt holders of $40,000 (ie $35,000) should be added to the statement of financial position liability, giving a total liability at 31 December 20X0 of $1,035,000.

(b)   **Convertible debentures**

The convertible debentures are compound instruments, as they have characteristics of both debt (the obligation to pay interest and to repay capital) and equity instruments (the right for the holder to have a share). The debt and equity elements should be classified separately as liability and equity as required by IAS 32. The split is based on measuring the debt element using market rates of return at inception for non-convertible debt of the same maturity date and value and treating the equity element as a balancing figure.

Consequently, the debt element of the convertible debentures should be reallocated as a current liability in this case. The annual return would be treated as finance costs until conversion/redemption.

3 Radost

(a)   **Notes to the statement of profit or loss and other comprehensive income**

Defined benefit expense recognised in profit or loss

	$'000
Current service cost	3,750
Past service cost	(6,000)
Net interest income [(10% × 45,000) − (10% x 52,000)]	(700)
	(2,950)

Other comprehensive income (items that will not be reclassified to profit or loss):
Remeasurements of defined benefit plans

	$'000
Remeasurement loss on plan liabilities	(4,750)
Remeasurement gain on plan assets	2,970
	(1,780)

Notes to the statement of financial position

Net defined benefit asset recognised in the statement of financial position

	$'000
Present value of defined benefit liabilities	(44,000)
Fair value of plan assets	64,170
Net defined benefit asset	20,170

Changes in FV of plan assets and PV of plan liabilities

	Assets $m	Liabilities $m
Balance at 1 January 20X3	52,000	45,000
Interest [(10% × 52,000) / (10% × 45,000)]	5,200	4,500
Contributions	12,000	-
Benefits paid	(8,000)	(8,000)
Current service cost	-	3,750
Past service cost	-	(6,000)
	61,200	39,250
Remeasurement gain on assets (bal figure)	2,970	
Remeasurement loss on liabilities (bal figure)		4,750
Balance at 31 December 20X3	64,170	44,000

(b)   Legally, the assets of the Radost pension scheme do not belong to Radost once the contributions are made. This is because to meet the definition of plan assets of a post-employment benefit scheme under IAS 19 *Employee Benefits* they must be held by an entity/fund that is legally separate from the reporting entity. This provides the employees with a measure of protection should the entity go bankrupt or should the directors fraudulently attempt to plunder the assets of the pension scheme.

Nevertheless, the substance of the arrangement is that the assets are held exclusively to pay the company's future defined benefit obligation and it is therefore logical that they should be shown in the company's statement of financial position reducing that liability.

In the case of plan assets that exceed the value of the associated obligation (as in Radost's case), a net asset would normally be recognised in the company's statement of financial position on the grounds that the definition of an asset ('a resource controlled by the entity as a result of past events and from which future economic benefits are expected to flow to the entity') is met. In this case the 'economic benefits' would be reduced future contributions payable, as the scheme is in surplus.

4   Share-based payment

(a)   **Accounting entries**

31.12.X1 $

		$	$
DEBIT	Staff costs	188,000	
CREDIT	Other reserves (within equity)		188,000

((800 – 95) × 200 × $4 × 1/3)

Being share-based payment expense for the year ended 31 December 20X1

31.12.X2

		$	$
DEBIT	Staff costs (W1)	201,333	
CREDIT	Other reserves (within equity)		201,333

Being share-based payment expense for the year ended 31 December 20X2

31.12.X3

		$	$
DEBIT	Staff costs (W2)	202,667	
CREDIT	Other reserves (within equity)		202,667

Being share-based payment expense for the year ended 31 December 20X3

Issue of shares:

		$	$
DEBIT	Cash (740 × 200 × $1.50)	222,000	
DEBIT	Other reserves (within equity)	592,000	
CREDIT	Share capital (740 × 200 × $1)		148,000
CREDIT	Share premium (balancing figure)		666,000

Being share issue

Workings

1   *Equity at 31.12.X2*

Equity b/d   188,000
∴ P/L charge   201,333
Equity c/d ((800 – 70) × 200 × $4 × 2/3)   389,333

2   *Equity at 31.12.X3*

Equity b/d   389,333
∴ P/L charge   202,667
Equity c/d ((800 – 40 – 20) × 200 × $4 × 3/3)   592,000

(b)   **Cash-settled share-based payment**

If J&B had offered cash payments based on the value of the shares at vesting date rather than options, the key differences would be recognising a liability in the statement of financial position rather than equity (reflecting the obligation to employees) and measuring it at the fair value at the year end date rather than the grant date (to reflect the best estimate of what will be paid).

In each of the three years a liability would be shown in the statement of financial position representing the expected amount payable based on the following:

| No of employees estimated at the year end to be entitled to rights at the vesting date | × | Number of rights each | × | Fair value of each right at year end | × | Cumulative proportion of vesting period elapsed |

The movement in the liability would be charged to profit or loss representing further entitlements received during the year and adjustments to expectations accrued in previous years.

The liability would continue to be adjusted (resulting in a profit or loss charge) for changes in the fair value of the right over the period between when the rights become fully vested and are subsequently exercised. It would then be reduced for cash payments as the rights are exercised.

5   KPG Bank

(a)   **Current purchasing power: explanation**

Why non-monetary items are restated and monetary items are not restated

The aim of current purchasing power is to measure profits as the increase in the current purchasing power of equity. Profits are therefore stated after allowing for the declining purchasing power of money due to price inflation. Changes in purchasing power are based on the general level of inflation using the General Prices Index (GPI).

Monetary assets and liabilities are not restated because the amount is fixed in $ by contract or statute e.g. cash, receivables, payables, loans. For example, if there is a trade payable of $100,000, the entity will have to repay $100,000 i.e. the amount agreed in the invoice. Therefore they are not restated for general inflation.

Non-monetary assets whose value is not fixed by contract or statute (e.g. inventories, non-current assets) should be adjusted for general inflation using the GPI because the purchase price will be out of date by the year end.

Holding gain or loss on monetary items

Gains arise from having monetary liabilities. For example, if an entity takes out a loan for $100,000 at the start of the year and the general rate of inflation for the year is 12%, if an entity were to take out an equivalent loan at the year end, it would be for $112,000. However, the entity only owes $100,000 as the amount is fixed in the loan agreement so a holding gain of $12,000 has arisen.

Losses arise on monetary assets. For example, an entity holding cash has a fixed value in nominal $ but if they continue to hold such assets, in times of rising prices, their purchasing power declines. In this situation the entity will make a loss.

(b) **Advantages of current purchasing power (only 2 of the points below are required)**

- The restatement of non-monetary asset values gives entities greater comparability, ie. all entities adopting current purchasing power measure their assets values at the same point in time (the year-end).

- The restatement of non-monetary assets to year end prices provides more relevant information to users of financial statements which helps with decision-making.

- Provided that the previous years' profits are re-valued into current purchasing power terms, comparability with prior years is improved.

- Profit is measured in 'real' terms and excludes 'inflationary value increments'. This enables better forecasts of future profits to be made.

- Current purchasing power provides a stable monetary unit with which to value profit and capital.

- Current purchasing power is based on historical cost data which can be easily verified. Inflation adjustments are also very auditable.

(c) **Alternative method of accounting in times of rising prices**

An alternative method of accounting to CPP in times of rising prices is current cost accounting. Current cost accounting requires adjusting for specific price rises (rather than general price rises). It takes into account operating capital maintenance i.e. the objective to maintain the operating capacity of the business in times of rising prices.

Non-monetary assets and liabilities in the statement of financial position are restated to their current cost. Current cost is their value to the business. For assets, deprival value is used. This is defined as the lower of replacement cost and the recoverable amount (the higher of realisable value and value in use).

Monetary assets and liabilities are not restated as they are already at current cost.

In the statement of profit or loss, adjustments are made to maintain the operating capacity of the business:

- Cost of sales adjustment – the difference between the historical cost of goods sold and replacement cost of goods sold.

- Additional depreciation adjustment – the difference between historical cost depreciation and current cost depreciation in the period (based on the current cost asset value).

- Monetary working capital adjustment – the effect of price changes on movement in monetary working capital (trade receivables less trade payables).

- Gearing adjustment – adjustment is also made to the statement of profit or loss and other comprehensive income to reflect the financing structure of the company, by adding back to profit the proportion of the above adjustments financed by debt rather than equity.

6 Group financial statements

Tutorial note. This is a general question to get you thinking about the nature of a group. The question strongly hints that there *are* limitations to group financial statements.

The objective of annual financial statements is to help shareholders exercise control over their company by providing information about how its affairs have been conducted. The shareholders of a parent company would not be given sufficient information from the financial statements of the parent company on its own, because not enough would be known about the nature of the assets, income and profits of all the subsidiary companies in which the parent company has invested. The primary purpose of group financial statements is to provide a true and fair view of the position and earnings of the parent company group as a whole, from the standpoint of the shareholders in the parent company.

However, group financial statements can be argued to have certain limitations.

(a) Group financial statements may be misleading.

(i) The solvency (liquidity) of one company may hide the insolvency of another.

(ii) The profit of one company may conceal the losses of another.

(iii) They imply that group companies will meet each others' debts (this is certainly not true: a parent company may watch creditors of an insolvent subsidiary go unpaid without having to step in).

(b) There may be some difficulties in defining the group or 'entity' of companies, although company law and accounting standards have removed many of the grey areas here.

(c) Where a group consists of widely diverse companies in different lines of business, a set of group financial statements may obscure much important detail unless supplementary information about each part of the group's business is provided.

7 Putney and Wandsworth

CONSOLIDATED STATEMENT OF FINANCIAL POSITION AS AT 31 DECEMBER 20X5

	$
Non-current assets	
Property, plant & equipment (135,000 + 60,000)	195,000
Goodwill (W2)	1,250
	196,250
Current assets (62,000 + 46,000)	108,000
	304,250
Equity attributable to the owners of the parent	
Share capital	50,000
Revaluation surplus (W3)	63,500
Retained earnings (W4)	124,750
	238,250
Non-controlling interests (W5)	8,000
	246,250
Non-current liabilities (14,000 + 12,000)	26,000
Current liabilities (18,000 + 14,000)	32,000
	304,250

Workings

1   *Group structure*

Putney

1.1.X1

Wandsworth Pre-acq'n ret'd earnings $10,000

2   *Goodwill*

	$	$
Consideration transferred		25,000
Non-controlling interest at acquisition (25,000 × 10%)		2,500
Net assets at acquisition:		
Share capital	15,000	
Retained earnings at acquisition	10,000	
		(25,000)
Goodwill at acquisition		2,500
Impairment losses to date		(1,250)
Goodwill at 31.12.X5		1,250

3   *Revaluation surplus*

	Putney	*Wandsworth*
Per question	50,000	15,000
Pre-acquisition	–	(0)
	50,000	15,000
Wandsworth – share of post acquisition revaluation surplus		
(15,000 × 90%)	13,500	
	63,500	

4   *Retained earnings*

	Putney	*Wandsworth*
Per question	90,000	50,000
Pre-acquisition	–	(10,000)
	90,000	40,000
Wandsworth – share of post acquisition earnings		
(40,000 × 90%)	36,000	
Less: goodwill impairment losses to date	(1,250)	
	124,750	

5   *Non-controlling interests*

NCI at acquisition (W2)	2,500
Share of post acquisition revaluation surplus (15,000(W3) × 10%)	1,500
Share of post acquisition earnings (40,000(W3) × 10%)	4,000
	8,000

8 Balmes and Aribau

BALMES GROUP
CONSOLIDATED STATEMENT OF FINANCIAL POSITION AS AT 30 JUNE 20X3

	$'000
Non-current assets	
Property, plant & equipment (97,300 + 34,400 + (W6) 1,400)	133,100
Goodwill (W2)	2,800
Other intangible assets (5,100 + 1,200)	6,300
	142,200
Current assets	
Inventories (43,400 + 14,300)	57,700
Trade and other receivables (36,800 + 17,400)	54,200
Cash and cash equivalents	700
	112,600
	254,800
Equity attributable to the owners of the parent	
Share capital	50,000
General reserve (W3)	5,100
Retained earnings (W4)	122,040
	177,140
Non-controlling interests (W5)	9,760
	186,900
Non-current liabilities	
Loan notes (10,000 + 4,000)	14,000
Current liabilities	
Trade payables (28,400 + 15,700)	44,100
Income tax payable (7,300 + 2,400)	9,700
Bank overdraft	100
	53,900
	254,800

Workings

1 *Group structure*

Balmes

1.7.X1   80%

Aribau   Pre-acquisition retained earnings = $25m
                Pre-acquisition general reserve = $2m

2 *Goodwill*

	$'000	$'000
Consideration transferred		28,500
Non-controlling interests at acquisition (fair value)		7,000
Net fair value of identifiable assets acquired:		
Share capital	5,000	
General reserve	2,000	
Retained earnings	24,000	
Fair value adjustments (W6)	1,500	
		(32,500)
		3,000
Impairment losses to date		(200)
		2,800

3   *General reserve*

	Balmes $'000	Aribau $'000
Per question	4,300	3,000
Pre-acquisition		(2,000)
		1,000
Aribau – post acquisition general reserve (1,000 × 80%)	800	
	5,100	

4   *Retained earnings*

	Balmes $'000	Aribau $'000
Per question	118,800	37,100
Revaluation gain on investment in Aribau cancelled on consolidation (35,500 – 28,500)	(7,000)	
Fair value adjustments movement (W6)		(100)
Pre-acquisition retained earnings		(24,000)
		13,000
Aribau – share of post-acquisition earnings (13,000 × 80%)	10,400	
Less: Group share of goodwill impairment losses to date (80% x 200 (W2))	(160)	
	122,040	

5   *Non-controlling interest*

	$'000
Non-controlling interests at acquisition (W2)	7,000
Share of post-acquisition general reserve (1,000 (W3) × 20%)	200
Share of post-acquisition earnings (13,000(W4) × 20%)	2,600
NCI share of impairment losses on goodwill (200 (W2) x 20%)	(40)
	9,760

6   *Fair value adjustments*

	At acquisition date $'000	Movement $'000	At y/e date $'000
Land (5,000 – 4,500)	500		500
Buildings ((14,000 – 5,000) – (12,500 – 4,500))	1,000	(100)*	900
	1,500	(100)	1,400

*Extra depreciation ($1,000,000 × 2/20)

9 Reprise

REPRISE GROUP – CONSOLIDATED STATEMENT OF FINANCIAL POSITION AS AT 31 MARCH 20X4

	$'000
Non-current assets	
Land and buildings	3,350.0
Plant and equipment (1,010 + 2,210)	3,220.0
Motor vehicles (510 + 345)	855.0
Goodwill (W2)	826.0
	8,251.0
Current assets	
Inventories (890 + 352 – (W5) 7.2)	1,234.8
Trade receivables (1,372 + 514 – 39 – (W6) 36)	1,811.0
Cash and cash equivalents (89 + 51 + 39)	179.0
	3,224.8
	11,475.8
Equity attributable to owners of the parent	
Share capital	1,000.0
Retained earnings (W3)	5,257.3
Revaluation surplus	2,500.0
	8,757.3
Non-controlling interests (W4)	896.5
	9,653.8
Non-current liabilities	
10% debentures	500.0
Current liabilities	
Trade payables (996 + 362 – (W6) 36)	1,322.0
	11,475.8

Workings

1 Group structure

R

| 75% ∴ non-controlling interests = 25%

E   Pre-acquisition retained earnings = $1,044,000

2 Goodwill

	$'000	$'000
Consideration transferred		2,000
Non-controlling interests (at fair value)		
(125,000 shares × $4.40)		550
Net assets at acquisition as represented by:		
Share capital	500	
Retained earnings	1,044	
		(1,544)
		1,006
Impairment losses to date		(180)
		826

3 *Consolidated retained earnings*

	Reprise	Encore
	$'000	$'000
Per question	4,225	2,610
PUP (W5)	(7.2)	
Pre-acquisition retained earnings		(1,044)
		1,566

Group share of post-acquisition retained earnings:		
Encore (1,566 × 75%)	1,174.5	
Group share of impairment losses (180 (W2) × 75%)	(135)	
	5,257.3	

4 *Non-controlling interests*

	$'000
NCI at acquisition (W2)	550
NCI share of post-acquisition retained earnings ((W3) 1,566 × 25%)	391.5
NCI share of impairment losses (180 (W2) × 25%)	(45)
	896.5

5 *Unrealised profit on inventories*

Reprise ———————▶ Encore

Unrealised profit included in inventories is:

$$\$31,200 \times \frac{30}{130} = \$7,200$$

DEBIT (↓) Retained earnings of Reprise $7,200

CREIT (↓) Inventories $7,200

6 *Trade receivables/trade payables*

Intragroup balance of $75,000 is reduced to $36,000 once cash-in-transit of $39,000 is followed through to its ultimate destination.

10 Fallowfield and Rusholme

CONSOLIDATED STATEMENT OF PROFIT OR LOSS AND OTHER COMPREHENSIVE INCOME FOR THE YEAR ENDED 30 JUNE 20X8

	$
Revenue (403,400 + 193,000 – 40,000)	556,400
Cost of sales (201,400 + 92,600 – 40,000 + (W7) 4,000)	(258,000)
Gross profit	298,400
Distribution costs (16,000 + 14,600)	(30,600)
Administrative expenses (24,250 + 17,800)	(42,050)
Profit before tax	225,750
Income tax expense (61,750 + 22,000)	(83,750)
Profit for the year	142,000
Other comprehensive income (net of tax) (20,000 + 5,000)	25,000
Total comprehensive income for the year	167,000
Profit attributable to:	
Owners of the parent	125,200
Non-controlling interests (W2)	16,800
	142,000
Total comprehensive income attributable to:	
Owners of the parent	148,200
Non-controlling interests (W2)	18,800
	167,000

Tutorial note: Intragroup dividend income from Rusholme has been cancelled out on consolidation.

STATEMENT OF CHANGES IN EQUITY

	Equity attributable to owners of the parent $	Non-controlling interests (W4/W6) $	Total equity $
Balance at 30 June 20X7	270,000 (W3)	48,000	318,000
Total comprehensive income for the year	148,200	18,800	167,000
Dividends (NCI: 25,000 × 40%)	(40,000)	(10,000)	(50,000)
Balance at 30 June 20X8	378,200 (W5)	56,800	435,000

Workings

1   *Group structure*

      Fallowfield

          | 60%   3 years ago

      Rusholme   Pre-acquisition reserves: $16,000

2   *Non-controlling interests (SPLOCI)*

	Profit for the year $	Total comprehensive income $
Per question	46,000	51,000
Less: PUP (W7)	(4,000)	(4,000)
	42,000	47,000
NCI share 40%	16,800	18,800

3   *Equity brought forward*

	Fallowfield $	Rusholme $
Per question	243,000	101,000
Pre-acquisition equity (SC 40,000 + Res 16,000)	–	(56,000)
	243,000	45,000
Rusholme – share of post acquisition (45,000 × 60%)	27,000	
	270,000	

4   *Non-controlling interest brought forward (SOFP)*

	$
NCI at acquisition (at fair value)	30,000
Share of post-acquisition retained earnings (b/f) (45,000(W3) × 40%)	18,000
	48,000

5   *Equity carried forward*

	Fallowfield $	Rusholme $
Per question	338,000	127,000
PUP (W7)	–	(4,000)
Pre-acquisition equity (SC 40,000 + Res 16,000)		(56,000)
	338,000	67,000
Rusholme – share of post-acquisition retained earnings (62,000 × 60%)	40,200	
	378,200	

6   *Non-controlling interest carried forward (SOFP)*

	$
NCI at acquisition (at fair value)	30,000
Share of post-acquisition retained earnings (c/f) (62,000(W5) × 40%)	26,800
	56,800

7   *Provision for unrealised profit*

Rusholme → Fallowfield

PUP = $40,000 × ½ in inventories × 25/125 mark up = $4,000

↑ Rusholme's cost of sales (& adjust NCI [SPLOCI] in (W2))

↓ Rusholme's retained earnings (in (W5))

↓ Group inventories (in SOFP)

11   Panther Group

PANTHER GROUP
CONSOLIDATED STATEMENT OF PROFIT OR LOSS AND OTHER COMPREHENSIVE INCOME
FOR THE YEAR ENDED 31 DECEMBER 20X4

	$'000
Revenue [22,800 + (4,300 × 6/12) – 320]	24,630
Cost of sales [13,600 + (2,600 × 6/12) – 320 + (W3) 10 + (W5) 5]	(14,595)
Gross profit	10,035
Distribution costs (2,900 + (500 × 6/12))	(3,150)
Administrative expenses (1,800 + (300 × 6/12))	(1,950)
Finance costs [200 + (40 × 6/12) – (W4) 20 cancellation]	(200)
Finance income (50 – (W4) 20 cancellation)	30
Profit before tax	4,765
Income tax expense [1,300 + (220 × 6/12)]	(1,410)
Profit for the year	3,355
Other comprehensive income for the year, net of tax [1,600 + (180 × 6/12)]	1,690
Total comprehensive income for the year	5,045
Profit attributable to:	
Owners of the parent (3,330 – 112)	3,229
Non-controlling interests (W2)	126
	3,355
Total comprehensive income attributable to:	
Owners of the parent (5,020 – 148)	4,883
Non-controlling interests (W2)	162
	5,045

CONSOLIDATED STATEMENT OF CHANGES IN EQUITY
FOR THE YEAR ENDED 31 DECEMBER 20X4 (EXTRACT)

	$'000
	Reserves
Balance at 1 January 20X4 (Panther only)	12,750
Dividend paid	(900)
Total comprehensive income for the year	4,883
Balance at 31 December 20X4 (W6)	16,733

Workings

1   *Group structure and timeline*

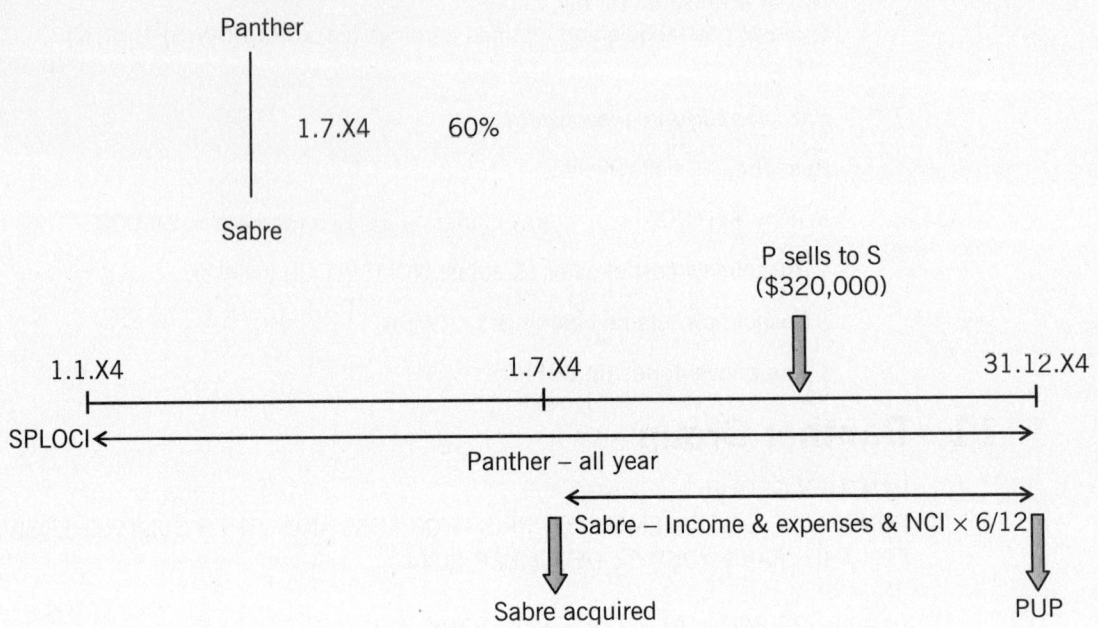

2   *Non-controlling interests*

	PFY $'000	TCI $'000
Per Q (640 × 6/12)/(820 × 6/12)	320	410
Additional depreciation on fair value adjustment (W5)	(5)	(5)
	315	405
NCI share	× 40%	× 40%
	= 126	= 162

3   *Unrealised profit on intragroup trading*

$$\text{Panther to Sabre} = \$60,000 \times \frac{20\%}{120\%} = \$10,000$$

Adjust cost of sales in books of seller (Panther).

4   *Interest on intragroup loan*

$800,000 × 5% × 6/12 = $20,000

Cancel in books of Panther and Sabre.

5   Fair value adjustments

	At acq'n 1.7.X4 $'000	Movement $'000	At year end 31.12.X4 $'000
Property	200	(200/20 × 6/12) (5)	195

6   Group reserves carried forward (proof)

	Panther $'000	Sabre $'000
Reserves per question	16,500	3,300
PUP (W3)	(10)	
Fair value movement (W5)		(5)
Pre-acquisition reserves [2,480 + (820 x 6/12)]		(2,890)
		405
Group share of post-acquisition reserves: Sabre (405 × 60%)	243	
	16,733	

12   Hever

CONSOLIDATED STATEMENT OF FINANCIAL POSITION AS AT 31 DECEMBER 20X4

	$'000
Non-current assets	
Property, plant & equipment (370 + 190 + (W7) 45)	605
Goodwill (W2)	8
Investment in associate (W3)	165
	778
Current assets	
Inventories (160 + 100 – (W6) 1.5)	258.5
Trade receivables (170 + 90)	260
Cash (50 + 40)	90
	608.5
	1,386.5
Equity attributable to owners of the parent	
Share capital	200
Share premium reserve	100
Retained earnings (W4)	758.5
	1,058.5
Non-controlling interests (W5)	168
	1,226.5
Current liabilities	
Trade payables (100 + 60)	160
	1,386.5

Workings

1   *Group structure*

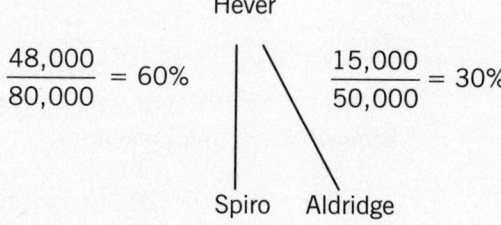

Hever

$\dfrac{48,000}{80,000} = 60\%$ $\dfrac{15,000}{50,000} = 30\%$

Spiro   Aldridge

Pre-acq'n reserves = $20k   = $150k

∴ In the absence of information to the contrary, Spiro is a subsidiary, and Aldridge an associate of Hever.

2   *Goodwill on consolidation - Spiro*

	$'000	$'000
Consideration transferred		128
Non-controlling interests (at 'full' fair value)		90
Net assets at acquisition:		
Share capital	80	
Share premium	80	
Retained earnings	20	
Fair value adjustments (W7)	30	
		(210)
Goodwill arising on consolidation		8

3   *Investment in associate*

	$'000
Cost of associate	90
Share of post-acquisition retained reserves (W4)	75
	165

4   *Retained earnings*

	Hever $'000	Spiro $'000	Aldridge $'000
Per question	568	200	400
PUP (W6)	(1.5)	–	–
Fair value movement (W7)		15	
Pre-acquisition retained earnings		(20)	(150)
		195	250

Group share of post acquisition ret'd earnings:	
Spiro (195 × 60%)	117
Aldridge (250 × 30%)	75
	758.5

5   *Non-controlling interests*

	$'000
NCI at acquisition (W2)	90
NCI share of post acquisition ret'd earnings ((W4) 195 × 40%)	78
	168

6   *Unrealised profit on inventories*

Hever ⟶ Spiro

Mark-up: $16,000 − $10,000 = $6,000 ∴ PUP = ¼ in inventory × $6,000 = $1,500

↓ Hever's retained earnings	$1,500
↓ Inventories	$1,500

7   *Fair values – adjustment to net assets*

	At acquisition	Movement	At year end
Property, plant and equipment	50	(5)	45
Inventories	(20)	20	0
	30	15	45

13 Armoury

BAYONET GROUP
CONSOLIDATED STATEMENT OF FINANCIAL POSITION AS AT 31 DECEMBER 20X9

	$'000
Non-current assets	
Property, plant and equipment (14,500 + 12,140 + 17,500)	44,140
Goodwill (W2)	3,580
	47,720
Current assets	
Inventories (6,300 + 2,100 + 450)	8,850
Trade receivables (4,900 + 2,000 + 2,320)	9,220
Cash (500 + 1,440 + 515)	2,455
	20,525
	68,245
Equity attributable to owners of the parent	
Share capital – 50c ordinary shares	5,000
Retained earnings (W3)	40,680
	45,680
Non-controlling interests (W4)	12,600
	58,280
Current liabilities (5,700 + 2,280 + 1,985)	9,965
	68,245

Workings

1   Group structure

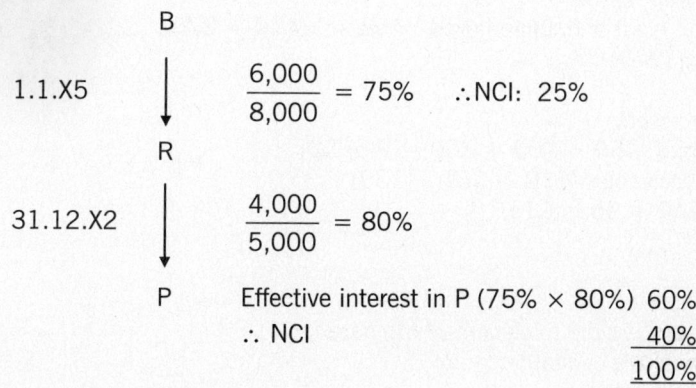

B

1.1.X5 $\dfrac{6,000}{8,000}$ = 75%   ∴NCI: 25%

R

31.12.X2 $\dfrac{4,000}{5,000}$ = 80%

P   Effective interest in P (75% × 80%) 60%

∴ NCI   40%

100%

2   Goodwill

	Rifle		*Pistol*	
	$'000	$'000	$'000	$'000
Consideration transferred		10,000	(9,000 × 75%)	6,750
Non-controlling interests (at fair value)		3,230		4,600
Fair value of identifiable net assets at acq'n:				
Share capital	4,000		2,500	
Pre-acquisition retained earnings	8,000		6,500	
		(12,000)		(9,000)
		1,230		2,350
			3,580	

3   *Retained earnings*

	Bayonet $'000	Rifle $'000	Pistol $'000
Per question	25,500	20,400	16,300
Retained earnings at acquisition		(8,000)	(6,500)
		12,400	9,800

Group share of post acquisition ret'd earnings:	
Rifle (12,400 × 75%)	9,300
Pistol (9,800 × 60%)	5,880
	40,680

4   *Non-controlling interests*

	Rifle $'000	Pistol $'000
NCI at acquisition (W2)	3,230	4,600
NCI share of post acquisition ret'd earnings:		
Rifle ((W3) 12,400 × 25%)	3,100	
Pistol ((W3) 9,800 × 40%)		3,920
Less: NCI share of investment in Pistol (9,000 × 25%)	(2,250)	
	4,080	8,520

12,600

14 Murder, Mystery and Suspense

MURDER GROUP
CONSOLIDATED STATEMENT OF FINANCIAL POSITION AS AT 31 DECEMBER 20X7

	$'m
Non-current assets	
Property, plant and equipment (2,458 + 1,410 + 870)	4,738
Goodwill (W2)	320
	5,058
Current assets	
Inventories (450 + 200 + 260 – (W5) 52)	858
Trade receivables (610 + 365 + 139)	1,114
Cash (240 + 95 + 116)	451
	2,423
	7,481
Equity attributable to owners of the parent	
Ordinary share capital	500
Share premium	250
Retained earnings (W3)	3,605
	4,355
Non-controlling interests (W4)	1,193
	5,548
Current liabilities	
Trade payables (1,130 + 418 + 385)	1,933
	7,481

Workings

1   *Group structure*

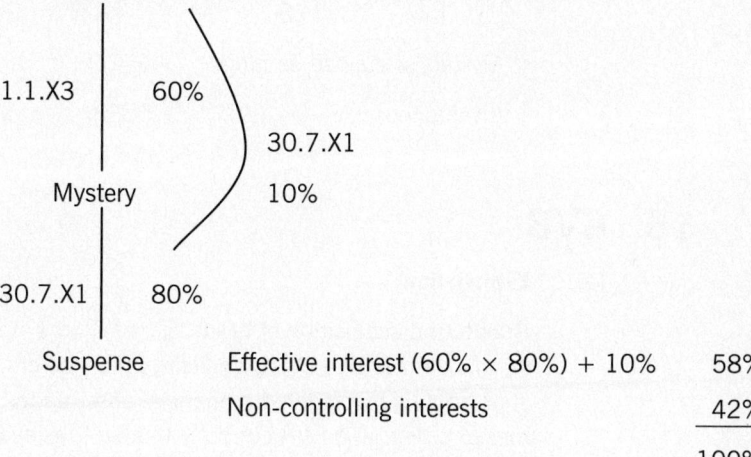

Effective interest (60% × 80%) + 10%	58%
Non-controlling interests	42%
	100%

2   *Goodwill (including step acquisition of Suspense)*

	Mystery		Suspense	
	$'m	$'m	$'m	$'m
Consideration transferred		900	(240 x 60%)	144
Fair value of non-controlling interests		536		210
Fair value of 10% equity interest in Suspense				50
Fair value of identifiable net assets at acq'n:				
Share capital	200		100	
Share premium	120		50	
Pre-acquisition retained earnings (1.1.X3)	950		100	
		(1,270)		(250)
		166		154
			320	

3   *Retained earnings*

	Murder	Mystery	Suspense
	$'m	$'m	$'m
Per question	2,805	1,572	850
P/L gain on investment in Suspense (50 – 27)	23		
Less: unrealised profit (W5)		(52)	
Retained earnings at acq'n (W2)		(950)	(100)
		570	750
Group share of post acq'n ret'd earnings:			
Mystery (570 × 60%)	342		
Suspense (750 × 58%)	435		
Group share of impairment losses to date	(0)		
	3,605		

4   *Non-controlling interests*

	Mystery	Suspense
	$'m	$'m
NCI at acquisition	536	210
Less: NCI share of investment in Suspense (240 × 40%)	(96)	
NCI share of post acq'n ret'd earnings:		
Mystery (570 (W3) × 40%)	228	
Suspense (750 (W3) × 42%)		315
	668	525
		1,193

5   *Unrealised profit on inventories*

Mystery $\longrightarrow$ Suspense

$$\text{PUP} = \$260m \times \frac{25}{125} = \$52m$$

↓ Mystery's retained earnings $52m

↓ Inventories $52m

15   CVB

(a)   **Explanation**

Prior to the acquisition of the 60% of FG on 1 April 20X5, CVB had a 15% shareholding in FG. As this did not give CVB significant influence or control over the relevant activities of FG, the 15% shareholding represented a financial asset under IAS 39 *Financial instruments: recognition and measurement* and CVB correctly treated it as available for sale i.e. at fair value with gains or losses recorded in other comprehensive income OCI.

On acquisition of the 60% on 1 April 20X5, CVB has a total shareholding of 75% and control of FG. Therefore FG should be treated as a subsidiary and consolidated in accordance with IFRS 10 *Consolidated financial statements.* At the acquisition is mid-year, the income, expenses and OCI would be pro-rated for six months in the consolidated statement of profit or loss and other comprehensive income.

In substance, on 1 April 20X5 CVB has 'sold' a 15% financial asset and therefore the financial asset should be derecognised with a profit or loss on derecognition recorded in profit or loss (and previous revaluation gains reclassified from OCI to profit or loss).

In substance, CVB has then 'acquired' a 75% subsidiary. IFRS 3 *Business combinations* requires goodwill on acquisition to be calculated at the date control is obtained i.e. on 1 April 20X5. Therefore goodwill should be calculated on the full 75% shareholding (with consideration being the cost of the 60% acquired plus the fair value of the previously held interest of 15%).

(b)   CVB – CONSOLIDATED STATEMENT OF FINANCIAL POSITION AS AT 30 SEPTEMBER 20X5

	$'000
Non-current assets	
Property, plant and equipment (22,000 + 5,000)	27,000
Goodwill (W2)	405
	27,405
Current assets	
Inventories (6,200 + 800 – 40 (W7))	6,960
Receivables (6,600 + 1,900)	8,500
Cash and cash equivalents (1,200 + 300)	1,500
	16,960
Total assets	44,365

EQUITY AND LIABILITIES
Equity attributable to owners of the parent
Share capital   20,000
Retained earnings (W3)   <u>8,629</u>
                                                                                              28,629
Non-controlling interests (W4)   <u>1,604</u>
                                                                                              <u>30,233</u>

Non-current liabilities
5% Bonds 2013 (3,900 + 132 (W6))   4,032

Current liabilities (8,100 + 2,000)   <u>10,100</u>
Total liabilities   <u>14,132</u>
Total equity and liabilities   <u>44,365</u>

Workings

1   *Group structure*

     CVB

          15% (1.5.X3) + 60% (1.4.X5) = 75%

     FG   PAR:

	$000
30.9.X5	5,000
Profits 1.4.X5 – 30.9.X5	
(3,000 x 6/12)	<u>(1,500)</u>
PAR at 1.4.X5	3,500

2   *Goodwill*

	$'000	$'000
Consideration transferred for the 60%		2,900
Non-controlling interests (at fair value)		1,250
Fair value of 15% holding at 1 April 20X5		800
Net assets at acquisition as represented by:		
Share capital	1,000	
Pre-acquisition retained earnings (W1)	<u>3,500</u>	
		<u>(4,500)</u>
		450
Impairment losses to date (10%)		<u>(45)</u>
		<u>405</u>

3   *Consolidated retained earnings*

	CVB	RG
	$'000	$'000
Per question	7,500	5,000
Profit on derecognition of available for sale investment (W5)	200	
Additional finance cost on bonds (W6)	(132)	
PUP (W7)		(40)
Pre-acquisition retained earnings (W1)		<u>(3,500)</u>
		<u>1,460</u>
Group share of post acquisition retained earnings:		
RG (1,460 × 75%)	1,095	
Group share of impairment losses (45 (W2) × 75%)	<u>(34)</u>	
	<u>8,629</u>	

4   *Non-controlling interests*

	$'000
NCI at acquisition (1 April 20X5) (W2)	1,250
NCI share of post acquisition retained earnings (1,460 (W3) × 25%)	365
NCI share of impairment losses (45 (W2) × 25%)	(11)
	1,604

5   *Profit on derecognition of financial asset*

	$'000
Fair value of 15% investment in FG at 1 April 20X5	800
Cost of 15% investment in FG	(600)
	200

6   *Bonds*

	$'000
At 1 October 20X4 (4,000 − 100)	3,900
Finance cost (8.5% effective interest × 3,900 b/f)	332
Interest paid (5% coupon × 4,000 par value)	(200)
At 30 September 20X5	4,032

Adjustment required:

↑ Finance costs (and ↓ CVB's retained earnings) [$332,000 − $200,000] $132,000

↑ Bonds (within non-current liabilities) [$4,032,000 − $3,900,000] $132,000

7   *Provision for unrealised profit*

FG ─────────────────▶ CVB

PUP = $400,000 × ½ in inventories × 20/100 margin = $40,000

↓ FG's (seller's) retained earnings $40,000

↓ Inventories $40,000

16 Holmes and Deakin

(a)   HOLMES CO
CONSOLIDATED STATEMENT OF PROFIT OR LOSS AND OTHER COMPREHENSIVE INCOME
FOR THE YEAR ENDED 31 MAY 20X3

	$'000
Revenue (1,000 + 540)	1,540
Cost of sales and operating expenses (800 + 430)	(1,230)
Profit before tax	310
Income tax expense (90 + 60)	(150)
Profit for the year	160
Other comprehensive income (net of tax) (20 + 10)	30
Total comprehensive income for the year	190

Profit attributable to:

Owners of the parent β	150
Non-controlling interest $(50 \times \frac{9}{12} \times 15\%) + (50 \times \frac{3}{12} \times 35\%)$	10
	160

Total comprehensive income attributable to:

Owners of the parent β	178
Non-controlling interest $(60 \times \frac{9}{12} \times 15\%) + (60 \times \frac{3}{12} \times 35\%)$	12
	190

(b)   HOLMES CO
       CONSOLIDATED STATEMENT OF FINANCIAL POSITION AS AT 31 May 20X3

	$'000
Non-current assets	
Property, plant and equipment (535 + 178)	713
Goodwill (W2)	80
	793
Current assets	
Inventories (320 + 190)	510
Trade receivables (250 + 175)	425
Cash (80 + 89)	169
	1,104
	1,897
Equity attributable to owners of the parent	
Share capital $1 ordinary shares	500
Retained earnings (W3)	507.5
	1,007.5
Non-controlling interest (W4)	157.5
	1,165
Current liabilities	
Trade payables (295 + 171)	466
Income tax payable (80 + 60)	140
Provisions (95 + 31)	126
	732
	1,897

(c)   STATEMENT OF CHANGES IN EQUITY (ATTRIBUTABLE TO OWNERS OF THE PARENT) AT 31
       MAY 20X3

	$'000
Balance at 31.5.20X2 (500 + (W6) 256.5)	756.5
Total comprehensive income for the year	178
Adjustment to parent's equity on disposal (W5)	73
Balance at 31.5.20X3 (500 + (W3) 507.5)	1,007.5

Workings

1   *Group structure and timeline*

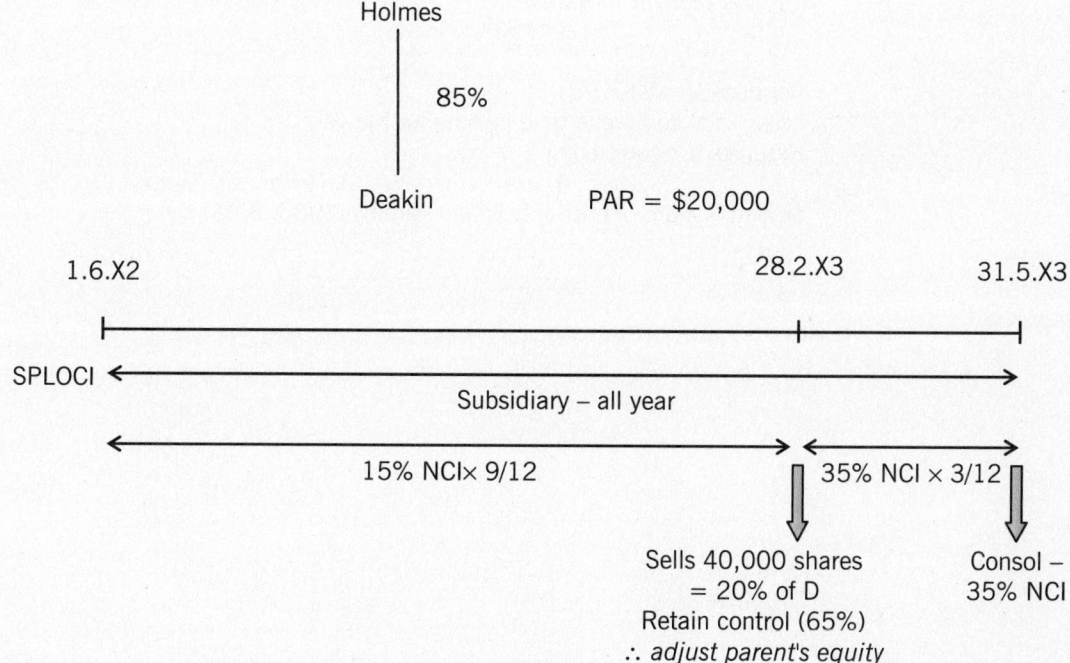

2   *Goodwill*

	$'000	$'000
Consideration transferred		255
Non-controlling interest (fair value)		45
Fair value of identifiable net assets at acquisition:		
Share capital	200	
Pre-acquisition retained earnings	20	
		(220)
		80

3   *Group reserves at 31 May 20X3*

	Holmes	Deakin 85%	Deakin 65% ret'd
	$'000	$'000	$'000
	310	155	170
Per question/at date of disposal $(170 - (60 \times \frac{3}{12}))$			
Adjustment to parent's equity on disposal (W5)	73		
Reserves at acquisition (W1)/date of disposal		(20)	(155)
		135	15
Group share of post-acquisition reserves:			
Deakin – 85% (135 × 85%)	114.75		
Deakin – 65% (15 × 65%)	9.75		
	507.5		

4   *Non-controlling interests (SOFP)*

	$'000
NCI at acquisition (W2)	45
NCI share of post-acquisition reserves to disposal (135 (W3) × 15%)	20.25
	65.25
Increase in NCI on disposal (65.25 × 20%/15%)	87
NCI share of post-acquisition reserves to year end (15 (W3)× 35%)	5.25
	157.5

5   *Adjustment to parent's equity on disposal of shares in group financial statements*

	$'000
Fair value of consideration received	160
Increase in NCI in net assets at disposal (W4)	(87)
	73

6   *Reserves brought forward*

	Holmes	Deakin
	$'000	$'000
Per question (31.5.X3)	310	170
Less: Total comprehensive income for the year	(130)	(60)
Reserves at acquisition		(20)
	180	90
Deakin – share of post-acquisition earnings (90 × 85%)	76.5	
	256.5	

17 Harvard

(a) HARVARD GROUP

CONSOLIDATED STATEMENT OF FINANCIAL POSITION AT 31 DECEMBER 20X5

	$'000
Non-current assets	
Property, plant and equipment (2,870 + (W2) 1,350)	4,220
Goodwill (W4)	146.7
	4,366.7
Current assets	
Inventories (1,990 + (W2) 2,310)	4,300
Trade receivables (1,630 + (W2) 1,270)	2,900
Cash at bank and in hand (240 + (W2) 560)	800
	8,000
	12,366.7
Equity attributable to owners of the parent	
Share capital ($1)	118
Retained reserves (W5)	3,018.7
	3,136.7
Non-controlling interests (W6)	1,070.0
	4,206.7
Non-current liabilities	
Loans	1,920
Current liabilities	
Trade payables (5,030 + (W2) 1,210)	6,240
	12,366.7

(b) CONSOLIDATED STATEMENT OF PROFIT OR LOSS AND OTHER COMPREHENSIVE INCOME
FOR YEAR ENDED 31 DECEMBER 20X5

	$'000
Revenue (40,425 + (W3) 25,900)	66,325
Cost of sales (35,500 + (W3) 20,680)	(56,180)
Gross profit	10,145
Distribution and administrative expenses (4,400 + (W3) 1,560)	(5,960)
Profit before tax	4,185
Income tax expense (300 + (W3) 1,260)	(1,560)
Profit for the year	2,625
Other comprehensive income:	
Exchange differences on translating foreign operations (W7)	316.7
Total comprehensive income for the year	2,941.7
Profit attributable to:	
Owners of the parent (2,625 – 600)	2,025
Non-controlling interests ((W3) 2,400 × 25%)	600
	2,625
Total comprehensive income attributable to:	
Owners of the parent (2,941.7 – 675.5)	2,266.2
Non-controlling interests [((W3) 2,400 + (W7) 302) × 25%]	675.5
	2,941.7

Statement of changes in equity for the year ended 31 December 20X5 (extract)

	$'000 *Owners of the parent*
Balance at 1 January 20X5 (118 + 1,452.5(W5))	1,570.5
Dividends	(700)
Total comprehensive income for the year (per SPLOCI)	2,266.2
Balance at 31 December 20X5 (118 + 3,018.7(W5))	3,136.7

BPP
LEARNING MEDIA

Workings

1   *Group structure*

   Harvard

   31.12.X2 | $\dfrac{1,011}{1,348} = 75\%$

   Krakow   Pre-acq'n ret'd earnings = PLN 2,876,000

2   *Translation of Krakow – statement of financial position*

	PLN '000	Rate	$'000
Property, plant and equipment	4,860	3.6	1,350
Inventories	8,316	3.6	2,310
Trade receivables	4,572	3.6	1,270
Cash	2,016	3.6	560
	19,764		5,490
Share capital	1,348	4.4	306.4
Retained reserves			
– pre-acquisition	2,876	4.4	653.6
– post-acquisition (14,060 – 2,876)	11,184	β	3,320
	15,408		4,280
Trade payables	4,356	3.6	1,210
	19,764		5,490

3   *Translation of Krakow – statement of profit or loss and other comprehensive income*

	PLN '000	Rate	$'000
Revenue	97,125	3.75	25,900
Cost of sales	(77,550)	3.75	(20,680)
Gross profit	19,575		5,220
Distribution and administrative expenses	(5,850)	3.75	(1,560)
Profit before tax	13,725		3,660
Income tax expense	(4,725)	3.75	(1,260)
Profit for the year	9,000		2,400

4   *Goodwill*

	PLN '000	PLN '000	Rate	$'000
Consideration transferred (840 × 4.4)		3,696		840
Non-controlling interests (4,224 × 25%)		1,056		240
Less: Share of net assets at acquisition:			4.4	
Share capital	1,348			
Retained earnings	2,876			
		(4,224)		(960)
Goodwill at acquisition		528		120
Exchange gain 20X3 – 20X4		–	β	12
Goodwill at 31 December 20X4		528	4.0	132
Exchange gain 20X5		--	β	14.7
Goodwill at year end		528	3.6	146.7

5 *Proof of retained reserves*

(i) At 31 December 20X5

	Harvard A$'000	Krakow A$'000
Per question/(W2)	502	3,974
Pre-acquisition (W2)		(654)
		3,320
Group share of Krakow post-acquisition (3,320 × 75%)	2,490	
Impairment losses to date	(0)	
Exchange differences on goodwill ((W4) 12 + 15)	27	
	3,019	

(ii) At 31 December 20X4 *(find as a balancing figure in the exam)*

	Harvard A$'000	Krakow A$'000
Harvard reserves b/d ((502 − (945 − 700))	257	2,538
Krakow net assets b/d (B$15,408 − 9,000 + 3,744)/4)		
Pre-acquisition net assets (B$ (W2) (1,348 + 2,876)/4.4)		(960)
		1,578
Group share of Krakow post-acquisition (1,578 × 75%)	1,184	
Impairment losses to date	(0)	
Exchange differences on goodwill (W4)	12	
	1,453	

Note: Net assets rather than reserves are used for the foreign subsidiary to incorporate exchange differences.

6 *Non-controlling interests*

	$'000
NCI at acquisition (W4)	240
Add: NCI share of post-acquisition retained reserves of Krakow ((W2) 3,320 × 25%)	830
	1,070

7 *Exchange differences arising during the year*

	SOCI $'000
On translation of net assets of Krakow:	
Closing NA at CR (W2)	4,280
Opening NA @ OR [(15,408 − 9,000 + 3,744)/4.0]	(2,538)
	1,742
Less: retained profit as translated ((W3) 2,400 − 3,744/3.90)	(1,440)
	302
On goodwill (W4)	14.7
	316.7

18 AH Group

AH GROUP CONSOLIDATED STATEMENT OF CASH FLOWS FOR THE YEAR ENDED 30 JUNE 20X5

	$'000	$'000
Cash flows from operating activities		
Profit before taxation	19,450	
Adjustment for		
Depreciation	7,950	
Profit on disposal of property	(1,250)	
Interest expense	1,400	
	27,550	
Decrease in trade receivables (W2)	470	
Increase in inventories (W2)	(3,100)	
Decrease in trade payables (W2)	(1,420)	
Cash generated from operations	23,500	
Interest paid (W4)	(1,480)	
Income taxes paid (W5)	(5,850)	
Net cash from operating activities		16,170
Cash flows from investing activities		
Acquisition of subsidiary, net of cash acquired (2,000 – 50)	(1,950)	
Purchase of property, plant and equipment (W1)	(11,300)	
Proceeds from sale of property	2,250	
Net cash used in investing activities		(11,000)
Cash flows from financing activities		
Repayment of interest-bearing borrowings	(1,000)	
Dividends paid (6,000 + (W3) 200)	(6,200)	
Net cash used in financing activities		(7,200)
Net decrease in cash and cash equivalents		(2,030)
Cash and cash equivalents at beginning of period		3,900
Cash and cash equivalents at end of period		1,870

Note. Dividends paid could also be shown under financing activities and dividends paid to non-controlling interest could also be shown under either operating activities or under financing activities.

Workings

1   *Property, plant and equipment*

	$000
B/f	44,050
Depreciation	(7,950)
Disposal	(1,000)
Acquisition of subsidiary	4,200
	39,300
Additions (balancing figure)	11,300
C/f	50,600

PROPERTY, PLANT AND EQUIPMENT

	$'000		$'000
Opening balance	44,050	Depreciation	7,950
Acquisition of subsidiary	4,200	Disposal	1,000
Additions (bal fig)	11,300	Closing balance	50,600
	59,550		59,550

2   *Inventories, trade receivables and trade payables*

	Inventories	Trade receivables	Trade payables
	$000	$000	$000
B/f	28,750	26,300	32,810
Acquisition of subsidiary	1,650	1,300	1,950
	30,400	27,600	34,760
Increase/(decrease)(balancing figure)	3,100	(470)	(1,420)
C/f	33,500	27,130	33,340

3   *Non-controlling interest*

	$000
B/f	1,920
SPLOCI	655
Acquisition of subsidiary (5,000 x 25%)	1,250
	3,825
Dividends paid (balancing figure)	(200)
C/f	3,625

NON-CONTROLLING INTEREST

	$'000		$'000
Cash paid (bal fig)	200	Opening balance	1,920
		On acquisition (5,000 × 25%)	1,250
Closing balance	3,625	P/L	655
	3,825		3,825

4   *Interest payable*

	$000
B/f	1,440
SPLOCI	1,400
	2,840
Interest paid (balancing figure)	(1,480)
C/f	1,360

INTEREST PAYABLE

	$'000		$'000
Cash paid (bal fig)	1,480	Opening balance	1,440
Closing balance	1,360	P/L	1,400
	2,840		2,840

5   *Income taxes paid*

	$000
B/f	5,450
SPLOCI	6,250
Acquisition of subsidiary	250
	11,950
Tax paid (balancing figure)	(5,850)
C/f	6,100

INCOME TAXES PAYABLE

	$'000		$'000
Cash paid (bal fig)	5,850	Opening balance	5,450
		Acquisition of subsidiary	250
Closing balance	6,100	P/L	6,250
	11,950		11,950

19 DM

(a) *Report to investor*

Date: October 20X5

This report has been prepared at your request based upon the financial statements of DM for the last two years to 31 December 20X4. A number of ratios have been calculated and these, together with some supermarket sector comparatives, are included in the appendix to this report.

Profitability – revenue

During 20X4 DM has opened 6 new stores which is an expansion rate of 17% although this has led to an increase in revenue of only 3%. It has also led to a fall in annual sales per store although the **annual store sales** for DM are still considerably higher than the sector average. However this may simply be due to the fact that DM has larger stores than the average. The reduction in annual sales per store may also be due to the fact that not all of the new stores were fully operational for the entire year.

Profitability – gross profit margin

Gross profit margin has remained the same for the last two years and is marginally **higher than the industry average**. In contrast the operating profit margin has increased 18% over the two year period although we have no sector comparative to compare this to. However we are told that the directors have reviewed the useful lives of the non-current assets and in most cases have increased them. This in turn will reduce the annual depreciation charge and therefore increase operating profit although there has been no real improvement in operating performance.

Profitability – net profit margin

Net profit margin for DM has increased from 2.9% to 3.7% and is now approaching the sector average. As the interest cost and tax expense have largely remained constant between the two years then this increase in net profit margin is due to the increased operating margin which in turn may be due to the change in depreciation charges.

Asset utilisation – asset turnover

The overall non-current asset turnover has **increased slightly over last year** but is still lower than the sector average. This increase could be due to the new stores although the non-current asset figure has remained almost the same as last year which is surprising due to the opening of the new stores. However it is possible that most of the capital expenditure on the new stores was actually incurred last year before the stores were brought into operation.

Asset utilisation – current ratio

The **current ratio is low** in both years as would be expected in a supermarket but has improved. There is also a distinct increase in the amount of cash being held. The inventory turnover period has not changed although there has been a slight increase in the payables payment period which will have a positive effect on cash flow. Finally the level of gearing has remained fairly constant and would not appear to be a problem.

Conclusion

DM has been **expanding** in the last two year and has appeared to **maintain and indeed improve its profitability** during this period. Its gross profit margin compares well with the sector average as do sales per store although the net profit margin has not kept pace with the sector average. It is possible, however, that the increasing operating profit margin and therefore net profit margin have been **manipulated** by the directors by the **increase in useful lives of the non-current assets** and therefore reduction in depreciation charges, This may have been done in order to encourage a high offer in any takeover bid that might be made. The directors would of course benefit personally from the sale of their individual stakes in the company at a high price but from the evidence we have it is not possible to state conclusively that this is the case. Further information would be required.

APPENDIX – RATIOS

	20X4	20X3	Sector
Gross profit margin	78/1,255 × 100 = 6.2%	75/1,220 × 100 = 6.1%	5.9%
Operating profit margin	57/1,255 × 100 = 4.5%	46/1,220 × 100 = 3.8%	
Net profit margin	33/1,255 × 100 = 2.6%	23/1,220 × 100 = 1.9%	3.9%
Annual sales per store	1,255/42 = $29.9m	1,220/38 = $32.1m	$27.6m
Non-current asset turnover	1,255/680 = 1.85	1,220/675 = 1.81	1.93
Current ratio	105/317 = 0.33	71/309 = 0.23	
Inventory turnover	47/1,177 × 365 = 14.6 days	46/1,145 × 365 = 14.7 days	
Payables payment period	297/1,177 × 365 = 92 days	273/1,145 × 365 = 87 days	

(b)   Limitations

Sector comparatives can provide useful information in ratio analysis but as with all comparisons there are both general and specific drawbacks. These include the following.

(i)   The sector figures are an **average** figure for the sector and therefore can be easily **affected by** just a **few abnormal** results or figures.

(ii)   The companies included in the sector figures may be of **different sizes** which may affect their sector results.

(iii)   The companies included in the sector figures may have **different year ends** which may affect the statement of financial position figures used in a variety of ratios particularly in the retail business.

(iv)   As with all comparisons the different companies in the sector may have **different accounting policies** which may mean that their results and resulting ratios are not strictly comparable.

(v)   There are a number of **different ways of calculating various key ratios** and if different companies in the sector calculate them in these different ways they will not be comparable.

20 Pilum

(a)   Earnings per share

	$
Profit for the period	1,403,000
Less: Preference dividends	(276,000)
Earnings	1,127,000
Earnings per share =	$1,127,000
	4,120,000
	27.4c

(b)   The first step is to calculate the theoretical ex-rights price. Consider the holder of five shares.

	$
Before rights issue (5 shares x $1.78)	8.90
Rights issue (1 share x $1.20)	1.20
After rights issue (6 shares)	10.10

The theoretical ex-rights price is therefore $10.10/6 = $1.68.

The number of shares in issue before the rights issue must be multiplied by the fraction:

$$\frac{\text{Fair value immediately before exercise of rights}}{\text{Theoretical ex - rights price}} = \frac{\$1.78}{\$1.68}$$

Number of shares in issue during the year

Date	Narrative	Shares	Time	Bonus fraction	Total
1.1.X4	B/f	4,120,000 ×	9/12 ×	1.78/1.68	3,273,929
1.10.X4	Rights issue (1 for 5)	824,000			
		4,944,000 ×	3/12 ×		1,236,000
					4,509,929

$$\text{EPS} = \frac{\$1,127,000}{4,509,929}$$

$$= 25.0c$$

(c) The maximum number of shares into which the loan stock could be converted is on the 31 December 20X5 terms of 90 $1 ordinary shares for every $100 of loan stock (90/100 × 1,500,000 = 1,350,000 shares). The calculation of diluted EPS should be based on the assumption that such a conversion actually took place on 1 January 20X4. Shares in issue during the year would then have numbered:

	$
Basic number of shares	4,120,000
Maximum number of shares on conversion (90/100 x 1,500,000)	1,350,000
Diluted number of shares	5,470,000

And revised earnings would be as follows:

	$	$
Earnings from (a) above		1,127,000
Interest saved by conversion (1,320,975 × 8%)	105,678	
Less: attributable tax (105,678 × 30%)	(31,703)	
		73,975
		1,200,975

$$\therefore \text{ Diluted EPS} = \frac{\$1,200,975}{5,470,000}$$

$$= 22.0c$$

Tutorial note:

Proof of liability component given in question:

	$
Principal ($1,500,000 x 0.681 [5 year 8% DF])	1,021,500
Interest ($1,500,000 x 5% x 3.993 [5 year 8% AF])	299,475
	1,320,975

21 STV

(a) Many entities carry on several classes or different types of business or operate in several geographical areas. Although the purpose of consolidated financial statement is to aggregate all of the information about a group into an understandable form from the perspective of the entire entity, if the financial statements are for a diverse group it is also useful to have disaggregated information in the notes about these different businesses or geographical areas.

To assess risks and returns

In an entity with different products or different geographical areas of operation it is likely that each business or area will have different rates of profitability, different opportunities for growth, different future prospects and different degrees of risk. The overall risks and returns of the entity can only be

fully assessed by looking at the individual risks and returns attached to each of these businesses or geographical areas.

To assess past performance and future prospects

Segment reporting should help investors to appreciate the results and financial position of the entity by permitting better understanding of past performance and thus a better assessment of its future prospects. It should also help investors to be aware of the impact that changes in significant components of a business may have on the business as a whole and to assess the risks and returns of the business.

(b)   **REPORT**

To: Investor
From: Accountant
Date: November 20X5
Subject: Segment analysis of STV

I have looked at the segment analysis note from STV's financial statements and have made the following analysis of the figures shown which may be of use to you. The detailed calculations upon which this analysis has been based are included in the appendix to this report.

From the segment analysis we can add more information to our overview of the results of the organisation.

Growth

Overall, revenue has grown by 6% in the year. The biggest growth has been in the newest segment, Secure Transport. However, this segment has the lowest margin. This is probably due to the start up costs of the segment as it was only established three years ago and will be suffering from high depreciation due to its investment in property, plant and equipment. The least growth has been in the largest segment, Road Haulage which makes up 68% of total revenue. This seems to reflect the strategy of changing product mix to focus on the new Secure Transport division and perhaps indicates market saturation in the area of Road Haulage.

Margins

The overall profit margin of the group has increased slightly from 24% in 20X4 to 25% in 20X5. This is largely due to the Secure Transport segment moving from an operating loss in 20X4 to an operating profit in 20X5. Although the Secure Transport segment has the lowest margin of the three segments, this is to be expected as it is a relatively new part of the business. If STV continues to expand in this market and the margin continues to improve, this is encouraging for the future. The largest segment, Road Haulage, has seen no change in margins and the most profitable segment, Air Freight has seen a slight improvement from 31% in 20X4 to 33% in 20X5.

Return on net assets

Overall the return on net assets has improved from 27% in 20X4 to 29% in 20X5. This is solely due to the Secure Transport division which is the only segment to have experienced an increase in return on net assets (from – 6.7% to 2.5%). Both Road Haulage and Air Freight have suffered from declining returns but the returns are still strong (Road Haulage: 37%; Air Freight: 52%). It appears that the Air Freight segment is using its assets most efficiently to generate revenue but it must be remembered that this ratio is influenced by the age of the assets. It could be that the Air Freight segment has older assets which may need replacing in the future whereas the Secure Transport segment has newer assets, causing a lower return.

Associates

The return on associates has improved from 14% (($12m / $84m) x 100%) in 20X4 to 19% (($16m / $85m) x 100%) in 20X5. It is a solid and improving return although lower than the Road Haulage and Air Freight segments. However, it is still a profitable investment.

Conclusion

Although the Secure Transport segment still only comprises a small portion of STV's overall business and has low profit margins, it is clearly improving as the investment in the infrastructure starts to feed through to profits. However, the performance of the other two divisions has seen little change which indicates that it is wise that the business has been diversifying.

APPENDIX

Key Ratios

		20X5	20X4
Profit margin			
Road haulage	169/653	26%	
	168/642		26%
Air freight	68/208	33%	
	62/199		31%
Secure transport	6/98	6%	
	(16)/63		-25%
Group	243/959	25%	
	214/904		24%
Return on net assets			
Road haulage	169/(805 – 345)	37%	
	168/(796 – 349)		38%
Air freight	68/(306 – 176)	52%	
	62/(287 – 178)		57%
Secure transport	6/(437 – 197)	2.5%	
	(16)/(422 – 184)		-6.7%
Group	243/(1,548 – 718)	29%	
	214/(1,505 – 711)		27%
Return on associates	11/85	19%	
	12/84		14%

Note to appendix. When the group ratios were calculated, the figures did not include unallocated expenses or assets/liabilities in order to be directly comparable with the segmental figures.

(c)   Even though segment reporting can be very useful to investors, it does also have some limitations.

Defining segments

IFRS 8 *Operating segments* does not define segment revenue and expense, segment results or segment assets and liabilities. It does, however, require an explanation of how segment profit or loss, segment assets and segment liabilities are measured for each operating segment.

IFRS 8 requires operating segments to be identified on the basis of internal reports about components of the entity that are regularly reviewed by the chief operating decision maker in order to allocate resources to the segment or assess performance.

Consequently, entities have discretion in determining what is included under segment results, which is limited only by their reporting practices.

Although this should mean that the analysis is comparable over time, it is unlikely to be comparable with that of another business.

Common costs

In many cases it will not be possible to allocate an expense to a segment and therefore they will be shown as unallocated expenses as in STV's segmental analysis. If these unallocated costs are material it can distort the segment results and make comparison with the overall group results misleading. Also if costs are allocated to segments on an arbitrary basis then this can distort the segment results.

Unallocated assets/liabilities

In a similar way to common costs, it may be that some of the entity's assets and/or liabilities cannot be allocated to a particular segment and must be shown as unallocated assets/liabilities as in STV. Again this can make the results and comparisons misleading. Finance costs

Finance is normally raised centrally and allocated to divisions etc as required. Therefore, the normal treatment for finance costs is to show them as an unallocated expense. However, if some areas of the business rely more heavily on debt finance than others, then this exclusion of finance costs could be misleading.

Tax costs

As with finance costs the effects of tax are normally shown as a total rather than split between the segments. If, however, a segment had a significantly different tax profile to other segments, again this information would be lost.

22 Current Issues

MEMORANDUM

To: The Chief Executive Officer of Clean
From: The Management Accountant
Date: 30 November 20X2
Subject: Current reporting practice

Introduction

This memorandum addresses the three issues raised in regard to current reporting practice in the context of Clean.

(a)   **IFRS and US GAAP**
       Convergence

       The US has traditionally adopted a rules-based approach to financial reporting standard setting, whereas the IASB's financial reporting standards are principles-based. The US has, in light of a number of major corporate scandals, now accepted that a principles-based reporting framework is more appropriate to current corporate reporting need.

       The IASB and US FASB (Financial Accounting Standards Boards) have undertaken the following joint steps towards convergence:

       •   The Norwalk agreement (October 2002) - a short-term convergence project to remove a variety of individual differences between IFRS and US GAAP.

       •   A 'Memorandum of Understanding' - a 'roadmap' of convergence between IFRS and US GAAP. Major differences were removed in the period 2006 – 2008 resulting in removal of requirement for non-US filers to prepare a reconciliation to US GAAP.

       •   'Roadmap for the Potential Use of Financial Statements Prepared in accordance with International Financial Reporting Standards by US Issuers' (November 2008) - milestones that could lead to adoption of IFRSs.

       •   Joint progress report (April 2012) – close to completing Memorandum of Understanding convergence programme and committed to complete the three remaining outstanding areas (financial instruments, revenue recognition and leases).

       At the time of writing, no final decision has been taken as to if or when US quoted entities will be required to adopt IFRS. Therefore, if Clean is acquired by a US quoted entity, Clean will have to convert its financial statements from IFRS to US GAAP for the purposes of the group financial statements.

Examples of differences between IFRS and US GAAP

Inventories

For determining cost of inventory, the LIFO (last in first out) method is prohibited under IFRS but allowed and widely used under US GAAP.

Revaluation of non-current assets

Under IFRS, revaluation of property, plant and equipment and intangible assets (in an active market) is allowed. Under US GAAP, it is generally prohibited.

Development costs

Under IFRS, development costs must be capitalised if certain criteria are met. Under US GAAP, they must be expensed.

Depreciation of property, plant and equipment

IFRS requires that separate significant components of property, plant and equipment with different economic lives be recorded and depreciated separately. US GAAP does not generally require the component approach to depreciation.

Impairment losses

Under IFRS, the impairment loss is based on the difference between the carrying value and the recoverable amount of the asset (the higher of fair value less costs to sell and value in use) and can be reversed (except for goodwill).

Under US GAAP, the impairment loss is based on the difference between the carrying value and the fair value of the asset and cannot be reversed.

Measurement of non-controlling interests at acquisition

Under IFRS, non-controlling interests at acquisition can either be measured at the proportionate share of net assets or at fair value. Under US GAAP, non-controlling interests at acquisition is always measured at fair value.

(b) **Environmental reporting**

Environmental reporting refers to a business' activities to maintain and enhance the environment.

There is no IFRS requiring environmental reports. However, many entities are voluntarily giving this information in their financial statements. The Global Reporting Initiative (GRI) have developed guidelines for those entities that wish to prepare an environmental report. These guidelines cover reporting on the economic, environmental and social dimensions of a business' activities, products and services.

There has been a greater trend towards environmental reporting for the following reasons:

- Public interest in pollution and other environmental issues
- Investor pressure
- Good public relations

Whilst a narrative environmental report is voluntary, environmental provisions and contingent liabilities are specifically covered by IAS 37 *Provisions, contingent liabilities and contingent assets*. Therefore if Clean's activities have environmental implications e.g. clean-up costs, it is possible that Clean may have to recognise a provision or disclose a contingent liability in accordance with IAS 37.

(c)   **Human resource accounting**

Competitive advantage is largely gained by effective use of people.

The case for regarding people as assets is as follows:

(i)   People are a resource which needs to be effectively managed.

(ii)   The organisation needs to protect its investment by retaining and developing its human assets, for example through training.

(iii)   Deterioration in employee motivation and attitude represents a cost to the business.

Nevertheless, there is a strong case against recognising employees in the statement of financial position, based on the IASB's *Framework*. The *Framework* defines assets as 'a resource controlled by the entity as a result of past transactions and events and from which future economic benefits are expected to flow'. Although there is a past event (the start of employment via an employment contract) which is likely to result in the employee generating future economic benefits as a result of their work for the entity, control cannot be proved. An employee is free to leave when they choose (subject to a notice period) and a contract of employment cannot and does not force an employee to work to provide benefits to the entity. Therefore the definition of an asset has not been met.

Furthermore, for an asset to be recognised, it has to be capable of reliable measurement. It is virtually impossible to objectively measure an employee's worth to the business. There would be too many uncertainties around specific economic benefits which may be regarded as attributable to employees. In addition, it would be very difficult to ascertain how would a human asset would be depreciated.

In conclusion, there are too many practical problems associated with human resource accounting for recognition of human assets to be allowed within financial statements.

Conclusion

If you wish to discuss these matters further, please do not hesitate to contact me.

INDEX

Note: **Key Terms** and their page references are given in **bold**.

Notes

Notes

Review Form – Paper F2 Financial Management (7/13)

Please help us to ensure that the CIMA learning materials we produce remain as accurate and user-friendly as possible. We cannot promise to answer every submission we receive, but we do promise that it will be read and taken into account when we up-date this Study Text.

Name: _____   Address: _____

_____

_____

How have you used this Study Text?
(Tick one box only)

☐ Home study (book only)

☐ On a course: college _____

☐ With 'correspondence' package

☐ Other _____

Why did you decide to purchase this Study Text? *(Tick one box only)*

☐ Have used BPP Texts in the past

☐ Recommendation by friend/colleague

☐ Recommendation by a lecturer at college

☐ Saw information on BPP website

☐ Saw advertising

☐ Other _____

During the past six months do you recall seeing/receiving any of the following?
(Tick as many boxes as are relevant)

☐ Our advertisement in *Financial Management*

☐ Our advertisement in *Pass*

☐ Our advertisement in *PQ*

☐ Our brochure with a letter through the post

☐ Our website www.bpp.com

Which (if any) aspects of our advertising do you find useful?
(Tick as many boxes as are relevant)

☐ Prices and publication dates of new editions

☐ Information on Text content

☐ Facility to order books off-the-page

☐ None of the above

Which BPP products have you used?

Text	☑	Success CD	☐
Kit	☐	i-Pass	☐
Passcard	☐	Interactive Passcard	☐

Your ratings, comments and suggestions would be appreciated on the following areas.

	Very useful	Useful	Not useful
Introductory section	☐	☐	☐
Chapter introductions	☐	☐	☐
Key terms	☐	☐	☐
Quality of explanations	☐	☐	☐
Case studies and other examples	☐	☐	☐
Exam skills and alerts	☐	☐	☐
Questions and answers in each chapter	☐	☐	☐
Fast forwards and chapter roundups	☐	☐	☐
Quick quizzes	☐	☐	☐
Question Bank	☐	☐	☐
Answer Bank	☐	☐	☐
OT Bank	☐	☐	☐
Index	☐	☐	☐

Overall opinion of this Study Text	Excellent ☐		Good ☐		Adequate ☐		Poor ☐

Do you intend to continue using BPP products?   Yes ☐   No ☐

On the reverse of this page is space for you to write your comments about our Study Text. We welcome your feedback. The BPP Learning Media author of this edition can be e-mailed at: yen-peichen@bpp.com

Please return this form to: Doug Haste, CIMA Publishing Manager, BPP Learning Media Ltd, FREEPOST, London, W12 8BR

TELL US WHAT YOU THINK

Please note any further comments and suggestions/errors below. For example, was the text accurate, readable, concise, user-friendly and comprehensive?